# Béla Bartók

# Béla Bartók

DAVID COOPER

YALE UNIVERSITY PRESS

NEW HAVEN AND LONDON

For information about this and other Yale University Press publications, please contact:
U.S. Office: sales.press@yale.edu   www.yalebooks.com
Europe Office: sales@yaleup.co.uk   www.yalebooks.co.uk

Typeset in Minion Pro by IDSUK (DataConnection) Ltd
Printed in Great Britain by Gomer Press Ltd, Llandysul Enterprise Park, Llandysul, Ceredigion, SA44 4JL

Library of Congress Cataloging-in-Publication Data

Cooper, David, 1956-
  Bela Bartók / David Cooper.
    pages cm
  Includes bibliographical references and index.
  ISBN 978-0-300-14877-0 (cl : alk. paper)
1. Bartók, Béla, 1881–1945. 2. Composers—Hungary—Biography. I. Title.
  ML410.B26C68 2015
  780.92—dc23
  [B]
                                                          2014047980

A catalogue record for this book is available from the British Library.

10 9 8 7 6 5 4 3 2 1

To Oliver and Ellie

# Contents

List of Illustrations      *viii*

Preface      *xi*

1 'Sweet was my mother's milk': 1881–1902      1

2 'Now I came from the battlefield': 1903–1904      22

3 'Two roads are before me': 1905–1906      43

4 'Because my love has forsaken me': 1907–1909      74

5 'Crossing the borders of Transylvania': 1910–1913      98

6 'To plough in winter is hard work': 1914–1918      131

7 'The time to rove has come': 1919–1925      167

8 'The forest rustles, the fields rustle': 1925–1928      207

9 'The wreath is wound around me': 1929–1935      237

10 'Stars, stars, brightly shine': 1936–1938      276

11 'From here is seen the graveyard's border': 1939–1942      309

12 'I see the beautiful sky': 1942–1945      345

Postlude      375

List of Works      *382*

Notes      *392*

Bibliography      *410*

Index      *417*

# Illustrations

**Figures**

1. Map of Hungary following the Treaty of Trianon, 1920s. Source:
   Robert Donald, *The Tragedy of Trianon: Hungary's Appeal to Humanity*
   (London: T. Butterworth Ltd, [1928]), frontispiece.                                  3
2. The second idea from 'Study for the Left Hand'.                                       28
3. The *Kossuth* leitmotif.                                                               32
4. Sonata for Violin and Piano, bars 10–14.                                              35
5. The first idea from the Piano Quintet.                                                38
6. The opening five bars of the Rhapsody for solo piano, op. 1.                          40
7. The motto theme and principal idea from the Scherzo
   (Burlesque), op. 2.                                                                    46
8. The opening theme of the first movement of the Second Suite.                          70
9. The opening theme of the first movement of the First Violin Concerto.                 80
10. The opening theme of the second movement of the First Violin Concerto.               81
11. The opening theme from the first movement of the First String Quartet, first
    and second violins.                                                                  91
12. Extracts from the First String Quartet.                                              93
13. Extracts from the first of Two Romanian Dances.                                      101
14. The first theme from *Bluebeard's Castle*.                                           112
15. Song number 47 from *The Hungarian Folk Song*.                                       113
16 Extracts from *The Wooden Prince*.                                                     134
17. The first seven chords from 'Az én szerelmem'.                                        141
18a and b. (a) Bars 6–7 of the fifth song from Five Songs op. 15; (b) 'Deine Zauber
    binden wieder' from the finale of Beethoven's Ninth Symphony.                         143
19a, b, c and d.  (a) and (b) The melody of bars 5–6 and 11–12 of the first
    movement of the Suite op. 14; and (c) and (d) their imagined folk-music
    source.                                                                              149
20. The opening motif and variants from the first movement of the Second String
    Quartet.                                                                             156
21. The opening of the second theme from the first movement of the Second
    String Quartet.                                                                      156
22. The main pitches of the three ideas in the first thematic group of the second
    movement of the Second String Quartet.                                              158
23 Extracts from the third movement of the Second String Quartet.                        160
24. The openings of the folk melodies of the Eight Hungarian Improvisations.             176
25. Extracts from the First Violin Sonata.                                               183
26. The principal theme of the first movement of the Second Violin Sonata.               191

27. The principal theme of the finale of the Second Violin Sonata.   192
28. The second idea of the finale of the Second Violin Sonata.   193
29. The main thematic material from the Dance Suite.   197
30. The three-note cells of the opening theme of the first movement of the Piano Sonata.   208
31. The opening of the fourth and fifth themes of the first movement of the Piano Sonata.   209
32. The openings of the rondo theme and the third episode from the finale of the Piano Sonata.   211
33. Part of the principal theme of the first movement of the First Piano Concerto.   215
34. The melody from the central section of the second movement of the First Piano Concerto.   216
35. The piano chords used in the ostinato accompaniment in the second movement of the First Piano Concerto.   217
36. The opening idea of the Third String Quartet.   222
37. The three principal ideas of the *seconda parte* of the Third String Quartet.   223
38. Extracts from the Fourth String Quartet.   228
39. Extracts showing thematic connections between *Cantata profana* and Bach's *St Matthew Passion*.   247
40. Extracts from *Cantata profana*.   249
41. Extracts from the first movement of the Second Piano Concerto.   252
42. The first two themes from the finale of the Fifth String Quartet.   271
43. The orchestral layout of *Music for String Instruments, Percussion and Celesta*.   278
44. The first theme of the opening movement of the Sonata for Two Pianos and Percussion.   291
45a and b. (a) The start of the opening theme of the finale of the Sonata for Two Pianos and Percussion as played by the xylophone and timpani; (b) the opening of the theme of the first of Beethoven's *Contretänze*.   295
46. The second and third thematic areas of the finale of the Sonata for Two Pianos and Percussion.   295
47. The main ideas of the third movement (*Sebes*) of *Contrasts*.   302
48. The model pseudo-folk-song structure and the first eight bars of the main theme from the first movement of the Second Violin Concerto.   305
49. Themes from the first and final movements of the Divertimento.   313
50. Extracts from the Sixth String Quartet.   317
51. The opening three bars of the first theme from the first movement of the Concerto for Orchestra.   347
52. The opening of the repeat of theme A from the fourth movement of the Concerto for Orchestra.   351
53. Extracts from the Third Piano Concerto.   367
54. Versions of the rondo theme from the finale of the Third Piano Concerto.   368

## Tables

1. The main tonal areas in *Bluebeard's Castle*.   114
2. The final structure of the one-act pantomime, *The Miraculous Mandarin*.   164–5
3. The structure of the first movement of the Sonata for Two Pianos and Percussion.   289
4. The outline of the structure to the finale of the Sonata for Two Pianos and Percussion.   294
5. Thematic correspondences between the first movement and finale of the Second Violin Concerto.   304
6. The structure of the finale of the Sixth String Quartet.   321–2
7. The structure of the outer sections from the second movement of the Concerto for Orchestra.   349
8. An outline of the structure of the finale of the Concerto for Orchestra.   354

# Preface

What a wee little part of a person's life are his acts and his words! His real life is led in his head, and is known to none but himself. All day long, and every day, the mill of his brain is grinding, and his thoughts (which are but the mute articulation of his feelings) not those other things, are his history. His acts and his words are merely the visible thin crust of his world, with its scattered snow summits and its vacant wastes of water—and they are so trifling a part of his bulk! a mere skin enveloping it. The mass of him is hidden—it and its volcanic fires that toss and boil, and never rest, night nor day. These are his life, and they are not written, and cannot be written. Every day would make a whole book of eighty thousand words—three hundred and sixty-five books a year. Biographies are but the clothes and buttons of the man—the biography of the man himself cannot be written.[1]

Samuel Langhorne Clemens, writing under his *nom de plume* Mark Twain in the preface to his own autobiography, brilliantly expresses the fundamental dilemma of the genre. No human life, even (or particularly) one's own, can be reconstructed and no personality delineated in more than the barest outline. As for the events and opinions of a book's protagonist, adduced as the objective points through which this profile is traced, their selection can reveal as much about the motivations of the biographer as his or her subject.

Although I have sought, wherever possible, the most credible sources for the Bartók revealed in the following pages, I must freely admit that this is but one of very many possible permutations of a narrative that could be constructed. The best one can hope is that this does not do him, or any of the other actors portrayed here, any serious disservice or injustice; and that this book communicates, albeit through a glass darkly, something of a life that was enormously rich and an output (as composer, performer, musicologist and pedagogue) that was extraordinary in terms of both its quantity and quality. There will, of course, be errors and mistakes, and for these I take full responsibility.

Bartók revealed himself not merely through his actions and words, but through his musical works. His scores are not timeless, ahistorical artefacts, but are contingent on the time and place of their composition. I thus took the decision to include the description and analysis of the pieces 'inline' with a discussion of contemporaneous events, because these provide an important part of the context in which the works were composed, in biographical, geographical and intellectual terms. This does, necessarily, break the narrative flow of the composer's 'outer life', but readers who are not interested in the technical niceties of a particular work can skim read or jump across these sections.

During the final year or so of Bartók's life, first Ditta (his second wife) alone and then both of them together, lived in an apartment on West 57th Street in Manhattan. Another émigré Hungarian couple lived in the same building, Pál and Erzsébet Kecskeméti, and Bartók had enormous affection for them. Pál was a sociologist and philosopher, and Erzsi was one of Bartók's former students who had apparently possessed one of the very few privately owned harpsichords in Hungary in the 1930s and had brought this with her to the USA. Pál, who would go on to work as a researcher for the RAND Corporation, had completed the first draft of his major work *Meaning, Communication and Value* in the early years of the Second World War, though it was not eventually published until 1952.[2] This was a consideration of the philosophical 'problem area . . . of evaluation and, more generally, of interpretation of meanings', and in Chapter Ten he examined the 'autonomous values': religious orthodoxy, truth, justice and beauty. Bartók receives no mention in this monograph, but behind Kecskeméti's theorisation of aesthetic value judgements one can imagine the conversations that took place between the two men.

While Kecskeméti accepts the apparent spontaneity of aesthetic experience, he goes on to note that 'There is a characteristic attitude which corresponds to this "aesthetic" element: that in which appearing forms are envisaged purely as such, divorced from practical and private associations.'[3] Developing his argument he comments that:

> the significance of the form of the aesthetic object may very well have representational and other associative factors. It is essential to the beauty of a landscape painting that it represent trees; but we do not perceive that beauty unless we go beyond the abstract, general idea that trees are represented and observe how beauty is achieved by the unique form of the trees in the picture. It is in this sense that we say that the significance of aesthetic form

is encompassed within a visible or audible or 'verbal' appearance. This consideration is also valid for any social or other 'message' that a work of art may convey. Such a message may be essential to the aesthetic value of a work; but what matters from the point of view of aesthetic experience is how the message is shaped by just this unique form.[4]

The ability of individuals to perceive the aesthetic significance of forms may be partly innate, but it needs to be developed through education. The significance of form 'is not timeless; it bears the mark of the historical occasion, the climate of its creation. Its appeal, however, is not limited to that historical location.' Paradoxically, however, 'Works bearing the signature of their time have timeless appeal.'

Kecskeméti recognises the need for 'immanent' criticism – the judgement of the work 'in terms of the body of doctrine underlying the style to which it belongs', but he accepts that there needs to be a balance between this and 'spontaneous sensibility and receptivity'. He concludes this section of his discourse on 'beauty' with the remark that:

A pattern of conformism–nonconformism, characteristic of every field of value, is closely connected with the relatively rational factor in the creation and appreciation of art. Basic practices, techniques, conventions, and principles of the various arts must be learned from masters; but in this field, too, pupils may emancipate themselves. They are primarily helped in this by some articulate doctrine. Innovators in art are often theorists.[5]

For Bartók, his 'masters' were, in particular, Brahms, Liszt, Reger, Busoni, Richard Strauss, Debussy and Stravinsky, and their 'forms' (in the widest sense of the term) reverberate through his output to the end of his life. As a theorist, unlike Schoenberg whose primary discourse was around tonal practice (in texts such as the *Harmonielehre, Structural Functions of Tonal Music* and *Fundamentals of Musical Composition*), Bartók's most important contribution was through the cataloguing and analysis of traditional music (of Hungary, Romania, Slovakia, Serbo-Croatia, Turkey and Algeria). His emancipation as a composer was entirely bound up with the theorisation of these repertoires and this impacted his scores in a technical sense from the tiniest detail to the largest element in terms of structure, tonality, phrase length, scale type, melodic contour, texture and sonority.

At the same time, Bartók placed himself and his music in a very direct feedback loop, taking on the role as his most significant early interpreter across Europe, Britain and the USA, either as soloist or accompanist. The critical responses to Bartók the composer were often closely bound up with reactions to Bartók the performer. Placing the descriptions of the 'immanent forms' (in Kecskeméti's terms) of his works side by side with the comments of his first reviewers will, I hope, offer some balance between Bartók's own views and those elicited by their 'spontaneous reception'.

The following twelve chapters will trace Bartók's career chronologically as composer, ethnomusicologist, pedagogue and pianist against three primary axes. On the first are the principal political and cultural developments in Hungary and Europe stretching from 1881 to 1945, and his responses to them; on the second are his ethnomusicological forays and collections (published and unpublished); and on the third are the personal and professional relationships that had the greatest influence on him (many are documented through letters of which, even now, only a fraction are readily available in English). Among the very many musicians who fell into his orbit in one way or another, and form members of the *dramatis personae*, were Jelly Arányi, Ernő Balogh, Frederick Delius, Ernő Dohnányi, Stefi Geyer, Philip Heseltine, Zoltán Kodály, Hans Koessler, Serge Koussevitzky, Yehudi Menuhin, Fritz Reiner, György Sándor, Tibor Serly, Zoltán Székely, József Szigeti and István Thomán.

There are very many people I must thank for their help and support. I would never have embarked on this project had it not been for the encouragement of Malcolm Gerratt at Yale University Press and throughout he has borne my slow progress with good grace and provided sage advice. Candida Brazil and the editorial team at Yale have provided excellent support through the production process, and I am particularly indebted to Richard Mason for his meticulous and sensitive editing. I am very grateful for the translations provided by Gergely Hubai and George Brassay, and Gergely's additional contextual information and correction of the Hungarian in the text has proved absolutely invaluable. My colleague Ian Sapiro has assisted in the technical work surrounding preparation of the manuscript. Malcolm Gillies offered very helpful advice and generously invited me to speak at the study day at the Royal Festival Hall in January 2011 for the wonderful Philharmonia Orchestra series *Infernal Dance: Inside the World of Béla Bartók*, which he curated. John Fisher, Deputy Vice Chancellor at the University of Leeds, ensured that I had time to complete the work. And finally, my wife Stephanie has put up with my absorption in the research and writing over the past five years, and has accompanied me on numerous occasions to obscure parts of Budapest, Bratislava and New York to follow up particular Bartókian associations.

# 'Sweet was my mother's milk': 1881–1902

Béla Viktor János Bartók was born on 25 March 1881 in Nagyszentmiklós (Great Saint Nicholas) in Torontál County of the 'Kingdom of Hungary within the Lands of the Crown of Saint Stephen'. At that point in the country's chequered history the town lay in the Bánát region of central Hungary and such celebrity as it had within Austria-Hungary largely resulted from the 'treasures of Nagyszentmiklós'. These comprise a group of first- and early second-millennium decorated golden vessels that were discovered in the town in 1799 by a Serbian peasant called Vuin Neru and taken to the imperial capital of Vienna, where they remain on display in the city's Kunsthistorisches Museum. Beyond this, Nagyszentmiklós was a relatively prosperous if unremarkable agricultural and market community. The population statistics for 1880 indicate that of its 10,836 inhabitants, around one third were ethnically Romanian and just over two fifths were German, with Hungarians and Serbs each forming slightly more than a tenth of the population;[1] in terms of religious affiliation, half of the inhabitants were Roman Catholic and most of the rest were Eastern Orthodox. This racial and religious mix reflected the diversity of late nineteenth-century Hungary as a whole, in which Magyars, the ethnic Hungarians, formed the minority in Magyarország, the country that bore their name.

The Hungary (or alternatively 'Transleithania') of the composer's early years was heterogeneous in terms of the racial origins of its inhabitants,[2] and in 1890 the Magyars formed just 42.8 per cent of a population approaching twenty million.[3] Romanians, Germans, Slovaks, Croats, Serbs, Ruthenians, Jews and Gypsies coexisted as the majority in a state that to at least some degree repressed and penalised them for their non-Magyar ethnicity. Jürg Hoensch has argued that the policy of Magyarisation adopted after the Ausgleich (or 'compromise') of 1867 effectively denied them full citizenship, for 'only Hungarian citizens "of a separate mother tongue" were formally recognised and nominally accorded equal civic rights, the unrestricted use of their native language in the lower levels of the administration, the judicial system, and elementary and secondary schools'.[4] In order to promote political integration, the primary language required to be taught in schools at every level was Hungarian, and schools serving the non-Magyar communities had to demonstrate their ability to teach in Hungarian or face the threat of closure. Social and political advancement was thus dependent upon assimilation.[5]

The process of integration of some non-Magyars appears to have been rather more spontaneous than some earlier historians have suggested. Géza Jeszenszky remarks that it was 'due to economic transformation, urbanization and "embourgeoisement"', resulting from 'the demands of society, the interests of the individual, and internal migration' rather than as a consequence of coercion.[6] For parts of the population assimilation was initially relatively unproblematic. In particular Jews, who had been emancipated in 1849 and 1867, rapidly adopted both the Hungarian language and the national ideals of the gentry.[7] Many were absorbed into the developing urban middle classes as doctors, lawyers, bankers and merchants, and by 1910 they formed around 25 per cent of the population of Budapest.[8] Although the government policy was actively to encourage integration and oppose anti-Semitism, anti-Jewish feeling was openly exhibited. As Iván Berend and György Ránki note:

> on this fertile ground of the antithesis of agriculture and industry, of countryside and town, of rural and urban values, nationalism flourished. It fed on hatred of aliens, both insiders and outsiders, and was conjoined to a kind of conservative, romantic anti-capitalism.[9]

Other ethnic groups, especially the Romanian peasantry of Transylvania (a region ceded to Hungary in 1867 as a result of the Ausgleich), regarded Magyarisation as a much greater threat. Demands increased for the restoration of the autonomy of the Transylvanian principality, either as a constituent of a federal 'Greater Austria' or in union with the kingdom of Romania (which had been part of the Ottoman Empire until 1878). These were fuelled in the first decade of the twentieth century by irredentist Romanian popular politicians who 'were openly proclaiming the annexation of Transylvania as the supreme object of the nation's policy'.[10]

Nagyszentmiklós held a liminal position, sitting almost exactly on what would become the border between Romania, Hungary and Yugoslavia after the post-war Treaty of Trianon of 1920. To the west and north, the population was predominantly Magyar, to the east, Romanian, and to the south, Serbian

Figure 1. Map of Hungary following the Treaty of Trianon, 1920s.

(Slavic), though with a very substantial pocket of ethnic Germans. This latter group, descendants in the main of the so-called *Schwabenzug* (the waves of German immigrants who arrived from many parts of Europe after 1723), tended to occupy a section of the town known as Németszentmiklós (German St Nicholas). Citizens of Nagyszentmiklós would naturally have been fully aware of issues of racial, ethnic and linguistic difference, but in the context of largely peaceful coexistence within county, kingdom and empire (Fig. 1).

The Bartók family name derives from Bartalan or Bertalan, the Hungarian form of Bartholomew, and the composer's ancestry can be traced over the previous five generations from the far north to the deep south of the country. His paternal great-great-grandfather, Gergely (or Gregorius, c. 1740–1825), was apparently a man of modest means – Tibor Tallián describes him as a serf[11] – and he lived in the village of Borsodszirák, close to Miskolc in northern Hungary.[12] Despite his poverty, as Denijs Dille notes, the fact that Gergely could count on a notary, a cantor (or precentor) and organist, and a priest among his three sons who survived infancy, suggests that he was likely to have been a man of at least some educational attainment.[13]

János (1785–1876), the eldest son of Gergely and his wife Mária (née Gondos, c. 1753–1820), was an adventurous youth. According to family lore, he left home when he was only eleven or twelve years old, and was present at

the Battle of Győr on 14 June 1809, when Napoleon's troops roundly defeated
the Austro-Hungarian forces. By 1822 János seems to have been employed as a
notary in Magyarcsernye (now Nova Crnja in Serbia), clearly an achievement
of note if he did come from such a humble background. Having survived into
his nineties, he died in the town of Nagybecskerek, three hundred kilometres
to the south. Baron József Eötvös de Vásárosnamény's three-volume novel, *The
Village Notary: A Romance of Hungarian Life*, both describes the nature and
significance of the notary in public life and elucidates the complex social hierarchy of the time.[14] An endnote from the first volume outlines the latter aspect:

> We will take this opportunity to say a few words about the terms 'nobleman'
> and 'peasant', which frequently occur in *The Village Notary*, and indeed in
> most Hungarian works. The term nobleman, in the general Hungarian
> acceptation, means neither more nor less than a freeman; and the peasant,
> as the unprivileged class of the population, may be said to be in a state of
> villanage. The privileges of the Hungarian constitution, namely, liberty of
> speech, freedom from unwarranted arrest, the privilege of not being
> subjected to corporal punishment, the right to elect their own magistrates,
> and a variety of similar immunities, are, in all the charters, described in
> terms which for a long time caused them to be confined to the ancient
> conquerors of the country, or to those persons who obtained the freedom of
> Hungary by a grant of royal letters patent.
>
> The rest of the community, the Jews, Razen [Serbs], gipsies, Russniaks
> [Ukrainians], and other tribes, are mentioned as 'hospites', guests or stran-
> gers, who have no political rights. Whether bound to the soil, like the peas-
> ants, or migratory like the Jews and gipsies, the 'hospites' were alike
> unprotected by law and at the mercy of all the whims, neglects, and cruelties
> of a legislature, which bears traces at once of the Turkish neighbours and
> the pedantic vindictiveness of the Hapsburgs. It was to break the yoke that
> for many centuries weighed down upon the unfortunate 'villains' and
> 'aliens' that the Reform party exerted itself against the Hungarian
> Conservatives and the Court of Vienna.[15]

Both János Bartók's son, who was also called János (1816–1877), and his
grandson, Béla (1855–1888), were educators by profession and were the headmasters of the Magyar Királyi Földműves Iskola (Royal Hungarian Agricultural
School) in Nagyszentmiklós. This school was established in 1800 by the local
aristocrat Kristóf Nákó (or Nacu) to serve the needs of the peasants on his
estate.[16] The era during which Bartók's father and grandfather served as headmasters of the agricultural school was a significant one. In 1868 the reformist

minister József Eötvös (author of *The Village Notary*) had introduced an Elementary Education Act that profoundly affected both the delivery of education and its impact on the ethnic minorities in Hungary. As Pál Bődy notes, 'This law assured organizational autonomy and self-government to all churches, associations, and school systems, with particular guarantees of freedom of choice in the language of instruction and religious education. The law also authorized townships to establish tax-supported public schools, where all children would receive instruction in their native language.'[17] Statistics published in 1876, in *The Year-Book of Education for 1878*, record overall literacy rates of 74 per cent for school leavers across the Hungarian system, some indication of the effectiveness of the government's policy.[18]

What kind of institution, then, was the Magyar Királyi Földműves Iskola in Nagyszentmiklós? Lajos Lesznai describes the composer's grandfather János rather grandly as 'Professor of Economics',[19] whereas for Tallián, both his father (Béla) and his grandfather were the headmasters of 'a college for local Swabian peasant boys having completed, according to the rules, four forms of elementary school, but who, for the most part, had finished only two. The headmaster supervised twelve resident pupils in a central building some three kilometres from the village.'[20] Writing in 1902, Alexander Vörös, the director of the Agricultural Academy in Magyaróvár, notes that such farming or tillage schools were intended to 'educate the sons of small farmers and peasants in a way which will enable them to make a living as managers of small farms, or as foremen and head-labourers on large estates. The course of these schools is of two years duration and of an entirely practical character.'[21]

Béla was the seventh of eleven children born to János and his wife Matild (née Ronkovics); Dille was not able to trace her date of birth accurately – it may have been 1825 or 1828 – but she is attested to have died in January 1885, when the composer was three.[22] It is quite possible, as Dille notes, that it was from his grandmother Matild that Bartók inherited his slight build as well as a familial peculiarity of the hand that has been labelled 'la main Bartók-Ronkovics'. This involves an average-sized hand having index, middle and ring fingers of almost equal length.[23] From the paternal side of the family he seems to have inherited a thumb that he could stretch an unusually large distance from his palm.

Béla senior's secondary education was at the Piarist high school in Budapest and the Kolozsvár (Cluj-Napoca) *reáliskola* (real school) 240 kilometres northeast of Nagyszentmiklós, and he studied for a year at the Agricultural Academy of Mosonmagyaróvár (near Győr, to the south of Pozsony). Two photographs present him as apparently somewhat distant and intense respectively. In the first he has his right hand thrust into his jacket in a vaguely Napoleonic pose, while he rests his head on his left hand and exhibits a rather glazed expression;

in the second, a three-quarter profile, his arms are folded on the back of a chair, his left hand lightly grasping his coat sleeve, and the body language suggests some unease. It is unwise, however, to draw too subtle a psychological reading from these portraits, for they are carefully staged and reveal the standard ploys of photographers of the day to avoid the blurring that resulted from movement during the relatively long exposures required. Certainly, though, a very clear physical likeness between Béla senior and his son is evident.

Dille remarks of the composer's father that:

> With lively manners, he had a typically Hungarian character: passionate, very cheerful, enjoying luxury and the good life, dancing and the distractions of company, always very neat in his appearance, dressing with taste and in a distinguished style (apparently a characteristic of the Ronkovics); he was spoken of as being 'all collar and cuffs', in the family. All in all, he was a gentleman such as was found in the middle class of the time.[24]

Despite, or indeed perhaps because of, his seemingly humble antecedents, Béla senior claimed ancestry from the Hungarian gentry that formed nearly 5 per cent of the population towards the end of the nineteenth century. This group sat in the middle of the highly stratified social pyramid which had at its top the nobility and at the bottom the agrarian proletariat, but with an extraordinary degree of granularity that included land-owning nobility, the *haute bourgeoisie*, the rich middle class, the gentry, lesser artisans, land-owning peasants and agricultural workers.[25] His position as a significant local figure may have encouraged Béla senior to feel that he needed to be able to demonstrate a rather more fitting social status, and the title he adopted was Szuhafői (indicating 'of Szuhafő', associated with the village of the same name, around twenty kilometres to the north-west of Borsodszirák). Although the composer apparently assumed the same title in his youth and would later encourage his own eldest son Béla to undertake genealogical research to verify it (even making use of it as late as 1923 in his marriage to Ditta Pásztory), there seems to have been no justifiable basis for it.[26]

The composer's mother, Paula Voit, was born on 16 January 1857 in Turócszentmárton in Turóc County (now Martin in Slovakia), some 200 kilometres north-east of Pozsony (Bratislava). She was the eighth of ten children born to Moritz Voit (1818–1873) and his wife Terézia (née Polereczky, 1821–1873),[27] who were of German stock. Both her parents had died by the time Paula was sixteen, leaving her to look after herself as a young woman. She trained as a teacher at the Pozsony Teacher Training College, developing as a reasonably proficient pianist, albeit one who does not seem to have particularly relished the public stage. She undoubtedly placed a very strong emphasis on personal integrity and modesty, characteristics she would instil in her children and grandchildren. The composer's youngest son, Péter, writes of his grandmother being responsible for his father's development 'both as a musician and a man of certain principles',[28] and he remembers how she invented an impossibly saintly imaginary child to act as a role model for him while he was growing up.

After graduating, Paula took up a teaching post in Nagyszentmiklós in 1876, having been invited to the town by a local dignitary called Adolf Kós. Her move to the south of Hungary was strongly influenced by the presence there of her brother Lajos, who was the steward on the estate of Count Géza Wenckheim in nearby Csorvás. (Lajos had befriended Wenckheim when they were both students at the agricultural school in Mosonmagyaróvár.) Béla Bartók senior took over as the director of the agricultural school when his father died in 1877, assuming at the age of just twenty-two the financial responsibility for his mother and his siblings. He met Paula as a result of the piano lessons she gave to his sisters and the pair married on 5 April 1880. Béla, their first child, was born on Friday, 25 March in the following year.

Béla senior took up the cello and organized an amateur band of his social peers, directed by a local Gypsy musician, to play dance music. There is little objective evidence to suggest that he exhibited any great prowess as a musician, and when he died his son was still rather too young to have been able to form a particularly sophisticated judgement of his ability. However, it seems that in retrospect his father's musical tendencies took on significance for Béla junior and in an autobiographical note written in 1921 he would remark that:

> My father, the director of an agricultural school, demonstrated quite considerable musical talent; he played the piano, organized an amateur orchestra, learnt the cello, so that he could perform in it as a cellist, and even tried his hand at composing dance pieces.[29]

Stefan Zweig, who was born in the same year as Bartók but on the other side of the Leitha river, describes the period in Austria leading up to the First World War as 'the Golden Age of Security'.[30] It was, he argues, a time when the state guaranteed stability, when 'every duty was exactly prescribed' and 'All that was radical, all violence, seemed impossible in an age of reason.'[31] The early years of the composer were certainly spent in an environment that was stable, comfortable and bourgeois, in which educational attainment was highly valued and music regularly performed. As one of two children (his sister Erzsébet Clementina Paula, affectionately known as Elza or Böske, was born on 11 June 1885), he would certainly have been likely to receive more individual attention from his parents than they could have had from theirs. He heard both the Hungarian and German languages spoken in his own household, but the sounds of Romanian and Serbian would also have been widely found in the community of Nagyszentmiklós, given its ethnic mix. Looking back to his childhood when he was almost fifty years old, in a letter to Octavian Beu the composer made it clear that he hadn't had any experience of what he would regard as folk music at this stage of his life, remarking that 'neither at Nagyszentmiklós nor at Beszterce or Nagyszőllős did I receive any folkloristic musical impressions'.[32]

In some respects Bartók was a rather slow developer as an infant and according to his mother, he was late learning to walk and was two and a quarter years old before he was able to talk. Yet he had shown, for some time before, a distinct interest in music and he responded positively to the singing of his nursemaid. In a study of his father's illnesses, Bartók's eldest son Béla junior noted that whereas his father was quite healthy at birth, he developed a very unpleasant rash on his face and body that lasted from the age of three months (as a result of a vaccination against smallpox) until he was five years old.[33] Bartók's son remarked that 'the permanent itchiness, the people shocked with the sight of the spots, and the many medical treatments without any result made him a reticent child, and this did not make the recovery much quicker either'.[34] A remedy for the eczema appears to have been finally found, in the form of arsenic-based drugs.[35] As a child Bartók also suffered from recurrent bronchitis, and in an attempt to resolve this condition when he was six years old he joined his father (accompanied by his Aunt Sarolta) for a 'cold water cure' in the spa town of Sankt Radegund bei Graz in Styria, Austria. In a travel diary Béla senior described the treatment (which was a modified version of the Preissnitz cure) in some detail. It sounds quite brutal, involving patients being woken at four o'clock in the morning, wrapped in a wet sheet, doused in cold water and dried in front of an open window, the sequence being repeated every twelve hours. Spartan as this regime may sound, it seems to have been effective and the bronchitis improved.

Although it is far too easy to indulge in crass psychological profiling based on limited objective evidence, there can be little doubt that these early developmental issues and illnesses must have had some impact on the formation of the young musician's personality. The death of his father (who suffered from Addison's Disease) as the result of a stroke on 4 August 1888 was inevitably a catastrophe for the family and left his mother in the position of sole breadwinner with two young children to support. Paula re-established her career as a piano teacher from another house in Nagyszentmiklós and in the following year she, her two children and her sister Irma moved to Nagyszőllős (now

Vynohradiv in the Ukraine, close to the border with Romania and north-eastern Hungary) to take up a post as a teacher. Nagyszőllős was a small town and in 1891 it is recorded as having 774 houses and 5,187 inhabitants (of whom 2,437 were Hungarian, 742 were German, and 1,947 were Ruthenian – Ukrainian – by ethnicity).[36] The family lived in a house that stood opposite Perényi Castle, the home of the eponymous aristocratic family, and Béla enrolled at the local civil school (polgár iskola) in September 1890.

As a result of his childhood illnesses, Bartók's relationship with his mother, as both parent and educator, was particularly close. In a letter written to her grandson Béla in 1921 about his father's upbringing, she described his early musical experiences and abilities: how he was able to tap out rhythms on a drum when he was only three; how he showed a particular interest in the occasional performances by Gypsy musicians in the town; how he was excited by her playing of dance pieces; and how he could pick out as many as forty tunes on the piano by the age of four.[37] He began learning the piano at her instruction when he was five years old and he seems to have developed extremely rapidly. By the age of eight he had considerable technical competence, attracting the attention of an organist called Keresztély Altdörfer who was visiting from the town of Sopron.[38] At the same time Bartók began his first steps in composition, writing in 1890 a number of little piano pieces, including *Walczer* (Waltz), *Változó darab* (Changing piece), *Mazurka, A budapesti tornaverseny* (Budapest gymnastics competition), the First Sonatina and *Oláh darab* (Wallachian piece). Works extant from the following year are largely dance tunes, especially polkas and ländler.

Drawing on the testimony of the sister of Endre Nagy, a friend of Bartók's in Nagyszőllős, as reported by Károly Kristóf in 1952 in the newspaper *Magyar Nemzet*, Serge Moreux asserts that Bartók did in fact gain some early (albeit limited) experience of traditional music of a sort while living there.[39] According to Kristóf, Endre, the teenage son of the schoolmaster Gábor Nagy, was given the task of minding Béla during the summer vacation. Endre had a holiday job as a harvest overseer for the Abony-Lator estate and the two boys were privy to the evening entertainments in the barn where the harvesters lived, and heard them repeating a folk song in macaronic verse (a mixture of various East European languages) while their vegetable soup bubbled in the pot. Bartók is claimed to have attempted to copy the song down in musical notation.

At the end of the summer of 1891 the ten-year-old Béla was sent off to study at the gymnasium in Nagyvárad (now Oradea in western Romania), almost 200 kilometres south of Nagyszőllős, living with his widowed aunt Emma Voit and her five children: Emma, Ottó, Lajos, Ernő and Ervin. Although there was no gymnasium in Nagyszőllős, it may seem curious given the very close bond with his mother that she should choose to send him to a school that was such a great distance away, but there can be little doubt that this was driven by a desire for Béla to have the greatest possible academic and musical opportunities. In Nagyvárad he was taught the piano by Ferenc Kersch, the organist at the Roman Catholic basilica, who had studied with Liszt and was also a composer. As early as 18 October 1891, Béla wrote to his mother that he had learnt Mozart's twelfth Sonata (K. 332 in F major) but that Kersch felt this was too easy for him and he was now studying the Fantasy and Sonata in C minor, K. 475/457. Other works he practised at the time included the Weber *Rondo Brillante* in E♭ major, and it was perhaps pieces such as this (which he got under his fingers very rapidly but with only partial technical grasp) that led his mother to suggest later that Kersch encouraged too superficial an approach. Béla's studies at the school run by the Catholic Premonstratensian order were short lived and not particularly successful – he was absent from 163 lessons during the time he was there because of illness – and he returned to Nagyszőllős in April 1892, suffering with an eye problem.[40] Paula (at least in retrospect) laid the blame for her son's relatively weak scholastic performance squarely on his teachers and was firmly convinced that they favoured children from wealthy backgrounds.

Béla's first appearance on the public stage as both pianist and composer took place on 1 May 1892, at the age of eleven.[41] Among the pieces he played at a charity concert to raise funds for poor students was the first movement of Beethoven's *Waldstein* Sonata op. 53, a work of considerable difficulty that gives an indication of just how technically accomplished he was by then.[42] He also performed an extended composition of his own that lasted for around twenty minutes – *A Duna folyása* ('The Course of the Danube'), which his mother had helped him to notate. *A Duna folyása* musically depicted the great river's progress from source to sea in nine programmatic sections (the arrival of the Danube in Budapest was musically denoted by a *csárdás*). While its musical language is redolent of Czerny and Diabelli, as Pierre Citron notes, it shows 'the influences of Haydn, Mozart and Schumann mixed with reminiscences of Gypsy dances and popular songs'.[43] Paula recalled Béla receiving a tremendous ovation and being presented with a number of bouquets.

Further driven by the desire to promote her son's education, Paula took up an offer made by a school inspector for a year's leave of absence and the family set off again in the autumn of 1892, this time for her home town of Pozsony. Béla began studying at the Katholikus Főgimnázium (the Catholic Grammar School) in a building in the Old Town that formerly housed a monastery of the Order of St Clare on Kapitulska. He took piano lessons with László Erkel (1844–1896), the son of Ferenc Erkel (the most successful nineteenth-century Hungarian operatic composer).

Unfortunately, his mother failed to find the permanent post she was hoping for and before the start of the next academic year the family upped sticks yet again and moved on, in September 1893. This time they went to the town of Beszterce towards the extreme east of Hungary, one of the seven fortified Saxon towns of Transylvania (now Bistrița in the Transylvanian region of Romania). As there was no Hungarian language school, Béla studied at the German gymnasium. The time spent at Beszterce seems to have offered little in terms of formative musical experiences, and his biographers (drawing largely on his mother's testimony) tend to note that he was the most proficient pianist in the town. He continued to practise the piano and compose, writing between 1890 and 1894 a number of small dance pieces (polkas, waltzes, mazurkas and ländler), two sonatinas, and an *Andante con Variazioni* in addition to *A Duna folyása*, and assigning them opus numbers running from 1 to 31. This was a relatively short-lived interlude, however, and in April 1894 Paula successfully applied for a post at the Teachers' Training College in Pozsony.

The period of stability that ensued from 1894 until 1899 – the first since his father's death – enabled Béla to develop intellectually and musically. He returned to the Catholic Grammar School in Pozsony in mid-April 1894 and despite a different curriculum to that in Beszterce, finished his academic year in the third form with excellent results (much to his mother's delight and relief). He took up again his studies in piano and harmony with Erkel at the beginning of the following school year, continuing until the latter's death in 1896.

As the most cultured Hungarian city outside Budapest, Pozsony offered Béla the opportunity to attend concerts and operas and hear musicians, both excellent and less good (as he would remark in an autobiographical note penned in 1918).[44] He worked with Erkel on such staple fare as Clementi's *Gradus ad Parnassum* and Bach's *Well-Tempered Clavier*, as well as pieces by Chopin and Liszt. He also developed an interest in orchestration, purchasing the score for Beethoven's *Leonore No. 3* overture with his pocket money; and at the same time he continued to compose, restarting his work list with a fresh set of opus numbers running up to op. 21 for the more elaborate pieces written between 1894 and 1898. Many of these have been lost, but they apparently included four piano sonatas, two string quartets, a piano quartet and piano quintet, two fantasies and a sonata for violin, and a number of piano pieces. A sonata for piano in G minor demonstrates the influence exerted by Beethoven on the young composer; as Günter Weiss-Aigner has pointed out, references to, or traces of, the Fifth Symphony, the 'Pathétique' Sonata in C minor (op. 13 no. 8) and the 'Tempest' Sonata in D minor (op. 31 no. 2) can be found in these works.[45]

Erkel's death in December 1896 was a further blow to the fifteen-year-old student, and he subsequently took instruction in piano and harmony from a teacher called Anton Hyrtl. Bartók began to play the organ in the school chapel in 1895 and it was around this time that he became disenchanted with the Roman Catholic faith to which he had previously been a pious adherent, a result it seems of the over-enthusiasm of his theology teacher's 'exhaustive instruction in the history, ethics, rites and dogmas of the Church'.[46] Sándor Albrecht (1885–1958) was a fellow pupil at the Catholic Grammar School, and would later follow him as a student to the Royal National Hungarian Academy of Music in Budapest. In a reminiscence published in the final year of his life, Albrecht looked back to the first time he met Bartók at grammar school.[47] He remarked on his deference to his teachers, a matter of significance because 'later on he was decidedly hostile to such polite practices, without ever actually erring on the side of bad manners'. These two interlaced elements – religious scepticism and a distrust of social formality and hierarchy (the bedrock of Hungarian society) – became increasingly distinctive personality traits. In an obituary, Ottó Gombosi remarked that 'he did not understand the little amenities of sociability or the innocent half-lies of daily life and rejected them with a child-like, brusque, perturbed amazement'. For Bertalan Pethő, Bartók would be characterised in adult life by 'orderliness, meticulousness, high level of aspiration, strict morals, rigid way of living, diligence, sense of duty, reliability [and] conscientiousness', attributes, he argues, that indicate the 'melancholic' personality type.[48] At the same time, the collecting, ordering and cataloguing of objects, both physical (butterflies, beetles, stones, peasant artefacts and so on) and musical (melodies and songs), would become a near fetish.

Such behaviours and mannerisms, among others, have encouraged a suggestion that Bartók may have exhibited the symptoms of Asperger syndrome, one of the so-called Autism Spectrum Disorders.[49] According to the *Diagnostic and Statistical Manual of Mental Disorders, Fourth Edition* (DSM–IV), published by the American Psychiatric Association, the criteria for diagnosis are:

Qualitative impairment in social interaction, as manifested by at least two of the following:

- marked impairment in the use of multiple nonverbal behaviors such as eye-to-eye gaze, facial expression, body postures, and gestures to regulate social interaction
- failure to develop peer relationships appropriate to developmental level

- lack of spontaneous seeking to share enjoyment, interests, or achievements with other people (for example, by a lack of showing, bringing, or pointing out objects of interest to other people)

- lack of social or emotional reciprocity

Restricted repetitive and stereotyped patterns of behavior, interests, and activities, as manifested by at least one of the following:

- an encompassing preoccupation with one or more stereotyped and restricted patterns of interest that is abnormal either in intensity or focus
- apparently inflexible adherence to specific, nonfunctional routines or rituals
- stereotyped and repetitive motor mannerisms (for example, hand or finger flapping or twisting, or complex whole-body movements)

- persistent preoccupation with parts of objects[50]

The psychologist Michael Fitzgerald, Henry Marsh Professor of Child and Adolescent Psychiatry at Trinity College Dublin, argues that a number of highly creative individuals have displayed Asperger symptoms according to these criteria – from Swift to Bruce Chatwin, Spinoza to A. J. Ayer, Mozart to Glenn Gould and Van Gogh to Andy Warhol. Fitzgerald indicates that Bartók largely meets the criteria as defined in DSM–IV, with the exception of demonstrating motor clumsiness. Of course, the evidence Fitzgerald draws on for his diagnosis is necessarily second-hand, limited in scope and chiefly taken from two principal sources – Stevens and Chalmers. While some of the finer detail may appear misguided or even misinformed, the broad conclusion merits further consideration and will be returned to in the course of this study.

Many of the works Bartók composed between 1895 and 1897 are no longer extant, but of those which are, the first of the 'Drei Klavierstücke', thought by Dille to have been written either in 1896 or 1897, is indicative of his progress by that juncture. It is a fleet-of-foot Presto in the spirit of the more sprightly of Mendelssohn's *Songs without Words* (such as the one in C major, op. 102 no. 3). Bartók's small-scale character piece largely concerns itself with the presentation of an attractive eight-bar phrase, which has something of the disposition of the first theme of the Scherzo from Mendelssohn's *Midsummer Night's Dream* music. In Bartók's Klavierstück this passage reappears untransformed three times and the piece concludes with a prolonged coda, though there is little attempt to develop the material significantly. While it is derivative in style – arguably as much pastiche as original composition – it is done very competently and demonstrates that by his mid-teens Bartók exhibited a considerable degree of musical sophistication as well as the ability to write effectively for the piano. Indeed, the notes lie sufficiently gratefully under the fingers as to suggest that the compositional process at this stage arose as much from the re-inscription of musical gestures learnt through the fingers as from conscious planning at the writing desk.

The *Scherzo oder Fantasie* in B major for piano of 1897 reveals the unmistakeable influence of Schumann and Brahms while also looking to the scherzos of Chopin. Although not particularly stylistically advanced, there is again considerable technical and musical assurance on display and a broader tonal palette. The initial eight-bar phrase commences with a figure in octaves that tentatively slides upwards before assertively leaping up a sixth over the arpeggiation of a dominant seventh, with a hemiola rhythm that calls to mind the main theme of the first movement of Schumann's Third Symphony. This rising shape is balanced by a steady descent to a closure in which a dissonant C$^\times$ in the right hand held over a B major broken chord in the left for a bar resolves to D$\sharp$. On its varied repeat the eight-bar phrase modulates to D$\sharp$ minor rather than the dominant or relative minor and there is considerable byplay between this tonal area (and its dominant, A$\sharp$/B$\flat$ major) and the tonic B major. A sustained trio that retains the hemiola rhythm of the first section is tonally mobile and has a developmental function, with a key signature that suggests B minor despite the repeated cadences on B major and the Brahmsian double thirds over a pedal B. The reprise is almost an exact repeat of the opening section other than the interpolation of four bars of dominant chords at bars 281–4, and finishes obliquely with a progression from G$^7$ (a renotated German sixth in B major) to the tonic.

During Bartók's final academic year at the Catholic Grammar School (1898–9), he prepared for advanced musical education and was accepted at the Vienna Conservatory after an audition in December 1898, with the offer of an imperial scholarship. However, after taking the advice of his friend Ernő Dohnányi (1877–1960), who was a native of Pozsony and regularly returned to perform there, he decided instead to apply to the Royal National Hungarian Academy of Music in Budapest (which at that stage was on Andrássy Avenue and called the Liszt Academy), where Dohnányi had been studying since 1894. Bartók successfully passed a private audition in January 1899, and was accepted for study with István Thomán (piano) and Hans Koessler (composition). He was subsequently required, however, to undertake a formal audition in front of the director of the Academy, Ödön Mihalovich, his two prospective teachers and Viktor Herzfeld (the professor of musical theory), before he could take up his place. In February he suffered another serious bout of illness, and Sándor Albrecht, four years his junior and taking piano lessons from him, reports how Béla's mother wrote to Sándor's father advising that her son had to stop teaching Sándor because of sickness and vomiting blood – something that appeared potentially life-threatening at the time. Fortunately, the symptoms proved much less serious than feared and Bartók recuperated in a resort close to Pozsony called Friedliche Hütte. His school studies were completed by the summer of 1899, with good examination results in most subjects, and he displayed particular excellence in mathematics, physics and history.

Bartók moved to Budapest during a period of enormous change and development for the city, which was to a large degree associated with the Hungarian millennial celebrations of 1896. Dorothy Barenscott has remarked how 'Looking out across the Danube River in 1894, from one side of Budapest to the other, one would have been greeted with the clamor, bustle, and din of a metropolis under accelerated construction.'[51] Major landmarks recently completed or being erected at the time of the composer's arrival included The Heroes' Square at the upper end of Andrássy út in front of City Park (in which the millennial exhibition was staged and which housed the newly constructed Vajdahunyad Castle), the Central Market Hall on Fővám tér, the immense St Stephen's Basilica (completed in 1905), the visually stunning Parliament overlooking the Danube (opened in 1902), and the new underground railway (only the second in the world) modelled on that of London. For Barenscott, 'With the simultaneous construction of the underground railway and the Hungarian Parliament building, the city of Budapest was articulated through built spaces at once devoted to the founding myths of Magyarization and to ideals associated with bourgeois urban modernity and cosmopolitan world exhibition.' Budapest was, at the same time, a city of immigrants, in which in 1890 fewer than 40 per cent of its nearly three quarters of a million inhabitants were local born, its population reflecting the ethnic and linguistic diversity of Hungary as a whole.

István Thomán (1862–1940), Bartók's piano professor at the Liszt Academy, had been taught by Ferenc Erkel (the father of Bartók's teacher in Pozsony), Robert Volkmann and most importantly, Liszt. According to Charles Hopkins, Thomán 'did much to assure the continuity of Liszt's artistic credo in his native country, laying particular emphasis on the elimination of extraneous artificiality in performance.'[52] In 1927, the year that Thomán celebrated his sixty-fifth birthday, Bartók recalled his time studying with him, writing about him with enormous affection and warmth. It seems that Bartók had made a considerable impression on Thomán at his audition, to the extent that a few months later Thomán generously invited him to attend a performance of Beethoven's Ninth

Symphony by the Budapest Philharmonic Orchestra conducted by Hans Richter, regarding this as an essential opportunity for an aspiring young musician.

When he began to study at the Liszt Academy in the autumn of 1899, Bartók had considerable technical proficiency but less finesse, and in his own words 'must have been a real "savage" as a pianist'.[53] He learnt from Thomán 'the correct position of the hands and all the different "natural" and "summarizing" movements' that his teacher had in turn been taught by Liszt, including 'the mastery of poetically colouring the piano tone'. Thomán believed his influence should be natural rather than artificial, by which he meant that the teacher should allow the individuality of his students to shine through, and his pedagogical approach was founded on demonstration rather than abstract theory. The stronger students, such as Bartók, would not simply emulate his performance, however, but take inspiration from it to develop their own individual and original interpretations. Bartók felt that Thomán was able to draw from students what was latent within them and wrote of his approach as being 'not to *impose* ideas on the pupil but to *awaken* the correct ones in him'.[54] However, and this is revealing in respect to the suggestion that Bartók may have displayed autistic tendencies, it was the warm-hearted, human side of his teacher that he particularly drew attention to in the final paragraphs of his celebratory essay, remarking that Thomán was a mentor and 'paternal good friend' to his students. And in summary, 'the harmonious entity made up of great circumspection, superior tact, deep love of mankind, and superb expertise are needed in order to achieve the results of István Thomán these past forty years'.[55]

In Thomán's pedagogical work, *The Technique of Piano Playing: Fundamental Exercises for the Mastery of Even and Virtuosic Playing*, he summarised his approach to the development of pianistic technique.[56] The exercises published there make little attempt to be musically interesting, but stress technical and physical development. At the same time Thomán was clearly pragmatic in his approach, noting for instance in his discussion of octaves that 'I do not prescribe any definite carriage of the hand for the octaves, since with great pianists who have a brilliant technique we can see that their wonderful octave passages are performed with totally different carriage of the hand. . . . The talented student will feel instinctively what sort of touch he has to use in certain octave passages'.[57]

Bartók's first public performance in Budapest took place on 31 March 1900 in a 'house concert' held in the Organ and Concert Hall of the Academy by students of Thomán, Dávid Popper, Adél Passy-Cornet, Jenő Hubay and Kálmán Chován. Here he played the first movement of Beethoven's third piano concerto, accompanied by his teacher.

It was on Thomán's recommendation that Bartók had been taken on as a composition student by the German composer Hans (János) Koessler

(1853–1926), who had joined the staff of the Academy in 1882. He was a cousin of Reger. Koessler's output was relatively slim, though it included two symphonies, concertos for violin and cello, several chamber works and the opera *Der Münzenfranz* (premiered in 1903). His chamber music in particular, including the four-movement F minor Sextet published in 1902, demonstrates the pervasive influence of the sound world of Brahms and to some extent that of Schumann. In this Koessler seems to have characterised the musical *zeitgeist* of the institution, and as a critic reported in January 1903, 'the general spirit at the Academy, no matter how they try to cover it up, is German. Brahms is their idol, and the young musicians are taught to worship him.'[58] Certainly, if Bartók showed Koessler the 'Drei Klavierstücke' he had composed in 1896/7, the elder composer would surely have been impressed by the aspiring student's success in assimilating the language of Brahms's mature small-scale piano works in his Intermezzo in C minor. Its velvety richness of harmony and voicing, its chromaticism and its control of pace go well beyond pastiche, and all betoken considerable technical and emotional maturity in its young composer.

One of the early works Bartók wrote under Koessler's tutelage was a group of songs composed in 1900, described on the title page as 'Liebeslieder'. These include lieder to texts by Nikolaus Lenau ('Diese Rose pflück ich hier', in E♭ minor) and Friedrich Bodenstedt ('Ich fühle deinen Odem' from the Orientalist collection of poems *Die Lieder der Mirza Schaffy*, in E♭ major). While the Schumann of *Frauenliebe und Leben* exerts some stylistic influence, so too do Brahms, Wolf and Strauss. Mendelssohn, as part of his op. 71, had also set 'Diese Rose pflück ich hier', and it is conceivable that Bartók could have been aware of this version, though his own setting is considerably darker in tone. Although they employ a relatively conventional late nineteenth-century Germanic musical vernacular, the songs certainly demonstrate substantial technical and emotional maturity in the young composer, a significant command of structure, harmony, and a grasp of effective vocal and piano writing. Two specific aspects are of interest in relation to the development of Bartók's later compositional language: in 'Diese Rose pflück ich hier' two three-bar phrases in 3/8 break up what is otherwise largely composed in regular four-bar phrases in 2/4; and in 'Ich fühle deinen Odem' there is a brief excursion into the flat mediant region of G♭ major.

Bartók fell seriously ill again in the summer of 1890, after a successful first year of studies at the Academy. On this occasion he suffered from pneumonia of the right lung and was coughing up blood as a result of haemorrhages, though the prognosis of his doctor, Gábor Pávai Vajna, as reported on 23 September 1890, was positive. He advised that Bartók should spend a significant period (four or five months) in 'a climatic resort of the south' rather than a sanatorium, 'considering his delicate, tender and oversensitive character'.[59] He was also insistent that Paula should accompany him as his nurse, and commented that 'that tender, loving, self-sacrificing mother, who because of the worries and anxieties and because of *sitting up so often at night* by the bed of her only, highly talented son, *is exhausted to such an extent*, that together with her son *she needs a holiday that lasts for several months*'.[60]

Among Bartók's fellow students at the Academy was a young woman called Felicitás (known affectionately as Felicie) Fábián, to whom he developed an amorous attachment. Felicie can be seen in a photograph with the other members of Thomán's class, taken on 6 June 1901. Her name is first mentioned in Bartók's letters to his mother on 16 January 1900, and she appears regularly in their correspondence up to February 1903. Towards the end of 1900 and the beginning of 1901 he composed a set of thirteen variations in E minor (*Változatok*) on a simple theme ascribed to her. This is a substantial work, 413 bars in length, that makes significant demands on its performer, including acrobatic leaps in the agitated third variation, rapid parallel chord structures in the fourth and tenth, virtuosic octaves in the eleventh, and Lisztian arpeggiated accompaniments in the twelfth. Although Brahms remains the most obvious stylistic influence, there are some quite daring harmonic touches, such as the Neapolitan F major chords that function as substitute dominants to the dominant and rhythmic/metrical quirks like the 15/8 bars that bring the first two phrases to an end in Variation 1. A harmonic sequence in Variation 8 that partially works through the cycle of fifths is an early manifestation of a gesture that makes an occasional reappearance in many of his later works, most famously perhaps in the *Intermezzo Interrotto* of the Concerto for Orchestra. On the whole, the variations have the flamboyance appropriate to a young man who wishes to make an impression on both his girlfriend and on concert audiences.

In composing a set of variations based on a theme by a female acquaintance, Bartók was emulating the approach of his friend Ernő Dohnányi, who had written a similar work in 1897, the year of his graduation from the Academy, and apparently played it widely at the time. In the case of Dohnányi, the Variations and Fugue on a Theme by G. E. drew its musical inspiration from Emma Gruber, who was born in Baja in March 1863, a talented and enthusiastic patroness of the arts. A member of the extremely wealthy and influential Hungarian-Jewish Schlesinger family (who had patriotically renamed themselves Sándor), she had married Henrik Gruber, a successful Budapest businessman who took an amateur interest in music. Emma's brother was the Hungarian liberal politician Pál Sándor (1860–1936), who had initially worked in his father's corn-trading business before becoming an executive of several major companies. Miklós Konrád has noted that 'at the turn of the [twentieth] century, the Jewish upper class controlled some 90 percent of Hungary's modern banking system and industrial plants', and Pál was a prominent representative of this very important stratum of society.[61]

Emma Gruber's salon was held in a first-floor apartment in 41 Andrássy Avenue, almost directly opposite the Opera – a prime position when it came to the many musicians and artists who visited her. These included the composer Ödön Mihalovich (the director of the Academy of Music), the conductor István Kerner (who would conduct the first performance of the Symphohnic Poem 'Kossuth' in January 1904), Bartók's piano tutor István Thomán, his composition teacher János Koessler (who was a friend of Emma's father), and the young virtuoso Ernő Dohnányi, who taught her the piano. According to Alan Walker, 'That she became enamoured of the attractive young man [Dohnányi] cannot be doubted and there is circumstantial evidence that much more than piano lessons took place in her salon.'[62] Emma Gruber's name begins to appear in Bartók's correspondence with his mother from May 1901, and in a letter written on 12 May in response to a visit to her salon he described her as 'a rather nice, knowledgeable, very musical, very outspoken, middle-aged lady' and observed that she had 'invited us on other occasions as well'.[63]

The health of the young musician had clearly improved during his second year in the Academy, and in the autumn of 1901 he performed the Liszt Sonata in a public recital at the Academy. Paula kept a copy of a review that appeared in *Budapesti Napló* on 22 October, the day after the concert, in which the reviewer noted that:

First, Béla Bartók played Liszt's B minor Sonata on the piano, with a firm, well-developed technique. This young man has developed his strength incredibly over the last 2 years. One and a half years ago his constitution was so weak that the doctors sent him to Meran lest the hard winter do him harm. And now he thunders around the piano like a little Jupiter. In fact, no piano student at the academy today has a greater chance of following in Dohnányi's tracks than he.[64]

In December 1901 Bartók performed in public again, at his first paid engagement, organised through the offices of Károly Gianicelli, the professor of double bass at the Liszt Academy (and a prominent supporter of Wagner's music as well as a regular member of the orchestra at Bayreuth). The concert took place in the hall of the beautiful Neo-Baroque Civic Lipótváros Casino (Lipótvárosi Polgári Kaszinó) on Nádor utca in Pest. The Casino was established in 1883 by Miksa Falk. It was an upper middle-class Jewish meeting place in the style of an English gentlemen's club that functioned as an important vehicle for performances of the musical and visual arts, and it would later play a significant role in the creation of Bartók's opera, *Duke Bluebeard's Castle*. It seems that the young musician gave his fee of ten gold pieces for the concert as a surprise Christmas present to his mother, a gift that seems to have made her extremely happy in its demonstration of his filial affection for her.

Thomán's record and attendance book itemises the repertoire Bartók studied in the academic year 1901–2. As well as the Liszt Sonata, in the first half of the year he worked on a number of Chopin Etudes and the C sharp minor Nocturne; Beethoven's Diabelli Variations and Brahms's Handel Variations; two Bach Preludes and Fugues; and several small pieces by Liszt. In the second half of the year, Bartók studied smaller-scale pieces by Beethoven, Chopin and Liszt, but the major work was the first movement of Brahms's monumental Second Piano Concerto, a clear indicator of the level of the young musician's technical competence.

Bartók's relationship with Felicie appears to have broken down early in 1903. Béla wrote to his mother on 10 February that:

> We have awkward and not very pleasant complications in the case of Felicie, which I have difficulty writing about. When all of this is resolved, I'll write about the final outcome. Otherwise I'm not in touch with them at the moment; I received a letter two weeks ago in which she told me that she was going to Vienna to become a student of Sauer and she bade farewell. There's no address in the letter, so I couldn't answer. Many things have happened since then, but I wasn't informed about anything; all of my information comes from Mrs. Gruber. They are in Budapest now; but I don't pay attention to that.[65]

Bartók's musical progress between the *Liebeslieder* and the works written in 1903 was considerable. A major transformational force that helped to move his compositional focus away from Brahms was hearing the first performance in Budapest of Richard Strauss's *Also sprach Zarathustra* on 12 February 1902 (nearly six years after its premiere in Frankfurt). Four days later he wrote to his mother to tell her both about this and about hearing Dohnányi's Sonata for cello and piano in B♭ minor (1899), which was performed on the previous Sunday. While the latter was, he felt, too Brahmsian, the former affected him greatly, and he reports to his mother that 'the whole thing speaks of enormous genius and it is truly original'.[66] He continues that it made him 'feel good to hear something entirely new again, which was truly modern, even more modern than Wagner ... I believe that Strauss is again somebody who has taken, that is, is taking the art of music one step further ahead.'

A direct outcome of hearing Strauss's *Also sprach Zarathustra* was Bartók's work on a four-movement Symphony in E♭, which was finished in short score by the end of December 1902 as he notes in a letter to Adila Arányi (to whom he had become romantically attracted); he also reveals his delight in receiving a signed photograph of Strauss from Gianicelli and a score of Strauss's *Death and Transfiguration* from Thomán. Although he made a start on the first movement, Bartók only completed the orchestration of the third movement, a scherzo, which was undertaken as an academic exercise later the following year (and played in a concert of graduating students at the Budapest Opera conducted by Kerner); the Symphony remained unperformed as a whole until 1968, when a completed version by Denijs Dille was performed. Günter Weiss-Aigner remarks how the work 'not only reflects the new inspiration of Strauss and the influence of other late-Romantic composers but also contains certain pointers to the national Romantic world of Hungarian music'.[67] The most pertinent aspects of Bartók's approach, Weiss-Aigner suggests, are his 'innate tendency to variation' supported by the employment of motives that interpenetrate the individual movements. The initial theme of the first movement, which begins in triple time with an arpeggiated figure following an upward trajectory, recalls similar ideas in Strauss's tone poems (including the second themes from *Also sprach Zarathustra, Don Juan* and *Don Quixote*, and the opening of *Aus Italien*). Yet one can also detect undertones of the Hungarian musical nationalism that would soon come to the fore in his work.

## CHAPTER TWO

# 'Now I came from the battlefield': 1903–1904

Bartók's earliest attempts to forge a musical language to express Hungarian national identity drew upon what has been described as the *verbunkos* tradition. The Gypsy-performed *verbunkos*, or 'recruiting dance', a hybrid of musical manners and motifs from various ethnic sources and stemming from the eighteenth century, originally had an entirely practical function – to attract an audience from which soldiers could be recruited for imperial service by means of an elaborate dance accompanied by popular music. Although the early history of the verbunkos was thus necessarily associated with the imperial state's apparatus, it was also held to strongly characterise the Hungarian nation.[1]

In fact, the affiliation between the gentry and Gypsy-performed music, and the process of Magyarisation that developed after the Ausgleich of 1867, were intimately connected. As noted earlier, in 1890, in a Hungary in which little more than 40 per cent of the population was ethnically Magyar and in which could otherwise be found an extraordinary diversity of Romanians, Germans, Slovaks, Croats, Serbs, Ruthenians, Jews and Gypsies, primary schools were required to teach in the Hungarian language or face closure. Ironically, as David Thomson has noted, Magyarisation actually functioned in the interests of the Dual Monarchy and the Emperor, for 'prevented by its origins and composition from finding any foundations in the solidity of national unity, the Empire ingeniously became a fabric held up by a scaffolding of officialdom and a precarious equipoise of national animosities both within and without'.[2] For the gentry, and in particular for that stratum of the upper classes which had lost its land after the abortive 1848 revolution and now ran the state apparatus through the civil service, the *verbunkos* tradition was (and still is) sometimes considered representative of the 'soul' of Hungary.

According to Bence Szabolcsi, 'everything known abroad since 1780 by the name of Hungarian music consisted without exception of the music of the "verbunkos" '.[3] It is therefore of some interest to find the British scholar, William Stafford, writing as early as 1830 in his *History of Music* about his perception of Hungarian music:

> Like all other half-civilized people, the Hungarians sang their national songs to tunes without time, key or harmony. They are fond of soft sounds and slow measures: and though this description of their music may be considered as rather more feminine than masculine in its nature, yet their patriotic songs frequently produced a surprising effect.[4]

Stafford's 'surprising effect' is the tendency of the songs to evoke responses in their audience of simultaneous lament and national fervour, and this 'weeping-rejoicing' bipolarity is inscribed on the music through the set of conventional codes employed by its composers and performers. Standardised features of the *verbunkos* have been catalogued by Szabolcsi and Jonathan Bellman, and include the use of the so-called Gypsy scale (arguably a harmonic minor scale with a sharpened fourth scale degree);[5] elaborately ornamented passage-work with considerable rubato in slower sections (described as *hallgató*, literally a 'listener' or 'person who is silent', when associated with instrumental renditions of vocal melodies);[6] contrasting slow (*lassú*) and fast or fresh (*friss*) sections; a clipped cadential figure called *bokázó* (meaning 'capering'); rhythms such as the choriambus, *alla zoppa* and Lombard; and melodic patterns such as the *kuruc* fourths with their alternation between the fifth and upper octave of the scale. Several pieces written by Bartók in 1903 illustrate the extent to which he had absorbed *verbunkos* features in his developing language: the vocal work 'Est' (which exists in two distinct settings, as a song in C minor and as a quite different unaccompanied male-voice choral work in F minor); four piano pieces; a sonata for violin and piano; and the symphonic poem *Kossuth*.

The song 'Est' ('Evening') was written in early 1903 (possibly in April) to a text by the poet Kálmán Harsányi. According to János Demény, the poet and the composer met in the summer of 1904 while Bartók was staying at the house of a friend in the village of Gerlicepuszta, situated in a predominantly Slovak region of Hungary around 150 kilometres north of Budapest.[7] It seems that Harsányi had already written, or was soon to write, a number of poems with explicitly nationalist themes, including 'Shadows of Rodostó' and 'The Thirteen of Arad', both of which he sent to Bartók in late August or early September 1904.[8] During the composition of 'Est' and *Kossuth* we find Bartók asking his sister to wear Hungarian national costume at a forthcoming piano recital, and to furnish him with the words of two 'folk songs' (*magyar nóták*, or popular

Hungarian songs), requests that are suggestive of the extent to which his own national consciousness was awakening at this time.[9]

The text of 'Est' in Hungarian with an English prose translation is as follows:

| | |
|---|---|
| **Est (Harsányi Kálmán)**[10] | **Evening** |
| Csöndes minden, csöndes, | Everything is quiet, quiet, |
| Hallgatnak a lombok, | The foliage is silent, |
| Meghalt a nap; ott a vérfolt, | The Sun is dead; there is a bloodstain, |
| Ahol összeomlott. | Where he fell. |
| | |
| Gyász van; mély sötét gyászt | There is mourning; |
| Ölt a táj magára, | The country has put on a deep dark |
| Harmatot sír a mezőnek | Mourning dress, all the flowers of the |
| Minden szál virága. | Meadows are weeping dew. |
| | |
| És susogják halkan: | And they whisper slowly: |
| 'Sose látjuk többé? | 'Will we never see him again? |
| Nem lehet az, hogy éj legyen, | It cannot be night from now |
| Most már mindöröké.' | For ever and ever.' |
| | |
| Várják, visszavárják, | And they are waiting, |
| Míg a láthatáron | Waiting for him to return, |
| Fölmerül a hold korongja | Until on the horizon rises |
| Halotthalaványon. | The disk of the Moon, pale as death. |
| | |
| Kisértetes fénytől | The horizon |
| Sápad az ég alja. | Is pale from the ghostly light. |
| Megborzongnak a virágok: | The flowers shudder: |
| 'Visszatért, de halva.' | 'He came back, but he is dead.' |

The morbid, symbolist quality of the language, which recalls Albert Giraud's *Pierrot lunaire* and Charles Baudelaire's 'Harmonie du soir', veils the potential political implications of the text,[11] and significantly, Bartók restates the opening words of the poem 'Csöndes minden, csöndes' ('Everything is quiet, quiet') as the subtitle of the final part of his *Kossuth* symphonic tone poem, completed later in the same year. The dramatic context of these words in the tone poem, according to the text draft sent to Bartók's mother sometime in 1903–4, is the silence following the defeat of the Magyar revolutionary leader Kossuth and the Hungarian army by the imperial forces in 1849. The inscription above the penultimate section of *Kossuth* is revealing: 'The country goes into deepest mourning. But even this is forbidden.'[12]

The first sentence of this 'explanatory inscription' resonates strongly with the line in the second verse of the poem, which reads 'There is mourning; the country has put on a deep dark mourning dress'. According to Ármin Vámbéry (author of the first English-language history of Hungary, a volume published in 1886), in the aftermath of 1848–9:

> wholesale massacres were committed throughout the country, until at last the conscience of Europe rose up against these cruel butcheries, and the court itself removed the sanguinary baron [the Austrian General Julius Jacob von Haynau] from the scene of his inhuman exploits. The best men in the country were thrown into prison, and thousands of families had to mourn for dear ones who had fallen victim of the implacable vindictiveness of the Austrian government. Once more the gloom of oppression settled upon the unhappy country.[13]

Can Harsány's text for 'Est' be taken to imply that nature has taken upon itself the prohibited role of mourner for the death of liberty and independence after 1849 and for the ensuing violent repression exercised by Haynau (or 'the hyena of Brescia' as he was known because of his cruelty)? If the real subject of the poem is in fact Lajos Kossuth, then the final line can be read literally, for in 1894, the year of his death, he did return to Hungary, or rather his mortal remains did, to enormous publicly expressed emotion.

This reading is supported by Bartók's use of a number of codes for Magyar nationalism in the song, including the Hungarian or 'Gypsy' scale. Bartók had experimented with this mode in a set of four *magyar nóta* influenced songs written in the previous year, and in the first of these ('Autumn Breeze'), a somewhat unassimilated adoption of the slow (*lassú*) musical manner can be detected.[14] A pervasive feature of the *verbunkos* repertoire, the Gypsy scale's most conspicuous element is its pair of augmented seconds (E♭-F♯ and A♭-B where C is the tonic), intervals that Bartók would later hypothesise to have found their way into Hungarian melody via Turko-Arabic music.[15] Interestingly, the succession of pitches in the first two bars of 'Est' (C-E♭-F♯-G-A♭), which outline the scale's most prominent characteristics, can also be found at the beginning of Mozart's C minor Piano Fantasy, K. 475. Bartók was certainly familiar with this work, and his use of that succession of pitches demonstrates the extent to which *style hongrois* mannerisms had become embedded within the Classical style.[16]

The opening vocal phrase of 'Est' is set with a pair of trochaic dotted quaver-semiquaver figures, characteristic of a number of Brahms's Hungarian Dances,[17] and a rhythmic idea which, as Bellman remarks, was 'all but universal in

*verbunkos* and a staple of Gypsy fiddlers as it provided an insinuating, attractive swing to melodies'.[18] Much later in his life, in the fourth of a series of
lectures delivered at Harvard University in 1943, Bartók described this same
rhythm as 'anti-Hungarian' because of its rare occurrence in *'genuine'*
Hungarian folk music.[19] His justification for this statement is the stress that is
normally placed on the first syllable of a polysyllable in the Hungarian language
– stressed short-long rhythmic units of the 'Scotch-snap' variety abound in
Hungarian peasant song, and are particularly common at line endings. Bartók
also draws on standardised Classical-Romantic codes for funeral music in 'Est',
for example in the quaver-dotted semiquaver-demisemiquaver figure of bar
five, which is used both to set and provide an underlay for the words 'Meghalt
a nap' ('the sun is dead'). A further prominent marker of the *style hongrois*
appears at the song's climax ('Until on the horizon rises the disk of the Moon,
pale as death. The horizon is pale from the ghostly light.'), where a chain of
double thirds over a dominant pedal tone is found in the piano accompaniment. Such parallel-interval writing is frequently found in Gypsy Hungarian
music, and can also be seen in some East European peasant music. For example,
it occurs in the extraordinary two-part Dalmatian melodies that Bartók transcribed in his final years from commercial recordings issued by Edison Bell
and that influenced the second movement of the Concerto for Orchestra.

   The Magyar codes of 'Est' are encapsulated within a late-Romantic musical
idiom that owes much to the harmonic approaches of Wagner and Richard
Strauss. The progression leading to the climax, for instance, involves a pivot-
tone harmonic sequence through implied A major, G♭ major, B♭ major and D
half-diminished seventh chords to a dominant triad. The piano postlude
provides an early example of the composer's penchant for harmonic connections by minor thirds, again probably under the influence of Strauss, and a
relationship that has become a central principle in Ernő Lendvai's theory of
Bartók's tonal language: broken chords of A major, G♭ major (enharmonic
equivalent of F♯ major) and E♭ major lead back to a tonic C which equivocates
between minor and major modes, eventually settling on the major.[20] Overall,
the song can also be seen to inhabit a similar lyrical space to the vocal repertoire of Hugo Wolf, who died in Vienna, Budapest's imperial twin city, in
February 1903.

   'Est' was composed in a social and intellectual context in which a developing Magyar nationalism was fostered by the Hungarian ruling classes in the
interests of promoting political and economic autonomy separate from Austria.
According to József Ujfalussy,[21] this was essentially divisive in nature in that it
encouraged antagonism between the native and non-native Hungarian working
classes. It was a type of nationalism that had little place for the essentially

marginalised peasantry, founded as it was on the notion of the aristocracy forming the entire 'Hungarian nation'.[22] More specifically in 1903, a new Imperial Army Bill was seen to be unfavourable to Hungarian interests, and resulted in a parliamentary filibuster which lasted for the best part of a year, until March 1904, and which Bartók mentions in the letter to his mother of 1 April 1903. These nationalist trends, which were in general anti-capitalist (and anti-bourgeois) in their orientation, were reflected by and were reflections of developments in the fine arts and literature, in which peasant art was seen as a potential source of symbols of national identity. Explicitly drawing upon the aesthetics of John Ruskin and William Morris, chiefly through the influence of a number of anglophile civil servants in the Ministry of Education and the Hungarian Royal Drawing School (Magyar Királyi Mintarajztanoda) in Budapest, Hungarian artists began to see folk art as 'the "pure source" of ancient national forms . . . reflect[ing] parts of the unspoiled character of the nation'.[23]

In 'Est', Bartók appears to be implicitly subscribing to the nationalist and *magyarist* programme espoused, in particular, by the lower strata of the nobility, a programme that was both racially and socially divisive, and whose resolution would be found in the 1920 Treaty of Trianon. Bartók's letter of 1 April, with its request for the words of the two folk tunes, which are in fact *magyar nóták*, reveals that he was consciously attempting to tap into the source of what he believed to be an authentic national music. Bill Ashcroft et al. note that 'the crucial function of language as a medium of power demands that post-colonial writing define itself by seizing the language of the centre and re-placing it in a discourse fully adapted to the colonized place'.[24] Musical language must equally be involved in this reorientation from centre (the Austro-German hegemonic style), to periphery, and Bartók's admixture of the techniques of the modernist Strauss and *style hongrois* mannerisms in 'Est' and in other works of this period, including the symphonic poem *Kossuth*, betoken his attempt to do so.

The Four Piano Pieces, DD 71 (which were published separately in 1904 by Bárd Ferenc és Fia), consist of an extended Study in B♭, two Fantasies (in C minor and A minor respectively) and a Scherzo in E minor. The influence of Magyarist musical codes is very apparent throughout these pieces, as is the imprint of Richard Strauss. Bartók had made a piano transcription of Strauss's tone poem *Ein Heldenleben* (1898) late in 1902 and played it to Emma Gruber on 15 November. He wrote to his mother on 17 January 1903, telling her how he had performed it from memory for Koessler in the concert hall of the Music Academy after his composition class. Although Koessler was immensely impressed by Bartók's skill in memorising it, he did not hide the fact that he disliked the piece. Nine days later, in his first public appearance outside

Hungary, Bartók performed his transcription for the Tonkünstlerverein (composers' association), which met at the prestigious Musikverein in Vienna.

Strauss's influence on Four Piano Pieces is seen most obviously in the first, 'Tanulmány balkézre' ('Study for the Left Hand', dated January 1903 in the published score), whose initial heroic arpeggiations capped by descending appoggiaturas follow trajectories that have some similarity to the opening of *Ein Heldenleben*. After this assertive gesture, a second idea is presented that describes an underlying descent with a syncopation at the phrase endings that place a minim on the second beat of the bar (Fig. 2). The rest of the piece involves an interplay between these two types of material, the heroic, assertive fanfares and the more subdued and inward-looking cantabile melody. Although titled 'study', it prioritises musical argument over the purely technical aspects normal to such a work. Nevertheless, if Strauss provides one of the basic genetic elements, Liszt also exerts a profound impact on its pianism, especially in the bravura octave work.

The first of the two Fantasies, in C minor, dedicated to Emma Gruber, moves beyond Brahms in the chromatic pitch space it inhabits, its melodic line opening with the notes F♯–F♮–C♯–D, in Forte pitch class terms, the set 4–7, to which theorist Larry Solomon gives the descriptive name of Arabian Tetramirror, highlighting its Orientalist aspects. While this collection of pitches most naturally arises in Western tonal music as the upper four notes of a harmonic minor scale (in this case, F♯ minor, where the F♮ is read as an enharmonic renotation of E♯), this is as remote from the tonic key of C minor as possible, despite the fact that the left hand prefigures and supports the opening F♯ with an arpeggiated dominant seventh in the home key. Bartók's continuation from the D is entirely chromatic, weaving its way down to B♭. Interestingly, the climax of the piece, on the penultimate page of the score, unambiguously projects G♭/F♯ major over an eight-bar passage that is bisected by a two-bar reworking of the opening chromatic figure, arguably placing this tonal area in tension with G, the true dominant. This dichotomy between 'natural' and altered dominant would remain an important aspect of Bartók's language throughout his career.

Figure 2.  The second idea from 'Study for the Left Hand'.

The second Fantasy, marked Andante and in A minor, is a much briefer affair. It is dedicated to Irmy and Emsy Jurkovics, sisters from Nagyszentmiklós of Serbian ethnicity who Bartók had known as a child and had reconnected with when performing a recital in his native town in April 1903. Certainly the musical tokens of Magyarism are to the fore again here, through allusion to the ornamented slow *lassú* style of *verbunkos* and the use of the Gypsy scale. At the same time, several elements emerge that point towards Bartók's mature style: the two opening phrases are in underlying five-bar units (though the second is extended to six with the addition of an echo of the final bar); and the tonal relations emphasise thirds, whether minor (at the beginning) or major (near the end).

Although the brisk and brilliant Scherzo that brings the set to its conclusion is basically in E minor, it employs a broad tonal palette, and on the second page of the published score the piece moves sequentially through the areas of C, E♭, F♯ and A minor, describing the relations between thirds that underpin Lendvai's axis theory of the composer's harmonic language. Bartók employs five-bar phrases, in this case at the beginning of the trio, and at the end of the section, as an innovatory notational touch, he superimposes discrete duple- and triple-time signatures in the two staves, with occasional compensatory shorter bars in the upper stave.

Bartók graduated from the Liszt Academy in the summer term of 1903 without having to sit formal final-year examinations. While, as he noted in a letter to his mother on 25 May, this was to the astonishment of his fellow students, it was a decision that apparently represented the unequivocal opinion of the teaching staff, and was a clear acknowledgement of Bartók's standing both as a pianist and a composer. He had completed the short score of *Kossuth* between April and May, and on 18 June he wrote to his mother that he had performed it on the piano for Koessler who had regarded it positively in the main. Bartók orchestrated the work between June and the middle of August that year, much of this time being spent in Passail in Styria. While staying in the resort town of Gmunden, on the edge of the Traunsee in the Salzkammergut region of Upper Austria, where the Dohnányi family had a holiday home, he met up with Koessler who told Bartók that he thought the instrumentation was 'very good, very modern' and advised him that 'it would sound very well'.[25] It seems that Koessler was particularly touched to discover that the score had been copied by the young man's mother and sister.

Bartók's nationalist inclinations particularly came to the fore during this period in Gmunden, and in an extraordinary and oft-quoted letter he wrote to his mother on 8 September, he set out his political stall, particularly in respect of language. He was less concerned about the public sphere of national politics, 'where there is plenty of enthusiasm for national ideals', but in the private, domestic, field he was deeply disturbed that 'individual members of the Hungarian nation, with insignificant exceptions, [were] so distressingly indifferent to everything Hungarian'. Quoting the comment of the chauvinist conservative politician Jenő Rákosi (editor of the newspaper *Budapesti Hírlap*) that 'It's all the same to us whether and how anybody speaks our unique and peerless language, instead we ourselves speak everybody else's language; we deride people who speak only Hungarian as uneducated, no matter how much they know; our girls, the mothers of future generations, we ruin at a tender age with foreign education . . ', it becomes clear that the specific focus of Bartók's concern is his own mother. He has made his personal choice between Magyar and Teutonic languages and cultures, noting in a rather high-minded tone that 'For my own part, all my life, in every sphere, always and in every way, I shall have one objective: the good of Hungary and the Hungarian nation. I think I have already given some proof of this intention in the minor ways which have so far been possible to me'. He fears, however, that his own immediate family was all too ready to fall back into German.

It seems that Bartók's greatest concern was that he might be regarded as a hypocrite and a fraud because of his family's linguistic laxity. Should any of his acquaintances who were aware of his nationalist views visit his household and hear members of his own family not speaking Hungarian, his credibility could be seriously undermined. That his mother spoke in German in order to converse with her sister, and companion, Irma, he could understand, but in sympathy with Rákosi's views he implored her to speak in Hungarian to his sister, Böske. He had transformed himself from bilingual speaker to monoglot, responding in Hungarian to those who spoke to him in German in shops or on the street as a political action. His mother, he avers, should do the same.

No doubt, Bartók would have later looked back on this letter with more than a degree of embarrassment. His wholehearted and passionate espousal of the Hungarian language over German would not have disconcerted him, nor perhaps the patronising and self-righteous tone he adopts with his mother. However, he would have cringed over his earlier enthusiasm for the writings of Rákosi, who in 1900 had demanded 'a total Hungarianness, when every man in Hungary will feel in his innermost soul that he had become a Magyar chauvinist', and who famously imagined a nation consisting of 'thirty million Magyars'.[26] It has even been suggested that, late in his life, in 1928, the by then ultra-conservative Rákosi met with Mussolini to discuss how the vacant throne of Hungary could be filled.

It was from this political milieu that the twenty-minute-long *Kossuth* came into being. A *Symphonische Dichtung* in the spirit of Liszt and Strauss, its ten sections involve a programme that traces Lajos Kossuth's involvement in the events of the 1848 revolution in Hungary and its aftermath. According to the programme note for the British premiere by the Hallé Orchestra in Manchester on 18 February 1904, which draws on the composer's own words:

> The year 1848 is one of the most eventful in Hungarian history. It was the year of the Hungarian revolt – a life and death struggle of the nation for freedom. The leader, the heart and soul of this struggle, was Louis Kossuth. As Austria saw, in 1849, that the war was going against her, she concluded an alliance with Russia. A crushing blow was inflicted on the Hungarian Army, and the hope of an independent Hungarian kingdom was shattered – apparently for ever. These events serve as the poetic basis of the Symphonic Poem, which may be considered as falling under twelve [ten] heads.[27]

The note goes on to identify the ten sections of the work, drawing attention through brief musical examples to the relationship between the thematic material and its programme:

I. 'Kossuth' – delineating the character of the hero.

II. 'What sorrow lies so heavily on thy heart?' Kossuth's wife, his faithful companion, sees the trouble written on her husband's countenance. Kossuth tries to pacify her mind, but he is no longer capable of dissembling his profound sadness.

III. 'Danger threatens the fatherland.' He loses himself in sorrowful recollections of the glorious days, now vanished, of his nation.

IV. 'A better fate than was ours.'

V. 'Yet this brief-lived happiness soon disappeared.' The theme depicts the servitude which regards no laws and which no freedom alleviates.

With the words:

VI. 'To the battlefield!' Kossuth tears himself away from these thoughts. He is resolved to win back by fighting [,] his natural right to freedom.

VII. 'Come, oh come, ye haughty warriors, ye valiant heroes!' – Kossuth's summons to the Hungarian nation to fly to arms.

> The hero theme appears (F minor).
>
> Kossuth repeats his inspiriting call to the assembled hosts. The Army swears a solemn oath.
>
> Some moments of fateful silence.

VIII. Then is heard the sound of the enemy's host, approaching nearer and nearer. It is characterised by the motive of the Austrian hymn.

The armies join in battle.

Assault after assault is made. At last the superior numbers of the enemy triumph. The catastrophe comes (fff on tympani and tam-tam). Only a few of the Hungarians, who have survived the conflict, fly before the vengeance of the victors.

IX. All is finished. Hungary lies in deepest woe, in deepest mourning.
X. A hopeless silence reigns.[28]

Bartók's orchestral palette is the large late nineteenth-century symphony orchestra of Strauss and Mahler. The work is scored for quadruple woodwind (including post-Wagnerian conventional doublings), eight horns, four trumpets (and bass trumpet), three trombones, two tenor tubas and bass tuba, timpani, untuned percussion, two harps and strings. Musically, it is structured using leitmotifs, and in particular it features a heroically configured motif (in Straussian terms) that represents Kossuth himself (Fig. 3). Like themes from 'Est' and the E minor Violin Sonata, this overtly references the 'Gypsy' scale through the sharpened fourth (D♯) in the first bar. Other allusions to Hungarian popular music involve aspects of orchestration, including the imitation of the tárogató;[29] rhythms such as the choriambus (long-short-short-long, familiar from the Hungarian rhapsodies of Liszt), syncopated short-long (like the so-called 'Scotch snap') and the Hungarian anapaest (short-short-long); the style of florid ornamentation labelled hallgató; and melodic ideas, for instance the rebounding 'Kuruc' fourths.

The premiere of Kossuth took place in Budapest on 13 January 1904 in a performance by the Budapest Philharmonic Orchestra under the baton of its chief conductor István Kerner (who had succeeded Sándor Erkel to the post in 1900). Kossuth was one of a pair of novel works that evening, the other being the First Violin Concerto by the Swiss composer Emile Jacques-Dalcroze, played by its dedicatee, Henri Marteau. The performance was very well received by the Budapest press and Bartók found himself immediately thrust into the limelight as a patriotic composer. The review published the following day by the music critic of Egyetértés (Accord) forgave Bartók for what were perceived

Figure 3. The Kossuth leitmotif.

as the work's shortcomings and for its excessive dissonance, because of his combination of patriotic aspiration and real genius. Similarly, the reviewer in *Esti Újság* (*Evening News*) pondered what future awaited this 'magnificent talent', who had previously been entirely unknown as a composer.

In the staunchly nationalist newspaper *Budapesti Hírlap* (*Budapest News*) of 14 January 1904, Aurél Kern drew attention to a specific chauvinistic touch on Bartók's part, that of turning up onstage to acknowledge the storm of applause at the work's conclusion, in national dress and wearing a Hungarian attila jacket. In his review Kern remarked that while Dohnányi adopted Germanic forms, following in the footsteps of masters such as Beethoven and Brahms, arguably creating a 'purer and more serene art than Bartók's', the latter's music was truer to Magyar feeling, through its lesser reliance on order, its impetuous-ness and outbursts, and its rhapsodic character. He said of the audience that 'Everyone was of the same opinion: Bartok is the first purely Hungarian symphonist.'

August Beer, in *Pester Lloyd*, felt that the Bartók of the *Kossuth* symphonic poem 'was a person of decided talent with surprising technical ability, an unusual colouristic sense, and a strong – indeed fiery – temperament', and described how he was called to the stage probably a dozen times at the work's conclusion. Bartók's passionate mutilation of the Austrian national anthem, 'Gott erhalte', in the boldest section of the work demonstrated to the critic of *Magyar Hírlap* (*Hungarian News*) that he had the courage to say what he believed and that this was one of the great hopes of his talent.

Bartók's distortions of the 'Gott erhalte' had created something of a storm among some members of the orchestra, and according to a news item in *Függetlenség* (*Independence*) on 16 January 1904 titled 'Politika a zenében' ('Politics in Music'), a number of Austrian players staged a demonstration during rehearsal of this section. Apparently Kerner brought the rehearsal to an abrupt end by laying down his baton and departing from the hall, leaving the musicians in confusion. Several performers – a report in *Pesti Napló* gives five – provided medical certificates to justify their subsequent absence, though despite the importance of their instruments to the ensemble, the premiere was able to take place.

Just over a month later *Kossuth* was performed again, this time by the afore-mentioned Hallé Orchestra in Manchester, conducted by its director, the Hungarian-born Hans (János) Richter. It appears that the eminent conductor may have met Bartók through Károly Gianicelli, who was an intimate of the Wagner family and like Richter a great enthusiast of Wagner's operas, and with Rákosi, who was a member of the committee that provided scholarships for Bayreuth. On 18 June 1903 Bartók had written to his mother telling her that

Richter was due to come to Budapest the following week; and on 7 July he communicated with János Batka in Pozsony (who had been a mentor to him while he had been at school there and was also close to Richter), thanking him for his kindness and his interest in his work and remarking 'how pleased I am to know that Mr Richter is sympathetically disposed towards me'.[30] Having set off for England around 10 February 1904, Bartók stayed at the Richters' home in Bowden, Cheshire, and wrote to his mother after his arrival describing to her 'the horrible state of English railway carriages, which is quite exasperating', and which, he claims, are worse than those 'on the most unimportant branch line in Hungary'.

In addition to *Kossuth*, the Hallé programme included Schubert's Eighth ('Unfinished') Symphony, Liszt's *Spanish Rhapsody*, orchestrated by Busoni, with Bartók as the soloist, and Dvořák's Suite for Orchestra, op. 39. Bartók also played two unaccompanied pieces, Volkmann's Variations on a Theme by Handel and his own Scherzo in E minor (the latter as an encore). The political and patriotic aspects of *Kossuth* were clearly much less significant or apparent to the English critics, though the deformation of the Austrian national anthem was seen by the reviewer (assumed to be Arthur Johnstone) in *The Manchester Guardian* of 19 February 1904 as 'ferocious and hideous', and 'the guying and degrading of the famous melody is altogether repulsive'. Considerable attention was paid to the Straussian influences, and Johnstone remarked that 'though the imitation of Strauss's "Heldenleben" extravagances is a mistake into which only a young man of very great talent would be likely to fall, it is nevertheless a very bad mistake'. It seems that although *Kossuth* was well rehearsed, it was received politely rather than ecstatically, the reviewer noting that 'If anyone thinks, however, that it really pleased the Manchester public, he is under a very gross delusion.'

The reviews in *The Manchester Guardian* and in *The Daily Dispatch* (also 19 February) were both positive about Bartók as a performer. For Johnstone of *The Manchester Guardian*, he played the solo part in Liszt's *Spanish Rhapsody* 'with technical power fully equal to its demands, and his rendering did not lack geniality and charm'. S.B. in *The Daily Dispatch* commented that 'It is a pleasure to be able to compliment Mr Bartok sincerely and unreservedly upon his talents as a pianist . . . . [he] displayed a very admirable technique, a beautiful, smooth touch, and, best of all, great expressive powers'.

*Style hongrois* characteristics that are so predominant in *Kossuth* are also present in Bartók's extended three-movement Sonata in E minor for Violin and Piano, but within a musical idiolect that still recalls his composition teacher's revered Brahms. Bartók had begun the work while still a student (and had performed the third movement during a concert at the Liszt Academy in June

1903) and brought it to completion through the summer of that year and during his extended stay in Berlin between October and December. A fairly regular sonata-form first movement emerges from the bass register of the piano in the subdominant with syncopated C–E dyads that are 'spiked' in the following bar by the transient addition of a dissonant F natural. The principal Magyar motif of the movement ($A_4$–$E_5$–$D\sharp_5$–$C_5$–$A\sharp_4$–$B_4$) then appears, accompanied by triple and quadruple stopped pizzicato chords in the violin. The piano writing in his passage is saturated by parallel thirds, a further 'Hungarian' effect that is as likely to have come through Liszt and Brahms as from any direct contact with the performance of Gypsy musicians. This figure interlaces a second idea that, like the main thematic material of the Study for the Left Hand (the first of the Four Piano Pieces from 1903), is built on a falling scalic pattern with further Magyar flourishes in the two pairs of quavers terminating the first full bar and opening the second (Fig. 4).

If the first idea references Brahms, then the somewhat quirky second subject suggests Schumann (recalling perhaps aspects of 'Verrufene Stelle' and 'Vogel als Prophet' from *Waldscenen*). The development section culminates with a fugato nominally in the remote tonal area of A♭, and although Bartók may have been drawing on the fugal section of Liszt's B minor Piano Sonata, his own working is rather regular. While chromatic, the fugal section completing the development has something of the student exercise about it, the movement heading to its conclusion with few major surprises, though exhibiting throughout beautifully conceived and executed piano writing.

The second movement, an Andante in A minor constructed as a theme-and-variation set, clearly exhibits Liszt's influence. If there are touches that appear to emulate the Gypsy style (for example, in the cimbalom-like fioriture accompanying the first, highly decorated, variation of the sombre theme in the high register), they have been filtered through Liszt's emulation of such music. It is notable that the second variation, an accelerating dance-inspired section that intimates the *friss* style of *verbunkos*, is in a triple hypermetre, its underlying phrase structure being in groups of three bars, a metric feature absorbed

[Allegro moderato (molto rubato)]

Figure 4. Sonata for Violin and Piano.

from the popular and folk traditions of Hungary that would reappear throughout Bartók's oeuvre. The most extraordinary and forward-looking of the variations is probably the penultimate one, in which the melody of the theme, now in triple time, is saturated by a single static harmony of B$^{\varnothing7}$ (the half-diminished seventh chord often described as the 'Tristan chord'), in various permutations and initially involving the interplay of sextuplet and quintuplet tremolandi in the piano.

The second and third movements might together be regarded as forming an enormously expanded *csárdás*, in which the overall *lassú* character of the second movement (allowing for the accelerating second variation) is matched by the *friss* of the finale in E minor/major. An expanded rondo, the finale's second theme bears an overt relationship to Kossuth's motif from the symphonic poem. Although largely conventional in approach (and reverting to the Brahmsian axis of the first movement), there are several elements of the finale that point forward to the mature composer. The most striking is found in the accelerating section of the transition to the reprise of the finale's first theme (from bars 371–6), in which whole-tone scales in the violin are underpinned by hammered-out tritones and octaves (E–A♯–E in the right hand on the strong beats and A♯–E–A♯ in the left hand on the off beats), the main beats being accented by D♯ acciaccaturas.

Bartók greatly enjoyed his time in Germany's capital, and in a letter to his mother on 3 December 1903 wrote 'I feel wonderful in Berlin – as I have never felt in any other city. There's no doubt that the climate and air here suit me better than in, say, Budapest.'[31] Eleven days later, on 14 December, he gave a solo recital at the Bechstein Hall near Potsdamer Platz, performing Schumann's F♯ minor Sonata, Dohnányi's *Passacaglia*, Chopin's C♯ minor Nocturne and C minor Étude, Liszt's *Spanish Rhapsody* and several of his own recent works – the Scherzo, Fantasy, and Study for the Left Hand. Writing to his old teacher Thomán two days later, Bartók gave him 'a faithful account of my recital'. He explained how he had been concerned that he might not have the physical capability to get through it, but was delighted to note how strong he felt. He was also particularly pleased about how well the Study for the Left Hand had been received by the audience, which filled the hall to two thirds of its capacity and included Godowsky and Busoni among its numbers. It seems that Busoni visited the young pianist in the green room to offer his congratulations, though Bartók reports hearing second hand that he had 'expressed some surprise that a player with such a fine left-hand technique, as he heard in the piece for the left hand, should then give an unsatisfactory rendering of Chopin's *Étude in C minor*'.[32] Bartók freely admitted that this was true and that his performance of the Chopin was poor, and he would rather not have played it.

The new Piano Quintet was begun in October 1903 while Bartók was living in Berlin and completed in the summer of the following year while he was staying in Gerlicepuszta. Peter Laki has said that its goal, like the Violin Sonata, 'seems to have been to fuse Brahmsian chamber music form with Hungarian elements, which, to Bartók at the time, still meant the nineteenth-century semi-popular style with which he had grown up'.[33] Of, course, as Laki points out, this is a synthesis that can already be detected to some degree in Brahms's own musical output. Written in four substantial movements, the work lasts more than forty minutes and follows a fairly conventional late nineteenth-century trajectory. Its extended first movement, in which an introductory Andante leads into an Allegro molto, is followed by a Scherzo, a broad Adagio and an accelerating Finale, the latter pair of movements conforming to some extent to the 'Hungarian' instrumental *verbunkos* model of consecutive *lassú* and *friss* sections, much as in the final two movements of the Violin Sonata in E minor. Other *verbunkos*-derived features of the Piano Quintet include the use of stereotypical rhythmic gestures (such as those founded on iambic and choriambic feet and the 'limping' *alla zoppa* figure), the Gypsy scale, rebounding 'Kuruc fourths', and the elaborate melodic/harmonic improvised decorative infill favoured by cimbalom players. In the spirit of Liszt, the work is integrated thematically by the use of a set of ideas that reappear in its course; Julie Richards has identified six such cyclic themes.[34]

Though the Piano Quintet is clearly still fundamentally tonal and notionally in C major, its harmonic milieu demonstrates a move beyond that of Brahms and Wagner. The opening gesture – a presentation of the first cyclic theme, which bears some passing similarity in melodic shape to the Tristan leitmotif – is tonally ambiguous and begins off-centre, its first full chord being interpretable equally as an A major triad with added sixth, or as an F♯ minor seventh in first inversion (Fig. 5). As the E in the second violin resolves down to a D♯, this transforms into a half-diminished seventh on the third beat, maintaining tonal uncertainty, and the immediate varied repeat of the rising figure retains this harmony at the start of the second complete bar, before sliding into the commonplace cadential progression of $V^7$ of $V/V^7/I$ in C. Richards has noted how the tritone relationship between F♯ and C permeates the work as a whole, but also how conventional functional relationships (dominant–tonic) are combined and alternated with tritonal ones (sharp subdominant/flat dominant to tonic). This is an early manifestation of a harmonic idiosyncrasy that would be found throughout the composer's career. Similarly, his penchant for chromaticism that results from the overlay of different modes sharing the same tonic also finds incipient expression here, for diatonicism, modality (in particular, the Phrygian mode) and the Gypsy scale coexist and interpenetrate.

Figure 5. The first idea from the Piano Quintet.

In very broad terms, the first and last movements can be seen as performing large-scale expository and recapitulatory functions, primacy being given to the first to third cyclic themes in the opening movement and the fourth to sixth in the finale. The rhythmic eccentricity of the scherzo results from a figure whose metre sounds to the listener to consist of the succession of three even beats and an extended fourth beat, a 2+2+2+3 pattern that looks forward to the 'Dances in Bulgarian Rhythm' from *Mikrokosmos*. Notated in 3/4 with a hemiola formed over the first two bars of each three-bar unit, this creates an interplay between triple and quadruple metres, and regular and irregular beat lengths, that takes some time to decipher aurally.

The metrical complexity disappears in the trio section, the melody of which has been seen as a variant of a *magyar nóta* titled 'Ég a kunyhó, ropog a nád' ('The Hut is Blazing, the Reed Crackles') in which the protagonist tries to decide which of two beautiful girls he favours, the brunette or the blonde:[35]

> The hut is ablaze, the reed crackles,
> how I love the dark one!
> Once I loved a blond girl,
> Didn't care the least for the dark one.
>
> Now I long for the blonde,
> just like I long for grapes;
> but I long even more for a dark one,
> like I long for a tart cider apple.[36]

Whether it is appropriate to imagine any autobiographical significance in this apparent musico-textual correspondence is moot. Bartók had certainly broken off with Felicie Fábián early in 1903 and had subsequently reconnected with the Jurkovics sisters during his trip to Nagyszentmiklós for a recital in April

1903. The dedication to them of the second Fantasy from the Four Piano Pieces on 12 October 1903 is perhaps indicative of the warm feelings he held for them (and for Irmy in particular), but beyond this must remain conjecture.

It is in the third movement, an Adagio replete with *style hongrois* filigree melodic decoration which commences with the first cyclic theme exposed at the beginning of the first movement (see Fig. 5), that the expressive and emotional heart of the work can be found. The pathos of the Adagio is balanced by a finale that draws on the virtuosic and heroic elements of the *csárdás* and places them in late nineteenth-century dress. Although there are some signs of the Bartók who would emerge from the cocoon of Hungarian chauvinism over the next few years, the language of the Piano Quintet is largely consistent with the musical status quo of the time. Indeed, in a letter written from Berlin in March 1904 to Lajos Dietl, a professor of piano at the Vienna Conservatoire, he would talk of discovering some 'beautiful' Strauss songs and remark in a mock-religious tone, 'Verily, verily, I say unto you: since Wagner there has been no composer as great as Strauss.'[37]

Bartók had two particularly influential musical experiences during 1904. In August he visited the shrine of Wagner at Bayreuth and attended various performances of his operas, including his Bühnenweihfestspiel *Parsifal*. While this didn't have quite the overpowering effect on him that *Tristan und Isolde* had, and he found the overt religiosity of *Parsifal* somewhat disturbing, he expressed his enthusiasm in a pair of postcards to his friend the poet Kálmán Harsányi, noting that he found it 'amazing that a man of 70 could write anything so fresh as the flower-maidens' love song in the 2nd act'.[38]

The second encounter was a true epiphany. While staying in Gerlicepuszta from May until November, at the home of the engineer and mine director, Karl Fischer, Bartók heard Lidi Dósa, the eighteen-year-old maid of Hedviga Fischer, singing songs from her Transylvanian village including 'Piros alma' ('The Red Apple'). He published a transcription of it in the Hungarian music journal *Magyar Lant* (*Hungarian Lyra*) on 15 February 1905, and the song later appeared as number 313 in his collection *cum* treatise *The Hungarian Folk Song*, which made its first appearance in 1924. Whereas in the latter volume Bartók gives the text simply as 'Piros alma leesett a sárba,/Ki felveszi, nem veszi hiába' ('The red apple fell into the mud,/Who picks it up will not be unrewarded'), in the version that he published as *Székely népdal* in 1905 there are three additional lines which continue the narrative as 'Én felveszem, kimosom a sárból/Elbúcsúzom a régi babámtól/Elbúcsúzom a régi babámtól' ('I pick it up and wash off all the mud/And say farewell to my old sweetheart'). For many European folk traditions the red apple is a symbol of virginity and fecundity, and indeed in some communities the bloodstained marriage sheets have been

ceremonially displayed to the groom's family after the wedding night, recipro-
cated by the gift of a bowl of red apples from the groom's parents to the bride's
parents. While there can be no doubt that the songs Lidi Dósa sang in Bartók's
earshot interested him because of their musical distinction from the *magyar
nóták* with which he was familiar, it is also possible that he was attracted by the
veiled sexual allusions of the text. The tune was modal in tonal orientation – a
blend of Dorian and Aeolian – and it must have seemed both austere and exotic
to the young man, pointing back to a much earlier tradition than the Gypsy-
disseminated *verbunkos*. Nevertheless, his published version involved a harmonisation that drew on contemporary harmonic trends, bearing some similarity
to the approach of Hugo Wolf (who had died in 1903).

If the sounds of Wagner were still fresh in Bartók's mind, it was to the
Magyarism of Liszt's Hungarian Rhapsodies that he returned in his own
Rhapsody for solo piano, op. 1 (dedicated to Emma Gruber), a large-scale work
lasting more than twenty minutes and the first piece to be published in his
mature system of work numbering (Fig. 6). The first five bars of the opening
*lassú* section yet again present the stock features of *style hongrois*, from the use
of the Gypsy scale, through the double-dotted rhythms, rapid broken chords
and rebounding *kuruc* fourths, to the modal ambiguity in the last bar. On the
following page the rhetorical and highly charged writing in the upper voices
involves parallelisms of thirds and sixths, recalling the approach of the
cimbalom player in a Gypsy band.

Figure 6.  The opening five bars of the Rhapsody for solo piano, op. 1.

While the Rhapsody is a work of considerable virtuosity, providing testimony to Bartók's technical accomplishment as a pianist and seeming as serious in intent and as politically motivated as *Kossuth*, it is still relatively conventional in its tonal ambit (albeit chromatically expressed). However, several incipient fingerprints of the composer's mature style can be detected in its course. Among these is the cyclic use of minor-third tonal relationships over the first few pages, in which stable areas of D minor, F major, A♭ major/minor and B major succeed each other. A more localised harmonic event that follows the underlying principle of harmonic substitution can be observed in the exchange of a chord of E♭ for a tonic (or possibly dominant) chord in C major in the eighth full bar. Modal flexibility is demonstrated by the alternation between major and minor versions of chords lying at points of closure, such that the A major chord in the fourth complete bar dissolves into A minor, and the C major chord in the ninth bar turns to C minor. Later, part the way through the *friss* section, Bartók places passages that lie a semitone away from each other side by side, causing an abrupt switch between G♯ minor and G major. Structurally and rhythmically, however, the Rhapsody does not stretch far from the familiar model of Liszt, a composer whose works Bartók had recently begun examining with greater diligence and enthusiasm. Among the pieces he prepared for a recital in Pozsony on 20 November 1904 were the *Funérailles* from *Harmonies Poétiques et Religieuses III*, the *First Mephisto Waltz*, and the variations on Bach's *Weinen, Klagen, Sorgen, Zagen*. In 1921 he would look back to this period and note how 'A really thorough study of Liszt's *oeuvre*, especially of some of his less well-known works, like *Années de Pèlerinage*, *Harmonies Poétiques et Religieuses*, the *Faust* Symphony, *Totentanz*, and others had, after being stripped of their mere external brilliance which I did not like, revealed to me the true essence of composing.'[39]

The opening and closing *lassú* sections of the Rhapsody are the most temporally extended and have the greatest emotional impact. Although they draw on standardised art-music reworkings of the Gypsy orchestra's performance practices, the influence of Liszt is audible in many of its details, including the contrapuntal passages in which entries of the opening theme overlap. As David Schneider notes, 'the climactic arrival in Bartók's Rhapsody generally fits Somfai's description of the "characteristically Hungarian culmination point"'. He distinguishes three specific aspects of this peroration in the major mode: 'there is a climactic reprise of music that has been heard before in a somewhat different form; the climactic passage occurs near the end of the movement but does not actually end it; and most important, this most exuberantly expressive passage of the work is densely packed with characteristically Hungarian markers.'[40] The Rhapsody's final bars are subdued rather than triumphant, indicative one might suggest of a political project that had not yet achieved its goals.

While he was still composing the Rhapsody, on 26 December 1904 the young composer wrote to his sister Elza a letter that brings together its composition and his new-found interest in traditional music:

> About me, I can tell that the rhapsody will be finished soon. It will be long and hard. I have a new plan now: collect together the most beautiful of Hungarian folk songs, and with the best possible piano accompaniment I will elevate them to the standards of an art song. This would be good because foreigners could learn about Hungarian folk music from collections like this. Our good Hungarians naturally don't deserve this. These are afraid of anything serious. They much prefer the usual Gypsy trash, which makes every musician and educated foreigner run away (*memento* Érsekújvár!).[41] If you accept me to your home for a short while, I'll play you the songs one by one; I'll have many of them finished by that point. – I need a little bit of help now; I especially want to know what's the continuation or the beginning of these songs? (their lyrics together with 2–3 bars).[42]

Bartók's request to his sister for information about tunes from the popular repertoire indicates his relatively limited knowledge at that stage. He would very soon develop a much more sophisticated understanding of Hungarian music through his interactions with people in the countryside for whom it was their vernacular, and he devoted much of the rest of his life to its collection, transcription and analysis. Although he may appear to have had a false start in his early musical developments and interests up to around 1905, in reality this laid the foundation for everything that was to follow.

In his first twenty-four years Béla Bartók had already achieved much. Despite the tragic early death of his father and the ensuing peripatetic lifestyle and frequent changes of school, he had completed his formal education satisfactorily, developed into one of the most technically accomplished pianists of his generation in Hungary, and had already found significant success and public acclaim, even notoriety, as a composer. He had set out the fundamental project for his life – to serve the native land he loved and to work to its benefit as a musician. And at the same time many of the personal and intellectual traits that would characterise him for the rest of his career had become apparent – scepticism about religion and authority figures in general, an interest in science and nature, a strong ethical sense, and a belief in the equality of men and women.

CHAPTER THREE

# 'Two roads are before me': 1905–1906

In their discussion of national and regional models of post-colonial literature, Bill Ashcroft, Gareth Griffiths and Helen Tiffin remark that:

> The study of national traditions is the first and most vital stage of the process of rejecting the claims of the centre to exclusivity. . . . Recent theories of a general post-colonial discourse question essentialist formulations which may lead to nationalist and racist orthodoxies, but they do not deny the great importance of maintaining each literature's sense of specific difference. . . . However, nationalism, in which some partial truth or cliché is elevated to orthodoxy, is a danger implicit in such national conceptions of literary production.[1]

It seems that sometime after his epiphany of 1904 Bartók started to recognise the 'cliché . . . elevated to orthodoxy' of the Hungarian national music performed by the Gypsy bands, and began to transfer his allegiance to the music of the rural peasantry. In so doing he was not merely abrogating the music of the German-speaking world, but that of the 'Magyar people' themselves. It should be remembered that traditionally the *natio Hungarica* or *populus* consisted of the nobility, Catholic clergy and city burghers alone, that social mobility was extremely restricted, and that in the countryside, semi-feudal conditions still largely prevailed. Bartók's advocacy of the music of the isolated villages would be seen as an act of treachery by some members of the gentry and nobility, as he noted on a number of occasions. The irony, of course, was that the very existence of this music was dependent upon the wretched conditions of the *misera plebs contribuens* ('the poor tax-paying population') of the country, which were largely created by the nobility and the rigid hierarchical structure of Hungarian society. While improvement in social and economic conditions would bring about greater mobility, it would thereby result in further 'corruption' of the music by the culture of the town.

By exploiting the codes of what he understood to be the most ancient and 'authentic' strand of Hungarian music, but within the context of a developing modernist style, Bartók was able, according to Max Paddison's reading of Adorno, to:

> span the gulf between, on the one hand, the ahistorical, epic 'natural community' (*Naturgemeinschaft*) of the pre-industrial world, where the 'individual' is represented by the hero, who speaks unproblematically for the community as a whole, and, on the other hand, the highly industrialized societies of the modern world, within which the individual, whose sense of the 'social whole' is now always partial and fragmented, exists in a state of alienation.[2]

In retrospect it is perhaps too easy to dismiss Bartók's early compositions as romantic 'blood and soil' nationalist works, and regard his output, particularly from 1908 onward, as their musical antithesis. Although critical of the repertoire of the Gypsy bands as shallow and superficial, he retained a certain affection for it throughout his creative life, noting in 1931 that 'the half-educated multitude of urban and semi-rural populations want mass products; let us be pleased that in music at least they are partial to domestic factory articles.'[3] The musical codes of the *verbunkos* never completely vanished from his language, and in the Concerto for Orchestra of 1943, a work full of both nostalgic reminiscence and confident forward-looking optimism, a number of them lie adjacent to codes inspired by peasant music. In Bartók's later output, however, the *style hongrois* gestures take on different meanings in their new context; no longer do they invoke the jingoistic Magyar nationalism of *Kossuth*, but symbolise the fragmentary and heterogeneous composition of society. Bartók had perhaps by then recognised that one had to return to the reality of the modern world with its complexity, ruptures and discontinuities.

One of Bartók's final compositions to be written in the early 'chauvinistic' style, but revealing intimations of the mature approach, was the Scherzo (Burlesque) op. 2 for piano and orchestra. This was completed towards the end of 1904 and it was intended that he should perform it in a programme of the Budapest Philharmonic Orchestra on 15 March 1905 conducted by István Kerner. However, this did not happen, as Bartók stormed out of the orchestral rehearsal, incensed both by the players' lack of preparation of the work and their failure to comprehend it, and he subsequently prohibited its performance. The premiere was finally given posthumously in 1961 and it was first published in that year.

The Scherzo is an extended concertante piece lasting around thirty minutes and is rhapsodical in style, drawing, at least in its early stages, both on familiar *verbunkos* gestures and the influence of Liszt and Richard Strauss. In a postcard sent by Bartók to his friend the poet Harsányi, he recounted how Hans Richter had described it as '*von und zu Übermenschen*' when he had played a draft of the work to him in Bayreuth in the summer of 1904.[4] He later wrote to István Thomán in September of that year (when the orchestration was still incomplete), describing the meeting in more detail. While Richter apparently thought it was 'a successful musical joke', he found it 'too grandiose, too complex, too "sparkling"' for such a plain title as Scherzo.[5]

Rooted in a modally and harmonically flexible E♭, it is notated without key signature and while the overall structure of the piece is straightforward – a scherzo and trio prefaced by a slow 'Hungarian' introduction and brought to a conclusion by a capricious coda – it is certainly more intricate than the scherzo of the incomplete Symphony in E♭ major (1902). The reprise from bar 597, marked 'scherzo da capo (ma poco variato)', brings the parenthetical burlesque aspects of the work's title to the foreground in a way that recalls the 'grotesque' aspects of *Kossuth* and in particular the deformation of the 'Gott erhalte', while presaging similar events in later works. For Julie Brown, 'many Bartókian moments lend themselves to description as musical "grotesquerie" according to its most common understanding as vulgar or bizarre sonic effect'.[6] Brown goes on to remark that 'Just as distinctions are not always precise between the syntactic categories of irony, satire, burlesque and the grotesque, so the grotesque in Bartók seems less than easy to pin down, overlapping as its characteristics do with other syntactic and figurative categories and concerns, including an interest in representations of transforming bodies'.

The introduction begins slowly and quietly, with a syncopated wave-like gesture (Fig. 7a) which, subtly transformed, acts as a motto theme to bind together the various parts of the work. During the course of this first section, from the end of bar 48, a change of metre to 6/8 signals the principal theme, which in outline involves a long looping descent and partial upward return (Fig. 7b).[7] Essentially harmonised in C minor in line with the underlying C Gypsy scale, it commences over the dominant seventh of C with the first and fourth quavers being harmonised with contextually dissonant augmented triads on E and D respectively; subsequent phrases involve the interplay between tonal areas of E♭, G and B major in a symmetrical trisection of the octave. Indeed, two particularly characteristic chord types employed by Bartók in the Scherzo are ones with whole-tone inflections and ones based on the half-diminished seventh 'Tristan' chord.

Figure 7. The motto theme and principal idea from the Scherzo (Burlesque), op. 2.

The burlesque treatment of the main theme in the scherzo da capo (bar 597 onwards) begins with alternating bars that are formed on the two mutually exclusive transpositions of the whole-tone scale (E♭–F–G–[A–]B–C♯ and E–[G♭–]A♭–B♭–[C–]D). While it is tempting to read Bartók's use of the whole-tone scale here as showing the influence of Debussy, it seems that he didn't start to study the latter's work seriously until 1907, following advice from Kodály. Bartók prominently employs a half-diminished-seventh chord (B–D–F–A) at the cadence of the section such that it resolves onto an E♭ triad, either as a type of 'mistuned' dominant or a chromatically altered and enharmonically renotated French sixth chord (the E♭ from C♭–E♭–F–A♮ being flattened to D♮).

At the same time, there remains the tendency noted in earlier works to place tonal areas that are separated by a semitone side by side. For example, the dominant seventh on B♭ established in bars 16–17 leads into a passage in E minor/major rather than the expected E♭ minor tonic; the B♭ that has been prepared in the passage leading up to bar 33 resolves to B major/minor in bars 34–5 before a slide back into E♭ minor; and the trio section in bars 498–596 is fundamentally in E major, a semitone above the work's tonic.

A sustained and graceful idea that seems to carry residual traces of 'Das Tanzlied' from Strauss's *Also sprach Zarathustra* (from bar 177) and the main theme of the scherzo proper (Fig. 7c), both derive from the motto theme. The latter is a simple variant that playfully alternates and superimposes 6/8 and 3/4 metres while retaining the harmonic ambiguity that underpinned its early presentation. From bar 303 the music presses forward with an accelerating section that, while acknowledging its debt to Gypsy music, prefigures the more acerbic and austere aspects of Bartók's mature style, and intimates his incipient reorientation from the Austro-German tradition. Built on the motto theme, this almost Stravinskian-sounding section opens with three five-bar phrases, the first of which is founded on an ostinato articulating a half-diminished-seventh chord (A–C–E♭–G). In the second phrase, placed a minor third higher than the first, Bartók employs a degree of modal flexibility such that the F supertonic is naturalised when ascending but flattened when descending. In contrast to the harmonically static initial phrase, first-inversion chords move in conjunct motion (E♭ minor – F major – G♭ major – F♭ major, etc.) against a pedal B♭, and such parallel writing remains a distinctive element of the composer's style as late as the Concerto for Orchestra and unfinished Viola Concerto.

In the course of the scherzo, the motto theme is further developed by means of irregular phrase length, and thus hypermetre – the higher-level metrical organisation – such that habitual four-bar units are largely avoided. As the expository section of the work drives towards its climax from bar 340, this irregularity is maintained as two six-bar phrases are followed by eight- and seven-bar phrases, dominated throughout by Hungarian anapaest rhythms in the piano part.

Although the Scherzo is a little-discussed work in the Bartókian literature and one that the composer himself suppressed and showed no subsequent interest in, it contains the rudiments or intimations of a number of the basic elements of the mature style: the use of symmetrical tonal areas; altered or 'mistuned' chordal functions; melodic contraction and expansion;

hypermetrical irregularity; and a marked tendency towards parody and the grotesque.

Between 1903 and 1907 Hungarian political life was dominated by a period of constitutional crisis. This began with what appears in retrospect to have been a simple piece of pragmatism by military leaders in late 1902 in relation to army bills in Austria and Hungary whose function was to increase the total number of recruits by some 21,000 men across the Dual Monarchy. Pending the approval of the legislation, supernumerary recruits beyond the currently mandated total, who would have been recalled once the bills were passed by the two parliaments, were required to remain in their barracks. Seizing its opportunity, the Independence Party (also known as the Party of 1848) led by Ferenc Kossuth, the eldest son of the great revolutionary leader, staunchly opposed the bill's progress in the Hungarian parliament. Employing filibustering tactics, the party refused to budge until the supernumerary recruits were allowed to return home. Although the recruits were discharged at the end of 1902, the Independence Party continued to press for concessions, particularly in relation to the use of the Magyar language (and other cultural aspects such as military music) by Hungarian troops. Innocuous as this may seem now, if the language of military orders had changed from German to Hungarian, the single line of control of the army would have been broken. As H. Wickham Steed, Walter Phillips and David Hannay noted a decade later:

> the crown considered [this] to be an encroachment upon the royal military prerogatives as defined by the Hungarian Fundamental Law XII. of 1867. Clause 11 of the law runs: 'In pursuance of the constitutional military prerogatives of His Majesty, everything relating to the unitary direction, leadership and inner organization of the whole army, and thus also of the Hungarian army as a complementary part of the whole army, is recognized as subject to His Majesty's disposal.' The cry for the Magyar words of command on which the subsequent constitutional crisis turned, was tantamount to a demand that the monarch should differentiate the Hungarian from the Austrian part of the joint army, and should render it impossible for any but Magyar officers to command Hungarian regiments, less than half of which have a majority of Magyar recruits.[8]

It was this aspect of the crisis which, at least in part, had stimulated Bartók to compose *Kossuth*, a work that had coalesced constitutional issues, the Hungarian army and Lajos Kossuth, and had encouraged him to proselytise the Magyar language and dress.

The Army Bill issue continued to be a major source of controversy and in March 1904 a partial, if short-term and coercive, resolution was found when the prime minister, István Tisza, threatened a guillotine motion. At the end of the following January, Tisza was defeated in a general election by a coalition of parties (including the Independence Party), though the Emperor refused to appoint them given the policies on which they had been elected, and the country was governed for a period by a non-parliamentary administration. It was only in April 1906 that the coalition agreed a pact that permitted it to take office and this was brought about largely by the threat of the introduction of universal suffrage (which would very likely have had a detrimental effect on the power of the Magyar nobility, given the demographics of Hungary). This was by no means the end of the affair, and in the following year further negotiation took place resulting in yet another pact. However, as Steed, Phillips and Hannay succinctly summarise:

> The agreement of 1907 had been but a truce in the battle between two irreconcilable principles; between Magyar nationalism, determined to maintain its ascendancy in an independent Hungary, and Habsburg imperialism, equally determined to preserve the economic and military unity of the Dual Monarchy. In this conflict the tactical advantage lay with the monarchy; for the Magyars were in a minority in Hungary, their ascendancy was based on a narrow and artificial franchise, and it was open to the king-emperor to hold *in terrorem* over them an appeal to the disfranchised majority.

Against this background of turmoil in his homeland and his previously expressed political views, it may seem a little strange that Bartók should choose to stay in the imperial capital of Vienna in the early months of 1905 if he still held such strong feelings about affairs of state. It is possible that Lajos Dietl, who was a professor of piano at the Vienna Conservatoire and one of his active supporters, was a factor in the decision to stay there. Bartók certainly wrote to him in December 1904 asking for advice about lodgings and suggesting that they meet up when he was in the city on 14 December. There can be no doubt, however, that for an aspiring composer and musician, even one of staunchly nationalist leanings, Vienna was the place to be at the beginning of the twentieth century.

Bartók was still keenly interested in the philosophy of Nietzsche, as a letter written to his sister Elza on 5 February amply demonstrates. He includes several quotations from *Human, All Too Human* and tells her that he is pleased to find Nietzsche articulating views he had held for some time. The first of these quotations is taken from section three of the first chapter, 'Of First and

Last Things', which is concerned with the failing of philosophers to see that man is not a constant, but like everything else, has 'become', and Bartók cites from the penultimate sentence, 'there are *no eternal facts*, just as there are no eternal truths'.

In the same letter he picks up the issue of women's rights, expostulating ' "Politics are unsuitable for women!" Who makes such an outrageous claim? What shall we make of it? That politics are fit for men, but not for women? Why and why not?'[9] He goes on to ask:

> And why should women not participate in certain matters, in the same way as men? It could be said instead that music and literature are not suitable for those engaged in agriculture, rather than that politics are not an appropriate subject for women. Nobody is going to compel an agricultural worker to listen to a concert, or give their opinion about a novel, but women are officially compelled to pay taxes, bring up their children in accordance with certain laws and so forth. What a narrow-minded attitude it is to exclude women from law-making, not even, indeed, to allow them an interest in politics, and yet at the same time make them subject to the laws that are enacted. In our country, of course, where there isn't even universal suffrage, it's laughable to express such sentiments.... I can understand the men's narrow-mindedness but in no way can I comprehend the women's complete calm. Where does this leave equality? Where indeed? How far are we still from that objective, we who make our wives our slaves; more servile than a servant because even divorce is only permitted in certain circumstances, under the laws enacted without their participation. On the other hand, of course, it's the husband's duty to take care of the women for life. And this is very good. And why not? For nearly two thousand years they have proclaimed this to be good. And what so many millions of men (amongst them many clever men, writers, poets, bishops and popes) claim to be good must indeed be holy writ! And this also is entirely just; the man supports his wife, and thereby assumes unlimited power over her. But there are, there will be exceptions to this. And what is now an exception will in a few hundred years become the norm. Women liberate themselves by earning in their own right. There's a strikingly enormous injustice here: woman is weaker than man, yet a double burden awaits her: bringing up children and earning a living. This injustice could be eased by adopting a certain social path. Yet it wouldn't be easy to bring in such fundamental reform.

On 18 February 1905 Bartók performed a solo recital at the prestigious Bösen-dorfer Konzertsaal in the Liechtenstein Palace on Herrengasse. His programme included Liszt's *Variations on a theme from Weinen, Klagen, Sorgen, Zagen by J. S. Bach, Funérailles* and *Spanish Rhapsody*; Schumann's Sonata in F♯ minor; Chopin's Ballade in F minor; and a Fantasy and the Scherzo from the set of four pieces Bartók composed in 1903. A few days earlier, on 15 February, the Budapest Philharmonic had performed Strauss's *Sinfonia domestica* under the baton of István Kerner and Bartók had penned an analysis which appeared in that week's edition of *Zeneközlöny* (*Music Gazette*), dealing with its broad structure and describing its principal motifs and their elaboration. Bartók's main intention, however, was to describe the non-musical narrative of a work that was a 'masterly depiction of the sentiments and moods of family life' and thus provide the programme that the composer had left unstated.[10] At the same time Bartók noted that:

> The classical simplicity of the work is astonishing, as is the complete lack of so-called cacophony. The subject of course demands such treatment. Excepting the introduction, the entire work might pass as a performance of absolute music, in which 'unity' and 'variety' are ideally blended.[11]

While staying in Vienna, Bartók worked on his First Suite for orchestra, a piece that for Antal Molnár 'constitutes the summit of his first creative period', as well as the culmination of the:

> 'Hungaristic' (all'ungharese, ungarisierend) musical romanticism, the chief exponents of which were Erkel, Liszt and Mosonyi. It also achieves the elevation of the well-known Hungarian national style, nourished on *verbunkos* and *csárdás* dance-tunes and popular drawing room ballads, to the purified sphere of absolute music. Drawing on the inferences of Erkel's and Mosonyi's vocal styles, of Liszt's interpretation of gipsy-music and his programme-music of Hungarian content, absorbing the worthwhile elements from native endeavours, Bartók succeeded in combining them all with the constructional methods prevailing at the turn of the century.[12]

The Suite is in five movements: Allegro vivace, a kind of compromise between sonata and rondo forms, with a reverse recapitulation; Poco adagio, a chain-like structure of four 'pictures'; Presto, a scherzo and trio; Moderato, a theme in three-bar phrases with what amounts to a set of variations; and Molto vivace, a brilliant Rondo finale that recalls several of the ideas from the previous movements. It is a work of symphonic proportions, lasting some thirty-five minutes, yet Bartók did not use the term 'symphony' to describe it and indeed avoided the term for the rest of his life despite his readiness to write concertos. (Significantly, his most substantial non-theatrical symphonic work not described as a suite would be the Concerto for Orchestra.) However, he did remark in a letter written to the Board of Directors of the Budapest Philharmonic Society on 10 December 1915, protesting about their performance of an attenuated version of the Suite in Vienna and Budapest, that it was 'not only symphonic: there is such a close thematic connection between the movements that certain bars of some of the movements cannot be understood unless one has already heard the preceding movements.'[13] The opening and closing tonalities of the work are E major, with the third and fourth movements relatively unambiguously focused on C major and A minor respectively. The second movement is more ambiguous, placing A minor and E major in tension, and it concludes on a chord of E major. Molnár has defined a set of three motifs that underpin the entire piece and help provide the thematic unity to which Bartók alluded: the first (a) is an articulation of a broken chord, falling then rising ($E_4$–$B_3$–$E_4$–$G\sharp_4$); the second (b) a scale segment and broken chord ($A_4$–$G\sharp_4$–$F\sharp_4$–$E_4$–$F\sharp_4$–$G\sharp_4$); and the third (c) a derivative of the first two ($F_5$–$E_5$–$D_5$–$C\sharp_5$–$D\sharp_5$–$E_5$).[14]

I have written elsewhere how the first theme of the opening movement bears a striking similarity to a *magyar nóta* tune collected and arranged by Francis (Ferenc) Korbay, and published in English and German by Schott and Co. Ltd in 1895, whose text reads:

> Good wine, youth and good health,
> Good wife make a man's wealth!
> Good and fair wife rare is,
> As a well-bred mare is;
> Both should ever young be.
>
> That girl! Why was she born?
> Lazy, sighing forlorn;
> Monday her health failing,
> Saturday still ailing,
> Sunday dancing is she!

Although there is no direct evidence for Bartók's awareness of this song, he was certainly still drawing on the *magyar nótá* repertoire for some time after hearing 'The Red Apple', as the letter to his sister on Boxing Day 1904 demonstrates, for he asks her for her assistance in finding the beginning or continuations of several tunes, including the very popular 'Az Egri ménes' ('The Herd of Eger'). According to György Kroó, in the original version of the Suite the second movement cited another well-known sentimental pseudo-folk song, 'Kék nefelejcs' ('Blue Forget-Me Not').

On a rather different tack, Benjamin Suchoff has suggested that the opening theme of the first movement is in fact a *verbunkos* transformation of the Austrian national anthem, the 'Gott erhalte'. During the time Bartók was staying in Vienna the sound of this melody would have been unavoidable, and it would be attractive to construct a post-colonial narrative that theorises such an apparent borrowing as a form of appropriation – 'the process by which language is taken and made to "bear the burden" of one's own cultural experience'.[15] However, while the thematic connection that Suchoff demonstrates between the two melodies is certainly plausible, one might presume that such an overtly political gesture would probably have elicited some comment from Bartók.

Whatever its stimulation – conscious or unconscious quotation, or mere coincidence – the first theme progresses with tremendous verve as a single enormous unbroken gesture, fifty-two bars in length. Part of its means of propulsion is the irregularity of the internal organisation of phrases such that the theme alternates unpredictably between three- and four-bar units. As I note elsewhere, this continually frustrates listeners' expectations, by simultaneously propelling and fragmenting the music.[16] The second theme, by contrast, has greater metrical regularity but is rhythmically asymmetrical, balancing long-held suspensions prefaced by a rising or falling major seventh in the first half of the phrase with more mobile figures in the second. Formally, Bartók elides a fairly straightforward sonata movement with elements of rondo, such that the blocks of thematic material can be interpreted as forming an ABA¹CA²BA structure, where the middle three sections effectively function as the development section. He would employ a not dissimilar tactic in the first movement of the Concerto for Orchestra nearly forty years later.

The second movement is perhaps the most interesting and unusual part of the work, and augurs the kind of textures that would be described as 'night music' in some of his later scores. Although Molnár also sees this movement as a kind of rondo, describing it schematically as A–B–C–A–B–D–C–A–B–A, it is perhaps as appropriate to see the prefatory decorated rising seventh of the 'A section', which invokes the opening of the second subject from the first movement, as a kind of promenade, like that of Mussorgsky in *Pictures at an Exhibition*, separating four 'portraits'. This initial gesture is, in itself, striking, as Bartók fills the seventh, not as might have been expected with pitches from a major or minor scale, but from a whole-tone scale (E–F♯–G♯–A♯–C–D–[D♯–E]). This is the first of a number of verbunkos gestures that pervade the movement, and in the first 'portrait' we hear the cor anglais, oboes and clarinets take on the role of the *tárogató* of the Gypsy band in an intense melody that draws heavily on the *lassú* performance style. The second of the 'portraits' (beginning at figure 9) is the most elaborate music Bartók had composed hitherto: over a bed of pianissimo tremolandos in the rest of the muted strings, and underpinned by the tritone G♯–D in the basses, the first violins and upper two desks of the seconds (soon joined by the flutes) play very rapid chromatic scales which interweave in conjunct and contrary motion to create a remarkable dense misty texture that may be taken to encode a rural landscape. Muted trumpets enter the scene, tapping out a rhythm in repeated notes, and are joined by woodwinds in moving towards a winding and impassioned melodic line. Overall, the portrait falls into two phases, the second a lightly varied reiteration one tone lower than the first. In mood and musical imagery this could be imagined to allude to the melancholy 'Lekaszálták már a rétet' whose singer, with the loss of his lover, sees himself like the yellowing autumn leaves with no hope of spring.

If the second 'portrait' draws on some of the most advanced modernist techniques of textural composition and orchestration, the third looks overtly to the popular song tradition. While its suave and somewhat maudlin melody (in E♭ major) is apparently an original composition of Bartók's, one could imagine that a song such as 'Kék nefelejcs' could well have been its model. Indeed, there are some correspondences, albeit tenuous, between the openings of the two tunes, both involving couplets with a falling minor third and a rising major second, separated in 'Kék nefelejcs' by a rising minor third (B♭–G–B♭–C) and in Bartók's tune by a falling major third (B♭–G–E♭–F). The movement is rounded off with a fourth portrait that has an element of recapitulation of the first. From rehearsal number 29, in a further modernist gesture, the dissonant notes D♯ and G♯ are repeatedly placed against the sustained A minor chord, and the final upbeat gesture brings the movement's rather unexpected cadence on E major.

Bartók returns to more familiar ground with the scherzo and trio that forms the centre of the Suite. This section takes up structurally where the Scherzo (Burlesque) had left off and interpolates into the trio a passage of development, a reminiscence of the textural music from the second movement and a new idea in duple time that has a certain Austrian character (though with the usual *style hongrois* codes such as dotted figures and 'scotch snaps'); perhaps this section provides some corroboration for Suchoff's suggestion of a possible connection to the 'Gott erhalte'. More significant for the composer's mature style is the modal flexibility of this idea – major and minor versions of the same chord being played in close succession (for example, in the first two bars of rehearsal number 30). The scherzo begins with the perfect fourths that characterised the first movement's main theme (Molnár's motif a), converting them into rebounding Kuruc fourths, and is propelled by a hemiola rhythm, an approach that Bartók had also taken in the 1897 *Scherzo oder Fantasie* and in the Piano Quintet. Here the first four bars of 3/4 effectively sound as if they are two bars of 3/2, with the following four bars restoring the primary metre. Despite this metrical irregularity, the movement as a whole is organised as a whole into eight-bar units.

The penultimate movement of the Suite can be regarded as a basic rondo form (ABA¹B¹A²), or alternately as a set of variations rather along the lines of the second movement of Beethoven's Seventh Symphony, given that the B sections develop the burlesque material from the A sections. Its phrase structure is regular, though the organisation of bars is in groups of three like Francis (Ferenc) Korbay's arrangement of the song 'Good wine . . .' (a common feature of much Hungarian popular music, whether formally composed or in the Gypsy-disseminated folk tradition, as Korbay's collection demonstrates). The opening idea is a further variant of the fourths-based motif, and the tonal organisation places the 'A' sections in A minor, A♭ major, A minor and A major respectively, a further example of the modal flexibility of the Suite. Despite the triple hypermetre, the movement has something of the spirit of the patriotic Rákóczi March (a melody that has often been regarded as the unofficial national anthem of Hungary).

With the finale, another rondo structure in the work's tonic key of E, many of the motifs outlined in previous movements are reprised in a bucolic and positive spirit. The major seventh that opens it, previously filled in with a whole tone scale at the onset of the second movement and having a rather ominous tone, is now turned into a B major scale. Although Bartók briefly establishes a 2/4 + 2/4 + 3/4 pattern (showing again an enthusiasm for additive rhythms well before the contact with Bulgarian and other Balkan music), this soon breaks down and, combined with the relentless syncopation, it becomes very difficult for the listener to predict or pin down the metre. The music briefly comes to a halt before the recall of an expressive *verbunkos* outcry from the second movement, and this is immediately converted into a fast *csárdás* with a syncopated accompaniment in C♯ minor. As the section progresses, the tonality slides through E major to G major, and after a passage of development in tonal flux, the tempo slows down at rehearsal number 19, in a section marked *molto sostenuto*, and briefly hovers around B♭ before returning to the pell-mell. The sequence of tonalities (C♯–E–G–B♭) lie on a diminished seventh and, as noted in Chapter 1 in respect of the song 'Est' and the Rhapsody op. 1, the discovery of such relationships, particularly in Bartók's mature music, encouraged the Hungarian musicologist Ernő Lendvai to develop his axis theory; these four tonal areas, according to Lendvai, function as substitute tonics. However plausible the broader theory is, in which each of the twelve tonal areas is accorded a function of tonic, subdominant or dominant (irre-spective of modal orientation), the application of tonal substitution across minor thirds, which Bartók presumably found through his studies of Liszt, Strauss and other *fin-de-siècle* composers, can certainly be observed in the finale of the Suite.

At rehearsal number 28, Bartók combines the final reprise of the main theme of the rondo contrapuntally with the opening theme from the first movement, initially in E in lower brass, bassoons and basses, before passing to trumpets, clarinets and violas in G, and then back to the trombones and tubas in B♭. In the run-up to the climax, the modal orientation shifts to whole tone, recalling the infill of the major seventh at the start of the second movement, and after a further brief recall of the mood of the Poco adagio, the finale comes to an end with a very lightly revised reprise of the final fifteen bars of the first movement's opening theme, restoring E major.

The first (incomplete) performance of the First Suite took place later that year on 29 November, appropriately in Vienna and performed by the Vienna Philharmonic under the baton of Ferdinand Löwe. In an autobiographical note he concocted in December, Bartók remarked that 'a week ago my orchestral suite, in all its Hungarian-ness, caused a sensation *in Vienna*'.[17]

One of the most important events for Bartók's later career was the introduc-tion to Zoltán Kodály. It is not exactly clear when this occurred. Denijs Dille places their first encounter at the end of 1904 or near the beginning of 1905, though they most certainly met on Saturday 18 March 1905 at Emma Gruber's salon in Budapest, three days after Bartók had performed Liszt's *Totentanz* with the Budapest Philharmonic Orchestra in the Vigadó concert hall, conducted by Kerner.[18] The programme had included the scherzo from his Symphony in E♭, and a postcard that Bartók sent to his mother after the concert reproduced the words 'Hans Koeßler bedauert sehr daß Sie heute nicht Zeuge des großen Erfolges Ihres Sohnes sein konnten' ('Hans Koessler regrets that you were not able to witness the great success of your son today'). Although Bartók and Kodály had been near contemporaries at the Academy of Music, surprisingly their paths had not crossed during their time there despite the fact that Koessler taught them both composition. It appears that Emma, who in 1910 became Kodály's wife, may have engineered their mutual introduction.

By this stage Kodály, who was Bartók's junior by a year, had studied Hungarian and German at the Péter Pázmány Catholic University in Budapest and at Eötvös College, as well as the Academy of Music. He was working on his doctoral studies, which would result in the PhD thesis *A Magyar népdal stró-faszerkezete* ('The Stanzaic Structure of Hungarian Folk Song') awarded the following April. The relationship that was established between Bartók and

Kodály on Saturday 18 March 1905 was remarkable. In 1921, at a very difficult period in Hungarian history, Bartók would write of him:

> I do not esteem Kodály as the best Hungarian musician because he is my friend; he has become my one and only friend because (apart from his wonderful human qualities) he is the best Hungarian musician. That it was I and not Kodály who realized the profit of this friendship merely proves once more his magnificent ability and self-effacing disinterestedness. In my career, which has not been entirely free of struggle, he has always stood by me bravely and openly, and has never spared trouble to further my success. . . . The experts know very well what a debt Hungarian musical folklore owes to him. His passion for research, his enduring diligence, his thoroughness, knowledge and clear vision have given him an unmatched knowledge of Hungarian peasant music. In this field nobody has come near him.[19]

Kodály set off on his first folk-song collecting trip in the summer of 1905, which took him to Galánta, a Slovak area that was then in the north-west of Hungary. He would later recall, in the introduction to the score of his 1933 orchestral work *Dances of Galánta* (*Galántai táncok*), how he spent 'the most beautiful seven years of his childhood' there. Meanwhile Bartók was preparing for the Fourth Rubinstein Competition in Paris, having entered for both the pianists' and the composers' prizes; he had also applied for a scholarship of 1,000 crowns for fieldwork in Transylvania, and he was notified in late May by the Academy of Music that this had been awarded to him. For part of June he stayed with his sister and her husband near the town of Vésztő in Békés County, in the south-east of Hungary, and the composer's son Béla claims he started transcribing some tunes from the area at that time. Over the course of Bartók's career, Békés would prove fertile ground, and of the 7,814 tunes identified as being collected by Bartók and six others (Kodály, Emma Kodály, Ákos Garay, László Lajtha, Molnár and Béla Vikár) in his 1924 monograph *A Magyar Népdal* (first published in English in 1931 as *Hungarian Folk Music*), 540 were discovered there (Bartók noting that 138 were collected from Vésztő alone).

The Paris competition proved a bitter disappointment, for Bartók failed to win prizes in either category. In a letter to his mother he makes it clear that he was not surprised that he had been unsuccessful in the piano section (which was won by Wilhelm Backhaus, who he describes in a later letter to his friend from Nagyszentmiklós, Irmy Jurkovics, as 'a truly fine pianist'), but was infuriated by the conduct of the judges in the Composers' Prize, for which he had submitted his Rhapsody op. 1 (describing it as a *Concertstück*) and the Piano

Quintet.[20] The Quintet was deemed too difficult to learn in the available time, and in its place Bartók substituted the Violin Sonata in E minor, which he played with the Russian violinist Lev Zeitlin who agreed to perform it at short notice. Bartók took the solo piano part in the Rhapsody with the Lamoureux Orchestra under the baton of the composer and conductor, Camille Chevillard and although he was generally happy with the performances, he was outraged that no composers' prize was awarded, and indeed that Attilio Brugnoli received the highest number of votes from judges for a 'certificate of merit'. With a tone of righteous indignation, he wrote to his mother 'I must say that Brugnoli's pieces are absolutely worthless conglomerations. It is quite scandalous that the jury could not see how much better my works are.' Later in the same letter he remarks that 'I wouldn't say a word if a composer of any worth at all had beaten me for the prize. But the fact that these dunderheads declared my works unworthy of the prize shows how extraordinarily stupid they were.'

Although the competition may have been a waste of Bartók's energy, he took the opportunity to investigate some of the major cultural landmarks and soak in the atmosphere of 'this heavenly godless city', including the Moulin Rouge (where the girls were '*comme il en faut*') and the Cabaret du Néant (the cabaret of nothingness), the Gothic night-club in Montmartre. While Bartók took great delight seeing the best-known masterpieces of fine art, it was Murillo's larger works in the Louvre that really impressed him, for he felt they:

> reveal a colour harmony such as you see in no other paintings. When I look at them, I feel as if I was being touched by a magic wand. It is an experience to be classed along with seeing a performance of *Tristan* or *Zarathustra*, attending the first Weingartner concert in Berlin, hearing Dohnányi play the Beethoven concerto in Vienna this year or catching my first glimpse of the Stephanskirche when I was in Vienna 3 or 4 years ago.[21]

Bartók does not specify the paintings by Murillo that particularly attracted him, but his reference to 'larger works' suggests it was probably the religiously inspired *The Angels' Kitchen* or *The Birth of the Virgin* rather than the smaller *The Young Beggar* (whose subject matter might have been deemed more attuned to the atheist composer's interests).

That Bartók could write to Irmy Jurkovics, a young woman whose father was a judge on the Nagyszentmiklós District Court, about prostitution, something that would certainly have been deemed a prurient issue, reveals how close their relationship was. Characteristically, however, Bartók notes that in so doing he is deliberately striking 'a little blow at R[ight] Hon[ourable] Convention'. After the descriptive elements of the letter he moves on to the issue of Hungarian music and talks about the high quality of the country's folk music compared to that of other nations. He tantalisingly alludes to a musical example that he has included with the letter (sadly since lost), which might possibly have been one he had collected in Vésztő a month or so earlier, and advises Irmy that 'if a peasant with the ability to compose tunes like the one enclosed had but emerged from his class during childhood and acquired an education, he would assuredly have created some outstanding works of great value'. One should not look to the intelligentsia who largely come from 'foreign stock' (and surely Bartók must have been aware of the irony of this statement, given his own ancestry on the maternal line), or to the aristocracy who are by and large incapable of understanding 'our national art'. What is required, Bartók claims, is 'a real *Hungarian* gentry', that middle stratum of society, as opposed to the 'haphazardly heterogeneous, rootless group of Germans and Jews' who formed the majority in Budapest: 'It is a waste of time trying to educate them in a national spirit. Much better to educate the (Hungarian) provinces.'

He then moves on, rather as he had with his sister, to philosophy, and draws on the metaphysics of Nietzsche with what has the appearance of a quotation, but as Dille points out, is probably a synopsis of aphorism 34 from *Human, All Too Human*: 'Each must strive to rise above all; nothing must touch him; he must be completely independent, completely indifferent. Only thus can he reconcile himself to death and the meaninglessness of life.'[22] Given the importance Bartók seems to accord to this statement, its apparent source merits detailed quotation from aphorism 34 ('On Tranquillity'):

> The whole of human life is deeply involved in untruth. The individual cannot extricate it from this pit without thereby fundamentally clashing with his whole past, without finding his present motives of conduct, (as that of honour) illegitimate, and without opposing scorn and contempt to the ambitions which prompt one to have regard for the future and for one's happiness in the future. Is it true, does there, then, remain but one way of thinking, which, as a personal consequence brings in its train despair, and as a theoretical [consequence brings in its train] a philosophy of decay, disintegration, self annihilation? I believe the deciding influence, as regards the after-effect of knowledge, will be the temperament of a man; I can, in addition to this after-effect just mentioned, suppose another, by means of which a much simpler life, and one freer from disturbances than the present, could be lived; so that at first the old motives of vehement passion might still have strength, owing to hereditary habit, but they would gradually grow weaker under the influence of purifying knowledge. A man would live, at

last, both among men and unto himself, as in the natural state, without praise, reproach, competition, feasting one's eyes, as if it were a play, upon much that formerly inspired dread. One would be rid of the strenuous element, and would no longer feel the goad of the reflection that man is not even [as much as] nature, nor more than nature. To be sure, this requires, as already stated, a good temperament, a fortified, gentle and naturally cheerful soul, a disposition that has no need to be on its guard against its own eccentricities and sudden outbreaks and that in its utterances manifests neither sullenness nor a snarling tone – those familiar, disagreeable characteristics of old dogs and old men that have been a long time chained up. Rather must a man, from whom the ordinary bondages of life have fallen away to so great an extent, so do that he only lives on in order to grow continually in knowledge, and to learn to resign, without envy and without disappointment, much, yes nearly everything, that has value in the eyes of men. He must be content with such a free, fearless soaring above men, manners, laws and traditional estimates of things, as the most desirable of all situations. He will freely share the joy of being in such a situation, and he has, perhaps, nothing else to share – in which renunciation and self-denial really most consist. But if more is asked of him, he will, with a benevolent shake of the head, refer to his brother, the free man of fact, and will, perhaps, not dissemble a little contempt: for, as regards his 'freedom', thereby hangs a tale.[23]

Freely admitting that he has not yet managed to elevate himself to this higher state, Bartók notes the paradox, which does seem to take on a personal significance, between the total indifference of the individual who has set himself free from ambition and the fervent desire he feels when he sees those who are still 'striving and struggling childishly for trivialities, incapable of rising higher', that all of humanity should 'rise to the same height'. Drawing further on Nietzsche, Bartók tells Irmy that he hopes this might stimulate a dialogue with her on the subject of religion. God, he asserts, is an invention of man and it is the material aspects of the body that are immortal, not the soul. And in another telling phase he notes the similarity of the vocations of priests and actors, both being preachers of fables. Unfortunately, we do not have Irmy's response to this letter, though Bartók ends with the complimentary closing 'hoping to hear from you'.[24]

He stayed in Paris until the first week of October 1905 and continued to take in the sights and soak up the atmosphere. On 10 September he wrote to his mother with some alacrity to advise her not to retire from her teaching job yet, and to tell her that he has hopes for a teaching job in the Music Academy once a new budget has been approved by parliament, though he is well aware that this may take some time because of the ongoing constitutional issues and what he describes as the Kaiser's policy of obstruction. Writing with surprising candour for a son to a mother, albeit taking a rather superior tone, he picks up the issue of equality, and perhaps thinking of his experiences of the courtesans at the Moulin Rouge he remarks that:

> Women should be accorded the same liberties as men. Women ought to be free to do the same things as men, or men ought not be free to do the things women aren't supposed to do – I used to believe that this should indeed be so for the sake of equality. However, after giving the subject a great deal of thought, I have come to believe that men and women are so different in mind and body that it may not be such a bad thing after all to demand from women a greater degree of chastity. These matters are too intimate to write about in detail.[25]

Clearly the philosophy of Nietzsche is still in his thoughts when he advises his mother that neither she, nor Bartók's sister Elza, should be concerned by solitude, and declares that 'spiritual loneliness' will be his destiny. He has been seeking his ideal life partner, but regards it as 'a vain quest' for 'even if I should ever succeed in finding someone, I am sure that I would soon be disappointed'. And in his final paragraph he recapitulates the theme he had exposed in the letter to Irmy Jurkovics:

> For solace, I would recommend to anyone the attempt to achieve a state of spiritual indifference in which it is possible to view the affairs of the world with complete indifference and with utmost tranquillity. . . . Sometimes I feel that for a brief space of time I have risen to these heights. Then comes a mighty crash; then again more struggle, always striving to rise higher; and this recurs again and again. The time may come when I shall be able to stay on the heights.

Over the next few months, Vienna became Bartók's base again, though in November he set off for England, to perform at the Free Trade Hall in Manchester with Richter and the Hallé Orchestra, playing Liszt's *Totentanz* and Bach's Chromatic Fantasy and Fugue. While his published letters are largely silent about the trip, and for all his talk about viewing the affairs of the world with complete indifference, there can be no doubt at all about the warmth of the concern he felt for his friends in the beautifully composed letter to Thomán, offering him his sincere sympathy in relation to a recent serious illness and surgery undergone by Mrs Thomán. Bartók's personal ennui shows through near the end of the letter, however, where he tells his old teacher that he suffers 'the same constant failure'.

His old flame and classmate Felicie Fábián had died at the age of twenty-one and was interred in the Wiener Zentralfriedhof on 8 October 1905 (where her name appears as Felizia). Although the cause of death was unclear, there has been some suggestion that it may have been suicide. Their relationship had broken down early in 1903 when she went to Vienna to study with the pianist and teacher Emil von Sauer. There are no further references to her in the published letters subsequent to February 1903 and indeed nothing to indicate that Bartók was aware of her death. However, between 1904 and 1905 he had arranged four *magyar népdalok* (Hungarian folk songs), of which one was posthumously published, by Dille in 1963. Perhaps coincidentally, this popular song called 'Lekaszálták már a rétet' ('The Meadow has been Scythed already') and discussed above in relation to the First Suite, speaks of the anguish of the jilted lover. Bartók's arrangement is in a similar vein to 'Est' written a year or so earlier and is predominantly harmonised in line with the Gypsy scale on C, with the fourth and sixth (final) lines being tonally more complex such that the lead-in to the cadence involves the progression $D\flat–A\flat–D^{o7}–D^7–G\sharp m–E–G$ [–Cm], an elaboration of the Neapolitan $\flat$II–V–I. Although the harmonic and tonal strategies of the accompaniment still do not stray far from the conventions of the time, it is striking how Bartók varies the time signature (including stretches in 5/8) to suggest the rubato singing style of the popular musician.

In November 1905, while still in Vienna, Bartók began work on a second orchestral suite, though this took much longer to compose than the first did and it wasn't completed (in its initial version) until September 1907, very slow progress in comparison with his previous swiftness. Hungarian folk music was exerting a greater impact on him now, forcing him to start to reconsider aspects of his musical language. He met Kodály once more at Emma Gruber's salon, early in January 1906, and heard about his trip collecting folk songs. The first fruits of their relationship would soon begin to be seeded through a project of twenty folk-song arrangements for voice and piano, the first ten by Bartók and the rest by Kodály, which would be published in December 1906 as *Magyar népdalok* (*Hungarian Folk Songs*). In the introduction jointly penned by the pair, they suggest that there are two main purposes for collecting folk songs: the first, to support scholarly study, is the production of a comprehensive corpus of material that functions like a dictionary; the second, to encourage the general public to be interested in this aspect of their culture, was to produce arrangements of the best of them, the 'pick of the crop'. Their collection was of this second kind, functioning as a taster for the broader genre, and in describing the approach they took in their arrangements the editors commented that:

> A meticulous selection is needed, and the choice pieces should be presented in a musical arrangement in order to make them more palatable to the taste of the public. If brought in from the fields into the towns, folk songs have to be dressed up. However, attired in their new habit, they might seem shy and out of place. One must take care to cut their new clothes so as not to cramp their fresh country style.[26]

The idealistic young composers acknowledged that it would take time to realise their vision of the songs finding a place in the musical life of the country, whether domestically or in the concert hall: 'The greater part of present-day Hungarian society is not Hungarian enough, nor naive enough and, on the other hand, not well-educated enough for these songs to find their way into the heart of these people.' Their expectation was not so much that the 'type of sham popular songs' would be entirely displaced, but that the 'ancient manifestations of the spirit of our folk' would at least sit on an even playing field with them.

The first half of 1906 was spent by Bartók sporadically touring as a concert pianist. Between January and March he was engaged for recitals in several cities and towns, including Graz, Pozsony, Temesvár (Timişoara) and Anklam (north Germany), before a more extended period in Spain and Portugal. Bartók attempted to act as an agent for both his own pianistic career and the jointly arranged collection of Hungarian folk songs. Writing at the end of January to Dr Lajos Posvék, a doctor who was the vice chair of Sopron's Literary and Artistic society, he described how he wished to develop 'a cultural link with the provincial towns of Hungary' and suggested that he might give a concert in Sopron 'possibly with one of the *better* local women singers'.[27] Although Bartók demonstrated that he had some understanding of the economics of concert organisation, proposing that local businessmen might take on the organisation with an appropriate percentage of the box office, and 'preliminary soundings' could be taken through advance bookings in order to 'discover whether the people of Sopron really like me', his approach was entirely unsuccessful. In March he wrote to Péter König, who was the director of the Szeged Music Conservatory, with a plea 'on a subject of national importance', namely that of encouraging subscribers from his students to the forthcoming collection of folk songs (described at this stage as being in two books, suggesting that he and Kodály intended to publish their arrangements in separate volumes). Again, this seems to have proved of very limited success given the very poor sales of the collection.

A more interesting activity, albeit involving 'mechanical musical work', was the series of recitals with the thirteen-year-old virtuoso violinist Ferenc Vecsey (chaperoned by his father, Lajos, also a violinist, with whom Bartók did not always entirely see eye to eye) in the Iberian Peninsula. Bartók arrived in Lisbon on 21 March, only to discover that the date of the first concert had been confused by the impresario and he almost immediately had to set off for Madrid, five hundred kilometres to the east, by means of a long and extremely tedious train journey on the 'abominable' Portuguese railway. A few days later, the pair were received by the Queen of Spain (Maria Christina of Austria, King Alfonso XIII's mother), for whom Bartók had very little respect. Commenting in a letter to his mother about Maria Christina's 'prize remark' that ' "Your King speaks Hungarian very well, doesn't he?" (Old Francis Joe!)', and on her request for them to perform some *csárdás*, he remarks 'if only she had known what a Hapsburg-hating republican she was speaking to!' Such inanities, he felt, would have been more bearable if she had been willing to pay them. Writing in 1944 to his great friend and collaborator, the violinist József Szigeti, Bartók recalled that while in Madrid, Vecsey's father had set up a meeting with Saint-Saëns for his son to play one of the concertos to him (Bartók couldn't remember which). It appears that under his father's instruction Ferenc performed the second movement at an excessively slow tempo and that Saint-Saëns stepped in to illustrate the correct speed before leaving, which Bartók commented 'made this otherwise boring (at least for me) piece at least tolerable'. It seems that after Saint-Saëns' departure and much to Bartók's amusement, the enraged Ferenc came out with the comment 'Oh, he does not understand, he is not a violinist!'[28]

Bartók's description of Lisbon, which he describes as a 'Demi-Afrique', shows just how entranced he was with its beauty and chaotic bustle, despite the poverty and degradation:

> It's not a place for nervous people, though. The streets are incredibly noisy, full of street-sellers all shouting their wares at the top of their voices. There are such a lot of mules, all overburdened with merchandise. And what ghastly filth in some quarters of the town! . . . And yet the general impression is indescribably pleasing. The sun does not shine in other lands with such kindliness as here; it transforms even the narrowest and most crooked streets. The city has a unique atmosphere.[29]

He was much less impressed with Madrid, which he saw as being rather similar to Budapest, and found the local custom of 'vin compris' – being given half a carafe of wine with each meal – while pleasurable, had left him feeling 'rather the worse for drink' every day.

Bartók's travels over the next couple of months can be reconstructed through the postcards and letters he sent to his mother, his sister, and to his old teacher and friend, István Thomán. On 11 April he visited the ancient Portuguese university city of Coimbra and spent much of the rest of April in the vicinity of Lisbon, with trips to Sintra and the seaside town of Cascais. At the beginning of May, he returned to Spain, staying for a little over a week in Madrid before going to Seville and Cadiz. Taking the ferry across the Mediterranean from Cadiz to Tangier in Morocco, he remained there for several days before returning to Europe by way of Gibraltar, sending his sister a postcard from there on 19 May. Back in Spain, Bartók returned to Madrid via Córdoba and finished the Spanish leg of his vacation in Barcelona (where in his estimation, Europe could be deemed to begin again). The royal wedding in Spain between Alfonso XIII and Princess Victoria Eugenie of Battenberg, due to take place on 31 May, offered a good reason to clear out of Spain with alacrity and he headed via Marseille to Venice, taking in much of the Mediterranean coast of France. A postcard to his mother from Venice, dated 26 May, tells her how he broke his journey by visiting the Milan World Exhibition (which celebrated the completion of the twenty-kilometre-long Simplon railway tunnel through the alps) and that 'the most beautiful thing I have seen on my trip to Spain – is Venice. It's divine!'[30] Bartók's final stopping point before returning to Budapest was the Free State of Fiume (which had the status of *corpus separatum* within the Kingdom of Hungary), round the Adriatic from Venice. From here the railway line created by the Fiumian Giovanni de Ciotta at the end of the previous century took the young composer back to Hungary's capital at the end of May, where for a brief period he could take a rest from travel.

Soon after returning to Budapest, Bartók was notified that he had been awarded the national music first prize of 1,600 krone by the Budapest Municipal Council in celebration of the anniversary of the coronation of the Emperor Franz Joseph (the second music prize went to the composer László Toldy).[31] Much of the following months would be spent in a further tour, however this time not performing but beginning the programme of work he and Kodály had set in motion – seeking out and collecting folk songs. Bartók's approach was pragmatic and heuristic, in that he generally stayed with family and friends and drew on their connections to come into contact with singers and musicians. Although, following the example of Béla Vikár (1859–1945), the great Hungarian pioneer of the phonograph as a tool for folk-music study, Bartók began to use the Edison machine to record songs and instrumental pieces, his method could not yet be described as having the 'scientific' rigour and fastidiousness that would characterise his later approach.

He commenced close to Budapest, staying for several weeks at the Vecsey's Witzenrad villa in the holiday village of Rákoskeresztúr, now in district XVII in the suburbs of Pest not far from the airport. It seems that the atmosphere at meal times was extremely formal and stuffy, and Bartók increasingly transformed himself during the period he stayed there into a bohemian in dress and manners, noting to his mother that 'as I have a taste for dissonance, I intend to invade this scene of awful orderliness wearing my summer shirt, without collar or cuffs, and my oldest shoes – just to shock them'.[32] From Rákoskeresztúr he visited the town of Tura some forty kilometres to the west, staying with the family of István Hajdu, Elza's brother-in-law, and managed to collect seventy-five songs in three days ('mostly old songs'), the Saturday evening and Sunday providing the largest trawl – with the wine flowing freely. It seems that István (or Pista as he calls him) was something of a religious fanatic, and Bartók informs his mother that he had to be very careful to restrain himself from making inappropriate comments.[33] He had meanwhile spoken to Willibald Seemayer, the director of the ethnography department of the National Museum (in part to see whether free rail travel could be organised for his collecting trips) and was enthusiastic about providing the museum with the materials. It was while collecting a second tranche of seventy-six songs from Tura that Bartók first used the phonograph systematically.

By 19 July 1906 Bartók was at the home of his sister and her husband, Emil Oláh Tóth (the manager of the Wenckheim family estate at Sziladpuszta in Békés County), around 180 kilometres to the south-east of Budapest. He was introduced to several farm managers who were to help him orient himself and find potential subjects. From here he visited the fair at the town of Gyula (the birthplace of Ferenc Erkel) on Friday 20 July, but with no success 'except as a dust swallower', for neither the farm manager from the estate who was supposed to guide him, nor a bagpiper called Vágássy who he had hoped would show up, appeared. In a letter sent to his mother on his return to Rákoskeresztúr, which is dated 15 July but was actually sent on 27 July (Bartók was characteristically conserving paper), Bartók tells her how the hotel he stayed in (the second best in Gyula and the only one with a vacancy) appeared to double as a brothel. The following day, in Benedek, proved equally futile, but finally on the Sunday he managed to collect some material from Fekete-ér puszta near the town of Sarkad. Thanks to the help of another farm manager called Franck, he visited the village of Doboz, bringing his phonograph with him, to meet some of the swineherds and shepherds, and he also recorded a domestic servant at Benedik. Singers were invited to supper and Bartók took the opportunity to record and transcribe a number of their songs. He indicates that he took down some eighty-seven melodies and made forty-seven recordings overall in the region, and thus what had initially seemed to have the makings of an unproductive trip proved eventually to be extremely worthwhile.

At some point in August, Bartók went to Tápiószele, a town fifty kilometres to the south-east of Budapest, and collected thirty-two songs. He also managed a further trip to Gerlicepuszta, up in the far north of Hungary (now in Slovakia), where he had previously stayed in the Fischer's house in 1904. This trip also proved highly successful and he recorded 120 songs in the local villages of which around one third were Hungarian. By the end of the third week of August, he was back in Rákoskeresztúr with the Vecseys, setting out his plans for the rest of the year, involving more folk-recording trips and concert activities. Towards the end of August, he again drew on old contacts, staying at the home of Mrs Gyula Baranyai, near Szeged. She and her husband, who was the principal of a school in Szeged, had taught in Nagyszőllős while the Bartóks were living there, and Bartók's mother, Paula, had remained in touch with her over the years. Bartók collected a number of songs in the region, dropping in to Nagyszentmiklós before returning to his temporary base at Rákoskeresztúr.

A diary entry by Béla Balázs (1884–1948) on 5 September indicates that Bartók met his future librettist during his stay in Szeged, while visiting his family home. Balázs had shared a room with Kodály at the Eötvös College in Budapest and it was through the latter that the introduction was arranged. In a private pen portrait which reads rather like character assassination, the young man described his mixed feelings about Bartók, whom he had joined in collecting folk songs, seeing in him a balance of fragility ('he is a weak, puny, sickly little man') and strength ('there exists in him an incredibly quiet tenacity'); modesty ('like a little girl') and vanity. Balázs comments that Bartók is prone to hyperactivity: 'He is inquisitive, impatient, unable to keep still, but seems to be searching for something whose *reality* he already senses'. Although he did not particularly take to Bartók as a person, Balázs could glimpse that he might be 'more than a grown-up Wunderkind composer'.[34] He noted that Bartók took a copy of one of his poems, titled 'Nocturne', from their meeting with the intention of setting it to music, though this does not seem to have materialised. (A 'Nocturno' by Balázs appears in the sixth number of the literary journal *Nyugat* for 1910.)

Clearly, very good progress had been made in finding material for the folk-music collection that Bartók and Kodály had planned earlier in the year. The two met together for three days in early September and plotted their previously discussed introduction in which, Bartók tells his mother, 'we have some harsh things to say about Hungarian audiences'.[35] He had personally collected ten of the eleven tunes that he set (the third song, 'Fehér László' appearing in two different versions), and only the eighth, 'Végig mentem a tárkányi sej', came from the collection of Béla Vikár (four of Kodály's songs were taken from this source). Of the tunes Bartók set, four (1, 3, 5 and 10) were collected in Gyula and Doboz in Békes County; two (2 and 9) came from Szeges and Szentes in the neighbouring county of Csongrád; two (4 and 6) from Tura in Pest County; and one (7) was transcribed from Lidi Dósa, the maid from Kibéd in Maros-Turda, whom he had first met in 1904 while staying in Gerlicepuszta.

Bartók's arrangements are carefully organised, so that the first pair share a melodic characteristic (a rising octave at the start of the tune); the second pair have the same texts, but different tunes; and the third pair are Dorian and Mixolydian variants of the same basic tune. Of the other tunes, number seven, taken from Lidi Dósa, is, with the exception of one B♭, a pentatonic melody. It is notable how many of the tunes are what Bartók would later describe as being 'architectonic' in form, having a reprise (whether varied or not) of the first line in the final line (2, 4, 5, 6, 8 and 10); and only one of them (number 8, from Vikár) is in three-bar phrases, a feature that would be of peculiar interest to Bartók in his own compositional technique.

Bartók's approach to the accompaniments was, on the whole, quite different to that taken in his earlier setting of 'Piros alma', where chromatic harmony was employed in a largely homophonic texture. The sparsest setting is of the first version of 'Fehér László', a song that can be found in a transcription and phonograph recording made of Zsuzsi Köteles in Doboz in July 1906 and narrates the story of its eponymous subject who is 'cast into the deepest dungeon' for the theft of a horse.[36] Here the left hand plays the song melody with occasional sustained dyads implying D minor, or open fifths on A, and a final pair of chords which give a cadence that has a half-diminished-seventh chord (E–G–B♭–D) in first inversion resolving on a D minor tonic. The other setting of 'Fehér László' was recorded in Tura by Mihályné Veszelka and appears as number 24 in *The Hungarian Folk Song*. One curious feature that appears neither in this publication nor in the setting in *Magyar népdalok* is Veszelka's performance of the final line, which is sung an octave higher than notated (but is shown at this pitch in the original transcription). Although the accompaniment is more elaborate than the first setting, the harmonisation is again simple, but with some novel touches, such as the doublings between hands in the third line and the almost parallel triads in the final line (A–B♭–C–F–B♭).

Bartók and Kodály were jointly responsible for funding the publication and had been trying to draw in subscribers with limited success. Bartók wrote in November from Pozsony to his friend and supporter in Vienna, the piano professor Lajos Dietl, informing him of a recital the following day in the city for the 'Tulip League' and complaining that he had had to 'force my fingers to play unimportant popular items', being so out of practice (it seems he'd arranged for a piano to be taken to Gerlicepuszta). He speaks of spending 'every evening for three weeks in Slovakian villages', transcribing 150 songs and phonographing 80. He then moves on to the issue of the *Magyar népdalok*:

> In a few days I shall be sending a scolding letter to those negligent people who have so far failed to send in their subscription lists. Kindly accept your share of the reprimand together with this letter. I have to let people know that if these lists are not sent in very soon, we shall suffer a considerable loss through not fulfilling our agreement with the publisher.[37]

As well as this concert, which included the Bach Chromatic Fantasia and Fugue, one of Chopin's Scherzos, and his own Rhapsody, Bartók performed Saint-Saëns' Second Piano Concerto in G minor in Budapest with the Philharmonic Orchestra under the baton of Kerner, a work for which, one may readily imagine, he did not have the greatest degree of enthusiasm.

Meanwhile what of his composition through this period of travel and discovery? He had started work on the Second Suite for small orchestra while staying in Vienna at the end of 1905, and had finished the first three movements, but put it aside before composing the fourth in 1907, completing the orchestration on 1 September of that year. However, this would not be his final word on the piece and he revised it substantially twice: in 1920 and again in 1941, the latter being published by Boosey & Hawkes as the 'revised 1943 version'. It is scored for a smaller orchestra than the First Suite, for double woodwind (with doublings on piccolo, cor anglais, E♭ and bass clarinets, and contrabassoon), three horns, two trumpets, timpani, percussion, two harps and strings. While the outer movements are in B♭, the scherzo which forms the second movement is, nominally at least, in G major, and the slow third movement ends on a chord of F♯ minor (with an added minor seventh), creating the rather curious overall tonal skeleton of B♭–G–F♯–B♭. As well as being in four rather than five movements, it is somewhat more compact musically, temporally and emotionally than the First Suite, and has the feel of a serenade about it; indeed Bartók used this very term to describe it on a postcard sent on 17 August 1907 to the pianist Etelka Freund (1879–1977), one of his few composition students and who had performed for Brahms and studied with Busoni (who apparently regarded her as his finest student).

In April 1910 Bartók wrote to Frederick Delius of the Second Suite's intended 'contradiction of the commonplace'.[38] Its commodious ternary-form opening movement (he specifically gives the tempo marking as *comodo*) certainly avoids the chauvinistic bombast of the Allegro vivace of the First Suite. Prefaced by a gentle ostinato outlining the tonic chord in the first harp, which deceives the ear through its hemiolas into imagining a tempo that is half the actual speed, the idea initiated by a solo cello (Fig. 8), which is initially elaborated in dialogue with the quadruple-divided violas, articulates a decorated arpeggiation of B♭. Allowing for the metrical changes, this five-bar figure (whose underlying four-bar pattern is extended by the varied repetition of the first bar) seems redolent of Brahms despite the overall influence of Richard Strauss. The cello's second phrase picks up the whole-tone implications of the French sixth in G (E♭–G–A–C♯), which underpins it harmonically, while introducing as a variant of the fifth bar of the theme a gesture of two short notes separated by a rest from a longer one (♫ ♪♩) – a version of a *style hongrois* figure that had appeared in the second theme of the first movement of the First Suite. In the third phrase the cello's line accommodates the half-diminished seventh (notated as E♭–G♭–A–C♯), a Wagnerian chord whose influence Bartók had still not escaped. The thirty-nine-bar opening idea cadences, not on the tonic of B♭, but a major third higher on the mediant chord of D major, and the varied repeat of the section closes on G major.

Figure 8. The opening theme of the first movement of the Second Suite.

The central section of the movement takes up the *style hongrois* figure first presented by the cello, now prefaced by a rapidly rising scalic gesture akin to that found in the second movement of the First Suite, and it is here that some of the more Straussian elements make their presence felt. Perhaps the most extraordinary section, prescient of several ideas that would appear in the Concerto for Orchestra, can be found in the reprise in B (a semitone higher than expected) from rehearsal number 15. Here the pair of harps repeat bare fifths (B–F♯) in a regular 3/8 rather than the hemiola rhythm that had opened the movement, and against this the first oboe plays a melody that improvisatorially oscillates around a dissonant A♯. The final part of the movement again begins off-centre, in D♭ major, and involves a further passage that Bartók appears to have half recalled in the Concerto for Orchestra, in the transition to the horn call in the recapitulation of the finale.

The second movement is a scherzo, written in a type of small-scale sonata form in which a fugal passage takes on the role of the development section. Its metre is irregular with many changes of time signature throughout its course. Although the melodic idea from rehearsal number 1, which is replete with rhetorical flourishes as it works its way to a D major triad, does have something of the triumphalism of the First Suite, overall it has a more ambiguous character and it feels as if it takes up from the burlesque reprise of the Scherzo op. 2. It is certainly quite difficult to hear the final triad of G as a tonic in the conventional sense, for although the movement is fundamentally tonal, it is very wide-ranging harmonically and the primary tonality is not strongly established, such that when unison Gs appear at the movement's climax (alternating with Fs) they seem to have the disposition of a dominant.

In the discussion of Bartók's Variations for Piano on a theme of Felicie Fábián in Chapter 1, there was an allusion to a compositional device that Bartók used at certain strategic moments in his mature works involving harmonic sequences that work their way through cycles of fifths, perhaps most famously in the cantabile theme of the fourth movement of the Concerto for Orchestra. An example of this approach can be found at rehearsal number 6 of the scherzo, where piccolos and E♭ clarinets initiate a downward spiral of arpeggios through winds and strings that dovetail together so that the root of one chord becomes the fifth of the next (E♭ min–A♭ min–D♭ min–G♭ min–B min–E min–A min). When this gesture is almost immediately repeated, it is distorted such that the subsequent fifth of the triad is a second lower than the root of the previous one (C♯ min–F min–A♭ min–C min–E min–A♭ min–C min).

The fugato section from rehearsal number 10, the opening of whose subject combines the falling arpeggio motif with a rising minor sixth and falling diminished seventh ($G_4$–$E♭_4$–$C_4$–$E♭_4$–$C_4$–$A♭_4$–$B_3$), may perhaps suggest the influence of Bach's Chromatic Fantasia and Fugue, which had become a mainstay of Bartók's solo recitals that year. But in fact, as Malcolm Gillies has noted, the model would appear to be the third movement of Liszt's 'Faust' Symphony as well as possibly being 'conditioned' by Liszt's use of fugal technique in his piano sonata.[39] At the climax of the section, the music becomes metrically complex and the combination of changing time signatures (including a number of bars in 5/8) and grouping running across bar lines makes the temporal organisation difficult for the ear to disentangle, while the sense of a regular hypermetre is temporarily lost.

Bartók gave the subtitle 'Scena della puszta' to the third movement in the two-piano reduction of the Suite he made in the 1940s. This Andante opens with an extended solo for the bass clarinet. Although it does not at first seem to demonstrate directly the influence of the traditional tunes that Bartók discovered at Gerlicepuszta (indeed one might question whether he could have been invoking the cor anglais solo that leads into the first scene of act three of *Tristan und Isolde*), there are three striking features which are exposed in this material. The first is a melody that is organised at the outset in three-bar phrases and starts in the Aeolian mode on F♯ before opening out chromatically; the second involves a descending perfect fourth played with a Hungarian Iambic rhythm and repeated note figure; and the third is a motif consisting of four of the five notes of a pentatonic scale that descends through an F♯m$^7$ chord (F♯–E–C♯–A–F♯). Bartók alludes to this idea in his 1928 essay 'The Folk Songs of Hungary':

> Because of the equal importance of the above-named degrees of the pentatonic scale, it follows that in pentatonic melodies the modal diminished seventh takes on the character of a consonant interval. This fact, as early as 1905, led me to end a composition in f♯ minor with the chord: f♯ a c♯ e. Hence in the closing chord the seventh figures as a consonant interval. At that time a close of this kind was something quite out of the ordinary. (Only in works by Debussy of approximately the same period could a parallel case be found.[40]

It was in 1907 that Bartók, through the mediation of Kodály, studied Debussy's music 'thoroughly and was greatly surprised to find in his work "pentatonic phrases" similar in character to those contained in our peasant music'.[41]

The pentatonic motif outlined by the bass clarinet halfway through its opening solo dominates the second section in which it is developed with increasing passion, reaching its climax at rehearsal number 3 in a long descending chain of thirds that covers the whole of chromatic space (if the D in the previous bar is taken into account). Two harps and tremolando strings move the tonality to B major (with an added major sixth) in the beautifully scored third part. This presents the melody from the beginning of the bass clarinet's solo in the lower woodwinds accompanied by trills and cascading fioriture in the upper woodwinds which pre-empt the later night-music style. A brief coda brings the movement to its conclusion with the closing pentatonic seventh chord.

Pentatonicism also suffuses the main theme of the finale, initiated by the first bassoon against a static harmony of steadily repeating thirdless chords of B♭. The movement as a whole is structured through the interaction of such harmonic plateaux with more tonally mobile material. In retrospect Bartók would find himself agreeing with Delius that this was the weakest movement of the Suite – 'rather lacking in invention'.

Quite a significant journey is travelled across the four movements of the Second Suite and the passage of time and experience is etched on its contours. Bartók's movement away from Richard Strauss is clearly audible, and elements of the mature style are beginning to come into focus. Of his early works, this seems to have been one for which he retained the greatest affection, and indeed traces of it can be faintly read in his final completed orchestral work, the Concerto for Orchestra.

## CHAPTER FOUR

# 'Because my love has forsaken me': 1907–1909

As 1906 moved towards its close, a year that had been one of almost continual activity and travel with no fixed base, neither professional nor domestic, the opportunity for some stability in Bartók's life began to emerge. His teacher and friend István Thomán had been compelled to resign from his teaching role in the Academy of Music. Bartók was subsequently appointed as professor of piano on a temporary basis on a salary of 4,500 krone per year and the position was regularised some two years later. At last he was able to settle down in Budapest and have a permanent home there. His concert activity was largely curtailed over the next three years as he spent his time teaching, composing and collecting folk music. In 1907 the Academy moved to its new building (which it still occupies) on Liszt Ferenc tér, below Teréz körút and near to the Oktogon. Bartók was afforded the privilege of being chosen to play in the inauguration of the concert hall on 13 May, a gala concert to the memory of the 'glorified' past masters, performing Volkmann's Piano Concerto in C. Bartók's First Suite was given in a concert several days later by illustrious former students, including Dohnányi, and the violinists Ferenc Vecsey and Stefi Geyer.

Geyer, born in Budapest in 1888, the daughter of a police doctor, was a child prodigy who had studied with Jenő Hubay at the Academy of Music. Bartók seems to have come across her while he was still a student and he refers to a concert by her in a letter to his mother on 4 March 1902. But it wasn't until 1907, when she was in her eighteenth year, that Bartók became completely infatuated with her. He visited the home of her uncle (a pharmacist) and aunt in Jászberény, eighty kilometres to the east of Budapest, on 28 June, ostensibly to collect songs, though Stefi averred in an interview with Denijs Dille in 1953 that the relative paucity of folk music in the area implied that the real reason must have been to see her. In fact, the Bartók complete online collection does identify eighteen songs that were collected in the town in the months of June and July, so it seems that the trip was not entirely in vain.[1] Bartók writes laconically in a postcard to his mother, in the house they were renting on Mária utca in Rákospalota in north-east Budapest, about the great heat, the dust, the mosquitoes and the hospitality. (Paula had moved from Pozsony to Budapest in May 1907 to join her son, but this first house proved entirely unsuitable and they rented an apartment at 17 Teréz körút in November of that year.)

Meanwhile Bartók finally set off on a tour to collect folk songs in the Hungarian region of Transylvania, an endeavour for which he had received funding in 1905. He left the Geyer's house in Jászberény on 1 July 1907 and took the train to Szolnok. Bartók reached Bánffy-Hunyad (now Huedin) in the Apuseni Mountains of Transylvania by 5 July. While staying there for one night he ordered a writing desk with rose designs from György Gyugyi Péntek, a master craftsman from the nearby village of Körösfő (Izvoru Crişului), a desk that matched cabinets he had previously purchased. These pieces of rural craftwork would be among the composer's most prized possessions, remaining with him during his various moves in Budapest. They can still be seen in the Béla Bartók Memorial House (based in the building he lived in between 1932 and 1940 in Csalán utca in Buda), his eldest son Béla having looked after them carefully during the war years. Bánffy-Hunyad lies around one hundred kilometres east of Nagyvárad (Oradea), where Bartók had lived between September 1891 and March 1892. Around this time the predominant language was Hungarian, most people being Calvinist by religion. The following day, 6 July, Bartók arrived at the city of Brassó (Braşov) further down the line from Nagyvárad. He greatly admired Brassó and took in the sights of the area, including the Csángó Hungarian 'seven villages' (Szecseleváros in Hungarian, now Săcele). He advised his mother that her next mail should be sent *poste restante* to the village of Csíkrákos (Racu), 160 kilometres to the north, the last stop on the railway line before it turned eastwards and at the centre of mountainous Csík County.

Baedeker's 1905 volume on Austria-Hungary said of the Hungarian inhabitants of Transylvania:

> The *Magyars*, who entered the land as conquerors, and settled mainly in the N.W. districts – The *Szeklers*; kinsfolk of the Magyars, who were settled in E. Transylvania at an unknown date, in order to act as 'Szekler', or guardians of the frontier, and who at one time erroneously regarded themselves as descendants of the Huns. The Magyars in Transylvania, including the Szeklers, number about 800,000 souls.[2]

Baedeker advised that there were in the order of 200,000 Saxons, nearly 1.5 million Romanians, and around 90,000 gypsies in the region. Clearly the issue of a relatively isolated ethnic Hungarian minority group within a territory in which Romanians formed the majority was significant at the time, and indeed it remains so to this day. Bartók had two potential advantages working with Transylvanian Hungarians (much as Cecil Sharp would have in his collections in the southern Appalachians of the USA): he was able to communicate with them without a language barrier and he had access to a repertoire that had been largely insulated from developments within other parts of Hungary.

The timing of his collecting activity over the next few weeks is not entirely certain, though a note in the so-called Black Pocket-Book, in which Bartók made sketches for compositions between 1907 and 1922, appears to indicate that he went from Brassó to Kolozsvár on 15 July. He definitely sent a postcard to the pianist Etelka Freund on 30 July from Csík-Karczfalva, a little way further up the valley from Brassó, telling her that the *poste restante* address for his mail would be Gyergyószentmiklós for the following twelve days. On 16 August he wrote to Stefi Geyer from Kilyénfalva in the Gyergyó region of Csík County in the form of a dialogue between the traveller (Bartók) and a peasant woman, and it appears that he had been there for some time. This letter very entertainingly describes the difficulties of collecting folk songs and his frustration, for his respondent (recommended by someone else in the village) first claims to know no old songs, and then says her singing days are over. On being whistled a tune by Bartók, she fails to remember the words, but when she eventually does start to sing, the songs are popular ones composed by the gentry and known throughout Hungary. Even worse, she offers him sacred songs – 'the gentleman has never heard anything more beautiful,' she tells him, and she finally suggests another local who 'knows a great deal, especially when she's had a drink or two'. At this stage Bartók breaks down:

> And so *da capo* from morning to night, Monday to Sunday (day after day)! I can't bear it any longer. Impossible!
>
> Endurance, perseverance, patience . . . to hell with you all . . . I'm going home.
>
> I can't do with this farce for more than 6 weeks at a stretch. Even in my dreams I hear 'Jesus keep you . . . Is she at home? . . . She's gone mowing . . . holy songs . . . Round is the forest . . . it doesn't fit in my pocket.'
>
> Terrible! Good-bye to you, high plain of Gyergyó, I shall not see you again till Easter.[3]

Perhaps things were not quite as soul-destroying and fruitless as Bartók suggested to Stefi Geyer, for the next day he wrote to Etelka Freund again, telling her that he had 'found examples of Székely tunes which I had believed were lost'.[4] A search of the complete collection of Hungarian folk songs brings up the large number that were written down by Bartók in Csík County in July and August 1907.

Stefi had obviously been playing heavily on Bartók's mind during his stay in Transylvania. Having gone to his sister's house at Vésztő on 6 September with the sole purpose of collecting a letter Stefi had sent him, he penned a long missive to her.[5] It seems quite characteristic of his epistolary approach to his female friends and relations that he should almost immediately get to the crux of the matter. He had been very much moved, in her letter, with the remark that 'There's so much beauty in nature – the arts – science', which reflected his own views (though he admitted that 'It is one of man's weaknesses that we only recognise the correctness of judgements when they correspond with our own – a pardonable judgement'). But when she had moved on to 'a weighty question', it became apparent to Bartók that she was 'God-fearing'. After explaining the route to his loss of faith – the zeal of a divinity master at Pozsony and his own later study (including astronomy) – he spends much of the rest of the letter dismantling the foundations of religion. Pouring particular scorn on the teleological argument for the existence of the universe, Bartók remarks 'Why don't we simply say: *I can't explain the origin of its existence* and leave it at that?' Reversing the standard religious tenet, he rhetorically enquires:

> What is the soul? It is the functioning of the brain and the nervous system. It develops by slow stages, from a pre-natal beginning (in conjunction with the development of the organs in question) and quite ceases to be at the moment of death. It is finite – mortal. The body, as matter, is 'immortal' indeed, for matter in this world is never lost; it only changes its form.

Realising that he has perhaps gone too far in his fevered response (but not so far that he might have thought it wiser to tear the letter up), he notes with a certain degree of self-awareness: 'But this is not at all how I intended writing on this subject – I meant to employ a mild melancholy key, avoiding all dissonance; and yet I've got carried away in the end. Mine is the domain of dissonances.' He finishes by moving on to his views of the purpose of life. He encapsulates his own attitude, rather bitterly, as 'on however small a scale, to give a few people some minor pleasures, on a bigger scale to work for the good of that set of corrupt demi-gentlemen we call the Hungarian intelligentsia by collecting folk-songs, etc., etc.' More broadly, he takes what can be conceived as an existentialist approach in the face of a universe in which everything will eventually decay and disappear in time. He declares that:

To be able to work, one must have zest for life, i.e. a keen interest in the living universe. One has to be filled with enthusiasm for the Trinity about which you write so eloquently in your letter; if I ever crossed myself, it would signify 'In the name of Nature, Art and Science . . .'

After all this high-flown rhetoric, the concluding lines seem almost perfunctory, and it is hard to understand what kind of effect Bartók could have imagined his letter would create. He was perhaps trying to test whether Stefi was capable of allowing her faith to be challenged. However, if the letter was a means of furthering a potential romantic relationship, it can hardly be seen as a sensitive or sensible approach.

Bartók's subsequent letter to Stefi makes it clear that she had not responded at all positively to his discussion of atheism and that he was taken aback by her dogmatism.[6] He did not give up, however, and continued to press his argument about the non-existence of the soul after death: 'It is memory alone that gives our existence a dimension in time.' Rather curiously, he claimed that 'People who do not understand serious music show in other spheres, too, that compared with those who can appreciate serious music, their intellects are not so well developed', going on to assert that 'there is no such being as an atheist with an uncultivated mind'. It seems that Stefi must have refused to accept the books he offered for fear that they might cause her to question her belief, which he found (and condemned as) a demonstration of her weakness. Perhaps the most disturbing section of the letter is a discussion of suicide, where Bartók claims that if he had no commitments (and his devotion to his 'poor, dear mother' was his principal obligation preventing him from conceiving of the possibility while she was alive), he would not see the act as cowardly. It may be that this was an allusion to Nietzsche's Aphorism 157 from *Beyond Good and Evil* ('The thought of suicide is a powerful solace: by means of it one gets through many a bad night'), but there had been no direct reference to suicide in the letter Bartók had sent to Stefi on 6 September.

Rather too late, it might appear, he suggested that they should drop the subject and moved on to composition, remarking that 'I have a sad misgiving that I shall never find any consolation in life save in music.' Quoting a brief musical fragment marked 'Adagio molto', in which the rising arpeggiation $C\sharp_4$–$E_4$–$G\sharp_4$–$B\sharp_5$ in the second complete bar is labelled 'this is your "Leitmotiv"', he describes the almost manic-depressive mood swings from elation to despair that Stefi elicits in him, enquiring of her:

What is to be the end of it all? And when? It is as if I am in a constant state of spiritual intoxication all the time. Just what one needs for work (composing)!

The letter concludes with a suggestion that they should meet again the following day, and in a postscript, an acknowledgement that they were 'both better at writing than at talking'. In total Bartók is known to have written some twenty-seven letters to Stefi between 1907 and 1908.

A string of new works would emerge in the wake of the relationship between the pair – the First Violin Concerto (1907–8), Two Portraits (1907–8), Fourteen Bagatelles (1908), Ten Easy Piano Pieces (1908), Two Elegies (1908–9) and the First String Quartet (1908–9). An early thirteen-bar sketch for the first theme of the two-movement Violin Concerto can be seen on the opening sheet of the Black Pocket-Book (on which Bartók has written 1907 jul. 1. Jászberény – Szolnok). The autograph full score gives the full dates of composition as 1 July 1907 (Jászberény) to 5 February 1908 (Budapest), and thus it appears that it was begun on the very day that Bartók set off from the Geyer's house for Transylvania.

The Violin Concerto's two movements, which he described as writing 'straight from my heart', can be read as portraits of Stefi: an idealized and intro-verted image in the first ('transcendent and intimate'), and an outgoing and confident one in the second ('gay, witty and entertaining').[7] It seems that Bartók had been considering a third movement which would have captured a third aspect, the 'cool, indifferent, silent Stefi Geyer', but rejected it.

In one of the letters he wrote to her sometime between the end of November 1907 and the beginning of February 1908 he explained to her that:

> This idealized picture has taken all my thoughts and feelings. I have never written such direct music before. I prefer it a hundred times, because it speaks about you and to you (only and solely). I really wrote it from my soul – I don't care if nobody likes it, only you should like it. The first movement is my confession to you.[8]

It is tempting to compare the main theme of the first movement (Fig. 9) with that of the slow movement of Rachmaninov's Second Symphony, which begins with the pitches $A_4$–$C\sharp_5$–$E_5$–$G\sharp_5$–$A_5$–$F\sharp_5$, exactly the same melodic contour. However, the symphony was composed between 1906 and 1907 and not premiered until February 1908, so any similarity between the two must be coincidental.

Bartók creates an amalgam of types of melodic material in this idea such that it begins overtly in D with a major-key version of the arpeggiated gesture that he described to Stefi as 'your "Leitmotiv"'; it then works its way through E♭ and F♯ in a rather more chromatic fashion before settling into what is effectively a pentatonic pattern in bars 5–6 (D–E–G–A–B/C). It may be significant that on

Figure 9. The opening theme of the first movement of the First Violin Concerto.

the page following his first sketch of this theme in his Black Pocket-Book, he notates a pentatonic scale on C and several folk tunes that employ this mode. The rest of the first movement is in a ternary form in which the main section has the character of a fugal exposition, with staggered entries of the subject (D bars 1 and 17; A bar 24; D bar 34; and A bar 46), followed by a sequential passage in 9/8 built from one-bar pentatonic phrases that become more chromatically inclined in the approach to the first climax. It is possible that the music of Reger had some on influence on Bartók in this movement, particularly in terms of his use of chromaticism and counterpoint – he certainly studied and performed several of the German composer's works over the following few years. In the gentler middle section, the material that functioned as a counterpoint to what might be regarded as the codetta to the first entry in conventional fugal theory is briefly developed before the solo violin enters with the subject in Fb major. The music gradually winds its way up (both in terms of dynamics and register) to a further peak that involves simultaneous ascending and descending versions of the leitmotif. The fleeting and ethereal closing section includes two final presentations of the theme: in the subdominant tonality of G major in violas, cellos and basses with a counter-melody played by the solo violin; and a final stratospheric, pianissimo rendition in the tonic.

In the technically challenging second movement, a sonata-form structure with three ideas and nominally in the tonality of G (retrospectively placing the first movement in a dominant relation to it), there is an increased sense of tonal strain, both at the level of harmonic progression and of individual chords. To commence the opening theme (Fig. 10), Bartók draws on a half-diminished seventh, the familiar 'Tristan chord', as its basis rather than the major or minor versions of the 'Stefi' leitmotif that underpin the first movement. Initially the theme is transposed a perfect fifth higher than in the first appearance in the

Figure 10. The opening theme of the second movement of the First Violin Concerto.

Prelude to *Tristan und Isolde* (where the pitches are $F_3$–$B_3$–$D\sharp_4$–$G\sharp_4$), and to demonstrate that this is no coincidence, Bartók cites the Tristan chord at its original pitch in bar 11, with a chromatically falling line in the violin in high register.

The four-note motif (or five-note, if account is taken of the *sf* $E_4$ in the following bar) is subject to a number of permutations in the course of the movement. At bar 14 it is transformed to $A_5$–$C\sharp_5$–$F\sharp_5$–$A\sharp_4$, coalescing the pitches of F♯ major and minor triads, a configuration, sometimes described as the major-minor chord, that would become a constant feature of Bartók's harmonic language. Subsequently the motif is found in such forms as a simple triad (bar 48); a half-diminished seventh (at the beginning of the development, bar 109); a dominant seventh (bar 122); and further major-minor chords (bar 196, beginning of the recapitulation and bar 257).

Richard Strauss has not yet been entirely abandoned in the suave, expressive, and whole-tone inflected second subject in B♭, whose first two phrases fall into three-bar units that switch between quadruple, duple and triple metres; or for that matter in the terse third idea, which closes the exposition and has a vague whiff of Strauss's *Don Quixote* about it. However, there is relatively little that could be said to demonstrate the influence of the folk music Bartók had collected. Although occasional hints at *verbunkos* gestures can be found, such as the figures in bars 175 and 177 (♪ ♪ ♫ ♫), most of the *style hongrois* mannerisms that suffused his previous works have been abandoned.

One curious feature is the brief quotation, from the German children's song 'Der Esel ist ein dummes Tier' ('The Donkey is a Stupid Animal'), that is cited just after the reprise of the third idea in the recapitulation (the autograph score indicates the date 'Jászberény, 28 June 1907' at this point).[9] Stefi recalls that she, Bartók and her brother (who was also a competent musician) sang three-part canons that were composed by Bartók for the occasion. Apparently these were rather complex, with difficult intervals and much chromaticism, and she eventually told him she wanted to sing something 'light and happy'. At this, in great good humour, he broke into 'Der Esel ist ein dummes Tier'. It may be relevant to recall remarks Bartók made to his mother in a letter sent on 18 January 1907, in which he talks about Dohnányi's enthusiasm for their collection of Hungarian songs and his frustration about the attitude of indigenous publishers and intellectuals, remarking that they should leave 'the donkeys and asses' in Hungary alone, and pursue any serious work abroad.[10]

Bartók included the following inscription in the copy of the score he presented to Stefi on her request: 'My Confession: For Stefi, from times still happy. Although it was only half happiness.'[11] At the end of the score he appended a poem by Balázs, writing 'In vain! In vain this poem fell into my hands'; the text, as translated by Carl Leafstedt from a copy of the manuscript score, appears in the second 'solo' section from Balázs's poem, published as 'Cantate' in the collection *A vándor énekel (The Wanderer Sings)*, and reads:

Vérzik a szívem,
Beteg a lelkem:
Emberek közt jártam.

Szerettem kínnal,
Kínszerelemmel
Hiában, hiában.

Lombotok borzad.
Ugye nem érttek
Testvérek, testvérek?

Nincsen oly távol
Csillag egymástól
Mint két emberlélek.[12]

('My heart is bleeding, my soul is ill: I walked among humans./I loved with torment, with flame love in vain, in vain!/No two stars are as far apart as two human souls!')[13]

It seems that the relationship finally came to an end on 13 February 1908, a little over a week after he had delivered the concerto to her. Although it remained unperformed until 1958, after the deaths of both Bartók and Stefi Geyer, the opening movement would later be reused as the first of the Two Portraits op. 5.

During this period of personal emotional turmoil, Bartók was preparing his first publication for *Ethnographia*, the Bulletin of the Hungarian Ethnographic Society. A selection of Székely ballads were to be published in the section

'Népköltészet és népzene' ('Folk Poetry and Folk Music'), and Bartók wrote to the co-editor Dr Gyula Sebestyén on 9 October 1907 to advise him that he was submitting twenty-three selected ballads. The final contribution, which appeared split across the first and second numbers of volume 19 in 1908 (on pages 43–52 and 105–115), consisted of fifteen ballads, five of which were given with variants (there are three versions each of numbers 5, 9, 10 and 12; and two of number 11). Although this paper appeared in a scholarly journal, the songs are presented with no commentary, contextualisation or scientific apparatus other than the brief note at the end remarking on the contingency of the relationship between texts and music, some basic information about the place of collection at the start of each tune, and the odd footnote. What was clearly significant for Bartók about these songs was the fact that several of the tunes were pure pentatonic (for example, the first version of 'Kádár Kata', the third version of 'Három árva', and the second and third versions of 'Úti Miska'), and others involved the modal inflection of a basic pentatonic melodic skeleton (such as 'Molnár Anna' and 'Magyarósy Tamás'). In 'Rokoly Katalin' each of the two melodic lines has a pentatonic foundation; the first is based on C–D–F–G–A in the upper register, which is transposed down a perfect fifth for the second (F–G–B♭–C–D).

Bartók's state of mind after the break with Stefi can perhaps be inferred from the rhetorical and rhapsodic elegy for solo piano completed in February 1908, which would later be paired with a second piece in December 1909 and published the following year as *Két elégia* (*Two Elegies*). Stefi's leitmotif makes an appearance in the fourth and fifth bars in a version that uses a diminished triad with a major seventh (C–E♭–F♯–B); on the second system of the second page of the score it is found a tone higher than in the quotation he sent to her on 6 September 1907 (D♯–F♯–A♯–D♮) marked *appassionato*, with its first three pitches grinding dissonantly against E minor harmony, the last alongside C⁷. The climax of the first section at bars 46–7 transforms the leitmotif into a grief-laden variant in which an arpeggiated and sustained D minor chord supports a C♯ played in octaves that falls to a C♮. This version of the figure underpins both the final angry climax, ten bars before the end, and the point of closure of the piece on a 'pentatonic' D minor chord with a minor seventh.

The first Elegy demonstrates a further development in Bartók's attitude towards tonality, and while it certainly could not be described as being atonal (indeed the composer observed that it was in D minor), it does show quite a considerable extension from the Second Suite. Its opening is highly chromatic: the first phrase (up to the start of the third beat of the fourth bar), which Benjamin Suchoff has compared to a motif from Liszt's Symphonic Poem, *Les Préludes*, merely omits A♯; the second, nearly parallel, phrase excludes G♮; and the third (to the end of bar 14) encompasses the entire chromatic space. Bartók immediately balances the flux of the opening with a more harmonically stable passage in which the melodic E♭ is circled by its nearest chromatic neighbours in a gesture that suggests grief, supported by decorated arpeggios first based on $G^9$, then on an augmented triad on F. The section reaches it high point on the last beat of bar 20 with a symmetrical black-note pentatonic chord ($D\sharp_3$–$G\sharp_3$–$C\sharp_4$–$D\sharp_4$ in the left hand, $F\sharp_5$–$G\sharp_5$–$C\sharp_6$–$F\sharp_6$ in the right).

From bar 53 the opening theme is developed, beginning very quietly with a pair of fugal entries that recall the opening gambit of the Andante sostenuto of the Violin Concerto. The theme progresses through another passionate outburst before settling into a reworking of material from the third phrase of the piece, against rapid broken-chord figures in the left hand. This melodic line soon takes on a whole-tone character, descending linearly from $B_5$ down to D♭. On the penultimate page a synthetic whole-tone-based scale (B♭–C–D–E–F#–G#–A) scurries above a further permutation of the motto in which it descends through $A_3$–$F\sharp_3$–$D_3$–$B\flat_2$. These elements are all symptomatic of Bartók's increasing ability to accommodate and consolidate many different types of tonal and modal material within a coherent framework that would later be described as polymodal chromaticism.

For all its developments, the first Elegy hardly prepares us for the extraordinary Fourteen Bagatelles (*Tizennégy zongoradarab*) for piano that Bartók composed from around May 1908. In a manuscript draft to his *Introduction to Béla Bartók Masterpieces for the Piano*, written in 1945, the composer remarks that:

> In these, a new piano style appears as a reaction to the exuberance of romantic piano music of the nineteenth century; a style stripped of all unessential decorative elements, deliberately using only the most restricted technical means. As later developments show, the Bagatelles inaugurate a new trend of piano writing in my career, which is consistently followed in almost all of my successive piano works.[14]

Each of these short pieces has its own discrete sound world, and the first seems emblematic of the new aesthetic in its combination of two key signatures (four sharps in the right hand, four flats in the left) — according to Bartók a 'half-serious, half-jesting procedure that was used to demonstrate the absurdity of key signatures in certain kinds of contemporary music'.[15] He argues against any bitonal or polytonal reading, however, regarding the combination of tones that results from combining the two modes as 'simply a Phrygian coloured C major'. The alignment of the two modes reveals the musical space that results from the superimposition of the modes (only D♮ is missing from the chromatic scale):

C♯  D♯  E   F♯   G♯  A    B
C   D♭  E♭     F   G   A♭     B♭

While the melodic idea in the right hand of the first bagatelle suggests the influence of traditional music, the fourth and fifth bagatelles are arrangements of tunes that Bartók actually collected. 'Mikor guláslegény voltam' ('When I was a Cowherd'), which formed the basis of the fourth bagatelle, was noted in Felsőireg in Tolna County in April 1907, and 'Ej, popred naš', used in the fifth bagatelle, was taken from Gerlicepuszta in August 1906. In both cases the artistic stance is different to that adopted in 'Three Pieces from the Csík District' ('Három csíkmegyei népdal') for piano, which was prepared in 1907, drawing on the tunes collected in Gyergyótekerőpatak that summer and published in 1910. The Csík pieces certainly display a clear effort to retain as much of the original melodic ornamentation as possible, and the accompaniment is quite sparse and extremely sensitively handled. But there is still some residue of late nineteenth-century harmonic practice in terms of the linear bass lines, chromatic voice leading in inner voices and cadential structures. The two folk-based bagatelles, by comparison, are more radical in approach, each working with a limited set of compositional principles. In the fourth, Bartók gives the pianist the problem of playing parallel perfect fifths with the thumb and little finger in the left hand, the lowest bass notes being almost a direct inversion of the melody, while requiring legatissimo performance. The repeat of this line is also concerned with parallel motion, but now of seventh chords within the prevailing Aeolian mode. It is only at the cadence point that Bartók briefly disrupts the modality with a colouristic accent on a G♯ which falls to F♯ before the D minor seventh chord that culminates the phrase. In the fifth bagatelle almost the entire tune in its first rendition is accompanied by reiterated chords of G minor seventh in first inversion in the right hand, with only the briefest deflection to a half-diminished seventh chord on A at bar 17. The rest of the piece investigates different permutations of ostinati, while retaining a limited range of chord types, mostly sevenths derived from the Aeolian or Mixolydian modes.

If the fourth and fifth bagatelles look to what Bartók would have seen as ancient Hungarian music, the second and third embrace the most contemporary trends. While he mischievously describes the second as being in D flat major in his 'Introduction to *Béla Bartók Masterpieces for the Piano*', and indeed the final struck pitches are low-register D flats (albeit against a sustained A♭

and B♭), the rest of the piece strays very far from the ambit of D♭, major or minor. This is one of the earliest experiments in melodic structures around an axis of symmetry, the melody chromatically rising above and falling below the axis formed by the repeated pitches of A♭ and B♭ (or later D and E, a tritone lower), with a rhythmic and gestural approach that recalls the burlesque sections of some of Bartók's earlier pieces. Stefi's motif, perhaps now beginning to be simply a stock melodic configuration as much as a conscious sign, can be found enmeshed in the falling arpeggiations in bars 7 and 14–17. The third bagatelle, more radical still and one that Bartók did not attempt to describe in tonal terms, segments the chromatic scale into two components: a rapid repeating five-note ostinato in the right hand using the pitches between G and B, and an austere melody largely in the left hand, with some of the rhythmic and structural characteristics of traditional melody using the residual pitches (with occasional borrowing of the pitches A and B from the ostinato).

In the slow and sparse sixth bagatelle, an experiment in simplicity, the melody, largely in steady crotchets, is accompanied in the main by chains of fifths or thirds. The seventh is capricious in its changes of tempo, accelerating and slowing across its course, and returns to the topic of chromatic complementarity found in the third bagatelle: for much of the time the left-hand melody is drawn from a black-note pentatonic set and the accompaniment from a white-note diatonic one. Perfect fourths predominate in the middle part of the piece, an element that Bartók extracted from the pentatonic scale, and their melodic use here is strikingly original.

The proto-expressionist eighth bagatelle has registration and voicing that suggest it could have been conceived for string quartet. It should be noted that Bartók had not yet come into contact with the music of Schoenberg, and indeed would not until 1912 when he was brought a copy of the Three Piano Pieces op. 11 by one of his students. Thus any apparent similarity to Schoenberg's style must be coincidental. Though still fundamentally tonal, the eighth bagatelle is highly chromatic, running through all twelve pitches in the course of the first two bars in which the melodic line painfully descends against a kind of acciaccatura pre-echo in the left hand. But this bagatelle also draws on brief gestures derived from Hungarian traditional music, such as the short-long figures in bars 8 and 9. Written largely for the hands playing the same line one octave apart, the ninth bagatelle is in three closely related sections and has a scherzando character. It opens with a figure that coalesces broken chords of C♯ min⁷ and E♭ min^{maj7}.

After the rhythmic and syncopated opening of the brisk, *marcato*, tenth bagatelle, a pattern of alternate Cs and Gs is established in the left hand, against which is placed a jagged and dissonant melodic line. This is succeeded by several other ostinato passages, including a version that adds the neighbouring minor seconds. Although not significantly longer than any of the other pieces, the power and virtuosity of the tenth bagatelle afford it a feeling of significant scale. The motoric ostinati perhaps indicate why Bartók might have later been attracted by some aspects of Stravinsky's music. More surprising still is the eleventh bagatelle, with its opening melody doubled in stacked fourths and its carefully notated short pauses between bars. Bartók is content in bars 9, 11 and 13 to leave suspended the quartal chord Eb–Ab–Db–Gb, perhaps betokening Debussy's influence. The presence from bar 27 of an octatonic-scale segment (alternating tones and semitones) may be fortuitous, for no attempt is made to follow up its implications. The twelfth bagatelle prefigures the night-music type material that would be found in a number of Bartók's mature scores. Here, accelerating repeated notes over static chords and brief flurries of notes domi- nate, and snatches of nocturne-like material occasionally come to the fore- ground. Such is the novelty of the piece that when the repeated pitch of A is played against the dyad F–C, the resulting F major triad sounds strangely unexpected.

A key referential sonority in the twelfth bagatelle is a minor triad with a major seventh, played harmonically, in conjunction with the half-diminished seventh 'Tristan' chord, and it seems likely that Stefi's presence is being symbol- ically indicated here. However, there can be no doubt that she was the subject of the final two pieces: the funereal 'Elle est morte' with its heartbeat rhythm on repeated triads that switch between Eb and A minor deep in the bass register, and a final reference in Db major to the leitmotif five bars from the end; and the acid 'Valse: Ma mie quie danse'. This final bagatelle would be later orchestrated and combined with the first movement of the Violin Concerto to form Two Portraits (Két portré), 'one ideal, one grotesque', published as op. 5.

The Fourteen Bagatelles were completed swiftly and in late June, Bartók (quite possibly drawing on Etelka Freund's connections) showed them to Busoni. He seems to have been very struck by the young Hungarian's new work, apparently saying 'Endlich etwas wirklich neues' ('finally something really new') and inviting Bartók to play them at his masterclass in the Vienna Conservatoire on 29 June. Busoni also wrote a glowing letter of recommenda- tion to the music publisher Breitkopf & Härtel, though they decided that they were unable to publish the work, as they found it 'ausserordentlich schwer und sehr modern' ('extremely difficult and very modern'). Almost immediately the publication was taken up by the Budapest publisher Károly Rozsnyai and the Fourteen Bagatelles appeared in print later that year.

Bartók completed a further set of piano pieces by the end of June, the peda- gogic Ten Easy Piano Pieces (Tíz könnyű zongoradarab). Although the title indicates ten items, in fact there are eleven, the first being a 'dedication' that draws significantly on Stefi's leitmotif, both in its opening gesture and an ethereal chordal version towards the end. As in the Fourteen Bagatelles, Bartók combines arrangements of authentic folk tunes (6 and 8) with pieces that are written in, or draw on, a folk style (1, 3, 5 and 10), and miniatures that experiment with radical techniques (2, 4, 7 and 9). As examples of the latter, the second piece, 'Painful Wrestling', employs an ostinato figure that decorates a perfect fifth with the pitches a semitone higher than the lowest note and a semitone lower than the highest, in its first manifestation reading D–A–E♭–G♯. This became an important musical device (both harmonic and melodic) for Bartók and it has been labelled the Z-cell in deference to Leo Treitler's use of the term 'cell Z' in relation to the use of the figure in the Fourth Quartet. 'Finger-Exercise' initially places complementary rising and falling whole-tone scale passages infilling C–G♯ and D♭–A in neighbouring bars. But Bartók still cannot escape from the Stefi motif, which in descending version dominates the second half of the piece, set in an alien tonal landscape. A tiny fragment at the end invokes a folk melodic-rhythmic figure with a terminal long-short gesture like a kind of shrug.

Much of the summer of 1908 was spent in Switzerland and France, and postcards to Etelka Freund allow Bartók's itinerary to be reconstructed. From Lucerne (where he says he had a bad time) to Zurich (where it was little better) he went to the alpine resort of Argentière and was delighted to find how beautiful it was: 'At last, no rows of "Grand Hotels", no hordes of idle, time-wasting Englishmen, no network of cogwheel railways ready to take you anywhere; here (well! *time is money*) poor yearning mortals can see Nature undefiled.'[16] By 31 July he was in Geneva and thence to Albertville, where he was thrilled to see a 'genuine folk-garment' and was pleased to find that for five francs a day he could eat as well as at the finest hotels, though his lodgings looked like 'a ruin on which someone has put a curse'. His next stopping points were Val d'Isère ('awesomely wild'), Pralognan-la-Vanoise (where he looked on the Dôme de Chasseforêt behind his hotel) and Chambéry. And on arriving at the Mediterranean seaside town of Saintes-Maries-de-la-Mer in early September he remarks to Etelka Freund with almost childlike excitement that he had 'reached the *ne plus ultra* of my desires: the sea' and that he had achieved three firsts: bathing in the ocean, walking barefoot and seeing a mirage. After a few more days back in Chambéry, he set off for home on 5 September.

Collecting folk music was not forgotten in 1908, and Bartók visited Körösfő (now Izvoru Crişului in Romania) in March where he collected some tunes (four examples appear in *The Hungarian Folk Song*). In October he travelled to the predominantly Hungarian commune of Torockó (now Rimetea), sixty kilometres south of Kolozsvár (Cluj-Napoca) where he 'made merry', over-looked by the imposing mountain called Székelykő ('rock of the Székelys').

The tunes Bartók collected were not simply of scientific value, for he was able to reuse eighty-five of them in his four-volume collection of pedagogical material *For Children* (*Gyermekeknek*), completed between 1908 and 1909 and published between 1910 and 1912 by Rozsnyai. The first two volumes (forty-two pieces) are based on Hungarian tunes, the final two volumes (forty-three pieces) on Slovak songs. Bartók was motivated by a desire to provide a reper-toire that had some intrinsic merit for students in the early stages of learning the piano and towards the end of his life he would remark that he selected folk tunes for this purpose to secure the thematic value.[17] These pieces are generally written in a much more conservative musical style than the Fourteen Bagatelles and Ten Easy Pieces, usually diatonic or modal, and support the development of techniques such as finger strength and independence, articulation, repeated notes, expression and so on. And of course, the pieces served the secondary, but very important function in these early years of the century of introducing middle-class Hungarians to a part of their tradition with which they were likely to be unfamiliar.

At the end of the year Bartók had another major coup, being invited by Busoni to conduct the Berlin Philharmonic Orchestra in the Scherzo from his Second Suite, his first (and last) outing as a conductor. The concert was to take place on 2 January 1909 in the Beethovensaal as the fourth item of an 'orchestra evening' of new and rarely performed works. Bartók was somewhat perturbed to be given the task of directing, remarking in a card to Etelka Freund that it would have been better if Busoni had wielded the baton. The movement contains numerous changes of metre and tempo and would have been daunting to a seasoned conductor, let alone a total neophyte. However, Bartók headed off to Berlin for rehearsal and wrote to István Thomán the day following the performance with enormous enthusiasm: 'Isn't it a wonderful experience to conduct an orchestra which responds exactly to what one wants!' He describes the two pro and anti 'camps' in the audience, hisses from one side and 'a storm of enthusiastic applause' from the other, and how he was called back on stage five times. For once he was totally content: 'The orchestra is splendid; every-thing sounds wonderful.'[18]

On 28 January he was able to report to Etelka Freund a further major devel-opment. He had completed a new string quartet the previous day that he had been working on since before his break-up with Stefi Geyer, and his postcard suggested that he would visit her on the following Saturday evening to intro-duce it to her. The Black Pocket-Book has sketches of several ideas for the first and third movements immediately after material for the first Dirge and the ninth and thirteenth ('Elle est morte') bagatelles, suggesting that the works were being conceived concurrently.

Composed in three movements (Lento – Allegretto – Allegro vivace) and lasting around thirty minutes, the First String Quartet op. 7 follows on stylistically from the Violin Concerto while revealing some of the experimentation of the Fourteen Bagatelles. The *style hongrois* devices have now been put to one side and Strauss no longer holds sway, though perhaps Reger can be detected as an influence on the counterpoint and wide-ranging chromatic harmony. At the same time, it has been suggested that the work looks to earlier models, and in a set of brief analyses of the quartets written by Mátyás Seiber and published by Boosey & Hawkes in the year of Bartók's death, Seiber commented that the first movement begins in the spirit of the opening of Beethoven's C♯ minor Quartet op. 131. Indeed, one might argue that there is an even more direct correspondence between Bartók's overlapping entries and his pairing of instruments and the approach taken by Beethoven in the Andante moderato e lusinghiero section of the fourth movement of op. 131.

The principal theme of the ternary-form first movement of the quartet draws on the contour of the four-note motif that is placed at the beginning of the second movement of the Violin Concerto, now reworked into the F min$^{\text{maj7}}$ harmonic context of the Stefi leitmotif and split between the first and second violins to form a compound melodic line (Fig. 11). The violins begin in close imitation, the second playing a perfect fourth below the first, and the seven bars can be heard almost as overlapping entries in a fugal exposition, an interpretation that is reinforced by the entry of the viola and cello at the eighth bar, one octave lower. From bar 21, against a strident figure in cellos and basses, the second violin doubles the first's mobile lines a major third lower, a striking sonority that evokes Debussy (one thinks particularly of the first five bars of the Prélude from *Pour le Piano*, and bars 17–20 of 'La Soirée dans Grenade' from *Estampes*). At the climax of the section, from bar 25, Bartók draws on the tonal symmetrical relations of the diminished seventh, such that the music moves from E♭ through F♯ to A.

The middle section completes the diminished-seventh cycle with a drone on $C_2$ and $G_2$ in the cello. To this the viola adds an impassioned and rhetorical figure formed on the pitches C♯–D♯–E–F♯–G♯–A, and on the repeat of the melodic fragment the first violin steadily reiterates the pitches $C_6$–$Eb_6$–$F_6$–$B_6$ floating high above in the upper register. By this stage, ten chromatic pitches are in play and the missing B♭ and D soon appear. In fact, the transition between the second and third section culminates with an elaborately textured chord of B♭ that is coloured by the pitches C♯, G♭ and A, forming the composite set of pitches (B♭–C♯–D–E–F–G♭–A) whose outer six pitches are symmetrically

Figure 11. The opening theme from the first movement of the First String Quartet, first and second violins.

disposed (with permutations of augmented and minor seconds), a result of the parallel major thirds between the second violin and viola.

At the climax of the movement Bartók picks up the version of the opening motif that had appeared at the close of the first section and quotes two measures from bar 14 of the finale of the Violin Concerto, at exactly the same pitch but played one octave higher by the first violin. Now the figure appears luminescent, clothed harmonically in a sequence of major seventh chords, and the movement dies away with a final, expressive and sombre reprise of the motif in A♭ minor, the melody divided between the first violin and viola.

Bartók turns to sonata structure for the triple-time second movement, though the proportions of exposition and recapitulation are quite different and material is developed throughout its course. The movement is restless and nervous, never settling and built on short fragments one or two bars in length that at times attempt to develop into cantabile passages but are usually thwarted. Several devices are notable in its course:

1. Repetitive passages that employ ostinatos whose pitch content slowly changes, such as between bars 20–30, 57–62 and 72–86;
2. A rhythmic tapping, like the increasingly heavy knock on a door that isn't answered, which begins with the cello at bar 45, runs through the ostinato passages from bar 55, is prominently played pizzicato by the cello from bar 103, is hammered out fortissimo by the entire quartet from bar 208, and is repeated two further times by the pizzicato cello in the recapitulation;
3. The use of the whole-tone scale in the first violin in bars 105–15, 319–24, 334–9 (first note) and 356–7;
4. The unexpected arrival on a major triad, such as with the F major chord on the second beat of bar 42 and the C major chord from 160–5.

Bartók continually changes the density of the textures and internal relationships between the *dramatis personae*, such that the opening pairings (viola and cello, first and second violins) give way at bar 45 to the second violin and viola playing the main theme in rhythmic unison (generally though not consistently doubled in major thirds), while the first violin plays an upper-register descant and the cello taps out its muffled knock. Later, from bar 103, after the second principal idea whose lilting expressive melody is performed by the middle pair of instruments against ostinati from the outer pair, these relationships are clarified; the second violin and viola sustain dyads while the cello raps and the first violin runs up and down the whole-tone scale with an idea that seems to encode emotional detachment.

It is tempting, and probably not unreasonable, to imagine that Bartók has placed his own character into the cello part and Stefi's into the first violin in this movement, and that an underlying narrative relating to their liaison is being played out. The 'Introduzione' that separates the second and third movements would seem to reinforce such a programmatic reading. After curtly hammered-out chords in the upper three parts, the cello has two passages of recitative which János Kárpáti has noted relate to Elemér Szentirmai's song 'Just a Fair Girl'. These become ever more agitated before a quietly expressive cadential figure in the violin that leads into a succession of variants of the Stefi motif.[19] At the final cadence, the first violin plays in the highest register with a gap of two and a half octaves from the rest of the ensemble, a suspended whole-tone chord (B♭–C–G♯–E) completing the section.

There is a significant change of mood for the finale, which begins with something of the character of the second, fifth and tenth bagatelles, and a theme that is derived from an idea from the second movement (Fig. 12). The fragmentation and uncertainty of the middle movement is replaced by vigour and regularity – almost a *moto perpetuo* for the first ninety-three bars. At this point, the tempo changes dramatically to adagio, and a brief reminiscence of a melodic idea exposed from bar 50 of the first movement ensues, now decorated with a prominent Hungarian short-long rhythmic pattern.

The highly syncopated and Lydian-inflected closing idea of the exposition, in A major, has the distinct flavour of a folk dance, and at its conclusion Bartók pounds out the quartally related pitches E–B–F♯ which pre-empt the fifth-based final chords. The rest of the movement conforms to a fairly conventional sonata structure, with elements of burlesque in the development as well as a regular fugal section with a vamping accompaniment. Kodály would later describe the work in terms of it indicating a return to life. This resurgence is made palpable in the finale whose final bars of closure first shoot up a three-octave whole-tone scale before the quartal ascent to the final three sustained chords, which are modally ambiguous but whose confidence and assurance is surely beyond question.

Figure 12. The First String Quartet (a) second movement, violin 1; (b) third movement, viola and cello.

Bartók's change of mood in early 1909 coincided with a much more successful romantic enthusiasm, in this case for one of his young piano students, Márta Ziegler (1893–1967). The daughter of Károly Ziegler, an inspector-general of police in Budapest, Márta and her sister Herma had begun to study with Bartók privately in 1907. Márta became a student at the Academy of Music in the autumn of 1908 and Bartók dedicated two piano pieces to her that year. One would eventually be published in 1912 by Rózsavölgyi as the first of Three Burlesques, titled '(perpatvar . . .)' in Hungarian and '(querelle)' in French. The other, 'Portrait of a Young Girl' (Leányi arckép), would be the first of the set of Seven Sketches (Vázlatok) published by Rozsnyai in 1911.

On 4 February 1909 we find Bartók writing to the sisters from Darázs in Nyitra (now Dražovce in Nitra in western Slovakia) to tell them about his collecting activities (he had previously collected there in October 1908). As well as describing the difficult conditions in the hut he was staying in, he discusses in some detail his artistic credo (as he had with Stefi):

> It is curious that in music until now only enthusiasm, love grief, or at most distress figured as motivating causes – that is the so-called exalted ideals. Whereas vengeance, caricature, sarcasm are only living or are going to live their musical lives in our times. For this reason, perhaps in contrast to the idealism manifested in the previous age, present-day musical art might be termed realistic, which without selection will sincerely and truly include all human emotions among those expressible. – In the past century we saw only a few scattered examples of this, in Berlioz's *Fantastic Symphony*, Liszt's *Faust*, Wagner's *Meistersingers* and Strauss's *Heldenleben*.

Bartók carries on to outline his disillusionment, which he fears may be life-long, but does find some solace in the possibility that every 'blow of fate' may make its impact on his art, for:

> I strongly believe and profess that every true art is produced through the influence of impressions we gather within ourselves from the outer world of 'experiences'. He who paints a landscape only to paint a landscape, or writes a symphony just to write a symphony, is at best nothing but a craftsman. I am unable to imagine products of art otherwise than as manifestations of the creator's boundless enthusiasm, regret, fury, revenge, distorting ridicule or sarcasm. In the past I did not believe, until I experienced it myself, that a man's works designate the events, the guiding passions of his life more exactly than a biography. We are speaking, of course, of real and genuine artists.[20]

Nine months later, on 16 November 1909, the day following a performance by Bartók and the orchestra of the Academy of Music of his Rhapsody op. 1, he and Márta were married in a very private ceremony. (It appears that even his mother was not aware of it and the extant letters make no reference to it.) On 22 August of the following year their son, Béla, would be born. Bartók had finally found the life partner he had thought might prove impossible — at least for a time.

As for the rest of 1909, it involved limited public success, but some further progress on the musical front. He was particularly delighted to receive a letter from the pianist Rudolph Ganz in February or March, which declared his enthusiasm for Bartók's work in contrast to the 'incredible number of attacks' the composer had to endure in Budapest as well as abroad on account of his piano pieces.[21] Bartók remarks in his reply that he has not yet encountered the music of Ravel, presumably recommended by Ganz, and indicates that he will seek it out. He also received good news about his String Quartet, which Rózsavölgyi had agreed to publish.

However, the most significant development for his career took place during the summer collecting trip. Bartók wrote to Etelka Freund on 17 July to tell her that he was 'off to work with the Wallachs'. (Wallachia, in the region that is now southern Romania, was united with Moldavia in 1859 to form the United Principalities, and in 1881 it became the Kingdom of Romania, Transylvania being ceded from Hungary as a result of the 1920 Treaty of Trianon.) He was accompanied on this trip by Ion Buşiţia (1875–1953), a teacher of drawing, geometry and music at the Romanian Uniate Grammar School in Belényes (now Beiuş) in Bihar County, and a man who appears to have been a local character with an enormous and eclectic range of hobbies.[22] Belényes was sixty-five kilometres south-east of Nagyvárad, the town where Bartók had stayed with his aunt, Emma Voit, between 1891 and 1892 when he was a student at the gymnasium. He was able to report to his mother on 17 July that he had visited Nagyvárad and found his aunt's house, though the area had changed considerably.

His friendship with Buşiţia, who was his guide, intermediary, translator and companion on this first Romanian foray, became very close and he remained in regular contact with him for the next quarter of a century. Illness limited Bartók's first stay to a fortnight, but by mid-August he was contacting Buşiţia again from his sister's house at Vésztő to arrange a second visit. At the end of August he went to Besztercc rather than Belényes, and wrote excited postcards to István Thomán and Etelka Freund about the songs and tunes he had found, telling Thomán that they are 'the most exotic I've ever heard' and revealing that in total he had collected '25 Hungarian, 20 Slovak and 320 Romanian songs'. On Freund's card he copied the tune of a *hora*, a fast round or circle dance, played by a peasant musician 'in the 3rd position on a violin tied with a string.'[23]

This would mark the beginning of Bartók's serious interest in Romanian folk music and over his lifetime it would result in some 3,500 tunes. Writing about Romania in 1933, he commented that:

> It was there that as recently as twenty years ago the folk music researcher was elated by the opportunity of coming into contact with pure, uncon-taminated material. . . . Such a wonderful state of things – from the point of view of the folklore researcher interested in uncontaminated material – could still be found in the North (Maramureş), Mid-West (Bihor), and central South (Hunedoara) portions of the Ardeal province. For miles on end, in these parts, there are entire villages with illiterate inhabitants, communities which are not linked by any railways or roads; here, most of the time the people can provide for their own daily wants, never leaving their native habitats except for such unavoidable travel as arises from service in the army or an occasional appearance in court. When one comes into such a region, one has a feeling of a return to the Middle Ages.[24]

His letter to Stefi Geyer with its 'dialogue in Gyergyó-Kilényfalva' can perhaps be better understood in the context of his experiences in ethnic Romanian areas. In the Magyar heartlands of Hungary it was becoming increasingly diffi-cult to find districts that were sufficiently remote that the music had not been rendered 'impure' or lost its appeal to the local communities, through contact with urban or gentrified music. Here Bartók had found a musical time capsule similar to that experienced by Cecil Sharp in the southern Appalachians of the USA a decade later. Bartók could not have been aware in 1909 how soon it would be before the world was turned upside down by war, and indeed how the entire territory that was his laboratory would be transferred to a neighbouring state.

In December 1909 he and his new bride headed off to Paris where he had enjoyed himself so much in 1905. This was an appropriately romantic venue for a honeymoon, though Bartók also intended to make the most of the opportunity to meet musicians who might be influential to his career. Busoni had provided a letter of introduction to Vincent d'Indy, but little came of it. Bartók noted with irritation in a postcard to Etelka Freund that the meeting 'was like when a celebrated professor condescends to meet a beginner and kindly gives him a few hints. *Enfin!* I've had enough of that and I'm not looking for more.'[25]

It will be recalled that one of the immediate outcomes of the break-up with Stefi Geyer had been the composition of an Elegy for piano. In December 1909 Bartók wrote a second piece with the same title, the set being published as Két elégia (Two Elegies) by Károly Rozsnyai in 1910. If the first Elegy was related to the Violin Concerto, the second evokes the experimentation of the Fourteen Bagatelles, and includes such radical techniques as a kind of tightly controlled aleatoricism, and limited polyrhythm (Bartók indicates 4/4 in the right hand and 3/4 in the left hand in the middle part). Although this is a virtuoso piece and there are elements of post-Lisztian rhapsodism, the tonal language is expanded and the opening section is fixated on the pitches A♯–C♯–E–G♯–A. Although this is derived from a descending variant of the Stefi leitmotif, the perfect fourths that had featured at the close of the First String Quartet are implied through the figure B♭[–C♭–D♭]–E♭–A♭. Furthermore Bartók recalls the insistent knocking from the second movement of the quartet with repeated octave As at the end of the first section, and repeated Ds at the centre of the Elegy. At its conclusion, the figure outlining a stacked pair of perfect fourths exposed at the start is placed against the strumming of the opening figure, rolled out by both hands and left suspended to fade into silence. The affair with Stefi, one might suspect, had been finally laid to rest.

As the first decade of the twentieth century, which had been a time of both progress and frustration for Hungary, moved to its conclusion, Bartók's position in cultural life had changed and he was no longer seen as the *wunderkind* composer and pianist who wrote patriotic music and bore the mantle of Richard Strauss. Approaching his thirties, he had a fixed and stable home, a wife who was expecting their first child, regular employment as piano professor in the Liszt Academy, and some musical and scholarly publications to his name; and he had already collected a very considerable quantity of folk music within the borders of Hungary. He had started to develop a novel set of compositional techniques, particularly in his Fourteen Bagatelles, and had completed a String Quartet that was arguably his first mature large-scale work. However, Bartók was being offered relatively few engagements as a solo pianist and he was finding increasing antipathy being levelled by the music critics towards his compositions. (He was already seen as a radical 'ultra-hyper-neo-impresszio-szecesszionista' by the newspapers that praised him as the composer of *Kossuth*, as he notes ironically in a letter to the Ziegler girls on Christmas Eve 1908.) Although the relationship with Stefi Geyer had proved stimulating to him musically, he had been emotionally scarred by it. And he had not as yet developed a truly scientific approach to the collection of folk music, which was still being organised largely on a piecemeal and empirical basis.

By no stretch of the imagination could the period since his graduation from the Liszt Academy be seen as a failure, but Bartók had not yet fulfilled the very high expectations that his early successes had created. The following decade would see a rapid advance in his achievements as a composer, including several masterworks for the stage. And as a result of the First World War everything would irrevocably change.

## CHAPTER FIVE

# 'Crossing the borders of Transylvania': 1910–1913

Count Pál Teleki's *Ethnographical Map of Hungary Based on the Density of Population*, which draws on statistical data from the 1910 census returns, reveals a marked change in the ethnic composition of the country in the period since Bartók's birth, at least as indicated by use of a primary language. Hungarians now accounted for nearly 55 per cent of a population that was just over eighteen million – a 13 per cent increase since 1881 – and this was the compound effect of Magyarisation (and more spontaneous assimilation), differential birth and mortality rates, and extensive emigration, particularly to the United States. Prosperous Germans had been specific targets for Magyarisation. In the throes of his early chauvinistic enthusiasms even Bartók had put pressure on his mother to forsake her German heritage and speak only Hungarian, to ensure that he wasn't embarrassed by any apparent lack of patriotism.

In 1905 the poet and writer Béla Balázs had spoken passionately to his friend Zoltán Kodály of his dream of 'a great Magyar culture that we must create'. In a diary entry for 22 August 1905 he describes how he told Kodály:

About the fight which must be waged against everything that exists . . . about an alliance which would have to be entered into by all those among the young who are born for greatness and who undertake to achieve greatness; those who do not want to be something, but to do something; those who stake their lives for their goals, whether in mathematics, law, music, architecture, poetry, or any other field, and if necessary lay aside every other value for their goal. Those who naturally, out of the depths of their hearts, hate that shallow, frivolous clique that burdens our science and art . . . A cooperative new 'Stürm und Drang', an intellectual revolution would clean up this garbage (newspaper-writer art and buffoon science) and build a great new, fresh art and science, a great new culture in its place.[1]

With the publication of his *New Poems* (*Új versek*, 1906), *Blood and Gold* (*Vér és arany*, 1907) and *On Elijah's Chariot* (*Az Illés szekerén*, 1908) the Hungarian poet Endre Ady (1877–1919) had demonstrated his desire to take up the challenge of redefining Magyarism. The poem 'I am not a Magyar?' from *Blood and Gold*, having set up the stereotype of 'the pain-fraught tested masterpiece/of a true unhappy god,/the child of the sun, a Magyar', asks:

> (And for the drowsy and dirty,
> for the mongrel and gaudy,
> for the half-alive and frothy-mouthed,
> for the magyarasters and fog-eaters,
> for the Hungarians come from Schwabs,
> I am not a Magyar?)[2]

In a similar tone, the narrator of the 'Song of the Hungarian Jacobin' from the section 'The Hungarian Winterland' of *On Elijah's Chariot*, declares that 'magyar, slav and roman sorrows/are issue of a single sorrow', and questions 'When shall we coalesce/and call out in one voice,/we the rabble and the homeless,/the magyars and non-magyars?'[3]

The establishment of the fortnightly literary journal *Nyugat* (*West*) in 1908 marked an important juncture for contemporary Hungarian culture. *Nyugat* was committed to the avant-garde, but was non-partisan in its approach and did not offer allegiance to any specific manifestation of modernism. It was fuelled by the antipathy of a generation of young Hungarian artists and intellectuals towards the conservatism and provincialism of conventional Hungarian culture, and its look to the West rather than the East was crucial. A poem by Ady titled 'A Sionhegy alatt' ('Beneath the Mount Sion') from *On Elijah's Chariot* appeared in the journal's first edition, on 1 January 1908, and his poems continued to feature very regularly up until his death. Béla Balázs's article on Hebbel ('A tragédiának metafizikus teóriája a német romantikában és Hebbel Frigyes'), which drew on his doctoral research on the playwright, can be found in the following issue, and like much material in *Nyugat*, served the pedagogical purpose of introducing important Western artists and their creative and aesthetic practices to the Hungarian public. As well as Ady and Balázs, both of whom would exert an influence on Bartók's output in the second decade of the century, many other important Hungarian writers of Bartók's generation featured frequently in *Nyugat*. These included Mihály Babits (1883–1941), Zsigmond Móricz (1879–1942), Gyula Juhász (1883–1937), Dezső Kosztolányi (1885–1936) and Árpád Tóth (1886–1928), testament to the enormous creative ferment of the time.

Bartók's pursuit of alternative, and as far as he was concerned, more authentic modes of signification of Hungary within a contemporary musical framework in the second half of the first decade of the twentieth century had resulted in his discovery of rural traditional music both within majority Magyar areas and in regions where ethnic Romanians and Slovakians predominated. From 1909 he had become interested in the music of the Romanian peasantry in its own right as much as in the music of the Hungarians and Székely people who lived in Transylvania.

Later in his life he would estimate that around 40 per cent of Hungarian music had non-Hungarian influence, and he reckoned that about 25 per cent of the Romanian material he had collected and analysed had been affected by Hungarian music.[4] This stance would create some personal difficulty for him, for once Transylvania was ceded from Hungary in 1920 by the Treaty of Trianon, and his own birthplace of Nagyszentmiklós had become part of Romania, he found himself embroiled in disputes about his findings and motives. Obviously drawing on his own experience, he looked back in 1937 to the problems faced by the idealist collector who considers the cultural output of neighbouring regions in order better to understand that of his own, and how 'His compatriots cry shame because he "wasted" his time on the study, collection, and preservation of a rival nation's cultural treasure.'[5] Even if the collector did not face censure, publishing would prove almost impossible as his compatriots would see no benefit in disseminating the materials of a neighbouring state, while the latter would be suspicious of the collector's approach and motivation. Bartók asserts that what was demanded of the researcher in this thorny situation was 'the greatest objectivity that is humanly possible' and that 'he must "do his best" to suspend his own national feelings as long as he is occupied with comparison of the material'.[6]

This was, no doubt, a lesson that Bartók had to learn over time, but one of the first compositions to bear the direct imprint of the 1909 trip was 'Két román tánc' (Two Romanian Dances) op. 8a, completed in March 1910 and published by Rózsavölgyi in July that year. In 1945 Bartók noted that these two pianistically demanding pieces were entirely his original material rather than being based on folk music he had collected.[7] The first is 138 bars long and is in a straightforward ternary form with fast outer sections and a slow middle part, and it dispenses with much of the melodic-motivic apparatus he had inherited from Brahms, Liszt, Strauss and Reger. Supported at the beginning by a percussive pulse in the left hand that oscillates between perfect-fifth dyads on B and the tonic C a semitone higher, the first section is built from four melodic units (Fig. 13a, b, c, d) that, drawing on aspects of folk performance, are played a variable number of times in different registers, and are transposed to several

Figure 13. The four melodic units (a–d) of the outer sections of the first Romanian dance (first two systems) of Two Romanian Dances; (e) the main idea of the middle section (third system).

tonal areas. As can be seen from Figure 13, the two fragments of (c) and (d) are related to those in (a) and (b) by approximate inversion, and the main melodic idea of the middle part of the piece (e) is a derivative of (b).

The four units (a–d) together fill almost the entire chromatic space and only the pitch B, which is a focus of the middle section, is missing. Although they can be read as implying C minor 'coloured' by the notes D♭ and F♯ (and on one occasion, E), a modal explanation may be equally plausible – the pitches of the first two fragments can be seen to emerge from the overlapping of the lower five notes of the Phrygian (C–D♭–E♭–F–G) and Lydian (C–D–E–F♯–G) modes on C, an example of the polymodal chromaticism that Bartók was consciously developing. He continues to employ the minor-third relations that were found in a number of previous works, such that the tonal areas of C, E♭ and G♭ are juxtaposed over the course of the first thirty-six bars, at which point C♯, E and G move into the foreground. The short-short-long rhythmic figure on the final beat of each of fragments (a)–(d) takes on an increasingly prominent role as the piece progresses, and at its conclusion, against open fifths of C and G it sounds out the configuration of unit (a) with its biting F♯ and D♭.

The second dance is a high-spirited motoric piece in a modally flexible G major. Although the Lydian mode is prominent, several other modes are employed and, whether intentionally or not, Bartók brings symmetrical structures into play in the left-hand melody that is heard on a number of occasions in the *più mosso* sections at bars 17–30, 47–60 and 96–103. The pitches of this idea (B–D–B–C–D♭–E♭–F / B–D–C♯–A–G–G–G) can be seen to result from the combination of the Lydian G pentachord G–A–B–C♯–D with its inversion (G–F–E♭–D♭–C). Inverting the entire Lydian mode generates the Locrian mode, and Bartók appears to be playing with the musical opportunities that this relationship offers, such as in the *Ancora più mosso* sections (bars 31–4, 64–8, 73–4 and 122–6) where descending passages encompassing the entire Locrian mode can be found.

Although the two dances were probably composed within a six-month period, there are signs of the progressive development of Bartók's musical language, the second dance appearing more consistent and confident in its use of the new resources than the first. This latter dance has a particularly raw and fresh quality, and there are aspects that suggest an affinity with Stravinsky (recalling that this piece pre-dates all of the Russian composer's major ballet scores). Bartók did not produce his own orchestral version of these dances, though his friend and compatriot Leó Weiner orchestrated them in 1939.

On 12 January 1910 Bartók wrote to his mother, sister and aunt in Vésztő to tell them of several exciting developments. Rudolph Ganz, who had contacted him the previous year, had played 'An Evening at the Village' and 'Bear Dance' from Ten Easy Pieces at a concert in Berlin and these were reported to have gone down very well with the audience. He was also able to tell them of a forthcoming pair of evening concerts devoted to himself and Kodály that were due to take place in mid-March. After a brief visit to Transylvania in February to collect folk songs for a week at Vaskoh (Vascău) in Bihar County, Bartók heard from the young Hungarian musicologist and teacher Sándor Kovács (1886–1918), who was resident in Paris, inviting him to take part in a *Festival Hongrois* to be held at l'Hôtel des Modes, Rue de la Ville-l'Évêque (off the Boulevard Malesherbes) on 12 March. This concert was to include a performance by Bartók and works of a number of other Hungarian composers. Writing to Kovács on 21 February, he lists the pieces he intends to play. They include most of his Fourteen Bagatelles (interestingly, Bartók describes the thirteenth as 'Ma mie qui danse' rather than 'Elle est morte' and appears to omit the doleful eighth piece), one of the Romanian Dances and the C♯ minor Fantasy. The rest of the programme consisted of works by Weiner, Szendy, Mihalovich, Dohnányi and Kodály (two movements from his cello sonata).

Fast on the heels of this event came a more significant pair of concerts in Budapest devoted entirely to works by Kodály (17 March) and Bartók (19 March). Bartók's programme consisted of his Piano Quintet written between 1903 and 1904, the First String Quartet op. 7 completed the previous year, and the Fourteen Bagatelles for piano. The string parts of the two chamber pieces were played by the recently founded Waldbauer-Kerpely Quartet (Imre Waldbauer, János Temesváry, Antal Molnár and Jenő Kerpely). In contrast to the weak and ill-prepared performances of some previous works, Bartók received excellent support from his fellow musicians who, he wrote to Sándor Kovács, 'played beautifully, like a first class string quartet'.[8]

Bartók's letter to Kovács comments particularly on the 'immense success' Kodály's concert had proved, and how he, hitherto quite an unknown man, had emerged from it 'as one of the first order'.[9] However, his own treatment by the press could not be seen as particularly favourable, if the review by Izor Béldi in *Pesti Hírlap* was remotely representative. Arguing that Bartók had completely lost his way subsequent to the Piano Quintet, which was 'so beautiful and melodious, so pure and simple, so naïve, natural, and immediate in its effect', Béldi found the String Quartet to be 'a sort of *Elektra* in chamber music form, a veritable orgy of eccentric sound effects and a rhapsodic piling up of a few incoherent musical thoughts'.[10] Bartók's music, he asserted, was the trigger of headaches, as 'it exhausts, torments and unnerves the listener'. In it, Béldi claimed, 'a logical train of thought is supplanted by arbitrary juxtapositions. Tangled musical threads suddenly broken, interesting thoughts suppressed almost as soon as they are born and continually mixed up with other themes in different keys and opposite moods – thus might we characterize the latest works by Bartók, a genius gone awry'.[11]

As might be expected, a very different view was expressed in the pages of *Nyugat* by Géza Csáth (the *nom de plume* of the psychiatrist and writer, József Brenner, 1887–1919), in a review published on 1 April. For Csáth, it was a curious coincidence that great artists often appeared in pairs. Bartók was 'a bolder, more active genius' and had an 'amazingly original musical mind'.[12] He closed with a description of the two men, Bartók and Kodály, taking the podium 'holding hands – as comrades, and even as comrades in arms'.

Bartók's third major achievement of the year took place in Zurich in May, at the second Tonkünstlerfest des Allgemeinen Deutschen Musikvereins (music festival of the General German Music Association). This involved a performance of the Rhapsody op. 1, under the baton of the Swiss conductor and composer, Volkmar Andreae (1879–1962), who was the director of the Tonhalle Orchester Zürich. The concert was a triumph from Bartók's perspective, and he wrote to Andreae after the event particularly to thank him for the care and attention paid to the preparation of his score, for the splendid performance, and for the great hospitality he had received. Even more enthralling was meeting Frederick Delius, whose *Brigg Fair* was included in the festival programme. Delius made an enormous personal impression on Bartók and he clearly felt a great affinity for him, writing on 7 June to express his pleasure. Given Bartók's general reticence, this is a remarkably heartfelt letter, in which he tells Delius 'I am very much alone here apart from my one friend, Kodály; I have nobody else to talk to, and I have never before met anyone to whom from the very first I could feel so close. This was something which made my time at the Zurich Festival one of the most beautiful periods of my life.'[13] Sometime after 17 August he contacted Delius again, partly to discuss a forthcoming performance of *Brigg Fair* in Budapest in February 1911 under Kerner. He was hoping that Delius might introduce him to Percy Grainger, as a fellow folk-lorist, but he opens up again about the difficulties of his professional life:

> We poor music teachers are so very much tied down – the school year lasts from the beginning of Sept. to the middle of June. If only they would give me the job of compiling a scientific collection of folk songs, I would apply myself to that with the greatest enthusiasm. But teaching the piano to untalented youngsters who look upon music as a means of earning their living is truly not a thing I feel any enthusiasm for.[14]

His own motivation for collecting folk music, he continues, 'is really not "the thirst for scientific knowledge"'.

Bartók had begun another set of piano pieces that was directly influenced by Transylvanian Romanian melodies in 1909, the *Négy siratóének* (Four Dirges) op. 9a. Sketches for the first and third dirges can be found in the Black Pocket-Book where they interlace with memos for the First String Quartet and the second of the Two Pictures. These brief pieces are very different in style to the Two Romanian Dances, ranging from the ethereal (with something of the simplicity and serenity of Satie's *Gymnopédies* and *Gnossiennes*) to a restrained passion, and Bartók demonstrates the confidence to put complexity and virtuosity to one side. Limited use of the octatonic scale, with its alternation of tones and semitones, can be found in the first and fourth numbers. Its application in the latter is the most elaborate, the melodic line of the first twenty-four bars alternating its way through two of the three possible permutations of the scale (C♯–D–E–F–G–A♭–B♭–B and C–D♭–E♭–E–F♯–G–A–B♭). Indeed, all of the pitches of the first five-bar phrase, including the accompanying chords, can be located in the first of these scales, each note appearing at least once, suggesting that this could not have been fortuitous. The opening and closing sections of the second dirge are suffused with pentatonicism and the initial seven-bar phrase has marked similarities in contour to the folk-like melody that opens *Duke Bluebeard's Castle*. The first four pitches of the opera's first phrase (F♯–C♯–B–C♯) are indeed a transposed rendering of the equivalent notes of the piano piece.

August 1910 also saw the completion of *Két kép* (*Deux Images*/Two Pictures) for orchestra op. 10, a work of around sixteen minutes' duration that was published by Rózsavölgyi in 1910. The title's nod to Debussy is indicative of Bartók's admiration for the French musician, as well as his enthusiasm for Gallic culture. Looking back in 1938, he described the very positive effect that Debussy had on several of the Hungarian composers of his generation, and how 'the revelation of his art' provided the focus for them to orient themselves away from Germanic musical culture. Although it would be unreasonable to suggest any causal relation between the two works, it is tempting to imagine that the 'dreamy poetry' of Delius's *Brigg Fair*, which Bartók had heard with such delight in Zurich earlier in the summer, offered a stimulus for his own rhapsodic pastoralism.[15] Given his wife's condition, 'En pleine fleur' ('virágzás', or 'in full bloom') is a particularly apposite title for the opening movement, a lush portrait of nature that anticipates similar aspects of both *Duke Bluebeard's Castle* and *The Wooden Prince*. Written in a ternary structure, its melodic lines insinuate folk music without directly quoting from it. Thus the first idea involves a four-section melody formed on a modified pentatonic scale (D–E–G♯–A–C), which passes between the woodwinds in counterpoint with a very quiet though restless line in the violas, cellos and basses. A more obviously Debussyan moment follows, in which birdsong is evoked in high-register flurries in the flutes and harps. The development of the first idea leads to the first climax on a chord of stacked fourths. The middle section introduces a second folk-inspired melody that starts with, and reiterates in its course, the familiar 'Hungarian' accented short-long rhythm. Many of the individual melodic elements are pentatonic, though they are continually reoriented according to the underlying harmonic context, and at the high point of the middle section Bartók crowns a major seventh chord on D with the descending perfect fourth figure, D♯–A♯–A♯–E♯. In the transition to the reprise of the first idea there is a brief reference to the half-diminished seventh 'Tristan' chord (A♭–C–D–F) in the horns, cellos and violas, and a repeated high D sings out in the oboe against the short-long rhythm. At the portrait's conclusion the modality changes, and apart from one stray E♭ in the clarinets and bassoons, the entire texture is permeated by the whole-tone scale.

'Dance Campagnarde' (*A falu tánca*, Village Dance), the second portrait, is outgoing and celebratory in tone and reveals the expansion of Bartók's musical

horizons since he completed the Second Suite. It has a similar atmosphere to
the Two Romanian Dances and draws on his experiences in the villages of
Transylvania. Written in an abridged rondo form (ABACA), the underlying
tonality is G, though the continual modal shifting can make it difficult to pin
this down. The opening idea is based on the pitches G–A–B–C♯–D–E♭–F–G, a
synthetic mode that combines a Lydian lower tetrachord and an Aeolian
(or Phrygian) upper tetrachord, and many of the ensuing fragments have
strong whole-tone inflexions. A sign of Bartók's increasing assurance in his
handling of the material is the unaccompanied unison writing found at
the beginning and several other places in the course of the movement, and the
avoidance of complex counterpoint or fugal technique. It certainly does not
appear to be coloured by the irony, burlesque or grotesquery of some earlier
compositions and sounds unforced and entirely sympathetic to its source of
inspiration.

The summer holidays of 1910 were spent in Graz, while Márta was in the
final months of pregnancy. Yet this did not seem to stop the couple from taking
strenuous exercise, including climbing the nearby 1,720-metre Hochlantsch
Alp less than a month before the birth of their son Béla on 22 August. Márta
suffered quite severe medical problems following the delivery and for some
time was receiving intensive treatment. This proved expensive and distressing,
as Bartók reveals in a letter to Delius.

Given that he had a young wife who had been seriously ill and a four-
month-old baby, it may seem rather strange that Bartók's next major collecting
trip should take place during the following Christmas period. However, this is
perhaps indicative of his lack of religious sentiment, his absolute commitment
to ethnographic research, and his desire to avail himself of the opportunity to
hear the seasonal music of the Romanians. He arrived in Transylvania on
Christmas Eve, and stayed in Abrudbánya (Abrud) from Christmas Day until
28 December before moving on. This proved too large a town to be fruitful (for
even the poorest people, Bartók says, wore bourgeois clothes), but in Kerpenyes,
five kilometres away, he had more success and transcribed forty-five pieces in
a thirteen-hour shift. Bartók found the countryside in its winter dressing and
covered in snow, truly beautiful, so much so that he told Etelka Freund, in a
postcard sent on 4 January 1911, that it would have been worth coming even if
he had collected nothing:

> We're making our way on foot, by sledge and sometimes by wagon – through
> pine forests and deep snowdrifts, and across rushing streams. All this is
> completely new to me; never before have I seen the wild wooded regions in
> winter. It is as good as a winter trip to Semmering or the Tátra Mountains.[16]

He worked his way further up into the mountains to Fehérvölgy (Albac) and among the musical discoveries along the way were the long alpine horns played by women and girls, and a wealth of instrumental music performed by rural musicians. On 31 December 1910 he informed Márta that in just five days he had collected a total of 150 tunes, the majority of which were dances and horn calls, and that he had now run out of blank phonograph cylinders.

In April 1910, Bartók had written to the Romanian musician Dumitru Kiriac-Georgescu to try to gain his support for the publication of the melodies he had collected in the area of Beiuş in Bihar County. Soon after his return to Budapest in early 1911 he discovered that the Romanian Academia Română in Bucharest had agreed both to publish the music and to support his work further. Replying to Kiriac-Georgescu on 20 February he told him that he now had 350 tunes from Bihar, 98 from Torontál County in the Bánát region, 110 from Szamosújvár (Gherla), and 330 from Topánfalva, Abrudbánya and around Zalatna. Typically, he requested only half the cost of collection as he had previously been supported by the Budapest Ethnographic Museum. He made it very clear that he wanted this to be a proper scientific publication, with commentary and texts, though without piano accompaniments.

The collection was eventually published in 1913 as *Cântece poporale românești din comitatul Bihor (Ungaria) (Romanian Folksongs from the Bihor District)*, and it includes a brief preface describing the sources, types of material, and Bartók's approach to their presentation and editing. As well as explaining the particular benefits to the collector of the phonograph (and remarking on the tendency of singers to be flummoxed by the presence of recording equipment and make extempore changes), he explicates his application of the system of Ilmari Krohn, a Finnish musicologist whose work on Finnish folk song was recommended to Bartók by Kodály. Following Krohn's methodology, Bartók notes:

> I have grouped melodies according to the final note of each line, and, in order to conform to this system, it was necessary for me – when transcribing the songs – to transcribe some of them in a previously selected tonality so that they would end on the note *sol* [g¹].[17]

At the same time, he was in discussion with a publisher in Turócszentmárton (now Martin in Slovakia), who had issued a folk-song series called *Slovenské Spevy (Slovak Songs)*, in the hope that they might publish the Slovakian tunes he had collected. The previous year Bartók had offered them 400 songs and he now included with his letter 134 songs from Nyitra County, mainly collected in Darázs (Dražovce). (It will be recalled that Bartók had written to the Ziegler sisters when he was staying in Darázs in February 1909.)[18] Despite a later contract with Matica Slovenská, which proved endlessly troublesome and which Bartók finally rescinded in 1939, the Slovak songs were not published until well after his death, and the third volume appeared only in 2007.

Bartók had meanwhile been assessing the Hungarian traditional music he had collected and his earliest polemical article on the subject appeared in the journal *Auróra*, in the first edition of the year. Gypsy music, and its adherents, is given a critical battering in this provocative piece, for from Bartók's perspective 'its main characteristics are the distortions of an immigrant nation'.[19] The gentry, he felt, were almost entirely ignorant of true Hungarian folk music, and the few indigenous tunes they knew were filtered from their peasant sources by the Gypsy musicians and 'unimaginably marred almost past recognition by their oriental fantasy'. At the same time, the gentry were incapable of noticing the difference between Slavonic and Hungarian tunes played by the Gypsy musicians, and 'the supercilious Hungarian squires pay their due to these [Slavonic] songs also with the compulsory national enthusiasm'. These same gentlefolk were totally uninterested in the 'recently discovered and very valuable ancient Hungarian melodies from Transylvania, which are unlike any folk melodies they have heard before'. The bulk of Hungarian musicologists (Bartók puts the term in quotation marks to show his utter disdain), who tried to suggest that Hungarian music could be written following melodic and rhythmic formulae derived from coffee-house Gypsy musicians, were no better. Not pulling his punches, he then went for the 'experts and critics', who detected the influence of composers such as Strauss, Reger and Debussy on the unfamiliar aspects of new Hungarian music and were incapable of hearing the impact of their own musical culture: 'God forbid that their ears would accept an ancient Hungarian melody; then music would be done with everything and would fall into decay!'

On a more positive note, Bartók's enthusiasm for Delius was further confirmed on 17 February by hearing a performance of his *Mass of Life* in Vienna. What he found most interesting about this piece actually involved a misapprehension that Delius was the first to use a wordless chorus as part of an orchestral texture, presumably being unfamiliar at that time with the use of a similar resource in Debussy's *Nocturnes* (or for that matter Tchaikovsky's *Nutcracker*). Bartók could envisage:

> what enrichment in terms of new colours and entirely new effects the further development of this technical device means. After all, music, too, is a very material art: what the means (instruments) are that we intend to

make use of, or what the material is that we dispose of, has great influence in shaping the ideas, the content.[20]

And he is surely thinking of himself as much as Delius when he says that when such novelties arise, 'it is as if the ideas of an age were suspended in air, so that the chosen artist – guided by his natural instincts – could reach up and realize them for the benefit of art'. But the bourgeois response is a shake of the head in shock and censure 'as if the previously unheard shatters the world, digs the grave of the arts, and so forth'.

The birth of Béla, his wife's illness, the trip to Transylvania and his own subsequent ill-health had all taken their toll. When Bartók was invited to play Liszt's Second Piano Concerto in Budapest with the Academy's orchestra, he found he had to work very hard indeed to return his fingers to concert readiness. More momentous, as he related to Delius on 24 March, was the news that he had started work on 'a difficult job – that is to say a one-acter' – his first reference to what would become known in English as *Bluebeard's Castle*. Carl Leafstedt has traced the chronology of Béla Balázs's play *A kékszakállú herceg vára (Duke Bluebeard's Castle)* as far back as 1907, when Balázs mentions it in a diary entry.[21] He worked on it between 1908 and 1910, and it was published in the journal *Színjáték (Stageplay)* on 20 April (the Prologue) and 13 June 1910 (the entire play) with a dedication to Bartók and Kodály.

Balázs had brought together his interest in modern symbolist drama with the language of (as Bartók would conceive it) the most ancient strand of Hungarian folk song. By drawing on folk ballads from the Székely region of Transylvania as models Balázs hoped to 'delineate modern souls with the plain primitive colours of folk songs', for in his and Bartók's belief 'complete novelty could be derived only from what was ancient, since only primeval material could be expected to stand our spiritualization without evaporating under our fingers'.[22] *A kékszakállú herceg vára* reflects this approach by being largely written in archaic-sounding octosyllabic lines organised into trochaic tetrameters, Bluebeard's dialogue with Judit near the start of the opera offering an example of this metric approach which, in Christopher Hassall's English translation, may recall the language of Longfellow's *Hiawatha*:

| | |
|---|---|
| Nem hallod a vészharangot? | Do you hear the bells a jangling? |
| Anyád gyászba öltözködött, | Child, thy mother sits in sorrow; |
| Atyád éles kardot szijjaz, | Sword and shield thy father seizeth; |
| Testvérbátyád lovat nyergel. | Swift thy brother leaps to saddle. |
| Judit, jössz-e még utánam? | Judith, answer, art thou coming?[23] |

Balázs's verse can be compared to numerous traditional song lyrics with eight syllables in each line. As an example of one collected by Bartók early in his career, the following was taken down in Felsőireg in Tolna County in 1906:

Erdők, völgyek, szűk ligetek,
Sokat bujdostam bennetek.
Bujdostam én az vaddakkal,
Sirtam a kis madarakkal.
(Forests, valleys, groves,/Long through you I fled,/Fled with the wild beasts,/
Wept with the little birds.)[24]

Versions of folk tales related to the Bluebeard legend can be found throughout the European tradition, including the Hungarian ballad 'Anna Molnár', though the most familiar and widespread is probably 'Lady Isabel and the Elf Knight'. In this, Lady Isabel, a king's daughter, is abducted by an elf-knight who takes her to the location where he intends to kill her, having told her that he has previously murdered six (or in some versions seven) princesses there. He instructs her to strip off her clothes and jewels, and she admonishes him that it is improper for him to see her naked and that he must turn away. At that point she kills him, either by decapitating him with his sword or by pushing him into deep water, and is returned to her family.

Given general familiarity with such folk narratives, Balázs is able to play with the audience's expectations in his telling of the Bluebeard story. The libretto begins with a scene-setting prologue spoken by a minstrel, before the introduction of the characters of Duke Bluebeard (bass), a figure familiar from Perrault's 1697 tale of Barbe Bleue, and his bride Judit (soprano). It is likely that her name was chosen because of its associations with the biblical figure of Judith who decapitated the Assyrian general Holofernes, and whose story was the subject of a play by Hebbel (the focus of Balázs's own doctoral studies). In the sphere of the visual arts in the imperial capital, the name was also associated with the figurehead of the Vienna Secession, Gustav Klimt, whose erotically charged painting *Judith and the Head of Holofernes* was completed in 1901. In his paper 'The Taboo of Virginity', which was first presented in 1917, Sigmund Freud would later take up the story of Judith and Holofernes as told by Hebbel, seeing in it the depiction of 'a woman whose virginity is protected by a taboo'. According to Freud, once she has been deflowered by Holofernes, her decapitation of him, which frees her people from their bondage, is an act of symbolic castration.[25] Elaborating on Freud's theme of the loss of virginity but in relation to the Bluebeard tale and its symbolism of keys and locked chambers, Bruno Bettelheim contends that:

The key that opens the door to a secret room suggests associations to the male sexual organ, particularly in first intercourse when the hymen is broken and blood gets on it. If this is one of the hidden meanings, then it makes sense that the blood cannot be washed away: defloration is an irreversible event.[26]

Symbolic reference to defloration is widely found in the folk cultures that Bartók and Kodály were recording and cataloguing, and Balázs establishes blood as one of the primary signifiers of his text.

The ensuing narrative, which has the structural simplicity of a ballad, reveals that Judit has abandoned her intended bridegroom and has followed Bluebeard to his bleak castle, whose walls, she feels, are shedding tears. She tells him that with her lips she will 'dry these weeping flagstones',[27] and that her love for him will prevail over his sadness. When Judit discovers the seven locked doors she requests Bluebeard to open them. While warning her of the rumours that surround them, he gradually acquiesces, allowing her to unlock the first six, each of which is associated with a specific colour of light. From the bloody-red torture chamber, yellow-red armoury and golden treasury that represent Bluebeard's power and authority, she moves to the blue-green of the garden, the dazzling white shining on his kingdom, and the shadowy lake of tears. Despite Bluebeard's warnings, Judit demands to see inside the seventh chamber, believing that all the other rooms, which were tainted with blood, pointed to the murder of his previous wives. But the opera ends with her discovery that they are all still alive inside the chamber, which is suffused with silvery moonlight, each of the women representing a time of the day and a period of Bluebeard's life: dawn, noon, twilight and finally midnight.

In 1915 Balázs wrote that 'My ballad is the ballad of the inner life. Bluebeard's castle is not a real castle of stone. The castle is his soul. It is lonely, dark and secretive: the castle of closed doors.'[28] In writing *Duke Bluebeard's Castle* there can be little doubt that he was aware of Endre Ady's poem 'A vár fehér asszonya' ('The White-Robed Woman of the Castle'), published in his 1906 collection, *New Verses*. The tone and mood of this poem seems so strongly connected to that of Balázs's drama that the relationship between them cannot be purely coincidental. Ady talks of his soul being an ancient 'castle of superstitions', haughty, mossy and deserted, with no light shining from its windows – two huge eyes looking out into the valley. Anton Nyerges translates the third stanza as 'Eternal is the mantling mist,/the cryptal balm and unlaid ghosts/ashiver in the shadowy vault,/and an accursed army moans'.[29] But occasionally, in secret night hours, a woman dressed in white walks through the castle and its eyes light up as she laughs through its windows. This, one might suggest, is one of

Balázs's starting points, for near the beginning of the opera, Judit sings 'I shall brighten your sad castle. . . . Bright as gold your house shall glitter.'[30] In elucidating his version of the story, Balázs writes of the castle that is Bluebeard's soul, 'When the woman walks in it, she walks in a living being. And the woman wants to break open every door. Her love and compassion make her do this.'[31] But as Joseph Zsuffa notes, rather than bringing the two closer, this attempt to know Bluebeard fully separates them further and Judit becomes part of his soul, a 'dream woman'.

Although Bartók worked on a first version of his score, which he dedicated to Márta, relatively quickly, completing it on 20 September 1911, he revised the ending in 1912 and again in 1918 for its first performance. It was not until 1921, ten years after its inception, that it settled into its final form. *Bluebeard's Castle* summarises the musical progress the composer had made up to his thirtieth year. Its opening melodic material (Fig. 14) is entirely pentatonic and reference has already been made to a similarity of contour to that of the second Dirge. The four lines of this theme, demarcated by pauses on the final pitches, are, in the terms he would adopt to theorise his folk-music collections, isometric (they have the same number of syllables in each line of a stanza) and 'non-architectonic' (the melody of the final line of the melody does not reprise the first). In reality, this opening theme probably does not conform to any actual Hungarian folk tune, as four-syllable lines are not idiomatic of the repertoire. Instead it can perhaps be seen as a skeletonised folk song and can be compared to Figure 15 ('Szép a leány ideig'), song number 47 from Bartók's *The Hungarian Folk Song* ('A girl is handsome awhile,/until she is eighteen;/But a boy is handsome so long/As he does not get married'). Although this melody is quite different from the theme presented in *Bluebeard's Castle* and there is no intention to suggest any causal relationship between them, if the repeated notes are imagined as being tied, it demonstrates how Bartók could have extrapolated the thematic shell from such a real or imagined folk song.

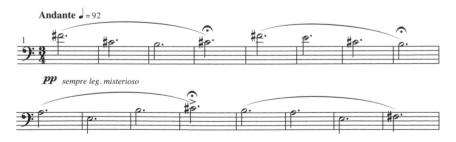

Figure 14. The first theme from *Bluebeard's Castle*.

Figure 15. Song number 47 from *The Hungarian Folk Song*.

If this archaic-sounding first thematic unit is understood to be a symbol of both the castle and Bluebeard, whose vocal lines are pervaded with pentatonicism, then the nervous idea that begins with a *style hongrois* shudder and is based on the collection A–B–C–D♯–E–F♯–G can be taken to refer to Judit. Contained within this matrix of pitches are three pairs of semitones, and Bartók employs this interval to encode the blood that Judit repeatedly sees or imagines in each of the chambers. This musical symbol is found at a number of places in the course of the opera: at rehearsal number 34 in the torture chamber; from the second bar of 45 in the armoury; at bar 58 in the treasury and 71 in the secret garden; one bar before 78 in Bartók's kingdom; throughout the agitated passage from bar 85; as the apex of the arpeggios symbolising the lake of tears from bar 91; and in the increasingly hysteria-laden build-up to the unlocking of the final door, bars 105–18. Judit's vocal lines are appreciably more chromatic than those of Bluebeard, and her opening musical gesture, calling out his name in Hungarian (Kékszakállú), inverts the Stefi Geyer leitmotif ($F_5$–$D\flat_5$–$A_4$–$G\flat_4$), from which one might reasonably infer an underlying personal narrative for Bartók.

Although he had occasionally utilised harmonically static ostinati in previous works, the extended passage from rehearsal number 8 to number 21 is remarkable for its reliance on the repetition of one-bar figures. At first these are pentatonic in orientation (based on G♯–A♯–C♯–D♯–F♯ from rehearsal numbers 8 to 11), but become increasingly chromatic from rehearsal number 11 onwards where a pentatonic scale is modified to B–C♯–E♯–F♯–A by the sharpening of the E. When the section reaches its climax at the tutti five bars after rehearsal number 17, as Judit sings 'I shall brighten your sad castle. You and I shall breach these ramparts', the minor triad with major seventh associated with the Stefi motif is fused with the pentatonicism of the work's opening.[32] These ostinati, which may be taken to insinuate Judit's nervous and agitated state, are almost entirely heard supporting her voice, and I have argued

Table 1. The main tonal areas in *Bluebeard's Castle*.

| Section | Tonality | Narrative |
|---|---|---|
| Opening | F♯–D♯–C♯–D–F♯ | Night/Castle |
| First door | F♯/C ~ C♯ | Torture chamber |
| Second door | F♯/D♯ ~ B ~ C♯ | Armory |
| Third door | D | Treasury |
| Fourth door | E♭ | Secret garden |
| Fifth door | C | Kingdom |
| Sixth door | A (min) | Lake of tears |
| Seventh door | C (min)–B♭–C–D (min)–F♯ (min) ~ | Former wives |
| Closing | B♭–F♯ (C♯) | Night |

elsewhere that their gradual tonal recontextualisation intimates that 'the transformation that she wishes to make, [is one] from dark antiquity to bright modernity'. [33]

Balázs's lighting scheme has its musical counterpart in the distinctive tonal organisation outlined in Table 1. In this, the primary areas of F♯ and C, which lie a tritone apart and are intended to signify darkness and light respectively, are elements in a cycle of minor thirds, the series being completed by E♭ and A, which appear in relation to the fourth and sixth doors.

In addition to the blood motif, Bartók draws on fairly conventional musical signifiers for the various chambers of the castle: a shuddering figure in the woodwinds and xylophone for the torture chamber; fanfares and galloping dotted rhythms for the armoury; glistening brass and metallic sounds, with arpeggios in the celesta and flutter-tongued tremolos in flutes, for the armoury; the Lydian mode and birdsong for the flower garden; parallel chords supported by the organ ringing out like church bells over Bluebeard's kingdom; and shimmering liquid arpeggios in the harp, celesta, flute and clarinet for the lake of tears. Bartók's subtly buried semi-quotation in the cor anglais of the *oboe da caccia* accompaniment to the alto recitative 'Ach, Golgotha' from Bach's *St Matthew Passion* as the seventh door opens is a rather curious piece of intertextuality. As an avowed atheist, it would seem odd that he should have felt it appropriate to refer to this contemplation of Christ's suffering at Golgotha. Its allusion, to 'the sinless' who 'here as sinner dieth', as Leafstedt notes, may offer an apposite commentary on the fate of Judit. However, one might question whether such a reading is entirely congruent with a symbolist drama in which the sympathy of the audience seems to be directed as much to the restrained and dignified Bluebeard as to the prying, passionate and demanding Judit. As the cycle of the drama is played out, is this perhaps intended to be seen as Bluebeard's own Golgotha before his castle, his soul, is reduced to eternal darkness?

Debussy's *Pelléas et Mélisande*, and Maeterlinck's symbolist play that it sets, were necessary precursors to *Bluebeard's Castle*, for both were psychological theatre in which the drama takes place as much within the minds of the audience as on the stage. It will be remembered that Balázs's intention was to 'delineate modern souls with the plain primitive colours of folk songs', and Bartók leavens the rather austere and hieratic language of his libretto with a score that is vibrant and colourful, and balances the address to modernity and tradition in musical terms.

In late March 1911 Bartók set off for Rome as part of an official Hungarian delegation attending the Congresso Internazionale di Musica that was being held from the start of April. He sounds somewhat frustrated in a postcard he sent to Etelka Freund from Rome on 9 April, for he had sacrificed his precious collecting time to be there, and although he had the opportunity to hear Ilmari Krohn speak, he found some of the other contributions rather less than enthralling. On his return to Budapest he became closely involved in the launch of an organisation called Új Magyar Zene-Egyesület (UMZE – the New Hungarian Music Society). Meticulous research by Lynn Hooker has revealed the range and remit of this society, which had initially showed great potential but lasted little more than a year.[34]

According to Hooker, the terminal decline of the National Symphony Orchestra just three years after its establishment encouraged the board of UMZE to lobby the Ministry of Culture for the funding of a new orchestra under its auspices. The composers on UMZE's board included Bartók and Kodály, as well as Ákos Buttykay (1871–1935, a piano teacher at the academy); Dezső Demény (1871–1937, an ordained priest who became the conductor of St István's Basilica in 1913); Pongrác Kacsóh (1873–1923, director of the high school in Kecskemét); Sándor Kovács (the musicologist whose acquaintance Bartók had made in Paris); and Leó Weiner (1885–1960). Almost immediately after it was formed, a rift appeared between the members of the board about its role, and Kovács (who had made a public announcement outlining what turned out to be his personal vision for UMZE in the journal *Zeneközlöny*) resigned as its secretary. On 11 May 1911 UMZE's remit was revised in *Zeneközlöny* to be 'the fostering and development of Hungarian musical life through the holding of lectures, establishment of a music library, and organization of concerts', and on 15 July 'the introduction of new and rarely heard music' was appended as a further goal.[35] Alongside its concert activities there was an aspiration for the society to 'hold lectures and seminars to popularize the scientific study of music'. The directors managed to attract some subsidies and sponsorship for the organisation, though their appeal to the Ministry of Culture to be allowed to take over the National Symphony Orchestra proved unsuccessful. Plans were made for a series of five concerts, which were to have included music by Schoenberg (his First String Quartet was to be performed in the fourth concert), and by Busoni and Kodály (piano pieces and songs in the fifth concert). However, only the first two of these concerts took place, in front of small audiences, on 27 November and 12 December 1911, and in each Bartók appeared as the piano soloist and accompanist to the singers. Ironically, the only 'contemporary' work to be performed in the opening concert was 'Old Hungarian Folksongs' (Bartók's arrangements), the rest of the programme being by Rameau, Couperin, Scarlatti and Beethoven. Incensed at Rózsavölgyi for cancelling a non-UMZE concert at short notice and their subsequent withdrawal from the concert planned for 12 January 1912, Bartók resigned from UMZE (though he was persuaded to take on an honorary presidential role).

Hooker demonstrates that the repertoire the UMZE had intended to put in place in its first season did not prioritise either Hungarian or contemporary music. Surprisingly, not a single original work by Bartók was listed, and even in the special 'all-Hungarian' replacement concert staged on 22 March 1912 neither his nor Kodály's compositions were programmed. As she remarks, 'The concerts UMZE planned did not tokenize or ghettoize Hungarian composers, but set them up as equal to the most modernist composers in Europe at the time; and folksong was used not as a token of nationalist pride, but as another way to let in the "fresh air" of new sounds and new worlds.'[36] Well intentioned as it was, UMZE proved a failure because of its inability to attract audiences, and as Bartók noted in his 1921 autobiographical note, 'we strove in vain, we could not achieve our aim'.[37]

In the course of 1911 Bartók published or completed several sets of piano pieces that were begun in the early stages of his relationship with Márta. He had written the graceful and tonally wide-ranging 'Portrait d'une jeune fille', the first of the seven Esquisses ('Vázlatok' or Sketches), in 1908; the second, whose Hungarian and French titles are 'Hinta Palinta' and 'balançoire' (seesaw) respectively, has the hands duplicating each other's lines a major or minor third apart for much of its course before gently oscillating and coming to a rest on Cs at the end, an octave apart. The notation suggests a kind of bitonality, the right hand seemingly being written in E while the left hand is in A♭, but this is another piece of polymodal chromaticism, in which Lydian and Phrygian modes of C are superimposed. Bartók wrote in Latin on the draft 'In everlasting memory of the hours 6, 7, 8, 9, 10, 11 p.m. 16 February 1909', but whatever occurred between Bartók and Márta at those times must remain in ellipsis.[38]

The third sketch is dedicated to the newlyweds Emma and Zoltán Kodály, who married on 3 August 1910. Although the gentle and limpid Lento, which has something of the feel of a barcarolle about it, is fundamentally in C, it toys with both pentatonic and whole-tone elements. While the rest of the *Esquisses* make relatively limited technical demands on the pianist, the extended and rhapsodic fourth piece, which opens on an implied $F^{maj7}$ and cadences in C♯ minor, is a rather tougher proposition. The Debussyan implications of the French title of the set of *Esquisses* are played out fully in this impressionistic piece that pre-empts Bartók's later nature pieces in its use of trills and arpeggios that could be taken to isomorphically encode birdsong over rippling water. Certainly these textures, the implied duet between bass and soprano that follows them, and the parallel seventh chords of the first page, seem to look to Debussy's *Images* for piano and in particular one could compare the latter's 'Reflets dans l'eau'.

The following pair of sketches turns to folk music, the fifth being a simple arrangement of the Romanian tune 'La toată lumeam plăcutu' that Bartók collected in Delani in Bihar County in 1909, played through three times with a modest accompaniment that does not intrude on the melody.[39] 'Oláhos' (à la manière Valaque, or in Wallachian style) is one of Bartók's synthetic folk pieces, a brisk dance in a polymodal C that invokes instrumental performance (presumably on the bagpipe). The piece involves variable drones that alternate between E and C, and rapid, glissando-like runs at the end of each phrase act as a kind of articulatory gesture. The serene final sketch, in 9/8 and marked *Poco lento*, opens with a decorated broken chord of B major. This is intercut with a whole-tone-inflected descending line that is harmonized with perfect fifths on F and then B♭; and as it works to its conclusion, whole-tone flurries surround the melody in parallel sixths between the hands. The piece ends with ten-note semi-cluster chords, the left hand playing the whole tones between A and E♯, the right hand immediately above, from F♯ to C×.

*Három burleszk* (Three Burlesques) would be published by Rózsavölgyi in 1912, the second piece being the last to be completed, in May 1911. The first Burlesque, subtitled '(perpatvar . . .)' in Hungarian and 'querelle' in French, wittily evokes a tiff with Márta that apparently took place on 27 November 1908. Bartók offered a range of alternative titles for this stormy scherzando, including 'Anger because of an interrupted visit'; and, with Beethoven's Rondo à Capriccio in G, 'Rage over a lost penny', obviously in mind, 'Rondoletto à capriccio'. The opening six-quaver figure (B♭♭–A♭–B♭♭–A♭–G–D♭) passes between the hands as a grumbling ostinato is joined after the ninth bar by a balancing idea that rises from the tonic up to an E before dropping back (C–G♭–B♭–E–D♭–C). The amalgamation and subsequent development of these two bars (which in combination can be seen as having fundamentally Locrian modal characteristics) drives the music on to bar 39. Three pairs of stamped-out and highly percussive chords built on the minor second between C and D♭ and spread over three octaves then briefly move the piece into a triple hypermetre (a three-bar phrase structure) in a rhythmic and metrical shift of gear. A brief, expressive, waltz-like figure that is mocked by sniping from the left hand gradually returns us to the opening material, first at half speed with an arpeggiated bass line and then at the original pace.

The second piece has the Hungarian subtitle '(kicsit ázottan . . . )', given in French as 'un peu gris' (slightly tipsy). Márta claimed that her husband entirely abstained from alcohol, and perhaps his experiences of 'vin compris' in Madrid discouraged him from alcoholic excess. Nevertheless, he regularly observed the effects of drink during his fieldwork, and this little character piece, in a Phrygian E, charmingly suggests light inebriation through its use of acciaccatura chords, erratic rubato, and very precise and detailed articulation. Bartók creates an extraordinary texture for the reprise with pianissimo staccato arpeggiated chords throughout, which roll downwards on the last two quavers of each bar.

For the daring final Burlesque, Bartók composed another capricious scherzo-like piece that has something of the fleet-of-foot pianism of 'Mouvement' from Book One of Debussy's *Images* or 'Feux d'artifice' from Book Two of the *Préludes*. Although the right-hand line can be understood as being in a Dorian E♭, the scale segments in the left hand sit a semitone lower, creating a very bright and incisive sonority. The central part of the piece settles for twenty-two bars into an almost static texture, like a strange mechanism with rapidly whirring figures in the treble, and staccato quavers in the left hand over a pedal $A_4$, and this becomes the matrix from which a vestigial melody emerges in the lowest voice.

Bartók's other major piano work of 1911 was the *Allegro barbaro*, which would first find its way into print, not in a publication of Rozsnyai or Rózsavölgyi, but under the auspices of *Nyugat* where it appeared in the opening issue of 1913 on 1 January. Whether fortuitously or by design, one of the poems by Endre Ady that appeared in the same edition was 'Régi énekek ekhója' ('Echo of Old Songs'), the third stanza of which reads, in Nyerges's translation:

So what if I dare to weep once more,
if my barbarism bursts forth, and the well-groomed laugh at
my unkempt life.[40]

This was not the first piece to bear this title, for the fifth of Charles-Valentin Alkan's *Twelve Etudes in Major Keys* op. 35 is also marked Allegro barbaro. In conversation with Denijs Dille, Kodály recalled that Busoni had told Bartók some of his music reminded him of Alkan, a composer with whom Bartók was unfamiliar at the time. Whether he was consciously or unconsciously recalling Alkan's use of the title, or was even aware of it, is not known, though the correspondence is striking.[41]

Benjamin Suchoff regards the *Allegro barbaro* as an amalgam of folk-music influences: Hungarian (the melodic pentatonicism), Slovak (the 5, 5, 7, 7 structure of the principal theme) and Romanian (the overall modality and tonality). The tonality of the piece is F♯ and all the pitches of the first fifteen bars can be found in the collection F♯–G–A–B♯–C♯[–D]–E, in essence the Phrygian mode on F♯, but with a sharpened fourth (B♯). The opening idea, following a four-bar introduction of vamped F♯ minor chords, can be understood as being built from three basis cells: a neighbour-note motif (AGA); a rising and falling minor third (AB♯A/ACA); and a falling three-note scale segment (F×E♯E/GFE). Overall, the piece involves a chain of closely related sections that manipulate these cells. In the opening part, the synthetic folk melody appears twice, first on the tonic F♯ and then a fifth higher, and this is followed at bar 34 by a new eight-bar idea that is repeated, punctuated sforzando by thirdless F♯ chords in the left hand. The forceful melodic passage in the right hand involves permutations of the three basic cells. The first is the most complex, the GFE segment transformed to GFA by modal transposition and rotation of its elements (GFE→AGF→GFA), the other two simply involving inversion and transposition (AGA becomes E♯F×E♯/FGF; F×E♯E/GFE becomes ABB♯/ABC).

For the third section from bar 58, the cell involving the falling three-note figure takes priority, gradually stretching out until at bar 76 it is extended to the pitches G–F♯–E–D♯–C♯–B–A. This is the Lydian mode with a flattened seventh that, following Lendvai's lead, has often been called the 'acoustic scale' in the Bartók literature, because its pitches can be derived from the fundamental and subsequent twelve overtones of a harmonic series once they have been transposed so that they lie within the same octave. In this guise the melodic line is supported for most of its course by triads of C major, a tritone away from the work's tonic. The *Allegro barbaro* moves to its conclusion by way of a sustained variant of the opening theme, first on F and then on B♭. By turns, further references to the material of the second and third ideas, hammered-out chords alternating an implied F♯$^{maj7}$ and an augmented triad on G♯, and a rising Lydian scale on F, return us to the F♯ minor vamp of the opening.

Although the proto-serialist technique implied above may seem far-fetched, this was precisely the kind of detail Bartók was noting in his transcriptions of folk tunes, where multiple variants of three- and four-note figures are often provided. Overall, one might be forgiven for imagining the influence of

Stravinsky in the *Allegro barbaro*, particularly in the pounding chords on the final page of the score, though it again pre-dates most of the Russian composer's most radical works and there is no evidence that Bartók had any familiarity with his music at all by that stage. However, it is worth remembering that *Petrushka* had been premiered in Paris on 13 June 1911, just a month before Bartók took a holiday in the city, and its reverberations would still have been felt. The clarity and simplicity of the *Allegro barbaro* is striking, and it has a consistency that suggests a composer who is fully confident of his materials and of his handling of them.

As for the rest of 1911, at the beginning of May the young couple moved out of central Budapest to Jókai utca in the Rákoshegy area of Rákoskeresztúr, which at that time was a town outside the boundary of Budapest. And on 13 May the premiere of Four Old Hungarian Folk Songs for male chorus was given in Szeged under the baton of Péter König, the director of the Music Conservatory there.

Leaving his family behind in the middle of July, Bartók headed off alone for Paris once more. He had been hoping to meet Delius again at Grez-sur-Loing, and show him the score of *Bluebeard's Castle*, but it was still not complete so their paths did not cross. His next port of call was to be the Swiss alpine resort of Zermatt where, despite marvelling at the grandeur of the Matterhorn, he decided that climbing it was beyond his ability. He took the mountain railway up the Gornergrat for its view of the mountain, but informed Márta that he was not as impressed as he thought he would have been, perhaps because of the lack of physical effort such an approach required. (Bartók was training Márta up as his copyist at this time, a role in which she would develop considerable competence. She had begun work on a vocal score of *Bluebeard's Castle* sometime in July, and on the full score from around 1 August.)

From Zermatt he went to the Lichtluftheim nudist colony at Waidberg, near Zurich, which was run by a Danish ex-army officer called Jørgen Peter Müller. The fare was vegetarian and conditions were Spartan. According to a contemporary newspaper report, while the residents of other such resorts in Switzerland were hidden from the public:

> at Waidberg it is otherwise. Here the followers of Nature can roam over hill and dale, swim lakes and rivers, and disport themselves at will in a state of almost complete nudity for many miles around Waidberg. . . . The furniture of a typical bedroom consists of an iron bedstead, a hard mattress, two sheets, no pillow, a wooden table, and chair. The walls and door are bare. An austere monk would be satisfied with such a room, but several of the Waidbergers find them too 'stuffy' and sleep on a mattress on the verandah

when it does not rain. If an ordinary person were to pass a night in one of the air huts he would probably be half-frozen by the morning, as there is no protection whatever against the cold and wind, and the only stove in the colony is in the kitchen!⁴²

The reporter, H. Devitte, conversed with one of the residents, who expressed sentiments that surely would have echoed those of Bartók: 'What would you, monsieur? When you have tasted all the pleasures and frivolities of life and found them only froth, and, tasting deeper, you come down to the dregs of the wine, no sincerity, no love, no natural feelings, but simply artificiality – a time come[s] when you wish to taste Nature herself and her simple joy.' Expecting 'fanatical freaks' among the vegetarian and teetotal colonists, Devitte found instead cultured and cultivated people from 'the diplomatic, military and social circles of several European capitals' for whom the sun and fresh air and austerity replaced their normally comfortable urban lifestyle. Days at Waidberg consisted of early exercises and a cold bath, followed by rambles, light meals, sports and gymnastics, reading and sunbathing, and eight hours sleep at night.

The Kodálys were also spending a holiday at Waidberg and the party was joined for a fortnight by Balázs and Edit Hajós. In his diary Balázs describes how Bartók would work long shifts on the score for *Bluebeard's Castle* in the solarium, wearing only his sunglasses, and remarks that he is 'A most moving and wonderful man. . . . He possesses an incredible magical dignity. . . . And how much innocence, how much charm he has. He travels with a knapsack and ten cigar boxes full of beetles and insects, which he collects with utmost pedantry and constant amazement.'⁴³ Balázs found 'a wondrous paradox in his appearance. His figure, face, movements are like a rococo prince's, and yet there is a certain titanic dignity about him. A rococo titan!' Throughout his life Bartók would try to maintain the principles he discovered at Waidberg and follow the exercises in Müller's book *My System* (first published in 1904 as *Mit System*). Indeed, in the year prior to his death he was photographed sunbathing with Tibor Serly.

Having completed the score of *Bluebeard's Castle* in September, Bartók submitted it to a competition for a new opera run by the Lipótvárosi Kaszinó in Budapest, to celebrate the centenary of Ferenc Erkel's birth. He also entered it into a second competition, with a later deadline, which was under the auspices of Rózsavölgyi, one of his main publishers. In the Lipótvárosi Kaszinó contest there were only two entries and it was announced in July 1912 that no prize was to be awarded. Towards the end of 1912 Bartók was to discover that, despite his connection with the firm of Rózsavölgyi, he had been no more successful in that competition. According to an announcement in *Zeneközlöny*,

Sándor Hevesi, who was the stage manager at the opera house, had ruled that both the score of *Bluebeard's Castle* and the other entry in the opera section were 'completely unsuitable for staged performance' and thus their musical qualities were not even considered.[44]

Just before the start of the Christmas period in 1911 Bartók set off for Transylvania to collect folk music in a group of villages between Nagyvárad and Belényes in Bihar County, while Márta and their infant son Béla stayed with her parents. Writing from Rákoshegy in January to arrange another ten day's collecting later in the month, he tells his Romanian teacher friend János Bușiția he had enjoyed his hospitality so much that 'with you I felt better than a king'. Bartók expresses concern about the trouble that he and his wife must have taken to entertain him, remarking with characteristic humility that 'it distresses me to know that anyone is putting himself out for me'.[45] The composer included his copy of Endre Ady's collection of poetry, *Az Illés szekerén* (*On Elijah's Chariot*), with his letter to Bușiția. He noted a number of his personal favourites among the poems, including the 'Song of the Hungarian Jacobin' (cited above) and 'The Hungarian Winterland', which appropriately talks of the poet looking out on the snow-clad fields from his train, 'homeword bound for Yule,/an aged stripling, but my soul/is there beneath the snow'.[46]

In February 1912 the Bartóks moved house once more, though this time they remained in Rákoshegy, settling just a few streets away on the other side of the railway line; this would remain their home until May 1920. Bartók also began collecting folk songs in Temes County, between Temesvár and Arad, in the middle of March. After a brief return home, the end of the month was spent in Bereg County. From Barkaszó (now Barkaszova in the Ukraine) he reported the usual variable success to Márta, telling her he found absolutely nothing – nobody was willing to open their mouth and sing to him. He had better luck at Rafajna-Ujfalu, and he wrote about possibly setting off for Nagyszőllős where he had lived as a child between 1888 and 1892.

Although Bartók still found succour in his 'scientific' work, the depression that resulted from his failure in the two recent competitions and the critical panning he regularly received for his compositions had taken their toll. In an oft-quoted letter to the composer and critic Géza Vilmos Zágon sent the following year, on 22 August 1913, he explained why he had decided to withdraw from public life. Zágon, who would assist Bartók in preparations for visiting Biskra in Algeria in June 1913, had suggested that Bartók might join him in a musical business venture. Bartók's reply was supportive and friendly, but in telling Zágon how his presence in such an enterprise would be counterproductive given his low status, he revealed his frustration and anger with the opinion formers in Hungary. These included his colleagues at the Liszt

Academy, the composer Ödön Mihalovich who was head of the Academy and the violin teacher Jenő Hubay (who had taught Stefi Geyer and would succeed Mihalovich in 1919). According to Bartók, 'a year ago sentence of death was officially pronounced on me as composer. Either these people are right, in which case I am an untalented bungler; or I am right and it's they who are the idiots.'[47] Between him and those who were deemed the country's musical leaders there could be no common cause or dialogue. Bartók continued, 'It therefore follows that since the official world of music has put me to death, you can no longer speak of my "prestige" - - - Therefore I have resigned myself to write for my writing-desk only.' His performances outside Hungary had been equally unsuccessful, he felt, and 'all my efforts during the last 8 years have proved to be in vain. I got tired of it and a year ago stopped pressing for that, too.' Only folk-song research must necessarily remain a public activity (composition can remain his private pursuit as 'neither recognition nor public appearances are required'), and he avowed 'I will do anything to further my research in musical folklore!' Perhaps suggesting a degree of paranoia, Bartók closed with the remark that 'Anything I support is pre-judged as suspect by official musical circles – and rightly so from their point of view.'

The one substantial composition that Bartók worked on in 1912 was *Négy zenekari darab* (Four Orchestral Pieces), which he drafted in a two-piano format but did not orchestrate for another nine years. He had originally conceived the work as another slow-fast pairing of movements (like Two Portraits and Two Pictures), namely a Prelude and Scherzo. But he decided to add a second pair – an Intermezzo and a Marcia funebre – to complete what is effectively a third suite. The beautifully sculpted ternary-form Prelude shares common ground with the music of *Bluebeard's Castle* that evokes the natural world, and it also prefigures the opening of the ballet, *The Wooden Prince* (1914–17). In the wash of sound at its beginning, an E major chord with added major sixth and seventh is sustained by strings, flute and timpani, and arpeggiated by harps and piano, to provide a lush setting for a melody in the horn in the Phrygian mode on E. Chains of sevenths follow, in ever-changing modal configuration over a pedal E, suggesting the influence of both Debussy and Delius. As the piece moves towards its centre, a chromatic line in the first flute is placed against a whole-tone sonority built on C in tremolando muted strings and harp arpeggios. From rehearsal number 4, in a further exquisite colouristic effect, filigree figuration in the piano based on the chromatic group of pitches between C♯ and E♭ rises and falls through octaves against *sul ponticello tremolandi* in the strings, a trait of the later 'night-music' style, leading first to F♯ major, then A♭ major sustained chords. The eclecticism of this piece suggests a composer who is not driven by the requirement for systematisation in his experimentalism.

The overtly grotesque elements of the Scherzo may be taken to look forward to (and in its orchestral guise, back from) Bartók's second dance work, the pantomime *The Miraculous Mandarin*. He had already shown considerable affinity for the Scherzo as a structure, finding it a suitable vehicle for his mordant wit. He had also, by this stage, become more familiar with the music of Stravinsky. Although the Scherzo should probably not be seen as an overt attempt to emulate the Russian composer, there are some technical aspects that do suggest his influence, as well as what might be deemed a certain primordial character. While nominally in B♭, the Scherzo begins off-centre, outlining and pounding out the tritone between D and A♭ before settling into the main idea in the brass, based on the pitches B♭–C♭–D–E♭–F–A♭–A. Accompanying this, strings and woodwinds play a gradually evolving motoric ostinato that employs the pitches A–B–C–C♯–D (atypically, the C natural used in generally rising contexts, the C sharp in falling ones); this regularly places the B♭s in the brass against A and B naturals, creating an extremely dissonant and incisive sonority.

At the fifth bar of rehearsal number 11 the music settles into one of its most Stravinskyan moments with an ostinato formed by the alternation of the chords E♭–A♭–D–B♭–E–A and F–B–E–A♭–D–G. These are constructed from four three-note chords, each of which has a perfect fourth and augmented fourth, a construction that Schoenberg particularly favoured and had used frequently from as early as 1903. Collectively, these chords encompass nine of the twelve chromatic pitches, and when a quintuplet idea appears in trumpets and trombone at rehearsal number 12, it provides two of the missing notes – C and D♭. Although the context is quite different, it is tempting to hear this as an echo of the quintuplet figure played by the trombones from rehearsal number 149 of the 'Danse sacrale' from Stravinsky's *Le Sacre du printemps*. A new six-note ostinato is set in motion at rehearsal number 14 against a melody that extends the perfect-plus-augmented fourth chords into what has become known as the Z cell, two overlapping diminished fifths/augmented fourths (here C–D♭–G♭–G). This would become another important fingerprint of Bartók.

The brief Trio is punctuated by references to the quintuplet rhythm, and the reprise of the Scherzo involves both attenuation and development of material from its first section. One specific technique used here is the alteration of phrase structure or hypermetre, such that passages previously in duple or quadruple hypermetre (groupings of two or four bars) are now placed in a triple hypermetre (three-bar groups) or in a state of flux. Thus, from rehearsal number 33 the groupings are 3+3+3; [34] 3+3+4; [35] 3+2+3; [36] 3+3+3; [37] 2+3+3+2+2+2+3.

In the opening material of the third movement, an Intermezzo in a limpid and graceful 3/4, Bartók might almost be referencing the music of his friend

Frederick Delius and his use of the term in the 'Walk to the Paradise Garden' intermezzo from the 1907 opera *A Village Romeo and Juliet*. Written in a modal G minor and mainly in a triple hypermetre, it is fundamentally Locrian (G–A♭–B♭–C–D♭–E♭–F) with an accompaniment that picks out every other note of the mode in a half-diminished seventh on G (G–B♭–D♭–F). The brief agitated and distraught outburst that emerges from the isomorphism of a shudder at the heart of the movement, climaxing on the 'major-minor' chord A–C♯–F♯–A♯, is immediately subdued by the reprise of the opening pastoral idea, perhaps a gesture of acceptance. The movement finishes on the half-diminished seventh with which it opened.

In the C♯ minor funeral march (Marcia funebre) that completes the set, Bartók returns to a musical genre he had previously explored in *Kossuth* and the Lento funebre thirteenth bagatelle, 'Elle est morte'. At its highpoint, what might be taken to be an allusion to the rhythm of Beethoven's 'fate' gesture from the Fifth Symphony in the brass (using cornets here rather than the trumpets of the rest of the work) is followed by a vestigial reference to Siegfried's funeral march from Wagner's *Die Götterdämmerung*. By 1921, when Bartók orchestrated the Four Orchestral Pieces, his language had moved on substantially, with the composition of the two ballets and Second String Quartet. Nevertheless, the work remains a powerful testimony to Bartók's troubled state of mind in 1912 and sits on the boundary between one creative phase and the next.

As he had noted to Zágon, the one thing that continued to give meaning and joy to Bartók, beyond his immediate family and his closest friends such as the Kodálys and Buşiţia, was traditional music and its performers. Bartók's essay on the subject, 'Comparative Music Folklore', was published in the January 1912 issue of the broadly based journal *Népművelés* (*Education of People*), which had taken on the title *Új Élet* (*New Life*) that year. This article is rather more temperate in tone than the one he published in the previous year, describing both the context of song collection and the method for indexing them. However, Bartók's discussion of Ilmari Krohn's methodology is somewhat confusing in its description of song cadences, and it would take a second article, 'Draft of the New Universal Collection of Folk Songs', jointly authored with Kódaly and published in *Ethnographia* the following year, to clarify the implementation of these cadences. In essence their approach involved the following iterative strategy to create a rational ordering:

1. All melodies were transposed so that their final note was G above middle C;
2. It was assumed that all melodies had four lines, and where there were three, for analytic purposes one was assumed to be repeated;

3. The final pitches of the first three lines were noted, as were the numbers of syllables in each line and the overall range or ambitus of the melody;
4. Tunes were initially filtered by the final note of the second line and then further
   sifted by the last pitches of the first and third lines in turn;
5. Each set of melodies resulting from stage 4 was additionally sorted by line
   length, from the shortest to longest;
6. Each subset resulting from stage 5 was further sifted by its range or ambitus
   from the fewest notes to the most.

At the end of this procedure, every melody was classified through these five
dimensions (the final pitches of the second, first and third lines, the number of
syllables per line, and the overall melodic range) into a group with similar
features. What was generated overall through this systematic process was a
kind of dictionary that allowed the search and retrieval of cognate melodies. In
his 1912 article in *Új Élet*, Bartók admits that although he and Kodály had
between them taken down some 3,000 melodies from within the territory of
Hungary, their collection was as yet unclassified and remained to be published.
Subsequent work would involve 'an investigation of the huge "virgin" territory
inhabited by Romanians', and the final purpose of the research was 'to establish
in a scientific way the types and characteristics of Hungarian folk song'.

 Back in June 1910, in his first letter to Delius, Bartók had written how he
could only yearn for the 'romantic regions' in Norway that the English
composer had told him about. In the summer of 1912, however, he was finally
able to able to visit Scandinavia for himself. This was, for once, a family holiday
rather than a concert tour or collecting trip, and their first port of call was
Stockholm, in Sweden's Olympic year. Fleeing from the crowds, they quickly
set off for Norway. Postcards to his sister tell of a coastal boat trip on the
Hurtigruten service (literally the fast route), which at that stage travelled
between Bergen and Kirkenes. Bartók was entranced by the partially snow-
covered mountains that stretched all the way down to the smooth sea of the
fjords and he was captivated by the wild seals on the Lofoten coast (the Lofoten
Islands being a highlight of the trip). However, the weather, as he reported on
26 August to Kodály (who was on retreat at Waidberg), was not clement, with
heavy rain and cool temperatures. Although Norway was beautiful, he sorely
missed the heat of the sun and vowed only ever to go south in future. At the
same time, the Scandinavians' liking for meat was in marked contrast to the
vegetarian diet he had been introduced to at Waidberg. As Bartók told Buşiţia
on a picture postcard displaying a family of Lapps (who are, he joked, 'our rela-
tives'), he was very disappointed to discover that folk music was moribund in
Norway. Even while on holiday, however, his own collecting work was never far

from his mind, and in several notes to Bușiția he rehearsed various issues and concerns that he had been pondering.

The Romanian composer and teacher Dumitru Kiriac-Georgescu, who had been very supportive in his interactions with the Academy of Science, had called on Bartók in Budapest on 19 June to seek his advice on a commission he had received from the Academy of Bucharest to record folk songs in Romania. He was particularly interested in the use of the phonograph, in which Bartók had developed considerable expertise. At the beginning of November, Bartók visited Bucharest to repay the compliment and he wrote to his mother that he had made friends with the Romanians (even if that was not possible at home).

For Bartók's annual winter collecting trip in December he returned to the southern Hungarian counties of Torontál and Temes (where he had spent part of his March trip). In a subsequent letter to Bușiția he described southern Hungary as a particular 'nest of ballads' and told him about his experience at the village known as Petrovoselo (Petre in Torontál, now Vladimirovac in Serbia, forty-five kilometres north-east of Belgrade). Here an aged *bakter* (a German loan word indicating either a night-watchman or a railway guard) 'sang 7 long ballads at one go, just as if he was reading them out. I was notating for 2 ½ hours without a break; I could hardly keep up.'[48] Bartók later discovered that two of the ballads were entirely unknown and one of them, 222 lines long, he felt was a 'real master-piece in the genre'. He also came across a 'quack-doctor' who played a kind of primitive six-holed oboe called a *cărabă* (the local name for a bagpipe) and used the instrument in his rituals. Bartók included ten of the tunes he recorded from the old man in the first volume of *Rumanian Folk Music*.

Driven by an almost insatiable desire to collect, no sooner was he back in Budapest at the beginning of January 1913 than Bartók set off again, this time to a majority Slovak region in Hont County, in the north of the country. He was assisted by Sámuel Bobál, a Lutheran pastor in Egyházmarót (now Kostolné Moravce, Slovakia). As had become his manner, Bartók was direct, precise and professional in the instructions he had transmitted to Bobál on 16 December 1912, to ensure that the brief time he had (just three and a half days) was spent as efficiently as possible. On this occasion he was particularly interested to find wedding songs and 'those with a jocular text, which often have a characteristic melody of their own'.[49] The enormous scale of his efforts over this period can be gauged from correspondence with Kiriac-Georgescu in March 1913, in which he tells him that over the winter he had collected 400 songs and dances in the Bánát (Torontál and Temes), and in the previous week alone, in Máramaros County, he had taken down 200. He was also working steadily to complete his first major published collection for the Academia Română, *Cântece Popolare Românești din Comitatul Bihor (Ungaria)* – with the French alternative title, *Chansons populaires roumaines du département Bihar (Hongrie)*. It would consist of 371 songs and appear later in the year. Bartók's preface to this work does provide some clarification of his use of cadence structure as a means of classification, though it still demonstrates an approach that was to some degree premised on a Western diatonic and tonal interpretation of the repertoire rather than a modal one.[50]

Despite his avowed withdrawal from public life, he did take on some concert activity, including a performance at a Kuruc evening organised by the Kecskemét Choral Society on 1 February at which he premiered the *Allegro barbaro* and played a number of his more recent piano pieces. Later in the same month, on 26 February, the Budapest Philharmonic performed Two Pictures.

Bartók's collecting trip in the summer of 1913 took him completely outside the borders of Hungary and involved a return to north Africa, which he had very briefly visited in 1906 at the end of the tour with the violinist Ferenc Vecsey. Some fifty years later, Márta recalled their trip to Algeria (at that stage a *département* of France), which proved something of an adventure for the pair.[51] Although Bartók had originally intended to go alone, he suggested that she should join him and they set off on 3 June, sailing from Marseille to the port of Philippeville (now Sakîkdah in Algeria) on the steamer 'Djurajura'. Following the advice in his Baedeker guide that the heat would be less extreme there, he had decided that their base should be Biskra, 300 kilometres inland, and when they arrived they commissioned the services of a local guide called M'hammed. Although he seems to have done his very best to be helpful, Bartók was by no means satisfied with the 'coffee house music' played by the group of musicians M'hammed had assembled for him.

He was all too familiar with the difficulties of finding willing performers – male or female – in Hungary, but he had the additional problem in Biskra of the social and religious customs relating to women. A rather novel solution was discovered. With the approval of the local police department, Berber women of the Ouled-Naïl tribes who earned their living in the town by dancing (and, it was suggested, prostitution), were permitted to enter Bartók's hotel to be recorded. Márta recollected visiting the street where the girls lived and to which they were normally restricted, and being fascinated to see the gazelles that they kept as pets. Surprisingly, perhaps, on 19 June Bartók told Zágon, who had assisted with the preparations for the fieldwork, that 'the work is going more easily than in Hungary';[52] and in October he commented to Ion Bîrlea (a Romanian priest who had accompanied him in Máramaros County) that 'The sheiks were most obliging; they simply ordered people to come in and sing. One very striking thing: there was no trace of shame in these people, not even the women.'[53]

From Biskra they headed off to Tolga in a hired car for three days. (The journey took longer than expected because Bartók could not resist searching for beetles for his collection.) They were provided with a room in a hotel to record the musicians, and those who turned up included a singer who played a kind of reed flute called a *gasba*, a player of the *rhaita* (or *ghaita* – a north African oboe), and various percussionists. Although the recording work was successful, the water in the hotel was bitter, the soup and tea were undrinkable, and the milk smelled like a goat pen! To add insult to injury, Bartók had uncharacteristically failed to check the cost of the accommodation and was shocked by the bill he received when they left. Returning to Biskra, they then drove to Sidi-Okba, eighteen kilometres south-east of Biskra, to hear more musicians. According to Márta:

> The recording of the songs took place in the most cheerful mood; elsewhere the singers were much more serious, almost sombre in mood. But here was a cheerful, slightly cross-eyed singer, a great artist who knew how to bring pleasure to the rest of the company.

The pair suffered an 'unpleasant incident' when the husband of one of the singers burst in and harangued his wife for singing to strangers, though apparently he calmed down somewhat when he saw that Márta was present.

Moving on to El-Kantara, on the road from Biskra back towards Constantine and Algiers, Bartók was struck down with gastroenteritis. He was suffering from fever and was extremely emaciated – his weight, Márta recalls, had fallen to just 47 kilogrammes – but they somehow managed to find their way back to Algiers. Here, to make matters worse, Bartók slipped in the hotel lift shaft and damaged his knee, forcing him to lie in bed for the majority of the final nine or ten days they spent there, with cold compresses to reduce the pain and swelling.

Despite the difficulties they had encountered, Bartók was extremely enthusiastic about the idea of returning the following year, suggesting that if he prepared himself properly in advance by undertaking a 'fattening diet' (of the type his sister regularly provided for him), it would permit him to lose a quarter of a kilogramme each day without ill effect. This second collecting trip proved unachievable, however, for in the following year the world political climate changed beyond measure and such trips outside Hungary became extremely difficult.

Bartók's scholarly write-up of the Algerian fieldwork appeared seven years later in 1920 in the paper 'Die Volksmusik der Araber von Biskra und Umgebung' ('The Folk Music of the Arabs of Biskra and Surroundings').[54]

Although he had done his best to prepare himself for the trip, including attempting to learn the language, his approach to the music comes through as that of an empiricist. He reports what he has found as an outsider using the tools at his disposal and tries to make sense of it, indeed, tentatively classify it. There is little or nothing in his paper, however, about Arab music theory (such as the employment of *maqams* and rhythm cycles) or a broader historical and social context. Rather than seeing this as a major contribution to the collection or theorisation of north African music, it is perhaps better to regard Bartók's paper as signalling a new compositional resource, a pool of material that would markedly influence his melodic and rhythmic imagination.

In December 1913 Bartók's Bihar collection finally made its appearance in print, and he immediately realised that he had made an error in the way that he had presented the melodies. He had followed Krohn's methodology, but had failed to organise his collection by the separate tune types: the *colinde* (Christmas carols), funeral songs, dance tunes, and the highly ornamented *doina* (known by the name of *hora* in the Máramaros). His intention was to remedy the fault in his next collection, which was to be devoted to Máramaros County, but this would not appear in print for a further ten years.

And so the first year of Bartók's 'exile' came to an end with the regular round of folk-music collecting over the Christmas holiday period, this time in Hunyad County, near Vajdahunyad. The outbreak of the First World War during the following summer would necessarily result in the adjustment of his familiar routines, but traditional music would continue to retain its central position in his creative life.

## CHAPTER SIX

# 'To plough in winter is hard work': 1914–1918

In his correspondence with Géza Vilmos Zágon in August 1913 setting out the reasons for his withdrawal from public life Bartók had remarked that although the Budapest Opera did not wish to perform *Bluebeard's Castle*, it had asked him to compose an hour-long ballet. Béla Balázs's libretto for his one-act dance piece *A fából faragott királyfi* (*The Wooden Prince*), written at the request of Bartók, was published in eleven sections in the final editionof *Nyugat* in 1912 (16 December). When he received a copy of the libretto, with its 'spectacular, picturesque, richly variegated actions', Bartók could see the opportunity to pair it with *Bluebeard's Castle*, whose performance was hindered by its lack of action – 'the plot offers only the spiritual conflict of two persons ... nothing else happens on stage'.[1]

Like *Bluebeard's Castle*, the narrative of *The Wooden Prince* has the simplicity of folk balladry. It is concerned with the rites of passage from childhood to adulthood and the ability to distinguish the profound from the superficial, nature from artifice. Balázs's libretto in *Nyugat* is accompanied by arch foot-noted comments which emphasise that this may well be a childish fairy tale but it is penned by a sophisticated and intellectual adult with a strong sense of irony. The ballet involves four principal dancers (the Princess, the Prince, the wooden Prince and the fairy of the grey veil) and in the 'grotesquely primitive' setting are two hills, each surmounted by a castle. In contrast to *Bluebeard's Castle* this is necessarily a work of stage business and action, and whereas the opera challenges the audience to interpret its opaque psychological drama, the ballet is overt and transparent.

As the curtain rises slowly, the young Princess is discovered dancing in the forest that lies at the foot of the hill below the Prince's castle and separates their two kingdoms. As he appears, having set off to explore the world, the fairy forces her to return to her own castle. Seeing the Princess, the Prince immediately becomes infatuated and attempts to join her. But the fairy prevents him by enchanting first of all the forest, which he eventually succeeds in passing through, and then the river, which rises to impede him, compelling the Prince to return through the forest. He endeavours to attract the Princess by placing his crown, clothing and eventually his hair, which he has cut off and formed into a wig, onto his staff. Intrigued by the wooden puppet, she comes down from her castle to investigate it. At this point the Prince interposes himself, to the terror of the Princess who starts to take flight from this 'ugly, bald man'. Fascinated by the puppet, however, which has now been animated by the fairy, she dances with it.

In his despair, the Prince falls asleep and the fairy now shows sympathy for his plight and comforts him, placing magic golden hair, a crown and a cloak on him. The natural world pays homage to the Prince who is handsome once again; he is 'King over the soul-comprehending' and thinks to himself, 'this is triumph, pomp and splendour! No more suffering, no more night.'[2] Meanwhile, the Princess has lost patience with the puppet, whose dance has become ever poorer. Seeing the Prince in his radiance, she attempts to entice him to dance with her. At first he rejects her, and mirroring the earlier action, she is kept apart from him by the forest. In her despair she disposes of her crown and gown, and cuts her own hair off. The Prince takes pity on her, and the two are united and embrace. The natural world returns to the unenchanted state of the ballet's opening, man having deserted it and returned to his own kind.

Bartók began sketching his score for *The Wooden Prince* in April 1914, though it took him nearly three years to complete it, for as will shortly be seen, the ensuing period was one of significant personal turmoil for him, let alone the havoc caused by war. According to Bartók, it was a performance of the Two Portraits by István Strasser on 20 April 1916 (in which 'Une idéale' was played by the violinist Emil Baré), and especially the grotesque aspects of the second portrait, that stimulated him to return to the composition.

Bartók extrapolated the following overall structure for his ballet from Balázs's libretto, with interludes connecting the main dances:

- Prelude (C Acoustic)
- Dance 1 (The Princess in the Forest) [11] (B♭)
- The Prince [19] (D Mixolydian)
- Dance 2 (The trees) [23] (C Locrian)
- Dance 3 (The waves)[39 + 9] (E min)
  - Dance 4 (The Princess and the wooden prince) [88 +5] (A min)
    - The Prince's despair and his coronation by nature [120–1] (C ~)
  - Dance 5 (The Princess pulls and plucks at the wooden prince [141 + 9. Dance 5 begins in score at 147] (B♭)

- Dance 6 (She tries to attract the Prince with a seductive dance) [156] (F)
- Dance 7 (The terrified Princess wants to come to him, but the forest stops her) [167] (B Locrian [♯7])
- Postlude [189] (C)

As can be seen from the synopsis, the plot involves some degree of mirror-symmetry with at its centre the apotheosis of the Prince from loneliness and bitterness to his coronation by nature. At the outset of the ballet, nature is encoded through a prelude in an extended passage in C (recalling the opening of Wagner's *Das Rheingold*, in E♭), built from the acoustic scale with its lower Lydian hexachord (C–D–E–F♯–G–A) and overlapping upper Mixolydian tetrachord (G–A–B♭–C). During the course of the prelude slow horn calls emerge as the music gains mass with the gradual accretion of further chromatic pitches, and it climaxes after four minutes in a remarkably dense swirling texture.

The appearance of the Princess in the first dance of the ballet is marked by a graceful and playfully undulating eight-bar melody in B♭ in the first clarinet, which like the music associated with Judit in *Bluebeard's Castle* is comparatively chromatic (Fig. 16a). For the arrival of the Prince on stage, Bartók provides a somewhat ponderous melody, which, while being in a Mixolydian D, can be seen as having a fundamentally pentatonic basis (Fig. 16b). The point at which the Prince's infatuation with the Princess becomes apparent is marked with what in the film-music world is often described as a stinger, a brief and tightly synchronised punctuating gesture (Fig. 16c) involving a B⁷ chord capped with a dissonant D♮, which moves via an acoustic scale on A to a B major chord surmounted with a G♮. Immediately following this an expressive motif appears in the clarinet that will later form the basis of the Wooden Prince's theme from rehearsal number 91.

With the overtly programmatic pair of dances, of the forest (from figure 23) and the waves (from the ninth bar of figure 39), Bartók produces some of his most elaborate and complex music, albeit the influence of Richard Strauss (in particular, the *Alpine Symphony*) and Stravinsky's scores for Diaghilev may be detected. (It should be noted that the Ballets Russes had brought *Petrushka* to Budapest in 1912.) In the highly chromatic textural music of the 'Dance of Trees', Bartók presents a semi-symmetrical accelerating and decelerating figure in the timpani that divides the beat into three, four, six, eight, five and back to three in the course of two 3/4 bars. Surrounding this is a dense wash of sound in the Locrian mode on C, from which a rhythmically incisive melody emerges in the brass articulated with 'Hungarian' short-long rhythms.

For the 'Dance of the Waves', Bartók places an alto and tenor (doubling baritone) saxophone in the limelight, a relatively early use of the instrument as

Figure 16. *The Wooden Prince* (a) the Princess's dance; (b) the Prince's dance; (c), the Prince's feeling of love.

providing mainstream orchestral colour (though Strauss did employ the family in his *Sinfonia Domestica*) in a chain of three melodic ideas that strongly suggest traditional music. The first (at rehearsal number 42) is a simple four-line Aeolian melody in B that has an AABB structure and the latent pentatonicism of an old-style Hungarian song; the second (from 45) is a pentatonic melody with an $AAA_1A_2$ structure; and the third (from 47) is a Dorian melody in C with an ABCD structure.

If the Budapest Opera was hoping for a work that would bring something of the notoriety and public attention of *Petrushka*, then in order to create a frisson the two big set pieces with the wooden prince would seem to have offered the ideal locations for an appropriate blend of modernity and accessibility. Bartók certainly availed himself of the colouristic resources available to him for these dances. These included the xylophone (which Saint-Saëns, Mahler and Strauss had previously used in an orchestral context) as a sonic signifier for the wooden puppet, untuned percussion, and the use of *col legno* technique in the strings in the increasingly grotesque and ironic-sounding fifth dance.

The central part of the ballet concerns the Prince's apotheosis and forms the expressive heart of the work, the slow movement of a symphonic structure around which the Princess's two dances with the wooden puppet are symmetrically disposed. One new dance is found in the final section of the work, which may have the whiff of Strauss's *Salome* about it, in which the Princess attempts to attract the Prince by dancing seductively for him. Here Bartók employs the symmetrical melodic configuration he had used in the Scherzo of the Four Orchestral Pieces in a pair of descending perfect fourths separated by a minor second – the so-called Z-cell (A♭–E♭–D–A) from the third bar of rehearsal number 157. As will be seen later, this seems to have had a specific extra-musical association for the composer and he sets this same succession of pitches (albeit a tone higher) to the text 'painful torture, blissful torture' in the erotically charged third song of the Five Songs op. 15. After the powerful climax, which follows the reprise of the dance of the forest, and with the couple finally united, there is a return to the 'nature' music of the Prelude, the work having come full circle.

The completion and orchestration of *The Wooden Prince* would take several more years and in 1914 Bartók's thoughts were primarily directed towards folk music. His collection of songs from Bihar County had received a very negative review in the Romanian ethnographical periodical *Șezătoarea*. The criticisms were multiple: that Bartók did not understand the Romanian language and culture; that he had not collected from fiddlers; that there were faults in the notation of words and music; that the interval of an augmented fourth was not actually sung; that Bartók could not have collected so much music in such a short time; and that in any case the music was not attractive. Bartók took a no-holds-barred approach in his response that was published in the journal *Convorbiri*, refuting every point in great detail and ensuring that the reviewer appeared both a dilettante and a chauvinist. He did, however, point out with remarkable integrity many of his own perceived faults that the reviewer had failed to see: the lack of attribution of songs; the failure to include a metronome mark for all of them; mistakes in the placement of some accented syllables; and the lack of classification by melody type. In conclusion he remarked:

> We categorically repudiate the charge hidden behind every line of the critic, namely, that the collector has erroneously notated the melodies. The collector is ready to go to any village whatever of the Bihar region, accompanied by whomever, and enter into competition in transcribing melodies; if incidentally,

there were someone who could note down quicker and better – on the spot –
the melodies performed by the peasants, this collector is ready to give up, once
and for all, any study of folk music.[3]

Perhaps the most interesting aspect of this well-argued, if angry, riposte is the
detail he provides on the process of collecting. Winter was deemed a particularly good time to collect because people were more likely to be at home and
activity could take place throughout the day and night. Each song took about
twenty minutes to record, split between the time taken for the singer to
remember the tune, the notation of it and the phonograph recording. As regards
the instrumentalists, transcription could proceed even more rapidly if they
were regular performers and knew their repertoire intimately. Bartók attested
that on one occasion he managed to note down 105 melodies in a single twenty-
four-hour period.

The rest of 1914 was dominated by the war, which broke out on 28 July
when Austria-Hungary declared war on Serbia as a result of the assassination
one month earlier of Archduke Franz Ferdinand (nephew of Emperor Franz
Joseph and heir to the throne) and his wife by Gavrilo Princip. Within days, as
a consequence of the domino effect of multiple pacts, all of the major European
powers were sucked into the conflict. The first Austro-Hungarian front would
be Serbia and operations there would prove much more difficult than expected.
Indeed the first major armed confrontation, the battle of Cer between 15 and
24 August, was a military disaster for the Austro-Hungarian army, which
incurred significant casualties.

Immediately before the outbreak of war, Bartók had been in France. He had
made plans the previous month to stay briefly in Paris, and while there to prepare
for his intended second north African trip. Having sought and found support in
Paris, he moved north to Normandy and wrote to Bușiția on 18 July about the
'wonder-country' of France and its beautiful cathedrals which he was 'feeding
on'. Clearly not aware of the extent of the crisis that was building up around him,
Bartók was still making plans for collecting more folk songs, including a trip to
Moldavia, jokingly observing that if a Hungarian spy is arrested near Bacău (in
the Moldavian region of Romania, to the west of Transylvania), it will be him.
He returned to Budapest from Paris at almost the last moment (indeed, if he had
remained longer Bartók might have faced internment as an enemy alien), on the
very day that the first hostilities were declared by Austria-Hungary. It must be
remembered that the Bánát region of southern Hungary – the counties of Temes
and Torontál – had been one of his major recent stamping grounds and had
proved a 'nest of ballads' for him; these counties were bisected by the Danube,
and lay immediately above the border with Serbia.

Ironically then, having declared himself *hors de combat* in terms of his public activity as a composer and pianist, Bartók's active participation as a collector was now also thwarted. Above all, he wanted to complete his work on Romanian folk music and especially that of Transylvania, but as well as the normal concerns about his immediate family, the composer was now extremely worried about his own potential conscription. On 30 October 1914 he was able to tell his collecting friend, the pastor Sámuel Bobál, that it was likely he would be rejected on health grounds. Yet it was a further month before he stood (naked) before the medical board, which he found a humiliating and terrifying experience, and heard officially that he had been declared unfit for military service.

Although in October 1914 Bartók had seriously wondered whether it would ever be possible to collect again with Pastor Bobál in Egyházmarót, once it was certain that he did not have to serve in the war effort, he began to think that it might after all be feasible. For the first time in many years Bartók didn't go away during the Christmas period of 1914. But in January 1915 he was able to collect tunes in his own neighbourhood of Rákoskeresztúr, and then during April in the Slovak area of Zólyom County in the north of Hungary he went to villages near the town of Besztercebánya. He was astonished to discover there that 'one could go on collecting exactly as in times of peace; the peasants are so merry and light-hearted, one might think they didn't have a thought about the war.'[4]

He also found a renewed interest in composition and wrote two sets of *Román kolinda-dallamok* (Romanian Christmas Carols), *Román népi táncok* (Romanian Folk Dances) and a brief three-movement Sonatina for piano, all entirely based on folk material.[5] Like the Ten Easy Piano Pieces, they served a pedagogic purpose and were more demanding technically than 'For Children' (written in 1908–9) and the pieces written in 1913 for Sándor Reschofsky's piano method, which would be published in 1929 as *Kezdők zongoramuzsikája (The First Term at the Piano)*. László Somfai deduces from the drafts that the works were probably composed in the order listed above (though the second set of Romanian Christmas Carols was written after the Sonatina).[6]

Bartók took three different approaches to the use of folk-related material in his compositions, which he described in an essay written in 1941. At the first level, the 'used folk melody is the more important part of the work. The added accompaniment and eventual preludes and postludes may only be considered as the mounting of a jewel.' At the second level, 'the importance of the used melodies and the added parts is almost equal'. And at the third level, 'the added composition-treatment attains the importance of an original work, and the used folk melody is only to be regarded as a kind of motto'.[7] As is the case with a number of his works written for the developing pianist, the Romanian Christmas Carols, Romanian Folk Dances and Sonatina fit into the first category.

Bartók had been particularly fascinated by the *colinde* (Romanian Christmas carols) sung by groups of waits or carollers on Christmas Eve, which he found to be very different from their often highly sentimentalised Western counterparts. Around a third of these carols were not connected with Christmas at all, but had texts that were a legacy of 'ancient pagan times'. These included the tale of the brothers who were turned into stags, which would later form the basis of his *Cantata Profana*. When they were invited into houses, carollers would split themselves into two groups, which would antiphonally alternate the verses of the *colinde*, employing a performance style that was 'fiery' and 'war-like' for the metrically irregular tunes. Bartók arranged twenty of the carols into two sets, carefully selecting and organising them in terms of their tempo and tonality to create a pair of tightly organised medleys arguably equivalent to the waltz sequences for the piano by Schubert and Brahms.

The seven instrumental tunes that Bartók arranged as a set of Romanian Folk Dances were collected between 1910 and 1912 in Máramaros, Torontál, Torda-Aranyos and Bihar Counties, and the work was subsequently scored for small orchestra in 1917. Sticking closely to the original transcriptions, the arrangements of the six dances (the last is based on two tunes) are similar in style to the Sonatina, with subtle harmonisation and extremely detailed indications of articulation and phrasing. The first, 'Jo[cul] cu bâtă' ('Stick Dance'), is a vigorous solo dance by young men that ends with them kicking the ceiling. In the second, 'Brâul' ('Waistband Dance'), the women hold onto the men's cloth belts. 'Pe loc' (literally 'On the Spot'), the third, is an energetic stamping dance for couples in which the woman places her hands on the shoulders of the man, who keeps his hands on his own hips. 'Buciumeana', the fourth, is alternatively a 'Dance from Bucium/Bucsum' or a horn dance, and the fifth, 'Poargă românească', is a Romanian polka. The final dance, a 'Mărunţel', is a couples dance in which the immobile female appears completely indifferent to the man's energetic actions that involve a jump on every fourth beat.

The opening movement of the Sonatina, which is in a simple ternary form, is titled 'Bagpipers' and derives from two bagpipe tunes. The first is an 'Ardeleana' in the composite Lydian/Mixolydian mode (or acoustic scale) on D (D–E–F♯–G♯–A–B–C–D), a dance performed by couples in columns facing each other, recorded in Feresd (Feregi) in Hunyad County in 1913. The second is a 'Jocul' recorded in Vaskohmező (now Câmp) in Bihar County. Bartók transcribed this tune (number 639 in the first volume of his scholarly edition, *Rumanian Folk Music*) in the Aeolian mode on B, but with a slightly flat major second above the tonic. He chooses to treat this as a minor second in the Sonatina, harmonising it initially as if it is in C major, but finishing the section on C♯ minor. For the extremely compact second movement, Bartók draws on a 'Bear Dance' in the Dorian A mode recorded from a Gypsy violinist in Váncsfalva (Onceşti) in Máramaros County in 1913, the tune appearing twice, first in the right hand and then the left. The finale again employs two fiddle tunes: a 'Jocul Ţurcii' in Mixolydian D mode, a dance performed by Christmas carollers that was recorded in Felsőrépa (Râpa-de-Sus) in Máramaros County in 1914; and a 'Babaleuca' also in Mixolydian D, collected in 1912 in Keviszőllős (Seleuş) in Torontál County.

Having discovered that collecting was indeed viable despite the war, Bartók spent a considerable amount of time in the area of Besztercebánya, returning in July and staying in the village of Hédel (to the north-east of Besztercebánya) until the last week of August. Márta and Béla junior joined him for a few days in early August, to allow the young lad to experience the mountains. An innovation in this trip was Bartók's experimental use of a camera to supplement the transcription and phonograph recordings, though the results were initially of limited success.

What appears to have happened over the next year was partially reconstructed by Denijs Dille many years later, and such evidence as exists relies on testimony that cannot be easily verified.[8] At some point during the summer of 1915, Bartók met the chief forestry engineer, József Gombossy, who was a relative of Ernő Dohnányi and lived in the village of Kisgaram (now Hronec), just outside Breznóbánya. Gombossy introduced Bartók to his teenage daughter Klára (1901–1980), an intelligent and strong-willed girl with a keen interest in poetry and literature, who was learning to play the piano. Despite the fact that she seems to have displayed little musical talent (her father hoped she would go on to study medicine), Bartók seems to have taken a close interest in her, offering advice and suggesting reading matter, no doubt in the attempt to introduce her to his philosophical and political interests, as he had done previously with several other young women.

Ten of Klára's poems were published in a local weekly journal called *Garamvidék*, edited by the poet Zoltán Rákosi, in the period between September 1915 and September 1916. Klára copied several of these by hand to give to Bartók, who was impressed with the aptitude she displayed, sharing them with Kodály. Although Kodály later felt that her poems might have demonstrated the influence of the poetess Jutka Miklós, Dille was not able to find specific models for them in her published work.

Bartók revisited the area in November and returned again for the Christmas period, Klára joining him between 27 and 29 December while he was collecting at Feketebalog, ten kilometres down the valley from her home. What, if anything, transpired while they were together cannot easily be ascertained. In Dille's account Bartók became so infatuated with Klára, who had then just turned fourteen (the age of consent in Austria-Hungary) though apparently mature for her years, that he proposed divorcing Márta in order to marry her. Klára, it seems, was not remotely interested in this man twenty years her senior, and Bartók then turned to her best friend, Wanda Gleiman, to try to persuade her. This proving equally futile, in October 1916 Bartók eventually broke off the relationship, which had created enormous psychological turbulence for him, though he remained in contact with Wanda and her sister Ani for a number of years.

A direct outcome of this ill-fated liaison was the set of Five Songs op. 15, posthumously published in 1958. No authorial attribution is given for the texts of the songs in the score, and indeed it was Bartók's demand that they should remain anonymous that proved the stumbling block for their publication during his lifetime. The five titles and dates of completion, in 1916, are respectively: 'Az én szerelmem' ('My Love'), 15 January; 'Nyár' ('Summer'), 5 February; 'A vágyak éjjele' ('Night of Desires'), 27 August; 'Színes álomban' ('In Vivid Dreams'), before 28 January; and 'Itt lent a völgyben' ('Down in the Valley'), 6 February. It is known that the texts for all but the third song were written by Klára; in communication with Dille, Wanda Gleiman claimed that this too was written by her, though Klára contended she may have drawn on a poem by Michi Rosenauer (who had formed the literary circle the girls attended) entitled 'Hangoló éjszaka'.[9]

Bartók later expressed his doubts about the literary quality of the poems in relation to the potential publication of the first three by Universal Edition as *Drei Lieder*, but this seems not to have been an issue for him when he composed the songs.[10] Klára's texts convey the feelings of an adolescent girl who has recently awoken to the sexual world and whose 'body is now alight with savage passion'. Perhaps Bartók heard a personal message in the fourth song's 'Speak, are you the perfect companion whom my soul has waited for?' Certainly its sentiments seem to spring from a similar source to *Bluebeard's Castle*, and the lines 'Say that you will accept my life from me: All its treasures are yours, all its glories' might well have come from Judit's lips. 'Night of Desires' is more overtly erotic (if at times voyeuristic) in tone, offering a frank description of a young woman's sexual tension and frustration as she lies in bed alone, yearning for a the kisses of a lover.

The set of songs seem to have been passed over in some embarrassment by a number of Bartók's critics, often along the lines that it is a pity that what are often musically interesting songs have such poor and gauche texts, making them unsuitable for the concert platform. While these songs express the feelings of young women who are not yet fully mature and are dealing with the hormonal changes of adulthood, by the standards of many of the traditional songs that Bartók collected, they were neither particularly naive nor technically deficient.

Bartók's setting of the first song bears a correspondence with the opening of *Bluebeard's Castle*, for while the text talks of the singer's love being like the 'flaring light of the mid-day sun', the music is surprisingly understated, resembling Judit's tentative description of leaving her father and mother to join Bluebeard. The chord sequence that supports this (Fig. 17) doesn't contain a single unadorned triad, and although an explanation can be made for a tonic of B for each of them, the overall logic of the progression is difficult to explain purely in tonal terms. While the song makes some use of pentatonicism, particularly in the brief postlude, there is a sense of tonal dislocation throughout that reinforces the controlled and almost detached passion of the vocal line, imbuing it with a reticence suggesting a dream-like state.

For the second song's invocation of the cloudless and airless summer, Bartók again composes an unobtrusive vocal line that has the rhythmic simplicity of a folk song and moves between pure pentatonicism (in the opening and closing bars) and more chromatic writing. The accompaniment is mainly written in bare intervals of perfect fifths and octaves (from bar 15 these briefly change to diminished fifths). An exquisite little interlude, a further Debussyan touch, leads to the song's final lines, which talk of the tree's shade briefly holding back the 'raging advance' of the summer.

The third song was completed several months later than the other four and is on a rather larger scale. Given the nature of the poem, with its feverish excitement and demand for 'csókolni' (kisses), Bartók's approach is suggestive rather than overtly graphic, the opening reiteration of interlocking major thirds in the right hand (notated as B♯–E and A–C♯) a subdued shiver rather than an outburst of ecstasy. The vocal line gradually extends in range and the words 'night of desires' are set to a chain of descending thirds ($D_5$–$B\flat_4$–$G_4$–$E\flat_4$–$C_4$), an extension of the falling major-seventh figure to which Judit had sung Bluebeard's name in the opera. From bar 22, as the poem describes the protagonist's

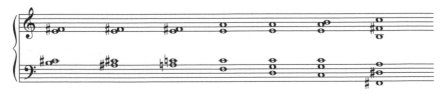

Figure 17. The first seven chords from 'Az én szerelmem'.

mounting excitement, the piano picks up the seventh chord as a rapid arpeggio divided between the hands and this is gradually transformed into an ostinato on the pitches C–D♯–E–G♯–A in the lead up to the words 'painful torture, blissful torture!' At this point Bartók introduces the motif of two falling perfect fourths separated by a minor second (E–B–B♭–F), a version of the Z-cell that was anticipated by the upper four pitches of the ostinato figure. This figure can be seen to derive from the major version of the descending Stefi/Bluebeard motif (E–C–A–F) through the flattening of the second note and the sharpening of the third, and from the pentatonic segment (E–B–A–E) through the raising of its two final pitches.[11] The Z-cell motif reappears on a number of further occasions in the course of the song, at bars 45–8, 64–5, and in the brief interlude at bars 66–74. With the restoration of the opening texture of interlocking thirds, the vocal line finishes in pure pentatonicism, entirely based on the pitches G–A–C–D.

'Színes álomban' ('In Vivid Dreams'), the penultimate song, begins and ends in a modally coloured C major, the music of the piano part at these points being based on the familiar Lydian/Mixolydian polymode (or acoustic scale). The recitative-like vocal line opens with pentatonic formations, but as the song progresses it moves through the Lydian F♯ mode (from bar 24) at the point where the poet offers the treasures of her life to her lover, to a more chromatic turn at the conclusion when she reveals that she believes him to be her 'soul mate'. Just before these final lines, at bar 33, the piano settles on, and reiterates, the chord F–C–F♯–B, a further manifestation of the Z-cell. The song concludes, as it had begun, in an implied C major, the voicing of the piano postlude picking up from bar 45 the harmonics from a C fundamental lying an octave below the lowest bass note.

Bartók had at one stage considered a cycle of songs around a seasonal theme, but only two of the published ones follow this path, the second ('Summer') and the final autumnal 'Itt lent a völgyben' ('Down In the Valley'), which contains some of the most radical piano writing of the set. The eight-note rolled chromatic chord running across three octaves and containing only the pitches D♭, D and E, which is repeated over the first four bars, is a truly original sonority. As a musical symbol it is obviously intended to suggest the death that autumn brings to the valley (and presumably also the death that war was currently bringing to Europe), and it can be seen as a close relative of the minor-second 'blood motif' of *Bluebeard's Castle*. If the tonic is taken as D♭, then the voice's first entry appears to have little in common with this tonality, outlining a fundamentally pentatonic melodic line from E (E–G–A–B–D, with a single passing C♯). The second phrase ('pale flowers await their fate'), underpinned by the chord B♭–B–C–F–F♯–G in the piano, has a surprising similarity to Beethoven's setting of the words 'Deine Zauber, binden wieder' – 'Your magic reunites (that custom strictly divides)' – of Schiller's 'An die Freude' in the Ninth Symphony (Fig. 18). This could, of course, be entirely coincidental, though the correspondence is striking and it could be construed as an ironic comment on Schiller's ode with its utopian vision that all men will become brothers in the haven of the wings of joy. In the following phrase, the descent of the vocal line and chords in the piano part, below inverted pedal tones of C♯–D in the right hand, isomorphically encodes the ground 'sinking like a boat into icy water'. Several brief references are made to the falling chain of thirds in the following verse, both in the prefatory gesture in the piano and the vocal line where it sings of the sods of earth weeping. The song, which concludes with an icy piano postlude, is suffused with a feeling of depression bordering on despair. One must always be cautious in assigning biographical explanation, but it is hard not to imagine that this reflected Bartók's state of mind at the time as did the coldly furious letter written to the directors of the Budapest Philharmonic Society on 10 December 1915, for their temerity in performing a 'truncated' version of his First Suite for orchestra. In his final paragraph he writes:

> I should be greatly obliged if you would never play any of my pieces again. I feel all the more entitled to make this request since the deplorable state of Budapest's musical life has forced me to forego all public appearances as a composer during the last 4 years and to withhold all my works written since then from public appearance.[12]

The Five Songs op. 16, to poems by Endre Ady, published by Universal Edition in 1923, were written between February and April 1916, in advance of the third song of op. 15. By 1916 Ady was widely regarded as the most influential poet in

Figure 18. (a) From the fifth song of Five Songs op. 15; (b) 'Deine Zauber binden wieder', from the finale of Beethoven's Ninth Symphony.

Hungary. Born in 1877 as the son of a Calvinist minister, Ady had contracted syphilis while working as a journalist in Nagyvárad between 1900 and 1903 and for most of his adult life he lived under its influence and threat. Anton Nyerges remarks that 'As a writer he was probably never mentally or spiritually free from the festering and fermenting effects of the illness, and not a single one of his main themes – love, death, God, genius, revolution – is without an intimate connection with its overpowering effects.'[13] Ironically, in a turn of events which curiously paralleled Dille's narrative of Bartók's relationship with Klára, in March 1916, at the same time that he was composing the songs, Ady, who was a notorious womaniser and alcoholic, began an affair with a girl of seventeen at the Városmajor Szanatórium in Budapest, while recuperating there from a bout of ill-health. Ady told his brother that he was going to divorce his wife (whom he had only married the previous year) but did not do so and died three years later from a ruptured aortic aneurysm.

Bartók had already revealed his enthusiasm for Ady in the letter he had sent to Buşiţia in January 1911. The composer was particularly attracted at this stage to the poems that chimed with his anti-Magyarist and anti-bourgeois feelings. Ady's position was complex and often confrontational. In a controversial piece published in the rival literary journal to *Nyugat*, the conservative *Új Idők* (*New Times*), which wished to draw him onto their writing team, he had strenuously denied being either a modernist or a revolutionary and indeed claimed spiritual kinship with the Magyars.

The poems Bartók chose to set talk of loneliness, discontent and sorrow, and pick up the autumnal theme of the final song of op. 15. All but the third poem are taken from the collection, *Blood and Gold* (1907), the first two from the group headed 'Kinsman of Death' and the final pair from 'Leda's Golden Statue'. For the central song, Bartók turned to Ady's *Longing for Love* (1909) drawing the poem from the group 'Ever Lengthening Days'.

In the first poem, 'Három őszi könnycsepp' (literally 'Three Autumn Tears'), which is given in the English translation by Nancy Bush in the 1939 Boosey & Hawkes score as 'Autumn Tears', Ady declares that in autumn noons and nights he is lost in silent and sorrowful weeping both.[14] Bartók's setting is a kind of lugubrious slow waltz in B in which the melodic structure of the vocal line of the first verse is transposed down a fifth for the second verse, and a linear rise and fall completes the third. The dragging two-bar piano introduction, which becomes the basis of the accompaniment for much of the first verse and can perhaps be regarded as the musical encoding of a sigh or moan, involves a low B followed by two chords, a more dissonant one acting as an appoggiatura to an eleventh on B on the third beat, whose pitches derive all from the Locrian mode (B–D–F–A–C–E). The vocal melody of the first verse initially rocks gently around the pitches of a C♯ minor triad before moving to a composite Mixolydian/Phrygian mode on G for its continuation. For the second verse Bartók transposes the melody down by an augmented fifth, though by the end of the section this has settled on a perfect fifth and is accommodated to the C Aeolian mode. The accompaniment to the third verse looks back to a technique found in 'Summer', the second song of the op. 15 set, where chains of diminished fifths moved in parallel motion. Here they become brittle-sounding octaves divided by tritones as the poet speaks of his weeping. One tiny, but telling, rhythmic gesture appears on the final word of each verse, through the use of the Hungarian accented short-long rhythm on the first two syllables of 'leányokra' (girls), 'csillagokra' (stars) and 'leborulni' (prostrations).

'Az őszi lárma' ('On Autumn Nights'), given as 'Autumn Echoes' by Bush, is a kind of ghost story: things go bump in the autumnal night and a long-buried man, who was joyless when alive, now wishes to see the stars. An expressionist-sounding song that could almost be taken as the work of the Schoenberg of *Pierrot Lunaire* and *The Book of the Hanging Gardens*, it is unselfconsciously eerie in tone. Bartók treats the vocal line like a recitative, developing the musical imagery in the piano part through an idea that is founded on pairs of perfect-fourth dyads placed a tritone apart (another Z-cell). The conjuring up of swirling mists through the wave-like patterns and arpeggiations of Z-cells and the rebounding of spectral footsteps matches Debussy in its colouristic use of the piano; and the final verse, in which falling and rising lines combine to signify the awakening of longing in the corpse, is quite extraordinarily powerful, pre-empting much cinematic horror music.

The third song, 'Az ágyam hivogat' ('Lost Content' – literally, 'My Bed is Calling Me'), seems to offer an ironic comment on the equivalent central song of op. 15, which was about erotic longing; for here the poet looks to his bed, which was previously a 'dream-place', a 'strength-well' and a 'kiss-pub', but has now become a coffin, a place of fear. In the second verse, which seems to betoken both physical and spiritual impotence, a moment of restored vitality ends in failure and shame. In her translation, Bush only partly takes into account Ady's unusual poetic scheme in which the final word or phrase of each line opens the next one, and the following literal translation by Gergely Hubai shows Ady's approach more clearly. The lines in square brackets are omitted by Bartók:[15]

**My Bed is Calling Me**
I lay down. Oh, my bed,
Oh, my bed, last year,

Last year you were different.
You were different: dream-place,
Dream-place, strength-well,
Strength-well, kiss-pub,
Kiss-pub, happiness,
Happiness. What have you become?
What have you become? Coffin,
Coffin. Every day,
Every day you're closing better,
Closing better. Laying down,
Laying down terrified,
Terrified wake up,
Wake up terrified,
Terrified I wake up.

To wake up, to look around,
To look around, to feel,
To feel, to realize,
To realize, to notice,
To notice, to hide,
To hide, to look out,
To look out, to get out,
To get out, to want,
To want, to feel sad,
[To feel sad, to determine,]
To determine, to break down,
[To break down, to feel ashamed,]
To feel ashamed. Oh, my bed,
Oh, my bed, my coffin,
My coffin, you're calling me,
You're calling me. I lay down.

The opening F major arpeggios, each coloured with an A♭ that functions as an appoggiatura to the major third, suggest a mood of resignation. As the poet recalls the former pleasure and potency associated with his bed, a troubled ostinato figure in the piano supports the vocal expression of the Z-cell (G–G–F♯–D♭–F♯–C) to the words 'álom-hely' (dream-place). With the recollection of the 'csók-csárda' (kiss-pub) Bartók moves to a pentatonic shape in the vocal line, the Hungarian short-long rhythm falling on 'vidámság' (happiness). In the increasingly agitated central section of the song, which deals with the emotional turmoil expressed by the second verse, the vocal line chromatically loops up to the climax whose text Bush translates as 'strength rises'. And with the return of the song's earliest gesture, the coloured major chord now a semitone lower, the opening insinuation of resignation and acceptance of fate seems to be made explicit and the song closes in F with the almost whispered 'I lay down' on the dominant.

For a significant period of his life, Ady was romantically involved with Adél Brüll, the wife of Paris-based Hungarian merchant Ödön Diósy. In Ady's poetry she is referred to as Léda, and the final two songs are taken from the group specifically devoted to her, 'Leda's Golden Statue' from *Blood and Gold*. 'Egyedül a tengerrel' ('Alone with the Sea'), arguably the most exquisite and developed number of the set, tells of the poet's loneliness in the hotel room he had shared with his mistress, embracing a flower she had left, whose perfume will soon vanish. While Bush's translation is direct and prosaic, Ady's original is allusive and elliptical, hinting rather than recounting. His poetic structure again involves repetition, the second line of each stanza being reiterated, though Bartók omits those in the third and fifth stanzas to enhance the musical flow.

A one-bar piano introduction conjoins two types of material, the pitches of a diminished chord with major seventh (F♯–A–B♯–E♯) and a pentatonic collection (C♯–D♯–F♯–G♯–B), and between them they provide the structural foundations for the song. They underpin the piano ostinati that Bartók conjures up for the first line of the third verse, translated by Nyerges as 'Like a fleeting kiss the perfumes soar' (a similar texture to that found in 'My Love', the first song of op. 15), and for the fifth verse, where the poet talks of lying on the couch listening to the savage sea and dreaming, interlaced dyads from the pentatonic scale alternate in the right hand against a variant of the seventh figure in the left, in which the F♯ is altered to a D♯.[16] Finally the two elements round the song off, rising by octaves as quiet arpeggios against a D♯ tonic. The opening and closing vocal lines are based on the pentatonic scale C♯–D♯–F♯–G♯–A♯, and the fourth verse's reference to the chanting of the sea ('come, my love') expands the pentatonic collection B–C♯–D♯–F♯ through the addition of G and A, effectively transforming it to the pitches of an acoustic scale on A.

In the final, succinct song, 'Nem mehetek hozzád' ('I Cannot Come to You'), each verse closes morbidly with the phrase 'S én meghalok' ('and I will die'). The poet laments to his 'great love, [his] sacred madness' that whereas others still enjoy the summer, music and love, the path he follows and his fate without her have become 'sad and awkward'. Bartók's music is spare and bleak, and he avoids the complex textures of the inner three songs, returning to the chordal approach of the first. Like 'Summer' from the op. 15 set, there is a tendency towards quartal writing with stacked-fourth chords moving in similar motion in the interludes between the first two verses. By the middle of the piece, the music seems to have lost any clear sense of tonality and from the second bar of the central Andante assai, five-part chords topped with composite perfect/augmented fourth chords slither around in parallel motion. Immediately before this, Bartók draws on the Stefi motif in its original rising minor form (E♭–G♭–B♭–D) in setting the words 'Mások mehetnek, törnek, élnek' ('free are others for living, loving'). The falling fourth in the last verse, to which the words 'Bús és balog' ('loss and sorrow') are set, fleetingly recalls the Z-cell used for 'painful torture, blissful torture' in the third song of op. 15. The final point of closure is an A minor seventh chord, which gradually replaces the Phrygian C modality that dominated the rest of the postlude.

Whether or not the two song cycles had any autobiographical significance for Bartók, they clearly demonstrate an enlargement of his musical horizons and an expansion of his musical resources. Unfettered as they were by the demands of a performer, the expectations of an audience, or the boundaries of musical convention, Bartók was at liberty to experiment, and he had moved to a position where it seemed that he might almost be on the borders of atonality.

At the same time that he was working on the song cycles, he composed his Suite for piano op. 14, a four-movement piece nominally in B♭ that was completed in Rákoskeresztúr in February 1916. Unlike the two sets of piano pieces based on Romanian tunes and the Sonatina, this is an example of the third level of folk influence in which residual traces of folk material perform the function of a 'motto' in what is otherwise an original piece. It appears that, like the song sets, this suite was originally intended to have five movements and an Andante was discarded. As it stands, the first three movements accelerate from a 2/4 Allegretto (crotchet = 120), through a 3/4 Scherzo in regular crotchets (dotted minim = 122), to a 2/2 Allegro molto in quavers (minim = 124). The slow fourth movement in 6/8 (with two forays into 9/8), marked Sostenuto (quaver = 120–110), brings the suite to its conclusion.

The first movement of the suite is in a straightforward ternary form with a truncated reprise of a principal theme that bears the traces of Romanian dance music without apparently quoting any actual material that Bartók had collected. After four bars of vamped B♭ chords, the movement proceeds with a two-bar pseudo-Romanian motif, from which the rest of the sixteen-bar melody and its immediate repetition an octave higher derive (Fig. 19). Mention has previously been made of the 'acoustic scale', which has a sharpened fourth and flattened seventh. The Hungarian musicologist Lajos Bárdos theorised an entire modal system parallel to the diatonic one, which he described as *heptatonia secunda*, of which the ascending melodic minor scale with its sharpened sixth and seventh can be regarded as the basic model and the acoustic scale one of its

Figure 19. (a) and (b) The melody of bars 5–6 and 11–12 of the first movement of the Suite op. 14; and (b) and (c), their imagined folk-music source.

seven permutations.[17] Modes from this system were found by Bartók (though he did not attempt to systematise them as Bárdos does) and he regarded the permutation whose first five pitches are configured like a major scale, but with a flat sixth and seventh, as a particular characteristic of the Bihar dialect. In the Allegretto, the thematic material at bars 5–11 is derived from a scale whose pitches are B♭–C–D–E–F♯–G–[A–]B♭, a version with the longest possible run of whole-tone intervals, making it a kind of super-Lydian mode.

The intonation (or pitch accuracy) of amateur musicians, particularly fiddlers who often have the greatest latitude in this respect, has long been a matter of interest for collectors of traditional music, and what may be regarded as a technical error by a player can often become a systematic element of their performance practice. Figure 19 (c) and (d) show a possible diatonic version of the melodic material in Figure 19 (a) and (b) to demonstrate how Bartók has introduced semitone shifts from the orthodox pitches, or 'mistunings', to employ a concept popularised in the Bartók literature by János Kárpáti. A conventional accompaniment for the first two bars in this diatonic version might involve a progression from the tonic in the first bar to the dominant seventh in the second. Instead, Bartók substitutes E major as a surrogate dominant to create a tritonal byplay that shifts to F♯ minor – C and D♯ minor – A minor in the second half of the sixteen-bar thematic unit. For the repeat of this unit one octave higher (from bar 21) Bartók employs the conventional alternation of the tonic and the actual dominant (as Fmaj⁷), setting the two different harmonisation strategies into relief. Reminiscent of the *Allegro barbaro*, the middle section takes on an increasingly motoric quality, with regular quaver pulsations articulated by octaves divided by tritones in the right hand, and chromatic semiquaver flurries interlocking with them in the left. In the distilled reprise of the first section, the whole-tone aspects of Bartók's scale are brought to the foreground, and extended to a complete whole-tone scale as a means of connecting the pseudo-dominant E to the tonic B♭.

Structured as a compact rondo, the percussive Scherzo is more systematic in its experimentation, its principal and central thematic areas investigating further the potential of the whole-tone scale. In the first section, Bartók splits each of the two versions of the mode (D♭–E♭–F–G–A–B and C–D–E–F♯–G♯–A♯) into pairs of augmented triads and interlaces them, for the first sixteen bars falling and then rising. In the central episode, after eight bars in which the tonality of C is established, he restricts his palette entirely to the whole-tone scale founded on C, as an ostinato to which a melodic line organised in six-bar phrases is added. The more tranquil and jocose 'B' sections alternate dyads in the left hand from the two whole-tone collections against pungent staccato minor seconds in the right.

Bartók turns his attention to the octatonic scale in the third movement in D, a *moto perpetuo* marked Allegro molto. He noted in a lecture given at Columbia University sometime between 1941 and 1942 that as well as bearing the imprint of East European traditional music, 'occasionally it may even be tinctured with oriental (for instance, Arabic) influences', and he cites this movement as an example of the latter.[18] Although he is probably thinking as much of the tendency to varied repetition as the specific tonal configuration, Bartók transcribed several pieces based on octatonic segments (for example, number 4a from 'Arab Folk Music from the Biskra District') and he found a *rhaita* whose scale was tuned more or less to an octatonic scale.

The octatonic scale has a structure of alternating tones and semitones, with only three possible different permutations (semitones are marked with a ^), though each can be rotated so they start on any of the eight pitches:

I. D–E^F–G^A♭–B♭^B–C♯
II. D^E♭–F^G♭–A♭^A–B^C
III. D♭–E♭^E–F♯^G–A^B♭–C

Characteristically, Bartók does not entirely restrict himself to the resources of any one of these three collections, but modulates between them. Thus, while the opening left-hand pattern for the first ten bars is entirely based on scale form I and the right-hand melody up to bar 20 on scale form II, each time the right hand plays an A natural, it is doubled by the left hand even though it does not fall within 'its' version of the scale. The reason Bartók does this is to maintain another systematic feature – the presence of either a perfect fifth on A♭, or an octave on A, on the second minim beat of every bar in the passage. From bar 21 he coalesces the lower five pitches of scale form I with the pitches of form II to create a composite longer version of the scale (D–E^F–G^A♭ and A–B^C–D^E♭–F^G♭–A♭^A), though this is not used entirely consistently and the E♭

occasionally appears in the lower octave. For the central *martellato* episode, Bartók moves to form III of the scale, firstly picking out and sustaining three of the triads that it contains (F♯, A and C minors). While the following thirty-four bars are almost entirely based on this form, Bartók does introduce a few stray pitches from outside it, demonstrating again that he will not permit a system to dictate his musical decisions.

The fourth movement, nominally in B♭, is marked *sostenuto* and is suffused with an air of melancholy. Its opening melodic idea, held within chords that otherwise contain the pitches D and F, is doubled an octave apart by a middle voice in the right hand and the upper voice in the left; it gradually opens out like a fan (B–C, B♭–D♭, B♭–E, A–E, A♭–F, G–F♯), something that would become another of Bartók's signature devices. A brief descent through a major-minor arpeggio of G♭ over a G major triad at bar 9 sets in motion a varied repeat of the opening idea in the left hand, mainly played by the thumb, the right hand reiterating the B♭ above it like the tolling of a bell. In a concise central section the falling arpeggio motif emerges again, followed by a succession of couplets in which major thirds in each hand slide towards each other chromatically, like sighs. With the varied reprise of the opening, the Z-cell that was hinted at in bars 16–17 is made manifest in the right hand in octaves against an F♯ major-minor chord and an F–D dyad in the left hand. This major-minor chord chimes out in the succeeding bars as the left hand moves downwards in tenths towards the tonic. The final bars submerge the B♭–D of a B♭ triad in a seven-note complex, the perfect fourths on C♭ suggesting a final expressive inhalation and exhalation.

In the summer of 1916 Béla junior was approaching the age of compulsory education. To avoid what his father perceived as his potential Roman Catholic religious indoctrination at school, Bartók decided to join the Unitarian Church which he had come across during his fieldwork in Transylvania, seeing it as the most liberal of the Protestant churches. Despite his avowed atheism, he was clearly willing to compromise these views to avoid difficulty for his son.

A much more substantial problem for Bartók arose from Romania's invasion of Transylvania on 27 August 1916. Zoltán Szász describes the disruption that ensued at that time:

> On the first day of the offensive, the Hungarian authorities took measures to evacuate the potential war zone south of the Maros River. Hungarian and Saxon townsfolk and the inhabitants of Székelyföld were instructed to pull back. Offices were transferred from Brassó to Földvár. Some two-thirds of the population of Nagyszeben moved out, and an even larger proportion left Csíkszereda, but the highways were also crowded with peasant carts and livestock. Over 200,000 people made the exodus. Refugees flooded into

Enyed, Torda, and Kolozsvár, and then into the districts of Temesvár and
Szeged as well. A large number of people sought temporary haven in
Budapest; due to the congested traffic and the shortage of railway cars, it
took them three to four days to reach the capital. Bishop Teutsch and other
Saxon Church leaders took refuge in Budapest, as did almost all of the
financial institutions, including the Romanian Albina bank. Most of the
Zsil Valley's miners were evacuated to Tatabánya.[19]

As luck would have it, and in an echo of the events at the start of the war, Márta
and her son were staying in Transylvania, in the town of Marosvásárhely (now
Târgu Mureş) in Maros-Torda County, at the time of the Romanian incursion.
The family had arrived at the end of July as guests of Márta's cousin, Dr Károly
Ziegler, and Bartók had taken the opportunity to collect songs from a number
of villages in the region. He set off for home early in the second week of August
1914 leaving Márta and Béla with Károly, completely unaware of the problems
that they were soon to face. A letter he sent to her on 31 August reveals that he
was particularly concerned about her safety, telling her 'Not on my account and
not even on account of the score, but rather because of the way things now are,
you should come home as a matter of the utmost urgency, by, I repeat, any way
you can.'[20] In what must have been a terrifying experience for the twenty-two-
year-old Márta, despite being accompanied by three companies of soldiers, by
14 September they'd still reached only as far as Nagyszalonta, forty kilometres
south-west of Nagyvárad. Eventually they made it home to Rákoskeresztúr,
though almost immediately Bartók set off again for Besztercebánya. In fact, the
invasion proved short-lived and the Romanian army was forced to withdraw
by the end of October, but it demonstrated the vulnerability of Transylvania to
attack and the extreme political sensitivity of the region.

Despite, or perhaps because of, Bartók's self-imposed withdrawal from
public life as a composer, the premiere of The Wooden Prince was keenly anticipated by the arts and theatre weekly Színházi Élet (Theatre Life) on 29 October
as the likely musical sensation of the season.[21] However, Bartók still had not
entirely completed his orchestration. This work would continue over the
Christmas and New Year period while he stayed at Tőkésújfalu (now Klátova
Nová Ves in Slovakia) on the country estate of Baron Lipót Haupt-Stummer.
Bartók had first come in contact with the Haupt-Stummer family in 1902 when
he was a student at the Liszt Academy; he had been recommended by Ödön
Mihalovich to Haupt-Stummer as a theory teacher for Ágost and Gertrúda, the
baron's youngest son and eldest daughter. Despite the presence of a pro-
German, monarchist and anti-Semitic widow who was staying with her chil-
dren, and despite a poor piano, Bartók did his best to entertain. He reports

progress on his work in a series of letters to Márta, quoting in one of them Ady's poem, 'A fekete zongora', which talks of the black piano, 'crazy instrument that cries, neighs and hums'. By Friday 5 January he had completed the second dance of the wooden puppet and advised Márta that he would be setting off for Pozsony on the following Tuesday. A month later the score of *The Wooden Prince* was completed and submitted to the Budapest Opera.

During this period Márta had been seriously unwell again, suffering from a lung infection, and this resulted in her staying for two months in a sanatorium at Újtátrafüred in the Tátra mountains. On 6 May, shortly before the premiere of *The Wooden Prince*, Bartók commented to Bușiția that he was anxious because she had still not recovered and that appropriate food for someone in her delicate condition was in short supply. At the same time, he complained about the frustrations he had with the Budapest Opera, describing it as:

> An Augean stable; a dumping ground for every kind of rubbish; the seat of all disorder; the pinnacle of confusion, where only one man is respected and has the right to make decisions, however trivial they may be: the Government Deputy; but this otherwise V.C.P.C. [Very Confidential Private Councillor] hardly ever looks in at the theatre. Now the first night is May 12th; and this is the last week of rehearsals. People are already sharpening their claws against me.[22]

A month and a half previously he had been fulsome in his praise to his mother of the ballet's Italian conductor, Egisto Tango, who had claimed that he would hold thirty rehearsals. Bartók was also extremely impressed that Tango wished to study the score thoroughly before he was willing to work on it with the orchestra.

Balázs asserts that he took on himself the major responsibility for the ballet's realisation, performing a much more substantial role in the technical aspects of the production than was ever normal for a librettist, and that he did this all for Bartók alone. In his version of events, Balázs maintains that he declared to Count Bánffy, the company's Intendant:

> Your Excellency, I have never in my life been on the stage. Entrust me with the production of the ballet. I have never heard how dancers are to be coached. Entrust me with the directing and coaching of the corps de ballet, or else *The Wooden Prince* will never be produced on the stage.[23]

For all Bartók's trepidation and hard labour (he professed that he 'worked for two months' and that his weight dropped by fifteen kilograms), the premiere proved to be a remarkable triumph for the composer if not for Balázs himself. Lasting for around fifty minutes, *The Wooden Prince* was performed as part of a triple bill including Gluck's one-act *opéra comique, Le Cadi dupe,* and a ballet called *Ámor játékai* (*Cupid's Games*) based on music by Mozart. Choreographed by Ottó Zöbisch, *The Wooden Prince* starred Anna Pallay as the Prince, Emilia Nirschy as the Princess, Boriska Harmat as the fairy and Ede Brada as the puppet prince. A major scandal was expected, but according to Balázs:

> It was a memorable night. After the last bars there was a deadly silence in the audience lasting for several seconds. There was not one sound of a handclap. But no whistling nor booing either. It was as if an invisible scale of gigantic proportions was being tipped first one way then the other. . . . Then the applause broke out in the galleries and like an avalanche swept down to the boxes and the stalls, carrying before it all the rabble of the press. Many reviews had to be rewritten that night. That was Béla Bartók's first tremendous success.[24]

A few weeks after the premiere, Bartók's admiration for Tango was unalloyed; the conductor was, he advised Buşiţia, the first professional musician who fully understood and embraced his music, and it was his perception and diligence that had ensured the work's musical triumph. Conversely, Balázs remained deeply irritated and upset that his contribution was insufficiently critically acknowledged, regarding the ballet's success as largely his making.

In the summer of 1917 Tango accompanied Bartók on his collecting activities in Arad County. Unfortunately, the conductor became seriously ill after a couple of weeks, which disrupted their plans and caused them to call on the hospitality of Buşiţia in Belényes. Typhus was suspected but it eventually turned out that Tango had contracted malaria and he was given the appropriate treatment. As Bartók reported laconically to his wife, poor Tango would not be leaving with the most favourable memories of the region.

There can be little doubt that Bartók's self-confidence as a composer and his willingness to present his music to the public was appreciably restored by his experience with the ballet. Brief sketches for several sections of the first movement of his Second String Quartet appear in the Black Pocket-Book sandwiched between ones for the first of the Two Pictures and for *The Wooden Prince*. According to the dates given at the end of the miniature score, the quartet was written between 1915 and 1917, and completed at Rákoskeresztúr. Márta reports his progress on the work to her mother-in-law on 11 November, by which point Bartók had completed the outer movements and had just told her that he would soon finish the central one.

Dedicated to the Waldbauer-Kerpely Quartet, who had premiered his first mature essay in the medium, Bartók's Second String Quartet is similarly in three movements, but with a quite different temporal trajectory. An inward-looking Moderato movement leads to a brilliant dance-influenced Allegro molto capriccioso, culminating with a Lento that moves between desolation and impassioned outcry. As well as the technical advances Bartók had made since his previous quartet, the second quartet reflects both the failures and more recent successes over this period. It began life as one of the works that was for 'his writing desk only'. Its spirit and language is rather closer to the Suite op. 14 and the sets of songs op. 15 and 16 than *The Wooden Prince*, showing little inclination towards compromise and fewer backward glances to earlier influences.

Although the quartet is still fundamentally tonal in orientation and is centred on A, there is a tendency to avoid unadulterated triadic diatonic harmony and to use all twelve chromatic tones freely. Superficially, the quartet's most conservative aspect is its structural approach, given that it employs sonata, rondo and ternary schemes. Yet the constant variation and development of material, combined with its tonal and harmonic intricacy, ensures that the work remains unpredictable and challenging. Bartók is particularly sensitive to the sonic and dramatic opportunities for interplay within the quartet and, as well as drawing on the full range of instrumental possibilities, from solo to tutti, he organises the instruments in varying pairs or with one voice set against the rest.

The initial idea of the opening movement involves two permutations of the Z-cell: the initial B♭ and E♭ in cello and second violin combined with the rising E and A in the first violin outlines the first permutation, and its continuation – the falling pattern D–C♯–G♯–G – the second. The arc of the first violin's motif is the generative model for much of the rest of the first theme, and the transitional passage between it and the expressive second theme (Fig. 20) begins with a series of overlapping entries of the version played by the cello in bar 20. As this thematic area moves to its culmination with a chain of rising triads played by the lower three voices, the first violin flamboyantly plays the pitch G over four octaves.

Bartók turns to the symmetrical whole-tone scale for the opening bars of the second theme (Fig. 21), and the succeeding passage embraces both poly-modality and the simultaneous use of major and minor thirds within a chord. Thus, from the fifth bar of rehearsal number 5 to the third bar of rehearsal number 6, the upper two parts are almost entirely white-note diatonic whereas the viola and cello are more chromatic. An unusual feature of this section is the use of polymetre, with the superimposition of 6/8 in the upper three

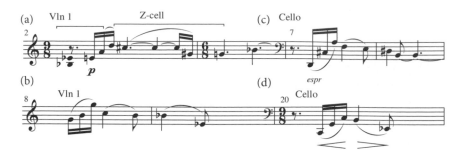

Figure 20. The opening motif and variants from the first movement of the Second String Quartet.

instruments and 3+4/8 in the cello for three bars, a compensatory 9/8 bar bringing the parts back into alignment. Bartók could have achieved precisely the same effect rather more conveniently for the players by beaming across the 6/8 bar lines, but the approach he adopted is symptomatic of his desire to extend the notational boundaries of music and to offer a challenge to his performers. The lyricism of the second theme permeates the closing bars of the exposition, which involves a gentle and pastoral-sounding diatonic idea in a modal F♯ played two octaves apart by the first violin and viola, the second violin and cello supplying chains of accompanying fifths.

The development opens in a more fragmentary fashion with the material that sutures the first and second subjects, and from this point on there are three main developmental components: a three-note motif in a long-short-long cretic metre that is passed around the quartet; a dramatic dialogue in inversion between the first violin and cello based on the cretic-metre motif, with inner voices playing an ostinato figure in thirds that oscillates around F♯ and A; and a more sustained passage that opens with chordal reiterations of the Z-cell.

Should there be any suspicion that the Z-cell's use in the exposition was accidental, the recapitulation makes it absolutely certain that this is a conscious and systematic element. Although the initial B♭ is no longer present, and the lower three voices now play what amounts to a French sixth in A (F–A–B–D♯)

Figure 21. The opening of the second theme from the first movement of the Second String Quartet.

– a further symmetrical structure – Bartók extends the melodic line with a series of repetitions of the Z-cell D–G–G♯–C♯ before moving through two other permutations of it (C–D♭–G♭–A♭♭ and E–A–B♭–E♭). The movement ends with a condensed reprise of the second subject and fragments from it, the pitches F–A–C♯ being left suspended over an E in the cello in the final chord, an A major second-inversion chord coloured with a minor sixth.

After the introspection of the first movement, the duple-time second movement, which combines and coalesces rondo and variation, is extrovert and effervescent, the caprice in its tempo marking referring both to the fluctuations of tempo and a more general musical quirkiness. The movement begins with an introductory flourish formed around the Z-cell B–E–F–B♭, before the tonic (D) and its fifth (A) are established over five octaves by the quartet, capped by octave E♭s that drop to D on the following quaver in a gesture that will function as an element of rhythmic and tonal punctuation. The opening melody of the chain of three ideas that forms the first thematic group is played by the first violin against rapidly pulsating D octaves in the second violin, and this owes much to the music Bartók had collected in Algeria. Indeed, the melody's pitch contour, with its multiple initiatory repetitions of the minor third between $D_4$ and $F_4$, is rather similar to that of 'Knab bâl Äši', one of the 'Knéja-melodies in "Tempo giusto"' published as number 15 in his article 'Arab Folk Music from the Biskra District'. This is based on a four-note scale consisting, in turn, of a minor third, a semitone and a whole tone. The same interval structure forms the underlying matrix of the first idea (I in Fig. 22) and its immediate repeat (D–F–F♯–G♯, bracketed in Fig. 22a), though it is gradually extended down to C♯ and up to A♯.

The punctuating two-quaver figure sets a second idea (II) into motion in the viola and cello, which moves the melodic matrix a tone higher onto E, against throbbing quaver octave dyads of D–E in the violins, and varies it by absorbing and extending the element marked with a dotted bracket in the second system of Figure 22. With the third idea (III), the tonal centre of D is restored and the cello and viola take turns holding the melodic line against a more dissonant accompaniment from the rest of the quartet, the melodic matrix assimilating the material marked with a slur from II.

This principal thematic group does not reappear in precisely the same format at any point in the rondo. Its first varied recurrence arrives after an idiosyncratic contrasting episode between rehearsal numbers 10 and 14, in which the tempo fluctuates erratically, intermittently slowing down with sustained chords spinning off in a flurry of rhythmic fragments and pizzicatos. For most of the powerful reprise of the first group between rehearsal numbers 14 and 19, the transformed melodic material is placed in the lower three voices

Figure 22. The main pitches of the three ideas in the first thematic group of the second movement of the Second String Quartet.

and draws on the collection D–F–F♯–A♯–C♯–E–G♯, the first violin supplying the drum-like repeated Ds.

At the heart of the rondo structure is an extended episode with a developmental function. Chromatic fragmentary interjections and pregnant pauses from rehearsal number 20 lead to the insistent reiteration of the falling motif D♯–A♯–E, which brings the first part of the movement to a close. Bartók's predilection for cycles of fifths has already been noted, and several partial series surface from rehearsal number 22, picking up the falling motif's fourths and extending them to perfect fifths, which interlace in chains, zigzagging up to a two-octave double-stopped dominant A in the first violin and a succession of exchanges from tonic to dominant. This culminates in a syncopated passage in which the first violin and cello outline a second-inversion G major chord, within which the second violin and viola articulate a first-inversion C♯ major chord (D–B–E♯–G♯–C♯–G). Whether this can be regarded as a covert reference to Stravinsky's infamous bimodal combination of F♭ and E♭⁷ in 'Les Augures Printaniers – Danses des Adolescentes' from *Le Sacre du printemps* is a moot point. Allusions to the minor thirds of the rondo's principal theme intercut a tranquil, serenade-like passage in which a gentle melody with strumming pizzicato accompaniment passes around the quartet before building up steam and spiralling off again.

In the final pair of varied statements of the rondo theme material, which begins four bars before rehearsal number 34, following a reprise of the first episode, the metre moves into triple time and the tonal centre migrates from G through F to C♯ before settling on a series of hammered-out chords containing the pitches E♭–A–G–C♯–F♯. A final Prestissimo in 6/4 acts as a coda that spirals upwards and then back down before honing into and settling on the germinal figure F♯–F–D, the latter two notes closing the movement.

After the excitement and *joie de vivre* of the second movement, the finale is a lament with occasional bursts of passion that subside into world-weariness. Musically and emotionally it has much in common with the final song of the Ady set, 'I Cannot Come to You'. The finale also uses contrary-motion fourth chords, unprepared and unresolved dissonances (such as the minor second in the opening two bars of the quartet), and several motifs including the falling minor second and perfect fourth, which in the Ady song sets the words 'Én meghalok' ('I die') in the first and fourth verses.

The motif played in bars 11–12 of the finale (Fig. 23a) returns to the opening theme of the first movement, and its overall melodic contour is like a reduced version of Ady's setting of the words, 'Here every fool has his summer'. The motif is repeated from bar 14 with most of its intervals compressed further such that it now spans an augmented fourth rather than the original diminished seventh. A cadential figure appears in the viola and cello at bars 19–22, consisting of the dyads $C\sharp_2/A_2$, $F_2/B_2$, $B_2/C_3$ and $A_2/C_3$, which will play a role throughout the rest of the movement. In the second phase of the movement, from bar 23, the falling part of the motif is developed as the music moves towards a brief moment of passion similar to that generated by the piano interlude that precedes the final verse of Ady's 'I cannot come to you'.

The middle part of the finale, marked Lento assai, opens with a four-part passage (Fig. 23b), the upper voice of which is predominantly Lydian. However, it is harmonised with pairs of perfect fourths moving in contrary motion, and comes to rest at bar 55, as it had begun, on a stacked fourth chord (C♯–F♯–B–E). At this point the first and second violins pick up the pentatonic implications of the chord and soar upwards, rather like the opening of Vaughan Williams' *The Lark Ascending*.[25] A varied repeat of the material outlined in Figure 23b follows, but two octaves higher and transformed into a searing melody, which, as it wanes, is underpinned by the dyadic cadential figure from the first section. This takes on an increasingly prominent role as it is intercut with pairs of major-third dyads that rise by a minor third in the violins (a figure that is a compression of the Z-cell with minor thirds separated by a semitones), leading to a further fortissimo outburst.

The restoration of the opening tempo brings a modified reprise of the principal idea in a free canon at the augmented fifteenth between the cello and first violin, its intervals largely smoothed down to thirds and sixths. It is subject to

Figure 23. The third movement of the Second String Quartet (a) upper system; (b) lower system.

further development that leads to a final climax on a chord of stacked fourths (A♯–D♯–G♯–C♯–F♯–B). The movement, and the work, comes to its desolate conclusion with an attenuated recall of the limpid falling motif from bars 23–5, and a final version of the dyadic cadential figure leads to pizzicatos on A and C in the viola and cello.

During the war Bartók and Kodály had taken advantage of the opportunity to record songs from soldiers, having received official sanction in March 1916, and by December that year they had accumulated around 350 items. Indeed, while the family was staying in Marosvásárhely in the summer of 1916, prior to Márta's evacuation, Bartók had collected songs from the local barracks. In 1917 he completed *Nyolc magyar népdal* (Eight Hungarian Folk Songs), a set of arrangements with piano accompaniment that he had begun ten years earlier, now supplemented by three soldiers' songs.

A public outcome of this activity was a 'Historical Concert' organised by the Musikhistorische Zentrale in the great hall of the Konzerthaus in Vienna, originally intended to take place on 15 December 1917 but moved on to 12 January 1918. In the second half of the concert, which was a grand-society affair (Bartók remarks to Bușiția, 'you can imagine what a galaxy of *Gotterhalte* backers, gem and decoration wearers and musical ignoramuses were present'),[26] he accompanied the tenor Ferenc Székelyhidy in a group of Hungarian soldiers' songs (including the final three items from Eight Hungarian Folk Songs). His *a capella* arrangements of five Slovak soldiers' songs for four-part male chorus were also performed, albeit and to his great annoyance, in German. If nothing else, at least 'there was an opportunity for "real" Hungarian folk-songs to be heard by those few Viennese musicians who accidentally dropped into that company of pluto-aristocrats'. The programme for the concert included a surprisingly detailed musicological exegesis penned by Bartók in which he differentiated between the old and new style of folk song.

A rerun of the programme was scheduled to take place in Budapest with Bartók's further involvement, but he withdrew. The musical direction fell to an old adversary, Emil Haraszti, who had charged Bartók with a lack of patriotism in a review of Two Pictures published in *Budapesti Hírlap* on 27 February 1913, describing him as a musical Scotus Viator; this was a reference to the pseudonym of the Scottish historian and activist Robert William Seton-Watson, who had authored the 1908 study of the Hungarian minorities, *Racial Problems in Hungary*. About Haraszti, Bartók would later say that he was 'a stupid and, in addition, a malicious man *who understands as much of music as a hen does an ABC*'.[27]

Traditional music formed the basis of two further piano works that Bartók had begun in 1914 but didn't complete until 1918, *Három magyar népdal* (Three Hungarian Folk Tunes) and *Tizenöt magyar parasztdal* (Fifteen Hungarian Peasant Songs). The first is written in a similar spirit to the Sonatina and Romanian Christmas Carols, as a set of relatively straightforward arrangements, 'mounting the jewels' of the songs. The opening one of the Three Hungarian Folk Tunes, 'Leszállott a páva' ('The Peacock Has Landed', now best known in Hungary as 'Fölszállott a páva'), was collected by Béla Vikár in 1899. The second, 'Jánoshidi vásártéren' ('On the Jánoshid Market'), and the third, 'Fehér liliomszál' ('White Lily'), were collected by Bartók in 1918. Whereas the first two involve straightforward repetition of the melody over the verses, the third is more developed, at least in the tonal sense, being taken through the Mixolydian modes of G, D and C before returning to G at the end.

In the much more substantial Fifteen Hungarian Peasant Songs, which sit at the second level of Bartók's hierarchical use of folk material, where 'the importance of the used melodies and the added parts is almost equal', he effectively creates a four-movement structure from the fifteen tunes. The first movement consists of a group of four old tunes; the second is a brief scherzo; the third is a set of variations on the tragic ballad of 'Borbála Angoli' whose melody is notated in 7/8; and the fourth is a finale involving a chain of nine bucolic pieces (the tenth and thirteenth marked 'quasi trio', each concluding with reprises of the previous tunes). An interesting feature of this finale is the selection of three tunes that have a triple hypermetre (7, 8 and 11) and one that operates in five-bar phrases, complicated further by the interplay between 2/4 and 3/4 (number 12). The last tune of the finale, the only number in the set that was recorded from an instrumentalist, is a brilliant evocation of a piper performing at a village dance. Bartók discussed this final tune in an essay that was revised on several occasions between 1911 and 1931, 'The Folklore of Instruments and their Music in Eastern Europe', describing it as 'the most beautiful Hungarian bagpipe tune, the most valuable from the musical aspect. The melody is a well-known hogherder's song.'[28]

Further successes for Bartók in 1918 included a contract with Universal Edition, which ensured the regular and ongoing publication of his compositions, and the first performance of the Second String Quartet by the Waldbauer-Kerpely Quartet on 3 March. This was 'an absolutely harmonious day' for the composer, yet although the rehearsal went beautifully, the concert performance was less perfect. And finally, seven years after the submission of *Bluebeard's Castle* to the competition of the Lipótvárosi Kaszinó and its rejection by the Budapest Opera, its premiere as a double bill with *The Wooden Prince* at the opera house took place on 24 May, conducted by Egisto Tango. Bartók was elated with this production, describing it in *Magyar Színpad* on the same day as first-rate, and remarking that Olga Haselbeck (who took the role of Judit) and Oszkár Kálmán (who played Bluebeard) 'sang their parts so perfectly that the performance completely came up to my expectations'.[29] Balázs was far less happy, for his libretto was critically lambasted. But more than this, he was distressed by Bartók's failure to acknowledge him and his part in the success in the *Magyar Színpad* article.

Bartók's mind now turned to a second ballet. Menyhért Lengyel (1880–1974), a writer with strong pacifist leanings who had moved to Switzerland on the outbreak of war, had published his libretto for a four-act 'Pantomime grotesque' called *A csodálatos mandarin* (*The Miraculous Mandarin*) in the first number of *Nyugat* in 1917, and was keen for Bartók's involvement. The two met on 21 June and Bartók agreed to compose the score for what turned out to be a one-act dance piece lasting around thirty minutes. Its Grand-Guignol scenario concerns three 'apaches' or 'thugs' who coerce a girl, Mimi, to attract clients into their den so that they can steal from them. An old rake and a student prove to have insufficient means, and are promptly turfed out. The third visitor is an impassive Mandarin. In order to arouse him, the girl dances seductively, but when he attempts to embrace her, she runs off in terror. At this stage, the thugs step in to rob the Mandarin, and then try to kill him by successively smothering, stabbing, shooting and hanging him. Each assault fails, however, and only after the girl relents and embraces him does he bleed to death in the ecstasy of passion. An outline of the structure of the score, with principal narrative events, tonal centres and thematic material, is given in Table 2.

It would be several months before Bartók started working on the score of *The Miraculous Mandarin*. First he stayed with his sister in Vésztő, embarking on one of his regular 'fattening diets' (increasing in weight from 46 to 49 kilos) and giving up smoking. He then visited Buşiţia in Belényes for a song-collecting trip, not realising that the region would soon be ceded to Romania; over the past nine years Belényes had become a second home to Bartók (and the Buşiţias, a surrogate family). And in the middle of August 1917 he stayed in the castle of the wealthy Jewish financier, industrialist and art connoisseur, Baron Adolf Kohner in Felsőszászberek, one kilometres east of Budapest. He describes the latter experience in letters to Márta and Buşiţia, being shocked and impressed in equal degrees by the lavish hospitality and opulence. Recounting the preparations for meals, Bartók tells Márta, who was staying in Marosvásárhely, 'So much ado, so much work, so much ceremony before each stuffing! What an artificial lifestyle! What highfalutin manners!'[30] And to Buşiţia he observes:

> Coaches, horses, food, baths, cigarettes, wine, real coffee – plenty of everything and everything of the best. And these people have such a gift of enjoying their affluence that one almost forgets to be angry at the unequal distribution of wealth.[31]

With the ambience of a grand hotel, there seems to have been a constant stream of people coming and going at the castle during this time, including György Kósa, one of Bartók's private students, and Wanda Gleiman (Klára's friend). Bartók, unsurprisingly, set himself up with the servants in the laundry, where he collected some songs, and he also managed to pick up fleas from some Slovak workers on the estate.

In a letter to Buşiţia on 14 September, Bartók tells him in an aside that he has just started setting to music Lengyel's libretto of *The Miraculous Mandarin*, and so this his final work for the theatre had now seen its inception. Twenty pages of the Black Pocket-Book are devoted to the preliminary sketches – around half of the eventual score – and concern the latter part: the Mandarin's pursuit of Mimi, his robbery by the tramps, their attempts to choke, stab and hang him, and the original ending.

It has been estimated that around sixteen million people died in the course of the First World War and that as many as one third of these were caused by the influenza pandemic, the so-called Spanish flu, that struck in January 1918.

Table 2. The final structure of the one-act pantomime, *The Miraculous Mandarin*.

| Action | Rehearsal numbers | Tonal centre | Principal thematic material |
|---|---|---|---|
| Introduction. | Up to figure [6] | G E [3] F [3] + 6 A♭ [5] | Derived from the overlap of G major and G♯ Aeolian scales. Three initial elements: a falling and rising scale pattern; repeated $D♯_5$ quavers with interspersed accents on B, E and F♯; and repeated and sustained C♯s with gradual introduction of lower E and upper D. From [5] dominated by quartal chords (with perfect + augmented intervals). |
| The tramps look for money and force Mimi to attract customers. | [6]–[13] | A♭, F♯ | Circular chromatic fragments frame rising and falling broken-chord figures. Rising perfect fourths G–C–F–B♭–E♭ from [9] + 6. |
| 1st decoy game (the old rake). | [13]–[21] | A/C♯ | Melodic lines develop perfect fifth plus semitone model (e.g. A–E–F–C–C♯–G♯) for the 'lure' motif. Chordal figures with decorative flourishes for the rake's character dance are varied at [18] + 8, and [20]. Settles around pitches D♯–F♯–G♯–B–D at [18] as the rake indicates that what matters is love not money. |
| The tramps throw the old rake out. | [21]–[22] | E | Descending diatonic seconds dyads. |
| 2nd decoy game (the shy young man). | [22]–[29] | C (/C♯) | Lure motif, perfect fifths + minor seconds model figures. Young man's character dance [24] + 7, falling perfect fourths and chains of thirds. 5/4 ostinato at [26] C♯–E–G–B–B♯ against an asymmetrical melody, initially focused on D–E♭–A–B♭ which gradually ascends and develops. |
| The tramps throw the young man out. | [29]–[30] + 5 | A | Descending seconds dyads. |
| 3rd decoy game (the Mandarin arrives). | [31] + 6–[37] | E/C? | Lure motif, perfect fifths + minor seconds model figures. [34] pentatonic figure (B♭–C–E♭–F–G) accompanied diminished fifth lower with chromatic figures above. Mandarin's character dance based on F–G♯–A–B. Closes with sustained B–D. |
| The tramps encourage the girl to lure the Mandarin in and she gradually draws his interest. She shudders as she sits in his lap. | [37]–[61] + 4 bars | E E♭ | 7/4 figure, G♯–F–B♭–D♭–A–E♭–E developed. Transforms into waltz from [44] + 4 that evokes Flower Maidens scene from Wagner's *Parsifal*. [59] + 5 chromatic melody built around G–C♯–D–E♭–F♯. |

| | | | |
|---|---|---|---|
| The chase. | [61] + 5–[71] | A (/A♭) ~* | Arab-influenced melody, largely symmetrical underlying pattern, basic pitches F–[F#]–G#–A–B♭–C#–D. Pitch centre moves from A to C at [64], F# at [66], C at [67], F at [68] + 1. |
| The Mandarin stumbles but resumes the chase. | [71]–[74] | A–F#–D# | [73] Syncopated figure based on pitches C#–D#–E–F#–A. |
| He catches her and a struggle ensues. | [74]–[76] | F | Arab-influenced melody as above. |
| The tramps jump out and grab hold of the Mandarin. | [76]–[78] | ~ | Asymmetrical metres, settles on G#–D. |
| They attempt to smother him. | [78]–[84] | C# | Repeated heavy chords (G–B♮–E♭–B♭–C) resolving onto C#/D♭ substitute. [78] + 6 F#. [81] Prominent half-diminished sevenths ('Tristan' allusion?). |
| He comes back to life. | [84]–[87] + 1 | D♭ ~ | Colouristic 'night music' (sustained notes and flurries, including piano and celesta). |
| They stab him. | [87] + 2–[93] + 2 | B♭ | Melodic major sevenths [88] + 4. Production of sword, repeated chords coalesce C minor and C# minor. Final section prioritises perfect fifths. |
| He comes back to life. | [93] + 3–[94] | F# | Interval sizes reduce from fourths through thirds to seconds. |
| They decide to hang him. | [94]–[101] | A♭ ~ B | Writhing Mandarin [95] intimated by the chromatically in-filled diminished fifths. Chords gradually move upwards to the point of the apparent death of the Mandarin (B–G–A♭ 'resolves' to B–C–F#–G). |
| His body begins to glow and they pull it down. | [101]–[103] + 3 | B–E | Swaying melodic minor thirds sung by a wordless chorus with chromatic decorations of rising minor thirds in the violas, which gradually expand in range as the other string parts join in. |
| He jumps on Mimi and she no longer resists his advances. | [103] + 4 [110] | E ~ | The melodic line elaborates a falling minor third E–C#, which moves to in-filled G–E over an F# major-minor chord from [106]. Reminiscent of the earlier 'Flower Maidens' passage from [44] + 4. Trombones and tuba enunciate a three-line marcato idea based on alternate perfect fourths and minor seconds, the third truncating the previous two varied sequential versions. |
| The Mandarin finally dies. | [110]–end | F | From [111], a falling sequence of fourths (A♭–E♭–B♭–F). Various chromatically coloured shuddering F chords lead to a resolution on F minor chords with an added major sixth. |

* The symbol '~' represents a tonally fluid section.

Over the next three years it would be contracted by a quarter of the world's population and up to fifty million would die as a result. The deadliest wave of infection reached its peak between October and December 1918, and Bartók succumbed to the Spanish flu on 8 October. For the next twenty-three days he was confined to bed, suffering from otitis and intermittently being unable to speak.

At the same time the world in which he had grown up was falling apart. With the impending capitulation by the Central Powers, there was a major demonstration in Budapest on 28 October calling for independence. This was declared the following day and on 30 October a popular uprising took place, spelling the end of the government. On 1 November, as a result of this blood-less revolution, Count Mihály Károlyi became the country's leader as head of its provisional government. A fortnight later, on 16 November, the Hungarian Democratic Republic was declared.

Having made significant progress in terms of his composition and folk-song collection during the war years, and having finally achieved recognition as one of Hungary's most important musicians, Bartók was about to enter a further period of turbulence and instability, both public and private. Soon, the Hungary that had given birth to him would be massively reduced in geograph-ical area and population, and the town of his nativity, all the places he had lived in while growing up and many of the sites of his folk-music collection, would be in the hands of foreign powers. He would enter this new era by staying in his own home, with his own family, over the Christmas period of 1918, for the first time in several years.

## CHAPTER SEVEN

# 'The time to rove has come': 1919–1925

On 28 October 1918 Bartók's friend and librettist Béla Balázs found himself embroiled in the fracas that followed a mass meeting outside the Károlyi Party building. The crowd, which had set off in the direction of the Chain Bridge to head up to the Royal Palace in Buda, was met with extreme brutality from the police, and almost by default from that point Balázs became a member of the Party's Military Council. He was immediately drawn into the preparations for what became known as the Aster Revolution on account of the flower worn by the supporters of the Social Democratic Hungarian National Council, which seized power on 31 October.

The following Sunday a 'Proclamation of the Hungarian Intelligentsia' appeared in the newspaper *Vildg* (*The World*), signed by one hundred of the country's leading thinkers. They included many of the regular contributors to *Nyugat*, among whom were the writers Ady, Balázs and Lengyel, and the composers Bartók, Kodály, Dohnányi and Molnár. This article advocated President Woodrow Wilson's 'fourteen points' which underpinned the Versailles peace treaty and particularly the tenth, that 'The peoples of Austria-Hungary, whose place among the nations we wish to see safeguarded and assured, should be accorded the freest opportunity to autonomous development.' Seeing Hungary as a nation renewed, the proclamation called for a democratic government and an alliance of free and equal states to emerge from the old Austro-Hungarian Empire; and it strongly emphasized the rights of speakers of minority languages within the state, which it was believed should be supported morally and intellectually as well as financially.

Meanwhile other countries were capitalising on the turmoil surrounding the fall of Austria-Hungary, and on 1 January 1919, Czechoslovak troops occupied Pozsony; the following month it was declared the capital of Slovakia, to the anger of the German and Hungarian majority, and a demonstration on

12 February resulted in troops firing on the crowd. Given that Bartók's mother and his Aunt Irma were living in the city, having moved back there again in 1910 after his marriage to Márta, he was extremely concerned for their safety and communication with them became very difficult for some time.

In the turmoil following the Aster Revolution, Dohnányi was appointed to the directorship of the Academy of Music in February 1919. Bartók was seemingly considered for a similar role in the Budapest Opera – perhaps with a degree of irony given his previous experiences with the company – but told Bușiția on 31 January that nothing had come of it, and that he was looking forward to an appointment to the Museum of Ethnography, where he felt that 'he would be very much in his element'.[1] Bușiția's young son had died as a result of contracting influenza, and Bartók wrote to him in this same letter with heartfelt sympathy. Aware that little could console a father's grief over such a tragic loss, he asked Bușiția to continue believing that he could serve his country, for 'After all, it is honest, strong, uncompromising men like you who are most needed everywhere.' Nothing came of the museum post, though in June he wrote to his mother that plans for a musical museum had been revised to accommodate the development of a musical folklore department within the auspices of the Museum of Ethnography, and it was intended that he should direct its work.[2]

Bartók's musical activities in the spring of 1919 included further drafting of *The Miraculous Mandarin* in February, and a performance of the Rhapsody with the Budapest Philharmonic Orchestra conducted by Dohnányi on 10 March. While it may seem odd that Bartók should still choose to play this early piece, which looked back to the old-fashioned musical chauvinism of his student days, the reality was that he did not have any alternative work for piano and orchestra – other than the Scherzo (Burlesque) – and his First Piano Concerto would not see the light of day until 1926. Márta reports to her mother-in-law that the Rhapsody was an 'elemental success' and that Bartók had broken from his usual practice by performing it from memory.[3] He also played the *Allegro barbaro* and the contrast between the two pieces must have revealed to the audience just how far his style had developed in the period since 1904.

With the resignation of Károlyi's government on 21 March 1919, eleven days after the concert, the Socialist Party of Hungary took power and declared a Soviet republic and the dictatorship of the proletariat under the leadership, in all but name, of Béla Kun, the Commissar for Foreign Affairs. A hard-line Marxist, Kun had argued in his polemical article 'Marx and the Middle Classes', published in *Pravda* on 4 May 1918, that 'Every compromise with the *upper* bourgeoisie is treachery to the proletarian revolution. Every compromise with

the *lower* middle-class after the victory of the revolution would mean the restoration of the supremacy of the upper bourgeoisie – the restoration of capitalist
rule.'[4] The only option, following Marxist theory, was 'the complete overthrow
of *all* sections of the capitalist class, and the dictatorship of the proletariat'. The
consequence of this in Hungary was the so-called *vörösterror* (red terror),
which followed the failed coup of 24 June, and the 'Lenin Boys' organized by
József Cserny, a gang of thugs who roamed the countryside, seeking out and
liquidating counter-revolutionary elements. A programme of nationalisation
of landholding, industry and finance was set in train, accompanied by the
abolition of aristocratic titles and the introduction of a number of universal
freedoms and rights. The Marxist philosopher György Lukács, a frequent
contributor to *Nyugat* and an admirer of Balázs's work, was appointed as the
deputy commissar of public education on the so-called Revolutionary
Governing Council, and he engaged Balázs as a member of the Writers
Directorate with a responsibility for Hungary's theatres. Dohnányi, Bartók and
Kodály were appointed to the Musical Directorate, where they were given the
remit of organizing concerts and other musical events directed specifically
towards the proletariat. In the field of film Béla Lugosi and Alexander Korda
held similar positions within the directorate, and both had to leave Hungary
later because of their association with the regime.

As for Bartók's own views about the new political order in the chaotic early
throes of the republic, the idealist within him could still caution his sister to be
patient in the confident hope that the Soviet system would be better for all
working people than the old one was, and that it had been achieved cheaply –
without the country falling into a civil war.[5] He went on to tell her what he
knew about the potential confiscation of assets – a matter of considerable
importance to her given that her husband Emil was employed on a large estate
– and perhaps slightly insensitively remarked on the country's need for teachers,
a role she could fulfil. Meanwhile, Kodály was apparently rather pleased that
some of the jewellery belonging to his wife, Emma, had been confiscated, as he
had been embarrassed by her wealth and this placed them on a more even
footing. While Bartók's own future position was not yet clear, he was confident
that art and science would be valued by the Communist government, and that
no longer would an Imre Kálmán (a popular operetta composer) or an Ödön
Mihalovich, for example, have praise lavished on them while an Endre Ady was
crucified.

It is difficult to imagine that the concert which took place at the Budapest
Academy of Music on Easter Monday, 21 April 1919, could have proved readily
accessible to a mass proletarian audience, for it consisted of some of Bartók's
most radical and demanding works: the op. 16 Ady song set, with the contralto

Ilona Durigo as soloist; the Second String Quartet played by the Waldbauer-
Kerpeley Quartet; and the composer himself performing the Suite for piano op.
14, the first Elegy, and the technically taxing and musically demanding Three
Studies, composed in 1918.

These studies took Bartók's experimentation with chromaticism, dissonance and metrical complexity further than any of his previous pieces. The
motoric first piece, a study in finger extension that stretches the hands up to
major tenths and beyond, is based on, and develops, a four-note chromatic
collection (initially F–G♭–G–A♭); the first study includes a *marcatissimo*
episode (that also concludes the piece) built on the energetic interplay between
the pair of chords G–A♯–C♯–F♯/G♯–G✕–B♯–E♯ dissonantly placed above the
chromatic ostinato transposed onto B (B–C–C♯–D). In the Andante sostenuto
second study long waves of impressionist non-diatonic broken chords are set
against a sustained, expressive melody, the hands swapping roles part the way
through; and in a cadenza-like passage the clashing six-part chords could
almost be taken for the work of Olivier Messiaen, a generation later. With the
first section of the capricious third study, Bartók outdoes Stravinsky in metric
inventiveness, the time signature changing almost by the bar and including the
use of 10/16, 11/16 and 15/16. The melody, which lies in an inner voice in the
more regular central part, is split between the hands, with perfect-fifth broken
chords and dyads supplying the accompaniment; and the varied reprise of
the opening material is approached through chains of three-note perfect/
augmented fourth chords.

Bartók examines the development of atonality in an article titled 'The
Problem of the New Music', published in the Berlin journal *Melos* in April 1920.
Here he talks about 'the decisive turn towards atonality', which, employing
concepts of liberty and egalitarianism he had used only months before in a
rather different context, involved 'the free and equal treatment of tones'.[6] He
remarks how 'nowadays one may even sound all the twelve tones simultaneously in the most varied combinations', and illustrates this with four musical
examples of atonal chords. As László Somfai has shown, two of these examples
are derived from the middle of the Three Studies: the second example, which is
described in terms of its 'sonorous daintiness' being taken from the start of the
varied reprise at bar 35; and the fourth example, in the low register it is notated
in, 'is near to a noise-like effect', though when transposed two octaves higher
(as it is in the study), 'its character alters and becomes more ethereal'.[7]

Bartók goes on to explain that:

One works in homophonic music – so to speak – with tonal masses that
sound simultaneously in a more or less quick succession, and with dense or

airy, massive or thin tone-patches whose features depend on the number of tones used, the absolute pitch, the relative (that is, open or close) position, and so forth. By means of these tone-patches which have an intensity of varied gradation that corresponds to the way in which they are combined, and whose single tones have different importance in accordance with the role they play in the vertical grouping, the consequence of those very differences makes possible the plan of the 'horizontal line' of atonal music. The perfection of the form of the entire work depends solely on whether the rise and fall of this line represents an harmonic entity.[8]

As a result of the lack of explicit 'rules', both composers and listeners currently have to rely on their instincts. This is not yet the moment for systematisation although Bartók does allow both for the 'blend' of homophony and polyphony, and for the occasional admission of tonal chords in a dodecaphonic context, albeit accepting the necessity of avoiding the most elementary tonal progressions. Equally, there seems no urgent need for further division of the tone into third- or quarter-tones as advocated by Busoni, though the time for this may come. However, Bartók deems the present system of notating pitches unfit for purpose in music in which all pitches are regarded as being of equal status, so that reform – whose inventor is awaited – becomes necessary. His own ideal, given that 'the eventual material of music consists of an indefinite number of tones of different pitch, from the lowest to the highest perceptible tone', is to 'utilize as means in art works an ever-increasing number of elements of this material'.[9]

Although the Hungarian Red Army achieved some military success in its attempt to regain territory that had been lost at the end of the First World War, defeat by the Romanian Army, which would occupy Budapest from 4 August until mid-November 1919, brought about the downfall of the Soviet Republic and the flight of Kun and other Communist leaders on 1 August. In their place, first István Friedrich and then Károly Huszár were appointed as acting Prime Ministers. Admiral Miklós Horthy (1868–1957), who had been head of the counter-revolutionary forces during the Soviet Republic and arrived in Budapest on 16 November at the head of his troops symbolically mounted on a white horse, took over as regent of the Kingdom of Hungary (in the absence of any monarch) and as the Head of State on 1 March 1920. With the manner of address 'His Serene Highness' he would hold this post until 1944, the year before Bartók's death.

A further and even more vicious period of violence, known as the White Terror and carried out by a particularly sadistic element called the White Guard, took hold between 1919 and 1921. Given that a number of the leaders of the Soviet Republic were Jewish, this took on a particularly anti-Semitic and proto-Fascist character. These were clearly very difficult times for those who were implicated in Kun's government: Kun himself escaped to Austria in August and Lukács at the end of September 1919. Balázs hid in Budapest, sought by the police, until late November when he managed to board a ship up the Danube to Vienna, then still a safe haven. Dohnányi was dismissed from his role as director of the Academy of Music and sent on leave, while Jenő Hubay made a triumphant return in November 1919. Kodály expected disciplinary action, though this was some time coming, and Bartók wrote in his support in early February 1920.

Meanwhile Bartók himself suffered no obvious or significant recrimination. He had previously been granted a period of six months' leave of absence in response to a request from Kodály (then the Deputy Director of the Academy) to the Ministry of Culture in September 1919. He was able to report in a letter to his mother on 23 October that although isolated and feeling in a state of siege, he was not being persecuted 'because they dare not'. However, he was strongly considering moving abroad to work – to Transylvania, Vienna or Germany, preferring the first of these options as it would be most like Hungary. Things had changed little by the end of November. His period of leave was to finish at the year's end and he intended to solicit an extension (which he felt the authorities would not wish to refuse), and Hubay was suggesting some kind of ethnomusicological post for him. Bartók was sufficiently realistic to accept that in this time of austerity the government could not bear the costs of his collecting work in phonograph cylinders alone, for their price had inflated twentyfold since before the war. In his letter he also expressed delight at the sugar that his mother Paula had sent them: 'We watched spellbound as the glistening, white lumps came into sight – we hadn't seen anything so marvellous for years.'[10]

By January 1920, Bartók was clearly fed up with the conditions in Rákoskeresztúr, as he complained to Lengyel (then in Berlin) that month. He had not managed to make further progress on the orchestration of *The Miraculous Mandarin*, nor had he given any consideration to a further project with him, a one-act opera titled *Seherezáde* (*Scheherazade*).[11] Despite the difficulties of transportation, he was able to make an extended trip to Berlin from the end of February for more than a month and sound out opportunities to work there. In early March he met the influential Austrian theatre director Max Reinhardt, who wanted Bartók to compose music for his production of Aristophanes' *Lysistrata*, forthcoming in June at the Grosses Schauspielhaus in Berlin. Although Bartók was apparently quite interested, nothing came of this proposal. On 8 March he performed in a concert at the Blüthner-Saal in Berlin, which included Kodály's Cello Sonata (the composer's name somewhat bizarrely spelt as Goldáy in the poster), Maurice Ravel's Trio, and several of his own piano pieces, including selections from the Bagatelles, the Elegies and the Burlesques.

His timing was unfortunate yet again, for on 14 March a general strike took place in Berlin, called by the trade unions in opposition to a putsch the previous day led by the Prussian right-wing activist Wolfgang Kapp and supported by the paramilitary Marinebrigade Erhardt. The strike brought the city to a complete standstill and this was a major factor in the rapid failure of the *coup d'état*, which came to an ignominious end on 17 March.

As a result of a meeting with César Saerchinger, the Berlin correspondent of the American journal, the *Musical Courier*, Bartók's analysis of the political situation in Hungary, and its ramifications for music there, was commissioned for its pages and appeared in an article published in the March edition, entitled 'Hungary in the Throes of Reaction'. In a country facing its darkest times, massively reduced because of the war settlement, 'the dictatorship of the military is crushing the intellectual life of the country, just as the dictatorship of the proletariat crushed its economic existence before'. Now shunned as a destination by most foreign musicians, Budapest's most important musical figure, Bartók asserts, was Dohnányi, who despite being seen as a pariah by the authorities, 'heroically continues his various activities, bringing comfort and joy to his countrymen'.

Claiming that they were 'not avowed Communists', Bartók argues that he, Kodály and Dohnányi took on their role within the musical directorate, to whose 'care was committed the guidance of the entire musical life', partly in the hope they could improve conditions and partly to prevent actions that might harm music-making or place 'musical parvenus' in a position of responsibility for it. The Communist regime proved hugely disappointing in its lack of a strategy concerning music and its institutions, and there was widespread relief when it fell at the end of July. Little respite came from the reactionary regime that took the Communists' place, for it was concerned with wreaking revenge and rooting out alleged Bolsheviks. Egisto Tango was sacked from the Budapest Opera and upped sticks to Romania, and the Academy of Music stood 'deprived of its best instructors'. According to Bartók, even the general director of the opera house, Emil Ábrányi, was (in a phrase ominous of later developments) 'accused of possessing too little marked a sense of "Christian Nationalism"' for engaging several Jewish performers and performing works by Jewish composers. Liberals and Jews were now both 'excluded as far as possible from all public activity'.

This was the first of a series of pieces written by Bartók about music in Budapest for the *Musical Courier* over the following couple of years (and also for the Italian magazine, *Il Pianoforte*). These articles gave him the further opportunity to press the suits of Kodály and Dohnányi to a broader international readership as well as express the difficulties that musicians were facing in Hungary. As he notes in the piece written on 2 June 1920, all musicians were poverty-stricken and could not afford to purchase new music. As a result they were not able to keep up with recent musical trends. The music written by Stravinsky since 1917, for instance, was completely unknown and performances of new works at the opera or by the Philharmonic Orchestra were inconceivable: 'The present economic position precludes the very thought of this, as we are only barely able to exist ourselves amid want and poverty.'[12]

Bartók had commented how Dohnányi would often end up having to walk home after his recitals and orchestral concerts because of the early closure of the transport system, a journey taking him an hour. He found himself in an equally difficult position in Rákoskeresztúr, with awkward transport connections to the city as well as concerns for their son's schooling (Béla junior was now high-school age), and it became imperative that the family move back into Budapest. Clearly not being in a position to afford this, thanks to the generosity of József Lukács (György's father) the Bartóks moved into a separate apartment in two rooms of his villa on Gyopár utca on 22 May and they stayed there for nearly two years. In fact, Gyopár utca is around ten kilometres from the centre of Budapest, due east of the northern tip of Margitsziget (Margit Island), and so hardly within close walking distance of the Academy. But it was in a quiet and safe neighbourhood near to the countryside, and it had functioning plumbing, sanitation and electricity.

At the same time that Bartók was moving house he was defending himself in the political newspaper *Szózat* (literally *The Voice*, whose title cites a famous poem by Mihály Vörösmarty, the musical setting of which by Béni Egressy is the secondary national anthem of Hungary). Charges had been laid against him in the Christian-Nationalist paper *Nemzeti Újság* (*National News*). The accusation had been made that the publication of his article 'Der Musikdialekt der Rumänen von Hunyad' in the German journal *Zeitschrift für Musikwissenschaft* was unpatriotic. That these allegations should have been made in print by Hubay, the director of the very institution that employed Bartók, was testament to the highly politicised environment in the months leading up to the Treaty of Trianon (June 1920). Bartók's belligerent response, which was unlikely to endear him to Hubay, is remarkable; presumably with the readership of the paper in mind, and some sense that he is 'untouchable', he asserts that in fact his ethnographic work both demonstrated Hungarian cultural superiority over Romanian and showed the country's concern for the minorities. It was the case, after all, that it required a Hungarian to collect and analyse the music, there being no one suitable in Romania. His closing thrust is to suggest that when it comes to a lack of patriotism, the boot is on the other foot:

Is not that man a 'malicious propagandist' who out of ignorance, malevolence or misrepresentation dares to forge the charge of unpatriotic conduct against an article which serves the cause of the Hungarian nation?[13]

The treaty signed in the Grand Trianon Palace at Versailles on 4 June had an enormous impact on the territory of Hungary. Under article 27 of its terms, borders were defined with Austria, Romania, Czechoslovakia and the Serb-Croat-Slovene State (Yugoslavia), the effect of which was to shrink Hungary to a third of its pre-war land mass and its population was reduced by thirteen million. Large numbers of ethnic Hungarians who lived in Transylvania now found themselves in Romania. Of the places that Bartók grew up in, Nagyszentmiklós, Beszterce and Nagyvárad were incorporated into Romania, and Pozsony into Czechoslovakia. Travel to them would now require a passport and an explicit declaration of preferred nationality.

Although 1920 was otherwise an unproductive year in terms of new works, Bartók did compose Improvizációk magyar parasztdalokra (Eight Improvisations on Hungarian Peasant Songs), one of his most experimental works based on traditional material, in which he believed he had reached 'the extreme limit in adding most daring accompaniments to simple folk tunes'[14] Elliott Antokoletz has demonstrated how Bartók in the Improvisations employs symmetrical harmonic structures derived from the folk modes, axes of symmetry to create tonal centres, intervallic cells (such as the Z-cell), and interactions between various different modes including the octatonic.[15] Allowing for these important technical innovations that are contingent upon, and extend, immanent properties of the folk melodies, the choice of the tunes and their settings seems to reflect the composer's mood, which moves through nostalgia and desolation to occasional points of elation. Only two of the old-style songs were actually collected by Bartók himself (the first and fourth, both from Tolna in 1907); the second, fifth, sixth and seventh were noted by Béla Vikár, the third by Ákos Garay and the eighth by László Lajtha. The sites of collection ranged across the pre-war territory of Hungary, from Csík and Udvarhely Counties in the extreme east, bounding Romania; Szerém on the southern border with what would become Yugoslavia; and Zala County on the western border. Overall, the piece is organised in four parts in which musically related tunes are connected without breaks, such that the first and fourth parts consist of two Improvisations each, the second of three, and the third of a single one (Fig. 24).

Figure 24.  The openings of the folk melodies of the Eight Hungarian Improvisations organised by their grouping and showing points of coincidence between tunes.

In the composite parts that consist of more than one tune, Bartók uses a *verbunkos*-inspired slow-fast scheme.

The text of the tune Bartók draws on in the spirited final Improvisation, 'Télen nem jó szántani', can in retrospect be taken to mirror the tone for the entire work and perhaps reflects on his virtual incarceration in Rákoskeresztúr, for it says:

> It's no good ploughing in the winter,
> Holding a heavy plough,
> It's better to stay in bed,
> Playing with the wife.[16]

The song that forms the basis of the serene first Improvisation, 'Sütött gyángyi rétest', describes the singer's cousin baking cakes and taking them into the garden in a red cloth, where 'Uncle followed her,/He was wearing a new cape,/And he kissed her/Right in the middle of the garden'.[17] The melody, in the Dorian C mode and played in the middle register by the left hand, is supported first by major second and then major third dyads, and the composure is briefly broken in the final strain by contextually dissonant Gb major and minor chords that presumably allude to the narrative events of the song. In contrast, the second Improvisation is energetic and capricious, with a balance between syncopation in the first part and regular, Stravinskyan-sounding ostinato figures in the middle. Although the folk melody is in the Mixolydian C mode, the repeated closing chords are of F♯ major in the left hand with the pitches C and A (enharmonically notated) dissonantly superimposed in the right.

The protagonist of the world-weary song that forms the basis of the third Improvisation sees a raven in a looming black cloud and asks it to take a message to her (or his) parents that 'I am ill,/and that in the churchyard/I long to find rest'.[18] Bartók clothes the tune, which is in the *heptatonia secunda* mode on D (D–E–F♯–G–A–B♭–C–D), in autumnal colours with figurations that bear comparison with the final song from op. 15 ('In the Valley) and the second from op. 16 ('Autumn Echoes'). Its initiatory and terminal gesture, consisting of an interlocking pair of perfect fourths a semitone apart (C♯–F♯–D–G), is not a Z-cell, but a close relative of it, with similar musical characteristics. The song underpinning the fourth Improvisation tells how when the wind blows from the Danube, it buffets the poor people, and the piece picks up this theme with little flurries in the right hand suggesting the gusts of air. Near the end, the Z-cell G♭–C–D♭–G (which has three pitches in common with the cell used in the previous number) makes an appearance in a little postlude, with final flutters in the right hand. This group is completed by a brisk number, with a folk melody that is in effect pentatonic (G–B♭–C–D–F), with occasional passing notes between the G and B♭. Crisp syncopated minor-second dyads on C♯ accompany the first statement of the tune and in the second the tonality shifts to A♭ and then F (with a descant placed above). The final version involves the fragmentation of the melody and an approach to the cadence point via a canonic treatment in which the entries are connected through the diminished-seventh B♭–D♭–E–G.

The isolated sixth Improvisation is a tipsily capricious setting of the pentatonic comic song, 'Jaj istenem, ezt a vént' ('O Lord, this Old Man'), which functions as a tiny scherzo, and in which the three statements of the tune work their way down the keyboard from the high to low register. In the prelude and postlude, white-note chords and dyads, either rolled, tremolando or as staccato quavers, are placed against the black-note melody.

Bartók dedicated the seventh Improvisation to the memory of Debussy, who had died in March 1918, and the piece was included in a *tombeau* for the composer published by *Revue Musicale* in a special supplement in the December 1920 issue, along with pieces from a number of other composers including Stravinsky, Ravel, Dukas and Satie. The underlying folk song is a lullaby that opens with the words 'Beli fiam beli' (according to Bartók, *beli* is a word found in cradle songs), recorded in Székelylengyelfalva in Udvarhely County in 1903 by Vikár. In this setting, the tune, whose modality veers between Aeolian and Lydian C, becomes an impassioned lament in which the reflection of complementary material between the hands is an underlying principle. Its partner piece, alluded to above, is in marked contrast, being boisterous and enthusiastic in tone – perhaps the positive counterpart to the 'Lost Content' of op. 16 no. 3, suggesting rebirth after the sombre expressions of the previous Improvisation. Following the opening A♭-inflected tetrads (C–E♭–A♭–D), the heavy chords in the left hand for much of the following passage are built from infilled major sevenths and minor ninths. A canonic presentation of the folk melody (at the augmented fourth) propels the piece towards its climax with pairs of the familiar Z-cell superimposed in a *sostenuto subito* interlude marked 'rumoroso' (noisy), and the final statement is entirely accompanied by five of the six possible permutations of the Z-cell. The ejaculation in the penultimate bar, which is prefaced by a G♭, and the final chord of the piece following the tonic C in the low register, overlay two versions of the Z-cell in eight-part chromatic chords.

At the end of November 1920 and over the subsequent year, Bartók wrote a series of letters to the eccentric English composer, musicologist and motorcyclist, Philip Heseltine (who was better known as his pseudonym, Peter Warlock). A particular link between the two composers was Delius (who was one of Heseltine's closest friends), though he appears to have been introduced to Bartók's music as early as 1913 by the composer Kaikhosru Sorabji, who was extremely enthusiastic about it. Heseltine was originally not convinced, telling Colin Taylor in 1914 that he thought the Ten Easy Pieces and 'For Children' were both disappointing and dull.[19] However, by January 1917, he had performed a complete volte-face. He now regarded Bartók as one of the world's three outstanding composers (the other two being Delius and Bernard van Dieren) and saw him 'pointing the road to the future'.[20] On 20 November Heseltine wrote to Delius:

> I hear from Hertzka and from Adila d'Arányi who has just returned from Budapest that poor Bartók is in very difficult circumstances and barely able to keep body and soul together. He is compelled to spend all his days teaching and has no time nor energy for composition any more. This is a great shame, for he is one of the finest creative minds in the musical world today. I have lately made a careful examination of all his published works and my love and admiration for his music increases with each new work I come across.[21]

Heseltine included an extremely supportive article on Bartók, penned by Cecil Gray, in the November 1920 issue of the journal *The Sackbut*, and on Adila Aranyi's advice was keen to organise a concert tour for him in England (which eventually took place in 1922). Bartók expressed his delight in the interest that Heseltine and Gray had shown, in his long letter dated 24 November (which, after the first paragraph, is composed in French). As well as bringing Heseltine up to date on his more recent works, he writes about his musical influences. He had detected in Heseltine's previous letter, and the copies of *The Sackbut* he had been sent, that there was an ongoing campaign in the journal against Debussy, Stravinsky and their followers. Bartók, while accepting that Debussy's imitators were unbearable, admitted that he admired his work greatly despite the limited purview of his creative power. Three pieces of Stravinsky's had made a substantial impression on him, namely the piano arrangements of *The Rite of Spring* and *The Nightingale* and the score for *Three Japanese Lyrics*. And as for Schoenberg, while Bartók considered that his music demonstrated unexpected new possibilities, he believed it was essentially quite different from his. The greatest influence on his style had undoubtedly been that of peasant music. In terms of his collecting activities Bartók remarks that 'our political and economic situation has changed so much since this year that I must forever abandon this work, which is so dear and important to me'.[22]

Bartók wrote enthusiastically to his mother in January 1921 about the article in *The Sackbut*, quoting sections of it to her that indicated how respected he was as a composer. He was obviously deeply pleased and reassured that there were musicians outside Hungary with whom he had no connections yet who loved his music. This suggested to him that he might have more success abroad if the situation did not improve at home.

In March, Heseltine and his friend, Gerald M. Cooper, set off together on a trip that took in Biskra, Venice, Rome, Vienna and Budapest, where they visited the Bartóks in Gyopár utca. In a letter to Delius from Budapest on 21 April, Heseltine remarks on the hospitality he received and describes Bartók as 'quite one of the most lovable personalities I have ever met'. He goes on to discuss the material difficulties Bartók and Kodály have suffered and the fact that 'the present Christian-Socialist [sic] government does not seem to be at all favourably disposed towards new music – or new art of any kind'.[23] Heseltine had previously expressed the hope that 'my generous host' Cooper 'may help Bartók to come to London and give some concerts. I hope so at any rate'.[24]

Bartók's interactions with Heseltine and Gray proved valuable to the dissemination of his output. His article, 'The Relation of Folk Song to the Development of the Art Music of Our Time', was published in *The Sackbut* in 1921. In 1922 he would perform twice in London and at Aberystwyth University, giving the premiere of the First Violin Sonata with its dedicatee, the Hungarian violinist Jelly d'Arányi, who had settled in London. Her two sisters were based there too: Adila was also a concert violinist, married to the barrister

Alexander Fachiri; and Hortense Emilia was the wife of the English economist and academic Sir Ralph Hawtrey. The girls' grandfather had married Joseph Joachim's sister. This connection was no doubt of interest to Bartók, who had given private piano lessons to Hortense (or Titi as she was known) when he was a student at the Budapest Conservatoire, and for a time in 1902–3 he seems to have had a crush on her older sister, Adila.

Meanwhile in May 1921 he reported his news to Busiția. Times were hard and although Bartók had been loaned the two-room apartment on Gyopár utca, the 'living expenses for the three of us are twice my year's salary. So I have to devote all my spare time to money-making.'[25] Even if he was in the right mood for composition (which he wasn't), he simply did not have the time. He was still buoyed by the response overseas to his work, not just in London, but in Paris in the *Revue Musicale*, in Austria in the *Anbruch*, and in various forth-coming publications. He had also had a number of performances including composer's evenings devoted to him, and book contracts related to his Hungarian, Romanian and Slovakian collections. All of this was well and good, but Bartók's greatest frustration was his inability to collect folk music – 'even if they were to make me the High Pope of Music, it would be no help to me as long as I remain cut off from peasant music'. He longed for the mountain air, which he hadn't been able to enjoy since 1918, and wrote about the possibilities for the summer holiday either in Belényes or in Slovakia.

In fact, visa difficulties meant that it was not possible to go to Romania, and Bartók ended up returning to the area of Anger, near Graz in Austria (where he had stayed eleven years earlier), writing regretfully to his mother that she, Márta and Béla could not be with him. The war had taken its toll and the food was certainly not as good as it was, but at least the mountains were quiet and free of people. He was working on the orchestration of the Four Pieces for Orchestra composed in 1912, though progress was not particularly rapid.

This trip appears to have been therapeutic, for on Márta's birthday, 19 October, she received the news – the surprise of which nearly made her 'jump out of her skin' – that Bartók was composing again. He was writing a violin sonata for Jelly d'Arányi. Although vowed to silence until it was complete, Márta felt she had to tell her mother-in-law, for she could conceive of no better birthday gift. She had been afraid that the wretched times they had lived through had paralysed her husband's ability to compose and was very grateful to Jelly for wakening what Bartók described as a long-dormant plan. And of course a violin sonata had advantages over a string quartet, for it only required the violinist given that Bartók could perform the piano part.[26]

A few days before this, in a letter to Cecil Gray, Bartók had asked him whether he was familiar with Michel-Dimitri Calvocoressi, whom he had met

in Paris in 1914. Now living in London, Calvocoressi had been in communication with Bartók since the summer and had offered to help organise concert
performances of his works.[27] On 24 September 1921 Bartók had told him of the
plan to perform with Jelly in London. When he wrote again on 20 October he
was able to tell him that he had now heard Jelly play and regarded her as excellent, and had hatched a plan to compose a sonata for her to perform in London.
Less than two months later, on 12 December, he had finished the composition,
though he reported to Titi d'Arányi that copying was not yet completed because
of a bout of illness that had run through the household. Rather curiously, the
premiere of the piece took place on 8 February 1922 in Vienna, not in the
hands of Bartók and Jelly d'Arányi, but by the Irish violinist and composer
Mary Dickenson-Auner and the pianist Edward Steuermann. In Paul Bechert's
review of the concert, published in *The Musical Times* in July 1922, he remarks
that:

To Mrs. Dickenson-Auner also fell the distinction of being chosen by Béla
Bartók for the first performance anywhere of his new Violin Sonata, which
is still in MS.[28] This composition, which has since been performed in
London as well, created a deep impression here by virtue of its strongly
personal and national touches. An equal share of admiration fell to the lot
of Mrs. Dickenson-Auner and to her partner, Eduard Steuermann, a
Viennese pianist from the Schönberg group, who, in their interpretation of
this piece, displayed remarkable technical resources and admirable interpretative powers. In spite of the heated discussion it has everywhere evoked,
this Bartók Sonata must be considered the most important addition to
violin literature in recent years.[29]

It seems that the d'Arányi sisters did most of the spadework organising the
British concerts. Bartók sent streams of detailed financial questions to them
(and to Calvocoressi), about the cost of living in England and whether, for
instance, £2 a night might be sufficient for a boarding house. These are not the
letters of an eminent public figure, but of a humble and very careful man who
has learned to make every penny count. He didn't need to concern himself with
the cost of accommodation, however, for he stayed with Titi (who had offered
to take some lessons from him to increase his income), and in one of his most
moving letters he wrote to her from Paris on 2 April:

please forgive me for having been in such low spirits, so downhearted, taci-
turn and sad yesterday evening. It broke my heart to leave London and your
cosy fireplace. Something was choking my throat so much that I could

hardly utter a word or two. Somehow I was having the feeling that perhaps I would never be able to return to London, to your lovely house I've become so fond of. Believe me, these three weeks were one of the most beautiful times in my life. This is what I wanted to tell you by phone this morning at 10 o'clock, but it seems better I didn't do so, it would have been more difficult – Jelly answered the phone instead of you, we chatted and time passed, I had to leave.[30]

He set off from home on 8 March, travelling via Vienna and Ostend, and arrived in London two days later, remaining there for three weeks. The British part of the tour included private concerts at the home of the Hungarian chargé d'affaires and that of Sir Duncan and Lady Wilson; a public concert in London at the Aeolian Hall on New Bond Street, at which Bartók and Jelly d'Arányi played the new violin sonata; a piano recital of his own music at Liverpool's Rushworth Hall; and a concert at Aberystwyth University that involved a Beethoven trio and several of his own works for piano.[31]

The British press showed considerable interest in Bartók and a report about the first private recital even found its way into *The Times*. Critics seemed to give him the benefit of the doubt and in H. C. Colles' lengthy review of the concert at the house of the chargé d'affaires, published on 18 March and titled 'Béla Bartók, Sonata for Violin and Piano: A Foreign Language', he tells his readership that the public concert 'should not be missed, because whether one likes it or not, there can be no doubt that it is new music'.[32] In saying this, he differentiates it from 'merely "modern" or "ultra-modern" music', which in time becomes 'commonplace', for he feels that this will not be the fate of this piece. 'Only a very clever or a very stupid person,' he declares, 'would profess to understand it at a first hearing, but quite an ordinary person may confess to being moved by it, and more than that, to having been kept moving [*sic*] the whole time.'

The temporal organisation of the three movements of the First Sonata for violin and piano, which Bartók seems to have conceived as being in C♯ minor, is rather more conventional than that of the first two string quartets. It involves a moderately fast and rhapsodic first-movement Allegro appassionato nominally in sonata form, a ternary Adagio, and a brilliant dance-inflected Rondo finale. It is a substantial piece, lasting around thirty-five minutes, and draws on and extends many of the approaches and techniques seen in works such as the op. 15 and 16 song sets, the Second String Quartet, the Suite op. 14, *The Miraculous Mandarin* and the Improvisations. The score is remarkable for the density of its markings of tempo, expression and articulation, and for its employment of almost every conceivable string technique. It is also unusual, as

János Kárpáti has noted, for the degree of thematic independence and autonomy of the two instruments.[33] Malcolm Gillies suggests a significant affinity between the sonata and various works of Szymanowski's that Bartók was investigating at the time, most especially the *Trois mythes* and *Notturno e tarantella*, and argues that several of the technical innovations of the violin sonata (including parallel double-stopping, strummed multiple-stopped pizzicati, and *ondeggiando* passages) can be seen to have their source in these pieces.[34]

Although the first movement notionally draws on the principles of sonata form, and there are three main thematic sections that can be discerned as appearing in sequence on three occasions in its course, as Paul Wilson points out, the absence of the conventional tonal cues from a single overriding tonic makes navigation quite complex.[35] He argues that the overall form could be symbolised as A A' A'', remarking that 'this is a perfectly worthwhile and viable design, with its own expressive meaning and impact, but it is certainly different from older and more forcefully directional kinds of sonata form'.[36]

The opening gesture in the piano establishes an arpeggiated texture spreading across three octaves, the pitch content of which is shown in order of appearance in the first ten notes of Figure 25 (arguably segmented into a C♯ minor triad with an added major sixth, and G maj[7] and F[7] chords). When the violin enters in the third bar, it completes the chromatic collection with its initial $C_5$ and the $E\flat_5$ acciaccatura in the following bar. Halsey Stevens heard an evocation of the cimbalom in the wash of sound in the piano (which bears comparison with the figure that permeates 'Alone with the Sea' from the Ady

Figure 25. First Violin Sonata (a) the opening pitches of the first movement; (b) the opening of the second movement; and (c) the start of the main theme of the finale.

songs). It is perhaps not stretching the imagination too far to imagine this opening passage as a highly stylised rendering of the slow *lassú* style of *verbunkos*, with the violin decorating around held notes, playing broken-chord figures and Hungarian accented short-long rhythms. While the principal idea restricts the violin line to low and middle registers, the second thematic area, from bar 16 begins in the highest part of its range and moves in great leaps, while the piano supports it with pairs of chords in a waltz rhythm that recalls the accompaniment to 'Autumn Tears' from the Ady songs. Two parallel passages in the violin from rehearsal numbers 3 and 4 restore the rhapsodism of the opening, while the piano establishes a pattern in chords with a strong rhythmic contour (♪ ♪ ♪ ♪ ♪ ♪ ♪ ♪ ♪ ♪ ♪.).[37] In the section from rehearsal number 6, Bartók deploys a semi-symmetrical figure in the piano, and such mirroring between the hands, along with parallel writing, becomes increasingly important as the movement progresses, most particularly in the 'development'. The third thematic area includes a passage of *sul ponticello* tremolandi in the violin from bar 82 that arches upwards in a pair of broken chords supported by an agitated three- semiquaver chordal reiteration in the piano. This leads to the high point of the exposition at rehearsal number 9 (bar 87) and a rapid unwinding to its closure on an F major/minor chord with added major sixth.

Whether one thinks of it in conventional terms as a sonata development, or as Wilson describes it as a variant of the exposition, the following section condenses the opening idea and places it in an entirely new ambience, with gently rocking figures in the piano gradually opening out mirror-wise, through seconds, thirds and fourths before moving up a fifth. It is perhaps too easy to imagine that every descending arpeggiation of a major seventh is a reference to the Stefi/Bluebeard motivic complex, but there are several very striking uses of a related figure based on a descending form of the 'major-minor' chord first heard in bar 8 of the exposition ($D\flat_5-B\flat_4-F_4-D_4$) and again from bars 51–3. Now, in bars 134–5 and 138–9, it takes on a particularly prominent role, and its unusual Italian marking, *risvegliandosi* – literally reawakening, as if slowly returning from the dreamlike state of the earlier part of the section before flying off – could be taken to stand for the entire piece.

In the tranquil reprise of the principal idea at bar 187, Bartók creates a wonderful crystalline texture from the opening sonority, holding back the A from the chromatic collection until the fourth bar where it takes on a prominent role. What is recapitulated, however, is the general rather than the particular, and the more capricious elements of the violin's melody are initially withdrawn. At the end of this section and in the reprise of the second idea from bar 214, fragmentary interjections bring the melody to a point of meditation before setting off again in a stretto with the tremolando third idea from bar 244. Here once more the music returns to an uneasy calm and in the final two bars all but two pitches of the chromatic collection (D and F♯) reappear, but in a context that seems to suggest B♭ minor rather than Bartók's notional tonic of C♯ minor.

Each main part of the exquisitely beautiful ternary form Adagio (Fig. 25b) is constructed from two pairs of subsections, the second of which varies the first. In the opening A section a cantabile chromatic melody in the solo violin with a distinctly pastoral quality that hints at the tonality of F♯ is placed adjacent to a passage of parallel triads in the piano, which opens on F and finishes on B♭, the violin introducing a descending cantilena part the way through. The central section of the movement begins at rehearsal number 4 with a limping tritone between F♯ in the piano and C in the violin, which decorates the fundamental pitch with figures that fleetingly insinuate the Phrygian mode and the Hungarian short-long rhythm. With the balancing passage, between rehearsal numbers 5 and 7, the density increases as the piano moves into the foreground, and an ever more insistent figure in cretic metre (long-short-long) reiterates the pattern G–F♯–C♯. After the varied restatement of this pair of ideas, Bartók restores the calm of the first section, though now the violin's melody is foreshortened and highly embellished, and the piano's parallel triads glitter with anticipatory grace notes formed from the triads lying a semitone above and below the main chord. As was the case with the first movement, the final cadence is somewhat obscure, the piano's low C♯ and violins in C being held against an F♯ minor chord with a major seventh.

The finale is a folk-inspired ABA'CA"BA"' rondo form in which the B section is a chain of three subsections, and overall the movement can be seen as taking on a role equivalent to that of the *friss* component of the *verbunkos*. Like the second movement of the Second String Quartet, this is an invented folklorism and in this case Romanian instrumental music is the pervasive influence. In the first volume of *Rumanian Folk Music* Bartók reports that the fiddle players in the Maramureş region were accompanied by a two-stringed guitar tuned to a perfect fifth that played in regular quavers, and this would seem to be the model for the theme of the A section (Fig. 25c), a fiery melody that avoids the regular four-bar phrases of the folk tune. In particular, one might compare this theme to the group of pieces called 'De băut' (drinking) or 'Bătută din pălmi' (hand clapping). Bartók remarks in volume 5 of *Rumanian Folk Music*, devoted to Maramureş county, that:

Although these melodies are neither called dances, nor are they danced to, they belong nevertheless in this category because of their pronounced dance character. The appointed musician plays them during the meal, while the guests call out 'dance-words' and give the beat by handclapping.[38]

Examples that seem most closely aligned to Bartók's tune include the two 'De băut' melodies, numbers 164d and 165, though similar features can also be found in dance tunes such as the 'Jocul fecioresc' (boys' dance).

The piano rolls down fifths-based chords on the off-beat, the pitch content of which is C♯–G♯–D–F♯–C♯–G while, given a C♯ tonic, the opening part of the violin melody lies within one of the *heptatonia secunda* modes (C♯–D–E–F–G–[A]–B). From rehearsal number 4 this turns into the interplay between the two versions of the whole-tone scale in the violin with the alternation in the piano of passages of fifths-based chords on the dominant (G♯–D♯–A–B–F–C) and on the tonic (the chord described above). Throughout the section, the piano interjects broken-chord figures that are generally based on the perfect and diminished fifths F♯–C♯–G, which function, perhaps, as the interjections of the audience to a 'De băut'.

The subsequent episode is in three sections, stretching between rehearsal numbers 8 and 22, at which point the main rondo theme makes its first reappearance. In the opening part (8–12) the tonality moves to E and the music becomes harmonically static, with quintuplet semiquavers in the piano clustering chromatically around E and the violin also locking on to this pitch before gradually introducing decorative flourishes that lead into 'Hungarian' short-long dotted rhythms. Then, in the second part, a three-note rising figure commences in the piano with the segment C–D–E♭ at rehearsal number 12 repeating and expanding like waves gaining momentum, setting off again in turn from A, B♭/E and E♭/F. The final section of the episode varies the first, the piano part centred around offbeat D major triads, the violin reiterating and embellishing the pitch A♯.

After the abridged reprise of the main rondo theme, initially underpinned by what can be understood as a D major/minor chord in the piano (F♯–A–D–E♯), to which an F major/minor chord (A–B♯–E♯–G♯) is soon appended, the middle episode begins at the fourteenth bar after rehearsal number 25. Here the incessant forward moment of the earlier part of the music is briefly checked as Bartók places the two instrumental characters into relief: heavy *marcato* chords in the piano set against a graceful if slightly quirky violin line. For a moment the two voices find themselves playing common material before the opening theme is reprised once more at rehearsal number 33 and is significantly modified and developed. At the end of the synoptic recapitulation of the B section, a fleeting recall of the two character types from the central episode leads into the brilliant final statement of the rondo theme in the closing bars, underpinned by a clear reference to a conventional dominant–tonic cadential strategy. The closing chord of the piece maintains tonal ambiguity by fusing C♯ major and minor triads and placing an added minor seventh in the upper voice.

In *Bartók in Britain*, Malcolm Gillies has examined in detail the response to the concert performance in the Aeolian Hall on New Bond Street on 24 March. In his estimation, 'final judgements of the evening were, on balance, mildly positive', though Bartók's music was seen by many as 'over academic'.[39] Gillies cites the views of E. A. Baugham in *Saturday Review*, in which he talks of 'the strangeness of workmanship [being] due to the cold self-consciousness of a theorist, and not to a tone-poet's instinctive search for the medium through which he can best express himself', and such allegations of musical academicism and a mathematical approach to composition would dog him for the rest of his life'.[40]

While in Britain, Bartók took the opportunity to hear the London Symphony Orchestra conducted by Albert Coates in a programme that included Stravinsky's *Firebird* suite, and the premiere of Delius's *Requiem* by the Royal Philharmonic Society. Bartók's trip to Wales involved spending some time in the company of Heseltine, whose motorcycle sidecar outfit apparently broke down, leaving the two of them temporarily stranded at the roadside.[41]

Overall the trip to Britain can be regarded as a considerable success, both musically and financially, and the tour continued with further activities in France organised by Henry Prunières, the founding director of the influential journal *La Revue musicale*. The composer and musicologist Egon Wellesz (1885–1974) had written to Bartók in February 1920 to tell him that Prunières had expressed interest in his music and that he felt Bartók would get more credit in France than in either Hungary or Austria.[42] In March 1921 the journal had published a piece on Bartók written by Kódaly and in November of the same year his article 'La Musique populaire Hongroise' had also appeared in its pages. Both of these usefully prepared the ground for Bartók's appearances in Paris: a symposium at the Sorbonne on 4 April; a private concert with Jelly as guests of the Duchesse de Clermont-Tonnerre on 5 April (Bartók is characteristically scathing about the gathering of aristocrats in a letter to his mother); and at the salon of the eminent Parisian hostess Madame Dubost on 9 April, with the main concert taking place on 8 April at the Théâtre du Vieux-Colombier.

After the recital that day, which Bartók felt had gone well, he had dinner at Prunières' house, where the other guests included Stravinsky, Ravel and Szymanowski; and later in the evening they were joined by Milhaud, Poulenc, Honneger and Roussel. A further performance of the violin sonata took place that evening after dinner, in front of 'half the "leading composers of the world"', a phrase he repeats to his mother with an equal mixture of pride and irony. Prunières was keen to organise a further visit and Bartók's main concern, hardly surprising given his circumstances, was the net profit that this would accrue. He also had lunch on 8 April with Georges Auric and Satie as the guest of Poulenc. The latter, a long-time enthusiast of Bartók's, remembered the *froideur* of the meeting, for 'like two birds who do not sing the same tune, Bartók and Satie observed each other with suspicion and maintained an overwhelming silence that Auric and I tried in vain to break. For me it is an extraordinary and symbolic memory.'[43] And in a letter to Bartók on 14 April, Poulenc talks of his 'marvellous *Sonata*' and the pleasure he has brought to young French musicians.[44]

While in Paris, Bartók seems to have become infatuated with Jelly d'Arányi, who her biographer, Joseph Macleod, suggests had a naturally flirtatious temperament. Although Jelly was chaperoned by her mother, Bartók tried to persuade her to take a romantic interest in him, and she thoroughly rejected his advances. In a letter to her father she was circumspect – he was 'a little difficult to be with', but to Titi she was forthright: 'B. has been making life beastly here for us. . . . It was a waste of time to help B. so much – he's an awfully disgusting character.'[45] Bartók's published family letters do not give any particular indication of his unhappy marital relations, though he and Márta had been used to spending significant periods of time apart in the past and had been forced into each other's company in the period of Bartók's sabbatical from the Academy.

Some would see Bartók's complete misreading of Jelly's signals (and those of several other women before her) as symptomatic of Asperger's syndrome, and indeed it is possible that this may be the case. However, he had suddenly been transported from a situation of material hardship and unfavourable critical reviews in Budapest into a world of glamour and celebrity in London and Paris – invited into the houses of the upper echelons, staying in high-class hotels, and fêted by some of the world's leading musicians. Despite his tendency to self-deprecation and disavowal of wealth and privilege, Bartók's reception as a composer must have deeply and positively affected his self-image. And at the same time, the musical partnership he had with Jelly was undoubtedly outstanding and they had had enormous onstage rapport. Adherents of crass popular psychology would no doubt suggest that Bartók was demonstrating the classic symptoms of a midlife crisis and that the fantasy-world he had been thrust into had amplified its effect. Whatever the case, this was certainly a signal that his marriage was not on a sound footing. A sad little domestic drama would play itself out over the following year.

Bartók's next port of call on his ten-week trip away from Hungary was Frankfurt, where the German premieres of *Bluebeard's Castle* and *The Wooden Prince* were due to take place on 13 May 1921. Before this he took part in a recital devoted to his music in the small hall of the Saalbau, the First String

Quartet played by a quartet led by Adolf Rebner (concertmaster of the Frankfurt Opera orchestra and former teacher of Hindemith), who also played the First Violin Sonata. Bartók was not impressed by the musicians of Frankfurt, later describing Rebner's performance to Calvocoressi as scandalous, and he wrote to Adila d'Arányi:

> Up until now I have spent time here, to little avail. The premiere took place yesterday; a mediocre performance (that in Pest was far and away better). The orchestra was bad and malevolent, Bluebeard was sick and completely out of tune. Reception: indifferent. Poor Szenkár really did his best but all his efforts have been jeopardised by too many obstacles. Well, I have had enough of Germans for quite a while! Terrible plebs![46]

The d'Arányi sisters appeared to have equally had enough of Bartók, for in a letter to Calvocoressi on 24 June, sent from his new apartment on Szilágyi Dezső tér (next to the Reformed Church on the banks of the Danube and looking over to the parliament building), he tells him that he has still not received any reply from Mrs Fachiri (Adila). He thus presumes they could not arrange a trip to London for the following winter.[47] Bartók was extremely grateful to Calvocoressi for his efforts and had sent him two autographs of pieces with the letter. One of these, ironically given his current marital problems that had been exacerbated by the concert tour, was the first of the Five Songs op. 15 – his setting of Klára Gombossy's 'My Love'.

The following months were spent on two particular tasks. The first was the ill-fated musicological study of Slovak folk material contracted for publication with Matica Slovenská. By the second week of October, Bartók was able to advise the publisher that the manuscript for the first volume, containing 763 tunes, was ready for submission, and that he hoped to have the other two volumes (containing 1,004 and 684 melodies respectively) completed by the following January. From July 1921 he had started work on the other project – a second sonata for violin and piano with Jelly in mind as its interpreter.

By 20 August he had made little further progress with his plans for another tour of Britain, and the d'Arányi sisters had continued to maintain a low profile. He therefore began trying out the First Violin Sonata with two other musicians – Imre Waldbauer, who had performed in Bartók's two string quartets, and Zoltán Székely (1903–2001), a violinist from Hubay's stable. Kodály had introduced Székely to Bartók in March 1921 and much to Hubay's annoyance they had performed together in two concerts that April, which included the Debussy Sonata and Beethoven's Kreutzer Sonata. In his review of musical events in Budapest between March and June 1921, published in *Il Pianoforte* in

Turin that September, Bartók described Székely as 'a young violinist but already eminent and of such musicality that we can hope the best for his future'.[48] In the last week of August 1922 he showed him the manuscript of the Second Violin Sonata, which he had completed as far as the recapitulation of the second movement (somewhere around rehearsal number 37), and the two played it through, Székely believing he was the first musician to see the work in progress. Although he was certain that both Waldbauer and Székely would be adequate to the task (and indeed the former would give its premiere in Berlin in February 1923 and the latter perform it in Amsterdam at the end of April), Bartók was still very keen for Jelly d'Arányi to play the piece, feeling he could not find a better interpreter then her. On 7 May 1923 his wish would be fulfilled in a recital of both his violin sonatas in a concert in London run by the recently founded International Society for Contemporary Music (ISCM).

In the spirit of the *verbunkos*, the Second Violin Sonata is in two parts, a slow and expressive first movement leading directly into a fast dance-inspired finale. It is also rather more concentrated than the first sonata, lasting just over twenty minutes. Although it terminates on a C major triad, it is often difficult to hear this as a tonic in any conventional sense. Most of the individual harmonic devices of the sonata are familiar from previous works. Many of them, such as the Z-cell, the major/minor chord, the stacked perfect-plus-augmented fourth, and the pairs of minor thirds whose lower notes lie a semi-tone and an octave apart (e.g. C♯–E–C–E♭), can be derived from the pitches of the octatonic scale.

The first movement is in a kind of abridged sonata form without a separate development section, but with considerable elaboration in the recapitulation. In the exposition, up to the bar before rehearsal number 9, Bartók lays out four thematic areas each with its own distinctive tonal, harmonic, rhythmic and textural characteristics. As László Somfai has noted, the principal theme embodies some of the elements of the highly improvisatory Romanian *hora lungă* melodies.[49] Bartók had analysed these in his *Volksmusik der Rumänen von Maramureş*, a monograph that would finally be published in 1923 by Drei Masken Verlag of Munich, ten years after the preliminary work had been completed.[50] Bartók described the form of the *hora lungă* as involving three phases: an initial sustained fourth or fifth degree that could be held or repeated up to eight times, followed by an embroidered underlying descent from the upper fifth and a 'declamatory cadence' on the final tone. Thus the movement opens with a low $F\sharp_1$ in the piano, arguably the movement's tonic, supporting an expressive reiterated $E_5$ in the violin (Fig. 26), and a highly decorated down-ward trajectory from $F\sharp_5$ leads to five repeated Bs in bar 13. The cantilena commences in a *heptatonia secunda* mode (F♯–G♯–A[–B]–C–D–E), though

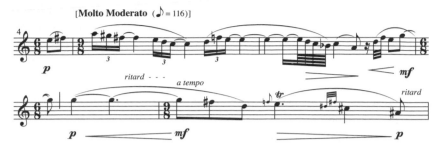

Figure 26. The principal theme of the first movement of the Second Violin Sonata.

the piano, soon expanding the modal frame and beneath the violin, plays dyads that are a mixture of fourths (both perfect and augmented), seconds, sevenths and sixths.

In the second part of the first movement (starting two bars before rehearsal number 3), the piano executes tremulous little figures against glassy harmonics on G, A and E in the violin that slide up the octave, contributing to the kind of texture that would later be described as 'night-music'. With the third thematic area, from rehearsal number 5, the duo begin in a 5:2 polyrhythm that is gradually disrupted, making the downbeat difficult to discriminate. Halfway through the section, at rehearsal number 6, the roles of the instruments are swapped, the overall trajectory of the lines being inverted and the metrical irregularities smoothed out. The final thematic element (from 7) involves chords that move against each other in partial symmetry in the piano with a syncopated rhythmic profile that begins as ♩♫ ♪ ♫ ♪ ♪ ♪ ♪, varying on each iteration; against this the violin plays long notes whose initiation and termination are decorated rather in line with the approach taken in the *hora lungă* theme.

Having assembled these four elements, the following part of the first movement acts both as development and reprise. Thus the first section gains figures in the piano that trace out a rapid parabola using the pitch content derived from four chromatic neighbour notes, and then rushes upwards combining white-note diatonicism and black-note pentatonicism; elements from the second and third sections are combined and varied in the subsequent bars from rehearsal number 11 to 15, a further intimation of the night-music style; and the fourth section is distilled to its essence, building to a substantial climax. The concluding twenty-one bars entail a concluding version of the principal theme that settles eleven bars from the end on a C♯–G♯ dyad played across two and a half octaves, the violin's high Fs briefly suggesting a C♯ major triad, though the movement ends in tonal ambiguity with a B–F dyad.

The finale brings together aspects of ternary, rondo and variation forms while involving the recapitulation of material from the first movement. At the largest level, the first part of a ternary structure stretches from the beginning to rehearsal number 21, and its varied reprise lies between numbers 35 and 56; a brief coda revisits the *hora lungă* of the opening movement. The principal melodic idea (Fig. 27) appears in the violin in the fifth bar, initially based on pitches derived from a *heptatonia secunda* folk mode on C (C–D–E–F♯–G♯–A[–B]), though these are gradually mixed with notes from other modes. It conjures up Romanian dance music (including the drinking and clapping tunes that are referenced in the First Violin Sonata) without directly citing any specific tune.

A contrasting passage one bar after rehearsal number 3 places the piano in the limelight (Fig. 28) with a rhythmic idea that embodies the principles of symmetry that Bartók had been exploring previously, the violin supporting the piano with repeated $D_4/E\flat_4$ dyads. The tonality at this point is ambiguous given that the pitch content of the first two chords conflates triads of G and A♭ major, though contextual cues tend to prioritise A♭. As this second idea progresses, it intimates the *colinde* that Bartók found so intriguing. Although it may be fanciful to hear the first part of the section (marked *lontano* – distant) as heralding the arrival of carollers, the asymmetrical additive rhythms from rehearsal number 5 in the piano (2+3+3, 2+3, 2+2+2, 2+3+3, 3+2+2, 2+2+2) are certainly redolent of the style.

The following pages develop and expand these two ideas, the passage from rehearsal number 7 to 15 concentrating on the first idea, and that between numbers 15 and 21 on the second. In the former, five variants are given in turn: from number 7 the melody is presented in semiquavers in G and at a rather faster pace; next, from number 8, the melodic ambitus is expanded by a semitone (G–A–B–C♯–D♯–E–F) with subsequent decoration around this new pitch;

Figure 27. The principal theme of the finale of the Second Violin Sonata.

Figure 28. The second idea of the finale of the Second Violin Sonata.

the linear ascent is extended further from number 9, rising up to D#$_6$; and at number 11 the violin melody is moved into the tonal area of B minor/D major; finally, at number 13 the tonality shifts to A♭ and the line momentarily fragments before spinning round and shooting upwards. Two versions of the second idea (from numbers 15 and 18) bring the first section to a close.

The middle part of the finale is marked by a change of modality, mutually exclusive five-note whole-tone 'clusters' alternating in the piano against a violin melody whose initial narrow range (G–A–B♭–C♭) is redolent of the Arab music Bartók collected in Algeria. Specifically, the 'Women's-*Knéja*' (number 12 from 'Arab Folk Music from the Biskra District') uses this scale and has some similarity in melodic configuration, and the piano's chords could be taken as a stylised imitation of the *darbuka*, including finger rolls and a resonant bass sound. Bartók plays with some of the symmetrical possibilities of an opened-out version of the scale (A–B–C–D) in the following section, and from the eighth bar of number 26 he establishes a rhythmic cycle in the right hand in the spirit of Arab drumming that takes fourteen quavers to complete. Played three times, the cycle eventually falls apart, and from number 29 three brief recollections of material from the first movement act as a frame for further material inspired by north African music, the opening of the *hora lungă* theme in harmonics functioning as a link to the concluding part.

With the reprise of the main section, Bartók further varies the two principal ideas, moving the metre initially to 5/8 and the tonality to C. Three versions of the first idea from numbers 35, 38 and 40 move the tonality up through perfect fifths via G to D, from which point the second idea appears twice, briefly re-establishing the tonic C at the fifth bar of number 46. Rather than culminating the movement in an extrovert way with the further development of the first idea that proceeds, the final bars of the work return to the *hora lungă* of the first movement, placing F♯ and C in relief and only allowing C to achieve the status of the tonic in the ethereal final couple of bars.

During the rest of 1922 Bartók engaged in sporadic concert activity. There were piano recitals on 10 October at Békéscsaba not far from his sister's home in Vésztő, on 22 November in Máramarossziget (Satu Mare), and on 20 December in the Academy of Music in Budapest when he was joined by Imre Waldbauer for the Hungarian premiere of the First Violin Sonata. Bartók gave further solo performances on Christmas Eve in Nagyvárad (Oradea) and on New Year's Eve in Kolozsvár (Cluj).

In February 1923 the Berlin journal *Melos* organised a series of concerts devoted to Bartók's complete chamber music involving the Waldbauer Quartet and the composer. In his review of the concerts Adolf Weissmann told the readers of *The Musical Times* that:

> Bartók himself is already too well-known in England to need any further introduction. That he is only one-sided in his art; that he lacks all sweetness of sound; in short, that he is all but a meridional [temperamentally southern] musician, is evident. But none can deny the convincing austerity and ever new solidity of his work, always bearing a stamp of its own. The limits of his musical capacity are the very limits of his human nature. The absence of sunshine in his art may lead his imagination to regions where no mortal will be able to follow him. This is shown by his second Sonata for violin and pianoforte, which, even though accompanied by the pianist-composer himself, could not impress all hearers with its value.[51]

A subsequent performance with Waldbauer in Kassa (Košice, Slovakia) had all the hallmarks of farce, as Bartók reported to his mother. On a tiny, rickety and poorly lit stage, which had to be mounted using a kitchen stool and a chair, and which creaked as they played, the performance was undermined by the page-turner knocking Bartók's music onto the ground and by Waldbauer forgetting to remove his mute so that the composer had to call out to remind him. Perhaps surprisingly, Bartók took this all in good heart and indeed commented that 'I was near to bursting with laughter'.[52]

In the following month, on 27 April, Bartók played the new Second Violin Sonata in Amsterdam with Zoltán Székely. Despite the latter's 'able assistance', *The Musical Times* correspondent, W. Harmans, found the piece heavy going, for 'At present he seems to have entered a stage of profound pessimism, which renders it almost hopeless to attempt to enter into the spirit of such works as his second Violin Sonata.'[53] When Jelly d'Arányi became the third interpreter (and dedicatee) of the work with Bartók at the ISCM event in London in May, *The Musical Times* critic E. E. (Edwin Evans) was rather more positive, remarking that like the earlier sonata, it 'displays the same purposeful expressionism, not easy to grasp unless the listener is prepared by previous acquaintance with Bartók's music, but singularly compelling the moment he is attuned to it'.[54] Jelly's performance, he felt, 'showed an amazing sensibility to its shades of emotion, which pass in quick succession'.

Bartók spent several weeks in May giving solo recitals in various parts of England: The Abbey girls' school in 'beautiful' Malvern Wells (three days before the ISCM event); the Highfield Assembly Hall in Huddersfield ('a nasty factory town' in his estimation) two days later; a private recital back in London; and finally at Normanhurst Court manor house in Battle, East Sussex, which had been converted into a girls' school after the war. These concerts were financially successful, netting the composer around £65, the equivalent of roughly 50 per cent of the average *annual* nominal earnings in the UK for 1923.[55]

During the first half of 1923 two events illustrated the contradictory position Bartók held in Budapest. The first was the commission by the City Council of new works from Dohnányi, Kodály and himself to celebrate the fiftieth anniversary of the union of Buda and Pest, which were to be performed in a gala concert on 19 November. The irony that the right-wing 'ultra-Christian' local government (as he perceived it) had chosen this group of composers was not lost on Bartók, for the trio had formed the Music directorate under Soviet rule. Perhaps this might be taken as an act of compensation on the part of the authorities, particularly for Dohnányi and Kodály, who had suffered more in the way of reprisals than Bartók had in the period after the regime collapsed. Almost simultaneously, Universal Edition had published Bartók's Five Songs op. 16, and he had dedicated the work to Béla Reinitz, 'with true friendship and love', dating it 1920. The composer and critic Reinitz was an active supporter of Bartók and Kodály, writing for *Népszava* and *Világ*, and in the role of Commissar for Artistic Affairs in the Communist government he had been involved in their appointment to the directorate. Reinitz fled the country after the counter-revolution and would not return to Budapest until 1931. Bartók's dedication may well have been deliberately provocative and it certainly raised a storm in the press for a time; as he commented on 27 May to Géza Révész, a Hungarian pioneer of music psychology, 'it even seemed at one moment that things were about to take a serious turn (official proceedings, etc.), but things have calmed down for the time being – perhaps for good'.[56]

*Táncszvit* (Dance Suite), Bartók's response to the commission, is in six sections and lasts for around twenty minutes. Scored for large orchestra, including a substantial array of percussion and piano, it marks a further development away from the Straussian orchestration of his earlier music, demonstrating great clarity as well as introducing some novel effects. A ritornello that sits before and after the second movement, between the fourth and fifth movement, and towards the end of the finale, helps to articulate what is effectively a fast–slow–fast three-part structure. All of the material is the composer's original invention, though it bears the strong imprint of various types of popular music. In a letter he wrote to the Romanian musicologist and critic Octavian Beu in January 1931, correcting errors the latter had made in a radio script, Bartók discusses the provenance of the various sources:

> No. 1 is partly, and No. 4 entirely of an Oriental (Arab) character; the *ritor-nell* and No. 2 are of a Hungarian character; in No. 3 Hungarian, Rumanian and even Arab influences alternate; and the theme of No. 5 is so primitive that one can only speak of a primitive peasant character here, and any classification according to nationality must be abandoned.[57]

In the same year, in a paragraph that he deleted from a draft essay on Hungarian music, Bartók further remarked that:

> The thematic material of all the movements is an imitation of peasant music. The aim of the whole work was to put together a kind of idealized peasant music – you could say an invented peasant music – in such a way that the individual movements of the work should introduce particular types of music. . . . In fact here and there is even a hybrid from these species. Thus, for example, the melody of the first movement is reminiscent of primitive Arabic peasant music, whereas its rhythm is of East European folk music.[58]

If the Budapest City Council or members of the audience at the premiere were expecting a piece that drew on the standard Magyarist musical markers, they may well have been somewhat taken aback to hear the sounds that emerged from the orchestra at the beginning of the Dance Suite. Certainly, if one of Bartók's intentions was to symbolise the eastern origins of the Hungarian tribes, it seems unlikely that many listeners would have made the connection between north Africa and the Urals (the putative homeland of their forebears, the Finno-Ugric tribes). He would later argue that there were commonalities between the *hora lungă* melodies of Romania that he had first discovered in 1912 and similar Ukrainian, Persian and Iraqi melodies; and in 1913 he had been surprised by the *hora lungă*'s apparent correspondence with the highly improvisational music he heard in Algeria, remarking that 'Although this similarity struck me at first hearing, I did not dare to see in it anything but a fortuitous coincidence.'[59] However, in 1923, he was as yet unaware of the Persian and Iraqi equivalents of *cântec lung*, and in any case this is not the genre that he invokes here.

Figure 29. The main thematic material from the Dance Suite. Numbers refer to the movements of the suite, R indicates *ritornell* in the version from rehearsal number 10.

The music Bartók had heard in north Africa had certainly been playing on his mind for some time and it had exerted its influence in the Suite op. 14, *The Miraculous Mandarin* and the Second Violin Sonata. In the main theme of the Dance Suite's first movement (Fig. 29 I) the idea presented by the bassoons against a perfect-fifth dyad over the movement's tonic of G employs a very narrow chromatic range similar to that of several of the melodies he had found in the Biskra district and it opens out through minor and major seconds to a minor third. Yet its rhythmic profile cannot be said to be comparable to any of the published tunes and, as the composer noted, it has an East European inspiration. A tranquil second idea in the cor anglais from rehearsal number 4 has the feel of Stravinsky about its repeated C♯s over off-beat chords of D minor with an added fourth played by *col legno* strings and piano, and this expands melodically before becoming involved in a kind of 'game of pairs' with the oboe. From rehearsal number 6 the tonality shifts to C and the outline of the first idea reappears in a new syncopated guise that leads to a climax and brief summary of the opening figure in tuba and trombone.

Bartók now introduces what is described as a *ritornell* in the Universal Edition score (following German usage), an Allegretto with a relaxed melody whose underlying pentatonicism is in marked contrast to the chromaticism of the previous material. As he had done in earlier sets of piano pieces based on folk material, Bartók establishes motivic connections between individual themes; in the pitches of the first two bars of the *ritornell* as they appear in Figure 29, there are two prominent intervals in common with the first dance: the major second and minor third, which in combination form the perfect fourth.

As was the case with the opening theme of the Second String Quartet, the subsequent Allegro molto stresses the minor third. The trombone glissandi between the B♭ and G, which act as a kind of refrain, are redolent of various passages in *The Miraculous Mandarin* and in particular the music associated with the Mandarin's ever more passionate chase of Mimi that precedes the tramps' attempts to kill him. This is a remarkable demonstration of Bartók's assurance in using the most elementary of musical materials; pared to the bone, the minor thirds, which predominate in the outer parts, sandwich syncopated rising and falling seconds and major thirds, and there is little that might be construed as conventionally developmental.

A second statement of the *ritornell* prefaces the animated and festive third movement, marked Allegro vivace, which is in the tonality of B major and coalesces rondo and chain forms in a structure that can be symbolically represented as ABACDA. In the pentatonic melody of the A section, the tessitura is expanded to an octave, with a pair of descending perfect fourths that may be understood to derive from the second and third bars of the *ritornell*. For the B section, more overtly Romanian influences are apparent in a metrically irregular tune in a *heptatonia secunda* mode on G (G–A–B–C♯–D–E–F–G), which evokes the *colindă* repertoire. A closely related idea (D) in the same modality, but beginning in a regular duple metre, appears after the reprise of the A section, and this is closely followed by a jaunty theme played by the piccolo in Mixolydian E♭. Accompanied by piled-up perfect fourths (C–F–B♭–E♭–A♭–D♭), this links motifs from the main theme and the *ritornell* and brings the larger section encompassing the first three dances to its conclusion.

There is a conspicuous change of mood for the fourth movement, marked Molto tranquillo, the first gesture of which presents the stacked-fourths motive in compact form (G–A–C–D) as a static texture. This alternates with a sinuous idea in the woodwinds that has the stereotypical characteristics of north African urban music with a narrow chromatic range and neighbour note embellishments. There are few points of correspondence with the published melodies, and arguably the role of this sinuous motif is as much cultural referent as the embodiment of musical principles discovered in the field.

Bartók establishes a symmetrical process around the unison melody such that the first four versions of it expand the number of pitches employed from four to five, to six and then eleven, before reversing the process:

I[II]/VII[VI]  F–A♭–B♭–C♭[–D♭]
III/V          G♯–A♯——C♯——D♯–E——F♯
IV             B—C♯–D–D♯——E♯–F♯–G–G♯–A–B–C

A fleeting statement of the *ritornell* paves the way for the final pair of dances. The brief fifth number, marked Comodo, which can be regarded as functioning as an introduction or structural anacrusis to the following dance, focuses on a simple rhythmic gesture grounded on a repeated E that builds up in layers through perfect fourths (E–A–D–G–C–F–B♭). A smoothed-out version of this figure also sets the finale into motion, now starting on C, with the entries overlapping and effectively running up through a cycle of ten perfect fourths. Much of what follows is varied recapitulation of earlier material, the trombones taking up the north African inflections of the opening dance at rehearsal number 48, the brass setting off with the rhythm of the second movement in stretto from number 49, and the main theme of the third dance appearing from number 53 before being developed. The presto at rehearsal number 56 leading to the first climax is again based on the second movement's minor thirds. After a moment of calm surrounding the final recall of the *ritornell*, the tension mounts again with trumpets and trombones revisiting the work's opening idea for the last time. The Dance Suite rushes to its enthusiastic conclusion by way of the third movement's pentatonic melody, and ends on the tonal centre of G.

Bartók completed the Dance Suite in Radvány (Radvaň, Slovakia) on 19 August 1923 at a time of great personal upheaval. His marital relationship with Márta had irretrievably broken down and he had become seriously attracted to one of his piano students at the Academy, Edith Pásztory (1903–1982). Ditta, as she was generally known, was the daughter of a high-school maths and physics teacher called Gyula Pásztory and his wife Kornélia (née Petrovics), a piano teacher. Ditta was born in Rimaszombat (now Rimavská Sobata in Slovakia). She had studied the piano at the Mór Somogyi private music school in Budapest from the age of fourteen, and graduated in 1921, taking lessons in the following year from Arnold Székely. She then began advanced training at the Liszt Academy in 1922 with Bartók as her teacher.

Bartók set off on 15 July to stay with Wanda Gleiman and her husband, Baron Antal Radvánszky, on their estate at Radvány. Three days later Márta penned a farewell letter to Bartók's mother, Paula, with whom she had had an extremely close relationship. She then joined Bartók at Radvány with Béla junior, so that they could explain their impending separation to the thirteen-year-old boy. On 26 July Márta wrote again to Bartók's mother, who was obviously deeply distressed by the situation, to tell her that 'On the same day [that they arrived] the little one heard about the change in our life from B; there were a few tears and he asked lots of question, but otherwise his healthy, cheerful disposition helped him to get over the sensational aspects of the matter relatively easily.'[60] Remarkably, despite the traumatic events she was dealing with, Márta continued working as Bartók's copyist and indeed there is a copy of the Dance Suite in her hand.

Bartók also contacted his mother to try to put her mind at rest and reconcile her to the divorce, telling her that 'I believe it will be well thus, it will be better than it has been up to now.'[61] He acknowledged that divorce would be much harder for Márta and that he could not have asked her to make the sacrifice. It seems, however, that Márta had proposed it, 'and I could not say no, after all, I was not the only one to be considered'. Divorce in Hungary was legislated by the 1894 Marriage Act, and according to a paper submitted to the Commission on European Family Law by Emila Weiss and Orsolya Szeibert:

> The acknowledgement of absolute grounds for divorce – which was the legislature's intention – resulted in the fact that in a system which is based strictly on fault in divorce the possibility of divorce based on the mutual consent of the spouses was established through the backdoor as the parties agreed to fabricate one of the grounds. However, one of the spouses had to be declared to be at fault in the divorce decree in these cases as well.[62]

Faults were of two kinds: absolute, which included adultery; and relative, which included 'serious violation of marital duties'. It must be presumed that some fault, absolute or relative, was admitted by Bartók, but whatever the case, the divorce was concluded swiftly and without overt acrimony. His marriage with Ditta then took place on 28 August 1923 in the Budapest District II registry office. Bartók and Márta remained on surprisingly cordial terms after the divorce and his remarriage. She stayed in contact with her former mother-in-law, and with Elza and her family.

The response of the audience to the Dance Suite at its premiere on 19 November under the baton of Dohnányi was by no means ecstatic (Bartók felt that the performance was weak) and Kodály's *Psalmus hungaricus* had a much warmer reception. However, by the end of 1925 the suite had been taken up widely and Universal Edition was able to boast in its advertising copy that it was to be performed in sixty cities in the following season.[63] It proved Bartók's first major international success and took his name to a much wider public than any of his previous works. His career as a performer, which was largely motivated by the need to supplement his core income from the Academy of Music, was also becoming busier. The winter of 1923 included a second trip to Britain, during which he performed on eight occasions. This included several recitals at girls' schools, in private houses, and for musical organisations, and public concerts in Bournemouth (at the Winter Gardens) and London. The most prominent of these, at the Aeolian Hall on New Bond Street, was organised by Gerald Cooper, who had been Philip Heseltine's (Peter Warlock's) travelling companion on his visit to Budapest. It brought to fruition Heseltine's hopes for Cooper's sponsorship of a Bartók concert.

This London concert included both of the violin sonatas played by Jelly d'Arányi. Edwin Evans's review in the January 1924 edition of *The Musical Times*, in which the critic just about manages to sit on Bartók's side of the fence, notes that:

Of the sharp contrasts presented by the plan of Gerald Cooper's chamber concerts at the Aeolian Hall, none was more pronounced than that on November 30, which brought Bartók into the centre of a scheme much occupied with gentle retrospection. Bartók stands for a mode of speech much less reticent. One of the greatest of his qualities is the absence of evasion. Musically, he calls a spade a spade without preparing his hearers for the truth or apologising for it afterwards. In his pianoforte writing and playing, he does not shirk the obvious truth that the pianoforte is an instrument of percussion. He accepts it, and plays and writes accordingly. Many of his most striking passages suggest a xylophone, except that in some curious, inexplicable, personal way he contrives to make percussive effects sound lyrical in significance.[64]

For Evans, Jelly's input was crucial to the success of the performances, for 'In the last year or two she has developed not only a breadth of expression, but a depth of insight that rank her among the elect of interpretative artists. I have heard other readings of this Sonata which provided an excuse for those who are not receptive to it, but as played by her with the composer it triumphs over its own spareness of conciliatory blandishments.'

Overall, the critical response in London to both Bartók's music and his style of playing was extremely mixed. The most caustic and damaging views were expressed by Percy Scholes, who was an important figure in British cultural life as music critic for both the *Observer* newspaper and the BBC. Scholes would later temper his judgement. In 1947, as editor of *The Mirror of Music, 1844–1944*, which surveyed the first century of *The Musical Times*, he described the mixture of 'puzzlement and delight' that resulted from the British premiere of the First Violin Sonata and continued with later works. However, 'amongst British musicians in general there is a deep respect for a composer whom they feel to be national, original, and sincere'.[65]

Ditta was by now expecting a child, therefore Bartók's concert activities in the first part of 1924 were relatively low-key and took place close to home, including Budapest and Komárno (Slovakia) in February; and Sopron, Timisoara and Oradea in March. The couple managed to take a holiday in Venice in April, Ditta being astonished by its beauty, and their only son, Péter, was born on 31 July. This was a further time of excitement for the Bartóks. For the first few weeks Ditta's mother supported her in their apartment at Szilágyi Dezső tér, while Péter spent much of the time crying (according to his father, at five weeks he had a head the size of a watermelon). There is considerable evidence that Bartók had very great affection for young children, perhaps because of their spontaneity and lack of artifice. However, given his need to work in silence, a newborn infant in the home of the forty-two-year-old composer could hardly have been conducive to serious work.

Bartók's most significant scholarly output of 1924 was the publication of his first Hungarian edition of the monograph *A magyar népdal* (*The Hungarian Folk Song*) by the publisher Rózsavölgyi és Társa. This was the composer's most substantial and detailed study of the subject thus far. In it he laid out the systematic basis of his taxonomy, which distinguishes three classes of melodies: the old style of Hungarian peasant music; the new style; and a catch-all miscellaneous group that itself is divided into seven sub-groups. Accompanying the theoretical first part of the book are 320 tunes that illustrate the various classes, notes about their sources or characteristics, song texts, and tables listing the places of collection. A German translation appeared the following year, and Bartók commissioned Calvocoressi to make the English translation that would finally be published in 1931 by Oxford University Press.

Since 1923 Bartók had been communicating with Baron Gyula Wlassics, the director of the Budapest Opera, about the company's desire to produce *The Miraculous Mandarin*, the orchestration of which he still had not completed. Wlassics had made him the generous offer of an advance to support his costs and an undertaking to follow his advice in artistic matters, with the intention of a performance early in 1924. But by May of that year Bartók had still only supplied a piano score and libretto and there was no sign of the orchestral material. At this stage he endeavoured to complete the first half by the middle of July and the rest by mid-August, but the task was much greater than he had given credit for in his current circumstances, and it was not completed until November or December.

The only substantial piece composed by Bartók in 1924 was *Falun* (Village Scenes), a work for woman's voice and piano based on Slovak melodies from Zólyom County (or Zvolenská in Slovakia as it now was). He completed the piece in December and dedicated it to Ditta. If he intended it as a kind of *Siegfried Idyll*, it was somewhat late for her birthday, for this fell on 31 October. Although there are similarities between its underlying theme (and to some degree, musical treatment) and Stravinsky's *Les Noces*, which was premiered in Paris in June 1923, there is no compelling evidence that Bartók was familiar with this work when he began to write Village Scenes, and his approach is largely consistent with previous developments in his musical language.

Seven folk songs are set in five sections, the first, second and fifth each being based on one tune, and the third and fourth on two. At the heart of the piece lies an exploration of the cultural traditions surrounding Slovak wedding celebrations, which were still deeply embedded when Bartók first visited the region. The English translation of the work as 'Village Scenes', rather than a more literal 'In the Village', reflects the fact that it sits somewhere between song cycle and operatic *scena*. However, it by no means presents an attempt to reconstruct the structure of a village wedding accurately and can perhaps be seen as a kind of rural *Frauenliebe und Leben*, working its way through haymaking (a site of courting), bridal preparations, wedding and childbirth, and ending with a celebratory young men's dance. Six of the source songs were transcribed between April and December 1915 at around the same time as Bartók's supposed infatuation with Klára Gombossy; the remaining one (the first song of the third section) was transcribed in December 1916, in Feketebalog (Čierny Balog).

Bartók sticks quite closely to the original song melodies for his vocal lines but adds modernist accompaniments and framing preludes, interludes and postludes that are subtly derived from the material of the songs. Previously, in a paper published in *Melos* in 1920, he had examined how tonal folk tunes could be placed in an atonal context, presenting Stravinsky's set of four songs, *Pribaoutki*, as an example of the effective integration of simulated Russian traditional material and Stravinsky's advanced idiom. He argued there that 'the obstinate clinging to a tone or a group of tones borrowed from folk music seems to be a precious foothold: it offers a solid framework for the compositions of this transition period and prevents wandering about at random.' The 'pure' traditional material (that is, uncorrupted by 'civilisation') should be seen as a 'natural phenomenon', functioning for the composer rather as 'bodily properties perceptible to the eye are for the fine arts, or the phenomena of life are for the poet'.

The symbolism of the text in the first song, 'Haymaking', is covertly sexual – ostensibly the dialogue of a couple, one of whom encourages the other to rake up the newly mown hay and admonishes (presumably) him for 'breaking his rake' through sleepiness. The melody is in Mixolydian G mode and involves a double tonic motion from the arpeggiation of an F major triad over the first three bars of each pair of phrases to closure on the G final. Bartók is very sparing with his use of triads in the accompaniment. He initially employs percussive rolled major second dyads (C/D) and then minor seconds (B/C), before expanding the harmonic range in the repeat of the melody a minor third higher with the use of major seventh chords (E♭–G–D) and various fourth-based chords.

In the beautiful moment of contemplation established by the second song, 'At the Bride's', the lyrics speak of a girl collecting peacock feathers to fill the pillows her lover's head will rest on. Here Bartók draws on a simple texture of major and minor thirds doubled between the hands that, in the course of the two verses (in the Mixolydian A mode), alternate with perfect fifths or fourths.

'Wedding', the third song, tells of the bride's dowry being transported to her new home and the bride's family setting off to meet their new in-laws in a different village. Elliptically describing her rite of passage through the marriage ceremony, the text informs us that the bride now no longer has a lover but a husband. While the words of one song declare that she will not fade away and wither like a rose, the other, as from her own mouth, says that when she has a husband 'petals drop and shrivel'. As her birth family joyfully returns from the festivities, she must stay with her new one. The overall structure of the song alternates two sections (ABABAB), but it is punctuated by an incisive rhythmic figure that articulates a pseudo-tonic chord of C♯ (G♯–C♯–D–E) and it supports the shrill ululations of the bride's supporters between the A and B sections on their first two occurrences. Much of the accompaniment derives from this collection of pitches, which is condensed from the notes of the vocal line or from the version lying a fourth higher in the central section (C♯–F♯–G–A). The two tunes are contrasted in metre and style – the first in 3/4 tends towards a waltz-like character, while the second in duple time is regular and unemotional. In a brief coda, the ululations are conflated with the residue of the first tune.

For the fourth song, 'Lullaby', two folk melodies are arranged as a pseudo-dialogue between a mother and her infant. She asks her baby son whether he will take care of her when she is old, and imagines him replying that he will, but only until he is married when he will leave her. In the exquisite imagery of the folk song, she tells him to 'Go into the green wood,/Wear your white shirt,/Let your white shirt twinkle/Through the dark green branches',[66] but asks him never to leave her. Bartók builds an AABBBA structure around the pair of melodies, in the underlying tonality of F. In the piano prelude he establishes a rocking figure in 5/4 with gentle harmonically generated accents on the second and fourth beats, which evokes the waltz-like accompaniment of the previous song. This latter element, and a static texture built from fourths, supports much of the first section, which, like the opening melody of the work, is based on a double tonic melody founded on the Lydian-inflected pitches F–G–A–B–C. An ostinato is then set in motion drawing on the pitches of two interlocking fourths (E–F–A–B♭) for the more anxious-sounding central part, whose melody lies in the Aeolian/Dorian B♭ mode.

Bartók surely had his own young son in mind in the final song, 'Lads' Dance', with its encouragement to the young goatherd to 'dance while life is free and new'. The tune itself is in Lydian E mode and has the most elaborate introduction of all the songs, alluding to bagpipe performance in the right-hand melody while the left hand vamps out its accompaniment. Similar material acts as an interlude between the second and third verses, and culminates the piece, supporting jubilant cries of 'hey ho'.

In February 1925 Bartók wrote to Calvocoressi in connection with his work on the translation of *The Hungarian Folk Song*. He told him that, because of family illness and other problems, the only piece of new music he had been able to complete was *The Miraculous Mandarin*, and even this had caused him great difficulty. Calvocoressi had previously suggested a possible collaboration with Bartók on a ballet project. But the composer felt obliged to advise him that his own current paucity of output meant that it really was not worth his while putting any effort into preparing a libretto.[67]

Much of the following month was spent on a concert tour in Italy – in Milan, Rome, Naples and Palermo – 'there's no need for me to tell you what a beautiful trip it was,' Bartók wrote to Buşiţia in May. He also informed him that he had been awarded the Bene Merenti 1st class by the Romanian government (in the previous October). Despite his usual concerns about such awards and prizes, he seems to have accepted this as token of the respect accorded to his work on Romanian music. However, a bronze Horthy ('signum laudis') medal, which was conferred on him weeks earlier, on 23 April, received no mention in this letter, nor indeed is it commented on in the published collections of his correspondence.

Bartók returned to Italy with Ditta in the summer for his annual holiday, staying at Chiesa in Valmalenco on the border with Switzerland. The couple had left Péter with Bartók's sister and Márta in Szőllőspuszta.[68] Unlike many of his previous holidays Bartók really does seem to have relaxed and did not attempt to compose any new works during this period. Domestic circumstances were soon to change again, however, with Márta's marriage to Károly Ziegler, the engineer son of her first cousin Dr Károly Ziegler. This involved her moving to Szekszárd, in the south of Hungary, while Béla junior joined the Bartók household in Szilágyi Dezső tér.

## CHAPTER EIGHT

# 'The forest rustles, the fields rustle': 1925–1928

In October 1925 Bartók embarked on a further brief concert tour of Holland in collaboration with Zoltán Székely (who now lived in Nijmegen). As well as playing sonatas by Bach, Brahms and Mozart, and a group of Bartók's piano pieces (including the *Allegro barbaro*), they performed Székely's own arrangement of the Romanian Folk Dances. The duo's recitals at Arnhem and Utrecht passed off successfully and Bartók also performed his Rhapsody op. 1 with the Concertgebouw Orchestra in Amsterdam, conducted by Pierre Monteux, in a concert that included the Dance Suite. The rest of 1925 was taken up with further sporadic concert activity and still no indication that Bartók's compositional fallow period was coming to its end; and in the first five months of 1926 he continued to perform the Rhapsody and the regular group of smaller solo pieces. A letter to Ditta in late June suggests that the problem was, at least in part, a mental block brought on by the plethora of new directions taken by the musical avant-garde that were being relentlessly reported and sloganised by the musical press. 'To be frank,' he tells her, 'recently I have felt so stupid, so dazed, so empty-headed that I have truly doubted whether I am able to write anything new at all anymore.'[1] Suddenly, however, the dam was breached and a sequence of new works flooded out: the *Szonáta* (Sonata for Piano) written in June; *Szabadban* (*Out of Doors*) between June and August; *Kilenc kis zongoradarab* (Nine Little Piano Pieces) completed at the end of October; and most importantly for his symphonic appearances, the long-awaited *I Zongoraverseny*, the First Piano Concerto, that he began in August and finished on 12 November. With good reason, then, 1926 has been characterised as Bartók's 'piano year'.

It has become commonplace to see the two key influences on these new compositions as that of Stravinsky and a group of contrapuntal keyboard composers who flourished prior to the time of J. S. Bach. In terms of the former,

Bartók had certainly attended the Philharmonic Society concert in Budapest devoted to the Russian composer that was held on 15 March 1926 in which Stravinsky had played the solo part in his Concerto for Piano and Wind Instruments, the programme also including *Petrushka* and *Le Chant du rossignol*. David Schneider has examined the contemporary critical response to this concert in Hungary and has noted the tendency to contrast what was perceived as Stravinsky's objectivity and absence of emotion with the classicism and expressivity of Bartók.[2]

On the surface, the three-movement Piano Sonata might appear to have been written under the shadow of Stravinsky. Its first movement, in particular, is characterised by ostinato figures, clean-cut rhythmic motifs and percussive piano writing. However, comparison with earlier works such as the *Allegro barbaro* of 1911 and the Suite op. 14 of 1916 demonstrates the logical development of their technique and spirit. Indeed, in 1945 Bartók wrote of the sonata's 'enlargement of the newly won means'.[3] This opening movement is written in a sonata form that is heavily weighted towards an exposition that accounts for exactly half its length and in which five distinctive themes inspired by folk music are presented in turn.

The first of these is a Lydian-inflected idea that begins with a dotted-rhythm motif connecting G♯ and B, with both natural and sharp versions of the intervening A, colouring the pitch and suggesting the equal division of the minor third into two three-quarter tones such as are found in Arab music theory and practice. This motif reappears on a number of occasions over the course of the movement as a linking device, and sets into motion the reiteration of the pitch B against an ostinato made from a pseudo-tonic to dominant vamp. As the theme progresses and becomes ever more animated, it works its way up the sequence shown in Figure 30, its fourteen tones including all twelve chromatic pitches.

The subdued second theme, from bar 44, has some of the characteristics of Hungarian folk melody, and more particularly it can be compared to the openings of number 71a ('Fekete füld termi a jó búzát') and 251 ('Hármat tojott a fekete kánya') from *The Hungarian Folk Song*. It begins in the tonal centre of A,

Figure 30. The three-note cells of the opening theme of the first movement of the Piano Sonata.

the melody harmonised in minor or major thirds doubled at the octave, and it has little rhythmic interjections of F♯–C♯ at the end of each phrase rather like the ululations of Village Scenes. This leads into a more assertive third theme (bar 55) that places the hands in contrary motion. The pitches in the right hand are entirely derived from a black-note pentatonic mode, those in the left hand from a white-note diatonic collection, providing another example of Bartók's carefully controlled usage of all the chromatic degrees.

A more restrained, if somewhat machine-like, fourth theme in G♯ minor, which opens out from a narrow melodic range at its inception at bar 76, is in two parts, the second a perfect fifth higher than the first. Its accompaniment (Fig. 31, upper system, first bar) is a further ostinato figure that can be seen to consist of a chain of thirds with an octave displacement (Fig. 31, upper system, second bar).

The minor third melodic cell also infiltrates the final theme of the exposition in E♭ (Fig. 31, lower system) that begins at bar 116, a descending version forming the basis of the melody played by the right-hand thumb (and mirrored in the left). This extends into a Mixolydian A mode apparently set bitonally against the E♭ triads.

In the development (from bar 135), Bartók focuses his attention on the first and second themes, and when the recapitulation arrives, it begins part-way through the first theme, the second quaver of bar 187 being the equivalent of the upbeat to bar 14. Neither the second theme (which was treated in the development) nor the third are reprised, and the fourth is substantially

Figure 31. The opening of the fourth theme (upper system) and fifth theme (lower system) of the first movement of the Piano Sonata.

foreshortened and played a tone lower than the exposition. After the second section of the final theme appears, a final syncopated allusion to the opening theme brings the movement to its close with a glissando from the dominant to the tonic of E.

The threnodic and austere second movement is in a three-part form that can be conceptualised as being AA'A", each section working with the same limited set of material. Its opening gesture, based on chords of A♭–E♭–F in the left hand, sounds like the tolling of a bell, while the repeated $E_4$s in the right hand resemble the dots and dashes of a Morse code message. Subsequently, a sharply etched figure with a pentatonic basis rises melodically through fourths and then seconds ($D_5$–$G_5$–$C_6$–$D_6$–$E_6$). Its stepwise three-note cell is briefly developed, switching between the inner and upper voices of a four-part texture that appears to bear witness to the composer's avowed interest in pre-Bachian polyphony, before descending in the lower register at the section's end.

The second part begins with an exploration of the pentatonic implications of the five-note figure. In its chordal manifestation it is subject to sequential repetitions from bar 24, played a tone lower each time and settling onto a pedal tone D in the bass, with a rising-scale pattern in the tenor voice and more chromatically oriented chords in the right hand. In the final part, after an abbreviated reprise of the first two ideas, the left hand settles on a gesture that oscillates through the minor third above and below $D_2$. The movement ends with the repeated $E_4$ above the chord of A♭–E♭–F heard at the opening, as an upbeat to a pentatonic phrase that closes on a C major/minor chord.

For the brilliant monothematic finale in the tonality of E, Bartók adopts an approach that fuses rondo (ABA'CA"B'A"') and variation forms, drawing on a folk-like theme in an irregular metre written in the spirit of the *colindă* (Fig. 32a) and in a *heptatonia secunda* mode on E (E–F♯–G–A–B–C♯–D♯–E). This reappears at bars 92, 157 and 227, and the intervening episodes (B at 53 and 205, and C at 143) are themselves variants of the principal theme. As László Somfai notes, they embody particular characteristics of folk performance practices.[4] Thus, for example, the C section (Fig. 32b), which is largely accompanied by alternating two- and three-note whole-tone sonorities in the left hand, is evocative of the style of the traditional flautist.

Perhaps the most novel pianistic elements of the finale are the percussive use of chromatic clusters (G–A♭–A–B♭) split between the hands in the first episode (bar 53) and its reprise; and the dense ten-, eleven- and twelve-note chords found at various places in its course. Overall the movement is a *tour de force*, balancing structural simplicity with sonic adventurousness.

An episode in the finale that imitated bagpipe performance was eventually removed by Bartók. Yet it found its way into a stand-alone piece, as the third

Figure 32. The openings of the rondo theme and the third episode from the finale of the Piano Sonata.

movement ('Musettes') of the two-volume set of five piano pieces, *Szabadban* (*Out of Doors*), written concurrently with the Piano Sonata. Somfai has demonstrated that the composition of the first two pieces of *Out of Doors* – 'Síppal, dobbal …' ('With Drums and Pipes') and 'Barcarolla' – preceded that of the third and second movements of the sonata.[5] The last two pieces, 'Az éjszaka zenéje' ('The Night's Music') and 'Hajsza' ('The Chase'), which formed the second volume, were written together, probably after the sonata was completed. They can be seen to function as a pair, Bartók's second autograph manuscript not providing a separate number for the final item.

According to Damjana Bratuž, the ternary-form first piece of the set, 'Síppal, dobbal …' ('With Drums and Pipes'), references the Hungarian children's song 'Gólya, gólya, gillce'. Its nonsense rhymes tell of a Turkish child cutting a stork's leg and making it bleed, and of a Hungarian child curing it with a pipe, a drum and a 'reed violin'.[6] This tune is still in wide currency and it was arranged by Kodály for children's chorus as 'Gólya-nóta' ('Stork Song') in 1929. The stork, which appears on the coats of arms of a number of the local regions of Hungary, can be regarded as something of a national symbol, and the words of the song hark back to enmities formed in the period of Ottoman rule. However, there is no indication that Bartók was intending any deeper significance through his veiled allusion to the text, nor indeed by the near quotation of the second line of the folk melody (which repeats the phrase F♯–F♯–E–F♯–G–F♯–E), close to the piece's beginning. At the heart of the piece, after percussive piano writing that conjures up the drums of the title through hammered-out low-register tone and semitone dyads, is a four-line melody with the character and structure of old-style Hungarian folk song.

'Barcarolla' pays its respects to the Venice that Bartók and Ditta had so enjoyed visiting. In the underlying tonality of G, its chromatic opening figure, built from rising and falling broken perfect-fourth chords, begins in the 6/8 of a conventional barcarole before locking onto a 4/8 + 3/8 metrical scheme that crests and troughs melodically like the gentle lapping of the waves. This acts as a frame for three strophes of a cantando melody played in G, D and A respectively, separating the first two statements (and a brief development) from the third.

As noted above, 'Musettes' originated as an episode in the Piano Sonata and while it evokes the performance of rural bagpipers, it is by no means a simple pastiche of a dance tune played by the *cimpoiu* (Romanian bagpipes). The Romanian and Hungarian pipes tend to have a chanter with a single-octave scale (usually Mixolydian), a tonic drone, and a middle pipe that is able to play both the tonic and dominant notes (and sometimes a third pitch); this feature permits the production of harmonic and rhythmic accompaniments. Bartók draws on many of these characteristics in the piece, much of which gives the impression of being prefatory and improvisatory, as if heard from a distance: he simulates the sound of the rather tentative piper filling the bag with air, suggests the tuning of the drone and middle pipe, and employs idiomatic short fingered trills. When a melodic thread appears at bar 41, it initially overlaps whole-tone (F♯–E–D–C–B♭–A♭) and octatonic (B♭–A♭–G–F–E) elements before taking on a more diatonic configuration. The second half of the piece can be seen as a varied repeat of the first in which, in the final passage, the now fully warmed-up and confident piper plays a dance-like melody in a *heptatonia secunda* mode on D (D–E–F♯–G♯–A–B–C). It involves the drone D, the middle-pipe fifth A, and the regular semiquaver rhythm characteristic of the 'real *Ardeleana* type' of Romanian tune, spiced up with rapid and brilliant runs.[7]

In some of Bartók's earlier works, attention has already been drawn to a type of atmospheric post-Debussyan textural music. Here he gives it a name for the first time – 'The Night's Music'. This piece involves three types of material, which interlace with each other in an almost cinematic way. The first of these is an impressionistic combination of rustling five-note chromatic clusters – an extension of the figure opening the autumnal final song of the op. 15 set, 'In the Valley' – which acts as a bed of sounds that suggest birdsong, the chirping of crickets and croaking of frogs. There is a marked simplification of the texture for the second section, from part the way through bar 17, where a four-line lament with a narrow chromatic range is punctuated by rolled chromatic clusters in the left hand, as the residue of the first section. After this melody has been repeated towards the extremes of the keyboard and a brief reprise of the opening material, Bartók introduces a third idea that sounds as if it had been conceived for the folk flute (comparable to a tune such as number 754 from volume 1 of *Rumanian Folk Music*) – the lonely performance of a shepherd tending his sheep. The three types of material are then superimposed from bar

48, the lament and flute melody coming into close dialogue from bar 61, and the extraordinary piece is rounded off with a varied restatement of the opening part of the movement.

The brilliant concluding piece, 'The Chase', can be compared to the dance in *The Miraculous Mandarin* associated with the Mandarin's pursuit of Mimi. If the title refers to the hunt, this seems more a Stravinskyan *Jeu de Rapt* than a Paganini-Lisztian *La Chasse*. Underpinning this Presto in F is an ostinato established in the fourth bar that is based on the pitches $F_2$–$G\sharp_2$–$B_2$–$C\sharp_3$–$E_3$, which appears in the left hand in quintuplet semiquavers and establishes a 3:5 polyrhythm against the right hand's quavers. Apart from the tonic F, the remaining notes of the ostinato lie a semitone away from the pitches of an F major triad. Above it the melody that begins in bar 14 involves the retrograde inversion of the *più mosso* idea from bar 41 of 'Musettes' with its overlapping whole-tone and octatonic elements (F–G–A–B–C$\sharp$–D$\sharp$–E–F$\sharp$–G[$\sharp$]). This idea forms the basis of the first, second and final sections of the piece, and in each, melodic points of arrival are oriented around the pitches of an $F^7$ chord (F–A–C–E♭). For the third section, Bartók turns to the semi-symmetrical melodic structures he had been exploring for some time, with wedge-like shapes opening out or turning inwards; and the fourth involves a 4:3 polyrhythm, the ostinato figure extended with the addition of three pitches from a G major triad to $E_3$–$B_1$–$D_2$–$G_2$–$A\sharp_2$–$F_2$–$G\sharp_2$–$C\sharp_3$. In both these sections the density of dissonance increases. The augmented octave, major ninth and minor tenth intervals in the right hand, as the piece progresses to the concluding section, place enormous strain on the player, to the extent that Bartók provides a less demanding *ossia* for six of the bars.

Bartók did not explicitly label the two volumes of character pieces as a suite and he regularly extracted individual items in his recitals. However, regarding the volumes as a suite makes considerable musical sense in aggregate and demonstrates a degree of symmetry, but without the rigorous application found in, for example, String Quartets Nos. 4 and 5.

*Out of Doors* and the Piano Sonata were certainly essential precursors to the much-needed First Piano Concerto in E that was completed between August and November 1926. This work is invested with folk influences from a wide range of sources, including that of the Arab music Bartók had first heard in Biskra in 1913. Its other crucial antecedent is Stravinsky's Concerto for Piano and Winds, which its composer had performed at the famous concert in Budapest on 15 March 1926 that was attended by Bartók. David E. Schneider has examined various points of correspondence between the first movements of the two concertos and he draws attention to the similar approach taken by Bartók in his introduction, principal theme and peroration.[8] Perhaps the most obvious connection, which may be a conscious act of deference on his part, is the total avoidance of string instruments in the introduction to the first movement (and subsequently, in the entire second movement).[9]

The first and third movements can be seen to reflect each other through their employment of analogous types of musical material; both are energetic and forceful, with a motoric quality similar to that found in the Piano Sonata's outer sections. For the introduction to the first movement, which is only slightly slower than the main tempo, Bartók takes a rather different approach to that of Stravinsky with his glance to the slow dotted rhythm of the French overture. Instead, Bartók presents the building blocks of the piece in their most elemental forms: a rhythmic idea founded on the dyad A/B with repeated quavers in the timpani; an acid chord built from perfect and augmented fourths (B♭–D♯–G♯–A); and an austere melody first played by the horns and then the bassoons, whose restricted range (D♯–E♯–F♯–G♯–A) and octatonic demeanour recall the tunes he had collected in north Africa. A cellular technique is employed in which most of the elements seem to derive from the 'germinal' motif outlined by the horns from rehearsal number 1.

The first subject of the opening movement is in a modally flexible D (the subtonic area) and is prefaced in the solo piano by fourteen double-octave repetitions of the pitch A that calls to mind Stravinsky's opening gambit in his Concerto for Piano and Winds. Although this subject may not have the structure of any specific peasant music, it employs characteristically Slovakian syncopated rhythms in a melody that grows out of the in-filled minor third of the Piano Concerto's inception (Fig. 33). This figure exhibits a kind of self-similarity in which the initial C–B–A is embedded at a higher level – the upbeat C, the downbeat B at the beginning of the second and third bars, and the thrice-repeated A. These patterns become increasingly prominent and the repetitions of the pitches B–C–D ever more insistent in the progress towards the second idea. Although this passage intimates Baroque influences, the highly elaborate *postludio* of a bagpipe piece collected by Kodály in 1911 in Salakusz, Nyitra County (now Salakuzy in Slovakia), which appears in Bartók's third volume of Slovak folk songs, shows the same unrelenting repetition of these three tones.[10]

When the second theme arrives, prefaced by a rising sequence of repeated notes and accompanied and surrounded by chains of parallel thirds that evoke J. S. Bach's keyboard writing, it is in the home tonality of E and is accompanied by fourth-based tonic chords (E–F♯–B). Again, Slovak influence can be detected in this folk-like idea, which shifts between registers as a duet, and its continuation provides a transition into the second part of the exposition. A varied reprise of the principal theme is placed in the tonality of F, and the section

Figure 33. Part of the principal theme of the first movement of the First Piano Concerto.

comes to a close with a new idea in G which simultaneously ascends and descends in stepwise motion and whose origins can be distinguished in the principal theme. In summary, over the course of the exposition the tonal centres progress through D–E–F–G.

The development section begins with sharply edged percussive chords in the piano in a brief moment of north African fantasy, before the closing idea of the exposition is picked up once more and this leads into a gradually accelerating dance founded on the movement's opening melodic gesture. Bartók's eclecticism is demonstrated by his willingness to move into much more diatonic territory with overlapping imitative passages in thirds five bars after rehearsal number 27. The dance becomes ever wilder as it builds towards the recapitulation and the section draws to its end with a number of variants of the principal theme. A relatively terse recapitulation places greater emphasis on the secondary theme than was the case in the exposition. In a sense the whole section can be understood as a kind of extended Phrygian cadence whose final resolution is onto the same E chord that originally accompanied the second theme, the supertonic F♯ replacing the conventional mediant.

If the outer movements attempt to reconcile the composer's mature style with his interest in Baroque techniques, the second movement is prescient of his Sonata for Two Pianos and Percussion of 1937, as its opening and closing parts are saturated with the sounds of percussion instruments. The instigation of the movement is related, in terms of mood and colour, to the 'night music' discussed above in relation to *Out of Doors*. The movement concentrates initially on the major and minor second intervals and fourth chords that permeated the Piano Concerto's introduction. At the same time, Bartók explores the colouristic opportunities of untuned percussion, utilising a new notation to discriminate their distinct timbres: side drums with their snares on and off are placed in timbral contrast with each other and, drawing on the technique of Arab tar and darbuka players, are struck at the centre or rim. In the passage from rehearsal number 4, in which Bartók first presents an idea that will later develop into a slow hypnotic dance at the centre of the movement, he hints at conventional tonal relations with the interactions of three types of chord: a D major-minor pseudo-tonic chord; a subdominant G with an inverted pedal F♯ and dissonant G♯; and a residual augmented sixth E♭–C♯.

The central part of the movement is dominated by the trance-like repetition and gradual elaboration of the fundamentally pentatonic nine-bar melody in a triple hypermetre (Fig. 34). Bartók accompanies this with an ostinato in the piano that expands on each repetition of the tune by means of the gradual infill of major seventh dyads with perfect plus augmented fourths, five-note and eventually six-note chords (Fig. 35).

In the assertive and primitive-sounding opening material of the third movement (which follows the second without a break, prefaced by rasping trombone glissandi reminiscent of the similar effect in *The Miraculous Mandarin*), Bartók substitutes the asymmetry of the corresponding theme in the first movement with much greater metrical regularity. Over a four-quaver ostinato figure in the strings entailing a falling and rising pattern of double-stopped perfect fourth dyads, the piano establishes an idea with two basic elements: a series of fortissimo double-octave tonic Es; and the decorated descent from G to E with a rhythmic profile that evokes some Romanian instrumental music (for example, the *mărunțel*). This latter figure, like its counterpart in the first movement, involves an element of self-similarity, embedding the Phrygian mode pattern G–F–E. Overall the three parts of the first thematic area can be construed as falling into a kind of AA′B bar form.

In the contrasting material that appears from rehearsal number 6 of this final movement, the descending third of the opening motif is expanded to a perfect fifth (G♯–F♯–E–D♯–E–C♯) and the underlying fall through sequential repetition of this fundamentally diatonic figure reflects the passages of superimposed linear ascent and descent in the opening movement (especially the one from the upbeat to rehearsal number 19 to the seventh bar after number 20). The percussive chords in the piano from rehearsal number 9 seem to emulate the sound of fingered rolls on the edge, and the resonant strike at the centre, of the darbuka. Beneath this new ostinato emerges an elaboration of the thematic material that appeared in the prelude to the first movement.

Figure 34. The melody from the central section of the second movement of the First Piano Concerto.

Figure 35. The piano chords used in the ostinato accompaniment in the second movement of the First Piano Concerto.

From rehearsal number 12 the music takes on a more pentatonic aspect, with prominent melodic fourths and a passing similarity to various motifs from the introduction to the first part of Stravinsky's *Rite of Spring*; and on one of only two occasions in the concerto Bartók employs a specific key signature, in this case five sharps. In the first part of this passage, the piano and orchestra contribute to a chromatic texture by operating in complementary tonal spaces, the largely 'black-note' music of the orchestra placed against the piano's 'white notes'. This leads into the closing idea of the exposition (rehearsal number 16), which draws on and further expands the motif of infilled fifths discussed above.

The development in the final movement is rather briefer than the equivalent section of the first movement. It begins with a two-bar ostinato rhythm on C underpinning little fragments that sound similar to some of the bagpipe motifs Bartók collated in the volume of instrumental melodies forming the first part of *Rumanian Folk Music*. At the heart of the movement the brass present a broad cantabile melody that displays more obviously the influence of Hungarian folk song, and this lyrical and fundamentally diatonic impulse dominates the rest of the section. Surprisingly, perhaps, the reprise of the first subject gives the impression of a structural upbeat rather than a major point of arrival. Throughout the recapitulation the tension continues to rise so that the climax of the movement, and the work as a whole, lies in its concluding bars.

Although this is undoubtedly a virtuoso work, Bartók did not feel the need to provide any cadenzas for the soloist; the piano and orchestra are presented as partners rather being placed in adversarial roles. The Concerto's integration of heterogeneous tonal material could be loosely equated to the blending of the abstract and the figurative in the sphere of visual art, or of the monochromatic and panchromatic in the field of film. While its symmetrically disposed movements do involve a high degree of motivic unity, the composer's predilection for the miniature (noting that its genesis was coincident with the composition of a number of short piano pieces) and for continuous development results in large-scale forms that have rather different structural dynamics to their Classical-Romantic models. The Piano Concerto certainly makes little further attempt to ingratiate itself with the audience than did the two violin sonatas. Early performances resulted in somewhat negative critical responses and slow adoption in the concerto repertoire.

*Kilenc kis zongoradarab* (Nine Little Piano Pieces) was completed at the end of October 1926, while Bartók was still working on the concerto. The nine works are organised in three books as two quartets of 'dialogues' and character pieces, and a stand-alone 'Preludio All'ungherese'. The opening four dialogues look to Bach's *Two-Part Inventions* rather as Paul Hindemith's much later *Ludus Tonalis* (1942) refers to *The Well-Tempered Clavier*. They are in E major, A minor, C major and E♭ major respectively, though in each case they press well beyond the diatonic territory normally demarcated by these key signatures. Perhaps for Bartók these contrapuntal pieces had the function of the compositional exercises that Brahms exchanged with Joseph Joachim. They arguably display an approach that resonates with the so-called Neue Sachlichkeit (New Objectivity), which in the musical field was particularly represented at that time by the works of Hindemith.

Although the titles of the four character pieces that follow (Menuetto, Air, 'Marcia delle bestie' and 'Tambourine') may seem to invoke the spirit of keyboard music prior to Bach, it sometimes sounds as if Debussy's reimaginings of the French Baroque have been distilled and refracted through Bartók's particular lens. László Somfai has remarked on Bartók's employment of a kind of interval expansion in the Menuetto, where the pattern C♯–D♯–C♯–D–C♯ in bars 3–4, over A♯–E tritone dyads in the left hand, is transformed in bars 9–10 to A–D–A–B–A through an increase in the relative interval size.[11] In the sparkling Air in A major, a piece that could easily have found its way into his pedagogical collection *Mikrokosmos*, Bartók invents a simple four-line melody much like folk song, which is played through twice with an unaffected and largely diatonic accompaniment. 'Marcia delle bestie' ('March of the Beasts') is a light-hearted and humorously cumbersome piece that begins predominantly in B♭ with the sharpened fourth and flattened seventh of the *heptatonia secunda* 'acoustic scale', though its employment is by no means consistent. It shares something of the approach of Stravinsky's Three Easy Pieces for piano and his *Histoire du soldat*, in its use of condensed military-march topoi and ostinati rhythms. 'Tambourine' is a fleet-of-foot miniature, the first half of which is unambiguously in the Mixolydian mode. It involves percussive rhythmic flourishes framing a brief melodic idea that stutteringly takes shape through a series of registral shifts and repeated notes before being placed an octave higher. In the second half reiterated B♭s in the left hand call to mind the principal thematic material of the Piano Concerto, and the coda brilliantly evokes Spanish rhythms associated with the tambourine.

The final 'Preludio All'ungherese' (in G♯ minor) entails the slow-fast structure of the *verbunkos* in a context that draws on the spirit of Hungarian rural rather than urban song. The Aeolian mode melody that is presented in five introductory bars forms the basis of both parts of the prelude. The melody is treated contrapuntally a little later in the opening Molto moderato section. It is then developed into a six-part pseudo-folk song with the ABB'A'B'A' form of a new-style tune, played twice as it gradually accelerates through the subsequent Allegro non troppo, molto ritmico. A particular feature of the second section is the use of strummed three-note chords in the left hand (initially G♯–A♯–D♯), a technique that recalls the use of the flat-bridge three-string violin in the Mureş region; and in the brilliant coda, the pentatonic implications of the melody and accompaniment come to the fore.

The most significant musical event of the final months of 1926 was the controversial premiere of the pantomime *The Miraculous Mandarin*, which finally took place in Cologne on 27 November. Bartók had been involved in fruitless discussions with the Budapest Opera earlier in the year and instead turned to Cologne for the first performance of his pantomime in the opera house on the Habsburgerring. It was placed in the hands of the conductor Jenő Szenkár and the director Hans Strohbach, with a cast led by Wilma Aug as Mimi and Gustav Zeiller as the Mandarin. Szenkár recalled both the difficulty of the work, which required much rehearsal, and also the public outcry that accompanied it: 'The uproar was so deafening and threatening that the safety curtain had to be lowered! We did not give up, however, and were not afraid even to go out in front of the curtain – at which the whistling redoubled!'[12] According to Hermann Unger's review in *Musikblätter des Anbruch*, 'Catcalls, whistling, stamping and booing which went on for several minutes, and did not even subside when the composer appeared, nor even after the safety curtain came down, and swelled to shouting when the composer and conductor stepped out of the little door in the safety curtain, must mean something for us.'[13]

Konrad Adenauer, the Mayor of Cologne (who would become West Germany's first post-war Chancellor), personally intervened and called Szenkár into his office, demanding of him how he could have thought it proper to 'perform such a dirty piece' and ordering that the show be cancelled forthwith. Despite Szenkár's best efforts to persuade Adenauer otherwise, he was compelled to acquiesce in the censorship; this was the ballet's solitary performance in Cologne. On 2 December Bartók wrote to his mother about these events with a certain wry humour, for he was clearly aware of the potential benefits of a ban in terms of promoting the piece.

During the first few months of 1927 the piano became a particular focus of Bartók's activities. He appeared as a soloist in Genoa, Venice and Kecskemét in January; in February and early March ensued a Romanian tour of Arad, Oradea (Nagyvárad), Cluj, Brasov and Sfântu Gheorghe (the Székely National Museum); he took part in a radio broadcast in Budapest on 9 March and in a performance of the Rhapsody in Barcelona in late March. Early Baroque music featuring in his repertoire during this time included works by the Italian composers Azzolino Bernardino della Ciaja (c. 1605–c. 1670), Benedetto Marcello (1686–1739) and Domenico Scarlatti (1685–1757), as well as the usual diet of Classical and Romantic works and his own compositions. In the March radio broadcast Bartók also included the theme and variations, 'Quodlings Delight' (sic), by the English composer Giles Farnaby (c. 1563–1640), from the *Fitzwilliam Virginal Book*, a somewhat recherché work for the time, even allowing for the other pieces he was playing.

These were relatively parochial concerts in comparison with the premiere of his First Piano Concerto on 1 July 1927 at the Frankfurt am Main Opera House under the baton of Wilhelm Furtwängler, as part of the events hosted by the International Society for Contemporary Music. Olin Downes was present at the concert and in a review published in *The New York Times* the following day he observed:

> Of the Bartok concerto it is not the time to speak in detail prior to the American performance, save to remark that it is essentially Hungarian in character, though highly modern in texture and rhythmical rather than melodic, and that the composer played it with superb virtuosity. In this he was admirably assisted by Wilhelm Furtwaengler, who had prepared the performance with much care and labour. There was also an ovation for Mr Bartok, a man of conservative demeanor, but who as an interpreter evinces a hot and boiling temper.[14]

According to Bartók's former piano student Ernő Balogh, who had moved to the USA in 1924, it was through his intervention that William Murray, the representative of the Baldwin Piano Company, offered a contract for a concert tour of America, claiming that 'At my suggestion, he showed willingness to invite Bartók to America, pay all his expenses, and guarantee the $3,000 honorarium for which Bartók was asking.'[15] In fact, it seems that Bartók had been involved in discussions with the Baldwin Company as early as December 1926 and had received more detailed correspondence from them on 17 April 1927; Downes also notes in his review that Bartók was due to play the concerto in the USA during the following winter. He most certainly met Murray at Frankfurt, for he contacted József Szigeti from Davos (where Ditta was being treated for tuberculosis at the Sanatorium Guardaval) on 7 August to tell him that Murray had offered a Sonata evening concert in New York. After the tour of America was completed, Bartók wrote to Balogh to thank him with great warmth for his hospitality in New York. But he also complained to him that 'either I didn't command the respect in America that I deserved, or the financial aspect of the matter had been poorly handled', noting that 'even someone like [Alexandre] Tansman made more money than I did'.[16] Such comments would surely seem more than a little insensitive (and very different in tone to the rest of the letter) if Bartók believed that Balogh really had played a major role in establishing the tour and its financial conditions.

A fortnight after the premiere of the First Piano Concerto, on 16 July, Bartók performed his Piano Sonata at the Deutsches Kammermusikfest in Baden Baden. In the following month, seeing his concert career bearing fruit through the forthcoming tour of America and his other European work, it is clear that he was starting to consider whether he might be able to afford to abandon piano teaching. In September, on his return to Budapest, he wrote to his mother about his intention to retire from the Academy after more than twenty years of service there. In reality this retirement proved to be temporary and within a year he had returned to his role in the Academy, finding himself again involved in an activity that he largely regarded as a drudge.

A first fruit of this period of withdrawal from the Academy was the two-movement Third String Quartet, composed in September 1927. In a similar approach to the Second Violin Sonata, this invokes the *lassú-friss verbunkos* model in which a moderately slow *prima parte* is linked directly to a brisk *seconda parte*, followed by a *ricapitulazione della prima parte* and closing with an Allegro molto coda that is closely related to the *seconda parte*.

Although the tonic of the quartet is notionally C♯, this is rarely expressed in a conventional tonal sense and sections that are virtually atonal are placed in tension with more overtly modal ones. In the svelte and almost waltz-like opening idea (Fig. 36), for instance, the symmetrically disposed chord sustaining $C\sharp_3–D_4–E_4–D\sharp_5$ supports a melodic line in the first violin that is drawn from the remaining eight pitches of chromatic space (though their pitch notation alludes to the tonic C♯). In contrast, the reprise of the first part of the A section of the ternary form *prima parte* (bar 87) places the tonic and dominant (C♯ and G♯) beneath a passage based entirely on the pentatonically related pitches C–D–E–G–A.

Each of the main divisions of the ternary form *prima parte* is constructed from two subsections of unequal length. In the first, which finishes in the bar before rehearsal number 2, the muted cantabile of the principal idea has a

Figure 36. The opening idea of the Third String Quartet.

rhythmic contour of three short syllables and a long one that could be conceptualised in terms of the Greek metrical foot called the *paeon* (˘˘˘ -). This is
succeeded by a gesture that outlines a rising fourth and falling third (G–C–A),
and the pentatonic potential of this figure is explored in the course of the
section. The tranquil second subsection picks up the *paeon* metre in a variant
of the opening melody a minor sixth lower; and when the three-note figure
reappears in the bar before rehearsal number 3, it is now based on the entirely
pentatonic set of pitches C♯–D♯–F♯–G♯–A♯, divided between the viola and first
violin and accompanied by three pitches from a complementary pentatonic set
(G–A–D) in the cello and second violin.

In the first part of the B section, Bartók places similarly complementary
pentatonic ostinati in the muted viola and cello, which insinuate a 'dragging'
sensation. Above these the violins play fragmentary and ghostly little gestures
*sul ponticello* that evoke the composer's 'night music' style. The music opens
out from rehearsal number 6 with overlapping cantabile phrases that are fundamentally pentatonic in constitution. The section then moves to the first climax,
culminating on a chord of C♯–G♯–D–A–E, a kind of distorted pentatonic
collection that combines two of the competing tonal areas of the movement.
For the second part of the section, Bartók returns to the *paeon* metre in a
phrase that is built on the pitches E–B♭–F–E♭ and passes around the quartet in
a stretto passage involving a falling cycle of perfect fourths.

As already remarked, the reprise of the A section summarises and clarifies
its material, placing together the C♯ tonic and what can be understood to be
the altered dominant of G. Indeed, the two phrases from rehearsal number 13
present a kind of large-scale pseudo-perfect cadence from the four-bar oscilla-
tion founded on G to the composite C♯/G that follows, the final three bars
revisiting the *paeon* metre of the opening melodic idea.

The *seconda parte* is a lively Allegro that follows without a break and can alternatively be read as a kind of truncated sonata form or as a rondo in which two
main elements alternate. Under a trilled D/E♭ in the first violin, the cello presents

a three-phrase melody in the Dorian mode on D that rises and falls in stepwise motion, extending the by now familiar *paeon* metre and playing in pizzicato open-voiced triads (Fig. 37a). The relationship between D and E♭ established by the opening trill (and encapsulated in the quartet's initiating gesture) is pivotal to the movement's tonal organisation. Little flurries in the Dorian mode on E♭ played by the first violin are interjected between renditions of the cello melody, pre-empting the contrasting (if closely connected) idea in the same modality in the first violin from rehearsal number 3 (Fig. 37b). While clearly related to the brack-eted section of Figure 37a, this new material is metrically irregular (initially switching between 5/8 and 3/8 before introducing 2/4, 6/8 and 3/4), and it has a more 'circular' melodic configuration than the cello theme, entailing a wave-like contour culminating on repeated E♭s. Beneath this, the cello alludes to its opening idea in an ever-rising line of pizzicato triads while the second violin and viola reinforce the D/E♭ polarity.

The opening paragraph of the movement (up to bar 74) focuses predomi-nantly on the second of these two ideas, inverting it at bar 40 and restoring its original orientation at bar 56. Bartók introduces a third idea at bar 75, which is closely aligned to the first two, in the familiar Lydian/Phrygian polymode (or acoustic scale) on A♭. Stamped out by the cello, chiefly using heavy downbows, this dominates the second paragraph.

The second major phase of the movement commences at bar 182 on E♭ (a pitch incessantly reiterated over the subsequent twenty-eight bars) with the combination and development of the second and third ideas; and for the fugato passage from bar 242, pairs of instruments (one arco, one pizzicato) join together to play the subject, which is itself a derivative of the original cello

Figure 37.  The three principal ideas of the *seconda parte* of the Third String Quartet.

theme. With the explicit return of the cello's theme in counterpoint with a version of the fugato subject at bar 284, and the third idea at bar 301 (whose interval structure becomes highly compressed from bar 316), the *seconda parte* works to its conclusion through smearing glissandi and rebarbative punctuating chords.

Bartók's formal innovation at this juncture is a highly modified reprise of the *prima parte* that picks up the open intervals from rehearsal number 6 of the earlier section in the cello in a sustained and serene duet with the viola. For much of the course of this 'movement' the approach to recapitulation is allusive rather than direct. Thus, from rehearsal number 3 of the *ricapitulazione* an idea is passed from the cello to the first violin, which recalls the various pentatonic phrases of the first part without explicitly restating them. The most unambiguous act of reprise arises in the final seven bars of the section, where there reappear the overlapping chains of figures involving a rising minor third and falling diminished octave originally heard from the upbeat to rehearsal number 11.

The ensuing Allegro molto coda effectively functions as a recapitulation of the *seconda parte*. It begins in what appears to be a kind of C minor with a series of *sul ponticello* stretto entries founded on the second idea (Fig. 37b). This soon gives way to a variant of the metrically irregular version on A that initially appeared at rehearsal number 5, and this is increasingly disrupted by the falling four-note figure E♭–D–C–B. The polarity between E♭ and D is revisited at rehearsal number 10 through the staggered pairs of rising octatonic scales founded on these pitches, and the third idea is performed powerfully by viola and cello in C♯. The conclusive return to the tonic C♯ is preceded by a pseudo-dominant chord on G♯ that includes the pitches G♯–A–D–F–G. The tonic itself, when it appears in the last five bars, is built from stacked perfect fifths (C♯–G♯–D♯–A♯), avoiding the conventional major/minor implications of common-practice tonality.

Not only is the Third String Quartet striking for its formal and tonal novelty, but also for its textural originality and its employment of a broad range of string techniques. These include harmonics; *sul ponticello, sul tastiera* and *col legno* bowing; multiple stopping (arco and pizzicato); extreme vibrato; and a variety of on- and off-the-string articulations. Some of these suggest the influence of the performance practices of traditional musicians, as indeed do aspects of the material itself. However, in line with Violin Sonatas Nos. 1 and 2, these are secondary to the musical integrity of the material in one of Bartók's most radical and modernist scores.

Bartók was busy as a performer during the autumn of 1927, including a BBC radio broadcast in London on 10 October comprising the Two Portraits, the Dance Suite and the First Piano Concerto accompanied by the Wireless Symphony Orchestra conducted by Edward Clark. Bartók subsequently played in Dessau, Prague, Warsaw, Budapest, Stuttgart and Munich, but it would be his first trip to America in mid-winter that would be of the greatest significance. On Monday 19 December 1927 *The New York Times* announced that Bartók had arrived in the United States the previous day, having set sail eight days earlier from Cherbourg on board the liner SS *Columbus*, the flagship of the Norddeutscher Lloyd line. The brief newspaper piece noted that he had largely been confined to his cabin as a result of seasickness that persisted for the first two days of the voyage. His first pair of concerts, with the New York Philharmonic Orchestra conducted by Willem Mengelberg at Carnegie Hall, was due on the following Thursday and Friday, and he was originally scheduled to perform his First Piano Concerto. However, a brief notice published in *The New York Times* on the Thursday indicated that instead Bartók would play the Rhapsody for his début. The American premiere of the Concerto would take place on 3 January 1928 with the Philadelphia Orchestra, Mengelberg seemingly having had insufficient rehearsal time to prepare the difficult piece properly.

Bartók's début appears to have been only a partial success. In his review of the first concert in *The New York Times* on Friday 23 December, Olin Downes registered some disappointment, for the Rhapsody, he felt, did not fairly represent the musical talent of the composer. The work was played again with the Philadelphia Orchestra under its guest conductor, Bartók's Hungarian compatriot Fritz Reiner. A week later, on his return to New York, the composer accompanied Jelly d'Arányi in a performance of the Second Violin Sonata on New Year's Day 1928, a concert which she had taken over from József Szigeti (at no fee). Two months of intensive concertising and touring ensued, taking the composer as far as Los Angeles on the west coast and thence to San Francisco, Seattle and Portland (Oregon). While staying in Seattle, on 18 January, he wrote about his experiences in the city to his mother, aunt and sister. By this stage he was already getting frustrated with the tedium of endless travelling and sitting around, which while not tiring in itself, made it 'impossible to get into the mood for creative work'.[17] A highlight of his time in the city was the opportunity to attend the Chinese theatre, where he 'was the only white man there apart from one attendant'. His recitals were relatively brief and undemanding, prefaced by a 'ten-minute address' in English, and including works such as the Suite op. 14, the Piano Sonata, and some of the shorter pieces (of which 'Bear dance' proved the most popular); he also played some of Kodály's piano works.

A forty-eight-hour train journey from Portland took him to Denver (Colorado), continuing to Kansas City (Missouri) and St Paul (Minnesota) before arriving in Cincinnati on 27 January. Bartók stayed here for five days to rehearse the First Piano Concerto with Reiner and the Cincinnati Symphony Orchestra. Finally, after several further solo and duet recitals, the time came for the US premiere of the Concerto, on 13 February at Carnegie Hall with the Cincinnati Symphony under Reiner. Downes contrasted the Concerto with the Rhapsody in his review in *The New York Times* the next day, hearing in the concerto 'the impress of post-war feeling in art, being stark and astringent in its manner, antiromantic and spare of ideas. These ideas are juggled with a kind of futile energy and gloom.' He did not regard it as being among the finest of the composer's works, however, observing that 'like too many other composers, his invention seems to flag as his mastery of technic [sic] grows. . . . He has become manneristic.'

The critical responses to the performances with Serge Koussevitzky in Boston (17 and 18 February) and Reiner in Cincinnati (24 and 25 February) were undoubtedly variable in tone, and Nicolas Slonimsky has published several of the most negative and vitriolic reviews in his *Lexicon of Musical Invective*.[18] These cannot be regarded as being entirely representative, however, as the review by Paul Rosenfeld (PR) in the *Daily Boston Globe* on 18 February demonstrates.[19] Rosenfeld (a significant supporter of contemporary music) pronounced the concerto as 'original and powerful' and 'one of the most interesting and important new works presented here in recent seasons', remarking that:

> The texture of Bartok's music is coherent. Its emotional and dramatic power comes largely from his mastery of the architecture of music. He builds up his piece measure by measure, page by page, always with the whole composition in mind. He writes with the sincerity, authority and imaginative power of a master, not with the perverse freakishness of the clever youth seeking to startle the conventional bourgeois listener.

Rosenfeld was particularly impressed with Bartók's ability to integrate the piano and orchestra, whereby he succeeded in overcoming this fundamental problem of concerto writing. In a pen-portrait of the composer Rosenfeld describes him as 'a small, delicately-built man, with finely modelled features, [who] has not a trace of the vanity and ostentation of the usual virtuoso pianist. His quiet self-possession and the extraordinary skill with which he played were noteworthy.'

It was fortuitous, perhaps, that while Bartók set out for the New World aboard the *Columbus*, he returned from his American tour, on 29 February 1928, on board a vessel named after one of the country's founding fathers, the

SS *George Washington*. Bound for Cherbourg, the liner docked on 8 March and Bartók finally reached home in Budapest a couple of days later. Despite the length of the tour and return journey, his concert activities continued apace, and he gave the Budapest premiere of the Piano Concerto with the Philharmonic conducted by Dohnányi soon after, on 19 March. It was, in his estimation, a first-rate performance. Further presentations of the work that followed included one in Cologne on 27 March with the Gürzenich Orchestra conducted by its Kapellmeister, Hermann Abendroth; and in Berlin on 20 April at the Kroll Opera House, conducted by Erich Kleiber, a musician whom Bartók described to Ditta as being excellent, both very clever and cheerful.[20] At the same time, Bartók continued to perform in solo recitals and radio broadcasts, including his own works and those of Kodály.

After this intense period of performance activity, in early June the Bartóks moved from their apartment on Szilágyi Dezső tér near the banks of the Danube, uphill and further north in Buda to 10 Kavics utca, roughly in line with Margitsziget. In this rather more tranquil part of the city he started work in July on his Fourth String Quartet, a work that he would later dedicate to the Belgian Pro Arte Quartet at their request. An early manifestation of Bartók's so-called arch form, its five movements are symmetrically disposed such that the first and fifth, and second and fourth, are closely related to each other, with a central slow movement. He adopts explicit organic imagery in his description of this structure, remarking that 'around the kernel (Movement III), metaphorically speaking, I and V are the outer, II and V the inner layers'[21] In fact, as László Somfai has noted, the sketches demonstrate that this *locus classicus* of the idiosyncratic Bartókian structural solution was something of an afterthought, as the fourth movement appears to have been drafted only after the other four were composed.[22]

Notionally 'in' C, the score manifests the most extreme and condensed development of Bartók's tonal language thus far, though his own analysis of the quartet stresses the more conservative aspects, describing the first movement in terms of sonata form and the other four as types of ternary structures.

The first movement and finale are directly connected through the transitional idea exposed from bar 15 of the opening Allegro (Fig. 38b), which becomes the principal theme of the last movement; and by the chromatic figure initially played by the cello in bar 7, which reappears in the middle section of the finale.

In the opening idea of the sonata-form first movement, comprising a pair of balancing two-bar phrases, the quartet's notional tonic of C is presented in a fully chromatic milieu. Bartók perhaps comes closer to an atonal approach here than ever before in his output. The melodic line in the first violin subtly

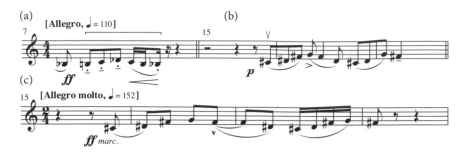

Figure 38. Fourth String Quartet (a) ritornello' motif from the first movement; (b) also from the first movement (c) the first bars of the principal theme from the finale.

weaves around the tonic, its arpeggiated descent in the second bar describing the pitches of major and minor tonic triads as the so-called major-minor chord $(E_5-[D]-C_5-G_4-E\flat_4)$. The following part of the theme reverses the direction of the first violin's closing C–D–E♭, piling up stretto entries, each a semitone higher than the previous one, with a little chromatic punctuating motif (Fig. 38a) in the cello that takes on an increasingly influential role in the course of the movement, functioning almost as a ritornello. It is this idea that brings the first thematic area to its close, in a canon at the octave by inversion played across the ensemble, an early manifestation in the quartet of Bartók's application of strict contrapuntal techniques.

The composer describes the passage from bars 14–29 as 'transitory', though rather than overtly involving conventional modulatory tactics, it builds up a largely static, if densely chromatic, texture through a succession of overlapping ostinati, each in its own distinct tonal/harmonic area. An underpinning figure employs the pitches C–D–E, first in the viola from bar 14 and then in the cello from the upbeat to bar 19. It is in the second bar of this passage that the cyclic theme makes its first appearance, involving a 'black note' pentatonic pattern surmounted by a semitone (C♯–D♯–F♯–G), a set of pitches that in Elliott Carter's usage is defined as an 'all interval tetrachord', embracing every possible interval.[23] The punctuating figure from the first subject, now in an even more dissonant version with each strand of the canon by inversion doubled a major ninth apart, brings the section to its close, leading to the A♭ that appears to be the tonic of the second theme.

Bartók makes every effort to connect each element of the movement thematically. The rhythmically vital and strongly syncopated second subject begins with the descending chromatic anapaest extracted from the 'ritornello' motif. Whole-tone and chromatic passages are placed in succession, or superimposed (from bar 40), and the theme generates overall a rather more 'open' feel than much of the preceding material. The multiple-stopped chords played in canon by the upper and lower pairs of instruments in bars 37–9, and the development of the ritornello figure played from the codetta beginning at the upbeat to bar 44, both seem to evoke the spirit of Stravinsky and in particular the violin writing in *The Soldier's Tale*.

The development section (49–93) is dominated by the all-interval tetrachord idea from the transition, played in canon by inversion by the viola and cello against harmonically static figures in the violins that could be imagined to simulate fingered rolls on the Arab darbuka. From bar 65 the four-note pattern extends to a composite melody by initially overlapping parallel tetrachordal segments (F♯–G♯–B–C/C–D–F–G♭). From bar 72 the violins present a distilled, three-note version of the figure, passing it through most of a cycle of fifths (F♯–B–E–A–D–G–C–F–B♭–E♭) that zig-zags downwards, the rhythmic thrumming continuing underneath in the cello. At the climax of the section, prefaced and surrounded by glissandi in all four instruments, Hungarian iambic rhythms ricochet around the ensemble, and the development closes with the cross-cutting of the fingered-roll figure and ritornello motif, which takes on an almost triumphant aspect at the junction with the recapitulation.

The overall sequence of events in the recapitulation mirrors the exposition, though somewhat truncated and with the melody of the second subject, from bar 119, moving into the cello, apparently in the tonality of B. In the coda, from bar 126, the ritornello motif is further developed and a figure that rises by minor and major thirds gradually emerges, by bars 147–8 traversing the pitches G♯–B–D♯–F♯–A–C–E♭–G. The modal ambiguity of the movement is maintained in the final permutation of the motif crossing the penultimate bar line (D–E♭–F/E♭–D♭–C), which brings together Gypsy and Phrygian modes, and a pseudo V–I cadence in C.

The Prestissimo con sordino movement that follows is a fleet-of-foot Scherzo and Trio in 6/8 in the tonality of E. Its opening nine-bar melody in the cello and viola involves a chromatically rising and falling wave-like idea whose tessitura becomes progressively attenuated as it is repeated. This is restated by the violins a perfect fifth higher and soon a second idea based on a turn-like figure (G♯–G♯–A–A♯–C–B) appears and is picked up in canon, each voice playing a tone lower (from bar 27). Before the canonic repeat of the opening idea on E, Bartók's penchant for symmetrical figures comes to the fore, with the major seventh between A and G♯ in the cello and first violin opening outwards with stacked perfect fourths and then infilled, resulting at bar 51 in an eight-note chord of B–E–A–D/E♭–G♯–C♯–F♯.

Bartók regarded the passage at bars 62–77, which ends with the chromatic polymetric ostinati in viola and cello covering the pitches between B♭ and D♭, as being 'transitional' in function. In the duet between the two violins that lies above this, the instruments decorate the inception of longer notes with chromatic figurations that surround them, and by bar 102 this has become what might be described as textural music, prefiguring the much later developments of composers such as Ligeti and Penderecki. Upwardly rising glissandi from bar 136 step up through whole-tone patterns and then work back down to their starting point of C, while a patchwork of scale segments lead to a canonic passage built on the symmetrical set of pitches D♯–F♯–G♯–A–B–D.

The reprise of the Scherzo is handled freely and introduces a degree of symmetry such that the material from bar 175 is closely related to that from bar 45 in the first part, though now transposed by a diminished fifth. When the main theme is recapitulated by the viola from bar 189 in the tonality of E, it is subtly varied in its configuration, and a series of entries follow in the first violin from B (bar 194), in the second violin from F♯ (bar 198), and in the cello and viola from A♯ and E respectively (bar 205). Supporting a final set of entries of a highly distilled version of the theme in the tonic by the upper three instruments, the cello slides up pizzicato triple-stopped fifth-based chords that chromatically glissando up a semitone, a brief polymetric moment that perhaps alludes to folk practice. Much of the final section of the coda (bars 223–50) is formed from the pitches of an octatonic scale on D (D–E–F–G–G♯–A♯–B–C♯) repeatedly played by the viola, acting as a surrogate dominant, and in the final cadence, glissandi sweep up the pattern F–G–A–B–E while the cello plays fifths chords founded on B, G and D, collectively implying a Phrygian E mode. Characteristically, the final chord (E–B–F♯ in the cello and E in the other instruments) is modally ambiguous.

As already noted, Bartók described the ternary-form central movement, marked *non troppo lento*, as forming the kernel of the quartet. With a tonal centre of A, it presents aspects both of the Romanian *hora lungă* and of his 'night music', and begins with a symmetrically disposed chord based on the pitches A–B–C♯/E–F♯–G♯ that is played initially without vibrato as it builds downward note by note, and then with vibrato as a chord. This shift between inexpressive and warm styles of playing continues to be a colouristic resource throughout the movement. At the centre of the chord the cello ululates around the D that completes the pitches of an A major scale in a manner that suggests lamentation. Gradually the cello works its way down to a cadential $A_2$–$E_2$ at bar 13 and the upper voices intone a new chord of G–C♯–D–E–G♯–A. The focus of the cello line now moves to $F_4$ and a further process of descent leads at bar 22 to the third sustained chord, on F–C–D–E–G♯–B♭ (whose upper five pitches are related through the whole-tone scale). Now the cello moves above the rest of the quartet to B$_4$, and this forms the focal point for the third phase of the section and the most impassioned and rhapsodic outpouring.

The subsequent subsection adopts the 'night music' style, the first violin playing rapid repeated notes and elaborately leaping figures – the stylised chirruping of birds, frogs or crickets, against a non-diatonic chord (C–B♭–D–E–G–C♯). After a brief agitated interlude that places the second violin into the spotlight, the music works its way back to the reprise of the A section through a chromatic passage that superimposes black-note pentatonicism in the first violin and cello over white-note diatonicism in the viola and then the second violin. The tranquil reprise (from bar 55) is quite different in tone and disposition to the opening, the expressive contrapuntal dialogue by inversion between cello and first violin being based on the final thoughts of the cello in the first section and articulating the set of pitches that formed the opening chord. A brief reminiscence of the night music leads to the restoration of the opening chord, now revoiced and fading into silence on a high D in the first violin as the individual pitches drop out.

As the tempo marking of the fourth movement (Allegretto pizzicato) suggests, strings are plucked throughout its course. As well as employing strummed (both downward and upward) and tremolo techniques that suggest other plucked chordophones drawn from the composer's fieldwork experience, so-called Bartók pizzicato are notated, in which a strong attack causes the string to rebound from the fingerboard with a distinct percussive slap. In essence, this movement reconstitutes the thematic material of the second movement (now based on A♭), and for the first section employs a process of interval expansion by which what originally encompassed a perfect fifth now covers an octave. This opening part is somewhat different in its detail, and effectively involves four entries of the subject moving through a sequence of perfect fifths on A♭, E♭, B♭ and F (the latter shadowed by a version on E♭), and a short canonic transition into the middle section. The two parts of the Trio (45–64 and 65–77) are quite closely aligned to the equivalent sections of the second movement, and a short transitional passage steers back to an abridged restatement of the A section. Finally, in the short codetta beginning at bar 102 the inversion of the main subject is presented canonically and then against its original orientation, and the work ends on an eleven-note chord (with nine distinct pitches) founded on the tonic A♭.

The finale (Allegro molto) returns to the overall tonic of C and presents the metamorphosis of ideas from the first movement to a fully fledged form. A ternary-form movement, the opening A section roughly divides into three parts whose tonal centres are C, A and F♯ respectively. The C tonality is established via percussive chords that spice the tonic and dominant pitches (C and G) with the addition of neighbour notes to a C major triad (F♯, D♭ and F). An additive rhythm develops in the cello and viola through 3+3+2 quaver patterns that traverse the bar lines. This accompanies a version of the transitional theme from the first movement, transformed into a 'folk' theme in four phrases whose total pitch content (C–C♯–D♯–F♯–G–G♯) is redolent of Bartók's discoveries in Arab music. From bars 47–74 the tune is stretched out to an octatonic melody (A–A♯–B♯–C♯–D♯–E–F♯–G) and this mode underlies the third phase of exposition at bars 76–151.

In the central episode, Bartók returns to another element of the first movement, the *cantabile* idea played by the first violin between bars 40 and 43. Now tonally reoriented and slightly adjusted in melodic configuration, the idea takes on a graceful if rather quirky persona. It is at first cross-cut with, then subsequently developed and superimposed on, the 'ritornello' motif as it moves towards the reprise of the principal section at bar 238.

Here Bartók picks up the opening material of the movement and after a version that is punctuated by repeated chords, offers a new 'open' variant based on the pitches A♯–[C♯–D♯–F♯–G]–A–C–D–E–F, that extends the white- and black- note pentatonic implications of the original idea (shown in square brackets).[24] The final few bars of a coda from bar 365 return to the equivalent point in the first movement and the terminal gestures almost literally repeat its cadential figure.

Although the Fourth String Quartet undoubtedly draws on influences from traditional music, these are secondary rather than primary musical components. A further work written in the summer of 1928, the *I Rapszódia* (First Rhapsody for violin and piano), dedicated to József Szigeti, is overtly composed from six tunes in Bartók's Romanian collection. He would make later arrangements of the piece for both violin and orchestra and for cello and piano, and it is a matter of interest that he should self-consciously adopt both the title and the two-part (*lassú – friss*) structure of the popular genre. He was, of course, looking to a rural rather than an urban manifestation of *verbunkos*. His individual instrumental sources included performances by the twenty-two-year-old violinist Ion Popovici from Râpa-de-Sus in April 1914 (the first and last tunes, *de ciuit* and *cuieşdeanca – joc fecioresc*); by the sixty-year-old Pătru Moş in December 1912 (the middle pair of melodies, *judecata* and *crucea*); by a certain János Balog, collected by Béla Vikár in March 1900 (the second tune, *árvátfalvi kesergő*); and by an anonymous forty-year-old Gypsy and his son in December 1912 (the penultimate dance melody, *pre loc*).

Bartók explicitly permitted the two sections of the Rhapsody to be considered as separate pieces and played independently, and they are structured as discrete entities. The *lassú* is a ternary-form movement in G major employing the first two tunes with a straightforward tonal accompaniment and little of the wayward tempo, sentimentality or quixotic character of the urban Gypsy band. The *friss* exists in two versions: the first – to be played when the complete Rhapsody is performed – begins the chain of melodies in E, and concludes with a reprise of the opening tune of the *lassú* restored to the work's overall tonic of G; the second (for the stand-alone version) finishes in E, employing a varied restatement of the *judecata* tune that opened the movement.

In October 1929 Bartók discovered that he had been awarded the substantial sum of $6,000 as the joint first-prize winner (with Alfredo Casella) of the Music Fund Society of Philadelphia competition, into which he had entered the Third String Quartet; as a mark of his gratitude he dedicated it to the society. He wrote to Reiner with some excitement in late October to thank him for his congratulations and remarked that he had completed his Fourth String Quartet, 'a much longer one this time', and queried drolly whether there might be any other competitions anywhere.[25] At roughly the same time, he wrote to Szigeti to tell him that he'd 'written a minor (12-minute) composition for [him] (based on folk dances)' and wished to discuss it with him. Strangely, the First Rhapsody actually lasts only nine and a half minutes in the complete version, whereas the Second Rhapsody (dedicated to Zoltán Székely), which was also composed in 1928, is of twelve minutes' duration. According to Székely, Bartók had already completed both of the rhapsodies in the late summer of 1928, and at a dinner party at Bartók's home, the composer had shown him the manuscripts for the two pieces and asked him to pick which he would prefer to be dedicated to him. Székely records that 'I happened to choose the Second Rhapsody because I preferred it, but that doesn't mean that the First Rhapsody was already dedicated to Szigeti. On the contrary, these works were not written specifically for a specific person.'[26] Whatever the case, Szigeti was clearly very proud of his dedication, for on every occasion on which he mentions it in his biography, *With Strings Attached*, he comments that it was written specially for him.

While the Second Rhapsody (in D) has tended to be the less popular of the pair, it involves a greater number of Romanian source tunes (ten) and is arguably the more technically demanding and complex in structure. For the *lassú* section, which is similar in character to the equivalent part of the First Rhapsody, three tunes that were collected in April 1914 are connected in an ABACA structure in a modal D minor: the first (*românie*) taken from a pair of gypsies, Iuon Lup and Ila Cacula; the second (*țiganeasca*) from Toma Tolofean; and the third (*'de-a sărită' joc fecioresc – körtánc*), which is close in style to the second, from Ion Popovici. Perhaps the most striking moment is at the first reprise of the opening melody, when the accompaniment rests on C♯–G♯, a semitone below the prevailing D minor tonality, suggesting that the solo violin has been transported into an alien landscape.

All but two of the seven tunes that follow each other sequentially in the cheerful *friss* section were originally collected in 1912 (the final pair being transcribed early in 1913), and five were taken from unnamed gypsy musicians. As is so often the case with his arrangements, Bartók selects tunes with related motifs or other characteristics that permit a logical musical ordering. Thus, the regular reiteration of a falling major seventh in the slightly tipsy-sounding first tune is also a feature of the second; the Lydian characteristics of the second tune are apparent in the third; and the latter's employment of a melodic 3–2–1–5 pattern finds a correlation in the brilliant fourth, which functions rather like a filmic dissolve. Underpinned harmonically by an octa-tonic segment (B–C♯–D–E–F) that alternates with a lower B minor pentachord after seven bars, this is somewhat redolent of the Stravinsky of *The Firebird*.

For the muscular and ebullient fifth melody, Bartók turns to a Ruthenian dance tune (*uvevanŷi*) collected from Szeklence in Máramaros County, the musical features of which (such as the prominent Lydian fourth and the offbeat quavers) are again consistent with earlier settings in the Rhapsody. The final two dances retain the festive mood, providing something of a coda to the proceedings with a brief passage of pizzicato quadruple stopping from the solo violin from rehearsal number 36, perhaps suggesting the *cobza* (a kind of lute) or guitar. The piece runs to its end in great good humour, but again without the histrionics of the popular style of the urban gypsy.

Bartók subsequently created orchestral arrangements of the piano accompaniments, which were published by Universal Edition in 1931. In this form they provided performers such as Székely and Szigeti with attractive concert works that represented the mature composer but were written in an accessible language. They also illustrated his re-accommodation and recon-struction of the prototypical Hungarian nationalist form of the rhapsody, employing what was now considered Romanian music (though when he collected it, Transylvania still lay within the borders of Hungary). Placing them next to the Rhapsody for piano and orchestra, which until recently had been a mainstay of Bartók's symphonic appearances, demonstrates the distance he had travelled, both musically and socio-politically, from his youthful chauvinistic enthusiasms.

Towards the end of 1928, Bartók was able to give the Piano Concerto a further series of airings, this time with the French conductor Pierre Monteux, who had collaborated with Stravinsky and Diaghilev in the premiere of *The Rite of Spring*, and was now the 'first conductor' of the Amsterdam Concertgebouw Orchestra alongside its long-term chief conductor Mengelberg.[27] The concerts in Amsterdam and The Hague took place on 9 and 10 November, and the composer was impressed with Monteux' skill and quickness of understanding.

The December 1928 edition of *The Musical Times* includes a review of the concerts in its 'Musical Notes from Abroad' section, in which the Yorkshire-born critic Herbert Antcliffe remarks:

> The Mengelberg concerts, under Monteux, are continuing in an even manner their high standard of performance. Béla Bartók has played his Concerto at these concerts at Amsterdam, The Hague, and Rotterdam, and has aroused alternate admiration, perplexity, and despair among the different classes of his audiences. His playing and personality in every case, whatever the opinion may have been of his music, have been exceedingly popular.[28]

In the same edition of this journal, a brief article based on an interview with Bartók appeared under the headline 'The National Temperament in Music'. Here the composer summarised his thoughts on the philosophy surrounding the approach that he and Kodály had taken to the collection of folk material:

> To get the right idea of national temperament we never looked for melodies written down or printed because, in general, we considered them to be dead material. To enter the true vibrating life of popular music by means of these tunes is an impossibility. Whosoever desires to enjoy the charms of genuine popular music must get into immediate contact with the peasants. And it is of equal importance to get acquainted with the surroundings from whence these tunes have sprung. It is necessary to see the peasant's mimicry, to be present at his dances, wedding festivities, Christmas celebrations, funeral ceremonies, because every occasion brings forth its special melodies which most advantageously reflect the national temperament. We wanted to feel the true spirit of this hitherto unknown music, and in conformity with this spirit – hard to express in words – we intended to create our own musical style. Therefore we betook ourselves to the original source of music – the soul of the peasantry.
>
> According to my conviction, the popular tune – using the term in a restricted sense – which shows the national temperament in its entirety, is a paragon of the highest musical perfection. In its limited scope I consider it as much a masterpiece as – in the world of larger scales – a fugue by Bach or a sonata by Mozart. Such a melody is a classical example of the infinitely condensed expression of a musical thought. It is true that such laconicism only seldom makes an impression upon the average musician. But the average musician regards as more important such accessories as accompaniment, development, &c., and is rarely able to appreciate fully the fundamental essence.[29]

Noting his own use of material from other regions – Slovak, Romanian and north African – Bartók's concluding comment is that 'internationalism is not only unimaginable but also injurious to music and to every other art'.

The decade that had passed since the Aster Revolution had seen substantial changes in Bartók's status, both as a composer and as a pianist. While in 1919 he was generally regarded as a Hungarian musician placed somewhat on the periphery of the European stage, by 1928 he had achieved considerable international celebrity and his music (although often admired and reviled in equal measure) was being performed in many of the major cities of the old and new worlds, by some of the greatest orchestras directed by major conductors. Similarly, his career as a solo pianist, both on the concert platform and through radio broadcasts, had blossomed, and he was increasingly receiving critical plaudits (as Antcliffe's review illustrates). Although his active collection of folk music had been largely put into abeyance because of the adverse circumstances, Bartók was ordering, cataloguing and preparing for publication the vast fruits of his earlier labours, and they was playing an ever more sophisticated role in his musical language. It was as a piano teacher that matters had changed least. While he had taken periods of furlough from the Academy of Music and undertaken significant concert tours, he had not managed to sever entirely his ties from an activity that in the main he regarded as a chore.

In the subsequent ten years leading up to the outbreak of the Second World War, Bartók would compose many of his masterworks, including String Quartets Nos. 5 and 6, the *Cantata Profana*, the Second Violin and Piano Concertos, the Music for Strings, Percussion and Celesta, the Sonata for Two Pianos and Percussion, *Contrasts* and the *Divertimento*. The foundations for these works, in which the composer would increasingly withdraw from the more radical position taken in the middle pair of quartets and the violin sonatas, were now firmly in place.

## CHAPTER NINE

# 'The wreath is wound around me': 1929–1935

In early 1919 Bartók had been involved, albeit in a minor way, in the Communist regime that took power in Hungary. Now, ten years later, in January 1929, he finally visited the Soviet Union for a solo concert tour that included Kharkov and Odessa in the Ukraine, and Leningrad and Moscow in Russia. The irony of the fact that he had been in Los Angeles just a year prior to this trip, where the average temperatures had been nearly thirty degrees Celsius higher, was not lost on him, though he didn't find the conditions in the Soviet Union particularly unpleasant in spite of the thermometer reading ten degrees below zero. Indeed he deemed the cityscape of Moscow attractive, describing to Ditta 'the roofs loaded with snow, so that they seem ready to cave in, and little one-horse sledges tinkling everywhere'; and he cited Maupassant's advice that the best time to visit the city was during the winter, for 'it is then that the country is at its most characteristic'.[1]

Despite, or perhaps even partly because of, the difficulties he faced, which included errors in the organisation of the tour resulting in the cancellation of a concert in Kiev, Bartók seems to have enjoyed the experience overall and was favourably disposed to many of the people he came across. The audience in Kharkov was enthusiastic and while in the city he had the opportunity to attend a performance of Rossini's *The Barber of Seville*; he was impressed by the mobile Constructivist sets. He went on to perform the Piano Concerto in Leningrad with Koussevitzky's former ensemble, the Philharmonic Orchestra, conducted by Aleksandr Gauk.

Bartók's verdict was that 'life goes on quite normally, but their way of life is entirely different from ours'.[2] Writing to his mother from Vienna on 29 January, after the tour was complete, he told her just how affecting he had found the experience and how beautiful the Soviet Union was – indeed, in three weeks he felt he had seen much more of interest than in the two and a half months he had spent in America. Of course there were many negative aspects that reminded him of the very worst of times in Hungary, including constant surveillance and poor communications across the country.

On his return from the Soviet Union he performed at the Musik Akademie Basel on 30 January. The programme included his Five Songs op. 16 to texts by Endre Ady (sung by the Hungarian contralto, Ilona Durigo, who taught at the Zürich Conservatory), a number of his piano pieces (including the Suite op. 14 and the ever popular *Allegro barbaro*), and the Second Violin Sonata. The violinist on this occasion was his old flame, Stefi Geyer, who, after the death of her first husband Erwin Jung in 1920, had moved from Vienna to Switzerland and married the Swiss composer and artist manager, Walter Schulthess. Based in Zürich, she now pursued a career as a professional musician while employed as a violin teacher at the Conservatory. Their concert was repeated in the Tonhalle in Zürich the following day, and in a duo recital at the Stadthaus in Winterthur on 1 February, Bartók accompanied her in a third performance of the sonata.

Later in February he visited Copenhagen and played his early Rhapsody at the Odd Fellow Palæet on Bredgade in the centre of the city with the ad hoc orchestra of the Musikforeningen conducted by its director, Ebbe Hamerik. Bartók gave a studio radio broadcast and an evening recital, also at the Odd Fellow Palæet. A subsequent brief foray to London entailed, on 4 March, a duo recital with Zoltán Székely at the Arts Theatre Club as part of the third series of 'BBC Concerts of Contemporary Music'.[3] The programme included his Second Violin Rhapsody, which was dedicated to Székely, and he commented to Ditta on 5 March that he felt the violinist had performed it very beautifully. In his review of the private concert, *The Musical Times* critic F. B. (presumably Ferruccio Bonavia) found himself not entirely convinced, remarking that:

> It gave an impression of light without heat, and of being music which keeps the interest alive by arousing expectations. This is one side of a composer's talent. The other side is in the fulfilling of expectations he has aroused, and in this I found Bartók's music wanting.[4]

Bonavia was of the opinion that Bartók's reliance on folk sources was an impediment, enquiring of the reader 'Is there nothing to be said for the poor man who seeks to express a personal mood or impression without the help of a folk-tune?'

In the same section of this edition of *The Musical Times*, D. H. appraised the first British performance of the Third String Quartet, given by the Hungarian Quartet at the Wigmore Hall on 19 February. This report similarly made reference to the composer's employment of a 'national idiom' and noted how 'the harshness of the music seemed at times deliberate to the verge of perversity', but recalled that further study of the equally perplexing First String Quartet had 'solved the difficulties and changed doubt to unfeigned admiration'.[5] While hoping that this work might reward similar examination, the reviewer went on to observe that 'The Quartet contains, in any case, passages of such strange beauty and emotional strength that one has little doubt that its difficulties will ultimately be smoothed away, and that we shall become reconciled to its discordance'.

En route to Budapest, Bartók gave further concerts in Aachen and Karlsruhe in the Rhineland (where he played the Rhapsody again), and in Paris he took part in a 'Béla Bartók Celebration' at the Conservatoire that included the First String Quartet given by the Roth Quartet and the Second Violin Sonata performed by Szigeti. The Fourth String Quartet, his most recent essay in the genre, was premiered together with the Third String Quartet by the Waldbauer Quartet in a further excellent performance on 20 March at the Budapest Academy of Music. This intense period of concertising continued unabated throughout the spring and early summer periods, and culminated in Rome in mid-April. Here, at the Accademia Nazionale di Santa Cecilia, Bartók accompanied Szigeti once more and commented on a postcard to Ditta that 'Poor Szigeti was quite shocked because the audience was rather noisy during my [second] violin sonata. He has never experienced such a thing before, but I'm pretty hardened in this respect'.[6]

In June the couple set off for their annual summer holiday, to Montana in the Valois region of Switzerland, where Bartók was able to walk extensively and climb in the mountains in glorious weather (including scaling the 2,995-metre Mont Bonvin, having set off at 6.00 in the morning, as he excitedly described the experience to Béla junior). Meanwhile his mother Paula, who was now seventy-two years old, had permanently relocated from Pozsony to Hungary along with her sister Irma, visiting Elza in the summer and settling in an apartment in Krisztina körút in Buda in October, an area that proved much more convenient for visits from her son and daughter-in-law.

The only substantial composition to be completed by Bartók in 1929 was *Húsz magyar népdal* (Twenty Hungarian Folk Songs) for voice and piano, published by Universal Edition in 1932 in four volumes of four, four, seven and five songs, respectively. All of the source tunes appeared in Bartók's 1924 monograph *A magyar népdal*, which Calvocoressi was translating into English for Oxford University Press as *Hungarian Folk Music* (subsequently reissued as *Hungarian Folk Song* and abbreviated in the following discussion as HFS). Although the Twenty Hungarian Folk Songs is one of the composer's lesser-performed works in the anglophone world (perhaps because of the lack of an edition with an English translation), it is a remarkable set of arrangements, and testament to Bartók's absolute mastery of compositional technique and his ability to successfully synthesise traditional song and contemporary musical language. It also demonstrates his continuing employment of conventional musical codes to heighten the expressivity of his settings.

Four 'sad songs' form the first group. 'A tömlöcben' (HFS 10 – 'In Prison') is sung by a husband to his wife from his gaol cell, and its old-style melody and accompaniment recall the mood of *Bluebeard's Castle*. The implied chiming of bells as an ostinato, drawing on the tune's underlying pentatonicism, ebbs and flows over the course of the song, and staccato major second dyads in the second verse can perhaps be taken to encode the falling of the man's tears. At the end of the fourth verse, the climax is supported by a variant that is almost entirely derived from an octatonic scale (A–A♯–B♯–C♯–D♯–E–F♯–G).

In the second song, 'Régi kerserves' (HFS 214, variant text – 'Old Lament'), the protagonist sings of his (or possibly her) loneliness. Here the settings of the two verses employ contrasting approaches: in the first, sustained perfect fifths are gradually piled up while staccato pricks of sound echo a semitone lower; and in the second, the melodic line in the right hand slowly circles around $E\flat_4$, with dyads in the left gradually opening out before a brief postlude restores the opening texture.

The third song, 'Bujdosó ének' (HFS 15 – 'The Fugitive'), again concerns isolation and despair, as an escapee relates his flight through woods and vales with wild animals, and his lamentation with the small birds. Almost all of the pitches of the piano accompaniment to the first two verses and postlude are derived from the octatonic scale that appears in the first song. The fourth, 'Pásztornóta' (HFS 7b – 'Herdsman's Song'), is sung by a cowherd who sleeps in his byre and wakes up late at night to discover that his animals have all disappeared. Bartók creates an agitated and dramatic texture for the first of the three verses, the bass octave Fs and tremolo E combining with the vocal contour to suggest an F major seventh chord. This gradually shifts, the bass rising chromatically over the course of the first verse and falling through a whole-tone progression in the second. The final bars, in a kind of modified Phrygian cadence, terminate on a warm E major triad with added ninth as the singer explains that he has discovered his love, the first part of the group thus ending in a rather more positive mood.

For the second set, Bartók draws on four dance songs. The opening pair of tunes, recorded from Székely musicians in the Csík region in 1907 and 1911, are a *lassú* (HFS 294) and a *friss* (HFS 196) respectively. In combination with the following couple of brisk melodies (HFS 302 and 11b) the entire group forms a rhapsodic structure. In the Phrygian-inflected, though essentially pentatonic, song that functions as the *lassú* section, 'Azt akartam én megtudni' ('I Wanted to Find Out'), the singer enquires whether it is permissible for him to fall in love with the sweetheart of another man and is disconsolate when he is told that it is not. 'Ne busuljon komámasszony' ('Cheer up, Godmother'), which follows, is a comical drinking song, the last verse warning an old woman to be careful in case the devil drags her to hell rolled up in a buffalo skin. For much of its course, bare fifths, like the open strings on a fiddle (D–A then G–D), are reiterated as incisive staccato chords in a 3+2+3 metrical grouping, while little clusters of faster notes in an Ionic metre (⌣⌣ - -) pick out a prominent melodic figure. The brilliant 'Kanásztánc' (Swineherd's Dance) is a setting of a pentatonic melody whose narrative describes the swineherd's sow and piglets getting lost in a field of wheat. The accompaniment for the third verse isomorphically references the grunts of the pigs with percussively articulated fioriture. To complete this dance-influenced group Bartók draws on the triple hypermetre tune, 'Six forint dance', whose second and fourth melodic lines virtually span a falling octave of a Dorian mode on D. Given the character of the melody, with its strong rhythmic impulse and melodic decoration, an appropriately 'instrumental' approach is employed.

While there are no overt narrative connections to be found in the larger set of seven 'diverse' songs (all but the last being representatives of the 'miscellaneous class' of *The Hungarian Folk Song* that forms the third part of the publication), there are motivic links between a number of the tunes, particularly through figures involving the stepwise pattern 1–2–3–2–1 and a falling perfect fourth or rising perfect fifth motif. In the first, 'Juhászcsúfoló', a shepherd's song (HFS 174), it is gradually revealed that he has failed to protect his flock from the wolf, the mood becoming darker and more intense through the course of the six verses which gradually work upwards tonally from G, through A♭ and B♭ to C♯, before returning to the tonic. In the final section (a repeat of the opening verse), the tolling middle C in the left hand over a minor seventh (C♯–B) supports the recurrent chromatic rise and fall between F and G, marked *senza colore* in the piano part. Meanwhile the words 'was there ever such a shepherd?' take on ironic import.

The humorous song, 'Két krajcárom volt nékem' (HFS 312 – 'I Had Two Pennies'), has as its incipit the melodic pattern 1–2–3–1–5, and the tune is transposed through the sequence B♭–F♯–D–A–E♭–B♭ in the course of its six verses. In the piano accompaniment, thirds are transformed into a brisk ostinato pattern of twelve *non legato* dyads in the right hand for the penultimate verse, whose rotations mirror the mill wheel that grinds the wheat described in the text. A pair of connected tunes follows. 'Sárga csikó, csengő rajta' (HFS 319

– 'Yellow Foal with a Bell') is a waltz-like song that imagines the journey to Róza Kocsis's courtyard and almost looks back to Richard Strauss or Hugo Wolf in its tonal language. It begins with the arpeggiation of an A major triad in the vocal line and is accompanied by bell-like sounds in the piano. The humorous 'Virágéknál ég a világ' (HFS 265 – 'A Fire is Burning at the Virags') describes a family cooking frogs' legs, and a visitor arriving so late that only the 'back parts' remained. This song's prelude recalls aspects of the main theme of the first movement of the Piano Concerto, and in a curious little gesture at its denouement it hints at the syncopated repeated chords in 'The Augurs of Spring' from Stravinsky's *The Rite of Spring*.

There is a distinct change of mood for the subsequent two slow songs. In the poignant and heartfelt 'Pár-ének' (HFS 240 – 'Alternating'), the beginning of which inverts the opening gambit of 'Sárga csikó, csengő rajta', the husband entreats his wife not to leave him when he has grown old and she responds that she will never forsake him. In 'Panasz' (HFS 258 – 'Complaint') the protagonist reveals that his sweetheart is very ill, perhaps close to death, and wishes that he could take on some of her suffering so they might share it. A two-bar phrase alternating F♯ major and minor, with the Hungarian snap on the down beat of the first bar suggesting a stab of pain, is established as an ostinato for much of the first verse, and this iambic figure continues to feature prominently in the second stanza. 'Bordal' (HFS 74b – 'Drinking Song'), which completes the group, is a high-spirited old-style melody in a triple hypermetre in which the singer doffs his hat to his beloved wine, arguing that one should drink until carried off to the graveyard.

The final five songs of the collection are new-style tunes (titled 'Lieder der Jugend' in the German version in the Universal Edition score) with 'architectonic' forms (generally ABBA or AABA). Bartók runs them together without breaks to create a continuous musical fabric whose modal finals follow the pattern F–C–B♭–F–D. These are generally briefer than the previous songs in the set, all except the last consisting of four-line verses in which the final pair are repeated. The first, 'Hej, édesanyám, kedves édes anyám' (HFS 119 – 'Hey Mother, My Dear Mother'), is an eerie setting accompanied by tremolando octaves and a curious figure that is a compressed version of the second and third bars of the melody (the falling vocal C–B♭–A♭–G–F becomes E♮–E♭– D♭–C–B♮). In this figure the singer – apparently conscripted into the Austro-Hungarian army – asks his mother to hang his mourning clothing on the wall for the three years of his military service.[7]

The mood gradually brightens with the second, 'Érik a ropogós cseresznye' (HFS 81 – 'The Crunchy Cherries have Come'), whose opening three pitches form the basis for the ornamentation of the almost Baroque-sounding accompaniment. In 'Már Dobozon, már Dobozon' (HFS 133 – 'Long Ago Snow Started Falling in Doboz') the singer fears that her lover may have fallen from his horse and be unable to clasp her to him. The tune, which is in Phrygian B♭, prominently features one of the characteristic rhythmic gestures of Hungarian popular music in which a dotted crotchet–quaver trochee is followed by its reversal as an iamb (- ⌣⌣ -). 'Sárga kukoricaszál' (HFS 133 – 'Yellow Maize Stalk'), the penultimate tune, intimates that as long as the crop remains to be harvested, the fair boy and dark girl will remain unkissed. It has an accompaniment that opens and closes with light chords, cadencing rather conventionally in F major. Finally, 'Búza, búza, búza, de szép tábla búza' (HFS 299 – 'Wheat, Wheat, Wheat, Great Field of Wheat'), the longest of the group and a tune still very widely performed in Hungary, rounds out the entire set of songs in a positive and almost anthem-like character. In Bartók's setting of the first verse, the opening tonic Ds, played throughout as a pedal tone, set in motion a rising chromatic scale in the left hand that ascends as far as the major seventh before gradually working down against chiming C–D dyads in octaves in the right hand. In the second verse, Bartók again avoids the commonplace in terms of harmonisation, though the song ends on a very solid D major triad.

The final few months of 1929, like the early part of the year, involved intermittent broadcasts, recitals and concert performances. In November two further premieres occurred, of versions of the Rhapsodies for violin but with orchestral accompaniment. They were played by their dedicatees, Szigeti and Székely, the first Rhapsody conducted by Antal Fleischer (director of the Magyar Királyi Operaház), the second by Ernő Dohnányi. In December, Bartók performed the Piano Concerto in Bremen and Danzig, and gave solo recitals in Königsberg and Berlin, entering the fourth decade of the twentieth century as a figure of considerable celebrity and indeed notoriety, across Europe and North America, both as composer and pianist.

In Malcolm Gillies' excellent study of Bartók's association with Britain, he notes that 1930 was the year in which his visits to the country were most frequent, with three separate tours in January, February and November.[8] On the first trip he performed the First Rhapsody for Violin and the Second Violin Sonata with Szigeti, and Hungarian and Slovak songs with the mezzo-soprano Mária Basilides, at the Arts Theatre Club. The second and third of the British forays involved performances with Sir Henry Wood and the BBC Symphony Orchestra at the Queen's Hall in London, the Piano Concerto featuring in February and the Rhapsody in November. The reviewer in the March edition of *The Musical Times* was obviously unaware that Bartók had previously performed the Concerto with Clark and the Wireless Symphony Orchestra in October 1927, remarking that it 'had apparently not been heard in England before. Some English critics and others had encountered it at one of the International Festivals, and on that occasion, we are told, it came as a quiet relief to some really contemporary music.[9] Now it was placed between Brahms and Tchaikovsky, in whose company it took on a more radical aspect, and the audience was apparently courteous rather than enthusiastic in its response. Although Bartók was undoubtedly pleased by the warm reception that the Rhapsody received in November, it also proved an irritation that it was his early work, totally unrepresentative of his mature style, which still proved most successful with audiences.

At the end of January 1930, Mária Basilides and Bartók gave the premiere of the Twenty Hungarian Folk Songs at the Budapest Academy of Music. Although this would be his last large-scale work for solo voice and piano, he arranged five of the songs (in the order 1, 2, 14, 11 and 12) for voice and orchestra in 1933 as *Magyar népdalok* (Hungarian Folk Songs). Around the spring of 1930 he was working on a further set of folk-song arrangements with the Hungarian title *Magyar népdalok*, in this case for unaccompanied mixed chorus, published in English as *Four Hungarian Folksongs*.[10] Once again, the five traditional tunes (the fourth chorus is actually built from two songs) were contained within the pages of *The Hungarian Folk Song*, and four were collected very early in his career, between 1906–7 in Tolna and Csík counties and on the edge of Lake Balaton. The settings are tonal, but clearly reveal the development of his language since the set of soldiers' songs, *Tót népdalok* (Slovak Folk Songs) for a capella male voice choir, and *Négy tót népdal* (Four Slovak Folk Songs) for mixed chorus and piano, all from 1917.

Like the first of the Twenty Hungarian Folk Songs, the opening old-style parlando-rubato melody is the song of a prisoner, in this case in dialogue with his mother, asking her to beg for his release, though she cautions him that she can offer him no reassurance and believes he is certain to hang. Suffused with an air of lamentation, the four verses cycle through the minor modalities of F, C and G, before returning in the last to the tonic, the piece exhibiting considerable rhythmic and harmonic fluidity, and textural variety, in its use of the double chorus. The second, a further parlando-rubato song, but this time in the Phrygian mode, begins with the words 'Ideje bujdosásimnak' ('It is the time to wander'), and concerns itself with the depressive thoughts of the incipient traveller, for whom dark clouds cast heavy shadows across his path, sentiments that might have come from the pen of Endre Ady. Bartók again establishes a tonal pattern of modal finals, in this case traversing A–E–F♯–G♯–E. The austerity of the opening verse, which is sung in unison by the altos, almost suggests plainsong. For the rest of the song, a common feature is the use of similar motion between voices in thirds or through parallel first- or second-inversion chords.

'Adj el, anyám' ('Finding a Husband') creates a positive change of mood, with a *tempo giusto* song that tells of a daughter who threatens to leave home unless her mother will find her a husband. She rejects the suggestions of a farmhand, a swineherd, a cowherd, a field-guard, a tinker or a Jew, but agrees that a shepherd would be acceptable, for, as Calvocoressi translates it in *The Hungarian Folk Song*, 'he who watches his flock/Will be a good educator for his wife'.[11] Here the choral writing looks to earlier genres, and indeed the balance of homophony and imitative counterpoint and the free-flowing rhythm rather recall the English madrigal tradition. The jovial final piece is a ternary-form composite of two tunes – 'Sarjút eszik az ökröm' ('My Ox is Grazing') and 'Az én lovam Szajkó' ('My Horse is Szajkó') – and in Nancy Bush's English version published in the Boosey & Hawkes edition this is titled 'Love Song'. In the first and final parts, the protagonist explains that his oxen are safely feeding in their stall and he can join his lover in her bed; and in the metrically irregular 'trio', the character Jankó explains that the shoes have fallen from his horse's hoofs and observes that his friend the blacksmith will repair the damage. Bartók subtly changes the rhythm of the first tune from its notated 7/8 as number 54b in *The Hungarian Folk Song* to reinforce its triple hypermetre, and places it in a largely homophonic context. By contrast with the enthusiastic and anthem-like tone of the outer sections in modal G, the middle part is more playful and set in B/F♯. Overall, the choral set can perhaps be seen to conform to the Hungarian *verbunkos* archetype, but with two slow sections preceding the two brisk ones.

The summer holiday of 1930 was spent in the beautiful little resort of Arolla, in the Valais region of Switzerland, at the end of the valley from Sion, two thousand metres up in the mountains. Bartók arrived there at the end of June, and soon after, on 2 July, wrote to his friend Constantin Brăiloiu to seek his advice on the orthography of a text of a *colindă* in Romanian that he had included with the letter, noting that he needed this for mid-August. The ballad tells the story of nine brothers who are magically transformed into stags when they go hunting in the woods. Their father finally finds the herd of deer while on a hunting trip and he is about to shoot, not realising that they are his offspring, when their leader, his dearest son, reveals them to be his children. The father begs them to return home with him to drink from the glasses their mother has waiting for them, but is told that they can never do so and must forever wander through the forest, drinking water only from the streams.

The folk ballad is essentially derived from the first of two variant texts (4a and b) of *colinde* that Bartók had collected in March 1914 in the Mureş-Turda region of Transylvania, the melodies of which would appear in 1935 in his monograph *Melodien der Rumänischer Colinde (Weihnachtslieder)* as numbers

12bb and 12i.[12] Bartók had perceived in its narrative the basis of a vocal and orchestral work and this was realised as the *Cantata profana* ('A kilenc csodas-zarvas' – the nine enchanted stags) for tenor, baritone, double chorus and orchestra. Although the poet József Erdélyi had published a Hungarian transla-tion of the ballad in the first edition of *Nyugat* in 1930, titled 'A szarvasokká vált fiúk', describing it as being based on a Romanian folk ballad collected by Bartók, the composer rejected this for his libretto because of various textual misunderstandings on Erdélyi's part. Instead he devised his own version in Romanian (it was this that he seems to have shared with Brăiloiu) and translated it into Hungarian.

As Julie Brown has remarked, *Cantata profana* has attracted its fair share of exegesis, much of which has focused on the metamorphosis of the young men and interpreted their assimilation into nature as a positive change. In fact Bartók's text stresses that the father had failed to instruct his sons in the crafts of husbandry or any other valuable work and had instead encouraged them to spend their time in pleasure and hunting.[13] He is punished for this negligence in an ironic twist common to many such folk narratives, by the transformation of his sons into the very quarry they had previously pursued and their consequent inability to return to the human world. Arguably the father could be taken to symbolise a modernity that has lost its connection with nature, regarding it as a resource to be plundered rather than cherished and nurtured. While it is perhaps an exaggeration to suggest that the theme of the *Cantata profana* is actually *labor omnia vincit*, one is reminded that the source of this phrase is the first volume of Virgil's *The Georgics*, a reflection on the value of agricultural labour. Bartók was undoubtedly concerned with the welfare of animals and the care of the rural environment, as was demonstrated by an episode in the early 1940s when he stayed on Agatha Fassett's Vermont estate and was apparently horrified by the condition of the horses and cattle on her neighbour's farm. Equally, he had little time for hedonism and even his holidays – supposedly times of rest and relaxation – were dominated by musical labour and strenuous exercise.

Bartók worked on the *Cantata profana* surrounded by the mountain scenery of Arolla, a fitting environment for the genesis of a score bound to themes of the natural world. The process of composition has been partially reconstructed by László Vikárius from the extant sources and other archival materials, and while the precise details still remain somewhat speculative, the piece was certainly completed by 8 September.[14] Bartók later told his friend and collabo-rator Sándor Albrecht of his plans to complete a trio of such cantatas on related themes, but the other two were never written.[15]

The three-movement secular cantata includes several references to pre-Classical musical techniques, though perhaps most explicitly to material from

Bach's *St Matthew Passion*. Both works treat the chorus as a means of contextualisation and narrative advancement, and as a source of commentary on the
events described. Thematic connections between the prologue to the *St
Matthew Passion* and the opening of the first section of *Cantata profana* (Fig.
39) are so explicit that it is difficult to regard them as other than intentional,
though drawing a narrative association between Christ's crucifixion and the
effective sacrifice of the nine treasured sons may seem unwarranted. While
Bach's two passion cycles conclude with Christ's death and entombment,
*Cantata profana* places the boys' transformation at its heart; and although the
Christ of the Gospels will subsequently return to his 'father's mansion', the sons
in the cantata may never do so.

Bartók's initial ostensible invocation of Bach follows directly from a four-
bar passage in the strings (supported by a pedal tonic D in the muted horns),
founded on one of the *heptatonia secunda* scale forms in D. This is constructed
from a lower Dorian or Aeolian tetrachord and an upper Locrian tetrachord
(Fig. 39a), a rotation of one of the most characteristic scales of the Bihar/Bihor

Figure 39. (a) Acoustic scale; (b) the Bach-inspired gesture from the first movement
of *Cantata profana*; (c) the opening of Bach's *St Matthew Passion*; (d) the main theme of
*Cantata profana*.

dialect. Rising and falling forms of this scale overlap with each other, immediately suggesting to the listener that the work may be less harmonically and tonally complex than the major concert works of the previous decade.

The principal melodic idea of the work (appearing first at bar 27) was one of the earliest gestures sketched by Bartók, setting the text translated into English in the 1955 Universal Edition full score as 'Whose treasure nine sons fair and sturdy was'. It employs the stereotypically 'Hungarian' choriambus metrical foot (long–short–short–long) with subtle dislocation between the rhythm and 9/8 metre (Fig. 39d), and is largely harmonised through mellifluous parallel diatonic chords in close voicings, building on the approach of the Four Hungarian Folk Songs. For the second part of the first movement, from bar 59, the pedal D in the horns is placed against a pentatonic inflected E♭ in an Allegro molto section that narrates the sons' hunt. This opens with a fairly regular fugue whose subject (Fig. 40a) places interlaced major seconds (e.g. E♭–D♭–C–D♮) in the foreground and reaches an initial climax with excited cries on a chord of D major sharp eleventh (D–F♯–A–C♯–E–G♯). A sequence from bar 126 is built from a falling diatonic cycle of fifths and the succeeding passage leads, at bar 164, to the moment of transformation as the boys cross an enchanted bridge and are turned to stags. This point of arrival is in essence an A$^7$ harmony, rendered more piquant by the addition of G♯ and A♯ in the stabbing chords in bars 164 and 167–8; and these latter two pitches, played by horn, timpani, harp and lower strings, provide an eerie undercurrent to the beginning of the beautiful final section of the movement.

Similar intertwining of rising and falling tones to that of the fugue subject underpins the unison idea that appears in bars 178–9 (Fig. 40b) with its rather matter-of-fact description of the metamorphosis; and the continuation, from bar 180 (Fig. 40c), employs a series of canonic entries, the sinusoidal contours of which correspond to the fugue subject by loose inversion.[16]

The narrative of the second movement of *Cantata profana* concerns the father's journey to find his sons and begins mysteriously with the lower strings developing the sinuous figure that closed the previous movement, harmonised in three-part chords, the basses and cellos moving in contrary motion to the violas. Here Bartók draws further on standard pre-Classical contrapuntal techniques, employing imitative entries and the inversion of an idea that is a close relative of the earlier fugue subject. From bar 22 he sets in motion a *stretto maestrale* in B♭ (prefiguring the climax of the development in the first movement of the Concerto for Orchestra). New entries arrive on each minim beat in a gesture that supports the text's 'Swiftly then their trail he followed' through its application of a conventional Baroque code.

Figure 40. *Cantata profana* (a) the fugue subject; (b) unison melody; (c) canon.

Once the section has reached its apex on what is effectively a chord of $G^7$ over an A♭ bass, the two soloists make their appearance: the tenor representing the eldest son and the baritone the father. In his surprisingly violent account, the tenor warns of the destruction that would befall the father if he attempted to shoot the stags. Over the course of its first twenty-eight bars, the tenor's line gradually ascends through a series of melodic loops. From bar 71 it makes two further ascents to the extreme high register, where the harmony settles in turn on three extended tonal plateaux involving the pitches B–D–D♯–F♯–A♯, the second adding G♯ as the bass of the chord and the third adding E♯.

For the father's appeal to his sons and the ensuing chorus, Bartók returns yet again to the material associated with the hunt (Fig. 40a), treated sequentially; and in the later part of the father's solo, from bar 129, he repeats a figure derived from a falling major seventh chord on C ($C_4$–$B_3$–$G_3$–$E_3$–$C_3$) six times in the course of thirty-one bars. The text describes the table spread with festive fare awaiting the return of the young men, and it is significant that Bartók should employ the hypermajor and the motif that was particularly associated in his early music with Stefi Geyer (here presented in a descending form).

In the highly expressive tenor solo that ensues, the son urges his beloved father to return home alone. Here the melody is constructed with a balance of consonant leaps and stepwise motion to create a line suggestive of the principles of *bel canto* while remaining in accord with the spirit of folk song. In Calvocoressi's English translation in the version of the score published by Universal Edition in 1951, the father's final interjection is given as 'O why forsake me?' set to a chromatically falling phrase. This resonates strikingly with Christ's words on the Cross as given in the King James version of St Matthew's Gospel: 'My God, my God, why hast thou forsaken me?' In the 1955 translation of the *Cantata profana* this is more prosaically translated as 'Oh, why? Oh, why not?'

The final movement of the work recapitulates the main narrative and thematic thrusts of the work in a simple ternary structure drawing on the themes associated with the description of the father's upbringing of his sons and their transformation into stags. And in the ethereal and ecstatic final moments, the tenor soars up an acoustic scale on D (the inversion of the scale form found at the inception of the first movement) in the upper octave of its tessitura and melismatically decorates the descent from its summit on $C_5$. A kind of plagal cadence from an A minor chord onto the tonic D brings the *Cantata profana* to its conclusion, fading into silence.

Later in 1930, the Corvin Wreath was awarded to Bartók, along with fifty-nine other recipients (the maximum number of simultaneous award-holders was sixty). This was one of three medals established by Admiral Horthy (the other two were the Corvin Chain and the decorative Corvin Badge restricted to non-Hungarians); it was intended to honour citizens who had demonstrated outstanding achievements in the fields of science, literature, art and culture. Both Bartók and Kodály received the lower of the two awards whereas Dohnányi and Hubay were decorated with the more prestigious Corvin Chain (there were initially to be only twelve holders of this latter medal at any time); the preference given to Hubay must have rankled as much with Bartók as would have receiving the award from the despised Horthy. In fact, Bartók diplomatically offered his excuses and did not attend the award ceremony, although he was recorded as a recipient.

The year approached its ending, as it had begun, with a further trip by Bartók to London. He undertook this in part for a BBC recital on 24 November, which included a performance of Mozart's Violin Sonata in A major, K 305, with Jelly d'Arányi as the soloist – any strain in their relationship now apparently healed. More importantly, he played with the BBC Symphony Orchestra conducted by Sir Henry Wood on the following Wednesday (26 November) in the Queen's Hall. Perhaps surprisingly, Bartók fell back once again on the Rhapsody for this concert, rather than playing the Piano Concerto, a demonstration that the latter had not satisfactorily filled the gap for his symphonic appearances. Indeed, in his review the following day the *Times* critic alluded directly to the age of the work (underestimating it by five years). In fact, Bartók had started on a new work in October. Nonetheless the Second Piano Concerto would be completed within the year and eventually premiered in Frankfurt by the composer with the Frankfurt Radio Symphony Orchestra, conducted by Hans Rosbaud, on 23 January 1933. This was just a week before Hitler was sworn in as Chancellor and would be Bartók's final performance as a soloist in Germany.

As Bartók noted in the schematic analysis he produced in 1939, he was all too aware of the difficulties of his first essay in the form, both for audiences and orchestras (no doubt recalling the problems surrounding the US premiere).[17] In response, this new concerto was intended to offer its listeners a work 'whose thematic material would be more pleasing', and this accounted for 'the rather light and popular character of most of the themes'.[18] Perhaps the most interesting formal aspect of the concerto, which is nominally in G, is its overall shape – a five-part structure pressed into three movements, in which the final one is a reworking of the first. The middle movement involves two slow sections surrounding a brilliant scherzo, creating a tempo structure of fast–slow–very fast–slow–fast for the entire concerto. This conceit of a pair of shells with an inner kernel as a formal model, drawn as it was from the natural world, similarly underpins the Fourth and Fifth String Quartets.

Like Stravinsky's Concerto for Piano and Wind Instruments of 1923–4, the opening movement is scored for piano, winds and percussion (the strings remaining silent throughout). The motif played by the first trumpet near its onset bears a striking similarity to the theme of the finale of Stravinsky's ballet, *The Firebird*, albeit speeded up considerably. It is not evident, however, whether these correspondences are in conscious homage to a much-admired fellow composer or are coincidental. Functioning as a binding idea throughout the first movement, the trumpet's diatonic fanfare-like idea appears on some nine occasions in different guises, generally played by brass instruments. The outline of the continuation of the principal theme in the piano (Fig. 41b) is closely related to this idea by approximate inversion. The anapaest-dactyl rhythm after the two semiquaver upbeats (♫ ♫) is occasionally found in Hungarian, Slovak and Romanian popular music. If it is imagined rebarred in duple time, it can be seen to resemble number 236 of the 'motifs of Class B' that Bartók gives in Appendix 1 of the first volume of *Rumanian Folk Music*.[19] In the introduction to this volume, he talks about the rhythmic characteristics of dance style in general and remarks that 'The supposedly-original pattern of eighths is transformed in instrumental performance; a pair of sixteenths is substituted for most of the single eighths. The result will give combinations of ♫♫, ♫, and ♫ patterns.'[20]

Bartók's enthusiasm for the keyboard music of the Baroque – of Bach and before – is also evident in this material, with contrapuntal and homophonic impulses alternating. However, despite his suggestion to the contrary, the piano

Figure 41. The first movement of the Second Piano Concerto (a) the binding idea; (b) the principal theme.

writing can hardly be said to be much less difficult than that of the First Piano Concerto, and passagework often demonstrates his personal facility in accommodating large spans.

For the second subject of the sonata-form movement, the tonality shifts to A♭, the dialogue between piano and percussion that initiates it seeming prescient of the Sonata for Two Pianos and Percussion, which Bartók would complete in 1937. As he had done in the slow movement of the First Piano Concerto, the composer notates the strike position on the unsnared side drum at the rim or centre, and a further colouristic innovation is the use of both wooden and metal sticks on the triangle. Subtly shifting from triple to compound duple time, this tranquil and graceful theme is effectively pentatonic in orientation though tonally mobile, shifting between modes and permitting passing notes that lie outside the gamut. As Bartók notes in his analysis, this theme reappears in three further guises in the course of the concerto: its intervals chromatically compressed in the recapitulation of the first movement; and in inversion and then tonally adjusted (in the direct form) in the finale.

The development section is much more concise than its counterpart in the earlier concerto and focuses chiefly on the principal theme. As the piano interacts with woodwinds, the heavy brass remain virtually silent and this reinforces the sensation of a divertimento-like movement rather than a large-scale symphonic adventure. In the recapitulation, the principal theme appears in inversion and initially, apparently off-centre on E♭, though it soon settles back onto the tonic as the brass present the inverted fanfare in a canon whose entries accelerate and then regularise at the distance of a crotchet. The cadenza that separates the reprises of the two main themes perhaps misleads the listener into imagining that the secondary theme will not be reprised. However, when it reappears played by clarinets and bassoons, it is both intervalically compressed and temporally truncated. Drawing on the opening fanfare for the final time, the movement comes to a firm conclusion on the tonic G.

The string section is introduced in the second movement, playing material with the character of a chorale whose tonal centre of C is only made manifest in the twenty-second bar. Slow, sustained, ethereal and other-worldly sounds built from stacked fifth chords, moving in contrary motion (played muted and without vibrato), are briefly interrupted by the piano playing a melody that entails the stylised use of Hungarian parlando-rubato rhythm, accompanied by quiet rolls on the timpani. After a second arching chorale from the strings, the piano attempts to reassert itself in a more extended passage that involves rhetorically repeated octaves As. But these grand gestures fall to silence with the return of the opening two bars of the string chorale, winding down sequentially and briefly cadencing on an implied C minor.

The fast and brilliant scherzo-cum-toccata employing the full orchestra, which forms the central part of the movement, is concerned as much with texture as with melody and can be conceived as another of Bartók's evocations of the nocturnal sounds of nature. Requiring considerable dexterity from the soloist, it presents some of the most innovative and experimental music of the work within a chromatic milieu that again owes much to Arab traditions. In this section the seeds of experiments by later composers such as Ligeti, Penderecki and Lutosławski can be heard. It provides a veritable compendium of contemporary piano techniques, from unison passages (bars 1–18), to major seconds in similar and contrary motion (bars 18–30), sixths and thirds (bars 31–59), and fourth-based chords (bars 61–74), to complementary chromatic textures in which the right hand plays only black notes against the left hand's white notes (bars 89–106). At the movement's heart are points of sound, textures and tiny rhythmic gestures, the entry of the first horn at bar 124 strikingly intimating a distant alphorn call. When the chromatic melody initiated by oboe and bassoon from bar 18 returns near the end of the scherzo (from bar 181) as a canon between strings (harmonised in parallel triads) and woodwinds, it is now in the ascending form, and gradually fades to silence.

Following a sharp punctuation from the piano, supported by trumpet and triangle, the opening section resurfaces as a ghost of its former self, with hushed tremolando strings and the piano dragging out its melody (now in descending orientation) as if suffering from great lassitude and transformed by the experience of passing through the nocturnal landscape of the scherzo. The solo piano finally reasserts itself through the repeated D♭s, before the final phrases of the string chorale bring the movement to a hushed conclusion on an implied C minor.

The finale reworks the music of the first movement with one additional ritornello-like idea, whose function Bartók likened to that of a framework. This new theme, generally written for piano, timpani and lower strings with a profile of repeated and infilled minor thirds, and Locrian modal characteristics (C–D♭–E♭–F–G♭), bears once more the strong impression of the Arab music that Bartók had collected in 1913 in Biskra. It appears four times in strategic positions, like the rugged walls of one of his beloved peasant cottages: in C (from bar 3); in F (from bar 73); in C and inverted (from bar 138); and finally in C♯ (from bar 207). Between the statements of this framework theme, Bartók's remodelling of material from the first movement, in which the rhythms have been smoothed out into triplet quavers, like a 9/8 'slip jig' (a common vernacular transformation of the ♫ and ♫ motifs, as he notes in the introduction to volume 1 of *Rumanian Folk Music*), focuses initially on the principal thematic area. Subsequently, after the third iteration of the ritornello, attention moves to the secondary theme, and the concerto concludes in brilliant style with a final restatement of the fanfare both in its original form and in inversion, the point of closure on the tonic triad being positive and absolutely unequivocal.

Serge Moreux, writing in the 1950s, considered the Second Piano Concerto as a 'compromise not a synthesis'. He noted that 'the professional musician is disconcerted by a certain heterogeneity of style in the melodic material . . . due to the intrusion of a neo-classical diatonicism within a chromatic framework which is very much modified by comparison with the chromaticism used by Bartók in other works written from 1926 onwards'.[21] Such accusations of compromise had previously been made by the musician and proponent of Schoenberg, René Leibowitz, in 1947 in his trenchant article 'Béla Bartók, ou la possibilité du compromis dans la musique contemporaine'; and in the decades following Bartók's death, critical views of the composer's later music would often draw attention to the supposed aesthetic problem of his adoption of a more accessible style in the 1930s.[22] For Moreux, Bartók was exhibiting a 'crisis in [his] creative consciousness' that resulted in a three-year period virtually devoid of original compositions and dominated by arrangements of existing folk material. These consisted of *Erdélyi táncok* (Transylvanian Dances, 1931) for orchestra, a version of the Sonatina for piano (1915); *Magyar képek* (Hungarian Sketches, 1931), orchestral transcriptions of early piano pieces; *Negyvennégy duó* (Forty-Four Duos, 1931), arrangements of folk tunes for two violins; *Székely dalok* (Székely Songs, 1932), settings for a capella male-voice choir; and *Magyar parasztdalok* (Hungarian Peasant Songs, 1933), based on nine numbers from Fifteen Hungarian Peasant Songs for piano of 1914–17.

Approaching the age of fifty, Bartók's international success as a composer did not encourage him, nor for that matter permit him, to reduce his activity as a concert artist. Throughout the winter of 1930–1 he continued to perform, at the end of November 1930 playing the Second Violin Sonata in Basle with Stefi Geyer, and in early 1931 as soloist in the First Piano Concerto in Frankfurt-am-Main. A three-week tour of Spain and Portugal followed from mid-January, including San Sebastián, Lisbon, Valencia de Alcántara, Madrid, Ovieda and Barcelona, though a bout of flu resulted in the cancellation of concerts in Granada and Palma.

Before setting off for Spain, Bartók had been in correspondence with the Romanian musicologist Octavian Beu about the content of the script for a radio broadcast that the latter had authored. Bartók rather took exception to the suggestion that he was a 'Rumanian composer', and offered a plain statement of his musical and ethical philosophy:

> My creative work, just because it arises from 3 sources (Hungarian, Rumanian, Slovakian), might be regarded as the embodiment of the very concept of integration so much emphasized in Hungary today. . . . My own idea, however – of which I have become fully conscious since I found myself as a composer – is the brotherhood of peoples, brotherhood in spite of all wars and conflicts. I try – to the best of my ability – to serve this idea in music; therefore I don't reject any influence, be it Slovakian, Rumanian, Arabic or from any other source. The source must only be clean, fresh and healthy![23]

A further instance of the composer's concerns about perceptions of his ethnic status and the status of his music appears in a letter to Constantin Brăiloiu. It appears that Romanian supporters of Bartók wished to erect a memorial plaque in his birthplace of Nagyszentmiklós (now renamed Sânnicolau Mare); his immediate response had been, characteristically, that people shouldn't be encouraged to waste money on such a tablet. On being advised that the money had already been raised, he had been willing to give his assent, but only on the basis that the plaque should be in both Romanian and Hungarian. In fact, the planned memorial did not appear in his lifetime, and it was only as late as September 1970, when Ceaușescu was Romania's leader, that a bilingual commemorative plate was finally erected in Sânnicolau Mare. This plaque does indeed make it clear that Bartók was Hungarian, but indicates that his multi-faceted activity contributed to the friendship between the Romanian and Hungarian people.

A major strand of his personal monument to the traditional music of Hungary eventually appeared in print in English in 1931 under the imprint of Oxford University Press, in Calvocoressi's translation and titled *Hungarian*

*Folk Music.* The critic Scott Goddard provided a brief review of it in the October edition of *Music and Letters*, though this focused principally on Calvocoressi's input, remarking almost parenthetically that he 'reiterated our sense of its worth for the student of folk music and to welcome its appearance in its present excellent form'.[24] Frank Howes, in his editorial notes of the *Journal of the Folk-Song Society*, published in December 1931, was more voluble in his praise, describing it as 'the most important publication of the year'.[25]

On 25 March 1931 Bartók turned fifty, the event not passing entirely unnoticed in the musical world. The Hungarian music critic László Pollatsek published a four-part study running across the May to August editions of *The Musical Times*, and in the final one he concluded with a powerful encomium:

> Bartók's tremendous creative power does not need any borrowing from former times. Instead of a renaissance of the glorious past, he is building the bridge of a new renaissance from the bleak present. He is the Asian Force of the primeval East knocking at the gates of the century, when the occidental art of music is helplessly writhing in its degeneration. Objective, mechanical, and jazz music are endeavouring to resuscitate the sick music of today by their injections. Bartók's music is the music of the age – mechanical, in so far as it is spanned by tremendous forces; jazz, because it throbs with rhythms of primeval roughness; objective, in that the formless individualism of the late romanticists is replaced in it by the collective forms of classicism. He is thus a phenomenon of the age, and in his fiftieth year is still a young giant, who is shaking in its foundation the ramshackle edifice of the music culture of a whole continent.[26]

The week before his birthday, Bartók's Fourth String Quartet had been played in New York by the New World String Quartet, in a performance that the *New York Times* critic Olin Downes took to be its American premiere. Downes was glowing in his review, for he heard in it a work that was 'strong, passionate, stark in its strength, stripped to the bone. . . . in spite of its exotic accent the music is classic in clarity, balance and insistence on sheerly musical ideas'.[27]

Despite these successes, a continuing source of frustration for Bartók lay in the fact that his pantomime *The Miraculous Mandarin* had still not been given its Hungarian premiere onstage, largely because of its perceived indecency, though Dohnányi had conducted the suite derived from it in 1928. Bartók made further revisions of the work in 1931 in the expectation of an impending performance at the Budapest Opera House, but there was further procrastination and a delay was announced until the autumn of that year. Predictably, this did not transpire and neither did a further attempt a decade later. Indeed, it was not until December 1945, shortly after the composer's death, that a Budapest audience could finally view it, choreographed by Gyula Harangozó who also danced the role of the Old Beau.

Bartók could already see around him the developing threat of fascism. Shocked by the treatment of the Italian conductor Arturo Toscanini, who had been attacked by Mussolini's supporters and had his passport briefly suspended because he refused to perform the fascist anthem 'Giovinezza' in a concert at Bologna on 14 May, he drafted a resolution to the ISCM on his behalf in May 1931 in the name of the UMZE (the New Hungarian Music Society).[28] And in Hungary, the right-wing soldier and politician Gyula Gömbös had been appointed Minister of Defence in 1929; in 1932 he would become Prime Minister and leader of the Szegedist 'Party of Hungarian Life'. The agenda and policies of this movement were utterly abhorrent to Bartók, aligned as they were to those of Hitler and Mussolini, and motivated by irredentism and the desire to restore Hungary's pre-Trianon borders.

If 1931 saw no new substantial compositions by Bartók, a flurry of journal articles, dictionary entries and reviews appeared in print on issues generally relating to folk music. Most of these were quite pithy, but collectively they articulated Bartók's ethnomusicological philosophy with the fruit of twenty-five years of accumulated experience. In 'What is Folk Music?', published in the popular Budapest weekly literary magazine *Új Idők* (*New Times*), he summarised his belief that '*peasant music of this kind* [belonging to homogeneous styles distinct from popular art music] *is nothing but the outcome of changes wrought by a natural force whose operation is unconscious in men who are not influenced by urban culture*'.[29] He went on to remark that 'The melodies are therefore the embodiment of an artistic perception of the highest order; in fact, they are models of the way in which a musical idea can be expressed with utmost perfection in terms of brevity of form and simplicity of means'. Of course, in positing this deliberately provocative thesis, he was drawing on a tradition that reached back a century and a half to the writings of Herder and demonstrated an essentialist attitude that tended to characterise the latent ethnomusicology of the early twentieth century.

His prestige as a musical figure was reflected through the invitation to join the League of Nations International Committee on Intellectual Cooperation, which had been established in 1922 and included in its membership (at various times) luminaries such as Albert Einstein, Henri Bergson, Thomas Mann, Marie Curie, Gilbert Murray and Paul Valéry. On his annual vacation in 1931, in the Austrian resort of Mondsee, Bartók wrote to his mother and Aunt Irma to tell them of his experiences during a meeting of the committee held in Geneva in July at which he was the only musician present. Clearly aware of the futility of many of the proposals coming forward from the committee, he was entertained by the proceedings, and was particularly amused by the excessive politeness of the delegates despite their tendency entirely to contradict each other's remarks. At dinner he enjoyed sitting next to, and conversing with, Thomas Mann, and Bartók performed 'Evening with the Széklers' and 'Bear Dance' from Ten Easy Pieces for the company. Later in the year, in the postscript of a letter to Buşiţia, he wrote scathingly, though with considerable perception and pragmatism, about his experience of the committee:

> We discussed many lofty notions there – the first session was in July; but what I'd like to say to those people is this: as long as one is unable to put the world in order economically and in other ways; as long as, for instance, currency restrictions make it difficult for even works of culture to pass the various frontiers, grandiose garrulity about 'intellectual cooperation' is completely useless. Even if I said it, it would, of course, be in vain.[30]

The time spent at Mondsee, staying at the modest Gasthof Koflerbräu, was not entirely a holiday, for he was engaged at the Austro-American Conservatory of Music summer programme from the middle of July until the end of August. This proved something of a farce, for the eight pupils he had been promised did not materialise and he ended up with just two *bona fide* students and two of the administrators (whom he rather uncharitably described as 'old hags' to his mother). However, there was still ample opportunity for walking, bathing and trips out, including to nearby Salzburg, and Bartók reported back by letter or postcard to Paula, Irma, Béla junior and Elza on a very regular basis.

Returning to Budapest he was still unable to escape the annual irritation of the entrance exams for the Academy of Music. More positively, however, performances of his orchestral music were given in the city by two of his fellow professors that autumn and early winter, including the First Suite conducted by the violinist and composer Nándor Zsolt with the Budapest Concert Orchestra, an ensemble Zsolt had formed the previous year; and a suite comprising three dances from *The Wooden Prince* directed by Dohnányi at the opera house. Shortly after this latter performance, the English popular musician Jack Hylton and his band visited Budapest and performed at the Academy, and Bartók took the opportunity to hear them, displaying a professional interest in the phenomenon of jazz. Ten years later, in the first draft of an essay given at Columbia University titled 'The Relation between Contemporary Hungarian Art Music and Folk Music', Bartók would note (though later cross out): 'I don't even shrink from [oriental (for instance, Arabic) influences] and even American influences (I mean of course the jazz)'.[31]

In his letter to Buşiţia cited above, Bartók had offered his belated thanks to his old friend for his congratulations on the award of Chevalier of the Légion d'Honneur on 17 September 1930, though characteristically he was rather unimpressed to be selected. After all, he wasn't the first Hungarian musician to receive the decoration (Liszt had been created Chevalier in 1845 and Officier in 1860); and in any case he would have preferred to have had more perform-ances of his music in Paris ('something which, I'm afraid, has happened very infrequently lately').[32]

The New Hungarian Music Society (UMZE), which had been disbanded shortly after its formation nearly twenty years earlier, had been revived in 1930, and as already noted Bartók had invoked its name in 1931 in a resolution in support of Toscanini. The first concert of the re-established organisation took place on 20 January 1932 and included pieces from *Negyvennégy duó* (Forty-Four Duos), which he had completed the previous year, symptomatic of the organisation's educational and cultural principles. Based almost entirely on folk tunes collected by Bartók and others from the Hungarian, Slovak and Romanian regions (and one from Algeria), the forty-four pieces are scored for two violins. They are graduated in difficulty over the two volumes in much the same way that those found in *Mikrokomos*, and they offer insight into the tradi-tional sources of some of the composer's more idiosyncratic metric and hyper-metric tactics.[33] Among them there are examples of five-bar phrases (no. 3); variable phrase lengths, 2+2+3+3 (no. 5) and 3+3+2 (no. 9); triple hypermetre (no. 6); additive metre, 3+3+2/8 (no. 19); as well as the metrical irregularity of four *colinde* tunes.

The early months of 1932 were spent by Bartók in familiar concertising activ-ities. After a radio broadcast in Frankfurt at the end of January, he headed off for England to perform in a duo recital with Szigeti in Oxford, including the Second Violin Sonata in the programme. A brief respite in Budapest was proceeded by a further northward journey, this time to Paris for the French premiere of the First Piano Concerto in the Salle Pleyel, with l'Orchestre Symphonique de Paris under the Russian conductor Nicolas Slonimsky. The initial rehearsal was not prom-ising, but the performance on 21 February seems to have fared better. Before returning to Britain, for a concert in Glasgow, he stayed as a guest of the Székelys in Nijmegen (in a villa owned by Mientje's mother) for five days. Székely describes how Bartók suggested for a bit of fun that they should play some of the early numbers from the Forty-Four Duos as though beginners, the composer literally so, the virtuoso violinist handicapped by having to play with his instrument reversed, held by the right hand and bowed with the left.[34]

Bartók's inaugural excursion to Glasgow (he would revisit it in the November of the following year) was at the invitation of the young Scottish

composer Erik Chisholm, who two years earlier had established The Active
Society for the Propagation of Contemporary Music, an organisation that
invited a number of 'radical' musicians to perform in the Scottish city.[35] Bartók
had little to say about this visit in his postcard home, other than that the Scots
were not notably good cooks but were very enthusiastic bagpipers! A few days
later he found himself in London once again, giving a broadcast of several solo
pieces by Baroque composers on 2 March and playing the Rhapsody in an all-
Bartók concert with the BBC Orchestra conducted by Sir Henry Wood. The
rest of this concert consisted of the First Suite and what was described in the
BBC programme listing in *The Times* as 'The Amazing Mandarin' (the suite
from the pantomime, *A csodálatos mandarin*). In his review in the 1 April
edition of *The Musical Times*, Edwin Evans pronounced that:

> The subject is a lurid, presumably symbolical, sex-drama. Taken seriously it
> might border on the unpleasant. Stripped of pretensions it is sheer melo-
> drama, and since Studio 10 is on the Surrey side one was prepared to meet
> it on that basis. For this mime-drama Bartók has composed appropriate
> blood-and-thunder music. He has treated the theme theatrically, with all
> his resources, and without trying to make it mean more than it need. As his
> resources are considerable, the result is correspondingly sensational. It
> makes Salome in retrospect nothing worse than a saucy minx. Such music
> can be, as this is, thrilling to hear once in a while. Its permanent value,
> detached from its subject, is more problematic.[36]

While in London, Bartók had taken advantage of the legal expertise of
Alexandre Fachiri, Adila d'Arányi's husband, to help sort out his visa to visit
Egypt in mid-March for what became known as 'The Cairo Congress'; this was
the first International Congress of Arab Music, to which he had been invited as
a delegate. The congress, which ran from 14 to 28 March, was inaugurated by
King Fu'äd I as a symposium and festival, and as well as musicians, artists and
theorists from across the Arab world, other European invitees included: the
composers Paul Hindemith and Alois Hába; the musicologists Erich von
Hornbostel, Curt Sachs, Egon Wellesz and Robert Lachmann; and orientalist
scholars such as George Farmer. It was intended that the congress would
'discuss all that was required to make the music civilized, and to teach it and
rebuild it on acknowledged scientific principles'.[37]

Delegates were permitted to choose which of seven strands of the congress
they wished to participate in. For Bartók this proved uncomplicated, 'as there
was only one section in question for me, that of the recordings, which I joined
with great pleasure'.[38] He was able to draw on his enormous knowledge of

recording, transcribing and cataloguing traditional music to advise the Institute of Arabic Music (which hosted the congress) on appropriate technologies and techniques, and to help select the performers to be recorded. This last activity put him in particularly close contact with the Arab musicians. The work of the recording section of the congress was eventually brought to fruition through the publication of more than 175 records by HMV, which as Ali Jihad Racy observes, 'was considered the first step toward reconstructing Arab music in its presumably ancient, uncontaminated, and distinctive form'.[39] As for Bartók himself, he was faced with the conundrum of discovering what appeared to be 'genuine' rural music performed within the urban context in the rituals of exorcism he came into contact with in Cairo. He mused on the implications of this in the final paragraph of his brief report published in *Zeitschrift für vergleichende Musikwissenschaft* the following year:

> The fact that this music of village character was only performed by city people seems to contradict the designation of village music. And one indeed had to weigh what would be the most suitable denomination for that kind of folk music, for genuine folk music is traditionally in existence as the spontaneous expression of the musical sentiments of the simplest national classes: peasants, herders, nomads.[40]

On his homecoming to Budapest, Bartók changed his address again, for the final time in Hungary; he now rented 27 Csalán utca, a house in a quieter area of district II, four kilometres further away, on the edge of the Buda hills, beneath Jánoshegy. Hungary had for some time been in the grip of a major economic downturn resulting from the Great Depression in the United States. Agricultural and industrial exports had diminished and levels of bankruptcy increased. Between 1930 and 1932 Hungary's GDP had fallen by nearly 10 per cent, and in 1933 the unemployment rate was running at more than 35 per cent. Inevitably these conditions took their toll on Bartók's immediate and wider family, and there would be no long holiday spent abroad that summer. To make matters worse, he went down with a very serious bout of influenza that kept him housebound from 31 August until the first week of October 1932.

Matica Slovenská's contractual publication date for his Slovak collection (more than 3,200 tunes) had passed in late June without its appearance in print. Bartók called on his old friend Sándor Albrecht, who lived in Pozsony and had collaborated with Anton Baník and Štefan Németh-Šamorínsky in supporting his fieldwork, to liaise with the publisher in repaying their advance to permit him to reclaim the 1,200-page manuscript. This was followed with a threat of litigation if they did not accede, though Bartók granted them a stay of execution and his ensuing illness limited his ability to carry out the threat. The publishers were now themselves in dispute with the latest editor they had appointed, the music critic Ivan Ballo, whose work on the collection Bartók respected. In late October he wrote to Albrecht, describing the situation and expressing his total lack of confidence in the company; and indeed this proved well founded, for the first volume of *Slovenské Ľudové Piesne* remained unpublished until 1957, twelve years after his death. Volume 2 of the collection appeared thirteen years later, in 1970, and the third as recently as 2007. Bartók would maintain regular correspondence with both Matica Slovenská and Albrecht throughout 1933, attempting to make progress, but he was perpetually frustrated.

Bartók's studies of traditional music resulted in a further honour in December, when he was admitted to the Romanian 'Order of Cultural Merit'. Naturally, given the tensions between the two states, this was a source of some embarrassment, particularly when it was picked up by the Hungarian press. Meanwhile, political issues of a different kind were to the fore in Germany. In the elections of July and November 1932, Hitler's Nazionalsozialistische Deutsche Arbeitpartei had won more than a third of the votes, and at the end of January 1933 he was appointed as Chancellor. In the week preceding this momentous event, Bartók had given the premiere of his Second Piano Concerto in Frankfurt, with the Frankfurt Radio Symphony Orchestra under Hans Rosbaud, a concert that passed without comment in most of the English-language musical press. According to the composer, it was more successful than the First Piano Concerto, though the performance was by no means exemplary.[41] His itinerary to Frankfurt passed through the Nazi heartland of Nuremburg. After Hitler's assumption of power Bartók would never again traverse it to perform in Frankfurt – nor indeed perform anywhere else in Germany.

In May 1933 Bartók and Kodály were invited as Hungarian delegates to the 'First International Music Convention' held in Florence. This attracted many of the world's leading musicians and critics, including such luminaries as Darius Mihaud, Richard Strauss, Alban Berg, Albert Roussel, Ernst Krenek, Alfred Einstein and Ottorino Respighi (though Stravinsky, Ravel, Schoenberg and Hindemith were missing from the roster). According to the convention's organiser Ugo Ojetti, as reported in *The New York Times* the following month, its purpose was 'to discuss, define and simplify the problems of musical creation, interpretation and criticism, as well as those of mechanical music, and the propagation of musical culture and international exchanges in a spirit of friendly accord'.[42] Bartók found the presentations and lectures rather tedious, though being in the company of the hero of his late adolescence, Richard Strauss, must have surely been of some consequence to him.

The Budapest premiere of the Second Piano Concerto on 2 June in the Vigadó concert hall was given, not by the composer, but by the Hungarian-Austrian pianist Louis (Lajos) Kentner (who had been a piano student of Arnold Székely and Leó Weiner at the Academy), with the Budapest Concert Orchestra under the baton of Otto Klemperer. Kentner played at Bartók's request and the performance was repeated in the Musikverein in Vienna five days later. The young cellist George Barati (György Braunstein) was a member of the orchestra and was present at both; in 1991 he recollected the events of the rehearsal and concert in Vienna:

Bartók was a very withdrawn, pure, naive, small-sized man, very timid and shy. We arrived in Vienna for a seating rehearsal, we called it a *sitzprobe* in German, a seating rehearsal to check how convenient the stage is, how it feels. The great concert hall in Vienna was unheated. Klemperer started conducting the Bartók concerto. There was Bartók at the piano. Klemperer as you know, was about six feet five, or six, enormous. Taller than I am by a half foot. And Bartók was tiny. There was Bartók sitting and Klemperer standing, enormous.

We started out the Bartók concerto which has very early in the piece a novel use of the then new machine timpani, the tunable, pedal timpani. Until then timpani had to be tuned by hand, and each note was fixed. This was a major innovation and a novel use by Bartók. A crescendo glissando could be played. So very early in the first movement was a glissando by timpani. There were no timpani. So Klemperer stopped and a great shouting scandal developed. 'Where are the timpani?' And nobody knew. 'Who is responsible?' Nobody said anything. Finally, our orchestra director said, 'I am the orchestra director. You know very well', nastily. He said, 'Where are the timpani? How do I know, I just came from Budapest.' And Klemperer said, 'No timpani. No concert. Goodbye.' And he left. And little Bartók just sat at the piano with his gloves on. There was no heat but he just sat for about twenty minutes. All of us got up and moved around or practiced or did something until the timpani arrived which had been used the previous night in a concert. Then a delegation had to go to Klemperer at his hotel to beg him to come back. And he came back. Then we rehearsed, and we went on with the concert. The concert was a great flop. The Bartók concerto had almost no applause.[43]

The only musical work by Bartók to emerge in 1933 was *Magyar népdalok* (Hungarian Folk Songs), and this was not new but an orchestral arrangement of five of the songs from the set of twenty he completed in 1929 for voice and piano (numbers 1, 2, 11, 12 and 14). They were first sung by Mária Basilides in a Gala Concert of the Philharmonic Orchestra celebrating its eightieth anniversary, held on 23 October, and conducted by Dohnányi. Kodály's *Galántai tancok* (Dances from Galánta) was also premiered in this celebratory event.

Bartók set off for Great Britain in November on a second trip starting in Glasgow, at the invitation of Eric Chisholm. By this stage the Scottish composer had married Diana Brodie, the secretary of the Active Society for the Propagation of Contemporary Music. Bartók stayed with the couple and their young daughter Morag, of whom he apparently made a 'great fuss'. According to Diana:

> He told us something of his experience in searching for and collecting the folk songs of his own country. Normally his face looked rather stern and taut, but his whole face lit up and his eyes became pools of liquid fire when recounting what was obviously the most vital of his life [*sic*]. At first he did make one feel he was unapproachable and distant. But when he found that he could relax, and was in no danger of being 'lionised' (the soul-searing penalty the celebrity pays for being a celebrity) and that he was among friendly, sympathetic people, his whole personality seemed to change, to become electrified.
>
> Then one became aware of the terrifically forceful personality of this seemingly quiet, shy, self-effacing musician. Here was someone with dynamic strength of will to achieve what he had set out to do with his life.[44]

He had the score of his Second Piano Concerto with him and showed it to Chisholm, who remarks that:

> I passed over some pages until I reached the presto section of this two-sided movement, which combines slow movement and scherzo, and raised my eyebrows enquiringly at my first sight of tone clusters. He smiled, then replied in that soft, almost inaudible voice of his: 'Not my invention, I'm afraid. I got the idea from a young American composer, Henry Cowell.' . . . [Cowell] told me, that when he was in London in 1923, Bartók accidentally overheard him playing some of his own music, which employed tone clusters. He was extremely interested in this new technique, and later wrote asking if he might be permitted to use similar tone clusters in his own compositions.[45]

For his visit to London in 1923, Bartók had been a house guest of Duncan and Freda Wilson. Cowell had stayed at the same time, on his first European tour.

It seems, then, that an encounter did take place between them, though the letter supposedly sent to Cowell has not yet been located.

After Glasgow (where he drew a reasonable audience of around 300 for his recital), Bartók took the train to London for a performance of the Second Piano Concerto with Sir Adrian Boult and the BBC Symphony Orchestra at the Queen's Hall. The anonymous critic writing in *The Times* the following day was extremely positive, remarking, apparently without irony, that 'it seemed to be one of the most arresting concertos which have appeared since composers made the discovery that the piano is a percussion instrument tuned in equal temperament and determined to act accordingly'; and 'wonder[ed] whether that "renunciation of romanticism" which we are told belongs to twentieth-century music is as complete as it is supposed to be'.[46]

Throughout the winter and spring months of early 1934, Bartók continued to take part in recitals and radio broadcasts as both performer and musicologist. One of these, on a Hungarian radio station (Radio Budapest) on 15 January, involved the illustrated talk on traditional music – 'Népzenénk és a szomszéd népek népzenéje' ('Hungarian Folk Music and the Folk Music of Neighbouring Peoples'). It was with obvious national pride that he concluded the journal article that resulted from this with the words 'The old and new melodies of the Hungarian villages constitute a specifically Hungarian spiritual treasure that we have not borrowed from our present-day neighbours; on the contrary, it is we who have given it to them.'[47]

The Second Piano Concerto had two further outings in Switzerland in March 1934, in Winterthur (conducted by Hermann Scherchen) and in Zurich (with Hermann Hofmann). On 25 May the *Cantata profana* finally received its premiere at Broadcasting House, London, in a radio broadcast given by the BBC Symphony Orchestra and the Wireless Chorus under the baton of the Australian conductor Aylmer Buesst, with the tenor Trefor Jones and the baritone Frank Phillips. Bartók appeared on the programme as soloist in his Second Piano Concerto and this received a rather warmer critical reception than did the choral work. According to the *Times* reviewer the following day, 'The "Cantata Profana" deals with a forest legend, but the chorus has to tell its tale in an interjaculatory style with the orchestra hampering them rather than elucidating the disrupted texture.'[48]

Bartók's extended period of compositional furlough would come to an end as a result of a telegram received from the Library of Congress on 5 June 1934. This indicated the commission of a new work to be funded by the Coolidge Foundation, the creation of the wealthy American patroness, Mrs Elizabeth Sprague-Coolidge. Before he began to compose what would be his Fifth String Quartet, Bartók departed with his wife and youngest son for a walking tour of

Sulden (near to Merano) in the South Tyrol. This was to be Péter's first Alpine trip with his parents and he writes both amusingly and movingly of the experience, describing his father's deep love of the mountains and of nature in his biographical study, *My Father*.

On Bartók's return home, having stopped in Venice en route for the Biennale, further good news awaited him – the long-awaited reprieve from piano-teaching duties at the Academy. This resulted from the offer of a post on the folk-music subcommittee of the Budapest learned society, Magyar Tudományos Akadémia (the Hungarian Academy of Sciences), in connection with the Hungarian folk-song collection to which he and Kodály had been major contributors, and which by this stage had reached some ten thousand melodies. It was apparently not until the following month, after Hubay's retirement, that the Academy of Music's management was made aware of the move; Dohnányi had just taken over as the director, and Bartók wrote him a long letter on 29 July explaining the situation and dealing with some of the practical issues. Although Dohnányi was clearly extremely disappointed to lose such a prestigious figure from his piano faculty, he could at least comprehend the magnitude of the role that Bartók was about to assume.

In the Fifth String Quartet, composed between August and September 1934, Bartók further extended the principles of symmetry that underpin the Fourth String Quartet and Second Piano Concerto. Its five-movement structure places a scherzo 'alla bulgarese' at its core, surrounded by an inner shell of related slow movements and an outer shell of substantial sonata and rondo forms. The principal tonality of the outer husk (and of the work as a whole) is B♭, the second and fourth movements being placed a third above and below this in D and G respectively, and the kernel in C♯.

The opening sonata-form movement is itself symmetrically disposed, with three contrasting thematic areas that are recapitulated in reverse order. In the first, a repeated note gesture enclosing a rising and falling major second acts as a kind of signal, returning on a number of occasions in different guises. Two melodic elements predominate: the measured rise by fourths from B♭ through E to A; and a pentatonically inflected figure that descends through the pitches A♭–G♭–E♭–D♭, the addition of F completing the lower pentachord of the major scale of D♭. A strong rhythmic impulse underlies the second theme, which is accompanied by a vamped accompaniment in the viola and cello in the local tonic of C. The metrically irregular idea in the violins has a chromatic melodic contour (entailing overlapping major seconds like those featured in *Cantata profana*) and is propelled by rising minor tenths from $C_4$. For the more lyrical third theme, Bartók draws on a simple stepwise rising and falling line that is embellished using polymodally derived variant pitches. The tonality eventually settles a tone higher on D, though this is only achieved at bar 55 as the outcome of the chromatic stepwise motion of a sequence of pedal tones from B♭ (bar 45), through B (49), C (53) and C♯ (54).

Bartók continues the logic of the tonal model established through the three principal polarities of the exposition, with its stepwise rise by tones (B♭– C–D), in the rest of the movement. The development begins with the 'signal' from the opening theme, now transposed to the level of E (a tonal area he describes as functioning like a 'dominant' in his own analysis of the quartet),[49] but soon moves on to the third theme, overlaying it with the first. At bar 86 the accompaniment to the second theme is developed, taking on what appear to be the rhythmic characteristics of a tango (complicated by realignment in the viola three bars later that places it a beat out of phase with the cello) and the upper strings explore the pentatonic fragment first heard in bar 9.[50] A sequence from bars 104–11 continues with the pentatonic motif, employing it contrapuntally and moving chromatically from $C_4$ to $E_4$ in falling versions, then descending from $A_4$ to $F_4$ in rising versions as a preface to an extended passage that is focused again on the tonal centre of E; from bar 126, E and F are coalesced in the first theme's rhythmic signal in preparation for the recapitulation. The three themes of the exposition now reappear in reverse order, varied and inverted: the third in F♯, the second in A♭, and the third (from bar 159) in B♭, completing the whole-tone scale pattern that forms the matrix for the main tonal areas of the movement. An extended coda drawing on material from the first subject brings the movement to closure on the tonic.

A group of three contrasting themes that are varied and reprised in reverse order to create a shell-like structure similarly underpin the Adagio molto second movement. The first is fragmentary, commencing with trills in the upper and lower registers before pithy melodic couplets (seconds or fourths) sound out over a descending melody in the cello. Subsequently, a chorale-like sequence of diatonic chords beginning on a C major triad accompanies a series of five-note phrases in the middle register in the first violin, the pitches of which for the most part chromatically complement those of the chorale. The third section, another manifestation of the textural 'night music' style, exploits tremolandi and alternates arco and pizzicato techniques (including plucking with the left hand fingernail). Melodic material based around the pentatonically related pitches G♭–D♭–E♭, which is established by the viola in bar 27, is passed around the quartet before the first violin introduces two more expressive variants, each falling and rising in a semi-symmetrical way. The section moves to its climax from the middle of bar 35 through a chain of overlapping entries of segments based on cycles of interlocking fourths that rise and fall in two waves (the first ascending through G♯–C♯–B–E–D–G–F–A♯ and then descending via the diatonic segment F–C–D–A–B–F–G–D–E; the second opening with D–G–F–B♭–A♭–D–C–F). Truncated variants of the second and first sections draw the movement to its conclusion on the tonic D.

Bartók's enthusiasm for the Scherzo stretches back to his earliest experiments as a composer. Here he brings together a well-tried and tested approach with the rhythmic discoveries from the Romanian *colinde* and from Balkan music, employing a compound time signature of 4+2+3/8 for the main section. Although the movement closes on a C♯ minor triad, it does take some time to arrive at a clear statement of this tonality, the accompaniment to the opening theme (based on broken-chord figures derived from the Dorian C♯ mode) starting off-centre on a vamped D♯ diminished/major, and the C♯ in bars 4–6 functioning as a seventh. The first point at which C♯ sounds as if it has been fully tonicised is at bar 24, with the arrival of the second thematic area. This is followed by passages from bars 30–2 in which C major triads appear prominently (with added seventh) and from bars 36–41, A minor (made more piquant with the addition of D♯). It is in bar 50, with the reprise of the first idea, that the Scherzo finally explicitly cadences onto C♯, though even this is rendered ambiguous by the closing minor third dyad on A that prepares for the trio.

A remarkable technical assurance is demonstrated in the near minimalist insistence on the chromatic one-bar ostinato figure (notated in the time signature 3+2+2+3/8) that dominates the Trio, played fourteen times in its first manifestation, with the sustained A and C that closed the Scherzo section in the viola intimating F major. This figure shifts up chromatically by stages and from bar 33 is repeated sixteen times on A, the inversion of the figure being added as a counterpoint from bar 41. With the restoration of the original version on F from bar 50 in the viola, the Trio section gradually comes to a halt. Bartók now makes some adjustment to the tonality of the theme and places it in dialogue with its inversion. The second idea also appears in inversion from bar 30 of the reprise of the Scherzo and the ensuing section develops the material, a contrapuntal chromatic passage from bar 58 leading to the climactic second-inversion tonic chord at bar 66 and gradual decline to the final pseudo-perfect cadence.

Although the second of the pair of slow movements, an Andante tonally orientated in G, appears on paper to be more substantial than the first, it is in fact somewhat briefer, lasting around a minute less in Bartók's own estimation of the durations. A variant of the second movement (and the parallel use of rehearsal numbers demonstrates the straightforward mapping between the two), it is more highly developed and intense, offering some of the most extraordinary sound combinations of the work. Pizzicato repeated notes replace the trills that had opened the second movement, and the cello's cantabile melody is truncated to its initial motif. With the repeated $G_3$s in the viola, the wispy, measured accelerating trills in the violins and the glissando pizzicato tritones in the cello, the texture again evokes the 'night music' mode; and the lyrical impulse of the imitative passage from bar 19 briefly evokes the performance style of the urban Gypsy band.

In the reworking of the 'chorale', rapid reiterations of seventh and ninth chords replace the sustained triads; and the expressive, chromatically complementary melodic material originally played by the first violin is transformed into stepwise figures in the cello, passed upwards through the viola and second violin. The modification of the third idea (from rehearsal letter B, bar 42) takes its basic raw materials (a repeated minor second interval, a rapid five-note figure, and a melody with pentatonic inflections) and moves them from a fragmentary state into one of greater continuity – as a regular pendulum-like repetition of minor seconds, a rising and falling seven-note pattern (D♯–E–F♯–G–F♯–E–D♯), and as an expressive melody whose first three phrases are played in fairly strict canon by the first violin and cello.

After the remarkable slithering chromaticism from bar 54, which can be considered as the elaboration of a half-diminished seventh on E with added major third (E–G–G♯–B♭–D), this chord becomes the explicit point of arrival at bar 60 as a shuddering tremolando. In the following pair of bars it punctuates a rhetorical 'Hungarian' gesture that gradually works up through the pitches F♯–A–C–F in unison. The subsequent section exploits material from the equivalent point in the second movement, now in inversion, with the violins playing a passionate, though modally ambiguous, four-phrase *parlando-rubato* melody imitatively and then in unison. Beneath this, the viola and cello provide textural underpinning, alternately scurrying up and down fundamentally chromatic figures that trace out the pitches of a G major/minor chord in the first pair of phrases, and moving this down a fifth to C major/minor from bar 73.

Residual traces of this chromatic parabolic pattern appear in the tranquil penultimate section in which the chorale material from the second movement is superimposed on the pianissimo arcs of the viola and iambic gestures of the cello. And at the culmination of the movement, the tonal ambiguity is retained by the B natural in the violin held against the cello's pizzicato G minor chord.

In his own analysis, Bartók describes the dance-like finale as a rondo, noting that it falls into a symmetrical $ABCB_vA_v$ form, and indeed this structure can be seen to summarise that of the entire quartet in an almost fractal piece of self-similarity. At the same time, the tonal scheme reflects that of the opening movement, following the trajectory B♭–C♯–E–G–B♭.

The movement is prefaced by a short passage that is loosely reminiscent of the gesture at the opening of Beethoven's Piano Sonata in C op. 111 and it takes on a framing function over the course of the movement, reappearing on three occasions and acting as a kind of ritornello. The principal theme itself begins off-centre tonally – after the three melodic B♭s in bars 18, 19 and 21 the next secure B♭ tonic does not appear until bar 54, appearing to move the tonality to G♭. This first theme is particularly permeated with overlapping major seconds (for instance, B♭–C/D♭–C♭ and E–F♯/G–F♮), manifestations of the so-called X-cell.[51]

Overall, the A section is constructed from four very closely related sub-units, and involves a symmetrical shape that might be labelled abb$_v$a$_v$. The first part leads from the start of the Presto in bar 14 (Fig. 42a) and the second, which opens with an inversion of the first five pitches of (a) from bar 55 (Fig. 42(b)). The two ideas are subsequently repeated in inversion and in reverse order: (b) in the violins from bar 75 and (a) in the cello and viola from bar 109 (the melody beginning in bar 116). As well as the modal flexibility – the underlying scale pattern can be considered as a *heptatonia secunda* mode on B♭ (B♭–C–D–E–F–G–A♭–B♭) that has been subject to chromatic embellishment (or 'mistuning') – the section is brimming with counterpoint, including several strict four-part canons as well as more informal imitative writing.

This contrapuntal spirit equally lies at the heart of the two central episodes: the rhythmic profile of the scurrying B section of three short notes followed by a longer one (the *quartus paeon* poetic foot), which was prepared in the preceding transition, is redolent of that of the transitional theme from the first movement, though its culmination at bars 347–8 with three F♯s falling to G sounds like a deliberate reference to Beethoven's Fifth Symphony; and for the even faster central section, Bartók transforms the principal theme from the first movement into a fugato supported by the local tonic and 'mistuned' dominant (E/B♭).

Having crossed the conceptual bridge at the heart of the movement, the final sections revisit earlier material, but with substantial variation. Although Bartók observed that the modified reprise of the B section is in G, this tonality is asserted somewhat obliquely and the general impression is one of musical whimsicality (for the passage from bar 485 the tempo marking is explicitly given as Allegretto capriccioso). And in the final part of the recapitulation of the A section (from bar 699) appears the famous 'barrel organ' episode, which Bartók marks Allegretto con indifferenza and indicates a mechanical style of performance, though he makes no reference to this in his own schematic analysis. This is a straightened-out version of the cello's theme from the A section (Fig. 42b) first diatonically in A major, then with the accompaniment in this

Figure 42. The first two themes from the finale of the Fifth String Quartet.

key superimposed on a version of the tune in B♭, the tonic of the quartet, in high register, as if the player had picked up a scordatura instrument. The gesture has been variously interpreted as gently humorous and bitterly sardonic, and as a comment on mechanised music. One might posit that a contrast is implied between the 'naïve' second violin, performing in a folk style in the lower register and using open A and E strings, and the sophisticated first violin, playing in the top register in the tricklier key of B♭, complete with terminal trill – indicating perhaps a dissonance between concert and vernacular readings of traditional music. Whatever the case, as with other similar musical effects, such as the Shostakovich parody in the Concerto for Orchestra, Bartók leaves it to the listener to determine and does not impose his own explanation.

With the coda at rehearsal letter N (bar 721), the quartet rushes to its conclusion beginning with the cello idea (Fig. 42(b)) enharmonically renotated in sharps. Gradually rising-scale patterns that coalesce the lower tetrachords of a major scale and that sitting a tritone higher (e.g. C–D–E–F/G♭–A♭–B♭–B♮), dominate the score and from this the opening 'Beethovenian' framing motif is restored, ever expanding in length. From bar 815, the figure C–B–A–G♯ is repeated ten times before landing on a chord of D major and from there making a final brilliant ascent to the tonic B♭.

Soon after completing the Fifth Quartet, Bartók began his work in the Hungarian Academy of Sciences, preparing the enormous collection of Hungarian folk music for publication. Taking the welcome opportunity to devote himself to this ethnomusicological work with open arms, he only performed in a couple of concerts during the rest of the year – the Second Piano Concerto in the Smetana Hall in Prague with the Czech Philharmonic Orchestra, conducted by Václav Talich in late November; and Beethoven's First Piano Concerto in Budapest's Municipal Theatre with Sergio Failoni, the director of the Hungarian State Opera. He briefly broke from his ethnographic labours to visit Holland with his wife for a fortnight from the last week of January 1935, playing the two violin sonatas in Amsterdam (the First Sonata) and Rotterdam (the Second Sonata) with Székely; a radio broadcast of a group of his piano pieces; and the Second Piano Concerto with the Rotterdam Philharmonic Orchestra conducted by Eduard Flipse. On this occasion the Bartóks stayed with the Székelys as the first house guests in their new home, called appropriately 'The Rhapsody', in Santpoort, near the coast to the west of Amsterdam.

Bartók agreed to be interviewed by a young music critic from the Amsterdam daily newspaper, *Algemeen Handelsblad*, who had arrived unannounced, and the long piece he wrote as a result was published on 29 January under the headline 'Béla Bartók Speaks: The Fable of the Faggot'. This curious title, which resonates with *A fából faragott királyfi* (*The Wooden Prince*), derived from a folk tale related by Bartók, which expressed metaphorically the necessity of dividing complex problems into their constituent components, and solving each separately:

> A father calls his sons together a gives them a bunch of branches and orders them to break them. One after the other tries it, but without success. Then the father takes the bunch apart and gives every son a branch which is now broken without effort.[52]

He was approached by another journalist the following week for the Amsterdam broadsheet *De Telegraaf*. Described as being initially shy and remote ('Bartók does not like to be treated as a celebrity, to be honoured as the center of attention'),[53] he gradually warmed up and spoke about the influence of folk music on young Hungarian composers. Discussing technical musical developments, he observed that:

> There was a time . . . that the direction seemed to be absolutely the atonality of the Austrians. Theoretically, it is considered possible, but the consequence is doubtful. I myself have never worked this way, and very likely you won't find anybody who does it this way in Hungary. Our folklore sources are still prolific.[54]

The concert in Rotterdam almost came to grief, the orchestra struggling to play the First Suite when Bartók entered the auditorium for the rehearsal. According to Mientje Székely, he was about to give up and leave but she managed to persuade him to remain. She recalled telling him bluntly 'Béla, the Concertgebouw doesn't even try it. The Hague doesn't even look at you, and now this small orchestra. . . . Flipse has worked hard to get this orchestra to play your difficult work and just now you can't wish more. He is very smart and I'm sure it will be better if you tell him what you want.'[55] Bartók apparently looked at Mientje 'as if [she] had said something terrible', but spoke to Flipse and they managed to turn the rehearsal round. She was impressed that he had been willing to listen to her petition for the conductor and that he been prepared to invest the effort to resolve the problems, remarking 'In this episode he was great'. After the concert she recollected that they went to a bar to eat, where a Romanian gypsy was playing the violin: 'He enjoyed that so much. He got so excited that he went to the man and talked to him about music. He asked him about the rhythm and the *glissandi* that he made since he liked that so much. I still remember his joy when he ran to that man.'

On 30 January 1935, while the Bartóks were still in Holland, the Budapest Opera opened its revival of *The Wooden Prince*, directed by Jan Cieplinski (whose production involved Cubist-inspired sets) and conducted by János Ferencsik, with six performances over the season. Meanwhile, he continued to perform as a pianist. Although his appearances became rather more sporadic and tended to be closer to home because of his folkloric work, he did accompany the celebrated cellist Emanuel Feuermann, the violinist Ede Zathureczky (who would later take on the directorship of the Academy of Music), and his long-standing collaborator, the soprano Mária Basilides, in various recitals.

Unfortunately, he was unable to attend the premiere of the Fifth String Quartet by the Kolisch Quartet in Washington at the Library of Congress on 9 April and despite best efforts to hear the subsequent radio broadcast, this also proved impossible. In Olin Downes's review of the concert, published in *The New York Times* on 14 April, he sang the praises of the ensemble, who opened with Beethoven's op. 130 quartet and the *Grosse Fuge* op. 133 as the finale, playing it entirely from memory, but he was somewhat disparaging about Bartók's piece, merely remarking that it was 'weak in invention but exacting in the demands of virtuoso performance'.[56]

Later that year, on 16 May, Bartók was elected as a corresponding member of the Hungarian Academy of Sciences by a large majority. Almost simultaneously, the first edition of his German-language scholarly study and collection of Romanian Christmas carols finally appeared under the imprint of Universal

Edition in Vienna, as *Melodien der rumänischen Colinde (Weihnachtslieder)*. His intention had been to publish this with Oxford University Press, to whom he had sent the manuscript almost a decade earlier, having completed it in September 1926. But as Bartók later noted in the draft of the preface to the first volume of *Rumanian Folk Music* (which remained unpublished in his lifetime):

> Their extremely interesting texts were supposed to appear in original as well as English. After several years of delay the translation into English prose was completed, one part in adequate archaic English, the rest (by someone else) in most unsuitable Kitchen-English. The publisher didn't wish to change this though. Result: I published the book at my own expense, however, only the musical part, because of lack of sufficient funds.[57]

His notation of traditional melodies had by this stage become much more elaborate than the earlier Hungarian collection and displayed an increasing attempt to delineate the finest details of a performance rather than simply presenting the bare outline of a melody. Five hundred copies of the book were printed, and subscribers had to be recruited to recoup the costs of publication. Bartók contacted many of his acquaintances to encourage them to purchase it at the price of five Swiss francs (including Imre Déak in Pasadena in the hope that he could persuade US libraries to buy it, and even Hubert Foss, his editor at Oxford University Press). During the rest of his lifetime, only three-fifths were sold and the enterprise proved far from a financial success.

Holidays were spent that year with Ditta and Péter in the northern Slovakian village of Csorba (Štrba) on the edge of the high Tátras. Two new choral works emerged during that summer, *Bartók Béla kórusművei: 27 két- és háromszólamú női- és gyermekkar* (27 Two- and Three-Part Choruses for Women's and Children's Choirs) and *Elmúlt időkből (From Olden Times)* for three-part unaccompanied male voices. Based on folk texts adjusted by Bartók, the material of the twenty-seven short unaccompanied pieces forming *Bartók Béla kórusművei* is original and the settings include eight more complex numbers explicitly written for women's voices. Kodály noted later that Bartók had developed an interest in the music of Palestrina, and these choruses can be seen to reflect this enthusiasm through their use of imitative counterpoint, controlled use of dissonance within a framework that prioritises consonant intervals (especially thirds, fifths and sixths), and a relatively simple rhythmic profile. The brief final chorus, simply labelled *Kánon* (Canon), is the most extraordinary, almost a summary or conspectus of the set of modal resources Bartók employs as a composer: its first two lines are octatonic (A–B–C–D–E♭–F–F♯–G♯); the third and fourth are whole tone (C♯–E♭–F–G–A); the fifth is pentatonic (C–D–E–G–A); the sixth a

synthetic pentatonic mode infilling a half-diminished seventh chord (C–D–E♭–
G♭–B♭); the seventh ambiguously chromatic; and the final Mixolydian (D–E–
F♯–G–A–B–C). Its text roughly translates 'I die for Csurgó,/But not for its
castle,/Just for one street;/But not for the street,/Just for one house,/And the one
who grew up there/My slim brown dove.'[58] It is not hard to imagine that Bartók
was thinking of Ditta when writing this, but another ('Lánycsúfoló' – girls'
teasing song, in which the boys tease the girls) is individually marked as '1935.
X. 31', and was certainly a birthday gift for her.

The triptych of three-part male-voice choruses in E, *From Olden Times*, is
organised with two substantial numbers with related titles surrounding a briefer
one. The first one's 'No-one is unhappier than the peasant' is transformed to
'No-one is happier' in the third number, with a final verse that lauds the peasant's self-reliance and absence of book learning. Bartók's choral writing in these
outer parts harks back to Renaissance music in its employment of imitative
techniques and carefully controlled balance of polyphony and homophony. The
energetic scherzo-like middle chorus traces out a cycle of exchanges that leads
from chestnuts to the bread given to his landlord, the story ending with the
protagonist being beaten with a stick by the recipient of the loaf.

The remainder of 1935 passed with few significant concert engagements.
Bartók's eldest son Béla, who had managed to get a job with MÁV (Magyar
Államvasutak), the Hungarian railway company, was married at the start of
December. A solo trip by Bartók to Winterthur followed, with a performance
of the Second Piano Concerto conducted by Scherchen in the Swiss city of
Schaffhausen. And plans were being hatched for a visit to Turkey through the
invitation of László Rásonyi, a Hungarian scholar at Ankara University, as
Bartók wished to pursue possible connections between the folk musics of the
two cultures. The year ended with a spat with the influential literary society,
the Kisfaludy Society of Budapest, who had awarded him their Greguss Medal
for his First Suite, written twenty-five years earlier. He advised them in a letter
written on 29 December to find someone better able to select their award
recipients. In a particularly sardonic tone he concluded with the words 'I take
the liberty of declaring that I do not wish to accept the Greguss Medal, neither
now, nor in the future, nor during my lifetime, nor after my death.'[59]

## CHAPTER TEN

# 'Stars, stars, brightly shine': 1936–1938

Bartók gave several performances of the Second Piano Concerto in Britain and Holland in early 1936. The first, on 7 January, was with Sir Henry Wood at the Queen's Hall in London. As he was appearing in Utrecht the following day, he travelled by air for the first time, flying to Rotterdam in a KLM Fokker XXII twenty-two-seater plane. He found the experience thrilling (even if the take-off was somewhat frightening) and wrote postcards to his mother and eldest son from his seat on the aircraft, describing the beautiful sky and the endless frilly clouds he could see below from an altitude of 2,400 metres. After the performance in Utrecht conducted by the young Dutch musician Willem van Otterloo, and a stop off in Santpoort, he returned to England again for a duo recital with Székely in the Rushworth Hall, Liverpool (for the Liverpool Music Society), and the Second Concerto in Birmingham, with the BBC Midland Orchestra conducted by Leslie Heward.

Bartók's inaugural lecture at the Hungarian Academy of Sciences on 3 February was, perhaps surprisingly, not directly about folk music, but was titled 'Liszt Ferenc' in the version published in the March issue of *Nyugat*, later appearing in print as 'Liszt Problems'. In a paper that re-appropriated Liszt as a radical composer he posed questions about the level of public understanding of his works, his technical developments and influence, his (mis)conception of Gypsy music; and his ethnicity. In the conclusion Bartók scored several points against some of his own more conservative fellow musicians and implicitly placed himself as an heir of Liszt's legacy, observing:

> there are important and publicly respected gentlemen in our musical life who are stubbornly opposed to everything new that has happened in Hungarian music since Liszt; who prevent, as far as they can, the following of Liszt's traditions; who, whether as composers or writers, spend their

whole lives crying down Liszt's artistic principles; who, in spite of all this, pharisaically call themselves supporters of Liszt, and pay homage to the memory of an artist whose whole life and work was in absolute opposition to their own. It is these who have the least right to take Liszt's name in vain, to claim him as a Hungarian and boast of him as a compatriot.[1]

In the same month that he was inaugurated into the Hungarian Academy of Sciences, Bartók defended himself from an extraordinary critical attack by the Romanian art historian, Professor Coriolan Petranu, in an article titled 'D. Béla Bartók şi muzika românească' published in the *Gând Românesc* (*Romanian Thought*). Clearly stung by the claims made in the article, Bartók's nine-page riposte, 'Antwort auf einem rumänischen Angriff' ('Response to a Romanian Attack'), appeared in the February edition of the Berlin scholarly journal *Ungarische Jahrbücher*. This was a point-by-point refutation of Petranu's assertions, including those about his supposed lack of impartiality and qualification to comment on the generality of Romanian music, as well as many detailed technical issues. Bartók concluded his polemic in a wounded, if resigned, tone with the comments:

> I am quite modest; I ask Mr Petranu to concede to me, a non-Rumanian, *just a quarter* of the liberty he does to a Rumanian. In the meantime, until that happens, I shall add to the thousands upon thousands of hours I have devoted to collecting, notating (the notation of a single, somewhat complex melody requires a work of several hours), classifying, and examining Rumanian folk music. And thousands upon thousands of hours toward additional research, not ever with the aim of being appreciated and rewarded (how right I was to discard this notion from the very beginning!), but to promote Eastern European folk music research: the international science to which I have dedicated and shall dedicate the greater part of my life.[2]

Bartók first met the conductor Paul Sacher, who had founded the Basler Kammerorchester in 1926 when he was just twenty years of age, in Basle in 1929. On 30 January that year, the composer had performed his Second Violin Sonata with Stefi Geyer in the concert hall of the Basle Conservatory of Music. Seven years later, in 1936, Sacher requested a new work from him for his orchestra, which specialised in contemporary and much earlier (generally pre-Classical) music. He had established a tradition of commissioning novel compositions since the ensemble's inception and his marriage in 1934 to Maja Hoffmann-Stehlin; she was the widow of Emanual Hoffmann, a member of the Hoffmann-La Roche family that owned the enormously successful Swiss pharmaceutical company, and she provided him with the means to become one of the most influential patrons of contemporary music.

In preliminary discussions, Bartók had been encouraged to write for a group of instruments in addition to a string orchestra. However, it seems that by 23 June, when Sacher contacted him to invite him to compose a new work to be performed at the Basle Chamber Orchestra's jubilee concert on 21 January 1937, he had already started work on a piece for strings.[3] He eventually settled on a double string orchestra that surrounded, on three sides, a piano, harp, percussion (pedal timpani, xylophone, bass, drum, cymbals, tam-tam and side drum) and celesta (Fig. 43), in the composition he titled *Music for String Instruments, Percussion and Celesta*. This arrangement that offered him interesting opportunities to explore both sonority and musical space.

Bartók moves away from the overtly symmetrical structures of the Fourth and Fifth String Quartets and the Second Piano Concerto, in a four-movement suite-like composition consisting of two slow-fast pairings. If these can be imagined to draw on the *verbunkos lassú-friss* model, then the tempo differential of the second pair of movements (Adagio–Allegro molto) is more extreme than that of the first pair (Andante tranquillo–Allegro). This coupling of tempi is reinforced by a tonal scheme built on minor third relationships that follows the overall trajectory A–C–F#–A, the key centres of the second and third movements alternately resting a minor third above and below the work's overall tonic.

The fugue that comprises the first movement is carefully contrived to traverse musical and physical space, the opening twelve entries working alternatively upwards and downwards by fifths in near-sinusoidal waves, and around and across the ensemble (reading from left to right):

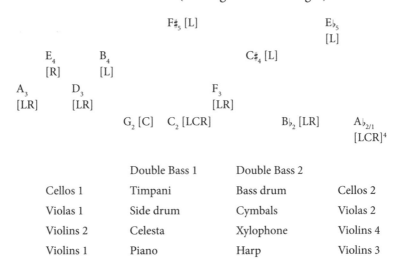

Figure 43. The orchestral layout of *Music for String Instruments, Percussion and Celesta*.

Built from four phrases, which operate as two related pairs, the fugue subject played by first and second violas entails chromaticism that results both from the polymodal writing and a kind of almost serial manipulation of four-note cells. The opening pitches can be understood to reference both a permutation of the 'Gypsy' scale on G ([G–]A–Bb–C#–D–Eb[–F#]), and the initial four notes of the Arab *Hijaz* tetrachord transposed to A (A–Bb–C#–D). With the addition of the falling dyad C♮–B♮, the first phrase (A–Bb–C#–C♮–B♮) encompasses the chromatic space of a major third. Through the course of the succeeding three phrases of the subject, a perfect fifth is negotiated and it is from the upper boundary (E) that the succeeding entry naturally emerges.

The movement progresses towards its climax from bar 52 by means of a recurring three-note pattern in the first and second violins, the initial pitch of which is shortened by one quaver on each of its two repetitions, as the cellos and basses descend through a chromatic scale. At bar 56 the pinnacle is marked by a hammered-out Eb (a diminished fifth higher than the tonic), which functions both as a mistuned dominant and the culmination of the process of ascending and descending cycles of fifths from A. In the closing section the celesta ripples out an ethereal twelve-note ostinato figure formed on the chromatic set C#–D–D#–E against the fugue subject in the tonic A, both in the original form and in inversion.

As a foil to the darkness of the first movement, the second is a bright and lively sonata-form Allegro that capitalises on the antiphonal opportunities of the two string sections. Prefaced by an upbeat minor third motif, the rhythmic profile of which pervades the movement, its principal idea involves a sequence of phrases built in turn on C, G, F and E before returning to C. Like the fugue subject (to which it is closely related) it melodically fills out chromatic space, in this case that of an augmented fourth. After the upbeat A, the version in the 'left' string section from bar 5 entails the pitches [C]–Db–C–D♮–E♮–F | [F#]–Eb–Db | [C]. With the response on G in the second orchestra, the upper pitches of the octave are encompassed, like a fugal answer. At the end of the section the piano picks out a fanfare-like summation (G–C–D–E–F–F#), a figure that will reappear on two subsequent occasions. It is almost in the guise of a framework theme (from bars 154 and 479), the perfect fourth that opens it being a particularly characteristic interval of the movement. In the ensuing material this is subject to interval expansion and over a pedal Ab the violas convert the music into a figure that shoots upwards (Ab | Cb–D♮–Gb–Bb | Db) with inversions and further extensions. The light and jovial second theme, in the dominant region, is again set in a chromatic milieu with a propensity to stress the flattened second and sharpened fourth degrees, and it is tonally ambiguous; the rhythm loosely recalls the vigorous final section of the 'Black Swan' *pas de deux* from

Tchaikovsky's *Swan Lake*, and indeed the whole movement seems pervaded by a terpsichorean temperament.

Near the start of the development, Bartók allows the music to settle on a complex ostinato played pizzicato by the second orchestra (joined by the basses from the first), utilising a five-quaver repeating pattern whose pitch content combines E♭ and A major triads. Against this, the piano and pizzicato upper strings from the first orchestra chime out an incisive little idea harmonised in first-inversion triads, which cycles from E♭ through A to F♯, tonal areas that Lendvai theorises are related to the tonic C along the axis system. In the following section (arguably a variant of the previous one, embracing the same three tonal areas) counterpoint again comes to the fore. After a moment of relative repose in E from bar 286 involving a series of overlapping scales combining Ionian and Lydian characteristics, a more regular fugal passage appears against a pedal F in the timpani. This propels the development towards its conclusion in a series of entries that at first rise by perfect fifths (E–B–F♯–C♯–G♯). The music then both ascends and descends scale-wise with entries both in the original form and inversion (D–E–F♯–G♯–A–G♯–F♯), the timpani and lower strings reiterating the tonic and dominant of C♯, a semitone higher than the tonic.

In the reprise, the first theme is rendered more metrically irregular, shifting between 2/4, 3/8 and 5/8, while the second theme (now conventionally restored to the tonic C) is in a consistent 3/8. A slight nod to the fugue subject of the first movement, and a further version of the piano's ritornello, lead to the final restatement of the principal theme and an unambiguous series of dominant-to-tonic cadential flourishes that bring this positive and highly accessible movement to its close.

Thanks in no small part to Stanley Kubrick's use of the impressionistic third movement – marked Adagio – in his 1980 horror film *The Shining*, it has subsequently taken on an independent musical and semiotic life. Written in a symmetrical ABCBA 'bridge' form, it is the apotheosis of the night-music style, with particularly prominent and effective use of the pedal timpani and xylophone. The fugue subject is exploited (in its original tonality) as a means of connecting together the various sections of the movement: the first phrase appearing in the first violas and cellos in bars 1–20; the second in the first violins, violas and cellos of the first orchestra between bars 33 and 34; the third in the upper violins and violas of the second orchestra (bars 60–4); and the final one in the piano and celesta from bar 73 to 74.

The opening (A) section is remarkable for its employment of an accelerating and decelerating figure on high F in the xylophone, a sound that recalls the click produced by the Northern Cricket Frog (*acris crepitans*), a native species of the United States. This call opens, closes and punctuates a section otherwise distinguished by the eerie use of glissandi in the timpani and an intensely lyrical and elaborately decorated melody. Initiated by the first violas, this is taken in turn by the second violins and passed to the second orchestra. Although the melody does not seem to be directly imitative of any of the Hungarian tunes that Bartók collected, it can be compared in its use of curt iambic rhythms (if not melodic contour) to several of the *parlando rubato* tunes in *The Hungarian Folk Song*, including number 259(e), 'Zúg az erdő' ('The Forest Rustles') an erotically charged song. The section reaches its high point through the piling up of entries of the final strain of melody in the second orchestra, and it closes with the 'rustling' C–F♯ in lower strings and timpani that has pervaded it.

After the first linking idea, the second section presents a new set of colours: a trilled whole-tone cluster in the upper strings of the second orchestra, and an ostinato of falling and rising major sevenths in the piano, doubled by glissandi up and down the intervals by the upper desk of second violins. Joined by tremolando versions of the sevenths in the first orchestra's violas and cellos, this provides an uncanny bed for a melody played by the celesta and two solo violins in the high register, a melody that slithers its way up to a climax on the tritone G♯–D.

The second phrase of the fugue leads to the middle section of the ABCBA 'bridge' form. A texture suffused with glissandi appears in the celesta, harp and piano, creating an entirely chromatic wash of sound over the pedal E♭. A melody that manipulates four-note chromatic cells emerges from this and brings the movement to its powerful climax at bar 45 (rehearsal letter C) on the collection of F–A♭–B–C♯–E–G (the amalgamation of D♭ major and E minor triads). Against this sonority appears what is effectively its 'chromatic complement' – the remaining pitches of the chromatic scale (excluding F♯) struck out in unison like the chiming of strangely tuned bells. This eleven-note set holds sway until bar 55 when the five-note cell is subject to overlapping imitation, the succeeding entries lying a fourth lower, eventually working down from C to E♭.

After the penultimate phrase of the fugue subject (in upper violins and violas of the second orchestra), the reprise of the B section entails the melody being played in canon at the diminished fifth, the upper three voices of the first orchestra leading the violas and cellos of the second, against arpeggiations and tremolandi of the pitches B♭–C–F in harp, celesta and piano. The final phrase of the subject leads to the briefest recollection of the opening section. The melody is reduced to a terse descending duet between the violins of the first orchestra, and if fades into silence with the first violas' restatement of F♯ against the timpani's C, and high F distantly clicking in the xylophone.

The Allegro molto finale is one of Bartók's finest symphonic dance movements. He described its structure formulaically as A+B+A, C+D+E+D+F, G, A, an admixture of ternary, rondo and chain forms in which the 'G' section is a version of the cyclic fugue subject. Against the downwardly strummed pizzicato chords of an unalloyed A major in the first orchestra, the violins and violas of the second orchestra play a unison melody in the Lydian mode with an additive rhythm. Bartók creates a slight rhythmic dislocation between the melody (which, although notated in 2/2, is articulated in groups of 2+3+3 quavers) and the accompaniment (whose rhythmic pattern is reversed to 3+3+2), so that collectively there is an event on every quaver in the bar. Such additive rhythms, often described as Bulgarian following the composer's own usage, are heard in Balkan traditional music (and can be widely found, for example, in Albania). More specifically, he transcribed them in several of the Romanian *colinde* melodies published in the previous year in his collection *Melodien der rumänischen Colinde (Weinachtslieder)*. The first four bars of the melody are stepwise in construction and isomorphically draw out a sawtooth shape that falls, rises and descends again. This is quite different from the second part, with its antiphonal overlaps, being more circular and restricted in register.

For the second theme, the tonality shifts to C♯/D♭ (timpani hammering out the tonic and dominant) and the sawtooth pattern of the opening theme is expanded, using perfect fourths, into a contour with a double rise and fall. The opening section closes with a summary of the principal theme and after a brief hiatus, moves onto the four related tunes of the following part. In the first theme (Bartók's C section), an amphibrach metre (short-long-short) gesture on B♭ sets into motion a metrically regular and largely white-note diatonic theme with prominent couplets; in the second (D) theme the tonality moves to F♯ for a syncopated and pentatonically inflected idea presented by the piano and varying the sawtooth contour of the movement's opening melody; and the third (E) theme modulates to Dorian E♭, the violas leading off with brisker material employing off-beat accents, giving the music tremendous impetus. The piano and harp now return to theme D, harmonised in F♯ minor, the strings responding antiphonally, initially with an ascending F Lydian scale. A rather cheekier idea in C♯, intimating children's taunting songs through its interplay between neighbour notes, provides the final new material of the movement (Bartók's section F). From bar 150, the repeated-note figure first exposed by the piano in bar 28 is restored, in a dissonant and percussive voicing.

The fugue subject makes its final expressive appearance from bar 203, with its intervals expanded, and an interlude from bar 230 places a solo cello from the first orchestra fleetingly into the limelight with a *verbunkos* gesture. The music spins off into what appears to be a summary of material in the rest of the movement as much as a recapitulation of the principal theme, and closure is achieved through parallel triadic motion onto the final A major triad.

Bartók completed work on *Music for String Instruments, Percussion and Celesta* on 7 September 1937. During the period of its composition he had spent some time on holiday at Ótátrafüred (now Starý Smokovec) in the Tátra mountains in northern Slovakia. While there he had also begun to prepare for his trip to Turkey, which finally took place in November 1936. He combined lectures to the Ankara branch of the Halkevi (an educational institution founded by the ruling Republican People's Party as part of its modernisation efforts), performances as a pianist, and a ten-day folk-music collecting foray to Adana and to several villages in the Mediterranean coastal area below Osmaniye (central southern Turkey, bordering on Syria); his visit lasted for most of the month. He was very ably supported by the Turkish composer and musicologist, Ahmed Adman Saygun, who acted as his interpreter and who notated texts.

Bartók's opening gambit on his arrival in Turkey was to examine the existing collection of recordings held by the municipal conservatory of music in Istanbul. He discovered that these had been unsystematically selected and lacked written versions of the texts. Unfortunately, he fell ill for several days in the early part of his time in Ankara and this affected the later progress of his own fieldwork. When Bartók, Saygun and two 'observers' from the Ankara music school (Necil Kazim and Ulvi Cemal) were eventually able to set off, they spent the first two days in Adana, relocating to Mersin on the third day before moving on to Osmaniye. As had often been the case in his previous collecting forays, Bartók had varying success in finding individuals who were willing to sing for them. In an article published the following year in *Nyugat*, he describes his particular joy in hitting upon an old man of seventy who:

> began to sing a tune for us in the courtyard without hesitation. It was an old narrative that he sang, about some war of the old days. I could hardly believe my ears, for it sounded just like a variant of an old Hungarian tune. . . . The second tune I heard from the old Bekir was again a variant of a Hungarian song. I was really much surprised at this. He sang this tune in the men's quarters, where the women are never allowed. Later on the old man's son and others present sang to us. We spent the whole evening in working, to my great satisfaction, but it was impossible to get a woman singer, and all the efforts of my companions to do so were in vain.[5]

As he noted to János Buşiţia on a postcard sent from Ankara on 18 November 1936, this was the first time Bartók had used a phonograph for field recording since 1917. That was nearly twenty years earlier, when he had collected tunes in Dumbrăviţa de Codru in Bihor County, Romania. Now, in Turkey in late 1936, after bad weather had caused travel difficulties, the team eventually arrived via Toprakkale at the winter quarters of the nomadic people from Tecirli in Tüysüz. With considerable effort they persuaded some of their number to sing.

Bartók's posthumously published monograph, *Turkish Folk Music from Asia Minor*, includes eighty-seven melodies, all but nine of which are vocal. His approach reveals a further emphasis on the 'descriptive' or 'etic', with such detailed Western notation of duration and ornamentation that some tunes become virtually unreadable. A significant intention of the research was to discover connections between this repertoire and that of Hungary, and he noted in the first and second of his conclusions that:

> (1) The seemingly oldest, most characteristic and homogeneous part of the material, representing its 43%, consists of isometric four section melodies with 8 or 11 syllabic text lines, in *parlando* rhythm, in Dorian, Aeolian or Phrygian mode, with descending structure, and in which traces of a pentatonic system appear, a system well known from Hungarian and Cheremiss folk melodies.
>
> (2) One part of the material as described under (1), that one with 8 syllabic sections is identical with the old Hungarian 8 syllabic material; the one with 11-syllabic sections is in near relation to the old Hungarian material. This points to a common Western-Central Asiatic origin of both the Turkish and Hungarian materials, and determines their age as of being at least 15 centuries old.[6]

The evidence for such grand assertions is of course rather meagre given the tiny sample, yet Bartók's micro-classification of the eighty-seven melodies into twenty groups suggests considerable musical heterogeneity.

Bartók remained in regular contact with Saygun while the two of them worked on the text of *Turkish Folk Music from Asia Minor*, and by 2 January 1937 he had transcribed a quarter of the tunes, which he found 'a most exhausting task, but at the same time, most interesting'.[7] He also informed Saygun about a radio talk he was due to give on 11 January that was to describe his experiences in Turkey, and this had obviously proved a stimulus to completing the transcriptions as rapidly as possible.

In the January 1937 edition of the journal *Music and Letters*, the American modernist poet Ezra Pound (who was by that stage a supporter of Mussolini) published a very favourable and cogent review of the performance of the Fifth

String Quartet at the previous year's Venice Biennale. In 'Ligurian View of a Venetian Festival', he commented that:

> Béla in music found himself in a mess similar to that which writers were in, back in 1905 and 1906. Somebody had to stir round, break moulds, try this, that and the other and generally get out of the slough of a partially dead and generally moribund idiom. Bartók was in the hinterland. There was abundant Magyar material, not quite as unstuck from the exploited European fields as was the Russian, or as the Russian had been forty years earlier, but still good.
>
> Bartók spent years in grasping. The anxiety shows, to my mind, in such of his works as I had hitherto heard. They were a mixture. In the fifth Quartet he has, I should say, come out on top of the rubble. I find the work whole, concrete, coherent. I think you could play it before or after or between any music you like and not damage it. It would hold its own and be different.[8]

Pound could see in Bartók a reflection of his own striving and effort, and he noted of the quartet in his *Guide to Kulchur*: 'It has the defects or disadvantages of my Cantos. It has the defects and disadvantages of Beethoven's music, or of as much of Beethoven's music as I can remember. Or perhaps I shd. qualify that: the defects inherent in a record of struggle.'[9]

The world premiere of *Music for Strings, Percussion and Celesta* took place in a concert held on 21 January 1937 conducted by Paul Sacher, to celebrate the tenth anniversary of the Basler Kammerorchester. It appears to have been a great success. According to Bartók, in a letter to his mother and Aunt Irma the following day, it received a tempestuous reception and Sacher repeated the finale as an encore.[10] The work rapidly became part of the standard orchestral repertory. Early performances included those in the Venice Festival, conducted by Fernando Previtali on 6 September, and the American premiere with the New York Philharmonic conducted by John Barbirolli at Carnegie Hall on 28 October.[11]

Basle involved endless socialising and Bartók was all too pleased to move on to Amsterdam and the Székelys. A radio broadcast the pair gave in Paris on 30 January proved amusing if irritating, as Bartók reported to his friend in Basle, the socialite Annie Müller-Widmann (who with her husband Oskar was a great collector of art). It seems that the announcer had confused the names of the two musicians, and they almost appeared as Zoltán Bartók and Béla Székely, their nationality supposedly Czech![12] Although there was little time to rehearse for a performance of the Second Piano Concerto in Brussels, Bartók was extremely impressed with the Flemish Radio Orchestra players' ability to sight-read, and 'delighted' with the performances of the orchestral version of the Second Violin Rhapsody, of *Village Scenes* and the suite from *The Miraculous Mandarin*.

As had become his custom over previous seasons, Bartók slipped over the channel with Székely to perform in England in a broadcast organised with a degree of deviousness by his agent Antonia Kossar, the BBC having become rather less interested in him as a commodity by that stage. On 9 February he gave the world premiere to the British section of the ISCM of several numbers from the pedagogic work, *Mikrokosmos*. He had commenced this in 1926 and would not complete it until 1939, by which point it would consist of 153 pieces in six volumes, taking the pianist from his or her first encounters with the instrument up to performance on the concert platform. Bartók's son Péter had begun learning the piano with his father in 1936. He describes how at first some pieces would be specially written for his lessons, though soon the speed with which Bartók composed them exceeded the boy's ability to learn them. The title, Bartók explained in a 1945 WNYC radio broadcast, 'can be inter-preted as a series of pieces in all of different styles [*sic*] which represents a small world. Or, it may be interpreted as a musical world for the little ones, for chil-dren.'[13] The ISCM concert in London's Cowdray Hall gave him the opportunity to play twenty-seven of the pieces in two groups (as well as the First Violin Sonata and Second Rhapsody, with Székely). M.M.S. (Marion Margaret Scott), the *Musical Times* reviewer, was generous in her praise of the performance of the violin pieces, 'which could be accepted as models of the[ir] interpretation', and she felt the slow movement of the sonata was 'rather lovely, in a half-frozen way: the violin solo is a masterstroke.'[14] As for his part in the recital, she considered that:

> The great event of the evening, however, was the 'first performance in any country' of pieces from 'Mikrokosmos', here arranged in two groups of seventeen and ten pieces each and played by Bartok with the firm – often fierce – touch he seems to like. Certainly his playing and these pieces (believed to have been originally written for a child's method of piano-playing) are bared of sensuous colour and atmosphere. Both have the clean-ness of steel. Each piece has a separate entity, much as Chopin's Preludes are separate – but Bartók makes them 'one-ideaed'. His ruthless logic strips away everything, save what is necessary to present and conquer the special difficulty chosen. The titles give an immediate clue to the contents: 'Five-tone Scale', 'Fourths', 'Melody', 'Syncopation', 'Minor Seconds', 'Major Sevenths' [*sic*] are typical examples. Occasionally Bartók relaxes to the grim

humour of 'From the diary of a fly' (it sounded like a portrait of the flies Mengelberg used to invite his guests to catch in the Val Sinestra!), but otherwise the pieces, if for children, must be for those of an iron age. To-day they require a strong man to get at their pith.

Bartók's enormous contribution to the field of Hungarian choral music was celebrated on 18 April 1937 by 'The Singing Great Plain' festival devoted to him and held in his presence at Kecskemét, the birthplace of Kodály. In this remarkable event, numbers from the Twenty-Seven Two- and Three-Part Choruses and *From Olden Times* were performed, and in total some twenty-one world premieres were given. A performance of the children's choruses in the following month had a particularly powerful effect on Bartók, as he explained to Annie Müller-Widmann on 24 May:

> It was a great experience for me when – at the rehearsal – I heard for the first time my little choruses coming from the lips of these children. I shall never forget this impression of the freshness and gaiety of the little ones' voices. There is something in the natural way these children from the suburban schools produce their voices, that reminds one of the unspoilt sound of peasant singing.[15]

In this letter he discussed his holiday plans and his intention of going to the region of Carinthia in Austria. His original scheme had been to holiday in Italy, but for his remarks that 'I have no wish, at least during my few week's holiday, to be continuously bothered by the aggressiveness of the Italians. Actually, they say that Austria has also been infected with the Nazi poison, but it is not so obvious there.'[16] On the same day he wrote to Paul Sacher about a further potential commission for a chamber piece. Bartók was concerned about the available time to complete a work by the following summer, and had several possible suggestions: a quartet for two pianos and two percussionists; a piano trio; or a piece for voice and piano. By 30 June he had decided that it should be the piece for pianos and percussion (not yet describing it with the published title), though it was the end of August before he was able confirm this. On 18 October he finally advised Sacher that it would be called Sonata for Two Pianos and Percussion, rather than Quartet, to allow for situations where it might require three rather than two players.

The musical seeds of the Sonata for Two Pianos and Percussion, which was composed between July and August 1937, can be traced back to earlier pieces by Bartók and in particular to the slow movement of his First Piano Concerto in which the piano subtly interlaces with timpani, side drums and cymbals.

Algerian Arab music that had provided the inspiration for this part of the concerto was obviously still exerting an influence on him. Since his trip to north Africa in 1913 he had been exploring the sonic potential of percussion beyond its basic functions in art music of articulation, or punctuation providing exotic colour. At the same time, it is conceivable that Bartók might have discovered in jazz how a 'traps' or kit player could interact creatively with a solo pianist. Certainly, in a short article published in *The Pittsburgh Press* some four years later, on 23 January 1941, he is quoted as admitting that jazz had influenced some of his more recent music.[17] Interestingly, although he was apparently happy to describe Benny Goodman (who commissioned *Contrasts*) as an excellent musician, Bartók had by that time 'not heard him play any popular music'. He had also demonstrated in *Music for String Instruments, Percussion and Celesta* how percussion could be successfully integrated into an orchestra lacking brass and woodwind, and it is arguable that he was making explicit in this work what had been implicit in some of his earlier piano music through its emulation of percussive sonorities.

Composed to supplement the two-piano repertory that he and Ditta performed in their duo recitals, the Sonata for Two Pianos and Percussion is in three movements. It neither exploits the symmetrical structures of the Fourth and Fifth Quartets and Second Piano Concerto, nor the large-scale variation form of the Second Violin Concerto. It is heavily 'front-loaded', the first movement being of around the same duration as the second and third in combination and bearing much of the emotional weight of the piece. Like Bartók's other music of the 1930s, the work's chromaticism is placed within a clear tonal context; indeed it looks to classical key relationships for the three movements, with a tonic of C for the outer pair and the central Lento, ma non troppo in the subdominant tonality of F. Bartók makes use of a relatively wide range of percussion instruments: three pedal timpani; xylophone; bass drum; two suspended cymbals; a pair of clash cymbals; two side drums (one with and one without snares); a tam-tam; and a triangle. He also uses some relatively unfamiliar (for the time) techniques, using beaters in non-standard ways and describing in detail which parts of the instruments' surfaces should be struck.

The composer provided his own analysis of the structure of the sonata in the Basle newspaper, the *National-Zeitung*, on 13 January 1938. In his description of the first movement he refers to two contrasting thematic areas and defines a third idea as alternately a 'codetta' in the exposition and 'a rather extensive coda (with a *fugato* beginning) built on the closing theme' (see Table 3).[18] The following discussion (also outlined in Table 3) offers an alternative sonata-form interpretation involving three distinct thematic areas and somewhat different structural proportions.

Table 3. The structure of the first movement of the Sonata for Two Pianos and Percussion.

| Bartók's analysis | | Alternative analysis | |
|---|---|---|---|
| Bar numbers | | Bar numbers | |
| 1–31 | Introduction | 1–31 | Introduction |
| 32–86 | Main theme group, consisting of two themes | 32–86 | Main theme group |
| 87–104 | Contrasting theme | 87–104 | Second theme |
| 105–74 | 'Codetta' (later described as closing theme) completing with brief reference to contrasting theme (161–74). | 105–32 | Third theme |
| | | 133–60 | Development of third theme |
| | | 161–74 | Development of second theme |
| 175–94 | Transition | 175–273 | Development of first theme |
| 195–216 | Development part 1 (ostinato in E) | | |
| 217–31 | Development part 2 (short interlude) | | |
| 232–73 | Development part 3 (ostinato in G♯ – inversion of part 1) | | |
| 274–91 | Recapitulation of main group | 274–91 | Recapitulation of main theme |
| 292–331 | Recapitulation of contrasting theme | 292–331 | Recapitulation of second theme |
| 332–3 | Coda | 332–432 | Recapitulation of third theme |
| | | 433–43 | Coda |

The energetic, if edgy, opening movement is prefaced by an introduction that acts as a structural upbeat, establishing F♯ in the role normally taken by a dominant. Surmounting three pentatonically related pitches presented in turn by the timpani (F♯–B–C♯), the first piano gradually unfolds, *pianissimo*, a chromatic figure (F♯–E♯–A/G♯–D♯–E/G♮–D♮/C♯) built on what can be conceived as the underlying harmonic progression I–v–♭II–V, which shifts metrically on each iteration. The second piano supplies the hitherto missing B♭ and B, and then completes the chromatic set with C♮, initiating a transposed repeat of the

figure in bar 5. The three phases of presentation and contrapuntal development of this idea are punctuated (in bars 6–8 and 10–11) by impressionistic
splashes of colour. With the second entry (in bar 8), versions on G and D♭ are
canonically superimposed, and played throughout in doubled minor sixths; a
consistent harmonic unit that emerges from this texture is the familiar bitter-
sweet 'major-minor chord', a first-inversion chord containing both major and
minor thirds (for example, D–F–B♭–D♭ on the first beat of bar 8). In bar 11 the
basic figure is inverted and the second piano begins to disturb the underlying
9/8 rhythm. From bar 18, the pace picks up, and against the upward arpeggiation of a substitute dominant chord (B–D–F–A♭–B♭) the rhythmic characteristics of the first subject proper are established.

The time signature of 9/8 is retained for the Allegro molto first subject, but
the metrical space is organised such that at times it can almost sound as if two
4/4 metres have been displaced by a quaver and overlaid. The material is played
by both pianos starting on the second quaver of the bar and has something of
the four-square rhythmic and tonal organisation of Hungarian folk song, but it
interlocks with the timpani to fill every quaver (TPT/PTP/TPP|P, where T
indicates timpani and P pianos). This can be heard as a reorganisation of 9/8
into units of 3/4 and 3/8 in which the timpani articulate the downbeats and the
pianos play on the offbeats (see Fig. 44). It is probably no coincidence that the
final phrase of the melody is related (by retrograde) to the arpeggio figure that
dominated the final six bars of the introduction. Arriving on the dominant, a
passage over a pedal G in the timpani involves the reiteration of quaver pairs
that alternate a perfect fourth E♭–A♭ and the quartal trichord C♮–F♯–B; and in
the first piano, a fragmentary figure derived from the three-note cells of the
introduction is heard on D and then in inversion on A♭. Taken together these
pitches add up to the Gypsy scale on C (C–D–E♭–F♯–G–A♭–B).

After a brief reprise of the first theme on A/F♯ (bar 61), and a series of overlapping entries of a five-note figure (A–G♯–F♯–E♯–D) in the second piano that
rises through a cycle of perfect fourths from D to A♭, the music settles into a
more tranquil mood for the second theme, beginning in E (though played over
a pedal D in the second piano); this has something in common in terms of
contour with the equivalent theme from the first movement of Beethoven's
'Waldstein' Piano Sonata in C op. 53. The linear rise and fall of this gentle,
though metrically irregular, four-phrase idea is harmonised by parallel first-
inversion major chords, articulated with acciaccaturas. It progresses through
F♯ and A♭ on its way to the B major-minor chord that underpins the third
thematic area (or codetta).

Accelerating from the calmer tempo of the second theme, the 9/8 metre is
now blurred by the tying of the B major chords across bar lines, suggesting

Figure 44. The first theme of the opening movement of the Sonata for Two Pianos and Percussion. The pitch material in the two pianos (replicated across four octaves) in the upper stave, the timpani part in the lower stave.

compound duple organisation. From bar 118 two effective 6/8 metres are superimposed, displaced by a dotted crotchet in the second piano part as the tonality moves to C. Up to this point, the melodic lines have been predominantly stepwise in motion so that the horn-call-like rising major sixths from the contextually dissonant D to B now stand out as an assertive new gesture. A characteristic sonority of this passage is the major-minor chord, and a sense of closure appears on a dominant G chord of this species, spiked with the falling major sixth from G to B♭ in the xylophone.

It is from this idea that, arguably, the development springs in bar 133, reversing the order of the themes in the exposition (though Bartók considered the material as far as bar 194 as still being expository or transitional). The third theme, faster still, sounds out over a base of quietly rolled glissandi in the pedal timpani, sliding first up and down the minor third from F$\sharp_2$ and then the major third (notated as a diminished fourth), the pianos playing in rough inversion. As this phase nears its end, the first piano takes up a rising linear progression of parallel second-inversion triads, and the second piano responds with a similar descending sequence. Parallel first-inversion triads harmonise the very brief development of the second subject in the first piano (beginning in E at bar 161), which is repeated in canon at the twelfth below by the second piano a bar later. The rest of the development is taken up with the first subject. In the first part (bars 175–94) the focus is on an oscillating semitone figure (the first two pitches of the introduction's chromatic idea), with the gradual accumulation of perfect fourths such that by bar 188 these have become eight-note quartal chords mirrored between the pianos. From bar 195 the motif from the intro-duction, transposed to E, forms an ostinato in the second piano that gradually evolves through the accretion of fourths from bar 204. Above this, fragments of the principal theme are developed by the first piano, disrupting the rhythmic stasis of the ostinato. A false recapitulation on A at bar 217 sets in motion a second phase of development in which a rather jazzy variant of the first theme's rhythm, played by the xylophone (♪♩♩♪♫♪|♩), comes to the fore; the ostinato figure reappears in inversion on G♯ from bar 232.

The return to the recapitulation (in which the material continues to be developed) takes the turn-like chromatic figure C–C♯–D–E–D♯ and transposes it upwards through a complete cycle of fourths from $C_1$. Each iteration overlaps with the previous one, up to the final dominant on G that leads to the tonic presentation of the first theme at bar 274.[19] Now assertive and even triumphant in mood, it is expanded and opens with bright third-less C chords and the residual trace of the earlier rhythm (♪♪♪♩. ♪♫). The change to quartal chords in the third phrase initiates the transition to the inverted second subject in A, with parallel first-inversion major chords in the second piano and a quietly glittering descant employing the pitches G♯, A and B♭ in the first piano. Shifting from F♯ through to C (tonal areas that Lendvai would regard, along with A and E♭, as substitute tonics), the section ends with repeated falling augmented fifths.

These are reflected as rising minor sixths (instead of the earlier major sixths) for the reprise of the 'horn call' third theme as a fugato in D in which the first set of entries rises by a sequence of fifths, and the subject is subsequently inverted and mirrored. From bar 383 a novel ostinato figure in the first piano is derived from the rising sixth motif ($A_2$–$F_3$–$D♭_4$–$B_2$–$G_3$–$E♭_4$). The figure is doubled a minor tenth lower, creating a motoric chromatic underlay for the fragmentary interjections from the second piano, analogous to the episode in the development at bars 195–216. After the section has reached its climax with twelve reiterations of the rising minor sixth A♯–F♯, the subsequent passage propels a further variant of the motif through a stretto in which the entries are related through a diminished seventh (G–A♯–C♯–E). The other pseudo-tonics for C are then asserted: E♭ (from bar 422), joined by A (from bar 426), and at bar 436 a repeated chord coalesces the pitch content from all four major chords of Lendvai's 'tonic axis' (C–C♯–E♭–E–F♯–G–A–B♭), an octatonic collection.[20] The final pseudo-perfect cadence is prepared from bar 437 with the alternation in the timpani between F♯ and C, and a reiteration of a figure (C–B♭–A♭–A♮–B♮) that picks out the alternative sixths and sevenths of the melodic minor scale of C; and the penultimate chord elides B and D♭ perfect fifth dyads over G, creating the altered dominant chord G–B–D♭– F♯–A♭ that slides by a semitone onto the perfect fifth on C which closes the movement.

In Bartók's own analysis, he comments that the second movement 'is in simple song form, A B A', though this description hardly does it justice. It is one of the most expressive and beautifully wrought examples of his 'night music' genre and capitalises on the sonic opportunities provided by the percussion instruments that set it into motion. The unison melody with a narrow tessitura initiated by the first piano winds chromatically around a series of pedal tones that gradually spell out a diminished seventh chord (B–D–F–A♭). The influence of Arab music is conspicuous in the compressed phrases that close on the tonic F in bars 8 and 13. For the middle part of this first idea (bars 14–21), Bartók inverts the opening four-note gesture, unfolding it as a descending and decorated half-diminished seventh (F♯–A–C–E) against a prevailing F♯ tonality. The reprise of the material from bars 5–8 closes the section and prepares for the more elaborate middle part of the movement.

Here a slow-moving motif (D–E♭–E–D♭) is established in the second piano. Above it the first piano plays a rhythmic gesture in staccato quintuplet semi-quavers enclosing a minor third (or later a minor second). This becomes ever more insistent in the approach to the first climax in bar 45, the xylophone and pianos alternating the figure on B♭. There is a winding back from bar 48, and at this juncture Bartók introduces another harmonic resource: the pitches of the ten-note chords in the first piano (in which the left hand reflects the right), which accompany the expressive melody outlined by the top notes, form complete octatonic collections; with the addition of the second piano an almost entirely chromatic texture is created. This dissolves into rapid contrary-motion writing leading to an ostinato (bar 60) from which emerges an instance of Bartók's nature symbolism, the isomorphism of sounds from the natural environment. A Debussyan sonic mist created by the superimposition of white- and black-note scales (later, glissandi in doubled thirds) supports the reprise of the material from the A section (bar 66), and now the melody is provided with a descant that is replete with *verbunkos* gestures – dotted rhythms and fioriture.

Table 4. The outline of the structure of the finale of the Sonata for Two Pianos and Percussion.

| Bars | Theme | Structure | Tonality |
|---|---|---|---|
| | | **Exposition** | |
| 1–43 | 1 | A₁ (1–17), A₂ (18–27), B (28–43) | C |
| 44–102 | 2 | A (44–55), A inverted (56–73), A original and inversion (74–102) | E |
| 103–33 | 3 | A₁ (103–14), A₂ (115–26), B (127–33) | G – Largely based on set (C♯–D–E♭–F♯–G–A♭–A♯–B–C) |
| | | **Development** | |
| 134–76 | 1 | Part 1 | E♭→A♭→D♭→F♯ |
| 177–228 | 2 | Part 2 | F♯→D→A→F♯ |
| 229–47 | 1 | Part 3 | B♭→G→E♭→C→A♭ |
| | | **Recapitulation** | |
| 248–68 | 1 | A (developed further) | C |
| 269–86 | 2 | A | E♭ |
| 287–300 | 1 | B | D♭ |
| 301–50 | 3 | A inverted, A inverted (harmonised in minor thirds→ first-inversion major chords→ major-minor chords→ second-inversion major chords→ minor sixths) | Set (E♭–E–F–A♭–A–B♭–C–C♯–D) with transposed versions |
| 351–419 | 1 | Coda | E♭–B♭–F–G–C |

In the coda there is an exquisite moment as the pianos arpeggiate descending octaves. A brief reprise of the middle section's quintuplet rhythms leads to the tonic F, with fifths dyads punctuated by acciaccaturas whose pitches are placed a semitone away from the sustained F and C. The xylophone's final gesture slows the quintuplet figure down and through the use of A♭ implies a minor mode point of closure.

Bartók describes the structure of the cheerful and energetic finale as a compromise between sonata and rondo; Table 4 outlines its overall form, the grey shading highlighting the porosity between the end of the development and the start of the recapitulation. If the second theme of the first movement seems to bear some resemblance to Beethoven's 'Waldstein' Sonata, then the finale's main theme has similarities – perhaps coincidental – with another of his works, the first of the *Zwölf Contretänze* (Fig. 45). While Beethoven's C major country dance is purely diatonic, Bartók's theme is formed on the acoustic scale in C. When compared to the first full four bars of Beethoven's work, its outline is stretched to six bars to accommodate the rising and falling perfect fourths in the timpani.

Figure 45. (a) The start of the opening theme of the finale of the Sonata for Two Pianos and Percussion as played by the xylophone and timpani; (b) the opening of the theme of the first of Beethoven's *Contretänze*.

The largely diatonic second thematic area of the Sonata for Two Pianos and Percussion involves the decorated reversal of direction of the first theme (Fig. 46a). The more chromatic third idea (Fig. 46b) involves a wave-like fall and rise that opens on the vamp between the tonic G and dominant augmented chord with major seventh (DM7[♯5]). The clusters of semitones in this latter figure A♯[B]C/C♯[D]E♭/F♯[G]A♭, which sit around the third, fifth and tonic in G, can perhaps be seen to relate to the augmented fourth, perfect fifth and minor sixth of the Hungarian 'Gypsy' scale.

Overall, the movement draws on a similar set of compositional resources as the first, and as well as the familiar polymodality, the following techniques can be found: static diatonic areas (for instance, the opening tremolando C major

Figure 46. The finale of the Sonata for Two Pianos and Percussion (a) the second thematic area; (b) the third thematic area.

chords); parallel diatonic chords (for example, bar 28 onwards, the accordion-like writing from bar 174, and in the coda, from the upbeat to bar 351); fourth chords; ostinato passages (in the third theme from bar 115); and contrapuntal procedures such as imitation, canon (from the upbeats to bars 160 and 229) and stretto.

The Sonata for Two Pianos and Percussion was one of the key works behind the formulation of Lendvai's golden-section theory. While there can be no doubt that the mathematical proportions Lendvai asserts exist in the piece are striking, there is no evidence that they were adopted consciously by Bartók either here or in his other works. At the same time, as I have noted elsewhere:

> If, as may be the case, some of Bartók's forms do conform to golden section principles, what are we to do with this information? Are we to assume that this manifestation of a ratio which is sometimes found in the natural world is an indication of some aesthetic quality? Is an 'authentic interpretation' (the term interpretation being as appropriate to the listener as the performer) one in which we are consciously aware of the proportions of the music? If this is the case, it suggests a mode of listening dependent on an awareness of the passage of chronological time, rather than the fluctuating, personal 'psycho-logical time' which usually holds sway in the apprehension of music.[21]

It is unquestionably of interest that Lendvai should find in the often sectional-ised forms of Bartók, with their careful demarcation by duration, the manifes-tation of organic principles. Such organicist tropes have been a feature of much of the subsequent scholarship and analysis of his music.

On 21 August 1937, Bartók wrote to his eldest son to update him on his news, telling him that he had been working during the summer on a second 'order' from Basle and that, hopefully, he had finished it. He also alluded to a further commission – the violin concerto he would be writing for Székely. It seems that the violinist had for some time wished that Bartók might write a concerto for him, and on 10 August 1936 he had made the request in writing.[22] In his response, a couple of months later, Bartók had indicated his interest. But he had also noted that his annual timetable, which normally placed composi-tional activity in the summer months, meant he could not possibly complete such a work before the beginning of the following autumn. Székely had asked for three years' exclusive rights to performance, and according to Claude Kenneson he believed:

> that their agreement would not constitute the acceptance of a commission or of a long-term business proposition. Rather, Bartók would write the new

Violin Concerto out of friendship – the honorarium offered, and accepted
[500 Dutch florins or guilders], would simply serve the purpose of compensation for the lack of performance fees that would have been paid to Bartók
by other artists during the time of Székely's exclusive performance rights.[23]

The commission fee was relatively modest for such a major work – it has been
estimated that 500 guilders in 1938 would have the equivalent purchasing
power of around €4,500 in 2013.[24] Although the agreement with Székely, which
Bartók sent him in May 1937, indicated that he would 'place a copy of the
work's score at Zoltán Székely's disposal by the end of 1937', according to the
dates given in the score, he did not actually start composing the work until
August 1937 (presumably after completing the Sonata for Two Pianos and
Percussion), and it was not finally completed until New Year's Eve, 1938.[25]

As for the rest of 1937, much of Bartók's time was spent on ethnomusicological work and preparing the following year's concert activities. In mid-
September he contacted Géza Voinovich, the Secretary General of the
Hungarian Academy of Sciences, to report on his progress with the folk collection. In the period since taking up the post in 1934 he had revised transcriptions of tunes held on phonograph (more than 1,000 items). As well as the work
on the Hungarian material, comparative study was required of the music of 'the
neighbouring peoples'. Bartók estimated that this would take a further three
years. In total he envisaged that the 12,000 songs would require a publication of
around 4,000 pages. It appears that the Academy of Sciences approached the
Ministry of Religious Affairs and Education for financial support for the project,
but this was rejected on the grounds that no money had been set aside for such
work in the budget for 1938–9.[26] Bartók was meanwhile also working on the
Second Violin Concerto. As he wrote in January 1938 to his former student
Wilhelmine Creel (who had studied with him between 1936 and 1937), it was
not yet finished, and this was 'a very oppressing burden on me'.[27]

The threats of Nazism and Fascism he alluded to in his letter to Frau Müller-
Widmann had encouraged Bartók to place a veto on the broadcast of his music to
Germany and Italy. He considered the matter in the newspaper *Pesti Napló* on
10 October 1937, and his rationale was carefully worded and judiciously explained:

I have never given broadcast performances for the radio networks of either
Italy or the Third *Reich*; what is more, I have never even been asked by those
two broadcasting corporations to perform directly for them. Under the
circumstances, I thought it would be unfair to allow the Hungarian Radio
to offer these two broadcasting corporations my recitals performances on
Radio Budapest as a sort of gift . . .[28]

It is easy to paint Bartók in the role of a political and moral idealist, as many of his early post-war biographers did. According to his youngest son Péter:

> It could be counted on that what he said reflected what he thought, there could be no doubt; there was no deception, not the slightest falsehood disguised as tact (whatever that is), you always knew where you stood with him. This applied also to those whose attitudes he detested for their insincerity or for other reasons; their recollections of my father are, perhaps, not the most pleasant. He was not good at hiding his sentiments.[29]

There can be no doubt that Bartók utterly despised Nazism and totalitarianism. But notwithstanding Péter Bartók's memories of his father as being totally incapable of artifice and guile, he does appear to have been sufficiently pragmatic to understand the need to preserve his family and work, and 'manage' his relationship with the political and cultural regime in Hungary. He commented in a letter to Annie Müller-Widmann on 13 April 1938 (a month after the Anschluss) that he believed the Hungarian government had taken the wrong track in November 1937. This was presumably an allusion to the discussions that took place on 25 November between Prime Minister Kálmán Darányi and Hitler, in which the latter discussed cooperation between the two countries to deal with Czechoslovakia, and in particular with the issue of the German-speaking parts known as the Sudetenland.[30] Bartók also asked the newspaper *Az Est* to print a 'declaration' that he hadn't sent any statement to the German authorities forbidding broadcasts of his work there in response to a piece published in March 1938.

The premiere of the Sonata for Two Pianos and Percussion, featuring the composer, Ditta, and the percussionists Fritz Schiesser and Philip Rühlig, took place in Basle on 16 January 1938; it was the tenth anniversary concert of the Basle Group of the Swiss section of the ISCM, for whom Paul Sacher had commissioned the piece. Although this passed with little comment in the English-language press, a high-profile performance subsequently took place in London on 20 June 1938, at the annual ISCM Festival. In the review of this concert in *The Times* the following day, the anonymous critic offered a very positive response to what would become an influential work for the post-war avant-garde:

> Easily the most exciting work in last night's programme was Bartók's sonata for two pianos and percussion, for the new sonorities disclosed by the unsuspected tonal affinities between pianos and tympani and xylophone (representing the treble and bass of a composite percussion instrument)

stimulated a first-class mind into thinking in a new way – the novel medium, that is, actually provoked individuality of thought. Stylistically the seven percussion instruments and the pianos hung together because they were all struck, and not stroked or blown; emotionally the music was mysterious in keeping with the evocative, non-thematic character of drums and such.[31]

A few days after the premiere of the Sonata for Two Pianos and Percussion in Basle in January, Bartók headed off to London to give what would be his final studio broadcast on British radio – including numbers from *Mikrokosmos* and from the Forty-Four Duos for two violins. With this and the June ISCM concert came to an end a relationship with Britain that had endured nearly thirty-five years, dating from 1904 and his first performance with Hans Richter and the Hallé Orchestra.

The impact of the Anschluss now dominated Bartók's thoughts, as his letter of 13 April to Annie Müller-Widmann demonstrates. In what is one of his most direct and anguished communications to any of his friends he accepts that the capitulation of Hungary 'to this regime of thieves and murderers' is only a matter of time: 'And how I can then go on living in such a country or – which means the same thing – working, I simply cannot conceive.' Feeling it will be his 'duty' to emigrate, he is desolate at the thought that at the age of fifty-eight he may have to return to piano teaching in a foreign country to earn a living, but he simply cannot countenance leaving his elderly mother. He explains to Müller-Widmann how both his publisher, Universal Edition, and the performing rights society A.K.M. (Autoren: Komponisten: Musikverleger), have been 'nazified'; the proprietors and directors of the former had been 'simply turned out' and the latter incorporated into the Nazi-dominated STAGMA (Staatlich genehmigte Gesellschaft zur Verwertung musikalischer Aufführungsrechte), which banned Jewish members. Having received AKM's 'unlawful questionnaire' that required him to say whether he was 'of German blood, of kindred race, or non-Aryan', Bartók's view was this question should 'remain unanswered'. He alludes to the possibility of both another publisher and performing rights society (but leaves them unnamed).

Most of the rest of the letter is concerned with three requests he has of Annie Müller-Widmann, taking up an offer of assistance she made on 23 March. The first was 'to give shelter to my manuscripts', which would be brought to her (Stefi Geyer is mentioned as a possible courier); a more mundane second request was to have copies made of the draft German translation of his Twenty-Seven Choruses; and the third was to act as an intermediary in a dispute he was having with AKM about his role in relation to the Five Hungarian Folk Songs (he was extremely irritated that they been 'demoted ... to the status of an "arrangement"'). His manuscripts were deposited with the Müller-Widmanns in several instalments during late May and early June 1938. Switzerland would also provide a place of tranquillity for the family's summer holiday in Braunwald in Glarus Canton.

On 11 August 1938, Szigeti wrote to Bartók to tell him that Benny Goodman ('the world famous jazz clarinet idol') had visited him in the Riviera on his European 'joy ride' to discuss a plan to commission a new work.[32] Bartók was to receive $300 (a threefold increase from the original suggestion of $100, on the advice of Szigeti's wife, Wanda) for an 'approx. 6–7 minutes long clarinet-violin duo with piano accompaniment'. Szigeti noted that 'if possible, it would be great if it is composed of two independent parts (and possibly playable separately, like the First Rhapsody for violin) and we hope that a brilliant clarinet and violin cadenza will be included too!'

*Contrasts* (*Kontrasztok*), which was completed on 24 September while Bartók was still composing the concerto for Székely, was thus originally conceived as a two-movement work rather in the mode of the two violin rhapsodies. It was in this format that the piece was premiered at Carnegie Hall, New York, on 9 January 1939 by Goodman, Szigeti and the pianist Endre Petri (who had been a student of Ernő Dohnányi). Indeed, in the review in *The New York Times* the following day, it is described as 'Bela Bartok's new Rhapsody for Clarinet and Violin'.[33] The first movement ('*verbunkos*') is at a moderate tempo and the finale ('*sebes*', meaning fast or speedy) is appropriately animated with a central section that involves a 3+2+3+2+3/8 'Bulgarian' rhythm; both are in relatively simple ternary structures, alternately in the tonalities of A and B♭.

Bartók decided to separate them with a slow movement labelled 'pihenő' (translated from Hungarian in the Boosey & Hawkes score as 'relaxation', but also meaning a break or a rest). In total, the duration of the three-movement version is around fifteen and a half minutes, and it may be that he felt the longer finale needed more substantial preparation than the first movement alone provided. This was certainly completed by 9 October 1938, as Bartók told Annie Müller-Widmann then that he had 'finished the Violin Concerto and two pieces (commissioned) for Szigeti and the American jazz clarinettist Benny Goodman (3 pieces, to be exact, 16 minutes altogether'.[34]

*The New York Times* critic at the premiere commented that:

In a sense, the Szigeti–Goodman collaboration was predestined, for it was at the suggestion of Mr Szigeti that Bartok wrote the composition for him and Benny. There is no indication that Bartok wrote the clarinet part for Benny's clarinet, so that jitterbugs reading this review have been simply wasting their time. The work is as Hungarian as goulash, and Mr Goodman was artist enough to restrain himself from any insinuation of swing.

There is undoubtedly some cross-fertilisation between *Contrasts* and the Second Violin Concerto, and both launch with material that explicitly or implicitly references *verbunkos*. The clarinet theme of the first movement of *Contrasts*, with its characteristic dotted rhythm and use of the Lydian/ Mixolydian polymode (A–B–C♯–D♯–E–F♯–G–A), is accompanied by open-voiced pizzicato chords in the violin that recall the approach taken by the Gypsy players whom Bartók heard in Mureş and parts of Torontál, in which close-voiced chords are strummed on a three-string fiddle. At the end of the first thematic unit at bar 11, the clarinet presents, like the Gypsy band leader, ever more elaborate embellishments from the tonic A, and its rapid arpeggiations support the violin's review of the theme.

A significant component of this opening section of *Contrasts* is the rising pattern of perfect fourths (C♯–F♯–B–E) that emerges in the violin from bar 21 and is elaborated in several phases during the reprise through the piano's sequential treatment of the opening motif (A–C♯–E–D♯) from bar 72, progressing cyclically up by fourths and reaching B♭ in bar 80. For the contrasting middle part, the tempo slows down and an insistent heartbeat rhythm is established in the violin. More relaxed versions of the Hungarian dotted rhythm (now permutations of triplet crotchets and quavers) appear from bar 39, and the climactic section from bar 45 involves flamboyant glissandi in the piano in imitation of the cimbalom.

'Pihenő' is a brief interlude exploiting some aspects of Bartók's night-music style. It opens with a type of limited *Klangfarbenmelodie*, the violin and clarinet intertwining and taking the upper melodic voice by turn. In the context of the ensuing section, which is supported by the piano playing increasingly agitated figures based on minor second oscillations, the pair of falling chains of thirds in the clarinet reverberate both with the 'Stefi motif' and the figure used by Judit to invoke Bluebeard's name. Towards the end of the movement, fragments based on interlocking fifths (E–F–B–C/D–E♭–A–B♭/B–C–F♯–G) grow logically from these earlier semitones and lead to the piano's mirrored major thirds, parallel fourths and terminal suspended B⁷ chord, redolent of earlier pieces that came under the influence of Debussy and Stravinsky.

For the brilliant finale of *Contrasts*, Bartók calls on a scordatura violin 'mistuned' to G♯–D–A–E♭, and the introductory fifths that result from playing the open strings have more than a whiff of Saint-Saëns's *Danse macabre* about them. Indeed, this relatively simple ternary-form movement could be taken more generally to represent the composer's 'grotesque' manner. In the first section, one manifestation of this is the continual change of strategies of accompaniment in the piano. They include unison linear writing in the opening 35 bars; superimposed perfect fourths (bars 3–42); major-minor chords symmetrically divided between the hands as triads (bars 53–64); vamped chords (bars 65–70, 75–80 and 94–9); parallel harmonic writing (bars 71–4 and 81–8); and reiterated chords (the G min⁷ underpinning bars 103–11, and the F min¹¹ in the subsequent seven bars). During this expository section the clarinet picks up the first of a group of dance themes (Fig. 47a), and two closely related ideas follow in due course: one exposed by the piano in bar 18 (Fig. 47b) and the other, the *grazioso* third idea (Fig. 47c), by the violin in bar 65. These three ideas are alternated over the course of the first part, and the familiar anapaestic rhythmic motif ♫ ♩ draws it to its end.

The 'trio' (Fig. 47d) introduces a theme very similar in melodic configuration to an idea that brings the slow movement of the Second Violin Concerto to its conclusion, though presented in a more complex metric context, drawing on 'Bulgarian' rhythm and structured as a four-line synthetic folk tune. Simultaneous stability and flux is generated by the regular pattern of 3+2+3+2+3 quavers generating its underlying 'pulse' and, as in the first part, there is considerable heterogeneity in the strategies of harmonisation, culminating in the use of five-note whole-tone clusters from bar 165.

Bartók continues to vary material in the reprise, the passage in the piano from bar 169 involving the sequential repetition of the first five pitches of the second thematic unit (Fig. 47b) as a staggered chromatic descent split between the hands; and a similar model is followed by the violin and clarinet

Figure 47. The main ideas of the third movement (*Sebes*) of *Contrasts*.

(in inversion) when they enter. The violin's cadenza is prefaced by further development of this figure as the clarinet derives an ostinato (or perhaps rather, in jazz terms, a riff) from it in the submediant (G), from bar 186. Against this, a piano vamp cycles through parallel major chords (G–A–B♭–A) in an almost Stravinskyan fashion, and the violin interjects a series of downbow octave C♯s that pre-empt the similar gesture in the 'Burletta' of the Sixth String Quartet. Following the cadenza, the movement rushes to its brilliant conclusion by way of the recapitulation of the opening pair of ideas. The final significant element is a long stream of repeated leading note As (with acciaccatura G♯s), with each voice entering by turn, and the piece closes in enormous high spirits on the percussively coloured tonic B♭.

Bartók was engaged in tortuous negotiations with Universal Edition during his final years in Hungary, as he attempted to move his works to Boosey & Hawkes. In September 1938 he observed in a letter to Székely, 'Neither while I am alive nor after my death do I want any German publisher to have any of my work, even if it means that no work of mine will ever be published again. This is for now what is fixed and final.'[35] He had by this stage scored the first two movements of the Second Violin Concerto and was close to completing the sketches for the finale; and in the same letter he tells his friend that he felt 'the third movement turned out very well, actually a free variation of the first (thus I got the best of you, I wrote <u>variations after all</u>).' In making this observation, Bartók was alluding to his original intention to write a work in variation form, something that Székely was not particularly enthusiastic about, preferring 'a big work in the traditional concerto form'.[36] And indeed this is what he got, for the piece is a very substantial three-movement concerto lasting thirty-two minutes in Bartók's own timing, though most performances tend to be longer, with an average duration of between thirty-five and forty minutes. This is a virtuoso work, written for a soloist who was both a very close personal friend and at the height of his powers.

The overall tonality of the work is B and while employing Bartók's usual modal flexibility, it strongly suggests the major mode, closing on a solid B major triad. As the composer noted to Székely, the overall structure employs variation on two levels: the finale reworks thematic material from the first movement in the new context (Table 5); and the second movement involves six variations and a reprise of the theme.

The prefatory six bars that open the movement involve the alternation of chords on the tonic B and the leading note (A⁹). Beneath these, pizzicato lower strings play a vestigial pentatonic idea that at first simply provides the root and fifth of the underlying harmony but will later take on a thematic life of its own in the development section. Influenced by the spirit of the Hungarian

Table 5. Thematic correspondences between the first movement and finale of the Second Violin Concerto.

| Thematic material | First Movement | Finale |
|---|---|---|
| Introductory idea (‖:B–F♯–A–E:‖ F♯–B). | Violas cellos and basses, bars 3–7. | Strings (with decorative infill), bars 1–5. |
| First thematic area, exposition. | Solo violin, upbeat to bar 7, 4/4, B. | Solo violin, bar 5, 3/4, B. |
| Transition to second area | Solo violin, bars 57–72. | Solo violin, bars 90–125. |
| Second thematic area, exposition ('twelve-note' theme: A–B–F–B♭–F♯–C♯–G–D♯–C–E–G♯–D). | Solo violin, bar 73, A. | Solo violin, bar 73, A, bars 129 onward (with internal repetition and reordering of pitches). |
| Inverted recapitulation of first thematic area. | Solo violin, bar 194, 4/4, G. | Solo violin, bar 260, 3/4, G. |
| Recapitulation of the first thematic area in original orientation. | Solo violin, upbeat to bar 213, 4/4, B (over F♯ pedal) . . . | Solo violin, bar 320, 3/4, C (over G pedal). |
| Recapitulation of second thematic area. | Solo violin, from bar 255, ambiguous. | Solo violin, from bar 423, G. |

vernacular tradition, Bartók gave the marking '*Tempo di verbunkos*' to the first section in a version of the solo part he provided to Székely. Figure 48 offers a putative 'traditional' model for the first eight bars of this idea, as a four-line old-style Hungarian tune with seven syllables per line. Obviously this is not a plausible vocal melody given its very wide range, but it suggests how the characteristics of traditional music could have been absorbed within it. In contour, the concerto theme involves the decoration of two underlying ascending and descending arpeggios, each four bars in length and stressing the tonic and dominant in their initial pitches.

After the orchestral exposition of the main theme from bar 43 and a transitional passage in which the soloist engages in rhapsodic passagework, the tonality shifts to A, for a new chromatic melodic idea. Bartók later explained to Yehudi Menuhin that he 'wanted to show Schönberg that one can use all twelve tones and still remain tonal'.[37] If the prime form of the 'set' is understood as the one given out from bar 73 by the violin solo (A–B–F–B♭–F♯–C♯–G–D♯–C–E–G♯–D), then the immediate repeat by the violins and violas in crotchets is a permutation in which the fourth and fifth pitches are swapped. The subsequent version in the violin, starting on D (presumably based on P5, the prime form transposed up a perfect fourth) at bar 79 divides the series into three

Figure 48. The first movement of the Second Violin Concerto (a) the model pseudo-folk-song structure; (b) the first eight bars of the main theme.

sub-units of four, three and five pitches respectively; the pitches are subject to internal reordering such that the relative positions of the fifth and sixth, eighth and ninth, and eleventh and twelfth are swapped. After this rather brief idea, the exposition picks up momentum again, with brisk sequential writing from bar 96 leading into the section's climax. A brilliant codetta bristles with the Romanian dance-influenced anapaest rhythms that featured so strongly in the finale of the Second Piano Concerto. They would also be an important ingredient of the finale of the Concerto for Orchestra.

The development opens neither in nor on the conventional dominant, but a semitone lower in a 'mistuned' F with the preludial material taking on an independent thematic role, first as a tranquil idea in the solo violin and then in the cor anglais in C minor. From bar 160 the tempo increases and the violin fires off with rapid semiquaver figurations that are placed in opposition to a syncopated figure with a tango-like rhythm (♪♪♪♩ – a device that can be found in some Hungarian folk material) in the woodwind and brass. This same rhythm appears again in the closing phases of the development as Bartók sets it against a 'straightened-out' version of the main theme.

In the recapitulation, from bar 194, a by now familiar Bartókian tactic is adopted with the presentation of the first theme in inversion by the soloist. This is no powerful point of arrival, however. Indeed the tonality is initially not the tonic, but the submediant G, the violinist being supported by an exquisite texture created by harp, celesta, high tremolos in the first violins, and gentle *sul ponticello* undulations in the violas. When the tonic is restored and the main theme is reprised in its original configuration from the upbeat to bar 213, after a momentary burst of enthusiasm drawing on ascending fragments of the anapaest rhythm, the mood remains tranquil.

A further build-up through a sequence ascending by perfect fourths leads to the superimposition of rising and falling versions of a fanfare-like variant of the main theme in the brass. Although the pace briefly settles down again for the twelve-note theme at bar 275, the music becomes ever more animated as it swirls off towards the brilliant cadenza. The final pages of the movement retain this positive and assertive mood, and a unison tonic brings it to its conclusion after further bravura work from the soloist.

Serenity and lyricism pervade the variations of the beautiful Andante tranquillo, which like the opening of the development of the previous movement is in G, the (flat) submediant tonality of the work. The Andante can almost be conceived as sharing the ethos of the first movement of Bartók's early First Violin Concerto written for Stefi Geyer, and it has the lucidity and clarity of the music of the young Benjamin Britten. Overall, the tonal organisation is cyclic, the variations gradually working down through a series of minor thirds: G (theme and variation one), E (variations two and three), D♭ (variation four), B♭ (variation five) and G (variation six and the reprise of the theme). The orchestra is reduced and the heavy brass remains silent, with chamber orchestral textures for much of the course of the movement.

After the unfolding of a G major triad in the harp and strings, the cantabile theme in 9/8 is played by the solo violin. Like the principal idea of the first movement it involves the decoration of arpeggiated figures, has Lydian modal characteristics, and is constructed in four two-bar phrases. Its closing pair of bars is repeated by the tutti, and Bartók harmonises this with a sequence running down through a cycle of fifths from E to A♭. This gesture is very strongly rooted in tonal practice and can be found in his compositional repertoire as early as the Variations for piano dedicated to Felicie Fábián.

The first variation, which lightly elaborates the theme using neighbouring notes, involves a skeletal thinning of the texture, initially with just timpani and basses before the gradual entry of the rest of the strings. In the second variation, the expressive impulse remains and the accompaniment includes exquisite decorative writing in the harp that picks up the Lydian fourth in its articulation of the 'acoustic' scale (the Lydian-Mixolydian polymode). The second and third variations form a pair, the third, marked *ruvido* (rough or coarse), acting as a dramatic and aggressive foil to its lyrical partner, the solo violin playing throughout in rhapsodic double stops.

A relaxation of tempo and a change to 4/4 herald a slow fourth variation that carries many of the markers of the *lassú* style of *verbunkos*, employing trills and rapid figurations in the violin, and Hungarian iambic rhythms in the clarinets. The melodic motion through perfect fifths that has been implicit in earlier variations is made explicit through the staged ascent from D♭ through A♭ to E♭. After a further upswing to a fourth plateau, on E$_6$, and a cadenza-like descent redolent of the performance style of the Gypsy band leader, the strings follow the soloist in a four-part canon descending by fifths that leads to a point of repose before the *scherzando* fifth variation. This brilliant section in B♭ has a somewhat similar identity to that of the Scherzo lying at the heart of the Second Piano Concerto, though it is very much briefer and placed asymmetrically within the overall structure. The final variation is again contrapuntal, the soloist providing a ghost-like decorative mirroring of the linear descent and ascent of the first violins, with the lower strings responding in canon. Subsiding through a wedge-like shape formed by simultaneous falling and rising scale patterns, the reprise of the theme ensues, though strikingly omitting the terminal cycle of fifths, the movement instead reducing to silence on the tonic G.

As already noted, the finale is a large-scale variation of the first movement and its key events and relationships are outlined in Table 5. Much faster in pace than its counterpart and in 3/4, this is a bravura movement that permits the soloist to show off both elaborate fingerwork and cantabile tone production. The tonal structure of the movement is perhaps less elaborate than some of Bartók's other works of the 1930s, the main thematic areas following the trajectory B–A–G–B across the exposition and recapitulation.

The closing moments of the Second Violin Concerto can be seen as a precursor to the Concerto for Orchestra in one specific respect: Bartók provided a second ending at the request of Székely. (The first version dispensed with the soloist and was thus deemed as being too symphonic in style from the perspective of its dedicatee.) After a mysterious-sounding move to an ostinato around A♭ from bar 450, it gradually accelerates and eventually shifts up a perfect fourth to D♭ (bar 497) before settling on a brief ethereal cadenza. The tempo whips up again, and as the music reaches a dominant pedal (F♯) the main theme is reduced to pure pentatonicism with an AABA idea akin to folk song encompassing three perfect fourths (C♯–F♯–B–E). In the second version of the coda, Székely was given his head and the violin part takes up a rhetorical figure involving a falling diminished seventh and falling seventh (B♭–G–E–C♯–E–D) before scurrying off with scale and broken-chord figures to the work's jubilant conclusion.

Although the two major compositions completed in 1938 were positive and optimistic in tone, the same cannot be said for Bartók's mood. In a letter to

Annie Müller-Widmann on 9 October, shortly after the signing of the Munich Agreement, he assessed the conduct of 'the scoundrel' Hitler and his total outmanoeuvring of Chamberlain. He remarked with prescience that 'the great settling of accounts must come, but later and under even more unfavourable circumstances'.[38] Despite Hitler's deception, Bartók was not particularly sympathetic to the Czechs, for he claimed that their authorities had 'used every kind of trick to try to deprive my mother of her citizenship and thus of her pension; they robbed my mother-in-law of a considerable part of her pension; and throughout these last 4 or 5 years *I have not had permission* to appear publicly in Slovakia'.[39] In conclusion he noted that:

> Two weeks ago, I really didn't know which I regretted more: my own and my family's ruin or the destruction of my entire work, etc. etc. – A war would of course ruin me, even if I wasn't hit by a bomb – and yet, I don't know if it wouldn't have been better to have it now than later![40]

Bartók took part in a series of concerts in Holland and Belgium in early November 1938, but the inexorable progress towards the outbreak of the Second World War would all too soon make such visits impossible. The great artistic collaboration and enormous friendship with Székely that had begun in 1921 would be severed by tragic international events. Sadly, Bartók would never have the chance of hearing his Second Violin Concerto played by its dedicatee, though Székely would go on to become one of its most successful interpreters.

## CHAPTER ELEVEN

# 'From here is seen the graveyard's border': 1939–1942

As the world entered its year of crisis, Bartók continued to examine his options. Székely's wife, Mientje, had suggested that he should consider moving to America, and the Anschluss had made Bartók all too aware of the inevitability of increasing difficulties, but he was not yet convinced. A letter to her on 10 January 1939 indicates he was concerned that he should be able to continue with his scientific work – the folk-music research – and didn't believe he could: 'If I can only "vegetate" there, then it would be of no use to change "domicile". I think it extremely difficult to decide something in that way and really I am at a loss what to do.'[1]

Several of his more recent compositions had achieved considerable success by the late 1930s – the British music periodical *Tempo* was able to report in its January 1939 edition that the *Music for Strings, Percussion and Celesta* had received some fifty performances in the 1937–8 season alone.[2] However, despite Bartók's international reputation as a composer and pianist, his existence was still relatively hand-to-mouth and relied heavily on his earnings as a performer to top up his pension and royalty income. A poignant letter written to the fourteen-year-old Péter by his parents on 24 August 1938 prepared him for the fact that the following academic year he was to move to the Lutheran school in Budapest (Fasori Evangélikus Gimnázium) where he was to board during the week and come home at weekends. This was because in the following year Bartók and Ditta intended 'to make very many longer journeys . . . needed for earning money, for the living of each of us'.[3] The broadcast he gave on 13 January 1939 for the Budapest radio station gives some idea of the level of earnings from such activities – the fee of 300 pengős equated to around $55, the relative value in 2013 being around $900 according to the historic standard-of-living measure.[4]

On the day before this broadcast he had written to the German pianist Hans Priegnitz, who was due to play his First Piano Concerto on the Nazi-controlled

radio in the spring and was labouring under the misapprehension that Bartók
had completed two further concertos not yet in print.[5] In response to Priegnitz's
query whether it would be possible to play them, Bartók made it clear that he
had in fact only composed two concertos and did his best to put him off playing
even the first by explaining the difficulty of the orchestral accompaniment and
the necessity of substantial rehearsal. And in a final sentence he remarked that
he was 'astonished that such "degenerate" music should be selected for – of all
things – a radio broadcast'.[6] This comment alludes to the infamous 'Entartete
Musik' ('Degenerate Music') exhibition held in Düsseldorf between 22 and 29
May 1938, organised by Dr Hans Severus Ziegler, in which a number of art
music composers (as well as popular and jazz musicians) were featured because
of their supposed degeneracy. According to *The Times* report published on 26
May 1938, 'The Press describes this exhibition as "presenting the appearance of
a veritable witches' Sabbath and of the most frivolous cultural Bolshevism; it
shows the triumph of sub-humanity, of Jewish impudence, and of complete
spiritual inanity"'.[7] Schoenberg, Stravinsky, Hindemith and Weill were singled
out for special consideration, with Schreker, Berg, Toch, Rathaus, Brand and
Hauer being described as 'petty Bolshevist giants'; but surprisingly Bartók was
spared any mention, presumably because of the good relations between
Germany and the pro-Nazi government of Hungary, and his absence from the
list of 'degenerates' was apparently a cause of irritation to him.

He had by this stage finally lost patience with Matica Slovenská, who had
failed to publish the collection of Slovak music, despite the further extension
they had been granted, the material having been in their hands since 1922. An
ultimatum was set with a termination of one month, within which the manuscript was to be returned and all publication rights rescinded resulting from
the publisher's breach of contract. Matica Slovenská responded robustly, and
while accepting that the company no longer wished to publish the collection
and would return the manuscript on receipt of Bartók's advance, they argued
that 'the work gives a one-sided picture of the actual character of the true
Slovak folk music, presents difficulties in the reconstruction of the texts, and
raises insoluble problems with regard to restoring the uniformly transposed
melodies to their original tonality'.[8] One can only imagine Bartók's sense of
outrage when he read this evaluation of his work, and he never deigned to
reclaim the manuscript from the publisher's possession.

By February 1939 the Sonata for Two Pianos and Percussion had
received six European performances. Corresponding with his former student
Dorothy Parrish in English, Bartók told her of further ones to come. He also
took up with her the concerns about his future that he had raised with Mientje
Székely:

The fatal influence of the Germans is steadily growing in Hungary, the time seems not to be far, when we shall become quite a German colony (as Cecho-Slovakia for instance has actually been turned into one). I would like best to turn my back on the whole of Europe, but where am I to go? And should I go at all before the situation becomes unsupportable, or had I better wait until the chaos is complete?[9]

Six additional performances of the sonata were scheduled by the Bartóks in a short tour: on 17 February in Zurich, 20 and 22 February in Lausanne, and 27 February in Geneva; and on 3 and 6 March in Paris. Back in Budapest in March he wrote to his indefatigable north European agent in Amsterdam, Antonia Kossar, to tell her that he needed a period of peace in the summer in order to recover and to compose, and that July, August and September were thus 'taboo'.[10] He also let her know that he was off concertising yet again, this time to Italy – to Parma, Florence and Rome with the violinist Ede Zathureczky (another great violinist from Jenő Hubay's stable), the programme including the Second Violin Rhapsody as well as sonatas by Mozart and Brahms. A final appearance in Venice, at Teatro La Fenice on 8 April, involved a further outing for the Sonata for Two Pianos and Percussion, coupled with Stravinsky's Concerto for Two Pianos. As well as a conductor (Nino Sanzogno, a young Venetian musician who had studied with Hermann Scherchen and later took on the role of chief conductor at La Fenice), there were apparently six percussionists on hand for this performance!

With Bartók's musical world gradually closing in around him, northern Europe had now become off limits. Like Britain, Holland had been one of his regular haunts, mainly because of the presence there of his most loyal advocate and interpreter, Székely. Bartók's final concert appearance in the Netherlands was in Scheveningen, one of the districts of The Hague, where on 30 June he played his Second Piano Concerto under the German Jewish conductor, Carl Schuricht, and The Hague Philharmonic Orchestra, in a programme that also included two great German masterworks, the Prelude to Pfitzner's opera *Palestrina* and Brahms's Third Symphony.

Writing to his eldest son, Béla, on 18 August 1939, from the Châlet Aellen in Saanen, Switzerland, Bartók commented that:

Somehow I feel like a musician of olden times – the invited guest of a patron of the arts. For here I am, as you know, entirely the guest of the Sachers; they see to everything – from a distance. In a word, I am living alone – in an ethnographic object: a genuine peasant cottage.[11]

He had completed the Divertimento for string orchestra the day before penning this letter, after a little more than a fortnight's work – a fair accomplishment for a score of some twenty-five minutes' duration – and his mind was already turning to another new piece, the Sixth String Quartet. The Divertimento was the second composition written by Bartók for the Swiss conductor Paul Sacher's ensemble, the Basle Chamber Orchestra. *Music for Strings, Percussion and Celesta* had rapidly turned into one of his most popularly successful works. According to the research of János Breuer, even in Nazi Germany this work received at least a dozen performances in the period between 1937 and 1942.

There can be no doubt that Bartók consciously composed the Divertimento against the backdrop of preparations for war. Germany would invade Poland on 1 September, a fortnight after his letter to his son, and he commented that 'the poor, peaceful, honest Swiss are being compelled to burn with war-fever', expressing his concern that he might not be able to get home 'if this or that happens'. Despite the connotations of the title 'Divertimento' (literally a diversion or an entertainment), this is in many ways a serious work, even in its apparently most cheerful moments. In the fundamental tonality of F (the middle movement is in C♯) and having a generally diatonic temperament though with a wide tonal purview, the interactions of solo instruments and the full ensemble recall the manner and spirit of the Baroque concerto grosso.

Supported by F major triads that are intermittently substituted by accented chords of F–G–B–C, the sonata-form first movement opens with a ritornello-like melody played by the first violins that coalesces folk inspiration and a neo-Baroque temperament, initially looping around $C_5$ (Fig. 49a). The sharpened fourths and flattened sevenths of the first four bars appear to imply the acoustic scale (the Lydian/Mixolydian polymode), though the arrival on A♭ in bar 5 (over a second-inversion chord of B♭) intimates a turn to the Aeolian mode. A modified version of the opening material in the dominant (C) leads into a more subdued passage in A from bar 25, a further variant of the principal theme's outline entailing the interplay between the solo strings and *ripieno*, the melody's metric complexities suggesting the influence of Romanian *colinde*. At the end of the section, a Morse code-like reiteration of unison Fs is tapped out by the full ensemble. This figure appears at crucial points in the rest of the movement, like a rapping on a door or a knocking on a table, attempting to impede the lyrical flow.

In the tranquil second subject from bar 42 this figure is taken up by solo violins and juxtaposed with a more reticent idea with anapaestic metre and modal flexibility in the tonality of D (Fig. 49b), though repeatedly interrupted by the fortissimo interjections in the *ripieno*. The exposition closes with the symmetrically disposed rhythmic gesture ♪♩.♩♪, which is treated as an ostinato.

Figure 49. Themes from the Divertimento (a) and (b) first movement; and (c), (d) and (e) from the finale.

At its outset, the development draws on the principal theme (now in B♭), before overlapping entries of a variant played by a solo quintet coil upwards by perfect fifths from D♭ (bar 95) and then downwards from G♯ (bar 101). The recapitulation is prefaced by: grinding chromatic versions of the ostinato figure that build up from bar 113; canonic entries in pairs of an intervallically compressed version of the first theme that slithers around (bar 122); and a final rebarbative series of dissonant chords articulating the symmetrical gesture (bar 125). In the recapitulation, the themes follow in the original order, both being abbreviated and subject to the composer's usual ongoing developmental strategies, the first reprised in the dominant form (compare bar 14) but in the harmonic context of D minor. A climactic version of the rhythmic motif is gradually reduced to silence like a series of echoes or aftershocks, and a final pastoral reprise of the first idea brings the movement to its conclusion.

The ternary-form second movement in C♯ (the last part of the work to be drafted) has something of the character of the 'night music' style. Muted second violins intone a sombre four-bar melody that opens with a rising diminished third and falling minor second, then slithers around like a life-form gradually emerging from a primeval swamp of chromatic lines in the lower strings; it is immediately repeated in canon by violas and first violins. In the second part of this expository section the music opens out of the chromatic morass through sequential writing that leads to a rhetorically repeated $D_6$ in violins (a standard *verbunkos* trope), marking the beginning of a middle part that is in three phases. The first of these phases has a slightly faster tempo and a prominent double-dotted iambic rhythm, initially played by the violas before being taken up by the second violins. An ostinato based on the pitches G–B♭–C♯–D–F, a pentatonic mode inflected by the Gypsy scale's sharpened fourth, supports the latter. In the second phase, more conventional pentatonicism employing the mode G♯–B–C♯–D♯–F♯ underpins a forceful two-bar ostinato that accompanies an ever more intense idea in the first violins. Working its way up to a climax at the centre of the movement with double-stopped grace notes and trills before gradually subsiding, the pitches in the first violins provide the chromatic complement of those of the accompaniment. The third phase is the briefest at just six bars in length and involves expressive chromatic figures derived from the opening string melody played by solo violins and viola surrounding agitated trills in the *ripieno*. The almost articulate lamentations of this section give way to a return of the gloom of the movement's opening, the reprise of the main section involving a textural change to a bed of tremolandi that suggest the ghostly trace of the first manifestation. After an impassioned *verbunkos* passage, which descends through fifths from $F\sharp_6$, the music subsides again, and after one final fortissimo iambic gesture, it dissolves to silence.

The finale presents an affirmative foil to the deep melancholia of the second movement. It too is marked by interplay between a solo subgroup and the full string orchestra, dashing on its way like a wild folk dance, and employing a modified rondo structure in which the central section fugally develops a subject derived from earlier material. An important means of generating the dynamism of the movement is the approach taken to hypermetric organisation in which thematic areas with regular three- and two-bar phrase patterns are established, juxtaposed and disrupted.

The principal idea, beginning at bar 14 (Fig. 49c), can be regarded as derivative of the opening theme of the first movement. This idea has been modified to the three-bar figure F–C–D | E♭–D–C | F, the opening twelve bars forming an ABAB synthetic old-style folk melody. Its triple hypermetre is disturbed by the subsequent two pairs of five- and thirteen-bar phrases (bars 36–61). At this point the triple hypermetre is restored as the idea first heard in bars 46–8 takes on a life of its own in a three-voice canon in a pure F major.

In a parallel approach to the first movement, Bartók establishes a syncopated repeated-note rhythm in duple hypermetre as the tonality settles on F♯

minor from bar 103. The reiterated As act as a kind of extended upbeat to a new asymmetrical melodic idea (Fig. 49d), the first three phrases extending from seven bars to eight and nine bars in length, before dropping back to six. When the opening idea reappears at bar 146 its apparent B♭ tonality is undermined by the Bs in the viola, and it is now hypermetrically irregular, alternating between two- and three-bar phrases. The end of the section is signalled by a chord that, as notated, coalesces five of the pitches of the Gypsy scale on G (G–A–B♭–C♯–E♭). The G can be understood to act as a modified dominant seventh to the tonality of A♭ of the ensuing fugal part of the movement (the A forms a sharpened 11th).

The eight-bar fugue subject (Fig. 49e) is given out by the full ensemble, the violas responding with a tonal answer, and the opening pitch of the third and fourth entries being slightly modified. From bar 214, a counter-exposition with the subject in inversion sets off, though this is interrupted after just three entries. As the tempo decreases, a solo cello and then a violin are placed in the limelight, the latter having a brief cadenza that connects across to the reprise. The opening ideas of the reprise are presented in inversion, the first from bar 268 and the second from bar 342. Original and inverted versions of the first theme are subsequently combined and a chromatically contracted variant appears at bar 436. After the music has come to a halt, a brief graceful interlude is presented from bar 513 based on the falling scalic material first heard in bars 62–81, counterposing triple and duple hypermetres. Piled-up ostinati then outline a whole-tone harmonic unit (B–C♯–E♭–F–G) that propels the movement into the final vivacissimo. Although the triple hypermetre is disrupted by the introduction of 3/4 bars, it is eventually re-established as the work moves to its final confident gesture in which a rising Lydian figure is complemented by a falling Phrygian scale, in the tonic F.

In the letter to his eldest son on 18 August 1939, Bartók had explained that he was about to start on another commission having completed the Divertimento, 'a string quartet for Z. Székely (i.e. for the "New Hungarian Quartet")'.[12] Székely had taken on the role as middleman for a young quartet of ex-students from the Liszt Academy who had performed the Budapest premiere of the Fifth String Quartet in March 1936. They had subsequently played it to great acclaim in the ISCM festival in Barcelona in the same year, and had taken it on a short European tour. Although the ensemble asked Bartók to compose his new quartet specifically for them, due to the war and the resulting breakdown in his communication with Székely, it was eventually dedicated to the Kolisch Quartet who gave its first performance in New York in January 1941.

A thematic memo for the four-movement Sixth String Quartet appears immediately after the draft of the Divertimento. This memo includes sketches for the ritornello or motto theme that ties together the entire work, for the opening idea of the first movement proper, and for the 'Marcia' section of the second movement. László Somfai has noted that Bartók's draft of the first movement did not originally open with the viola solo or the subsequent ten bars leading into the Vivace, but with the solo violin's principal theme.[13] Benjamin Suchoff evidences the apparent development of the motto theme by reverse in stages starting from the final five bars (19–23), followed by the central five bars (14–18) and eventually the first seventeen bars.[14] It seems that the overall shape of the quartet took some time to clarify in Bartók's mind. Indeed, the finale originally involved a slow introduction (bars 1–45 of the existing fourth movement) that led to a fast concluding part.

In the final version of the quartet, which is in the overall tonality of D, the ritornello makes four appearances: as the *mesto* viola solo beginning on G♯; in two parts (the upper three voices playing in unison) with the theme in the cello and starting on E♭, as a preface to the Marcia section; taken by the first violin on B♭ in three distinct parts before the Burletta (the viola doubling the first violin an octave lower from its midpoint); and as the basis of the entire *mesto* finale, the first pair of entries being on C (first violin) and F♯ (cello).

Although the viola's lugubrious melody (Fig. 50a) is chromatically orientated, each pitch of the chromatic set appearing on at least two occasions in its thirteen bars, it is significantly weighted towards the notes G♯, D, E and G/F♯ by their greater total durations; D (the principal tonal centre of the work) and G♯ form the two pivotal pitches of the melody. More broadly, the set of tonal relations connected by the diminished seventh chord (G♯–B–D–F) underpins the entire quartet: the tonality of the second theme from the sonata-form first movement is F; the tonal centre of the second movement is B (its trio emerging on a repeated A♭); the third movement closes on F; and the finale coalesces D and F in its final gesture.

Bartók organises the thematic material of the first movement so that it flows logically from the ritornello, the pitches marked in bold emerging from its coiling terminal notes (G♭–**G**–F♭–**A♭**–**E♭**) and taken up in unison by the ensemble. The version in the viola and cello is immediately transposed and played in retrograde to give A–D–C♯, and from this springs the almost Beethovenian first idea (Fig. 50b). If the opening phrase of this first subject is understood to be a decorated version of a figure that loops up through $A_4$–$D_5$–$C_5$–$F_5$–$A_5$, then the next phrase (from bar 31) reverses the direction of travel, spiralling downwards through $D_6$–$A_5$–$B_5$–$E_5$–$G♯_5$–$C♯_5$. The material of the first two phrases is immediately developed contrapuntally, and in the passage from bar 60 an ostinato derived from the first two bars briefly emerges in the cello in the transition to the second subject.

Figure 50. The Sixth String Quartet (a) ritornello theme; (b) first movement opening theme; and (c) second theme.

Here, the principles of polymodal chromaticism are overtly displayed in the gentle linear material exposed by the first violin (Fig. 50c) over pedal Cs with trills and offbeat pizzicati: the falling pentachord (C–B♭–A♭–G♭–F) and the subsequent ascending line (F–G–A–B–C) are alternately derived from Phrygian and Lydian modes on F. From the third and fourth bars, variants gradually accrue and the thematic area concludes with a cyclic succession through fifths (C–F–B♭–E♭–G♯–C♯–F♯). A much faster closing theme initially takes up fragments from the ritornello and the exposition closes on F triads.

Much of the development section in the opening movement is concerned with the principal theme, and in the first part the ensemble is continuously reorganised. The upper and lower pairs of instruments function together in bars 166–79; an ostinato is established in the outer pair (first violin and cello) from bar 180 using the Lydian set F–G–A–B, while the inner pair (second violin and viola) play fragments derived from the second half of the motif shown in Figure 50b; and from the upbeat to bar 194 duos and trios are organised around the pizzicato ostinato in F♯ in the viola. Further harmonically static areas are instituted by the cello on B♭ (bar 206), B (bar 213) and C (bar 217), and these accelerate chromatically upwards, with broken chords on C♯, D, D♯ and E (bars 222–5). After the climax in bar 226, in which descending interlocking perfect fifths are presented in the first violin as the expansion of the next phrase of the first subject, F is set up as a further local tonic, the second violin introducing a quartal figure in symmetrical tonal space

(F–B♭–E♭ | E–A–D). A transposed version of this gesture (C–F–B♭ | B–E) leads to a pianissimo point of repose on a C♯ min$^7$ chord (bar 268), and hence to the retransition to the recapitulation (bar 287).

The three thematic areas now reappear in the original order, though the very brief restatement of the first subject is followed by a curious vivacissimo passage based on minor thirds separated by semitones (F–A♭–A–C–C♯–E) – a kind of compressed version of the quartal figures of the development. Rather than reprising in the tonic (D), the second subject is offset by a major third in F♯, and the codetta/third subject reverses the trajectory of the exposition, the first violin initially decorating a chromatic descent. A return to the original configuration (bar 345) leads to a long held D major triad and the tempo gradually relaxes. A further point of harmonic stability in G major (bar 363) involving plucked chords against the sustained triad supporting a final version of the principal theme inflected in the subdominant, together with the final resolution onto a tonic triad of G, suggests a plagal cadence.

The following two movements, a march and a burlesque, could be seen as character pieces in the mould of some of the early piano works. After the spectral rendering of the *mesto* ritornello in the cello with the unison counterpoint spread across three octaves, a terminal gesture (D♯–F♯–A–G♯) prepares for the main idea of the Marcia, a *verbunkos*-inspired movement with a similar morphology to the first movement of *Contrasts*. The opening section of the Marcia has three main phases. The first (bars 1–42) exposes the dotted idea in B and is bisected by rebarbative chords with iambic rhythm and melodic rising thirds. In the *risoluto* second phase (from the upbeat to bar 43 until bar 58) an assertive idea with an underlying rising trajectory is introduced, the cello ascending from C♯$_2$ to A♯$_4$ over the course of five bars with support or response from the other instruments (for example, through the chain of major second-inversion chords from bar 44). After a passage that gradually unravels, the varied reprise of the first section, with glissandi, trills and tremolandi, entails a melodic line whose path ascends by perfect fourths in the first violin, from D♯ (bar 67) up to F♯$_6$ in bar 69, and superimposed on this final pitch, the rise from B$_4$ to E$_5$ in the second violin.

The Marcia section closes on tonic B major chords surrounding a sustained G♯$_3$ in the viola. This pitch, transposed up an octave and enharmonically notated as A♭$_4$ in the cello, initiates the trio with an accelerating rhythmic pattern. This prefaces an impassioned and agitated lament utilising alternating semitones and minor thirds, which brings together aspects of Gypsy performance with the spirit of the Romanian *hora lungă*. For the accompaniment, Bartók incorporates a tremolando sonic wash in the violins (beginning with C major-minor chords) and accelerating quadruple-stopped strummed triads in the viola. As the section progresses, the tonality of the chords gradually shifts. It arrives at a trilled perfect fifth dyad on B at bar 98 over which the first violin commences a broad melody with chains of thirds, the accompanying fifths rising to D♯–A♯ and gradually subsiding chromatically to B♭–F. The final subsection is described in the score as a 'quasi cadenza' and involves overlapping entries of rapid arpeggiated figures that constitute minor mode versions of the first four pitches of the Marcia theme. These eventually form a repeating string of four minor seventh chords in third inversion (B–D–F♯–E) that gradually subsides.

While the reprise follows the overall course of the first part, it is substantially transformed in terms of texture, the dotted theme being antiphonally recapitulated with block chords (cello and second violin) and octaves (viola and first violin). Bartók then inverts the material of the *risoluto* middle part, the violins descending to the C♯ as a point of stasis at bar 168; and in the final subsection the first violin's rising-fourth glissandi climax on the tonic $B_6$, shadowed by the second a major ninth lower, before reversing back down. At the end of the movement, following fragmentary references to the opening *verbunkos* idea, the sustained G♯s in violins are left suspended after the concluding $B^9$ pizzicato chord has faded away.

The third, three-voice, iteration of the ritornello begins on B♭ in the first violin, the second violin picking up the G♯ that closed the previous movement as A♭ supported a major third below by the cello's $F♭_4$. Against the largely chromatic descent to $B_2$ in the cello, the upper strings focus on the first five-note phrase, sequentially ascending to the climax in bar 14. Now the first violin and viola, which are meshed together as a single voice, playing the principal melodic voice in octaves, begin a rapid descent over pedal B–F. The diminished fifth acts as a surrogate tonic, and the second violin's final gesture leaves an $E_5$ suspended above it.

'Burletta' is a piece of Bartókian grotesquery, a ternary-form movement whose outer sections are pervaded by a sardonic humour. It particularly recalls the second of the three Burlesques for piano, 'un peu gris' (a little tipsy), written nearly thirty years earlier in May 1911 – and to some degree the first movement of the Suite for piano op. 14. Fundamentally in F, the opening section of the Burletta is in three main parts with four prefatory bars that display several species of 'comic' gesture: in the first part (bars 21 and 23), a kind of pseudo-dominant ($V^{13}$ in F minor) to tonic motion is punctuated by accented and locally dissonant Bs; in the second part, eight quavers with rising semitone acciaccaturas are all played with heavy downbows. Supported by a vamp in the lower pair of instruments beginning on $E^7$, the violins play a brief idea that picks up the repeated downbows, but with a rising glissando minor third, doubled a quarter tone lower as a further burlesque touch suggesting a mocking response. This idea could certainly be taken to signify music from the Hungarian tradition. Although the melodic contour is not particularly idiomatic as it stands, it is tempting to connect it to the old-style tune number 58 from *The Hungarian Folk Song*, 'Asz [azt] hittem, hogy nem kellek katonának' ('I was sure I should not have to be a soldier'), collected by Bartók in Békés County in 1906. In this tune the narrator tells how he had hoped to be able to stay at home looking after his mother, but has been conscripted into Franz Joseph's imperial army.

In the second part of this section, from bar 33, the tempo increases slightly and the strings operate together in upper and lower pairs as the material becomes more syncopated. Starting in an octatonic mode (F–G–G♯–A♯–B–C♯–D–E), the members of each duo generally play a tone or ninth apart from one other, the couples being placed in contrary motion, joining together in unison for an intermittent rising perfect fourth figure (C♯–F♯). The double-stopping in the violins in the third part (from bar 46) recalls Stravinsky's use of the instrument in *L'Histoire du soldat* (especially in 'Music to Scene 1'), and the perfect fourth motif provides a syncopated accompaniment to the chromatic lower violin part. From bar 50, the texture becomes more complex, the second violin's material doubled a ninth higher by the first violin, the viola's accompaniment doubled a tone lower by the cello; and from bar 55 the ensemble is reoriented with the first violin playing versions of the perfect fourth from the pentatonic set F–G–B♭–C–E♭ against the syncopated idea in the other three instruments. After thirteen brusque repetitions of a second-inversion half-diminished seventh (the enharmonic equivalent of the chord D♯–F♯–A–C♯), development of the initial idea from the first bar of the Burletta brings the first part of the movement to its close.

Mockery is put to one side in a moment of pastoral repose in the gentle Andantino trio, and two basic ideas alternate (ABA'B'A"), slightly extended on each reappearance: the first idea, in D, involves a decorated descent from tonic to dominant (D–C♯–B–A–B♭–G–A); the second idea, in B♭ (and subsequently B), is rhythmically (and to some extent, melodically) comparable to the 9/8 theme from near the opening of *Cantata profana*, to which the chorus sings 'Whose treasure nine sons fair and sturdy was'. The tranquillity is interrupted by the reprise of the first idea, subject to substantial development. In a codetta (bar 135) three attempts by the 'Cantata profana' theme to restore the peace of the trio are curtailed with heavy repeated chords. The movement then comes to its conclusion with a cadential structure that tonicises F, though 'spiked' with a B natural.

Bartók had closed his Second String Quartet with a slow movement and he follows a similar model here (though, as already noted, this appears not to have been his initial intention). In a luminous piece of polyphony, which largely eschews colouristic effects until the final page, the slow finale of the Sixth String Quartet intertwines versions of the ritornello theme with the principal ideas from the first movement. The underlying harmony of the slow movement is often triadic, with brief points of repose on C minor (bar 13), a half-diminished seventh on A♯ (bar 22), and a diminished triad (bar 45); and with the reprise of the second subject from the first movement a succession of minor triads appears – on F, A, B♭ and B. The final harmonic event of the slow movement is ambiguous. It brings together the overall tonic (D) and the F major of the contrasting theme from the first movement, so that it hovers between a D minor seventh and an F with added sixth, undermining the clear D major on the cello's first triple-stopped chord in bar 85. The movement's individual elements are outlined in Table 6.

Completed in November 1939, it is hard not to regard the entire Sixth String Quartet as Bartók's personal response to the unfolding tragedy of war.

Table 6. The structure of the finale of the Sixth String Quartet.

| Bars | Material | Initial pitch | Instrument |
|------|----------|---------------|------------|
| 1–4 | Ritornello, first eleven-note phrase. | C | Violin 1 |
| 3–6 | | F♯ | Cello |
| 4–7 | | F♯ | Violin 1 |
| 6–9 | | B♭ | Cello |
| 7–12 | Sequential versions of first five pitches of ritornello. | A–B–C♯ | Violin 1 |
| 13–16 | | G♯–F♯–E | Cello (inversion) |
| 16–21 | Overlapping entries. | G–A–B | Viola |
| | | F–G–A | Violin 2 |
| | | E♭–F–G | Violin 1 |
| 22–30 | Three overlapping variants of the opening eleven-note phrase starting on the second note. | Implicit G♯ | All |
| 31–8 | Bars 5–9 of the ritornello at the original pitch, the final seven notes played one semitone lower and the last five pitches repeated twice. | C♯ | Violin 1 |
| 40–5 | Ritornello, first eleven-note phrase (slowed down). | C | Violin 1 |

(Continued)

| Bars | Material | Initial pitch | Instrument |
|------|----------|---------------|------------|
| 46–54 | Movement 1, first theme, original pitch (cf. bar 24). | A | Violin 2/1 |
| 55–63 | Movement 1, second theme *senza colore*, original pitch (cf. bar 81). Inverted from bar 59. | C | Violin 2 |
| 63–72 | Movement 1, climax of development (bars 222–9). Melodically compressed and reworked, ending with sinusoidal quartal figure. | E (63) E (65) G (67) | Viola Violin 2 Violin 1 |
| 72–5 | Sequential version of first five pitches of ritornello (the final one completes the first phrase) | E–F♯–G♯ | Violin 1 |
| 75–81 | E♭ and C♯ major/minor chords separating chromatic fragments from the ritornello (pitches 8–10) in various transpositions; alternation of major second dyads rising by fourths with the D min♯⁶ chord. | – | All |
| 81–6 | Ritornello, first eleven-note phrase. | G♯ | Viola |
|  | First five pitches of ritornello harmonised with triads D–B♭–E min–F, under perfect fifth dyad D–A. | F♯ | Cello |

The last movement in particular sounds like a threnody for a way of life that seemed as if it was about to disappear for ever.

Bartók did manage to maintain some concert activities during the final months of the year. He performed variously with the violinist Ede Zathureczky, as soloist with the Budapest Concert Orchestra (in Beethoven's Second Piano Concerto), and in two-piano repertoire with Ditta during a short Italian tour in early December (Florence and Rome). Bartók's last appearance as a soloist in Europe was playing his Rhapsody in Turin.

On 19 December 1939, soon after he arrived back in Budapest, his mother died after a long period of gradually worsening health. Although this must have been expected, it was an enormous and a terrible blow to Bartók. Paula had been the most important and constant influence on his life and he had been entirely devoted to her. He had succumbed to a fever in Italy, which prevented him from attending her funeral (or perhaps gave him a pretext not to have to face the reality of her death). One of his earlier communications after her departure was with Sándor Albrecht in Bratislava on 10 January 1940. In a rather understated letter Bartók tells him: 'What I feared the most had happened. I had a very sad Christmas. We must accept the unchangeable if we can't be at peace with it.'[15] He was certainly racked with guilt that he had not given more time to his mother in her final years. As he wrote to Annie Müller-Widmann from Naples on 2 April 1940, he was still overwhelmed with grief: 'Three and a half months have passed since I lost my mother, and I still feel as if it had just happened yesterday.'[16]

Despite the undoubted anguish, his mother's passing did mean that one of the most compelling reasons to remain in Hungary no longer pertained. He had previously planned a trip to America from the beginning of April 1940, the highlight of which was to be a recital with Szigeti. Before his mother had died Bartók had resolved not to go, but he was subsequently persuaded by Szigeti that he should; he departed from the port of Naples and arrived in New York on 11 April. Back in mid-January Bartók had written to his former student, Dorothy Parrish (employed since 1938 as a piano teacher at Juniata College, Huntingdon, Pennsylvania), to clarify part of his upcoming schedule; she wished to have some lessons with him and was to arrange for him to give a recital in the college's Oiler Hall.

Bartók departed somewhat later than he originally intended, given that the letter to Annie Müller-Widmann from Naples was written the day before he set sail and the liner was not due to arrive until 11 April. Just two days after disembarking, he performed in Washington at the Coolidge Auditorium of the Library of Congress, as part of the ninth festival of chamber music of the Sprague Coolidge Foundation. In this morning recital, he and Szigeti performed the First Rhapsody and Second Violin Sonata along with Beethoven's sonata op. 47 and the Debussy Sonata. The Second Violin Sonata did not find particular favour with *The New York Times* critic Howard Taubman in his review the following day. According to him, 'The themes and rhythms are scrappy, and the least agreeable elements of the violin are singled out for emphasis.'[17] In his pen portrait of Bartók as performer Taubman described how the 'frail little man with a sharp, tense face, proved to be an accomplished pianist. Aside from an occasional swollen tone – probably because he underestimated the carrying qualities and the excellent acoustics of the auditorium – he played with a musician's imagination.' A few days later, Eugene Ormandy paid Bartók a minor tribute by performing his *Deux Images*, composed thirty years earlier, at Carnegie Hall with the Philadelphia Orchestra. The composer was not present on this occasion, however, for almost immediately after the Library of Congress recital he had set off from Washington on the 250-mile journey to Huntingdon as previously arranged with Dorothy Parrish. Before returning to New York, he continued to Pittsburgh and Chicago, travelling some 750 miles on this outward stage of his trip, and performed in both cities.

Much was made in the press of the fact that Bartók had not visited America since 1928. When he appeared onstage in a concert at Town Hall in New York after the intermission on 21 April to accompany Szigeti in the First Rhapsody, he was apparently met with 'a prolonged ovation'; at the end of this work, his only advertised contribution to the programme, 'the audience would not let him go until he had given two groups of encores'.[18] Noel Straus, *The New York Times* reviewer on this occasion, was deeply impressed, remarking that 'Mr Bartok was one of the first of the modernists, and the importance of his artistic output and his influence on the music of this century can never be over-rated.'

In the subsequent couple of days he was in Boston, giving a lecture at Harvard University titled 'Some problems of folk music research in East Europe', and in Philadelphia, performing at the Casimir Hall of the Curtis Institute of Music where Fritz Reiner held a conducting post. At the first event Bartók became aware of the Milman Parry Collection of Serbo-Croatian folk material held at Harvard, through Albert B. Lord, who had been in the audience for his lecture. Recently awarded a Junior Fellowship at Harvard, Lord was a scholar of Slavic and Comparative Literature and had accompanied the linguist Milman Parry on his two collecting trips to Yugoslavia between 1933 and 1934; after Parry's tragic accidental death in 1935, Lord was the academic best acquainted with the collection of some 2,500 double-sided records of epic poetry and women's songs. He wrote to Bartók on 23 April, giving him a brief description of the material and encouraging him to contact the Hungarian-born musicologist George Herzog (formerly an assistant to Erich von Hornbostel), currently Assistant Professor of Anthropology at Columbia. The opportunity offered by the Parry Collection to further his ethnomusicological aims would very strongly influence Bartók's decision to return to the USA later in the year.

New York's Museum of Modern Art (MoMA) was the venue for a League of Composers' concert on 24 April in which Bartók performed. The programme included the First String Quartet, performed by the Philharmonic Quartet (members of the New York Philharmonic Orchestra); a group of Hungarian songs arranged by Bartók and sung by the Irish-Hungarian contralto Enid Szantho (of the Metropolitan Opera Company); several pieces from *Mikrokosmos* (garbled as 'Mokrokosmos' in Olin Downes's review in *The New York Times*); and the *First Rhapsody* with Szigeti (the latter piece being more to Downes's taste).[19] On the following day, as part of the Eastman School of Music's American Music Festival, the Second String Quartet, a group of Bartók's songs, a couple of his piano pieces and an arrangement of the First Rhapsody for cello and piano were broadcast on the radio station WQXR; one of the pianists was Ernő Balogh, a figure who would exert an important influence in the final years of the composer's life. And in a repeat of the MoMA concert, Bartók performed with the same group of performers at the McMillin Academic Theater of Columbia University on May Day.

In a remarkably sophisticated and erudite piece of newspaper journalism, published in *The New York Times* on 5 May, the Hungarian expatriate musicologist Otto Gombosi (who taught at the University of Washington, Seattle) provided 'An estimate of the music of a contemporary who is on visit here.'[20] The latter part of this piece found Gombosi asking himself the question, 'What has Bartók given to modern music?' He responded by summarising the composer's technical achievements:

> First, a richness of new harmonic possibilities. The influence of Debussy did not lead him into coloristic effects, but to an ingenious and daring extension of tonality to the utmost limits. Then he gave to modern music a kind of rhythm which seems to incorporate the elemental powers of nature – a rhythm creating form. He gave to modern music a flourishing melody, which grew up from assimilated elements of folklore to a quite individual richness and individuality. He gave examples of formal perfection, growing organically from the material. And finally, he gave to modern music a ripe polyphony that has little to do with 'neoclassicism' and which is formed with an iron consistency that reaches extreme possibilities.

For Gombosi, 'In its deepest fundamentals, Bartók's music is of an elemental strength; it is chthonic and orgiastic in its severity and its visionary poetry.' He suggested that the composer's already broad musical horizon would continue to expand in the future.

When the US liner *Manhattan* sailed for Genoa and Naples on 18 May with Bartók as one of its passengers, he must surely have looked back on the experience of his second American tour with a degree of satisfaction. Not only had his concerts proved successful and received critical acclaim, he had been courted by several of the country's most prestigious academic institutions. He had also interacted with a number of Hungarian expatriates who held influential positions in America's musical life and could provide a potential support structure for him. The day prior to his departure Bartók had written in English to Dorothy Parrish to provide her with a personal reference. He told her that 'There are plans (excepted concertising) to make it possible to me (and to my wife too, of course) to stay here longer, perhaps for several years. I am not authorised to give details, but I hope these plans can be turned in reality.'[21] And on the same day, in a note to Reiner, Bartók told him that 'I hope I can get back to the "free" country by October at the latest.'[22]

As soon as he had got back home to Budapest, Bartók bit the bullet and started planning his next trip to America in earnest. He was not able to attend the premiere of the Divertimento in Basle on 11 June, but on 11 August *The New York Times* was reporting that the composer would be attending its US premiere in St Louis on 9 November; the St Louis Symphony Orchestra would be playing it, conducted by Vladimir Golschmann. The article continued that later, in January 1941, its first performance in New York at Carnegie Hall would be given by Ormandy and the Philadelphia Orchestra. It was noted that as well as the Bartók duo (himself and Ditta) playing his 'new sonatas' [*sic*] for two pianos and percussion at a concert of the New Friends of Music' on 3 November, he would 'appear as soloist with many orchestras, and will lecture at a score of universities, colleges and clubs'.[23]

Corresponding with Annie Müller-Widmann on 6 September, Bartók elaborated his travel plans and detailed the issues he had been facing in sorting out US and transit visas through France, Switzerland and Italy en route to Lisbon where he and his wife would board ship. He asked for her specific help and advice in sorting out some of his arrangements, being characteristically comprehensive and precise in his requirements in terms of costs and timing, the fruit of many years of touring as a professional musician. He also told her about the considerable pain he had been suffering from the peri-arthritis in his right shoulder (a long-term problem), which was making it almost impossible for him to play the piano. A month later, having already started on his final departure from Europe, he wrote to her again from Geneva and described the last concert that he and Ditta had played in Budapest on 8 October with János Ferencsik, including three concertos: he performed the Bach A major, his wife the Mozart F major, K. 459 (he comments 'this was her first solo appearance, and she played beautifully'), and together they played Mozart's double piano concerto.[24]

This poignant letter (echoed in another note to Paul Sacher sent on the same day) speaks of Bartók's anxiety for the future, particularly given his health concerns, but also of his heartfelt pain on saying farewell to his friends – to Stefi Geyer, who had spent the day with them, to Annie and her family, and indeed to Switzerland itself ('this wonderful country, your country'). He finishes with the remark that 'This voyage is, actually, like plunging into the unknown from what is known but unbearable. . . . But we have no choice; it isn't at all the question whether this has to happen; for it must happen.'

The couple faced many frustrations in their early days in America. Their luggage had become stuck in transit; the six large trunks included their clothing and music, requiring them to purchase new concert wear for their forthcoming performances. Bartók was only able to report the final reappearance of the trunks almost four months after their departure, on 11 February 1941, fortunately without loss or damage. Mail was often very slow and intermittent, meaning that news did not come through from Hungary regularly. This was particularly worrying, because their youngest son Péter was still in Budapest completing his schooling and would not join them in America until April 1942.

Soon after their arrival Bartók and Ditta spent an evening at Ernő Balogh's apartment. Among the guests was another Hungarian expatriate, Ágota (Americanised as Agatha) Illés. She worked in New York as a piano teacher and owned a cottage in Riverton, Vermont, which according to Sylvia Parker:

> became her 'Mountain View' summer residence and the vacation destina-
> tion of her many visitors, particularly music acquaintances. Thus it
> continued its role, in the view of one local Vermonter, as a bed-and-breakfast
> for the rich and famous. Guests, often eight or ten at any one time, would
> arrive at the Riverton train station and be brought up Erhardt Hill just
> above it to the cottage with its beautiful views, healthful country setting,
> and relaxing atmosphere.[25]

Described by neighbours as 'eccentric, warm, smiley, a bit theatrical, and sp[eaking] with a distinctive Hungarian accent', Agatha Illés (later Fassett, when in 1947 she married Stephen Fassett, the owner of Fassett Recordings in Beacon Hill, Boston) remained a particularly close friend of Ditta. Her contri-bution to the Bartók literature, *The Naked Face of Genius: Béla Bartók's Last Years*, recounted her interactions with the composer more than a decade later and in a style that at times comes rather close to popular fiction.[26] It is far from clear how she could have recorded conversations in the detail in which they are presented even if she had noted them down immediately afterwards. Nevertheless, allowing for possible lapses in memory and some artistic licence in the reconstruction of dialogue and events, Agatha's underlying portrait of Bartók does seem to have a considerable degree of consistency with the testi-mony of others. According to Peter Bartók, it was faithful to his father's character.[27]

After spending the first month in The Buckingham Hotel in midtown Manhattan, on 7 December 1940 the Bartóks moved into the first of their New York apartments, 110–31, 73rd Road, Forest Hills, Long Island, between the Queens Boulevard and the railway line and very close to the subway station. By this stage he had received an honorary doctorate from Columbia University (25 November). He had also played several concerts in New York (including the Sonata for Two Pianos and Percussion at Town Hall on 3 November; a solo recital at the New Jersey College for Women in Hackettstown on 5 November; and two piano recitals at Swarthmore College and again at New York's Town

Hall on 8 and 24 November), and embarked on an eight-day concert tour of Cleveland. In the latter city on 5 December in Severance Hall he gave the US premiere of the Second Piano Concerto with the Cleveland Orchestra, conducted by Artur Rodziński, and he repeated it two days later. Although Bartók apparently found the weather in Cleveland 'nasty' and 'uninspiring', he told the readership of *The Plain Dealer* that 'Still you're lucky. You have plenty of fuel and good lodgings. That is more than we have in Europe. I like it here. I am happy.'[28] The Cleveland critics played the usual cards in their reviews: in the *Cleveland News* Bartók's music was deemed to be 'modern music of the mathematical sort, rather empty'; and in the *Cleveland Press* it was described as 'elemental, barbaric, almost brutal rhythmic dynamism with an intellectual approach to thematic development, and some occasionally rather remarkable sophistications of tone color'.[29]

Writing to their two sons on Christmas Eve, the Bartóks were able to tell them of the new life they were living, and the discoveries, particularly linguistic and geographic, that they had made. The janitor of their apartment block in Forest Hills was a Slovak who could speak good Hungarian and seems to have taken a shine to them, driving them out to the seaside on one occasion and preparing lunch for them on another. Bartók amusingly recounts his own failure to find the correct stop on the subway to transfer lines when attempting a visit to the most southerly part of New York, ending up travelling backwards and forwards for three hours before giving up and returning home. The cultural transition was certainly difficult, however, and there were aspects of the American lifestyle to which he could never fully adapt.

On 20 January 1941 the Sixth String Quartet was premiered at the Town Hall in Manhattan by the Kolisch Quartet in the composer's presence, programmed along with Mozart's C major quartet, K. 465, and Schubert's 'Death and the Maiden'. Howard Taubman, reviewing the concert in *The New York Times* the following day, sensed extra-musical significance in Bartók's quartet, especially the ritornello theme that appeared to him to be 'grief-laden, resigned'.[30] Summarising, Taubman commented that 'Throughout the impression is of simplicity, not a radiant, natural simplicity, but a simplicity that comes from rigorous, intellectual discipline.'

The following day Bartók set off for Pittsburgh, by way of Huntingdon where he had offered to give Dorothy Parrish four or five hours of lessons in the twenty-four-hour period he was staying there. Two performances ensued of the Second Piano Concerto, on 24 and 26 January, with Reiner and the Pittsburgh Symphony Orchestra at the city's 'Syria Mosque'. The reviewer for the *Pittsburgh Post-Gazette*, Donald Steinfirst, was extremely appreciative. It was, he felt, 'a work of extreme importance that must command the attention of every pianist', though it was accessible 'to even the uninitiated'.[31] Steinfirst remarked on the composer's authoritative performance with its 'crisp and percussive' tone, and submitted that 'Bartok's music will live and be played when the Schoenbergs and the Bergs are gathering dust, for this is modern music with intelligence and culture, exciting to hear and with something to say.' Ralph Lewando for *The Pittsburgh Press* was much less convinced about the Second Piano Concerto in terms of its 'direct appeal' to the general public. Yet he admitted 'there is a brilliance of instrumentation, remarkable rhythmic and dynamic effects and marvellous use of percussion instruments that make this concerto at times thrilling'.[32] Bartók's performance (playing from the score) 'displayed amazing virtuosity which he encompassed with characteristic unaffectedness'.

While Bartók had been away from New York, Douglas Moore, the Head of Columbia University's Department of Music, had written to him to confirm a role as Visiting Associate for the spring semester, with an honorarium of $1,500. Bartók was not required to undertake any teaching as part of this honorary position and the duties were to be agreed between himself, Moore and George Herzog. The approval of the post (albeit just for one semester in the first instance) supported by the Alice M. Ditson Foundation (a bequest of $400,000 to Columbia in the will of the widow of music publisher Charles Ditson), gave Bartók a very useful additional source of income from concert fees, performance rights and publishers' sales. He would find Columbia a very amenable place to work, as he would report to Kodály in December 1941. Not only was the equipment excellent:

> It feels almost as if I continued my work at home in my Academy of Science office, yet under different circumstances. Even the surroundings are of the same kind of 'noble' dignity. Evenings, when I pass through the campus, it is as if I walked on one of the great historic 'Commons' of a European city.[33]

Two days after the second performance of the Second Piano Concerto in Pittsburgh, on 28 January 1941, the Divertimento was introduced to New York and Carnegie Hall by Ormandy and the Philadelphia Symphony. On this occasion Noel Straus was the critic for *The New York Times*. Obviously greatly impressed, he commented that 'Every page of the score was absolutely sincere and filled with vitality.'[34] It was the slow movement that particularly captivated Straus, who found it 'a deeply moving adagio, which in itself would be enough to lend real import to this latest creation of the Hungarian genius'. The composer was in the audience, and Ormandy's performance 'brought on an ovation at the end not to be stilled until Mr Bartok acknowledged the applause from the platform'.

*Contrasts* was premiered in the complete three-movement version by Bartók, Goodman and Szigeti on 4 February at the New England Conservatory's Jordan Hall in Boston in a concert replacing a scheduled appearance by the Busch Quartet. Goodman's more familiar status as a jazz musician was acknowledged by one C.W.D. in the following day's *Daily Boston Globe*:

> For his first appearance in Boston as a classical musician, Mr. Goodman played Debussy's Rhapsody for clarinet and piano, partnered by Mr. Bartok, and joined him and Mr. Szigeti in Mr. Bartok's 'Contrasts'. When the 'King of Swing' shuffled amiably upon the stage, midway of the program, he was faced not with a crowd of stamping, whistling hep cats, but the dinner coats and evening gowns of a Bostonian audience trained to sit up attentively during a Mozart Sonata and who know better than to applaud between the movements.[35]

On 13 February Bartók departed on a month-long tour taking in St Louis, Denver, Provo, San Francisco, Seattle and Kansas City. Despite the fact that by rail this is a distance of nearly 7,000 miles traversing east to west of the United States, then north and back east, he felt able to write to Béla junior that this was 'not a great deal for four weeks, of course, but at least it won't be tiring'. The concerts were a mixture of solo and duo performances (the latter with Szigeti or Ditta) and mainly took place in universities.

Bartók's ethnomusicological activity at Columbia commenced in March. On 2 April he informed his eldest son that 'since March 27th I have been deriving a good deal of pleasure from my work on the Yugoslav material'.[36] A report to Douglas Moore a fortnight later gave more information about the contents of the collection and its importance, as well as suggesting the approach to its examination. Two components were proposed: the notation of 'the most important samples of the epic material'; and 'the transcription of the other materials . . . for an inclusive picture of Yugoslav folk music'.[37] Bartók estimated that it would take a year to complete this labour in addition to the semester he had already embarked upon.

Carl Paige Wood, head of the Music Department at the University of Washington (Seattle), wished to encourage Bartók to take up an equivalent visiting professorship there. Wood wrote to him on 22 May offering similarly open terms of appointment to those of Columbia at a salary of $300 per month. Hans Heinsheimer, a representative at the New York office of Boosey & Hawkes, replied on Bartók's behalf to say that he was interested. However, the extension of the Columbia appointment for a further year, which had now been agreed, meant that he would not be in a position to take up the position in Seattle until the summer or autumn of 1942. Bartók was soon formulating plans to transcribe the Native American ('Indian') music held at the University of Washington, to give a six-week cycle of one-hour lectures on the collection and the approach to folk research, and to train students in the skills of transcription. It appears he was aware of the collection of wax cylinders and discs covering the Pacific Northwest region of the North American continent, recorded by Melville Jacobs, Viola E. Garfield and Arthur C. Ballard. According to Jacobs' paper, 'Survey of Pacific Northwest Anthropological Research, 1930–1940', published in the *Pacific Northwest Quarterly* in 1941, 'So little has been done in the music-dance aspect of Pacific Northwest culture, apart from the recordings deposited with the writer, and the time remaining for research in this material seems so short, that energetic effort should be put into some program to secure early pursuit of field studies.'[38] However, Bartók had little real enthusiasm for this repertoire, telling Béla junior on 20 June that 'it is a field of study very remote from the folklore areas I have dealt with so far, and to start now would mean frittering away my energies'.[39]

The post was confirmed by Wood on 19 June, and soon agreement was reached that it could be held over to the following year, with more advantageous terms approved in a letter of 20 August from the college president, L. P. Sieg (a salary of $3,600 along with the title Walker-Ames Lecturer in Music). Bartók was also permitted a period until March 1942 to come to a decision whether to join the university in January 1943 for a calendar year or for the full academic year 1943–4, depending on whether Columbia extended the duration of his post there. When Sieg responded to Bartók on 4 March 1942, he commented that the change in the political situation since the attack on Pearl Harbor in December 1941, and the subsequent American entry into the Second World War, had created uncertainty about the university's financial situation in relation to its investment income; he therefore suggested that the post be put in abeyance until the spring of 1943. Although Bartók's ill health would eventually prevent him from taking up the lectureship, as late as November 1943 he was still in detailed discussions with Wood about the possibility of coming to Seattle in January 1945.

With his main tour of the 1940–1 season now completed, Bartók performed a few further concerts and informed Béla junior in his letter of 2 April that 'Our biggest success so far was in Detroit – the audience seems to have been delighted with our programme.' He and Ditta had been joined on this occasion by the cellist Georges Miquelle (principal cellist of the Detroit Symphony Orchestra) in an arrangement of the First Violin Rhapsody.

Bartók had by now begun to find the apartment in Forest Hills intolerable, due to the noise of radios and pianos from neighbours, automobiles from the streets outside, and the regular rumble from the subway. Coupled with these irritations was the significant distance he had to travel to Columbia. So the couple moved on again, this time to 3242 Cambridge Avenue in the Bronx, on the middle floor of a three-storey house with quiet neighbours above and below. This building had something in common with 10 Kavics utca in Budapest, where the Bartóks had lived from 1929 to 1932, and he seems to have found the surrounding area (with the attractive nearby Ewen Park) much more conducive and relatively inexpensive.

Meanwhile Péter was still in Budapest, his move to America hampered by his father's need for a non-quota immigrant visa. The application process was slow and complex, as Bartók described to Béla junior. Under the terms of the 1924 Immigration Act, non-quota status included 'an immigrant previously lawfully admitted to the United States, who is returning from a temporary visit abroad'. Bartók's Washington solicitor appears to have been drawing on this clause in making his case (which it was maintained would require him temporarily to visit Canada and return to the USA from there).[40] Bartók was also very concerned about the following season's concert schedule and was unsure whether this was the fault of his agent or simply the wartime atmosphere. If matters did not improve, 'we should then have to return to Hungary, no matter how the situation develops there. By that time things won't be much better even here. . . . if things are bad everywhere, one prefers to be at home.'[41]

That summer the Bartóks vacationed in Agatha Illés's Riverton cottage, Ditta having spent a few days there earlier in July. Fragmentary episodes from the period are reported in a somewhat sentimentalised, if often quite illumi-nating, way in *The Naked Face of Genius*: Bartók's concern for Agatha's lost cat Lulu and her kittens; his work on the Romanian collection; his horror at the neighbouring farmer Matthew's poor management of his estate; his joy at eating with the Spanish neighbours, the Gonzales, and his praise for Mr Gonzales's husbandry; his pleasure in swimming in a deserted lake when out for a picnic; his frustrated attempt to teach Agatha a Romanian dance, in which the woman shows complete indifference to her suitor; and his discomfort and anxiety at an air-raid practice that caused him to leave Riverton early and return to New York alone.

While staying in Riverton, Bartók had been further distressed by the discovery that Aunt Irma, his mother's sister and lifelong companion, had now also died, on 22 July at the age of ninety-two. A letter that Ditta and Bartók had written to Irma on 19 July, but which she did not live to receive, poignantly expressed just how much the couple were missing both her and 'our beautiful

Hungary'. Ditta also had described the wonderful two weeks she had previously spent with Agatha (and another girlfriend called Duci) at Riverton. Bartók's physical condition was a particular cause for concern during the stay. As noted earlier, he had suffered from shoulder problems since 1940, and while at Riverton he had been troubled with bursitis on the left shoulder. Despite largely ineffective X-ray treatment, this was still causing him pain by the middle of October, though he was still able to play the piano.

As already observed, advance bookings were far fewer than Bartók had hoped for. He confided to Wilhelmine Creel that the only concerts he had in the diary for the following season were 'one orchestra-engagement, three two-piano recitals, four minor engagements (piano solo or lecture)', which made their financial condition even more precarious and reliant on the income from Columbia.[42] Meanwhile, he had been working on an arrangement for two pianos of the Second Suite op. 4, to enlarge the repertoire he and Ditta performed in their duo appearances (and presumably increase the number of works from which he could obtain royalties). Although this idiomatic and often brilliantly arranged version of the Suite demonstrates just how far his language had developed since 1905–7 when he had originally conceived it, the roots of his more recent style can nevertheless be discerned in it.

The orchestral engagement mentioned to Mrs Creel was with the Chicago Symphony Orchestra, involving two performances of the Second Piano Concerto on 20 and 21 November 1941. They were conducted by the symphony's long-term music director, the German expatriate Frederick Stock, who had been at its helm since 1905. Two years earlier, Storm Bull had given the American premiere of the concerto with the same orchestra and conductor, so the Chicago audience now had the opportunity to compare the two interpretations. While Bartók was impressed with the orchestra, he certainly did not feel that he played at his best.[43] He followed this concert with a lecture and recital at Stanford University in Palo Alto, California. Bartók then continued on to Seattle, where he had arranged to speak to Professor Wood at the University of Washington in order to discover more technical information about the 'Indian' collection.

In the autumn of 1941 Bartók had played several solo recitals and given ethnomusicological lectures – at Wells College in Aurora, New York, Reed College in Portland, Oregon, and the University of Oregon in Eugene. And in January and February 1942 he and Ditta performed two piano recitals at Northwestern University in Evanston, Illinois, and at Amherst College, Massachusetts. In these duo concerts, they included the three-movement piece *Balinese Ceremonial Music*, a transcription made by the New York-based Canadian composer and ethnomusicologist, Colin McPhee, who had conducted extensive fieldwork in Indonesia. A recording of the work made in 1941 exists, played by McPhee and Benjamin Britten (who for a time shared a house with McPhee and W. H. Auden in Brooklyn); proto-minimalist scores such as this (and the forty or so others that McPhee made) would exert a significant influence on Britten and a later generation of composers. Bartók had previously referenced Indonesian music in number 109 of the fourth volume of *Mikrokosmos*, 'From the Island of Bali'. This draws on the Balinese *Tembung* mode, a five-note subset of the *Slendro* scale (D–Eb–G#–A–Bb) that is closely aligned to the familiar Z-cell.

Bartók was able to summon up a degree of darkly ironic amusement in his correspondence with Wilhelmine Creel about the critical response to the Evanston concert (at which he and Ditta played the new arrangement of the Second Suite). He felt they had played well enough, but one review was 'as bad as I never [*sic*] got in my life. Just as if we were the last of the last pianists. So you see your choice of piano-teacher was a very bad one!'[44] He did at least have some good news for her: Péter was now on his way to America and had arrived in Lisbon on 10 February, though he faced problems getting a sailing permit;[45] and Bartók's Columbia post had now been extended until the end of December 1942. While this musicological work provided basic support, Bartók avowed that there had been no previous time in his adult life when he had faced such serious financial difficulties. Ditta wanted to add to the family income by taking on some piano teaching, but the couple were somewhat at a loss how to proceed and sought Creel's advice. Characteristically looking on the black side, Bartók was deeply pessimistic, having 'lost all confidence in people, in countries, in everything'.[46] To add insult to injury, the Baldwin piano company, who had loaned him two pianos, had decided to recall the upright and he had insufficient funds to hire a second one.

A couple of days later, on 4 March 1942, Bartók corresponded with his other American student and confidante, Dorothy Parrish, along similar lines. He noted that the salary from Columbia would not be sufficient to support three people when Péter arrived and asked for her guidance about working with agencies to find students for Ditta. It may seem astonishing that one of the world's greatest musicians should be writing in such a way, even allowing for the very difficult international situation. Of course, the Japanese attack on Pearl Harbour had taken place just three months earlier, on 7 December 1941, and the US Congress had declared war against Japan the following day. Hitler had responded on 11 December by declaring war on America, whereupon Hungary, as a client state of the Axis powers, necessarily followed suit. Bartók's sister, Elza, his eldest son, Béla junior, and their families remained in Hungary, and communication with them would unavoidably become ever more difficult;

his youngest son Péter was probably still trapped in Europe and facing an arduous and dangerous Atlantic crossing. Bartók was by nature pessimistic, and back in 1940 had told Annie Müller-Widmann that he did 'not approve of the *"keep smiling"* attitude'.[47] Given his emotional situation, can it be any surprise in the circumstances that his mood should be so bleak?

To compound matters, his physical condition had further deteriorated and in April 1942 he had begun to develop fevers, his temperature remaining at a higher than normal level for an extended period. Gyula Holló, who had been Bartók's doctor in Budapest but was now a leading physician at the Goldwater Memorial Hospital in New York (as a Jew he had fled Hungary and the threat of Nazism), apparently suggested 'atypical myeloid leukaemia' in his case notes at this early stage. Yet this was never communicated to Bartók.[48]

There was some good news that month, however. Bartók's publisher, Ralph Hawkes (of Boosey & Hawkes), wrote from London on 17 April to tell him about the 'extremely well received' performance of the Sixth String Quartet (played by the Laurance Turner Quartet) two days earlier at the Wigmore Hall, and to propose some new compositions.[49] He had two specific ideas: an orchestral work of ten to fifteen minutes, most likely based on folk music and technically not too difficult; and a series of concertos for solo instrument and string orchestra rather in the line of Bach's Brandenburg Concertos, featuring piano, violin or flute. Hawkes also released Bartók from his company's Artists Department, in response to the composer's expressed concern that he was not being well served by them. The tenor of Hawkes's letter is gracious and respectful throughout, and suggests a publisher wishing to remain on the most amicable terms with a composer who was of considerable value to his company.

Three days after this letter was sent and before Bartók could have received it, Péter finally arrived in New York from Europe. The remarkable chance meeting between father and son as the latter was on his way to his parents' house is described by Péter: 'As I was searching for a taxi at 231st Street, I found instead a white haired man with a familiar type of briefcase who looked from the back just like my father. What a small place New York is!'[50] Péter's journey, which is described in *My Father*, was itself an extraordinary ordeal, taking some four months in total, including three weeks on board a freighter as one of two passengers. His safe arrival removed at least one major cause of anxiety for his father.

The last concert of the season took place under the auspices of the ISCM at the MacDowell Club in New York (a women's club that promoted art and music). Beyond its announcement, the concert passed without comment in *The New York Times*. In the programme were the Second Rhapsody for violin, played by Rudolf Kolisch; the two-piano arrangement of the Second Suite played by the Bartóks; and *Contrasts*, performed by Kolisch, the composer and Eric Simon, the Austrian émigré clarinettist. Simon had given lessons to Benny Goodman between 1940 and 1941, and presumably had been recommended by him.

In the meantime Bartók had become drawn into the 'Movement for Independent Hungary' established by the politician Tibor Eckhardt, head of the Independent Smallholders' Party. Eckhardt had arrived in America in August 1941 with a remit to create an organisation that could represent Hungarian interests after the defeat of Hitler. Five million dollars had reportedly been transferred to a New York bank in 1940 by the Hungarian government to support the mission. After assuming the role of president of the Executive Committee of 'Independent Hungary', Eckhardt had issued a series of anti-Nazi proclamations. In one he declared that 'In this intolerable situation, we Hungarians living outside of Hungary, fortunate in being able to express our views freely, have not only the right but also the sacred duty to give voice to the genuine convictions of the Hungarian people and to take up the fight against Nazi domination.'[51] Bartók had written in June 1942 to the Hungarian-American professor of comparative literature at Western Reserve University in Ohio, Joseph Reményi, to encourage him to join a 'Commission of the Arts and Sciences' of Independent Hungary, which he now chaired. In a follow-up letter Bartók described the structure of the commission and named some of those who had been contacted. They included Pál Henry Láng (professor of musicology at Columbia University, and influential in Bartók's appointment there), Eugene Ormandy and Ernő Balogh. Although Eckhardt had been successful in gaining publicity and support for the movement from the main Hungarian-American organisations, his motives were distrusted in American governmental circles: he had been dogged by accusations of racism and anti-Semitism, and it was widely understood that the mission had actually been approved by Miklós Horthy. Eckhardt resigned the leadership of the committee on 9 July 1942. According to Steven Béla Várdy, 'Thereafter the Movement for Independent Hungary – nominally under Béla Bartók's leadership – gradually petered out and died.'[52]

Another expression of Bartók's political consciousness appeared in the article 'Race Purity in Music', which featured in the League of Composers journal, *Modern Music*. His dark mood can be inferred from the first paragraph, which fails to strike a hammer blow against the notion of race purity (a notion of some significance for the USA, given its racial segregation, and not only for Nazi Germany and its allies). Perhaps he was writing out of respect for the country that had given him a home:

There is much talk these days, mostly for political reasons, about the purity and impurity of the human race, the usual implication being that purity of race should be preserved, even by means of prohibitive laws. Those who champion this or that issue of the question have probably studied the subject thoroughly (at least, they should have done so) spending many years examining the available published material or gathering data by personal investigation. Not having done that, perhaps I cannot support either side, may even lack the right to do so. But I have spent many years studying a phenomenon of human life considered more or less important by some dreamers commonly called students of folk music. ... In the present period of controversy over racial problems, it may be timely to examine the question: Is racial impurity favourable to folk (i.e., peasant music) or not?[53]

Drawing on his experience of traditional music in several Eastern European cultures, he describes the 'continuous give and take of melodies, a constant crossing and recrossing', which results in great variety; thus 'the "racial impurity" finally attained is definitely beneficial'.

Bartók was able to discuss his work on the Parry Collection in some detail in an article published in *The New York Times* on 28 June. He made the explicit comment that 'One of the reasons for my return to the United States was the possibility of a careful study of this material, which I had badly missed in Europe.'[54] Six specific qualities of the collection are listed:

- Its scale – 'it is in fact the richest recorded collection [of Yugoslav folk song] enumerated';
- Its completeness – unlike Bartók and his compatriots, Parry had been able to record all the verses of a song, 'even of ballads as long as forty to fifty stanzas';
- Its recording media – the aluminium disks were robust and of high fidelity;
- The unbroken nature of the recordings – 'Theoretically, every piece, however long it be, could have been recorded without any interruption';
- The additional recordings of conversations with singers – 'you really have the feeling of being on the spot, talking yourself with these peasant singers';
- The presence of second recordings of some performances by the same singer at a later time.

In his conclusion (and in words echoing those of the collector George Petrie writing almost a century earlier about the potential loss of Irish music due to the Great Famine), Bartók writes:

The work was done in the twelfth hour. Already in 1934 and 1935 there were signs of slow and constant deterioration in the life of heroic poems. Heaven knows if and how they can survive the present disastrous events at all.

These poems seem to be the last remnants of a folk usage at least several thousand years old, expressed in words and music, leading back perhaps to antiquity, to the times of the Homeric poems.

In August 1942 Bartók was still reporting his raised temperature that had begun in April, and he told Reiner that 'the wise men of medicine' had not been able to determine its cause.[55] The rest of the autumn yielded no further concert activity from him, but he opened correspondence with Yehudi Menuhin on 7 October, in reply to a letter from the young violinist telling him that he had started to learn the Violin Concerto. In his biography *Unfinished Journey*, Menuhin describes how, during an evening of chamber music with the conductor Antal Doráti at the latter's house in New York, Doráti:

> spoke of Bartók, pressed me to discover the music for myself, and played excerpts from various works at the piano. Like all important revelations, it seemed clear, obvious, even familiar, once it had been made. Deriving from the East, Bartók's music could not but appeal to me, but in his greatness a local heritage had been absorbed, interpreted and recast as a universal message, speaking to our age and culture and to every other.[56]

Menuhin determined to play both the Violin Concerto and the First Violin Sonata. Plans were hatched for a performance of the concerto with the Minneapolis Symphony conducted by Dimitri Mitropoulos, and of the sonata in Carnegie Hall during the following year (1943–4 season).

On the final day of 1942, Bartók wrote to Wilhelmine Creel to catch up on the year's events. He told her that he was still running a temperature of around 100° F and that his doctors still had not been able to diagnose the root cause. He was to cease work at Columbia University ('dismissed') the following day, a cause of great irritation, because his work on the folk collection was far from complete, but he had been given some teaching work ('a certain number of conferences and lectures') at Harvard. There was only one other engagement in his diary, a concert with the New York Philharmonic in January 1943. Nevertheless, his ethnomusicological work had progressed satisfactorily, with the book on Serbo-Croatian music due to be published by Columbia University and the two volumes of Romanian music now apparently finished with 'the hope that it will be published'.[57] Noting ironically that he was 'gradually advancing to the position of an English writer', he concluded pessimistically that 'my career as a composer is as much as finished: the quasi boycott of my works by the leading orchestras continues, no performances either of old work[s] or of new ones. It is a shame – not for me of course.'

What turned out to be Bartók's final public performances took place in early in 1943. On 22 January, under Reiner and the New York Philharmonic, he and Ditta premiered his Concerto for Two Pianos and Orchestra (an arrangement he had made of the Sonata for Two Pianos and Percussion of 1937). The programme was also repeated the following day. The title 'Concerto' is perhaps something of a misnomer. This is in effect a quite conservative arrangement of the sonata in which the orchestra for the most part doubles lines in the piano parts, provides some harmonic underpinning, and adds colour, while the work involves no significant concertante interplay between soloists and ensemble. During the first performance of the concerto, Bartok seemed to depart completely from the score for several moments. Agatha Fassett recalled what happened afterwards backstage:

> After a while Reiner came in, looking grim and disturbed. He did not speak at first, but finally walked over to Bartók.
>
> 'What on earth came over you, Béla?' he said in a voice that was cold, but somehow compassionate too. 'How could you endanger everything, risking disaster for a momentary whim? Didn't you realize what an impossible task it was, trying to follow you through your wanderings? For all of us, not to mention Ditta!'
>
> Bartók looked up at Reiner and did not say anything, and seemed to remain detached and undisturbed.
>
> He held his brooding silence in the taxi on the way to Riverdale, and we were already going up the hill when he sat up straight and turned to Ditta.
>
> 'The tympanist,' he said, 'the tympanist is the one who started everything. He played a wrong note, suddenly giving me an idea that I had to try out, and follow through all the way, right then. I could not help it – there was nothing else for me to do.'[58]

As for Olin Downes's review in the following day's edition of *The New York Times*, this was hardly enthusiastic; indeed he felt that the concert would have been best if it had ended after the first item, Haydn's Symphony no. 102 in B♭:

> The addition of the orchestra furnishes more instrumental color than the first scoring. Yet it is questionable if this was what the composer most desired, since the tendency in his last period is all toward a beauty which is

not sensuous, a treatment of line and rhythm that is severe and often barbaric in atmosphere – a modern Hungarian primitive might be the word for it.[59]

Downes detected a conflict between the 'primitive' folk source and 'a modern intellectuality which does not merge with the older idea or convincingly produce new beauty'. Although personally disappointed, he did report that 'by a large section of the audience it was cordially received'.

No doubt a result of his mother's upbringing and his ingrained belief in self-sufficiency, Bartók was deeply antipathetic to anything that suggested patronage, nepotism or charity. According to Fassett, he became suspicious that his and Ditta's part in the Carnegie Hall concert was due to their friendship with Reiner. Bartók's attitude was well understood by his publishers, agents and his friends, who would often have to engage in considerable subterfuge to ensure that their well-meaning attempts to support him financially were not summarily rejected. This would prove challenging at times in the following three years.

The hole in Bartók's income left by termination of the work at Columbia University was to be filled by an honorary post at Harvard University. This was created at the invitation of Arthur Tillman Merritt, the dynamic new chairman of the music department. It was initially intended that Bartók should deliver a series of 'conferences' with students at Harvard beginning in mid-February 1943. Bartók had suggested two series of 'informal lectures'. The first series would provide participants with an understanding of contemporary Hungarian music, especially his and Kodály's, while the second series would cover the 'scientific approach to folkmusic'.[60] Merritt was supportive of this plan but proposed that Bartók should conduct eight conferences instead of the first lecture series, and six public lectures in Paine Hall (subsequently advising that the lectures should begin in the fifth week to fit into the teaching term). As part of his duties Bartók was also to perform in a recital. He duly recommended Louis Krasner (who had commissioned Berg's Violin Concerto) to join him, on the strength of Krasner's reputation. Krasner wasn't available, however, so instead Bartók invited Rudolph Kolisch.

The lectureship was supported by the Horatio Appleton Lamb Fund, Bartók receiving an honorarium of $2,000 from Harvard and given rooms in Eliot House. On 12 February 1943 a piece in the university daily newspaper, *The Harvard Crimson*, titled 'The Music Box' had provided readers with a potted biography of the composer. The article furnished information about the attendance at the first conference (it was presented in front of 'a small but appreciative audience') and gave a brief review:

Bartok's lecture Tuesday was not an exciting affair, but it was an extremely competent introductory talk to a course on folk and modern music. Clarity, good organization of material, a quiet but effective sense of humor, frequent and excellent illustrations on the piano, and a sincere desire on his part to please all speak for a highly successful association between Bela Bartok and those who would like to gain the benefits of his presence at this University.[61]

On 18 February a further article in *The Harvard Crimson*, presumably intended to encourage attendance, had explained that Bartók was 'considered the greatest of Hungary's modern contributors and now lecturer on music at Harvard'.[62]

Bartók had completed only the first three of his conferences when his poor health made it impossible for him to continue. On 8 March a note was posted that the opening public lecture had been postponed, but gave no indication that he might not be able to return:

The first lecture to be given on 'The Scientific Approach to Folk Song' by Bela Bartok, visiting lecturer under the Horatio Appleton Lamb Fund, which was scheduled for this Thursday, has been postponed. The series of six lectures will ordinarily meet on Thursday at 3:30 o'clock in John Knowles Paine Hall in the Music Building. Bartok will also give a program of his own music on March 26 in Sanders Theater.[63]

He had managed to find his way home from Cambridge after giving the third lecture. Because of the seriousness of his condition, however, Bartók was persuaded to go to Mount Sinai Hospital for tests (from 5 March). From Agatha Fassett's account he refused to allow an ambulance to be called (as ambulances were, in his estimation, only for the seriously ill), and he went instead by taxi. By 10 March he had returned home, with a diagnosis – the confirmation of polycythaemia, the elevation of red blood cells in the plasma.

Clearly concerned, Merritt drew on his contacts at Harvard and started to investigate physicians who might be able to offer better advice to Bartók, coming up with the name of Dr Bernard S. Oppenheimer at Mount Sinai Hospital and recommending him to Ditta. She discussed the matter with Dr Holló, the family doctor, and he was keen to progress with this course of action, though Ditta explained to Merritt in a note written on 16 March that 'it would be impossible for us to meet the financial requirements of a consultation'.[64] Merritt then took control of the situation, writing to Oppenheimer himself to explain the situation and saying that 'I am willing to stand behind them and would appreciate it if you would send the bill to me rather than to them'. He added 'Our resources here are not very large either, but since this is a very important human question to me, I hope you will do your best.'[65]

Oppenheimer met with Bartók and Holló on 19 March, urging the composer to return to Mount Sinai for further tests. He was certainly back in the hospital by 22 March, remaining there for a week. Under Oppenheimer's care he had finally agreed to have a chest X-ray taken (which he had previously refused). This led to the diagnosis of a flare-up of tuberculosis as the primary cause of the high temperature, along with the secondary polycythaemia previously discovered. Oppenheimer gave an account of the investigations to Merritt on 28 March, the day before Bartók was due to be discharged. He told Merritt that rest was essential for his patient, and that Bartók 'was in a deplorable condition the first time I saw him, but now he has picked up physically and is definitely more optimistic'.[66] The fact that the composer's weight had dropped to 86–7 pounds was, Oppenheimer asserted, largely due to Bartók's fussiness and his 'peculiar ideas on what he will or can eat'.

On returning to his apartment Bartók tendered his resignation from the visiting Harvard lectureship and continued to work on the manuscript of his Turkish music study. Ditta, at her wits' end as his situation deteriorated and his doctors expressed concern about his chances of recovery, approached Bartók's friends for assistance. Ernő Balogh contacted the American Society of Composers, Authors and Publishers (ASCAP), whose president was the composer and music journalist Deems Taylor. ASCAP was responsible for licensing the musical performances of its members' works and collecting and distributing royalties on their behalf. It had a fund designed to support 'sick, infirm, needy or deserving member[s]' and it was to this source that Balogh turned. He was fortunate in having Taylor's support, for Bartók was not (and as a non-citizen of the USA could not be) a member. James Pegolotti comments that Taylor 'had heard Bartók's music and shared with the Hungarian his great interest and joy in the folk music of many lands'.[67] ASCAP stepped in without delay to pick up Bartók's medical expenses, and after further hospitalisation and tests under the direction of Dr Israel Rappaport, the composer's recuperation at the resort of Saranac Lake. Rappaport was another expatriate Hungarian, who had looked after Endre Ady twenty-six years earlier. Although the investigations he directed appeared to have made little significant progress in resolving the diagnosis and treatment, Bartók's condition did start to show some signs of improvement. When Péter wrote to his brother on 7 November 1945, some time after his father's death, describing the illnesses of his final three years, he told him that though the doctors by this time 'knew – or at least thought – that it was a leukaemia, they told us it was a polycythaemia'.[68]

While Bartók was in Mount Sinai Hospital, a further supportive gesture resulted directly from his friends' intervention. This was the commissioning of a new work under the auspices of the Koussevitzky Music Foundation, founded in 1942 in memory of the wife of Serge Koussevitzky, conductor of the Boston Symphony Orchestra. A letter from Koussevitzky was sent to Bartók's Riversdale address on 4 May 1943, informing him that he had been awarded $1,000 for the composition of an orchestral work. Payment would be made in two equal instalments, the first when the award was accepted, the second when the work was completed.[69] Koussevitzky concluded with the remark 'I look forward to an opportunity to talk this matter over with you in the near future.' Grants to Bartók, Stravinsky and William Schuman for symphonic works were announced in *The New York Times* on 13 May, and three days later Koussevitzky penned an article titled 'Justice to Composers: Koussevitzky Speaks for Need of Support for Those Who Create'. Although he does not mention Bartók directly, it is evident that Koussevitzky's thoughts lay with him, and indeed it may all have been part of a scheme to ensure the composer could not regard himself as the recipient of charity. Looking back on the unjust treatment of the great composers in previous centuries who 'were ignored by their contemporaries and allowed to die of heartbreak and misery', Koussevitzky argued that 'the contemporary composer is forced to go out and teach, lecture and crowd his days with trifling obligations which kill his time, his energies, his creative art'.[70] Proposing the establishment of a composers' fund, he saw this as an imperative that was consistent with American culture and tradition. With a rhetorical flourish, he concluded: 'Whatever action we take now will lay the groundwork for the impelling and just cause of the composer. Embracing that cause, we shall ascend to new heights; we shall gain in confidence, in self-esteem and in fortitude.'

Ditta mentioned the meeting between conductor and composer in his hospital ward when she wrote to Szigeti on 23 May. Although Bartók initially seems to have been interested in composing a work for chorus and orchestra (perhaps he had in mind a companion piece to the *Cantata profana*), 'they agreed on a purely orchestral work'.[71] She was delighted that Bartók was now considering composition again, and that 'Béla's "under no circumstances will I ever write any new work —" attitude has gone. It's more than three years now —'. She went on to express her heartfelt gratitude to the person she felt responsible, Szigeti himself.

The couple terminated the lease on their apartment in the Bronx and put their furniture into storage, setting off on 1 July for a three-month stay at Saranac Lake, a village that sits within Adirondack Park in New York State. At the time, the resort had a world-leading reputation for the treatment of tuberculosis. It also attracted luminaries such as Albert Einstein, who spent many summers there from 1936 onwards. On the advice of the ASCAP physician Dr Henry Leetch, the Bartóks stayed at 32 Park Avenue, in the heart of the village, in a cure cottage owned by Mrs Margaret Sageman who lived in a nearby bungalow. She seems to have got on very well with both Bartók and his wife, and she later described him as 'brilliant, kind, humble, and with a good sense of humour'.[72]

Although investigations into Bartók's illness continued and various diseases were proposed, by the middle of August his doctors remained baffled as to his underlying condition. Nevertheless in Saranac Lake he started to make a partial recovery and began the final and enormously rich creative period of his life.

## CHAPTER TWELVE

# 'I see the beautiful sky': 1942–1945

The bulk of the composition of the Concerto for Orchestra, Bartók's response to Koussevitzky's commission, took place between 15 August and 8 October 1943, the dates that appear at the end of the first version of the Boosey & Hawkes score. His autograph full score, written on twenty-four-stave Parchment Brand paper, only includes the last date. For the sketches of the concerto Bartók used a field music notebook that had accompanied him on his trip to Turkey in 1936. As Klára Móricz has demonstrated, these evidence the 'micro-chronology' of the work's composition, in which the second movement seems the first to be fully conceived, followed by the others in their final order.[1]

Perhaps in describing his new work as a Concerto for Orchestra, Bartók was thinking back to the suggestions Ralph Hawkes had made the previous year, though it seems significantly larger in scale than the Brandenburg-type pieces his publisher had envisaged. This was not the first contemporaneous composition to bear this title, however, for in 1925 Paul Hindemith had written such a work, and Albert Roussel had composed a Concerto for Small Orchestra. Stravinsky's Concerto in E♭ (*Dumbarton Oaks*) had appeared in 1938, and this may well have been the kind of work that Hawkes had been imagining. However, the most likely precursor was Kodály's single-movement Concerto for Orchestra, the score of which Bartók had brought with him on his 1940 visit in order to pass it over to the Chicago Philharmonic Society, which had commissioned it.

In his 'Explanation to Concerto for Orchestra', Bartók clarified the work's title in terms of 'its tendency to treat the single instruments or instrument groups in a "*concertant*" or soloistic manner'.[2] The overall mood, he observed, 'represents – apart from the jesting second movement – a gradual transition from the sternness of the first movement and the lugubrious death-song of the third, to the life-assertion of the last one'. He had employed five-movement structures as early as the First Suite, and the Fourth and Fifth String Quartets were notable examples of this approach, the symmetrical opportunities such structures offered being explored particularly systematically. In the Concerto for Orchestra, drawing on Bartók's metaphor of a seed, the outer shell (the testa or seed coat) is rapid in tempo, the inner shell (the endosperm) moderate and the kernel (the cotyledons and radicle) slow. The overall tonality is F, and those of the five movements are, in turn, F, D, C♯, B and F, all except the central C♯ falling onto Lendvai's tonic axis.

As much as in any other of his works, Bartók forges close connections between almost all the musical ideas of the work. Through the course of the slow introduction to the first movement, he establishes a sequence of pedal tones: C♯–F♯–D♯–E–G–E♭. When these are placed in scale order (C♯–D♯–E–F♯–G) they spell out the first five pitches of an octatonic scale. The opening figure in cellos and basses (C♯–F♯–B–A–E–F♯–C♯) is pentatonic in configuration and includes rising and interlocking falling fourths; and when upper strings appear in bar 6 they present a wedge-like shape that includes all the chromatic pitches between $A\flat_4$ and $E_5$ in its course. Along with the usual range of diatonic modes, these three elements – the octatonic, the pentatonic and the chromatic – underpin much of the work's material.

A diverse range of folk sources is also brought into play in the concerto, referencing many of the cultures from which Bartók had collected in the course of his life. The opening pentatonic fragment might be taken to invoke a new-style Hungarian tune that Bartók collected in 1907 from Felsőireg, 'Idelátszik a temető széle', whose text appropriately reads 'From here is seen the graveyard's border/Where rests she who was light of my eyes./The grave holds her, whom I would hold./Now I know how thoroughly I am orphaned'.[3] This passage also recalls the bleak pentatonicism at the beginning of *Bluebeard's Castle*. Two further Hungarian-influenced ideas follow, projected against the ostinati that are generated from the opening pentatonic idea: a parlando-rubato melody in the trumpets from bar 39 that signifies the old melodic style without replicating the morphology of any specific tune (and indeed, the pauses on the fourth and eighth syllables are not particularly idiomatic of the repertoire); and a *verbunkos*-like passage from bar 51.

Although the first movement of the Concerto for Orchestra can be seen to be in a fairly regular sonata form with reversed recapitulation, it might also be taken to allude to Baroque concerto structure, with the presentation of the principal idea as a quasi-ritornello on five occasions over its course. The opening nine pitches of this theme segment into octatonic and pentatonic groups, though if the B♮ is disregarded as a passing note, the whole figure can be seen to lie in the F Dorian or Aeolian modes. I have pointed out elsewhere

Figure 51. The opening bars of the first theme from the first movement of the Concerto for Orchestra.

that the first six pitches (F–G–A♭–B♭–B♮–C) appear frequently throughout number 27c of *Serbo-Croatian Folk Songs* (pages 158–9), 'Polećela dva vrana gavrana' ('Two Black Ravens Flew'). This is one of several elements that may have been influenced by Bartók's work on the Parry Collection.[4]

The first phrase, the antecedent of an almost Beethovenian sentence structure, is three bars in length, with a 3+3+2 metric scheme. This reveals an interplay of regular and irregular features, both temporal and acoustic, that is apparent across the concerto. One particular instance is the use of triple hypermetres, whether consistent (as in the continuation of the first theme from bar 110), or metrically more complex (as in the 'Bulgarian' 3+3+2 groupings of Fig. 51, or the 3+3+4 from bar 192).

For the tranquil second theme played by the oboe (from the upbeat to bar 155), Bartók seems to returns to north African Arab music, and as Yves Lenoir has proposed, 'the scarcely modulated chants of the bards of the desert accompanied by the two-string rabab'.[5] However, Bartók also found examples of melodies with similarly narrow range in his research for the introduction to *Serbo-Croatian Folk Songs*, leaving as an open question whether there might be any connection between the two repertoires.[6] The tonality shifts to B (a semitone lower than the 'true' dominant, C) and the hypermetre is initially quintuple, though it adjusts to triple for the varied repeat in the clarinets.

The development falls into three main phases. In the first, between bars 231 and 271, Bartók focuses on the first theme, splitting it into its two components, and he takes each in turn, concentrating on the octatonic elements. Thus, from bar 248 the interlocking perfect fourths are extended into an octatonic framework (A–[B–]C–D–E♭–F–[G♭–]A♭), and from bar 254 these work through all three permutations of the octatonic scale. The second phase of the development is in A♭, is more subdued and in triple hypermetre; it can be seen to derive from the second theme, though reconfigured in the sway of the quartal passages that preceded it. (It is notable that although the clarinet resolves on C, the viola's

B♭ beneath it in bar 273 completes an interlocking fourths figure, A♭–D♭–E♭–B♭.) In the final phase, starting with a further iteration of the 'ritornello', there is a fugal exposition in B♭ founded on a further derivative of the interlocking fourths idea and what is effectively a counter-exposition in C with the subject inverted. The climax of the development falls on a long sustained unison A♭.

The order of thematic events is reversed in the recapitulation and after the A♭ slides up into an A–E dyad, the second subject is restored, initially in a regular triple hypermetre and then, after the tonality has descended again, now to G, in a 3:4:5 polyrhythmic texture. With the climax on D♯ minor at bar 438, Bartók introduces the novel timbre of strummed harp chords played with 'an appropriately shaped wooden (if possible metal) stick'. In a transitional passage, chains of parallel second-inversion major triads are presented, a further manifestation of a technique that had been in his repertoire since his early discovery of Debussy. Fragments of the second and first ideas intermingle in the accelerando leading to the restoration of the primary theme at bar 488, which functions equally as recapitulation and culmination point, the triple hypermetre now initially regularised by the modification of the 2/8 bars to 3/8. In the subsequent passage, Bartók breaks the hypermetric regularity just established and long chains of falling thirds with rising scales superimposed culminate in a final rendition of the pentatonic fanfare that formed the fugue subject in the development and a pseudo-perfect cadence in F.

'Giuoco delle copie' ('Game of Pairs'), the jovial and bucolic second movement, was originally marked by Bartók as 'presentando le coppie' (pairwise presentation). It is in a ternary form in which the outer parts are constructed from chains of five sections, each of which involves pairs of wind instruments playing in similar motion separated by a largely constant interval and with a distinct character (Table 7). It seems that this general approach may have been suggested by his Yugoslavian music research, for he notes on page 62 of the section of *Serbo-Croatian Folk Music* devoted to morphology that:

> in Dalmatia, besides the 'normal' part singing, there is an extremely peculiar kind of 'two-part' singing – in major seconds. . . . There are available (or at least there were before the Second World War) some commercial disks with such two-part songs of Dalmatia. Listening to those records, one may hear the major seconds sometimes 'degenerate' into minor thirds. Nevertheless, since these deviations seem to be more or less due to chance, this kind of performance may be called 'part singing in major seconds'.

Bartók further comments in a footnote on the same page about 'instrumental preludes on the commercial disks, which for technical reasons invert the melody played on two sopels (a kind of oboe), that is, there appear minor sevenths instead of major seconds. These minor sevenths are never changed into any other interval.' He makes use of these interval pairs as well as sixths, thirds and perfect fifths in the course of the movement.

In the course of the five sections the harmonisation and voicing moves from being largely diatonic and triadic in the first section to whole-tone in the fifth. Binding the movement together, a side drum without snares acts as master of ceremonies, opening and closing the outer chains and playing through the caesuras in the chorale-like trio; and brief linking passages in the lower strings connect the sections from B to E.

The important role given to the side drum is, of course, entirely consistent with the treatment of percussion in a number of Bartók's later works, including the Sonata for Two Pianos and Percussion, but it may be that he was also referencing the use of drums in a folk context. He had come across a single-sided drum called the *dobă* in a couple of villages in Transylvania, and the *davul* in Turkey. It is possible he was also aware of an instrument related to the *davul* found in Serbia, Macedonia and Bulgaria and known as the *tapan*, which accompanied the round dances collectively called *kolo* that Bartók mentions in *Serbo-Croatian Folk Music*.

Table 7. The structure of the outer sections from the second movement of the Concerto for Orchestra.

| Section | Instruments | Interval | Reprise | Modifications |
|---|---|---|---|---|
| A<br>8–24 | Bassoons | Sixth (mainly minor) | A'<br>165–80 | Third bassoon added, scale and arpeggio figures in counterpoint. |
| B<br>25–44 | Oboes | Third (both major and minor) | B'<br>181–97 | Two clarinets in inversion with oboes. |
| C<br>45–59 | Clarinets | Minor seventh | C'<br>198–211 | Two flutes in sevenths interlock with clarinets, creating stacked fourths chords. |
| D<br>60–86 | Flutes | Perfect fifth | D'<br>212–27 | Oboe, then clarinet added, creating parallel first-inversion major chords. Second oboe from bar 216 doubles upper voice an octave lower. |
| E<br>87–124 | Trumpets | Major second | E'<br>228–63 | Harp glissandi, string whole-tone tremolandi octave higher. |

Yves Lenoir has suggested that the trio in B has a correspondence with the chorale 'Nun komm der Heiden Heiland' ('Now come, Saviour of the Gentiles'); while the organ-like, five-part setting is certainly consistent with this proposition, it would be stretching the degree of similarity between the two to regard it as a quotation.[7] Indeed, there are other potential models within the Hungarian folk repertoire. The first strain of several variants of the tune for 'Fehér László' (which tells the story of the horse thief László Fehér, who is 'cast into the deepest dungeon' for his crime) has a similar melodic configuration to the opening six bars of the 'chorale'. After the varied reprise, the final point of closure is on a repeated and then sustained chord of $D^7$ that fades to silence as the side drum draws the movement to its conclusion, disappearing into the distance.

At the heart of the concerto lies the 'Elegia' described by Bartók as a 'lugubrious death-song': an elegy arguably for his mother, for Hungary and for humanity. Framed by two 'night music' sections, which are prefaced and terminated by references to the interlocking fourths idea from the introduction to the first movement, sit three impassioned chain links. The first and third of these develop folk-inflected material originally heard in the *Introduzione*. Although the opening bars give priority to an idea that rises and falls by alternating perfect fourths and minor seconds, the texture of the first 'night music' is built from a 1:3 scale (C–E♭–E♮–G–A♭–B♮) juxtaposing alternating minor thirds and minor seconds. A chromatic idea in the first oboe no doubt recalls Berber Arab music, but again Bartók draws connections with his recent Yugoslavian research; in *Serbo-Croation Folk Songs* he demonstrated musical similarities between the chromatic melody he notated in Tolga, Algeria, in 1913 and a two-voice Dalmatian song he transcribed from commercial disks.[8]

A transitional passage, also based on the 1:3 scale, now shifts the tonality down from C through B♭ to A♭, and a series of Hungarian anapaests and iambs descend through a minor triad with major seventh (another allusion, perhaps, to Stefi's motif). Bartók then revisits the material first heard at bar 39 of the *Introduzione*. Now played by the tutti in a heroic *verbunkos* mode, replete with iambic rhythms in the first trumpet and cascading scales with ever-changing modality, it is subsequently developed by inversion before landing on a harmonically static texture bounded by the tritone F♯–C and chromatically infilled by oboes, clarinets and cellos. The second chain link, the emotional core of the *Elegia*, is also highly chromatic, and the searing four-strain viola melody has the keening quality of Transylvanian funeral laments; one could usefully compare number 628a from the second volume of *Rumanian Folk Music*. On its repeat, the closing note of each strain is harmonised by a major triad, and these descend through E♭, via D and C, to the climax on A♭, the third of the latter chord treated with a Baroque unprepared suspension and resolution (D♭–B♭–C).

A variant of the overtly *verbunkos* theme from the *Introduzione* is reprised in the tonality of E♭ as the third link in the chain, and it climaxes with a passage overladen with the musical symbols for grief, though it rapidly subsides. In the subsequent 'night-music' section, the flutes and clarinets arpeggiate 1:5 model scales (alternate perfect fourths and semitones) with a piccolo superimposing isolated notes, trills and couplets that clearly suggest birdsong. The brief coda from bar 112 takes the movement to its end. Here there is an ambiguous cadence on C♯ in the timpani by means of interlocking perfect fourths figures subtly harmonised, as well as fragmentary, increasingly distant recollections of the piccolo's birdcall and the horn's heroic Hungarian gestures.

After the unabashed and overt outpouring of sorrow in the 'Elegia', the fourth movement, 'Intermezzo interrotto' (which has the overall structure ABA' – 'interruption' – B'A"), turns to brutal irony in the disturbance that splits apart its gentle character. The tonality and basic pitch content of the first section are pre-empted in the first four pitches, played positively by the strings: B–A♯–E–F♯, the tonic, subdominant, dominant and leading note of B major. When the opening idea arrives, its rhythmic contour suggests some of the Romanian *colinde* repertoire, with their varying metres and the solo oboe's melody (supported for the first seven of its eight bars by what is effectively a dominant seventh chord of B major that resolves to the tonic on the eighth bar) gives the impression of effectively being based on a pentatonic mode (B–C♯–E–F♯–A) in which the A has been sharpened (Fig. 52, upper stave). On its repeat, beginning in bar 12, the approximate inversion of the melody in the first bassoon (Fig. 52, lower stave) is configured rather like one of the composer's pedagogic piano pieces (for instance, number 141 from the sixth volume of *Mikrokosmos*, 'Subject and Reflection'); and following a brief modulatory section, a third version of the A theme appears with a simple descant in the first flute.

At bar 42, Bartók introduces the second idea, in which a broad melody is played first by violas and repeated by the first violins and cor anglais, against an

Figure 52. The opening of the repeat of theme A from the fourth movement of the Concerto for Orchestra.

accompaniment that works down through a partial cycle of fifths. The material has some similarity in configuration to the main theme of the aria 'Szép vagy, gyönyörű vagy Magyarország' ('You are beautiful, you are lovely Hungary') from the operetta *A hamburgi menyasszony* by Zsigmond Vincze. As always with Bartók, however, this is by no means a literal quotation and after the first thirteen notes he goes his own way; even the pitches in common with the aria are set quite differently in terms of rhythm and harmony from those of Vincze. Although Bartók normally had little time for such 'popular art music', whose role, as he commented in his 1930 essay 'Gipsy Music or Hungarian Music?', was 'to satisfy the musical needs of those whose artistic sensibilities are of a low order', he does not seem in this instance to be presenting it in a particularly ironic sense.[9]

On the other hand, there seems to be no doubting his parodic intentions in the interruption that follows the reprise of the A section. With the move to E♭ major and the vamped accompaniment comes a simple linear melody that appears to burlesque the march theme from the first movement of Shostakovich's Seventh Symphony (which it has been suggested is itself in part a lampoon of the aria 'Da geh' ich zu Maxim' from Franz Lehár's operetta *Die lustige Witwe*). In one of his most brilliant orchestral effects, worthy of the hero of his adolescence, Richard Strauss, Bartók simulates cackling laughter, has the trombones blowing raspberries, and after placing the melody in a fairground ambience, musically imitates shrieks of derision.

There are at least two elucidations of this interlude that have been ascribed to the composer. Antal Doráti recalled Bartók discussing with him how his irritation at the success of Shostakovich's Seventh Symphony had caused him to 'g[i]ve vent to my anger'. The composer explained that 'The melody goes on its own way when it's suddenly interrupted by a brutal band-music, which is derided, ridiculed by the orchestra. After the band has gone away, the melody resumes its waltz [*sic*] – only a little more sadly than before.' Peter Bartók effectively confirms this interpretation, remembering his father's comment after the first radio broadcast of the Shostakovich symphony: 'It's not just that repetition of a theme so many times is excessive under any conditions. But of such a theme!'[10] He had apparently suggested that a parody might be in order and was encouraged to provide one by his son, but nothing further was said of the matter.

The second version derives from the Hungarian pianist György Sándor, as reported to the conductor Ferenc Fricsay, and involves a rather different interpretation. As I have noted elsewhere, in this reading 'it is not the Shostakovich/ Lehár music which is being ridiculed by the orchestra, but culture and civilization itself by a drunken mob who sing a debased music'.[11] Sándor describes how 'a young lover, an idealist, brings his beloved a serenade' and explains that 'the serenader personifies a nation, and the ideal to which he sings is his fatherland'. At this stage a drunken mob arrive led by a boot-boy, 'a rough possessor of power, who leaves ruin and waste behind him wherever he goes; he whistles a trivial melody, a gutter song that has considerable similarity to a Lehár melody'.[12] Although the young man attempts to take up his serenade again with his 'broken instrument' after this violent and brutal disturbance, he falters and fails.

Bartók did not provide any clarification of the narrative content of the interruption in his writings or letters. Although there is a tentative thematic connection between the linear descent of the Shostakovich/Lehár idea and the ascent of the cantabile theme purportedly influenced by Vincze, it is difficult to escape the feeling that it is intended to express something beyond the purely musical; however, this remains open to individual interpretation. The movement ends with condensed recapitulations of the B and A sections. Yet there is one further interpolation in a fleeting cadenza for the solo flute built around stacked perfect fourths evoking birdsong, a moment of isolated reverie.

Writing to Péter on 26 September 1943, his father tells him that he has enjoyed twenty-six days without high fever and 'feel[s] virtually normal, the constant tired feeling is gone, the rheumatism-like pains are gone'.[13] He is also able to give his son news about the composition of the concerto, informing him that he is 'struggling with the last one [movement]; this is the most difficult for certain reasons. This kind of thing involves a lot of fussy work, although still less than the writing of a scientific work. I would like to be able to finish it while still here.' Klára Móricz has examined the process of composition of this substantial finale, which accounts for nearly 50 per cent of the printed score, and remarks that 'Bartók's struggle with the movement, especially with the end, signifies that his intended program, – a 'life-assuring' finale in the form of a series of folk-dances – did not match unproblematically with the sonata para-digm. In the process of composition, sometimes the former, sometimes the latter principle seems to have determined the formal procedure.'[14]

The overall structure of the finale is outlined in Table 8, though this cannot convey either the complexity or the level of coherence of this brilliant and viva-cious movement. Almost all of the musical resources and techniques that Bartók had hitherto developed – tonal, harmonic, rhythmic, metric, contra-puntal and colouristic – come into play with a control, confidence and degree of integration that is extraordinary given the parlous state of his health when he had begun work on it. Two characteristics call for special mention. The first is the pair of fanfare-like ideas that recall the alphorn calls and collectively act in the role of framework themes. The second is the principal idea (first heard in bars 5–49), which draws closely on the spirit and style of a Romanian *horă* (a round dance seen as the most characteristic of the country, 'symbolic of national brotherhood and unity');[15] Bartók had come across the *horă* from a recording given to him by Constantin Brăiloiu.[16] The source tune involves a mode with sharpened fourth and minor seventh, the same Lydian/Mixolydian (acoustic) scale that underpins Bartók's theme.

Table 8. An outline of the structure of the finale of the Concerto for Orchestra.

| | Bars | Tonality | Section | Folk resources |
|---|---|---|---|---|
| **Exposition** | | | | |
| | 1–4 | F Lydian/Mix-olydian | Horn call 1 | Romanian alphorn calls |
| | 5–49 | A Acoustic | First subject group, part 1 | Romanian *Horă nemțească* (Germanic) |
| | 50–95 | F Acoustic (after dominant preparation) | First subject group, part 2 | *Horă* (59–73) |
| | | | | *Mărunțel* (74–95) |
| | 96–118 | D ~ A | First subject group, part 3 | *Horă* |
| | 119–47 | A–F–D–F–[A/D/G] | First subject group, part 4 | *Horă* |
| | 148–87 | A♭ ~ | Horn call 1 (transition) | Alphorn calls |
| | 188–255 | D♭ | Second subject/horn call 2 | Hungarian-style bagpipe tune and (Slovak?) alphorn call |
| **Development** | | | | |
| | 256–316 | C♭/B | Development part 1, three-voice fugato based on horn call 2 | Alphorn, Balinese/Javanese gamelan |
| | 317–83 | ~ C♯ | Development part 2, based on horn call 2, contrapuntal | Alphorn |
| **Recapitulation** | | | | |
| | 384–417 | F♯/F acoustic | First subject group, part 1 | *Horă* |

| 418–48 | F | First subject group, part 2 (cf. 74–95) | Mărunțel |
| 449–81 | D–A–G–F– G–A | Transition (decorates pitches from horn call 1) | Alphorn |
| 482–555 | A♭–F♯ ~ C | Horn call 1 | Alphorn |
| 556–625 (alt. ending) | ~ F | Second subject (horn call 2) | Alphorn, triple hypermetre pseudo-folk tune based on 1:3 scale |

It is impossible to know whether Bartók's improved health – his temperature had dropped close to normal since the beginning of September and many of the rheumatic symptoms had vanished – was the result of his 'lazy lifestyle' at Saranac Lake, or part of the progression of the disease.[17] The advice of his principal physician, Dr Rappaport, was to remain in a 'resting lifestyle' on return to New York and 'settle in a "nursing facility" similar to the one here, and continue a similar existence. At the ASCAP's expense of course.'[18]

Less than a week after completing the Concerto for Orchestra, Bartók found himself the centre of attention in New York with three performances of the Second Violin Concerto at Carnegie Hall, on 14, 15 and 17 October. The soloist was Tossy Spivakovsky, concertmaster of the Cleveland Symphony, who performed with the New York Philharmonic under its newly appointed conductor Artur Rodziński. Bartók's financial concerns caused him to worry that the hotel Péter was staying in, where Bartók also hoped to rent a room for a few days, was too far uptown in Manhattan and that he would not be able to afford the taxi fare to attend the concert! This proved to be no problem, however, as ASCAP picked up the composer's bill for a suite in the Hotel Woodrow on West 64th Street, near Central Park and just a short distance from Carnegie Hall.

In his review of the first of these concerts, Olin Downes reported the audience's enthusiastic response – 'it was very well received', Bartók was 'called repeatedly to the stage after the performance', and 'the orchestra rose in [his] honor'.[19] As well as commenting on 'the independence and logic of his writing, the characteristic rhythmic energy, and, at moments, the lyrical beauty of ideas', Downes acknowledged the sincerity, profundity and mastery of the composer. Spivakovsky seems to have been particularly well attuned to the work and not only received a critical accolade but the composer's admiration. A month after the concerts Bartók sent him a manuscript of some sketches of the concerto, but made it clear that he was unlikely to be able to write a further violin concerto. Instead, he suggested that Spivakovsky investigate the Second Violin Rhapsody and the first of the Two Portraits, which he told him was intended as the first movement of a concerto (though he made no reference to Stefi Geyer's role in that work).

Violinists had been Bartók's companions and inspirations from his late adolescence – Stefi Geyer, Ferenc Vecsey, Jelly d'Arányi, Zoltán Székely, József Szigeti, Imre Waldbauer, to name but a few. In November 1943 another of the world's great soloists joined this group: Yehudi Menuhin. It will be recalled that Menuhin had been in correspondence with him in October 1942, and that he had decided to perform both the Violin Concerto (with Mitropoulos in Minneapolis) and the First Violin Sonata in Carnegie Hall that year. In the brief gap between the two concerts, a meeting was arranged at the apartment on Park Avenue belonging to Mrs Lionello Perera, a patron of music and friend of Menuhin. Bartók was already present when Menuhin and his pianist Adolph Baller arrived. In the violinist's own words Bartók was:

> Seated in an armchair placed uncompromisingly straight on to the piano, with score laid open before him and pencil in his hand . . . There were no civilities. Baller went to the piano, I found a low table, put my violin on it, unpacked, tuned. We started to play. At the end of the first movement Bartók got up – the first slackening of his rigid concentration – and said, 'I did not think music could be played like that until long after the composer was dead.'[20]

On that same afternoon, Menuhin suggested a commission, nothing substantial, 'just a work for violin alone'.[21]

In the middle of December, and still supported by ASCAP, Bartók set off by himself for Asheville in North Carolina for the continuation of his treatment. He would stay in the Albemarle Inn before returning to New York on 26 April 1944. Clearly because the composer was still believed to be suffering from the effects of tuberculosis, the physician in Asheville engaged by ASCAP to treat him, Dr C. Hartwell Cocke, was a pulmonary specialist.[22] At this stage, Bartók's health seemed to have improved significantly, his temperature was normal, and he had gained weight – to a 'stout' seven and a half stone, as he informed József Szigeti – and he was able to undertake gentle walks in the forests and mountains.[23] Personal reminiscences of Bartók's time in Asheville were later recorded by two local musicians, Dr Arnold Dann and Mrs Grace Carroll.[24] Dann, an Englishman who had settled in Asheville, appears to have got on particularly well with the composer, meeting with him regularly, giving him access to his piano, and conversing together about Shakespeare; and he was treated to

Bartók's gentle and mischievous humour. In Dann's recollection, Bartók was by then incapable of playing the piano with any proficiency. It was probably an acceptance of this fact that caused him to cancel two concerts projected for April, though he advised Péter that 'The risk would have been too much. The practising facility is also meagre here. – So it was not worth it.'[25]

During his time in Asheville, he engaged in three specific musical activities: producing a piano reduction of the Concerto for Orchestra for a fee of $500; working on the translation of 'Wallachian' song texts, the final element of his magnum opus on Romanian music; and composing the Sonata for Solo Violin commissioned by Menuhin. The Concerto for Orchestra arrangement was intended for a ballet to be choreographed for the American Ballet Theatre by Antony Tudor, who had bought an option on the stage rights; for the composer this was probably little more than hackwork.[26] When Dann questioned the playability of part of the transcription, Bartók apparently remarked that 'nobody will ever see this, nobody will ever take the trouble to look at it. I don't think anybody will ever try to play it. But if they do I have set them a puzzle.'[27] The 'unplayable' section is in the finale, in bars 482–556, where the music is spread over three and four systems, though in his notes Bartók suggested either a second player or leaving out the lower part entirely. As this arrangement pre-dates the first performance, it only includes the original ending. A later edition by György Sándor provides the revised version.

The Romanian song texts clearly afforded the composer much more amenable and interesting work, as he commented to Szigeti at the end of January. Bartók was particularly entertained by the curse texts, which were 'amazing, quite Shakespearean in their fantasy', and the obscenities which were 'quite extraordinary. Not disgusting urban army stuff but full of surprising ideas.'[28] These latter texts were provided with ellipses in the English translations for the extremely sexually explicit words that remained unexpurgated in Romanian (and could not have been published in English). They certainly demonstrate that Bartók was no prude.

Compositional work on the Sonata for Solo Violin began sometime in February and was completed by the middle of March 1944 (the score is dated 14 March). In order to sketch the piece Bartók turned to the field music book that had accompanied him on his Arab trip. This reveals that the first ideas were for the third movement ('Melodia'), with a draft of the first section of its ternary form.[29] The opening 'Tempo di ciaccona' movement and the subsequent 'Fuga' are interlaced in the pages of the sketchbook, and followed by the completion of the 'Melodia' and the entire Presto finale (the initially drafted part of this movement being the first folk-influenced episode from bar 101 of the published score).

Baroque forms are overtly referenced in the nomenclature for the movements of Bartók's Sonata for Solo Violin, the fundamental tonality of which is G. The four-movement Sonata in G minor BWV 1001 by J. S. Bach is a very obvious model, its initial pair of movements functioning as a prelude and fugue, after which the gentle melodically driven Siciliano in B♭ leads to a Presto finale. Bartók's opening chaconne insinuates both the final part of Bach's D minor Partita for solo violin BWV 1004 and the rhapsodic first movement of Kodály's Sonata op. 8 for unaccompanied cello. Like the Kodály sonata, it is superficially conceived in fairly conventional sonata form (the development beginning at bar 53 and the recapitulation at bar 91), though development is continuous throughout the movement. The chaconne does not conform to its usual structure either by the use of a ground bass or of a repeated underlying harmonic progression. However, there are aspects of its workings that go some way beyond the employment of the stereotypical rhythmic patterns of the chaconne. These include the tendency towards (though by no means exclusive use of) eight-bar units; and the reflection of four-bar antecedent phrases a fifth higher in consequent phrases to be found in both the principal theme (bars 1–16) and the secondary theme (bars 32–52).

The violin writing in the first movement is extremely demanding, extending up to the extreme high register. In combination with almost continuous double, triple and quadruple stopping, shifts of register and chromaticism, the writing requires from the player extreme accuracy of intonation. While allusions to pre-Classical mannerisms are certainly evident, gestures derived from folk music are much less apparent, though there are prominent examples of iambic rhythms in both main themes.

Virtuosity at the highest level is also required in the four-voice fugue. In its narrow melodic range and chromaticism the resolute subject in C seems to bear witness to the Arab music contained in the earlier pages of the sketchbook. The exposition is fairly regular, with the first episode from bar 21 focusing on rising scale patterns and falling sixth dyads. In the set of entries that follow from the end of bar 37, the subject is played in F♯, initially in the original orientation with a florid accompaniment and then inverted with the rhythm smoothed out from the end of bar 44. A tonally mobile second episode (bars 50–62) gives prominence to E♭, before leading to a further set of entries on E (from bar 62), A (from bar 66), F (in inversion from bar 70), and in a heroic version on C (from bar 76). The passage from bar 85 outlines a falling diminished seventh F♯–D♯–C–A (the set of tonal relationships underpinning the entire movement), before settling on a doubled-stopped D–A inside which the chromatic space is gradually filled. A brief attempt to restate the subject in both original form and inversion is abruptly cut off, and from bar 98 a final adapted entry in four voices brings the movement to its conclusion.

The exquisite Melodia is a simple ternary-form movement. The first part is organised in four phrases, each terminated by a brief and quiet refrain that subtly changes on every occurrence, a ghostly echo of the material it follows. At the movement's centre is a mysterious-sounding episode involving a kind of minimal night music that links to the reprise of the A section through a trace of birdsong. The melodic and rhythmic contour between the pair of five-bar chorale-like passages on B♭ and E beginning the middle section is similar to the second idea of the finale of Brahms's Violin Sonata in A major op. 100, which may well be entirely coincidental. Yet the correspondence is striking and it is tempting to imagine that Bartók is making covert reference to this piece that connects back to his youth. In the return of the first section, the overall melodic orientation is reversed and a parabola is drawn out that starts and finishes in the upper register, the final B♭–F dyad sounding at a stratospheric height.

Bartók reserved his most radical technical innovation for the original version of the rondo finale, through the use of microtones in the ritornello passages at bars 1–100 and 201–69. Menuhin remarked that:

> Bartok gave me the option of playing these passages in half tones, and given that I had only weeks to prepare the Sonata, I found the demand of accurate quarter tones in fast tempo too intimidating and chose his alternative. I am still doubtful whether quarter tones would allow the music sufficient clarity, but I regret not having included the quarter-tone version in the published edition.[30]

The *scorrevole* ritornello does not, in fact, seem to have been the first part of the movement to be drafted. Instead, the folk-inspired episode from bar 101, with its pentatonically inflected melody and hemiola rhythms, appears before it in Bartók's sketchbook. In its rhythmic configuration, this theme returns to a gesture he had explored almost half a century earlier in his *Scherzo oder Fantasie* for piano of 1897. Its internal structure is characteristically ternary, the outer parts (bars 101–17 and 163–200) being variants of each other and the middle section moving the hemiola to the end of a pair of five-bar phrases. After a series of stuttering iambic rhythms and scale passages, Bartók seems to allude to another popular work of the solo violin repertoire, Paganini's ninth Caprice in E major (known as 'La Chasse'), suggesting its double-stopped horn calls.

On its abbreviated reprise, the ritornello is transposed from the tonic G up to E♭, with its melody doubled a perfect fifth higher. This leads to a further episode in A♭, which has a lyrical character and is in three phases; the second phase (bars 282–91) more or less inverts the first (bars 270–81), and the third phase initially restores the orientation of the first and then its tonality. Bartók returns to the opening pair of ideas, and starting with the folk-like episode, develops them alternately before intertwining elements of both of them. In the coda a brief recall of the third, lyrical idea on B♭ and a long ascending scale in the same tonality brings the sonata to its close with an unambiguous perfect cadence in G major.

Menuhin may have got more than he expected from his commission in at least two respects: this is a fiendishly difficult work that presents the player with the severest of technical challenges; and because it does not compete in the crowded world of the concerto, but the much more sparsely populated field of solo violin music, the piece occupies a niche position. It is arguably the most important contemporary work in the repertoire and has become a standard companion to Bach's masterpieces.

Bartók spent the period of four months in Asheville away from Ditta, who had remained in New York, staying first with Agatha Illés and then moving into a small apartment on 309 West 57th Street. He was briefly visited by Péter, however, who went down a storm with the other 'inmates'. Bartók arrived back in New York on 28 April and stayed at the Hotel Woodrow for the next couple of months. While there, towards the end of May, more sinister medical symptoms relating to his spleen developed; he had suffered some rib pain during his time in Asheville, though this had dissipated and blood tests revealed that his white cell count was very high (some 28,000 per microlitre as compared with the normal range of 4,500–10,000).[31] He set off for Saranac Lake on 5 July, to spend the summer again in the cottage at 32 Park Avenue. Ditta joined him on 18 July and they remained together for much of the time.

Compared to the summer of 1943, the weather was extremely hot and the nights were unpleasantly sticky. However, unlike the previous year, this was not a time of feverish compositional activity for Bartók. Instead he continued to work on his introduction to the volume of Romanian song texts as well as dealing with the proofs of the volume of *Serbo-Croatian Folk Music* for Columbia University Press; the punctilious copy-editor had sent him numerous corrections, which he tells his good friends Pál and Erzsébet Kecskeméti (living in the same apartment block as Ditta) had 'often gone too far'.[32] He had by now recovered the ability to play the piano, which seemed to have been seriously affected when he was in Asheville, and he went as far as proposing some recordings to Ernő Balogh, including the *Allegro barbaro*, the Suite op. 14 and the Sonatina.

It gave Bartók particular joy to hear about the liberation of Paris and the German surrender there on 25 August 1944. He wrote to Péter on 1 September,

'I always adored and adore all France, especially Paris. Paris was for me the unique city in the world; when I went to Paris I felt as if going home.'[33] He had no obvious home to go to when he returned to New York and gloomily told Péter, who had offered to lend him his savings, 'Here am I with my "world-fame", and in such misery. Of course, one can not fill one's stomach with world-fame!'[34] On 5 October he settled into Ditta's apartment on West 57th Street and was reasonably satisfied with it; she certainly saw an improvement in his physical and mental state – 'he is friendly to people, it is possible to discuss, arrange everything with him nice and calmly'.[35]

The premiere of the Sonata for Solo Violin, which took place on 26 November 1944, was a truly remarkable success. Olin Downes of *The New York Times* headed his review 'Menuhin Thrills Capacity Crowd'. As well as a packed audience in the auditorium, several hundred soldiers were seated on the stage of Carnegie Hall for a concert that made very few compromises, the sonata 'being a test for the ears, the intelligence, the receptiveness of the most learned listener'. Despite this, Menuhin held all present in the palm of his hand and 'The immense audience accepted the sonata whole, as it were, and applauded it, while Mr Menuhin led the composer back and forth upon the stage to receive the tribute.'[36] Downes acknowledged how rewarding the interpretation must have been for Bartók, 'who has had his share of the difficulties of the radical innovator in modern music', and the technical prowess of Menuhin, who had put his heart and soul into the performance. But Downes was unable to offer a 'definitive' judgement of this work in Bartók's 'most boldly dissonant style' after one hearing. The composer was certainly impressed. He commented later to Wilhelmine Creel that Menuhin's interpretation of what he had feared might be too long a work for an audience to cope with was 'wonderful'.[37]

At the end of November Bartók prepared to travel to Boston to attend the final rehearsals and premiere of the Concerto for Orchestra. Although the composer did finally receive his doctor's permission, Rappaport took quite a bit of persuasion. Bartók later observed to Péter that:

All went very well, rehearsals, performances; the orchestra, together with Koussevitzky, outdid themselves. Koussevitzky is enthusiastic about the piece, he repeatedly declared it to be the most significant orchestral work of the last 20–25 years. As someone else told me: 'he is raving about the piece'.[38]

On the day before the concerto's public inauguration, Winthrop P. Tryon had prepared his readers for it in an article published in *The Christian Science Monitor* of 30 November. Although Bartók had titled it 'Concerto', Tryon argued that the work amounted to much the same as a symphony and that the score had 'all the traits of something written by a master musician'.[39] He concluded by questioning whether it really was 'an original piece of music to want to make itself heard once and again, or . . . one more brilliantly contrived example of orchestral craftsmanship?'

The answer would come the following day, 1 December, with the first of six performances by the orchestra in Boston and New York over the period of a month and a half (the second pair in Boston was on 29–30 December, including a radio broadcast). Critical reception for the premiere was, by and large, extremely positive. Rudolph Elie Jr. of the *Boston Herald* hailed it as 'the composer's masterpiece, which is to say it must rank among the masterpieces of recent years'.[40] From Elie's review it is apparent that the audience was by no means ecstatic in its response. However, he felt that Bartók, 'whose music has withheld its innermost secrets from the general public', should not be concerned by this, for 'If a composition of transcendent musical art may be defined as one which, in its own way, is a summation of all that has gone before, then the Orchestra Concerto is a work of art . . . and a great one.'

Warren Story Smith was a little more muted in the *Boston Post* on 2 December, but remarked that 'the new Concerto should win many friends',[41] regarding it as a 'different sort of symphony'. Cyrus Durgin of the *Daily Boston Globe* noted on the same day that 'you find practically nothing of the harmonic sourness or the rigorously intellectual patterns of a prominent modernist whose previous music has earned him, among some people, the scorn of such words as arid and eccentric'.[42]

The performances at the end of December were equally well received. Elie advised his *Boston Herald* readers on 30 December that 'no doubt about it, it is a masterwork, and certainly Bartok's masterpiece'.[43] Durgin remarked in the *Daily Boston Globe* on the same day that the concerto's length was 'no deterrent to whole-hearted enjoyment of matter and style'.[44] After the New York premiere in Carnegie Hall on 10 January 1945, Olin Downes gave his most unambiguously positive review of any of Bartók's works. Laying aside any suggestion that the composer might be pandering to popular taste by adopting a simpler style, Downes saw his 'striking out, in late years, in new directions' as an act of courage and 'an emergence from the pessimism which might pardonably have engulfed him, as it has so many leading artists of today'.[45] Wondering whether this was merely 'a temporary divagation from the road Bartok so consistently has traveled', Downes claimed the audience was enthusiastic. It seems from Bartók's letter to Péter the same day, 11 January, that the piece did not receive quite such a warm reception, for he was in agreement with the critic of the *Herald Tribune* who had observed that 'It was disheartening that the audience received this fine composition with a coolness which amounted merely to polite applause'.[46]

Sometime after the New York premiere, probably in February or March 1945, Bartók produced an alternative ending to the Concerto for Orchestra (as he had done for the Second Violin Concerto) at the request of Koussevitzky. In this version the five-note segment from the second horn call (C–C–C–E♭–C) is given prominence at its culmination. This could be seen to create a rather more positive and assertive conclusion, rounding the movement off by reflecting its opening horn call and synoptically referencing aspects of the work in the pentatonic and acoustic scale.

Meanwhile his financial situation had seen some improvement, for Boosey & Hawkes had agreed to advance him $1,400 each year for the following three years against royalty payments. And in a letter to Péter on 8 February 1945 Bartók told his son that:

> Three people (independent from one another) would like to commission works from me: one a viola concerto, another a piano concerto, the third one a two piano concerto. They would pay 1000+1500+1000, total 3500 . . . Well this is very nice, the only problem is, that I do not know where and when I could write this enormous amount of sheet music. Hardly here in New York.[47]

A fortnight later, he wrote to Péter again, this time explaining that he had decided not to take on one of the commissions (as the 'commissioner is an unreliable "nobody" '),[48] but he was keen to bring to fruition a plan to compose a concerto for Ditta as a birthday present. He remarks that 'If she could play this at 3–4 places, that would already mean as much money as the one rejected commission.'[49]

As far as the Viola Concerto was concerned, this commission came from the Scottish violist William Primrose who had established a successful career as a soloist. He had contacted Bartók at some point in late 1944 with the proposal for a concerto (this was the $1,000 alluded to in the letter to Péter), and met him in his apartment in the spring of 1945 for further discussions.[50] Bartók initially seems to have been uncertain about taking the work on because of lack of familiarity with the viola's potential. As part of his preparations he therefore asked Hans Heinsheimer, the New York representative of Boosey & Hawkes, to help him lay his hands on a copy of Berlioz's *Harold in Italy* which features a viola obbligato. Primrose suggested Bartók listen to the Walton Viola Concerto, which Primrose was to play with Malcolm Sargent and the NBC Symphony Orchestra, and it seems that the composer acquiesced after hearing the broadcast on 11 March.

Bartók chronicled his illnesses throughout the spring of 1945 – colds and bronchitis, dental problems, asthma, peri-arthritis, bursitis and influenza (which Rappaport treated with the very expensive new drug, penicillin, at three-hour intervals for four days). Rappaport put his improvement from influenza down to the penicillin. Bartók, however, was less convinced, having decided (despite being a lifetime smoker) that he could have been intolerant to tobacco. He was now 'adhering stubbornly to the stopping, because I have been infuriated for a long time by this artificial cigarette-shortage'.[51]

Yehudi Menuhin invited the Bartóks to stay with him in California for much of the following summer. In April, Bartók gratefully accepted the offer, saying that he would arrive with Ditta in mid-June and stay for three months. However, by 6 June he had decided that this would not be possible after all, indicating to Menuhin that illness (both his and Ditta's) made him unwilling to undertake the very long journey. It seems that Bartók was unable or unwilling to foot the train fare (he had presumed ASCAP would have paid, but they refused); he had apparently estimated that he could cover transportation and rent a cottage at Saranac Lake for two months for less than half the $466 it would have cost to travel to California.[52]

The situation in Hungary was also very much on Bartók's mind and he scanned the newspapers daily for photographs of Budapest, looking for signs of damage to its landmarks. In late April he discovered that he, along with three other exiles including former President Count Mihály Károlyi, had been 'elected' to the Hungarian parliament as non-party members of the Provisional National Assembly – a brief piece appearing to that effect in *The New York Times* on 28 April 1945. Although he was gratified, Bartók was bewildered as to why and by what means he had been elected. In the same letter in which he tells Péter this news, another side of his character can be seen in his falling out with Hans Heinsheimer, 'this time once and for all –. At times he is so brazenly impertinent and flippant that I am not willing to put up with this and I wish not to meet him or talk with him ever.'[53]

Gradually, word came through about familiar places and people in Budapest. A heartbreaking note to Péter on 6 June revealed the depth of Bartók's depression. In response to Péter's enquiry about the possibility of returning to Hungary he replied:

> Oh, how can you imagine that?! There will probably be no conveyance even in a year's time that would carry one home. Waiting, waiting, waiting and – weeping, weeping, weeping, weeping – this is all we can do. For news has slowly begun to trickle over here and these [sic] are rather alarming. Shocking. In my estimate conditions will not be suitable for civilized human existence within 5 years.[54]

His mood remained black a fortnight later, not improved because Ditta had managed to allow herself to be cheated by a shopkeeper out of their sugar and meat coupons for the following three months. Turning his venom on the Allies, who had been too late in defeating the Nazis 'on account of the isolationist Americans, negligent English, the gambling Russians', Bartók observed bitterly that while the First World War had demonstrated that it was not worth saving money, the Second had shown 'that there is no point accumulating anything else, that is, it is not worth to work more than what is needed for daily subsistence'.[55]

With Ditta he set off for Saranac Lake at the end of June, staying this time in a primitive rustic cabin in the grounds of a house at 89 Riverside Drive, right on the edge of Lake Flower. Soon after their arrival, Bartók wrote to the expatriate Hungarian film orchestrator, Eugene (Jenő) Zádor, who had been attempting to commission a movement from him for a collective work for narrator, chorus and orchestra called the *Genesis Suite*, which drew on new material from several contemporary composers; these included Schoenberg, Stravinsky, Tansman, Toch, Castelnuovo-Tedesco, Milhaud, Toch, and the Hollywood composer, orchestrator and arranger, Nathaniel Shilkret, who conceived the work. Although Bartók accepted the commission in principle at this stage, he later withdrew and returned the advance of $250. Simultaneously he contacted Arthur Merritt at Harvard University's music department, agreeing to take up the lectureship again at the beginning of the spring term in 1946.

Before he could start working seriously on the Third Piano Concerto and the Viola Concerto, Bartók had briefly to pay a brief visit to Canada in order to attend to his US immigration status. After staying overnight in the border town of Plattsburg, fifty miles north-east of Saranac Lake, it took him nine and a half hours of queuing the following day to obtain his visa (he tells the Kecskemétis that 'I loafed, loitered and sat around in that Consulate, consumed with anger and anxiety').[56] Surprisingly, given the stress of the situation, he seems to have quite enjoyed Canada – there was plenty of meat and tobacco on offer (indicating he may after all have returned to smoking) – and he found Montreal rather attractive and 'more Europe-like'.[57]

Bartók worked on the Third Piano Concerto, intended as a birthday present for Ditta, between July and mid-September 1945, mainly at Saranac Lake and partly back in New York.[58] He managed to score all but the last seventeen bars, which remained in draft when he died, the Hungarian word *vége* (meaning 'end' or 'it's all over') being written after the double bars. The full score was completed by Tibor Serly, a routine task involving little creative input.

In the overall tonality of E (with a strong orientation towards modes having a major third as mediant) and in three movements, the concerto is lyrical in temperament and has relatively little ostentatious virtuosity – there are no cadenzas, for example. But this should not suggest that it is technically unde-manding. It was certainly made to measure for Ditta (whom Bartók had taught before they married in 1923), no one knowing her strengths and weaknesses as a pianist better than he did. There is much unison writing in the first move-ment, often with the hands separated by one or two octaves or some other consonant interval such as sixths or thirds. The octave and chordal passages in the finale tend to keep the hands in relatively relaxed positions, and avoid more extreme stretches (such as the tenths which were a signature of his own tech-nique), with wide-scale application of diatonic, close-position voicing of chords. Such rapid fingerwork as there is generally eschews awkward and precarious hand movements.

The relatively short opening movement, a relaxed Allegretto, has two contrasting thematic areas (Fig. 53, first and second staves). Influenced by the *verbunkos* in a similar way to the opening movement of *Contrasts* and the 'Marcia' from the Sixth String Quartet, the first idea is announced by the piano over rustling couplet dyads in second violins and violas, and repeated by the orchestra. Indeed, overlaying the opening theme with the 'Marcia' reveals just how closely aligned they are, the former almost appearing to be a variant of the latter despite the difference in modality and time signature. For the orchestral restatement of the theme, the tonality moves to G and from there by turns to D♭ (bar 24) and B♭ (bar 35), working round the 'tonic axis' (E–G–B♭–D♭), before briefly stabilising in an acoustic-scale flavoured E♭ (bar 37).

A succinct second theme (Fig. 53b), marked *scherzando* and in G, is more quixotic and rhapsodic in style, a solo clarinet engaging in dialogue with the piano; the exposition then ends after a mere seventy-four bars with the addition from the horn of an E♭ to the soloist's sustained G–B. Treating this augmented triad as a replacement dominant, Bartók opens the development section with a lyrical variant of the principal theme in A♭, now rhythmically regularised with its upbeat figure converted into a turn and accompanied by broken-chord figures (Fig. 53c). During the rest of the section a series of harmonic plateaux ascend by whole-tone step through B♭ (bar 87), C (bar 99), D (bar 102), and very briefly on E (bar 104) before stabilising again on F♯ (bar 105). A very simple transition leads to the recapitulation from bar 117. This follows the outline of the exposition, the restatement of the principal theme now in C, and the second theme restored to the tonic. The movement ends smartly, with neither cadenza nor extended coda, but just a tiny interplay between the flute's rendition of a fragment from the second strain of the principal theme and a closing pianissimo altered tonic to dominant couplet repeated in the piano.

Figure 53. The Third Piano Concerto (a) and (b) the principal themes of the first movement; (c) the opening of the development.

Given Bartók's rejection of conventional religion in early adulthood and his atheistic or at best agnostic views, it may seem rather surprising that he should mark the exquisite second movement 'slow and religious'. However, he does appear to be deliberately referencing the 'Heiliger Dankgesang eines Genesenen an die Gottheit in der lydischen Tonart' ('a convalescent's holy song of thanksgiving to the deity, in the Lydian mode'), from Beethoven's String Quartet in A minor op. 132. This was perhaps an indication that Bartók felt he was in a state of recuperation and recovery, albeit his 'Dankgesang' may have been an offering of thanks more to nature than to any divinity.

Like the equivalent movement in the Second Piano Concerto, the second movement of the Third Piano Concerto takes on a simple ternary form: the first part, opening in G, interlaces a placid Mixolydian-mode polyphonic idea in the strings with an austere homophonic five-line chorale in the piano as a kind of chorale prelude; the second part is a faster 'night-music' section that imitates the sounds of the natural world; and the third is a varied and decorated reprise of the first part. Incorporating a piece of birdsong (bars 60–7), which Bartók transcribed during his stay at Asheville and labelled 'Parting in Peace' in the source, the middle section is particularly interesting for its use of chromatic cluster chords in the strings.[59] Curious echo effects from bar 72 involve the pentatonic figures of the birdsong being reproduced at three metric levels by woodwinds, lower strings, and piano and xylophone. The piano's figuration of the reprise of the chorale (the first four phrases of which are now played by woodwinds) and its cadential flourishes in the reprise are a further tribute to pre-Bachian polyphony; for instance, one can usefully compare the writing

Figure 54. Versions of the rondo theme from the finale of the Third Piano Concerto.

with that found in Frescobaldi's Toccata in G for organ, F 3.05, which Bartók transcribed and edited for piano.

The finale follows without any break. It is structured as a broad ABA¹CA² coda rondo form in which the B section is a fairly conventional fugue, while the C section is organised as a ternary shape in which a graceful neo-Baroque idea with prominent suspensions and resolutions surrounds a further fugato. The movement begins with the soloist scampering up a pentatonic inflected arpeggio to introduce a lively 'Hungarian' theme almost in the heroic Lisztian tradition of his youthful works – with a characteristic short-long, long-short rhythm and a hemiola accompaniment that fills the rhythmic gaps in the 3/8 metre to create a regular stream of quavers (Fig. 54a). The Hungarian musician and theorist Lajos Bárdos has suggested that a putative model for the melody in Bartók's folk-music transcriptions can be found in 'Hërvadj, rózsám, hërvadj' ('Fade away, rose, fade away'), number 159 from *The Hungarian Folk Song*; this is a 'bagpipe tune' that he collected in 1910 in Nagymegyer, though it is quite different rhythmically and in its overall contour from the melody in the finale.[60]

A passage in the timpani changes the hypermetre from quadruple to triple and leads directly into the initial fugal section in C♯, led off by the piano with the first presentation of the subject and a tonal answer. The fairly regular exposition continues with a subsequent subject-answer pair in first violins and violas, and after a brief episode (bars 269–83), a set of middle entries. Subsequent to the piano's F minor entry, woodwinds overlap pairs of inverted versions on G♯ and direct versions on E, and a further episode leads to the final set of entries. The subject's reprise on C♯ in unison strings clarifies the triple hypermetre (the subject had previously involved a 3+5 bar structure), and a four-voice *stretto maestrale* concludes an almost copybook fugue, demonstrating Bartók's mastery of the genre.

At this stage a variant of the rondo theme (Fig. 54b) is restored with the timpani's triple hypermetre signal on E again acting as a bridge to the middle part of the movement. Bartók's approach to varying this theme is clearly indicative of the influence of one specific aspect of his taxonomic work, in which distinct versions of the same underlying tune, recorded at different times and in different places, are placed side by side for comparative purposes. This is particularly evident in the large group of songs beginning at number 1,185 of volume three of the Slovak collection, *Slovenské L'udové Piesne*, in which more than fifty tunes share the same 'genotype' but are expressed with a great diversity of 'phenotypes'.

Starting in B♭, the beautiful neoclassical idea that ensues is almost Bachian in its employment of suspensions and decorated resolutions, the piano's harmonised rising B♭ scale being echoed with a falling version in D♭. Bartók now introduces a second fugal passage with a more austere subject that melodically unfolds the chromatic descent of perfect fourth and perfect fifth dyads from A♭ to C♯, with direct entries of the subject on A♭, E and C, the latter overlapping with an inverted version on A♭. During its course the piano embellishes the texture with rising scale patterns in the main, and picks up a chromatically inflected version with the subject on B superimposed in direct and inverted forms at bar 452.

The reprise at bar 527 involves yet another variant of the rondo theme (Fig. 54c) presented in the harmonic context of C♯ with alternation between C♯[7]and F♯[7] chords. After further development of this material, the movement works towards its final climax by way of a presto section in 3/4 whose combination of diatonic chords and chromatic motion almost looks back to the Lisztian tradition. Bartók now restores the original tempo and metre, while maintaining interest by shifting gear partway through, from triple hypermetre to the four-bar phrases starting at bar 748. The piece comes to a close with a series of dominant (expressed as B min[7]) to tonic exchanges.

Almost simultaneously with the Third Piano Concerto, Bartók worked on the Viola Concerto commissioned by William Primrose. On 5 August 1945 he drafted a letter to the violist, which was never sent, outlining the state of play. He reported that 'there stirred some viola concerto ideas which gradually crystallised themselves, so that I am able to tell you that I hope to write the work, and maybe finish at least its draft in 4–5 weeks, if nothing happens in the meantime which would prevent my work'.[61] He thus expected a draft to be completed by the beginning of September and the score by the end of that month or the following one. At this point he believed it would:

> be in 4 movements: a serious Allegro, a Scherzo, a (rather short) slow movement, and a finale beginning Allegretto and developping [*sic*] the tempo to an Allegro molto. Each movement, or at least 3 of them will [be] preceded by a (short) recurring introduction (mostly solo of the viola), a kind of ritornello.[62]

Bartók subsequently wrote to Primrose on 8 September, on his return to New York, with a revised version of the draft of this letter. It is apparent that he had made considerable progress with the concerto and was able to tell Primrose that 'the main work – the rather detailed draft – I am through; and the remaining work is a rather mechanical one, I repeat it'. He remarked on the influence of the 'sombre, more masculine character' of the viola on the disposition of the piece. Bartók also described some of the technical issues he had encountered, declaring that 'The orchestration will be transparent, more transparent than in a violin concerto'. The description of the structure of the concerto found in the draft letter of 5 August was no longer provided, reflecting the changes in his views about the overall shape of the piece that had transpired over the intervening month.

Bartók left the Viola Concerto unfinished on his death. It fell to his friend Serly to complete it, the published Boosey & Hawkes score including on the title page the words 'Prepared for publication from the composer's original manuscript by Tibor Serly'. As László Somfai has commented, the draft, which was written on four bifolia manuscript sheets in short score, was left in a 'preliminary form'. It clearly could not go through the numerous revisions and amendments that Bartók would normally make, though it did include three versions of the opening of the first movement.[63]

As the work now exists, it is in the tonality of A and in three movements: a Moderato in sonata form, and an Adagio religioso and Allegro vivace (both in ternary forms). Some controversy has surrounded the inclusion of two fragments in Serly's score: a fourteen-bar Lento parlando section, placed between the opening two movements (with an additional four bars) as an interlude; and an Allegretto lasting twenty-eight bars that connects the second and third movements. Donald Maurice has removed the Lento parlando section in his version of the concerto, seeing it as a rejected draft of a slow movement that proved too brief. The Allegretto has been truncated by eight bars in Serly's completion, and a repeat apparently intended by Bartók has been removed. Despite these issues and several questionable decisions made by Serly (including the transposition up by a semitone of a passage starting at bar 114 of the finale), the concerto has found a welcome place in the viola repertoire.

Many of the elements found in the Concerto for Orchestra and Third Piano Concerto are present in the concise though cheerfully concluded Viola Concerto, and as Yves Lenoir has demonstrated, folk music (from various sources) is also a constant influence. The principal theme of the first movement involves a similar octatonic/pentatonic interplay to its equivalent in the Concerto for Orchestra. It is based initially on an octatonic scale on A (A–B–C–D–E♭–F–G♭–A♭), before it turns at bar 10 to a pentatonic scale on C (C–E♭–F–A♭–B♭) and then to a black-note pentatonic collection (D♭–E♭–G♭–A♭–B♭). Largely built from a series of in-filled falling fifth fragments, the second theme (from bar 61) is more chromatic in orientation.

The development (beginning at bar 81) is in four main sections, its expressive heart lying in the second (bars 102–11). In this, the consequent phrase of the concerto's opening idea is extended into a synthetic four-line old-style Hungarian melody in B. Although the fairly terse recapitulation follows a normal course, the double-dotted and dotted rhythms in the reprise of the second subject have given cause to some commentators to see this as a Scottish touch in deference to Primrose. However, none of the 'Scotch snaps' that are such a feature of the Strathspey tradition is to be found.

Following the Lento parlando interlude mentioned above, the second movement proper (in E) involves, like its opposite number in the Third Piano Concerto, a night-music section surrounded by chorale-like passages. In the first of these, the viola plays an expressive cantilena in the Mixolydian mode, accompanied by sustained chords, the middle part becoming more impassioned with an ever more insistent iambic rhythmic gesture that emphasises the pitches C and E♭. This latter idea initially disrupts the reprise of the viola's cantilena before the opening theme of the first movement is restored as a kind of ritornello.

While it is impossible to know whether Bartók would have retained the Allegretto, which in Serly's version links the slow movement to the finale, in any subsequent revision of this interlude the quartal harmony and employment of stacked fourths in the solo part from bar 70 do not seem particularly consistent with the music that precedes and follows it. The last movement itself is positive and jovial in mood. Like the finale of the Concerto for Orchestra it draws strongly on Romanian dance rhythms and begins with the same Lydian/Mixolydian polymode (A–B–C♯–D♯–E–F♯–G–A) that underpins its primary theme. The initial *horă*-like idea and a series of variants are followed by a dance similar to the Romanian Mărunţel or Ardeleana from bar 51. Thereafter the underlying rhythmic characteristics of these two types of material are juxtaposed.

In the middle section, perfect fifths drones in a syncopated rhythm in the strings accompany a new idea that it has been claimed demonstrates Scottish influence (an affinity with 'Comin' thro' the Rye' has been proposed). However, Eastern European bagpipe music might seem a more obvious source. Indeed, the first volume of *Rumanian Folk Music* (instrumental melodies) contains many examples of bagpipe tunes with comparable melodic shapes. It was the first twenty bars of this theme that Serly transposed from A♭ to A, a curious decision that distorts the tonal organisation of the movement. In the reprise, the overall order of the dances is reversed, the Mărunțel/Ardeleana material taking the lead and placed in an octatonic guise from bar 189 (C♯–D–E–F–G–A♭–B♭–[C♭]). After a final brief reference to the bagpipe tune from the middle section, superimposed on the *horă* melody, the movement rushes to its concluding perfect cadence and closes on a thirdless tonic chord of A.

How then, should the Viola Concerto be regarded? Although it may not present Bartók's final intentions, the reconstruction by Serly, with the various revisions of Atar Arad, Csaba Erdélyi, Peter Bartók and Donald Maurice, is undoubtedly a sincere and skilful attempt to create a coherent performing edition of the draft. It has many attractive moments and unquestionably affords the listener an extremely valuable insight into Bartók's mental state during the last few months of his life. Yet it must remain a moot point whether he would have regarded this reconstruction and the accompanying revisions as an authentic part of his oeuvre.

When Bartók, Ditta and Péter left Saranac Lake for the three-hundred-mile train journey back to New York on 30 August 1945, neither Bartók nor Ditta were in good health and he was running a temperature again. He wrote briefly to Dorothy Parrish that day, and told her that 'I began to write some works in Saranac, could unfortunately not finish them, and am wondering whether it will be possible to continue the work in N.Y.'[64] In the apartment on West 57th Street, Bartók's physical condition rapidly declined. Although suffering great discomfort he continued to work, as much as he could, on the Viola Concerto and Third Piano Concerto. Apparently aware that his time was running out, Bartók tried to explain to Péter how his affairs would be conducted after his death, and the role of Victor Bator as the executor and trustee of a new will he had signed in 1943. Yet Péter was unable to accept that his father could be so seriously ill that this was necessary.

A sudden drop in Bartók's temperature on 21 September was regarded by Dr Rappaport as a very sinister development, and after some persuasion the composer agreed to be taken to the West Side Hospital, on this occasion by ambulance. It was here that he spent his painful final week, kept alive with grape sugar. Bartók's close friends and fellow residents of his apartment block, the Hungarian sociologist and philosopher Pál Kecskeméti and his wife Erzsébet, provided a moving description of his condition:

> Only occasionally was he conscious, but everyone at his bedside had the impression that his spirit was fully present. This dissociated manner seemed not unusual to those who knew Bartók for actually he would bow thus on the concert stage before an audience of a thousand. In his face there no longer was anything to suggest man's physical nature. It seemed a death mask at the moment of resurrection, when the first trumpets sound. The last day they kept him alive under an oxygen tent.[65]

Bartók's final words, to his friend Dr Henry Lax, are generally regarded as being 'What I most regret is having to leave with a full trunk' – reflecting the fact that he had not managed to complete his final two concertos, make progress on the Seventh String Quartet requested by Ralph Hawkes, or publish the Romanian, Slovak and Turkish collections. He died on the morning of 26 September 1945 at the age of sixty-four.

Two death notices appeared in the following day's obituary section of *The New York Times*, the first simply announcing:

> BARTOK – Bela, on Wednesday, Sept. 26, beloved husband of Edith Bartok, father of Bela and Peter Bartok. Services at 'The Universal Chapel', Lexington Ave., at 52d St., on Friday, Sept. 28, at 2 P.M.

The second was from Deems Taylor as president of ASCAP and it reads 'We announce with profound sorrow the death of the distinguished composer, Bela Bartok, in New York on Sept. 26, 1945.'[66] And in the same edition of this newspaper Bartók received a long and fulsome obituary, which began by remarking that he was 'one of the most important composers of modern music, he was also an outstanding specialist in musical folklore and a teacher of wide repute'.[67]

According to the Kecskemétis, the funeral was well attended by his friends and it was 'a ceremony in the ancient sense of the word, where everyone present joined a mystic act whereby a community accompanies one of its members to the gates of the other world'. The interment took place at Ferncliff Cemetery in Hartsdale, Westchester County, around twenty-five miles from the funeral chapel. Forty-three years later Bartók's body would be reinterred in Farkasréti Cemetery in Budapest and his remains now lie with the rest of his immediate family – his mother Paula, Ditta, Béla junior and wife Judith, and his sister Elza and her husband.

Ditta's psychological and physical condition had been very fragile during their final years in America and her husband's death was an unbearable blow for her. She returned to Budapest soon after, living in isolation and poverty for the following fifteen years. When Peter (who had by now adopted the English spelling of his name) believed he had discovered that she was not benefiting appropriately from the trust set up by Bartók in his will and managed by Bator, he set in motion a very long-running legal battle that was eventually settled in the family's favour.[68] Ditta made a limited return to the concert platform in the 1960s and indeed recorded her husband's Third Piano Concerto. In a review of the disc in *The New York Times* on 11 May 1969, Robert T. Jones noted of her performance that 'Mme Bartok sounds as if her hands are made of steel. Her technical accuracy is absolute – and the playing is cold as charity. She plays with a chill perfection that one might expect in Bach but hardly in this usually romanticized concerto.'[69]

# Postlude

What manner of person, then, was Bartók himself? For some he was, cold, remote, lacking emotional intelligence, mathematical, detached, unfriendly, pedantic, caustic and humourless; for others who managed to pierce his outer shell and come close to him he was warm, friendly, passionate, good humoured, caring and engaged. How could the same man elicit these entirely contradictory responses? There are some attributes that both his detractors and supporters generally appear to agree about: his honesty and integrity (sometimes taken to an extreme), fastidiousness, egalitarianism, industriousness and lack of motivation by material success. He could certainly be extremely direct, but he was canny enough to know when he should remain silent or when it was sensible to retreat. Indeed, the move to America was one such strategic withdrawal, when the odds were stacked against there being any benefit from remaining in Hungary and trying to work in defiance of the regime from within (or tacitly acquiescing with it). He, his family and his acquaintances would have certainly suffered if he had taken this approach, and he typically managed to find a subtle way of leaving his homeland without appearing to flee from it.

One of the most interesting and persuasive descriptions of Bartók is provided by his long-time family doctor, Gyula Holló, who observed that:

> the finest qualities of the folk manifested themselves in the fashion in which he handled others. In the peasant attitude there always has been a certain elegance and this characterized Bartók on a higher artistic plane. He hated all things artificial. . . . He lived very simply and this wasn't just a matter of principle with him. Nothing could hold his interest which had anything in the way of prestige value. He was utterly indifferent to material comforts. It was quite impossible to wrangle with him. He was patient and

understanding. However, there was a great deal of distant reserve, and I can imagine that this often pained those who loved him. Despite his modesty and courtesy, he was completely aware of who he was. He hated to accept anything from anyone.[1]

On one hand his life's work could appear almost superhuman: the compositional output alone would be deemed sufficient by many successful composers; but in addition, there are few ethnomusicologists who can claim to have collected, transcribed and classified such an enormous quantity of traditional music from so many different sources; and he maintained a very successful, if not outstanding, international circuit as a concert pianist until the final few years. And, of course, all of this activity was conducted in addition to the essential, if rather despised, day-to-day grind of teaching the piano for a large part of his career. Yet despite all of this success and achievement, Bartók was a down-to-earth, practical and highly self-reliant individual who, contrary to some readings of him, was interested in the mundane as well as the high flown (as his letters to family and close friends clearly demonstrate).

There is considerable evidence that he displayed the 'common touch' though not, I would argue, in a condescending or affected way. In general, it appears that Bartók simply treated people as he found them and wasted little effort in unnecessary niceties with those to whom he did not feel drawn. Some might regard this as being indicative of a degree of social dysfunction – even as an autistic trait. I am not competent to make a clinical judgement but would suggest that, to employ a somewhat unfashionable term, he was demonstrating an authenticity to his personality moulded through (among other environmental factors) the vicissitudes and stresses of his childhood and upbringing (including his father's untimely death, periods of debilitating illness, frequent moves and financial insecurity); a dominant maternal influence; and the challenges of an intense musical education. Such authenticity was refined from his third decade as a result of his close interactions with the rural proletariat. This same sense of authenticity underpins his music, which despite its heteroglossia and heterogeneity, is in general able to establish and maintain stylistic coherence. In his lifetime, Bartók's reviewers sometimes criticised his music as being inhuman – as cold, dry and 'mathematical'; with the passage of time we may now more readily discern its 'humane' aspects – its passion, warmth, humour and essential sincerity.

It was perhaps not entirely coincidental that Bartók's sons should be employed within the two industries that mediated his life and work: public transportation (Béla junior worked for the Hungarian railway company MÁV) and audio recording (Péter was a sound engineer and producer). Without these two key inventions of modernity, the railway train and the phonograph, Bartók would have found it vastly more difficult to travel to collect traditional music; and 'scientific' transcription, analysis and classification would have been rendered near impossible (however fine an ear he had, on-the-spot notation from performers with such a fine resolution of pitch and rhythm would not have been achievable). Ironically, of course, the preservation of the cultural artefacts of the pre-industrial era was enabled by the very technologies that would contribute to their decline as the shared cultural substrate of rural communities.

Not only has the world whose traditional music Bartók sought to preserve and catalogue long ceased to exist, both the Hungary that was his home and the one that ensued as a socialist state under Soviet hegemony have also disappeared into history. Hungarian popular music and dance (both in the forms that Bartók actively advocated and essentially spurned) are certainly widely performed and attended in the country, but their wholesale adoption by the tourist industry as marketing collateral has rendered their status somewhat ambiguous. At the same time, the right-wing Jobbik Party (established in 2002) has all too keenly embraced 'Magyar' folk art and music as national identity markers, politicising their performance and dissemination. In a speech given to an Azerbaijani audience in 2011 by Márton Gyöngyösi, an economist educated at Trinity College Dublin who at that time was leader of Jobbik's foreign affairs committee, he rehearsed the familiar notion of Hungary occupying an ambiguous position between Europe and Asia, commenting that.

> Hungarians are – geographically speaking – unquestionably and integrally part of the West as one of the oldest nation states of the European continent; nonetheless, Hungarians are Asian, Turanian people with strong and deep Asian roots. Would anybody dare question the validity of this identity, who knows Hungarian folk music, folk dance, folk tales and mythology, who speaks our language or tasted our cuisine? Or, who is familiar with the most recent genetic, anthropological or archaeological research?[2]

That there may appear to be some correspondence between the views expressed by Bartók about the sources of the old Hungarian musical style, and the Turanist persuasions of the contemporary far right, is illustrative of the very short distance between well-intentioned idealist scholarship and insidious ideology. Nevertheless, the value assigned by the hard right to Hungarian folk culture demonstrates just how far the stock of traditional music has risen over the century or so since Bartók, Kodály and other musicians began to collect it.

Volumes devoted to Bartók's ethnomusicological work are still appearing seventy years after his death; Lujza Tari's edition of the Hungarian instrumental transcriptions, *Bartók Béla hangszeres magyar népzenegyűjtése* (*Béla Bartók Hungarian Instrumental Folk Music Collection*), was published only in 2011, and at the time of writing, a supplementary fourth volume of Slovak material has not yet surfaced. The magnitude of his achievement, therefore, even when judged simply in terms of the labour he expended, becomes ever more apparent. It must be remembered that ethnomusicology did not exist as a term when Bartók started collecting traditional music (it only gained currency in the 1950s). His approach at that stage (and indeed for the rest of his life) was consistent with Guido Adler's 1885 definition of comparative musicology, which had 'as its task the comparison of the musical works – especially the folksongs – of the various peoples of the earth for ethnographical purposes and the classification of them according to their various forms'.[3] To judge Bartók's work by the highly interdisciplinary, and often deeply sociologically informed, field of contemporary ethnomusicology that has surfaced since his death may be misplaced, though his overall project was undoubtedly in keeping with the fundamental mission of the domain as defined by The Society for Ethnomusicology: 'the study of music in its cultural context'.[4]

Nevertheless, in spite of the enormous extent of his collections, there are certainly weaknesses and idiosyncrasies within its methodology. For instance, as Alica Elscheková and Oskár Elschek have pointed out, the Slovak collection (which contains more than 3,400 vocal and instrumental melodies and 4,500 texts) is geographically limited and 'doesn't present a complete view on the Slovak song tradition, because [Bartók] concentrated his interest to four regions: to Nitra, Hont, Zvolen and Gemer without taking into account especially West, North and East Slovakia'.[5] Similarly, his method of ordering Hungarian folk song contrasts with Kodály's primary focus on the relative pitches of structural tones within a melody (the cadential notes at line endings). Bartók's method emphasises the rhythmic and syllabic aspects of the songs, and is premised upon a (perhaps not unreasonable) assumption of an evolutionary cultural process in which more complex heterogeneous structures postdate simpler and more homogeneous ones. It is expressed through three classes of melodies (old, new and 'mixed'), the ragbag 'mixed' class being selected by means of negative rather than positive criteria – these songs are neither old nor new. Thus, rather than producing the logically ordered 'dictionary' originally envisaged, Bartók created a kind of musical 'ice core' which displays his estimation of the development of musical style. In this, as László Dobszay remarks, he demonstrates that 'stylistic insight was more important . . . than lexicographical consistency'.[6]

Bartók has sometimes also been criticised for an over-elaborate approach to the transcription of melodies (which by the terms of the pioneering American ethnomusicologist Charles Seeger would be deemed 'descriptive' rather than 'prescriptive'), particularly in the later collections. However, in adopting this painstakingly detailed methodology Bartók acknowledges the transience and fragility of the medium of the phonograph cylinder as the primary source. Long before the development of the personal computer and routine digitization of audio material, his method might be deemed an attempt to encode, to translate accurately from one medium to another, every nuance of an individual rendition and to introduce as little 'noise' into the ensuing encoding as possible.

Turning to Bartók's status as a performer, while his concert repertoire was quite varied, he is now probably best known as a pianist through the recordings of his own music. Here we find a similar willingness to trade off consistency and insight as in his cataloguing of Hungarian folk music. Thus, as Marilyn Garst discovered in her examination of Bartók's recordings of several of the smaller piano pieces, despite the exactitude of his notation and apparent expectation that it should be followed literally by his interpreters, he rarely played repeats in the same way as the original version. He would also introduce unmarked changes of tempo, his articulation of types of touch such as non-legato was subject to considerable variation, and he would often arpeggiate chords in deference to the Romantic pianistic tradition.[7] That no obvious 'school' of Bartókian pianism after his death has appeared may be connected to this discontinuity between description and action. Whatever the case, his own technique and interpretation continue to be spoken of with enormous respect and admiration by some of the world's greatest pianists, as private conversations with Radu Lupu, András Schiff and Murray Perahia have revealed.

A core sample taken down through Bartók's compositional career would reveal from top to bottom two parallel strands of influence: in the first strand are a number of art music composers, perhaps most significantly Stravinsky, Debussy and Richard Strauss, down to a bedrock including Brahms, Beethoven and Bach; in the second strand are traditional forms of music from various ethnic and national sources, including Serbo-Croatia, Turkey, Romania, Slovakia, North Africa and Hungary. The development of Bartók's compositional style traces out the interactions and interpenetration of these fundamental resources. Although the basic structures and techniques he was introduced to in his youth (sonata, rondo, variation, ternary form, fugue and so on) continued to hold sway throughout his career, they were continually refreshed and revised in the light of experience. While his most familiar formal innovations may be the bridge forms (often found in association with the 'night music' genre), the thematic chains grafted onto more conventional forms (for example in the finale of the Concerto for Orchestra) and the symmetrical disposition of movements found in several of the larger works, Bartók responds in rather different ways to the norms and possibilities of the conventional formal models he employs at different stages of his career. The nature and function of the expository, developmental and recapitulatory stages of sonata structure are contingent upon the material employed. Thus, for example, in the mature violin sonatas and middle quartets, which stray furthest from the tonality of common practice, rather different solutions are adopted compared to the later concertos. Jonathan Bernard has noted that analysts have adopted two approaches to Bartók's own schematic and conservative form descriptions – to ignore them or 'accept them more or less at face value'. He comments that 'it may well be that Bartók had recourse to traditional form, not only for the sake of orienting his readers/listeners usefully to something they already knew, but also to provide a useful analogy for his own purposes, for what he was attempting in a formal sense, even if his own forms, in the final reckoning, really worked in quite different fashion'.[8]

Since his death, Bartók has attracted music analysis on a near industrial scale, and the attempt to establish the means by which overall coherence is achieved in his works has been tackled in a plethora of ways. They include (among others) the application of pitch-class set theory; the examination of symmetries and interval cycles; the consideration of proportionality; pitch space and neo-Schenkerian prolongation; and metrical and rhythmic analysis. That these approaches often offer interesting and valuable insights, but fail to be revelatory on the broader scale, may be symptomatic of Bartók's simultaneous interest in aspects of systematisation and his willingness to sacrifice such systematic processes to higher-level considerations, whether formal, tonal, narrative, or whatever.

In January 2011 *The New York Times* critic Anthony Tommasini published his personal list of the 'top 10' classical music composers. He placed Bartók in tenth position and described him 'as an ethnomusicologist whose work has empowered generations of subsequent composers to incorporate folk music and classical traditions from whatever culture into their works, and as a formidable modernist who in the face of Schoenberg's breathtaking formulations showed another way, forging a language that was an amalgam of tonality, unorthodox scales and atonal wanderings'.[9] It is difficult to find an appropriate index of a composer's reception that provides a measure of their current popularity beyond such value judgement. ArkivMusic, one of the largest American distribution companies of classical recordings, enumerates their holding of recordings of each composer from a catalogue of around 120,000 titles. While the number of titles held for a composer does not indicate the level of either sales or auditions, it provides some evidence of the relative status of individual composers in the commercial environment, at least to the extent that companies feel it valuable to maintain the availability of recordings of their works. The 1,001 Bartók titles held in July 2014 (an arbitrary sampling date) by ArkivMusic are fewer than those of Debussy (2,840), Ravel (2,309), Rachmaninov (2,166), Prokofiev (1,754), Shostakovich (1,631), Mahler (1,524), Stravinsky (1,322), Britten (1,132) or Sibelius (1,090). Yet they exceed those of most of the other twentieth-century composers by some margin (for instance, only 534 are listed for Schoenberg, 366 for Berg and 217 for Webern).[10]

Bartók's multifaceted career has ensured that he still retains a broad and prominent public profile: young pianists and string players are routinely introduced to his pedagogical works at an early stage of their development; the six string quartets continue to be perceived as important musical and technical challenges by amateur and professional groups; simpler orchestral arrangements such as the *Transylvanian Dances* and *Hungarian Sketches* have proved attractive for school and amateur orchestras, while the Concerto for Orchestra has become routine fare for the most proficient youth orchestras; and the piano and violin concertos are standard options for finals of the world's leading instrumental competitions. Bartók's musical language has influenced composers writing for both the concert stage and for film and television, and the timbral resources (particularly in the area of string technique) he introduced have become widely accepted and extended. His contribution to the study of traditional music and its integration within a compositional language that is grounded in an indigenous culture, but not in a chauvinistic way, continue to provide a positive ethical model for composers and ethnomusicologists.

Thus, in the second decade of the twenty-first century, seventy years after his death, the status of Bartók's music appears secure. A number of his compositions retain an aura of extreme difficulty and challenge, and are still acknowledged, in Tommasini's words, as the work of 'a formidable modernist'. After Bartók's death, some commentators argued for the organic integration of his mature music. I would contend, to the contrary, that the great strength of his output is its very ability to accommodate difference and to permit integrative and disruptive forces to coexist. Much like his personality, his output absorbed antinomies without entirely resolving them: bourgeois and anti-bourgeois; urban and rural; conservative and radical; tonal and atonal; naive and sophisticated; free and constrained; passionate and detached; rooted and rootless; and rational and empirical.

# List of Works

BB = Béla Bartók Thematic Catalogue number
Sz = Szőllősy number
W= Waldbauer number
DD = Denijs Dille number
Opus = Bartók started three sets of opus numbers, the first between 1890 and 1894; the second between 1894 and 1898; and the third from 1904 to 1920. Titles in Bartók's second set were mainly given German titles by the composer.
Works marked with an asterisk are believed to be no longer extant.
Titles of the works written from 1903 onwards are given in Hungarian (where appropriate) with English translation on the first appearance. Subsequent versions or arrangements are generally given in English.

| Name | BB | Sz | W | DD | Opus | Year | Instruments/ voices used |
|---|---|---|---|---|---|---|---|
| *Walczer* (Waltz) | 1 | 1 | | 1 | 1 (list 1) | 1890 | Piano |
| *Változó darab* (Changing piece) | 1 | | | 2 | 2 (list 1) | 1890 | Piano |
| *Mazurka* | 1 | 2 | | 3 | 3 (list 1) | 1890 | Piano |
| *A budapesti tornaverseny* (Budapest gymnastics competition) | 1 | | | 4 | 4 (list 1) | 1890 | Piano |
| Sonatina No. 1 | 1 | | | 5 | 5 (list 1) | 1890 | Piano |
| *Oláh darab* (Wallachian piece) | 1 | | | 6 | 6 (list 1) | 1890 | Piano |
| *Gyorspolka* (Fast polka) | 1 | | | 7 | 7 (list 1) | 1891 | Piano |
| 'Béla' Polka | 1 | | | 8 | 8 (list 1) | 1891 | Piano |
| 'Katinka' Polka | 1 | | | 9 | 9 (list 1) | 1891 | Piano |
| *Tavaszi hangok* (Voices of Spring) | 1 | | | 10 | 10 (list 1) | 1891 | Piano |
| Jolán-Polka | 1 | | | 11 | 11 (list 1) | 1891 | Piano |
| Gabi Polka | 1 | | | 12 | 12 (list 1) | 1891 | Piano |

| Name | BB | Sz | W | DD | Opus | Year | Instruments/voices used |
|---|---|---|---|---|---|---|---|
| *Nefelejts* (Forget-me-not) | 1 | | | 13 | 13 (list 1) | 1891 | Piano |
| Ländler No. 1 | 1 | | | 14 | 14 (list 1) | 1891 | Piano |
| 'Irma' Polka | 1 | | | 15 | 15 (list 1) | 1891 | Piano |
| *Radegundi visszhang* (Radegund echo) | 1 | | | 16 | 16 (list 1) | 1891 | Piano |
| *Induló* (March) | 1 | | | 17 | 17 (list 1) | 1891 | Piano |
| Ländler No. 2 | 1 | | | 18 | 18 (list 1) | 1891 | Piano |
| *Cirkusz polka* (Circus Polka) | 1 | | | 19 | 19 (list 1) | 1891 | Piano |
| *A Duna folyása* (The Course of the Danube) | 1 | 4 | | 20 | 20 (list 1) | 1891 | Piano (also for Violin and Piano) |
| Sonatina No. 2 | 1 | | | 21 | 21 (list 1) | 1891? | Piano |
| Ländler No. 3* | 1 | | | 22 | 22 (list 1) | 1892 | Piano |
| *Tavaszi dal* (Spring song) | 1 | | | 23 | 23 (list 1) | 1892 | Piano |
| *Szöllősi darab* (Szöllős piece)* | 1 | | | 24 | 24 (list 1) | 1892 | Piano |
| Margit Polka | 1 | | | 25 | 25 (list 1) | 1893 | Piano |
| Ilona Mazurka | 1 | | | 26 | 26 (list 1) | 1893 | Piano |
| Loli Mazurka | 1 | | | 27 | 27 (list 1) | 1893 | Piano |
| *Lajos valczer* (Lajos Waltz) | 1 | | | 28 | 28 (list 1) | 1893 | Piano |
| Elza Polka | 1 | | | 29 | 29 (list 1) | 1894 | Piano |
| Andante con Variazioni | 1 | | | 30 | 30 (list 1) | 1894 | Piano |
| X.Y.* | 1 | | | 31 | 31 (list 1) | 1894 | Piano |
| Sonata No. 1 in G minor | 2 | | | 32 | 1 (list 2) | 1894 | Piano |
| Scherzo in G minor | 2 | | | 33 | | 1894 | Piano |
| Fantasia in A minor | 3 | | | 34 | 2 (list 2) | 1895 | Piano |
| Sonata No. 2 in F major | 4 | | | 35 | 3 (list 2) | 1895 | Piano |
| Capriccio in B minor | 5 | | | 36 | 4 (list 2) | 1895 | Piano |
| Violin Sonata in C minor | 6 | | | 37 | 5 (list 2) | 1895 | Violin and Piano |
| Sonata No. 3 in C major* | 7 | | | 38 | 6 (list 2) | 1895 | Piano |
| Pieces for Violin* | 7 | | | 39 | 7 (list 2) | 1895 | Violin |
| Fantasia for Violin* | 7 | | | 40 | 8 (list 2) | 1894 | Violin |
| Fantasia* | 7 | | | 41 | 9 (list 2) | 1895 | Violin |
| String Quartet No. 1 in B flat major* | 7 | | | 42 | 10 (list 2) | 1896 | String Quartet |

| Name | BB | Sz | W | DD | Opus | Year | Instruments/ voices used |
|---|---|---|---|---|---|---|---|
| String Quartet No. 2 in C minor* | 7 | | | 43 | 11 (list 2) | 1896 | String Quartet |
| Andante, Scherzo and Finale* | 7 | | | 44 | 12 (list 2) | 1897 | Piano |
| Drei Klavierstücke | 8 | | | 45 | 13 (list 2) | 1896/7 | Piano |
| Piano Quintet in C major* | 9 | | | 46 | 14 (list 2) | 1897 | Piano Quintet |
| Two Pieces* | 9 | | | 47 | 15 (list 2) | 1897 | Piano |
| Great Fantasy in C* | 9 | | | 48 | 16 (list 2) | 1897 | Piano |
| Violin Sonata in A major (draft incomplete)* | 10 | | | 49 | 17 (list 2) | 1897 | Violin and Piano |
| *Scherzo oder Fantasie* | 11 | 8 | | 50 | 18 (list 2) | 1897 | Piano |
| Piano Sonata | 12 | | | 51 | 19 (list 2) | 1898 | Piano |
| Piano Quartet in C minor | 13 | 9 | | 52 | 20 (list 2) | 1898 | Piano Quartet |
| Drei Klavierstücke | 14 | 6 | | 53 | 21 (list 2) | 1898 | Piano |
| Three Songs | 15 | 10 | | 54 | | 1898 | Voice and Piano |
| Scherzo in B minor | 16 | | | 55 | | 1898 | Piano |
| String Quartet in F major | 17 | | | 56 | | 1898 | String Quartet |
| Tiefblaue Veilchen | 18 | | | 57 | | 1899 | Soprano and Orchestra |
| Scherzo in Sonata Form | 19 | | | 58 | | 1899–1900 | String Quartet |
| Scherzo in B flat minor | 19 | | | 59 | | 1900? | Piano |
| Six Dances for Piano | 19 | 54 | | 60a | | 1900 | Piano |
| *Valczer* (Waltz) | 19 | | | 60b | | 1900 | Orchestra |
| Piano Quintet fragments | 19 | | | B10 12 | | 1899 | Piano Quintet |
| Three mixed choruses | | | | 61a | | | Mixed Choir |
| 'Was streift vorbei im Dämmerlicht' for four-part male choir | | | | 61b | | | Male Choir |
| Liebeslieder | 20 | 13 | | 62 | | 1900 | Voice and Piano |
| Scherzo ('F.F.B.B') in B flat minor | 21 | | | 63 | | 1900 | Piano |
| *Változatok* (Variations on a Theme by F.F.) | 22 | | | 64 | | 1900–1 | Piano |
| Scherzo in B flat major | | | | 65 | | 1901 (?) | Orchestra |
| Tempo di minuetto | 23 | | | 66 | | 1901 | Piano |
| *Négy dal Pósa Lajos szövegeire* (Four Songs to texts by Lajos Pósa) | 24 | 15 | 1 | 67 | | 1902 | Voice and Piano |

| Name | BB | Sz | W | DD | Opus | Year | Instruments/ voices used |
|------|-----|-----|-----|-----|------|------|--------------------------|
| Symphony in E flat major (only the Scherzo was completed) | 25 | 16 | 2 | 68 | | 1902 | Orchestra |
| Duo for two violins | 26 | | | 69 | | 1902 | Two Violins |
| Albumleaf (Andante) in A major | 26 | | | 70 | | 1902 | Violin and Piano |
| *Négy zongora darab* (Four Piano Pieces) | 27 | 22 | 6 | 71 | | 1903 | Piano |
| Violin Sonata in E minor | 28 | 20 | 4 | 72 | | 1903 | Violin and Piano |
| 'Est' (Evening) for Voice and Piano | 29 | | 5 | 73 | | 1903 | Voice and Piano |
| 'Est' (Evening) for Male Choir | 30 | 19 | 5 | 74 | | 1903 | Male Choir and Orchestra |
| *Kossuth. Szimfóniai költemény nagyzenekarra* (Symphonic Tone Poem for large orchestra) | 31 | 21 | 3 | 75a | | 1903 | Orchestra |
| *Gyászinduló. Marche funèbre* (Funeral march from *Kossuth*) | 31 | 21 | | 75b | | 1903 | Piano |
| *Négy dal* (Four Songs) | 32 | 18 | | 76 | | 1903 | Voice and Piano |
| *Zongoraötös* (Piano Quintet) | 33 | 23 | 7 | 77 | | 1903–4 | Piano Quintet |
| *Székely népdal* (Székely Folk Song), *Piros alma* | 34 | 30 | | | | 1904 | Voice and Piano |
| Scherzo (Burlesque) | 35 | 28 | 9 | | 2 (list 3) | 1904 | Piano and Orchestra |
| *Rapszódia* (Rhapsody) | 36a | 26 | 8 | | 1 (list 3) | 1904 | Piano |
| *Rapszódia* (Rhapsody) | 36b | 27 | 8 | | 1 (list 3) | 1905 | Piano and Orchestra |
| *Magyar népdalok* (Hungarian Folk Songs), 1st series, 1–4. | 37 | 29 | | | | c. 1904–5 | Voice and Piano |
| Petits Morceaux (from BB 37/2 and 24/1) | 38 | | | 67/1 | | 1905, 1907? | Piano |
| *I Szvit* (Suite No. 1) | 39 | 31 | 10 | | 3 (list 3) | 1905, rev. c.1920 | Orchestra |
| *II Szvit* (Suite No. 2) | 40 | 34 | 12 | | 4 (list 3) | 1905, 1907 rev. 1943 | Small Orchestra |
| Children's Songs ('For the little "tót"') | 41 | 32 | 11 | | | 1905 | Voice and Piano |
| *Magyar népdalok* (Hungarian Folk Songs), 1st series | 42 | 33 | | | | 1906, rev. BB97 1928 | Voice and Piano |

| Name | BB | Sz | W | DD | Opus | Year | Instruments/ voices used |
|------|-----|-----|-----|-----|------|------|--------------------------|
| *Magyar népdalok* (Hungarian Folk Songs) (nd series) | 43 | 33a | | | | 1906–7 | Voice and Piano |
| *Két magyar népdal* (Two Hungarian Folk Songs) | 44 | 33b | | | | 1906 | Voice and Piano |
| *Gyergyóból. Három csíkmegyei népdal* (From Gyergyó. Three Folk Songs from the Csík District) | 45a | 35 | 14 | | | 1907 | Recorder and Piano |
| Three Hungarian Folk Songs from Csík | 45b | 35a | 14 | | | 1907 | Piano |
| *Négy szlovák népdal* (Four Slovak Folk Songs) | 46 | 35b | | | | 1907 | Voice and Piano |
| *Nyolc magyar népdal* (Eight Hungarian Folk Songs) | 47 | 64 | 17 | | | 1907 (1–5) 1917 (6–8) | Voice and Piano |
| *I Hegedűverseny* (Violin Concerto No. 1) op. posth. | 48a | 36 | 15 | | | 1907–8 pub. 1956 | Violin and Orchestra |
| *Két portré* (Two Portraits) | 48b | 37 | 16 | 5 (list 3) | | 1908–9 | Violin and Orchestra |
| *Két elégia* (Two Elegies) | 49 | 41 | 21 | 8b (list 3) | | 1908–9 | Piano |
| *Tizennégy zongoradarab* (Fourteen Bagatelles) | 50 | 38 | 18 | 6 (list 3) | | 1908 | Piano |
| *Tíz könnyű zongoradarab* (Ten Easy Piano Pieces) | 51 | 39 | 19 | | | 1908 | Piano |
| *I Vonósnégyes* (String Quartet No. 1) | 52 | 40 | 20 | 7 (list 3) | | 1908–9 | String Quartet |
| *Gyermekeknek* ('For Children'), 4 volumes | 53 | 42 | 22 | | | 1908–9 | Piano |
| *Vázlatok* (Seven Sketches) | 54 | 44 | 23 | 9b (list 3) | | 1908–10 | Piano |
| *Három burleszk* (Three Burlesques) | 55 | 47 | 24 | 8c (list 3) | | 1908–11 | Piano |
| *Két román tánc* (Two Romanian Dances) | 56 | 43 | 25 | 8a (list 3) | | 1910 | Piano |
| *Két roman népdal* (Two Romanian Folk Songs) | 57 | | 25 | | | c. 1909 | Female Choir |
| *Négy siratóének* (Quatre nénies/Four Dirges) | 58 | 45 | 26 | 9a (list 3) | | c. 1909–10 | Piano |
| *Két kép* (*Deux Images*/ Two Pictures) | 59 | 46 | 27 | 10 (list 3) | | 1910 | Orchestra |

| Name | BB | Sz | W | DD | Opus | Year | Instruments/ voices used |
|---|---|---|---|---|---|---|---|
| *Négy régi Magyar népdal* (Four Old Hungarian Folk Songs) | 60 | 50 | 30 | | | 1910–12, rev. 1926 | Male Choir |
| Romanian Dance (BB 56/1) | 61 | 47a | 25 | | | 1911 | Orchestra |
| *A kékszakállú herceg vára* (*Duke Bluebeard's Castle*), opera in one act | 62 | 48 | 28 | | 11 (list 3) | 1911 rev. 1912 & 1917 | Voices and Orchestra |
| *Allegro barbaro* | 63 | 49 | 29 | | | 1911 | Piano |
| *Négy zenekari darab* (Four Orchestral Pieces) | 64 | 51 | 31 | | 12 (list 3) | 1912, orch. in 1921 | Piano/Orchestra |
| Nine Romanian Folk Songs | 65 | 59 | 40 | | | 1915 (or earlier) | Voice and Piano |
| Piano method (with S. Reschofsky) | 66 | 52 | 32 | | | 1913 | Piano |
| *Kezdők zongo- ramuzsikája* (*The First Term at the Piano*) | 66 | 53 | 32 | | | 1913 | Piano |
| *Román kolinda- dallamok* (Romanian Christmas Carols), Series I–II | 67 | 57 | 38 | | | 1915 | Piano |
| Román népi táncok (Romanian Folk Dances) | 68 | 56 | 37 | | | 1915 | Piano |
| *Szonatina* (Sonatina) | 69 | 55 | 36 | | | 1915 | Piano |
| *Szvit* (Suite) | 70 | 62 | 43 | | 14 (list 3) | 1916 | Piano |
| *Öt dal* (Five Songs) | 71 | 61 | 41 | | 15 (list 3) | 1916 | Voice and Piano |
| *Öt dal* (Five Songs), E. Ady | 72 | 63 | 44 | | 16 (list 3) | 1916 | Voice and Piano |
| *Szlovák népdal* (Slovak Folk Song), 'Krutí Tono vretena' | 73 | 63a | | | | 1916? | Voice and Piano |
| *A fából faragott királyfi* (*The Wooden Prince*), ballet in one act | 74 | 60 | 33 | | 13 (list 3) | 1914–17 | Orchestra |
| *The Wooden Prince Suite* | 74 | | | | 13 (list 3) | 1921, 1924? | Orchestra |
| *II Vonósnégyes* (String Quartet No. 2) | 75 | 67 | 42 | | 17 (list 3) | 1915–17 | String Quartet |
| Romanian Folk Dances for small orchestra (from BB 68) | 76 | 68 | 37 | | | 1917 | Orchestra |
| *Tót népdalok* (Slovak Folk Songs) | 77 | 69 | 46 | | | 1917 | Male Choir |

| Name | BB | Sz | W | DD | Opus | Year | Instruments/ voices used |
|------|----|----|---|----|----|------|--------------------------|
| *Négy tót népdalok* (Four Slovak Folk Songs) | 78 | 70 | 47 | | | 1916 or 1917 | Mixed Choir |
| *Tizenöt magyar parasztdal* (Fifteen Hungarian Peasant Songs) | 79 | 71 | 34 | | | 1914–18 | Piano |
| 'Leszállott a páva' | 80 | | 35 | | | 1914 | Piano |
| *Három magyar népdal* (Three Hungarian Folk Tunes) | 80b | 66 | 35 | | | 1914–18 rev. 1941 | Piano |
| *Etüdök* (Three Studies) | 81 | 72 | 48 | | 18 (list 3) | 1918 | Piano |
| *A csodálatos mandarin* (*The Miraculous Mandarin*), pantomime in one act | 82 | 73 | 49 | | 19 (list 3) | 1918–19, orch. 1924 | Orchestra (w. Choir) |
| *The Miraculous Mandarin* Suite | 82 | 73 | | | 19 (list 3) | 1918, completed in 1927 | Orchestra |
| *Improvizációk magyar parasztdalokra* (Eight Improvisations on Hungarian Peasant Songs) | 83 | 74 | 50 | | 20 (list 3) | 1920 | Piano |
| *I Szonáta* (Sonata for Violin and Piano No. 1) | 84 | 75 | 51 | | 21 (list 3) | 1921 | Violin and Piano |
| *II Szonáta* (Sonata for Violin and Piano No. 2) | 85 | 76 | 52 | | | 1922 | Violin and Piano |
| *Táncszvit* (Dance Suite) | 86 | 77 | 53 | | | 1923, piano 1925 | Orchestra/piano |
| *Falun: Dedinské scény* (Village Scenes) | 87a | 78 | 54 | | | 1924 | Female Voice and Piano |
| *Falun; Tri dedinské scény* (Three Village Scenes) | 87b | 79 | 54 | | | 1926 | Four or eight women's voices with chamber orchestra |
| *Szonáta* (Sonata for Piano) | 88 | 80 | 55 | | | 1926 | Piano |
| *Szabadban* (*Out of Doors*), five piano pieces | 89 | 81 | 56 | | | 1926 | Piano |
| *Kilenc kis zongoradarab* (Nine Little Piano Pieces) | 90 | 82 | 57 | | | 1926 | Piano |
| *I Zongoraverseny* (Piano Concerto No. 1) | 91 | 83 | 58 | | | 1926 | Piano and Orchestra |

| Name | BB | Sz | W | DD | Opus | Year | Instruments/ voices used |
|---|---|---|---|---|---|---|---|
| *Három rondó népi dallamokkal* (Three Rondos on Folk tunes) | 92 | 84 | 45 | | | 1916, 1927 | Piano |
| *III Vonósnégyes* (String Quartet No. 3) | 93 | 85 | 60 | | | 1927 | String Quartet |
| *I Rapszódia* (Rhapsody for Violin and Piano No. 1) | 94a | 87, 88 | 61 | | | 1928 (Cello transcription BB 94c, 1929) | Violin (or Cello) and Piano |
| Rhapsody for Violin and Orchestra No. 1 | 94b | 86 | 61 | | | 1929 | Violin and Orchestra |
| *IV Vonósnégyes* (String Quartet No. 4) | 95 | 91 | 62 | | | 1928 | String Quartet |
| *II Rapszódia* (Rhapsody for Violin and Piano No. 2) | 96a | 89 | 63 | | | 1928 rev. 1935 or 1944 | Violin and Piano |
| Rhapsody for Violin and Orchestra No. 2 | 96b | 90 | 63 | | | 1928, rev. 1935 or 1944 | Violin and Orchestra |
| Five Hungarian Folk Songs (revision of BB 42) | 97 | | | | | 1928 | Voice and Piano |
| *Húsz magyar népdal* (Twenty Hungarian Folk Songs), vols 1–4 | 98 | 92 | 64 | | | 1929 | Voice and Piano |
| Four Hungarian Folk Songs | 99 | 93 | 65 | | | 1930 | Mixed Choir |
| *Cantata profana. A kilenc csodaszarvas (Cantata Profana. The Nine Enchanted Stags)* | 100 | 94 | 67 | | | 1930 | Tenor, Baritone, Double Choir and Orchestra |
| *II Zongoraverseny* Piano Concerto No. 2 | 101 | 95 | 68 | | | 1930–1 | Piano and Orchestra |
| Sonatina for Violin and Piano (arr. BB 69) | 102a | 55 | 36 | | | c. 1930 | Violin and Piano |
| *Erdélyi táncok* (Transylvanian Dances), BB 69 and 102a | 102b | 96 | 36 | | | 1931 | Orchestra |
| *Negyvennégy duó* (Forty-Four Duos) | 104 | 98 | 69 | | | 1931–2 | Two Violins |
| *Mikrokosmos*, vols I-VI | 105 | 107 | 59 | | | 1926, 1932–9 | Piano |
| *Székely dalok* (Székely Songs) | 106 | 99 | 70 | | | 1932 (and 1938?) | Male Choir |
| *Magyar parasztdalok* (Hungarian Peasant Songs) (arr. BB 79/6–15) | 107 | 100 | 34 | | | 1933 | Orchestra |
| Five Hungarian Folk Songs (from BB 98) | 108 | 101 | 64 | | | 1933 | Solo Voice and Orchestra |

| Name | BB | Sz | W | DD | Opus | Year | Instruments/ voices used |
|------|----|----|----|----|------|------|--------------------------|
| Hungarian Folk Songs, vols I–II (based on transcriptions of eleven pieces from BB 53 by T. Országh) | 109 | 42 | 22 | | | 1934 | Violin and Piano |
| *V Vonósnégyes* (String Quartet No. 5) | 110 | 102 | 71 | | | 1934 | String Quartet |
| *27 két- és háromszólamú korus* (Twenty-Seven Two- and Three-Part Choruses) | 111 | 103 | 72 | | | 1935–6, with orchestra 1937–41 | Children and Women's Choir (without and with orchestra) |
| *Elmúlt időkből (From Olden Times)* | 112 | 104 | 73 | | | 1935 | Male Choir |
| Petite Suite (arrangement of BB 104) | 113 | 105 | 69 | | | 1936 | Piano |
| *Zene húros hangszerekre, ütőkre és celestara (Music for Strings, Percussion and Celesta)* | 114 | 106 | 74 | | | 1936 | Strings, Percussion and Celesta |
| Sonata for Two Pianos and Percussion | 115 | 110 | 75 | | | 1937 | Two Pianos and Percussion |
| *Kontrasztok (Contrasts)* | 116 | 111 | 77 | | | 1938 | Violin, Clarinet and Piano |
| *II Hegedűverseny* Violin Concerto No. 2 | 117 | 112 | 76 | | | 1937–8 | Violin and Orchestra |
| Divertimento | 118 | 113 | 78 | | | 1939 | String orchestra |
| *VI Vonósnégyes* (String Quartet No. 6) | 119 | 114 | 79 | | | 1939 | String Quartet |
| Seven Pieces from *Mikrokosmos* (BB 105) | 120 | 108 | 59 | | | 1939–40 | Two Pianos |
| Concerto for Two Pianos and Orchestra (arrangement of BB 115) | 121 | 115 | | | | 1940 | Two Pianos and orchestra |
| Suite for Two Pianos (arrangement of BB 40) | 122 | 115a | 12 | 4b (list 3) | | 1941 | Two Pianos |
| Concerto for Orchestra | 123 | 116 | 80 | | | 1943 | Orchestra |
| Sonata for Solo Violin | 124 | 117 | 81 | | | 1944 | Solo Violin |
| *A férj keserve (Goat Song/The Husband's Sorrow)* | 125 | 118 | 83 | | | 1945 | Voice and Piano |
| Three Ukrainian Folk Songs | 126 | | 82 | | | 1945 | Voice and Piano |
| Piano Concerto No. 3 | 127 | 119 | 84 | | | 1945 | Piano and Orchestra |

| Name | BB | Sz | W | DD | Opus | Year | Instruments/ voices used |
|---|---|---|---|---|---|---|---|
| Viola Concerto (sketches only) | 128 | 120 | 85 | | | 1945 | Viola and Orchestra |

BB 129 contains sketches of unrealised compositions.

Sources: Denijs Dille, *Thematisches Verzeichnis der Jugendwerke Béla Bartóks 1890–1904*; László Somfai, *Béla Bartók: Composition, Concepts, and Autograph Sources.*

# Notes

The following abbreviations are used in the notes:

*Apám*    Béla Bartók jr., *Apám életének krónikája* (Budapest: Zeneműkiadó, 1981)
*BBcl*    *Bartók Béla családi levelei* (Budapest: Zeneműkiadó, 1981)
*BBE*    *Béla Bartók Essays*, ed. Benjamin Suchoff (London: Faber and Faber, 1976)
*BBL*    *Béla Bartók Letters*, collected, selected, edited and annotated by János Demény; trans. Péter Balabán and István Farkas; translation rev. Elisabeth West and Colin Mason (Budapest: Corvina, 1971)
*BBlev*    *Bartók Béla levelei* (Budapest: Zeneműkiadó, 1976)

Pitches are given in ASA notation where C4 = middle C.

## Introduction

1. 'Second Preface, in Three Parts: Paragraph 6', in *Autobiography of Mark Twain*, vol. 1 (2010, 2008) <http://www.marktwainproject.org/xtf/view?docId=works/MTDP10362.xml;style=work;brand—tp;chunk.id=d1e9128#d1e9149> accessed 4 January 2014.
2. Paul Kecskeméti, *Meaning, Communication and Value* (Chicago: The University of Chicago Press, 1952).
3. Kecskeméti, *Meaning, Communication and Value*, 289.
4. Kecskeméti, *Meaning, Communication and Value*, 290.
5. Kecskeméti, *Meaning, Communication and Value*, 292.

## Chapter 1

1. 'Erdély etnikai és felekezeti statisztikája (1850–1992)' ('Transylvania's Ethnic and Denominational Statistics [1850–1992]'), *Varga E. Árpád* <http://varga.adatbank.transindex.ro/?pg=3&action=etnik&id=3625> accessed 18 November 2008.
2. Transleithania ('across the Leitha' – a river running to the south and east of Vienna roughly parallel to the Danube) is the name given to Hungary in the Dual-Monarchy period from 1867 to 1918. It neatly underlines the relationship between the two states, for the perspective is that of Austria (Cisleithania or 'this side of the Leitha').
3. Raymond Pearson, *The Longman Companion to European Nationalism: 1789–1920* (Harlow: Longman, 1994), 239.
4. Jürg Hoensch, *A History of Modern Hungary, 1867–1986* (London and New York: Longman, 1988), 28–9. The compromise gave a degree of autonomy to Hungary, though the Imperial Habsburg dynasty retained control over all military and diplomatic matters.
5. Versions of this and the following paragraph originally appeared in my essay 'Béla Bartók and the Question of Race Purity', in *Musical Constructions of Nationalism: Essays on the History and Ideology of European Musical Culture, 1800–1945*, eds. Harry White and Michael Murphy (Cork: Cork University Press, 2001), 16–32 (16–17).

6. Géza Jeszenszky, 'Hungary Through World War I and the End of the Dual Monarchy', in *A History of Hungary*, eds. Peter F. Sugar, Péter Hanák and Tibor Frank (New York: John Wiley & Sons, 1994), 274.
7. Hoensch, *A History of Modern Hungary*, 32. By 1910 the first language of 75 per cent of Jews was Hungarian.
8. Iván T. Berend and György Ránki, *East Central Europe in the Nineteenth and Twentieth Centuries* (Budapest: Akademiai Kiado, 1977), 33, indicate that nearly half of all doctors and lawyers were Jewish by extraction.
9. Berend and Ránki, *East Central Europe in the Nineteenth and Twentieth Centuries*, 33.
10. Carlile Aylmer McCartney, *Hungary: A Short History* (Edinburgh: Edinburgh University Press, 1962), 202.
11. Tibor Tallián, *Béla Bartók: The Man and His Work*, trans. Gyula Gulyás, rev. Paul Merrick (Budapest: Corvina, 1981), 8.
12. Ferenc Bónis, *Béla Bartók: His Life in Pictures and Documents*, trans. Lili Halápy, rev. Kenneth McRobbie (Budapest: Corvina, 1972; New York: Belwin Mills Publishing Corporation, 1972), 30. The composer's connection with the village is recognised by the Béla Bartók Kultúrotthon.
13. Denijs Dille, *Genealogie sommaire de la famille Bartok* (Antwerp: Metropolis, 1977), 9.
14. József Eötvös de Vásárosnamény, *The Village Notary: A Romance of Hungarian Life*, trans. Otto Wenckstern (London: Longman, Brown, Green, and Longmans, 1850).
15. Eötvös, *The Village Notary*, 283–4.
16. Alexander Vörös, 'Agricultural Education in Hungary from Times Past Down to the Present', in *Agricultural Industry and Education in Hungary: Being an Account of the Visit of the Essex Farmers' Party to Hungary in May and June, 1902*, compiled by T. S. Dymond (Chelmsford: County Technical Laboratories, 1902), 136. The school fell into disuse, but reopened in 1855.
17. Pál Bődy, 'The Rumanian-Hungarian Confrontation, 1840–70', in *Transylvania: The Roots of Ethnic Conflict*, eds. John F. Cadzow, Andrew Ludanyi and Louis J. Elteto (Kent, OH: The Kent State University Press, 1983). At <http://www.hungarian-history.hu/lib/transy/transy10.htm> accessed 1 February 2009.
18. Henry Kiddle and Alexander J. Schem, eds., *The Year-Book of Education for 1878* (New York: E. Steiger; London: Sampson Low & Company, 1878), 81.
19. Lajos Lesznai, *Bartók*, trans. Percy M. Young (London: J. M. Dent and Sons, 1973), 3.
20. Tallián, *Béla Bartók*, 9.
21. Vörös, 'Agricultural Education in Hungary', 137.
22. To distinguish the three generations of Béla Bartóks, the composer is indicated as Béla, his father by the addition of 'senior' and his son by 'junior'.
23. Dille, *Genealogie sommaire de la famille Bartok*, 23.
24. Dille, *Genealogie sommaire de la famille Bartok*, 35. 'De manières vives, il possédait un caractère typiquement hongrois: passioné, très enjoué, aimant le luxe et la bonne chère, la danse et les distractions de société, toujours très soigné dans sa mise, s'habillant avec goût et de façon distinguée (une caractéristique des Ronkovics à ce qu'il paraît); il était tout col et manchettes, disait-on dans la famille. En somme, c'était le gentleman tel qu'on rencontrait dans la bourgeoisie de l'époque.' (author's translation)
25. Jeszenszky, 'Hungary Through World War I and the End of the Dual Monarchy', 275–7.
26. Béla Bartók Jr., 'The Private Man', in *The Bartók Companion*, ed. Malcolm Gillies (London: Faber and Faber, 1993), 18–29 (22).
27. Dille, *Genealogie sommaire de la famille Bartok*, 38.
28. Peter Bartók, *My Father* (Homosassa, FL: Bartók Records, 2002), 51.
29. 'Bartóks Selbstbiographie aus dem Jahre 1921', in *Documenta Bartókiana*, Heft 2, ed. Denijs Dille (Budapest: Akadémiai Kiadó, 1964), 117. 'Mein Vater, Direktor einer landwirtschaftlichen Schule, zeigte ziemlich hohe musikalische Anlagen; er spielte Klavier, organisierte eine Dilettantenorchester, lernte Cello, um darin als Cellist mitwirken zu können und versuchte sich sogar in der Komposition von Tanzstücken.' (author's translation)
30. Stefan Zweig, *The World of Yesterday* (London, Toronto, Melbourne and Sydney: Cassell and Company Ltd, 1943), 13.
31. Zweig, *The World of Yesterday*, 13–14.
32. János Demény, ed., *Béla Bartók Letters* (Budapest: Corvina Press, 1971), letter 151 to Octavian Beu (10 January 1931), 199–205 (200).
33. Béla Bartók Jr., 'Béla Bartók's Diseases', *Studia Musicologica Academiae Scientiarum Hungaricae* 23 (1981), 427–41.
34. Béla Bartók Jr., 'Béla Bartók's Diseases', 427.
35. For a contemporaneous discussion of the use of arsenic-based drugs in the treatment of eczema, see Charles D. F. Phillips, *Materia Medica and Therapeutics: Inorganic Substances* (New York: William Wood & Company, 1882), where it is described as 'empirical, as opposed to rational', vol. 2, 80.

36. 'Szőllős', *Kislexikon* <http://www.kislexikon.hu/szollos.html> accessed 26 February 2010.
37. Béla Bartók Jr., ed., *Bartók Béla családi levelei* (Budapest: Zeneműkiadó, 1981), 315–24.
38. In a letter to his mother on 18 October 1891, Bartók calls him 'Uncle Altdörfer'.
39. Serge Moreux, *Béla Bartók*, trans. G. S. Fraser and Erik de Mauny (London: The Harvill Press, 1953), 14–17.
40. Béla Bartók Jr., 'Béla Bartók's Diseases', 429.
41. According to Moreux, Bartók performed in a night-time event at his school in Nagyszőllős to celebrate the 1848 revolution, presumably on 15 March 1891, and played a waltz of his own composition.
42. Otto Gombosi claimed that the work performed was not, in fact, the 'Waldstein' Sonata, but Beethoven's Sonata op. 2 no. 3 in C major, and draws on Bartók's personal testimony in 1943 for this assertion. See Benjamin Suchoff, *Béla Bartók: Life and Work* (Lanham, MD: Scarecrow Press, 2001), 268 fn. 18. In either case, these were both demanding works.
43. A concert review published in the local paper *Ugocsa* on 8 May 1892 gives the title of the work as *A Duna falyását*. See also Pierre Citron, *Bartok* (Paris: Éditions du Seuil, 1963), 5.
44. 'Bartóks Selbstbiographie aus dem Jahre 1918', *Documenta Bartókiana*, vol. 2, 113.
45. Günter Weiss-Aigner, 'Youthful Piano Works', in *The Bartók Companion*, ed. Malcolm Gillies (London: Faber and Faber, 1993), 101–9 (102).
46. *BBL*, 75. Letter 45, to Stefi Geyer, 6 September 1907.
47. Malcolm Gillies, *Bartók Remembered* (London: Faber and Faber, 1990), 9.
48. Gillies, *Bartók Remembered*, 201; Bertalan Pethő, 'Béla Bartók's Personality', *Studia Musicologica Academiae Scientiarum Hungaricae* 23, no. 1 (1981), 443–58 (444).
49. See, for example, Michael Fitzgerald, 'Did Bartok have High Functioning Autism or Asperger's Syndrome?', *Autism – Europe Link* 29 (2000), 21; Michael Fitzgerald, *Autism and Creativity: Is There a Link between Autism in Men and Exceptional Ability?* (East Sussex: Brunner-Routledge, 2004); Ioan James, *Asperger's Syndrome and High Achievement: Some Very Remarkable People* (London and Philadelphia: Jessica Kingsley Publishers, 2006).
50. *Diagnostic and Statistical Manual of Mental Disorders*, Fourth Edition (DSM-IV) (Washington, DC: American Psychiatric Association, c. 1994), 77.
51. Dorothy Barenscott, 'Articulating Identity through the Technological Rearticulation of Space: The Hungarian Millennial Exhibition as World's Fair and the Disordering of Fin-de-Siècle Budapest', *Slavic Review* 69, no. 3 (Autumn 2010), 571–90 (571).
52. Charles Hopkins, 'Thomán, István', *Grove Music Online, Oxford Music Online* <http://0-www.oxfordmusiconline.com.wam.leeds.ac.uk/subscriber/article/grove/music/27855> accessed 9 July 2010.
53. Benjamin Suchoff, ed., 'About István Thomán', in *Béla Bartók Essays* (Lincoln, NE: University of Nebraska Press, 1992), 489–91 (490).
54. *BBE*, 'About István Thomán', 490.
55. *BBE*, 'About István Thomán', 491.
56. István Thomán, *The Technique of Piano Playing: Fundamental Exercises for the Mastery of Even and Virtuosic Playing* (*A zongorázás technikája*), 6 vols. (Budapest: Editio Musica, 1982).
57. Thomán, *The Technique of Piano Playing*, vol. 4 (octaves), 5.
58. Quoted in David Schneider, *Bartók, Hungary and the Renewal of Tradition: Case Studies in the Intersection of Modernity and Nationality* (Berkeley and Los Angeles: University of California Press, 2006), 30.
59. Medical record of Dr Gábor Pávai Vajna, head physician of the state hospital, Pozsony, cited in Béla Bartók Jr., 'Béla Bartók's Diseases', 23 (1981), reprinted with revisions in Gillies, *Bartók Remembered*, 12–14.
60. Gillies, *Bartók Remembered*, 13–14.
61. Miklós Konrád, 'Jews and Politics in Hungary in the Dualist Era, 1867–1914', *East European Jewish Affairs* 39, no. 2 (2009), 167–86 (175).
62. Alan Walker, 'Ernst von Dohnányi (1877–1960): A Tribute', in *Perspectives on Ernst von Dohnányi*, ed. James A. Grymes (Lanham, MD: Scarecrow Press, 2005), 5–6.
63. *BBcl*, 35 (12 May 1901), 44, trans. Gergely Hubai, who notes that a literal translation would be 'half-old', which he interprets as 'middle-aged' (personal communication).
64. Gillies, *Bartók Remembered*, 14.
65. *BBcl*, 85 (10 February 1903), 86, trans. Gergely Hubai.
66. Tibor Tallián's translation in *Béla Bartók: The Man and His Work*, 30. See *BBcl*, letter 50, 56.
67. Günter Weiss-Aigner, 'Youthful Orchestral Works', in *The Bártok Companion*, ed. Malcolm Gillies (London: Faber and Faber, 1993), 441–53 (441).

## Chapter 2

1. Bence Szabolcsi, *A Concise History of Hungarian Music* (Budapest: Corvina, 1964), contains a consideration of the rise of *verbunkos* in Chapter 6.
2. David Thomson, *Europe Since Napoleon* (Harmondsworth: Penguin Books Ltd, 1970), 487.
3. Szabolcsi, *A Concise History*, 56.
4. William C. Stafford, *A History of Music* (Edinburgh: Constable and Company, 1830, reprinted by the Boethius Press [New York], 1986), 255.
5. In C this would include the pitches C, D, E♭, F♯, G, A♭, B, C.
6. David Schneider provided me with the following very useful information about the term *hallgató*: 'While hallgató does mean "student", its more literal meaning is "listening" (students are supposed to do this!). Thus, when used in the context of *verbunkos*, the hallgató is the "listening music", that is the music people just listened to as opposed to the music they danced to, thus I usually translate it as "music for listening". It's hard to dance to this music because it doesn't have a steady beat. The term "hallgató" to describe this music is of mid- to late-nineteenth-century origin (I'm not 100 percent sure when it was established), so some Hungarian scholars insist on the not very colourful "slow introductory music of irregular pulse" or some such.' (Personal email)
7. *BBL*, 378. Bartók stayed at the house of Karl Fischer between May and November 1904. According to Dille, Bartók was already in regular correspondence with Harsányi. See Denijs Dille, *Béla Bartók: Regard sur le passé* (Louvain-la-Neuve: Institut Supérieur d'Archéologie et d'Histoire de l'Art, Collège Érasme, 1990), 110.
8. *BBL*, 378–9. The title 'The Thirteen of Arad' refers to the thirteen generals who fought on the Hungarian side against Austria and were executed on 6 October 1849.
9. *BBL*, 22, letter to his mother dated 1 April 1903.
10. Translated from the Hungarian by László Kiss, translation edited by the author.

A further poetic translation was supplied to the author by Steve Frankl:

**Evening**
Everything is silent, so silent,
The lofts hearken
The Sun has just died; A bloodstain is where
He collapsed.

Mourning, deep dark mourning,
Is cast on the landscape.
The Flowers on the meadow
Cry tears of dew,

And rustle in silence:
'Will we ever see You again?'
It's not possible for the night to fall,
For the night to fall, and stay forever,

And They are waiting.
Awaiting His comeback,
Till the deathly pale disk of the Moon
Is rising above the horizon.

Ghostly lights have turned
The skies as pale as death,
The flowers are thrilled:
He is back, but dead.

I would also like to thank Ferenc Gerlits for his translation, his note that the title more accurately translates as 'E'en', and that as there are no genders for pronouns in Hungarian, the sun could be masculine, feminine or neuter.

11. One is reminded of Baudelaire's line from 'Harmonie du soir':
    'Le soleil s'est noyé dans son sang qui se fige.' ('The sun is drowning in its congealing blood.') (author's translation)
12. *BBL*, 37.
13. Arminius Vámbéry, *Hungary in Ancient, Mediaeval, and Modern Times* (London: T. Fisher Unwin, 1886), 434.
14. Bartók gives the tempo marking in Hungarian, using the term *Lassan* (slowly).

15. See, for example, Benjamin Suchoff, ed., 'The Bartók-Möller Polemical Interchange', in *Béla Bartók Studies in Ethnomusicology* (Lincoln, NE, and London: University of Nebraska Press), 144–5.
16. In fact, this configuration of pitches is also found in the first line of Elemér Szentirmay's 'Play on, Gipsy . . .' in Korbay's arrangement.
17. For example, the openings of no. 1 in G minor and no. 5 in F minor.
18. Jonathan Bellman, *The 'Style hongrois' in the Music of Western Europe* (Boston: Northeastern University Press, 1993), 116.
19. *BBE*, 'Harvard Lectures' (1943), 384. My emphasis.
20. The pedal-tone sequence is C♯/D♭ (A major to G♭ major), B♭ (G♭ major to E♭ major) and G/E♭ (E♭ major to C minor).
21. József Ujfalussy, *Béla Bartók* (Budapest: Corvina, 1971), 43.
22. Judit Frigyesi, 'Béla Bartók and the Concept of Nation and Volk in Modern Hungary', *The Musical Quarterly* 78, no. 2 (Summer 1994), 255–87. Quotation from David Cooper, *Béla Bartók: Concerto for Orchestra*, Cambridge Music Handbook (Cambridge: Cambridge University Press, 1996), 8.
23. Ilona Sármány-Parsons, 'Hungarian Art and Architecture, 1896–1914', in *A Golden Age: Art and Society in Hungary, 1896–1914*, ed. G. Éry and Z. Jobbágyi (Budapest, London and Miami: Corvina, Barbican Art Gallery, Center for the Fine Arts, 1990), 37.
24. Bill Ashcroft, Gareth Griffiths and Helen Tiffin, *The Empire Writes Back: Theory and Practice in Post-Colonial Literatures* (London and New York: Routledge, 1989), 38.
25. *BBL*, 28.
26. John Lukacs, *Budapest 1900: A Historical Picture of a City and its Culture* (New York: Grove Press, 1988), 128.
27. David Clegg, 'Das Englische Programm der *Kossuth-Symphonie*', in *Documenta Bartókiana*, vol. 1, ed. Denijs Dille (Budapest: Bartók Archiv, 1964), 70.
28. Clegg, 'Das Englische Programm der *Kossuth-Symphonie*', 70–3.
29. This was a shawm-like instrument whose use was apparently banned because of its association with the war of independence, though it was replaced in the final decade of the nineteenth century by a new invention that was related to the clarinet family.
30. *BBL*, 7 July 1903, 25.
31. *BBL*, 3 December 1903, 34.
32. *BBL*, 16 December 1903, 35.
33. Peter Laki, 'Violin Works and the Viola Concerto', in *The Cambridge Companion to Bartók*, ed. Amanda Bayley (Cambridge: Cambridge University Press, 2001), 134–5.
34. Julie A. Richards, 'The Piano Quintet of Béla Bartók: Context, Analysis and Revisions', DMA Dissertation, University of Houston (2009), 21–2.
35. Benjamin Suchoff, *Béla Bartók: Life and Work* (Lanham, MD: Scarecrow Press, 2001), 40.
36. Translation from Louise O. Vasvári, 'A Comparative Approach to European Folk Poetry and the Erotic Wedding Motif', *CLCWeb: Comparative Literature and Culture* 1, no. 4 (1999) <http://docs.lib.purdue.edu/clcweb/vol1/iss4/1> accessed 4 March 2012.
37. *BBL*, 38.
38. *BBL*, 41.
39. *BBE*, 408–11 (409).
40. David E. Schneider, *Bartók, Hungary, and the Renewal of Tradition: Case Studies in the Intersection of Modernity and Nationality* (Berkeley and Los Angeles: University of California Press, 2006), 59.
41. Presumably Bartók is alluding to the siege of Érsekújvár.
42. *BBcl*, letter 126, 125, trans. Gergely Hubai.

## Chapter 3

1. Bill Ashcroft, Gareth Griffiths and Helen Tiffin, *The Empire Writes Back: Theory and Practice in Post-Colonial Literatures* (London and New York: Routledge, 1989), 17.
2. Max Paddison, *Adorno's Aesthetics of Music* (Cambridge: Cambridge University Press, 1993), 38. Adorno was writing in 1921.
3. *BBE*, 'Gipsy Music or Hungarian Music?', 207.
4. *BBL*, 41.
5. *BBL*, 43.
6. Julie Brown, *Bartók and the Grotesque: Studies in Modernity, the Body and Contradiction in Music* (Aldershot: Ashgate, 2007), 2.
7. The $B_5$ and $A♭_5$ are melodic infill.
8. H. Wickham Steed, Walter Alison Phillips and David Hannay, 'A Short History of Austria-Hungary and Poland', *Encyclopaedia Britannica*, 11th Edition (London: The Encyclopaedia Britannica Company, Ltd, 1914).

9. *BBcl*, 126–7. Translated by George Brassay.
10. *BBE*, 437–45.
11. *BBE*, 445.
12. *First Suite*, pocket score (Budapest: Editio Musica Budapest, 1956), xiv.
13. *BBL*, 132.
14. *First Suite*, pocket score, xv.
15. Ashcroft *et al., The Empire Writes Back*, 38.
16. David Cooper, 'Bartók's Orchestral Music and the Modern World', in *The Cambridge Companion to Bartók*, ed. Amanda Bayley (Cambridge: Cambridge University Press, 2001), 45–61.
17. *BBL*, 54.
18. Denijs Dille, 'La Rencontre de Bartók at de Kodály', in *Béla Bartók: Regard sur le passé* (Louvain-la-Neuve: Institut Supérieur d'Archéologie et d'Histoire de l'Art, Collège Érasme, 1990), 199–204.
19. *BBE*, 'Zoltán Kodály', 470.
20. In *BBL*, 44, this is given as 8 August, but as the competition took place on 9 August this cannot be correct. *BBcl* queries it as 9 or 10 August.
21. *BBL*, 48.
22. Denijs Dille, 'Bartók, lecteur de Nietzsche et de la Rochefoucauld', *Studia Musicologica Academiae Scientiarum Hungaricae* 10, no. 3/4 (1968), 209–28.
23. Friedrich Nietzsche, *Human, All Too Human: A Book For Free Spirits*, trans. Alexander Harvey (Chicago: Charles H. Kerr & Company, 1908). It is likely that he did not have his copy of the Nietzsche volume with him in Paris.
24. Although Dille believes some thirty-two letters between Bartók and the Jurkovics sisters were extant in 1945, only this one letter has survived.
25. In *BBL*, 53–4.
26. Benjamin Suchoff, *Béla Bartók: Life and Work* (Lanham, MD: Scarecrow Press, 2001), 52.
27. *BBL*, 59.
28. *BBL*, 331.
29. *BBL*, 61.
30. *BBL*, 64.
31. Béla Bartók Jr., *Apám életének krónikája* (Szombathely: Helikon Kiadó, 2006), 85.
32. Tibor Tallián, *Béla Bartók: The Man and his Work*, trans. Gyula Gulyás, rev. Paul Merrick (Budapest: Corvina, 1981), 57.
33. *BBcl*, 158.
34. Trans. Carl S. Leafstedt, *Inside Bluebeard's Castle: Music and Drama in Béla Bartók's Opera* (New York and Oxford: Oxford University Press, 1999), 17–18.
35. *BBL*, 67.
36. See Béla Bartók, 'Hungarian Folk Songs (Complete Collection)', Online publication by the Hungarian Academy of Sciences Institute for Musicology <http://db.zti.hu/nza/br_en.asp> accessed 13 September 2012. Known as the Bartók System.
37. *BBL*, 68–9. In September he had collected traditional music close to Lake Balaton. As well as revisiting Gerlicepuszta in October as described in this letter to Dietl, he went to his sister's house again in November, but Doboz yielded little on this occasion.
38. *BBL*, 105.
39. Malcolm Gillies, ed., *The Bartók Companion* (London: Faber and Faber, 1993), 463–4.
40. *BBE*, 334–5.
41. *BBE*, 408.

Chapter 4

1. Denijs Dille, 'Angaben zum Violinkonzert 1907, den Deux Portraits, dem Quartett, op. 7 und den Zwei rumänischen Tänzen', in *Documenta Bartókiana*, vol. 2 (Budapest: Akadémia Kiadó, 1964), 91–102.
2. Karl Baedeker, *Austria-Hungary, Including Dalmatia and Bosnia: Handbook for Travellers* (Leipzig: Karl Baedeker, 1905), 403.
3. *BBL*, 74.
4. *BBL*, 74.
5. *BBL*, 75–83.
6. *BBL*, 83–7.
7. György Kroó, *A Guide to Bartók* (Budapest: Corvina Press, 1974), 40.
8. Benjamin Suchoff, *Béla Bartók: Life and Work* (Lanham, MD: Scarecrow Press, 2001), 58.
9. Günter Weiss-Aigner, 'The "Lost" Violin Concerto', in *The Bartók Companion*, ed. Malcolm Gillies (London: Faber and Faber, 1993), 468–76 (475).

10. *BBcl*, 176.
11. Suchoff, *Béla Bartók*, 59.
12. Béla Balázs, *A vándor énekel – Versek és novellák*, ed. Sándor Radnóti (Budapest: Magyar Helikon, 1975), 134–6.
13. Trans. Carl S. Leafstedt, *Inside Bluebeard's Castle: Music and Drama in Béla Bartók's Opera* (New York and Oxford: Oxford University Press, 1999), 19.
14. *BBE*, 432–3 (432).
15. *BBE*, 432–3.
16. *BBL*, 89.
17. 'Contemporary Music in Piano Teaching', *BBE*, 426.
18. *BBL*, 93–4.
19. János Kárpáti, 'Early String Quartets', in *The Bartók Companion*, ed. Malcolm Gillies (London: Faber and Faber, 1993), 230.
20. *BBcl*, 187–8, in Tibor Tallián, *Béla Bartók: The Man and His Work*, trans. Gyula Gulyás, rev. Paul Merrick (Budapest: Corvina, 1981), 76–7 and 88–9.
21. *BBL*, 148–9. Suchoff gives the date as 'the beginning of 1910'. Suchoff, *Béla Bartók*, 67.
22. *BBL*, 390–1.
23. *BBL*, 95.
24. *BBE*, 120–1.
25. *BBL*, 96.


Chapter 5

1. Lee Congdon, 'The Making of a Hungarian Revolutionary: The Unpublished Diary of Bela Balazs' (sic), *Journal of Contemporary History* 8, no. 3 (1972), 55–74 (59–60).
2. Anton N. Nyerges, trans. and introduction, *Poems of Endre Ady* (Buffalo, NY: Hungarian Cultural Foundation, 1969), 112. For a detailed consideration of Ady's influence on Bartók, see the second part of Judit Frigyesi, *Béla Bartók and Turn-of-the Century Budapest* (Berkeley: University of California Press, 1998).
3. Nyerges, *Poems of Endre Ady*, 170.
4. 'Answer to the Petranu Attack', *BBE*, 227–36 (235).
5. 'Folk Song Research and Nationalism', *BBE*, 25–8 (28).
6. 'Folk Song Research and Nationalism', *BBE*, 28.
7. Benjamin Suchoff claims that these can be regarded as 'level 4' arrangements and that similar features can be found in several of the Romanian folk tunes Bartók collected, though these points do seem rather tenuous. See 'Fusion of National Styles', in *The Bartók Companion*, ed. Malcolm Gillies (London: Faber and Faber, 1993), 124–45 (134–45).
8. *BBL*, 99–100.
9. *BBL*, 99.
10. Peter Laki, 'The Gallows and the Altar: Poetic Criticism and Critical Poetry about Bartók in Hungary', in *Bartók and His World*, ed. Peter Laki (Princeton: Princeton University Press, 1995), 79–100 (82–3).
11. Laki, 'The Gallows and the Altar', 82.
12. Géza Csáth, 'Bartók Béla és Kodály Zoltán', *Nyugat* 3, no. 7 (1910) <http://epa.oszk.hu/00000/00022/00053/01450.htm> accessed 9 October 2012. (author's translation)
13. *BBL*, 104.
14. *BBL*, 105.
15. 'A Delius Première in Vienna', *BBE*, 449–50 (449).
16. *BBL*, 107.
17. Benjamin Suchoff, ed., *Béla Bartók Studies in Ethnomusicology* (Lincoln, NE, and London: University of Nebraska Press, 1997), 4. G1 is the G in the octave beginning with middle C.
18. *BBL*, 173.
19. *BBE*, 301–3.
20. *BBE*, 450.
21. Carl S. Leafstedt, *Inside Bluebeard's Castle: Music and Drama in Béla Bartók's Opera* (New York and Oxford: Oxford University Press, 1999), 20.
22. György Kroó, 'Duke Bluebeard's Castle', *Studia Musicologica Academiae Scientarum Hungaricae* 1, parts 3/4 (1961), 251–340. And see David Cooper, 'Béla Bartók's *Bluebeard's Castle*: A Musicological Perspective', in *Bluebeard's Legacy: Death and Secrets from Bartók to Hitchcock: New Encounters: Arts, Cultures, Concepts*, ed. V. Anderson and G. Pollock (London: I. B. Tauris, 2009), 53–68 (55) where I have already argued these points.
23. Béla Bartók, *Bluebeard's Castle*, Full score. English trans. Christopher Hassall (Vienna, London and New York: Universal Edition, nd), 5.

24. Béla Bartók, *The Hungarian Folk Song* (London: Oxford University Press, 1931), 113.
25. Sigmund Freud, *On Sexuality: Three Essays on the Theory of Sexuality and Other Works*, The Pelican Freud Library, vol. 7 (Harmondsworth: Penguin Books Ltd, 1997), 269.
26. Bruno Bettelheim, *Uses of Enchantment: The Meaning and Importance of Fairy Tales* (London: Penguin Books, 1978), 300–1.
27. Bartók, *Bluebeard's Castle*, 17–18.
28. Béla Balázs, 'Duke Bluebeard's Castle: Notes on the Text', in Carl S. Leafstedt, *Inside Bluebeard's Castle: Music and Drama in Béla Bartók's Opera* (New York and Oxford: Oxford University Press, 1999), 201–3 (202).
29. Nyerges, *Poems of Endre Ady*, 61. See also Frigyesi, *Béla Bartók and Turn-of-the Century Budapest*, 180–1.
30. Bartók, *Bluebeard's Castle*, 21–2.
31. Joseph Zsuffa, *Béla Balázs, the Man and the Artist* (Berkeley, Los Angeles and London: University of California Press, 1987), 69.
32. Bartók, *Bluebeard's Castle*, 20–1.
33. Cooper, 'Béla Bartók's *Bluebeard's Castle*', 68.
34. Lynn Hooker, 'Modernism on the Periphery: Béla Bartók and the New Hungarian Music Society of 1911–1912', *Musical Quarterly* 88, no. 2 (Summer 2005), 274–319.
35. Hooker, 'Modernism on the Periphery', 281.
36. Hooker, 'Modernism on the Periphery', 297.
37. 'Autobiography', *BBE*, 410.
38. Suchoff, 'Fusion of National Styles', 139.
39. Vera Lampert, *Népzene Bartók műveiben – A feldolgozott dallamok forrásjegyzéke* (Budapest: Helikon Kiadó, 2005), 91.
40. Nyerges, *Poems of Endre Ady*, 374.
41. Denijs Dille, 'L'Allegro barbaro de Bartók', *Béla Bartók: Regard sur le passé* (Louvain-la-Neuve: Institut Supérieur d'Archéologie et d'Histoire de l'Art, Collège Érasme, 1990), 205–12.
42. H. Devitte, 'The Simple Life at Waidberg: An Extraordinary Colony', *The Advertiser* (Adelaide), Saturday 17 September 1910, 16–24 (16).
43. Zsuffa, *Béla Balázs*, 38.
44. Leafstedt, *Inside Bluebeard's Castle*, 150.
45. *BBL*, 113.
46. Nyerges, *Poems of Endre Ady*, 171.
47. This and the following quotations are taken from *BBL*, 123–4.
48. *BBL*, 115. Both this source and *BBL* give the date as November–December 1912. However, as all the melodies from Petrovasile (as Bartók gives it) in volumes 1 and 2 of *Rumanian Folk Music* are dated XII, 1912, the earliest the letter could have been written was the last few days of December 1912. Bartók talks about checking the melodies when he got home, and as *Apám* gives the date of visiting Petré as 29 December, the letter must have been sent no earlier than 1913.
49. *BBL*, 119.
50. Bartók presumes a cadential structure to the final section of the song that is either perfect (V–I) or plagal (IV–I) and introduces a third category (III–I) to accommodate the many tunes that finish with a falling major or minor third. See page viii of the Romanian-language preface to the collection.
51. Márta Ziegler, 'Bartók's Reise nach Biskra', in *Documenta Bartókiana*, vol. 2, ed. Denijs Dille (Budapest: Akadémiai Kiadó, 1965), 9–13.
52. *BBL*, 122.
53. *BBL*, 126.
54. *Zeitschrift für musikwissenschaft* 9 (November 1920), 489–522.

## Chapter 6

1. 'About *The Wooden Prince*', *BBE*, 406.
2. Nicholas John, series editor, *The Stage Works of Béla Bartók*, Opera Guide 44 (London: John Calder, 1991), 77.
3. 'Observations on Rumanian Folk Music', *BBE*, 195–200 (200).
4. *BBL*, 130.
5. Tunes discussed below are identified in Vera Lampert, *Népzene Bartók műveiben – A feldolgozott dallamok forrásjegyzéke* (Budapest: Helikon Kiadó, 2005), 94–5. Following Lampert, Romanian names have been given in brackets.
6. László Somfai, *Béla Bartók: Composition, Concepts, and Autograph Sources* (Berkeley and Los Angeles: University of California Press, 1996), 191.

7. 'The Relation Between Contemporary Hungarian Art Music and Folk Music', *BBE*, 351–2.
8. See Denijs Dille, 'L'Opus 15 de Béla Bartók', in *Belá Bartók: Regard sur le passé* (Louvain-la-Neuve: Institut Supérieur d'Archéologie et d'Histoire de l'Art, Collège Érasme, 1990), 257–78.
9. Dille translates this as 'nuit flamboyante' – 'flaming night', though the Hungarian word for 'flaming' is *lángoló, hangoló* meaning 'tuner' or 'tuning'.
10. See Somfai, *Béla Bartók*, 307. It is of note that Márta copied the first two songs and Bartók the third for this printer's copy. According to Somfai, the final page of Bartók's score for the first song was published in facsimile in the avant-garde journal *Ma (Today)* in 1917.
11. In fact this is the one version of the falling sevenths figure that Judit does not sing in the opera.
12. *BBL*, 132.
13. Anton N. Nyerges (trans. and introduction), *Poems of Endre Ady* (Buffalo, NY: Hungarian Cultural Foundation, 1969), 23.
14. Nancy Bush was the wife of the composer Alan Bush and sister of Michael Head. Presumably '*délben*', meaning 'noon' or 'afternoon', is given as 'morning' by the translator for prosodic reasons.
15. The author is extremely grateful to Gergely Hubai for providing this translation.
16. Nyerges, *Poems of Endre Ady*, 140.
17. Lajos Bárdos, 'Heptatonia secunda – Egy sájastágos hangredszer Kodály műveiben', *Magyar Zene* 3–4 (1962–3).
18. 'The Relation Between Contemporary Hungarian Art Music and Folk Music', *BBE*, 350.
19. Zoltán Szász, 'Political Life and the Nationality Question in the Era of Dualism (1867–1918)', in *History of Transylvania*, vol. 3, ed. Zoltán Szász (New York: Columbia University Press, 2002) <http://mek.oszk.hu/03400/03407/html/431.html> accessed 9 October 2012.
20. Translation by George Brassay.
21. *Apám*, 74.
22. *BBL*, 135.
23. Ferenc Bónis, *Béla Bartók: His Life in Pictures and Documents*, trans. Lili Halápy, rev. Kenneth McRobbie (Budapest: Corvina, 1972; New York: Belwin Mills Publishing Corporation), 106.
24. Bónis, *Béla Bartók*, 106.
25. This work was only available in the violin and piano version at that time and despite his connection with Delius, it is extremely unlikely that Bartók would have been aware of it.
26. *BBL*, 137.
27. *BBL*, 202.
28. *BBE*, 262.
29. Carl S. Leafstedt, *Inside Bluebeard's Castle: Music and Drama in Béla Bartók's Opera* (New York and Oxford: Oxford University Press, 1999), 13.
30. Peter Laki, ed., *Bartók and His World* (Princeton: Princeton University Press, 1995), 208. Translation of a letter to Márta, probably sent on 24 August.
31. *BBL*, 140.

## Chapter 7

1. *BBL*, 143.
2. *BBcl*, 298.
3. *BBcl*, 291.
4. Béla Kun, *Revolutionary Essays* (London: BSP, nd [1919?]), 12–17 (14).
5. *BBcl*, 292.
6. 'The Problem of the New Music', *BBE*, 455–6.
7. László Somfai, ed., *Documenta Bartókiana*, vol. 5 (Budapest: Akadémiai Kiadó, 1977), 28.
8. 'The Problem of the New Music', *BBE*, 457.
9. 'The Problem of the New Music', *BBE*, 458.
10. *BBL*, 143.
11. The libretto for *Seherezáde* eventually appeared in *Nyugat* in the final edition (24) of 1923, dedicated to Bartók.
12. 'Musical Performances in Budapest, March–May, 1920', *BBE*, 466.
13. 'Reply to Jenő Hubay', *BBE*, 203.
14. 'Harvard Lectures', *BBE*, 375.
15. Elliott Antokoletz, *The Music of Béla Bartók: A Study of Tonality and Progression in Twentieth-Century Music* (Berkeley and Los Angeles: University of California Press, 1984), 55–62, 103–9, 154–7 and 213–29.
16. Translated by Gergely Hubai, who notes that the word '*jáccani*' suggests a heavy rural tone – in standard spelling this would be *játszani* (personal communication).

17. Béla Bartók, *The Hungarian Folk Song* (London: Oxford University Press, 1931), 123.
18. Bartók, *The Hungarian Folk Song*, 123.
19. Barry Smith, ed., *The Complete Letters of Peter Warlock* (Woodbridge: The Boydell Press, 2005), 370.
20. Smith, *The Complete Letters of Peter Warlock*, 524–5.
21. Smith, *The Complete Letters of Peter Warlock*, 677. It was not the case at this point that Bartók was devoting his time to teaching, as he was on a period of leave from the Academy of Music.
22. Somfai, *Documenta Bartókiana*, vol. 5, 139–40. There is no letter to Bartók in the complete letters, but it appears that this is a response to previous communication from Heseltine, and Bartók remarks that he's just received the second letter sent on 20 November.
23. Smith, *The Complete Letters of Peter Warlock*, 693.
24. Smith, *The Complete Letters of Peter Warlock*, 689.
25. *BBL*, 154.
26. *BBcl*, 325.
27. Adrienne Gombocz and László Somfai, 'Bartóks Briefe an Calvocoressi (1914–1930)', *Studia Musicologica Academiae Scientiarum Hungaricae* 24, nos. 1–2 (1982), 199–231.
28. She had also recently performed Reger's Violin Concerto, reported in Bechert's previous review.
29. 'Musical Notes from Abroad: Vienna', *The Musical Times* 63, no. 953 (July 1922), 515.
30. Adrienne Gombocz and László Vikárius, 'Twenty-Five Bartók Letters to the Arányi Sisters, Wilhelmine Creel and Other Correspondents. Recently Acquired Autograph Letters in the Bartók Archives', *Studia Musicologica Academiae Scientiarum Hungaricae* 43, nos. 1–2 (2002), 151–204 (169).
31. Bartók also performed at a further private concert on 17 or 18 March, and on 19 March after a reception at the home of the German-born businessman and musical philanthropist Robert Mayer (who was married to the soprano Dorothy Moulton and involved in the formation of the International Society for Contemporary Music). See Malcolm Gillies, *Bartók in Britain: A Guided Tour* (Oxford: Clarendon Press, 1989).
32. H. C. Colles, 'Béla Bartók', *The Times* (London), 18 March 1922, 8. *The Times Digital Archive*, accessed 29 November 2012.
33. János Kárpáti, *Bartók's Chamber Music* (New York: Pendragon Press, 1994), 289–320.
34. Malcolm Gillies, 'Stylistic Integrity and Influence in Bartók's Works: The Case of Szymanowski', *International Journal of Musicology* 1 (1992), 139–60.
35. Paul Wilson, 'Violin Sonatas', in *The Bartók Companion*, ed. Malcolm Gillies (London: Faber and Faber, 1993), 243–56.
36. Wilson, 'Violin Sonatas', 247.
37. This is notated with the rhythmic groupings as indicated by Bartók.
38. Béla Bartók, *Rumanian Folk Music, Volume Five, Maramureş County*, ed. Benjamin Suchoff, text trans. E. C. Teodorescu, preface trans. Alan Kriegsman (The Hague: Martinus Nijhoff, 1975), 23.
39. Gillies, *Bartók in Britain*, 42.
40. Gillies, *Bartók in Britain*, 42–3.
41. Smith, *The Complete Letters of Peter Warlock*, 726.
42. Denijs Dille, ed., *Documenta Bartókiana*, vol. 3 (Budapest: Akadémiai Kiadó, 1965), 109.
43. Carl B. Schmidt, *Entrancing Muse: A Documented Biography of Francis Poulenc* (Hillsdale, NY: Pendragon Press, 2001), 113.
44. Dille, ed., *Documenta Bartókiana*, vol. 3, 118.
45. Cited in Gillies, *Bartók in Britain*, 139.
46. Gombocz and Vikárius, 'Twenty-Five Bartók Letters to the Arányi Sisters, Wilhelmine Creel and Other Correspondents', 173. Jenő Szenkar (1891–1977) was the conductor and he went on to give the Cologne premiere of *The Miraculous Mandarin* in 1926.
47. Gombocz and Somfai, 'Bartóks Briefe an Calvocoressi (1914–1930)', 214.
48. 'Musical Events in Budapest, March–June, 1921', *BBE*, 480.
49. László Somfai, 'Bartók Béla: 2. Hegedű-zongora szonáta', *A hét zeneműve* (1977) <http://www.mr3-bartok.hu/component/option,com_alphacontent/section,5/cat,18/task,view/id,206/Itemid,52/> accessed 5 December 2012.
50. Published in English as Béla Bartók, *Rumanian Folk Music, Volume Five, Maramureş County*.
51. Adolf Weissmann, 'Musical Notes from Abroad: Germany', *The Musical Times* 64, no. 961 (March 1923), 211.
52. *BBL*, 162.
53. W. Harmans, 'Musical Notes from Abroad: Amsterdam', *The Musical Times* 64, no. 964 (June 1923), 433.
54. Edwin Evans, 'London Concerts: Contemporary Music Centre', *The Musical Times* 64, no. 964 (June 1923), 424.

55. 'The Annual RPI and Average Earnings for Britain, 1209 to Present (New Series)', *Measuring Worth* <http://www.measuringworth.com/datasets/ukearncpi/result2.php> accessed 7 December 2012.
56. *BBL*, 163.
57. *BBL*, 202.
58. Cited in Tibor Tallián, *Béla Bartók: The Man and His Work*, trans. Gyula Gulyás, rev. Paul Merrick (Budapest: Corvina, 1981), 133.
59. 'Why and How Do We Collect Folk Music?', *BBE*, 11.
60. *BBcl*, 342. Translated by Frank Finlay (personal communication).
61. Cited in Benjamin Suchoff, *Béla Bartók: Life and Work* (Lanham, MD: Scarecrow Press, 2001), 100.
62. Emila Weiss and Orsolya Szeibert, 'Grounds for Divorce and Maintenance Between Former Spouses: Hungary' <http://ceflonline.net/wp-content/uploads/Hungary-Divorce.pdf> accessed 12 December 2012.
63. Malcolm Gillies, 'Dance Suite', in *The Bartók Companion*, ed. Malcolm Gillies, 496.
64. Edwin Evans, 'London Concerts: Jelly D'Aranyi and Bartók', *The Musical Times* 65, no. 971 (January 1924), 71.
65. Percy Scholes, ed., *The Mirror of Music, 1844–1944: A Century of Musical Life in Britain as Reflected in the Pages of the Musical Times* (London: Novello & Co. Ltd and Oxford University Press, 1947), 459.
66. Béla Bartók, *Village Scenes*, English trans. Martin Lindsay, new edn., Universal Edition, 1994, rev. Peter Bartók, UE8712.
67. Gombocz and Somfai, 'Bartóks Briefe an Calvocoressi (1914–1930)', 221.
68. Bartók's sister and her husband had moved to Békéssámson, 90 kilometres south-west of Vésztő in September 1921. The nearest town was Orosháza and Bartók addresses letters here to Szöllős Puszta.

**Chapter 8**

1. Cited in Tibor Tallián, *Béla Bartók: The Man and His Work*, trans. Gyula Gulyás, rev. Paul Merrick (Budapest: Corvina, 1981), 140.
2. David E. Schneider, *Bartók, Hungary and the Renewal of Tradition: Case Studies in the Intersection of Modernity and Nationality* (Berkeley and Los Angeles: University of California Press, 2006), 153–6.
3. 'Introduction to *Béla Bartók Masterpieces for the Piano*', *BBE*, 432.
4. See László Somfai's discussion of this aspect in 'The "Piano Year" of 1926', in *The Bartók Companion*, ed. Malcolm Gillies (London: Faber and Faber, 1993), 177–8.
5. László Somfai, *Béla Bartók: Composition, Concepts, and Autograph Sources* (Berkeley and Los Angeles: University of California Press, 1996), 176.
6. Damjana Bratuž, 'On the Shaman's Trail: Béla Bartók's Szabadban (OUTDOORS)', *Ninth International Congress on Musical Signification* 'Music, Senses, Body' 'La Musica, i Sensi, il Corpo', 19–23 September 2006, Università di Roma Tor Vergata, <http://www.damjanabratuz.ca/bartokiana/abstracts/on_the_shamans_trail.htm> accessed 8 January 2013. The word *gilice* has been variously interpreted as a nonsense word, or the Hungarianisation of the Latin word for stork, *ciconia*. While the similarity with the Turkish word *gizlice* may be a coincidence, its invocation of furtiveness, secrecy and deviousness seems appropriate in this context.
7. Bartók describes this dance in *Rumanian Folk Music, Volume One, Instrumental Melodies*, ed. Benjamin Suchoff (The Hague: Martinus Nijhoff, 1967), 47.
8. Schneider, *Bartók, Hungary and the Renewal of Tradition*, 153–73.
9. See, for example, scale number 29 in 'Arab Music from the Biskra District'.
10. Béla Bartók, *Slovenské L'Udové Piesne*, vol. 3 (Bratislava: Vydavateľstvo Slovenskej akadémie vied, 1959), 678. Tune number 1618.
11. Somfai, 'The "Piano Year" of 1926', 173–88 (184).
12. Malcolm Gillies, *Bartók Remembered* (London: Faber and Faber, 1990), 111.
13. Ferenc Bónis, '*The Miraculous Mandarin*: The Birth and Vicissitudes of a Masterpiece', in *The Stage Works of Béla Bartók*. Opera Guide 44. Series editor Nicholas John (London: John Calder, 1991), 81–93 (86).
14. Olin Downes, 'Dissension Marks Music Festival', *The New York Times*, 2 July 1927, 20.
15. Peter Laki, ed., *Bartók and His World* (Princeton: Princeton University Press, 1995), 257–8.
16. Laki, *Bartók and His World*, 259.
17. *BBL*, 184–5.
18. Nicolas Slonimsky, *Lexicon of Musical Invective: Critical Assaults on Composers Since Beethoven's Time*, 2nd edn. (Seattle and London: University of Washington Press, 1969).
19. Paul Rosenfeld, 'Bartok Soloist at Symphony Concert', *Daily Boston Globe*, 18 February 1928, 5.

20. *BBcl*, 434.
21. 'Structure of the Fourth String Quartet', *BBE*, 412–13 (412).
22. Somfai, *Béla Bartók*, 100–1.
23. Minor and major seconds and thirds, and perfect and augmented fourths, are directly present, the remaining intervals being the inversions of these.
24. The upper F5 only appears very briefly and the underlying upper G–A–C–D–E is pure pentatonic.
25. *BBL*, 189–90.
26. Claude Kenneson, *Székely and Bartók: The Story of a Friendship* (New York: Amadeus Press, 1994), 113.
27. Mengelberg also served as music director of the New York Philharmonic and had conducted the performance of the *Rhapsody* with Bartók earlier in the year, having aborted the US premiere of the Piano Concerto.
28. Herbert Antcliffe, 'Musical Notes from Abroad: Holland', *The Musical Times* 69, no. 1030 (December 1928), 1134.
29. Béla Bartók, 'The National Temperament in Music', *The Musical Times* 69, no. 1030 (December 1928), 1079.

### Chapter 9

1. *BBL*, 192.
2. *BBL*, 193.
3. The review in the April 1929 edition of *The Musical Times* gives the date of this concert as 2 March.
4. Ferruccio Bonavia (?), 'London Concerts: Béla Bartók', *The Musical Times* 70, no. 1034 (April 1929), 351–2 (352).
5. D. H., 'London Concerts: Hungarian String Quartet', *The Musical Times* 70, no. 1034 (April 1929), 352.
6. *BBL*, 194.
7. I am grateful to Gergely Hubai for his help in understanding this text.
8. Malcolm Gillies, *Bartók in Britain: A Guided Tour* (Oxford: Clarendon Press, 1989), 76.
9. 'M', 'London Concerts: BBC Symphony Concerts', *The Musical Times* 71, no. 1045 (March 1930), 259.
10. László Somfai, *Béla Bartók: Composition, Concepts, and Autograph Sources* (Berkeley and Los Angeles: University of California Press, 1996), 57. However, Bartók dates the songs as 1929 in a letter to Octavian Beu written on 5 November 1930.
11. Béla Bartók, *The Hungarian Folk Song* (London: Oxford University Press, 1931), 170.
12. This truncated version of a text completed in 1926, omitting the complete texts of the songs, eventually became the fourth volume of the posthumous *Rumanian Folk Music*, ed. Benjamin Suchoff, text trans. E. C. Teodorescu (The Hague: Martinus Nijhoff, 1975).
13. Julie Brown, *Bartók and the Grotesque: Studies in Modernity, the Body and Contradiction in Music* (Aldershot: Ashgate, 2007), 78–9.
14. László Vikárius, 'Béla Bartók's "Cantata Profana" (1930): A Reading of the Sources', *Studia Musicologica Academiae Scientarum Hungaricae* 35, no. 1 (1993–4), 249–301.
15. *BBlev*, 446.
16. Such interlacing of major seconds is also widely found in the Fourth String Quartet; see, for example, the passage in the second movement, bars 195–212.
17. 'Analysis of the Second Concerto for Piano and Orchestra', *BBE*, 419–23.
18. 'Analysis of the Second Concerto for Piano and Orchestra', *BBE*, 419.
19. See, for instance: Bartók, *The Hungarian Folk Song*, 169; Bartók, *Slovenské ľudové piesne*, vol. 3 (Bratislava: Vydavateľstvo Slovenskej akadémie vied, 1959), 1259b, 1442a and 1510; and Bartók, *Rumanian Folk Music, Volume One, Instrumental Melodies*, ed. Benjamin Suchoff (The Hague: Martinus Nijhoff, 1967), p. 598, number 236.
20. Bartók, *Romanian Folk Music, Volume One*, 42.
21. Serge Moreux, *Béla Bartók*, trans. G. S. Fraser and Erik de Mauny (London: The Harvill Press, 1953), 164–5.
22. *Les Temps modernes* 3, no. 25 (October 1947), 705–34. Published in English as 'Bela Bartok: Or the Possibility of Compromise in Contemporary Music', *Transition Forty-Eight*, 3 (1948), 92–122.
23. *BBL*, 201.
24. Scott Goddard, 'Review of *Hungarian Folk Music* by Bela Bartók, trans. M. D. Calvocoressi', *Music and Letters* 12, no. 4 (1931), 419.
25. Frank Howes, 'Editorial Notes', *Journal of the Folk-Song Society* 8, no. 35 (1931), 304.

26. László Pollatsek, 'Béla Bartók and His Work: On the Occasion of His Fiftieth Birthday (Concluded)', *The Musical Times* 72, no. 1062 (1931), 699.
27. Olin Downes, 'New Quartet Gives Novelties', *The New York Times*, 18 March 1931, 33.
28. Toscanini's passport was subsequently returned after an international outcry on 4 June 1931.
29. 'What is Folk Music?', *BBE*, 6. Bartók's emphasis.
30. *BBL*, 221.
31. *BBE*, 350.
32. *BBL*, 220.
33. Two pieces (35 and 36) are based on original tunes by Bartók in folk style.
34. Claude Kenneson, *Székely and Bartók: The Story of a Friendship* (New York: Amadeus Press, 1994), 139.
35. In a paper by Erik Chisholm delivered in 1964, excerpts of which are published in Malcolm Gillies' *Bartók Remembered* (London: Faber and Faber, 1990), the memories of Chisholm's first wife, Diana, surrounding his two visits seem to have been conflated, for the pair were not married until November 1932, and her daughter Morag (for whom Bartók apparently showed great affection) was not born until 1933.
36. Edwin Evans, 'London Concerts: Contemporary Music', *The Musical Times* 73, no. 1070 (April 1932), 359.
37. Ali Jihad Racy, 'Historical Worldviews of Early Ethnomusicologists: An East-West Encounter in Cairo, 1932', in *Ethnomusicology and Modern Music History*, ed. Stephen Blum, Philip Bohlman and Daniel Neuman (Chicago: University of Illinois Press, 1993), 69.
38. *BBE*, 38.
39. Racy, 'Historical Worldviews of Early Ethnomusicologists', 73.
40. *BBE*, 39.
41. *BBcl*, 537.
42. RH, 'Florence Music Convention', *The New York Times*, 11 June 1933, x4.
43. George Barati, *George Barati: A Life in Music*, interviewed and edited by Randall Jarrell <http://library.ucsc.edu/sites/default/files/userfiles/barati.pdf>, 18–19, accessed 26 October 2013.
44. Erik Chisholm, *Béla Bartók* <http://www.erikchisholm.com/writings3.php> accessed 26 October 2013.
45. Chisholm, *Béla Bartók*.
46. Anon., 'Bela Bartok at Queen's Hall', *The Times* (London), 9 November 1933, 10. *The Times Digital Archive*, accessed 26 July 2013.
47. Benjamin Suchoff, ed., *Béla Bartók Studies in Ethnomusicology* (Lincoln, NE, and London: University of Nebraska Press, 1997), 199.
48. Anon., 'B.B.C. Concert', *The Times* (London), 26 May 1934, 10. *The Times Digital Archive*, accessed 26 July 2013.
49. 'Analysis of the Fifth String Quartet', *BBE*, 414–15.
50. Though as noted later, this rhythm can be found in Hungarian traditional music.
51. See Elliott Antokoletz, *The Music of Béla Bartók: A Study of Tonality and Progression in Twentieth-Century Music* (Berkeley and Los Angeles: University of California Press, 1984), 71–2.
52. Kenneson, *Székely and Bartók*, 149.
53. Kenneson, *Székely and Bartók*, 150.
54. Kenneson, *Székely and Bartók*, 151.
55. Kenneson, *Székely and Bartók*, 153.
56. Olin Downes, 'The Kolisch Quartet: Debut in Washington is Outstanding Event of Coolidge Festival', *The New York Times*, 14 April 1935, x5.
57. Benjamin Suchoff, 'Bartók's Folk Music Publication', *Ethnomusicology* 16, no. 2 (1971), 220–30 (221).
58. Translation by Gergely Hubai (personal communication).
59. *BBL*, 245.

Chapter 10

1. *BBE*, 510.
2. *BBE*, 235–6.
3. László Somfai, *Béla Bartók: Composition, Concepts, and Autograph Sources* (Berkeley and Los Angeles: University of California Press, 1996), 117.
4. The note name and octave number represent the opening pitches of the subject (where $C_4$ is middle C); the letters LCR stand for left, centre and right respectively.
5. *BBE*, 140–1.
6. Béla Bartók, *Turkish Folk Music from Asia Minor* (Princeton and London: Princeton University Press, 1976), xxx–xxxi.

7. *BBL*, 254.
8. Ezra Pound, 'Ligurian View of a Venetian Festival', *Music and Letters* 18, no. 1 (1937), 36–41 (39).
9. Ezra Pound, *Guide to Kulchur* (London: Faber & Faber, 1938), 135.
10. In the poster for the concert (which also included premieres of works by Conrad Beck and Willy Burkhard), the Bartók is simply listed as *Musik für Saiteninstrumente* and no reference is made to the additional resources.
11. Olin Downes' review of the Carnegie Hall performance was negative in tone, and registered his disappointment about what he regarded as a formulaic work. *The New York Times*, 29 October 1937, 18.
12. *BBL*, 255.
13. Peter Bartók, *My Father* (Homosassa, FL: Bartók Records, 2002), 38.
14. M.M.S., 'London Concerts: Béla Bartók', *The Musical Times* 78, no. 1129 (March 1937), 267.
15. *BBL*, 257.
16. *BBL*, 257. The Bartóks visited Velden am Wörthersee in June–July 1937.
17. Anon., 'Bartok Admits Jazz Influence in Compositions', *The Pittsburgh Press*, 23 January 1941, 15.
18. *BBE*, 417.
19. The retransition from the upbeat to bar 229 to bar 273 was rewritten in 1939 and it is this version that appears in the score.
20. The F♯ appears from the second chord.
21. David Cooper, *Bartók: Concerto for Orchestra*, Cambridge Music Handbook (Cambridge: Cambridge University Press, 1996), 71.
22. Claude Kenneson, *Székely and Bartók: The Story of a Friendship* (New York: Amadeus Press, 1994), 158.
23. Kenneson, *Székely and Bartók*, 159.
24. Calculation performed using 'Value of the Gilder/Euro', *International Institute of Social History* <http://www.iisg.nl/hpw/calculate.php> accessed 17 September 2013.
25. Kenneson, *Székely and Bartók*, 179.
26. *BBL*, 424.
27. *BBL*, 265.
28. *BBL*, 426.
29. Peter Bartók, *My Father*, 196.
30. See András D. Bán, *Hungarian-British Diplomacy, 1938–1941: The Attempt to Maintain Relations* (London: P. Frank Cass Publishers, 2005), 26–7.
31. Anon., 'International Festival', *The Times* (London), 21 June 1938, 14. *The Times Digital Archive*, accessed 17 September 2013.
32. Denijs Dille, ed., *Documenta Bartókiana*, vol. 3 (Budapest: Akadémiai Kiadó, 1965), 226.
33. G.G., 'Goodman Assists in Szigeti Recital: Band Leader Carries Clarinet Part with the Violinist in Bartók Rhapsody', *The New York Times*, 10 January 1939, 23.
34. *BBL*, 272.
35. Kenneson, *Székely and Bartók*, 191.
36. Kenneson, *Székely and Bartók*, 186.
37. Yehudi Menuhin, *Unfinished Journey* (London: Macdonald and Jane's, 1976), 164.
38. *BBL*, 271.
39. *BBL*, 272.
40. *BBL*, 273.

## Chapter 11

1. Claude Kenneson, *Székely and Bartók: The Story of a Friendship* (New York: Amadeus Press, 1994), 203.
2. Anon., 'Music in the Making', *Tempo* 1 (1939), 3–7 (3).
3. Peter Bartók, *My Father* (Homosassa, FL: Bartók Records, 2002), 268.
4. Value assessed using 'Purchasing Power of Money in the United States from 1774 to Present', *Measuring Worth* <http://www.measuringworth.com/ppowerus/> accessed 6 December 2013.
5. Denijs Dille, ed., *Documenta Bartókiana*, vol. 3 (Budapest: Akadémiai Kiadó, 1965), 232–3.
6. *BBL*, 274.
7. 'Our Correspondent', 'Anti-Jewish Exhibition in Germany', *The Times* (London), 26 May 1938, 18. *The Times Digital Archive*, accessed 6 December 2013.
8. Benjamin Suchoff, 'Bartók's Odyssey in Slovak Folk Music', in *Bartók Perspectives: Man, Composer and Ethnomusicologist*, ed. Elliott Antokoletz, Victoria Fischer and Benjamin Suchoff (Oxford: Oxford University Press, 2000), 15–27 (26).
9. *BBL*, 276.

10. *BBlev*, 619.
11. *BBL*, 278.
12. *BBL*, 278.
13. László Somfai, *Béla Bartók: Composition, Concepts, and Autograph Sources* (Berkeley and Los Angeles: University of California Press, 1996).
14. Benjamin Suchoff, 'Structure and Concept in Bartók's Sixth Quartet', *Tempo* 83 (Winter 1967–8), 2–11.
15. *BBlev*, 643. Thanks to Gergely Hubai for this translation.
16. *BBL*, 281.
17. Howard Taubman, 'Bela Bartok Plays Own Compositions', *The New York Times*, 14 April 1940, 44.
18. Noel Straus, 'Ovation to Bartok at Szigeti Recital', *The New York Times*, 22 April 1940, 18.
19. Olin Downes, 'Bartok is Honored Here', *The New York Times*, 25 April 1940, 27.
20. Otto Gombosi, 'The Art of the Hungarian Composer Bartok: An Estimate of the Music of a Contemporary who is on a Visit Here', *The New York Times*, 5 May 1940, 160.
21. *BBL*, 283.
22. *BBlev*, 649.
23. Anon., 'Notes of Musicians Here and Afield: Bela Bartok to Return to the United States', *The New York Times*, 11 August 1940, 106.
24. *BBL*, 284.
25. Sylvia Parker, 'A Riverton Retreat: Royal Charter to State Forest', *Vermont Historical Society* (2010) <http://vermonthistory.org/journal/78/VHS780105_95-111.pdf> accessed 27 December 2013.
26. Agatha Fassett, *The Naked Face of Genius: Béla Bartók's Last Years* (London: Victor Gollancz Ltd, 1970).
27. Peter Bartók, *My Father*, 90.
28. Donald Rosenberg, *The Cleveland Orchestra Story* (Cleveland: Gray & Company, 2000), 173.
29. Rosenberg, *The Cleveland Orchestra Story*, 173–4.
30. Howard Taubman, 'Bartok Quartet Heard in Premiere', *The New York Times*, 21 January 1941, 18.
31. Donald Steinfirst, 'Bartok Work is Presented by Symphony', *Pittsburgh Post-Gazette*, 25 January 1941, 5.
32. Ralph Lewando, 'City Symphony, Composer Give Brilliant Performance: Bela Bartok, Noted Hungarian, is Soloist for His Own Ultra-Modern Music', *The Pittsburgh Press*, 25 January 1941, 7.
33. Letter to Kodály, 8 December 1941, cited in 'Alice M. Ditson Fund, Research Award', *Columbia University Libraries/Information Services* <http://exhibitions.cul.columbia.edu/exhibits/show/music-centennial/ditson-fund/bela-bartok> accessed 30 December 2013.
34. Noel Straus, 'Bela Bartok Work Introduced Here', *The New York Times*, 29 January 1941, 21.
35. C.W.D, 'Benny Goodman and Clarinet Go Classical Here', *Daily Boston Globe*, 5 February 1941, 19.
36. *BBL*, 299.
37. *BBL*, 301.
38. 32, no. 1 (1941), 79–106 (90).
39. *BBL*, 306.
40. 'The Immigration Act of 1924' <http://www.upa.pdx.edu/IMS/currentprojects/TAHv3/Content/PDFs/Immigration_Act_1924.pdf> accessed 31 December 2013.
41. *BBL*, 306–7.
42. *BBL*, 317.
43. *Apám*, 217.
44. *BBL*, 320.
45. A later letter from Ralph Hawkes (of Boosey & Hawkes) reveals that he had contacted the British Foreign Office on Bartók's behalf and had been advised that they were aware of the situation and were confident that there should not be any appreciable delay. Dille, ed., *Documenta Bartókiana*, vol. 3, 256.
46. *BBL*, 320.
47. *BBL*, 282.
48. Béla Bartók Jr., 'Béla Bartók's Diseases', *Studia Musicologica Academiae Scientiarum Hungaricae* 23 (1981), 427–41 (438). See also Anon., 'Holló Gyula', *BANATerra* <http://www.banaterra.eu/magyar/H/hollo_gy.htm> accessed 31 December 2013.
49. Dille, ed., *Documenta Bartókiana*, vol. 3, 256–7.
50. Peter Bartók, *My Father*, 86.
51. Tibor Eckhardt, 'Proclamation', *The American Hungarian Federation* <http://www.americanhungarianfederation.org/images/AHFHistory/IndependentHungaryProclamation_Eckardt.gif> accessed 9 January 2014.
52. Steven Béla Várdy, 'Hungarian Americans during World War II: Their Role in Defending Hungary's Interests', in *Ideology, Politics and Diplomacy in East Central Europe*, ed. M. B. B. Biskupski (Rochester, NY: University of Rochester Press, 2003), 120–46 (133).

53. *BBE*, 29.
54. Béla Bartók, 'Parry Collection of Yugoslav Folk Music: Eminent Composer Who Is Working on It, Discusses Its Significance', *The New York Times*, 28 June 1942, x6.
55. *BBlev*, 688.
56. Yehudi Menuhin, *Unfinished Journey* (London: MacDonald and Jane's, 1976), 164.
57. *BBL*, 324–5.
58. Fassett, *The Naked Face of Genius*, 261–2.
59. Olin Downes, 'Reiner Conducts Haydn Symphony; Performance of B-Flat Work is Feature of Concert by the Philharmonic; The Bartoks on Programme; Concerto for Two Pianos They Composed Presented in New Form', *The New York Times*, 22 January 1943, 24.
60. Vera Lampert, 'Bartók at Harvard University as Witnessed in Unpublished Archival Documents', *Studia Musicologica Academiae Scientiarum Hungaricae* 35, 1/3 (1993–4), 113–54, 125.
61. Anon., 'The Music Box', *The Harvard Crimson* (1943) <http://www.thecrimson.com/article/1943/2/12/the-music-box-pbela-bartok-noted/#> accessed 10 January 2014.
62. Anon., 'HGC to Offer Modern Work: Compositions by Williams, Bartok in Sanders Concert', *The Harvard Crimson* (1943) <http://www.thecrimson.com/article/1943/2/18/hgc-to-offer-modern-work-pbesides/> accessed 10 January 2014.
63. Anon., 'Bartok Talk Postponed', *The Harvard Crimson* (1943) <http://www.thecrimson.com/article/1943/3/8/bartok-talk-postponed-pthe-first-lecture/> accessed 10 January 2014.
64. Lampert, 'Bartók at Harvard University', 138.
65. Lampert, 'Bartók at Harvard University', 139.
66. Lampert, 'Bartók at Harvard University', 142.
67. James A. Pegolotti, *Deems Taylor: A Biography* (Boston: Northeastern University Press, 2003), 270.
68. Béla Bartók Jr., 'Bartók's Diseases', 440.
69. Dille, ed., *Documena Bartókiana*, vol. 3, 258.
70. Serge Koussevitzky, 'Justice to Composers: Koussevitzky Speaks for Need of Support for Those Who Create', *The New York Times*, 16 May 1943, x5.
71. *BBL*, 326.
72. Julia Frank, 'Great Composer Lived Here: Mrs Sageman Remembers the Bartoks', *Adirondack Daily Enterprise*, 18 August 1970 <http://localwiki.net/hsl/Bartok_Cabin> accessed 2 February 2014.

Chapter 12

1. Klára Móricz, 'New Aspects of the Genesis of Béla Bartók's "Concerto for Orchestra": Concepts of "Finality" and "Intention"', *Studia Musicologica Academiae Scientiarum Hungaricae* 35, no. 1/3 (1993–4), 181–219 (189).
2. *BBE*, 431.
3. Béla Bartók, *The Hungarian Folk Song* (London: Oxford University Press, 1931), 131.
4. David Cooper, *Béla Bartók: Concerto for Orchestra*. Cambridge Music Handbook (Cambridge: Cambridge University Press, 1996), 36.
5. Quoted in Cooper, *Béla Bartók: Concerto for Orchestra*, 41.
6. Béla Bartók and Albert B. Lord, *Serbo-Croatian Folk Songs: Texts and Transcriptions of Seventy-Five Folk Songs from the Milman Parry Collection and a Morphology of Serbo-Croatian Folk Melodies* (New York: Columbia University Press; Oxford: Oxford University Press, 1951), 54.
7. Yves Lenoir, *Folklore et transcendance dans l'oeuvre américaine de Béla Bartók (1940–1945)* (Louvain-la-Neuve: Institut Supérieur d'Archéologie et d'Histoire de l'Art Collège Érasme, 1986), 358.
8. Bartók and Lord, *Serbo-Croatian Folk Songs*, 63.
9. *BBE*, 206.
10. Peter Bartók, *My Father* (Homosassa, FL: Bartók Records, 2002), 174.
11. Cooper, *Béla Bartók: Concerto for Orchestra*, 54.
12. Ferenc Fricsay, *Über Mozart und Bartók* (Copenhagen and Frankfurt am Main: Wilhelm Hansen, 1962), 59–61, translated in Cooper, *Béla Bartók: Concerto for Orchestra*, 54–5.
13. Peter Bartók, *My Father*, 277–8.
14. Klára Móricz, 'Operating on a Fetus: Sketch Studies and their Relevance to the Interpretation of the Finale of Bartók's *Concerto for Orchestra*', *Studia Musicologica* 35, nos. 3–4 (1995), 461–76 (475).
15. Liner notes for album FE4419, 'Folk Music of Rumania from the Collection of Bela Bartók', Folkways Records, 1950 <http://media.smithsonianfolkways.org/liner_notes/folkways/FW04419.pdf> accessed 19 January 2014.
16. See Lenoir, *Folklore et transcendance*, 395–401.
17. See letters to Peter of 23 August and 26 September 1943 in Peter Bartók, *My Father*, 276–7.

18. Peter Bartók, *My Father*, 277.
19. Olin Downes, 'Rodzinski Directs Berlioz Symphony; Bartok Violin Concerto also Heard – Spivakovsky Soloist with The Philharmonic', *The New York Times*, 15 October 1943, 22.
20. Yehudi Menuhin, *Unfinished Journey* (London: Macdonald and Jane's, 1976), 164.
21. Menuhin, *Unfinished Journey*, 166.
22. Carl Leafstedt, 'Asheville, Winter of 1943–44: Béla Bartók and North Carolina', *The Musical Quarterly* 87, no. 2 (Summer 2004), 219–58 (233).
23. *BBL*, 330.
24. Leafstedt, 'Asheville, Winter of 1943–44: Béla Bartók and North Carolina', 234–9.
25. Peter Bartók, *My Father*, 282.
26. Cooper, *Béla Bartók: Concerto for Orchestra*, 25.
27. Leafstedt, 'Asheville, Winter of 1943–44: Béla Bartók and North Carolina', 235.
28. *BBL*, 330.
29. László Somfai, *Béla Bartók: Composition, Concepts, and Autograph Sources* (Berkeley and Los Angeles: University of California Press, 1996), 75–8.
30. Menuhin, *Unfinished Journey*, 166–7.
31. Peter Bartók, *My Father*, 285.
32. *BBL*, 334.
33. Peter Bartók, *My Father*, 287.
34. Peter Bartók, *My Father*, 290.
35. Peter Bartók, *My Father*, 292.
36. Olin Downes, 'Menuhin Thrills Capacity Crowd: Violinist Features New Bela Bartok Sonata in Recital at Carnegie Hall', *The New York Times*, 27 November 1944, 16.
37. *BBL*, 342.
38. Peter Bartók, *My Father*, 298.
39. Winthrop P. Tryon, 'Dr Koussevitzky to Present Work at Symphony Concerts', *The Christian Science Monitor*, 30 November 1944.
40. Cooper, *Béla Bartók: Concerto for Orchestra*, 25.
41. Warren Story Smith, 'Symphony Concert', *Boston Post*, 2 December 1944, np.
42. Cyrus Durgin, 'Music, Symphony Hall, Boston Symphony Orchestra', *Daily Boston Globe*, 2 December 1944, 6.
43. Rudolph Elie Jr., 'Symphony Concert', *Boston Herald*, 30 December 1944, np.
44. Durgin, 'Music, Symphony Hall, Boston Symphony Orchestra', *Daily Boston Globe*, 30 December 1944, 4.
45. Olin Downes, 'Bartok Concerto Introduced Here: Boston Symphony, Directed by Koussevitzky, Plays New Work at Carnegie Hall', *The New York Times*, 11 January 1945, 18.
46. Peter Bartók, *My Father*, 304.
47. Peter Bartók, *My Father*, 307.
48. Peter Bartók, *My Father*, 308. According to Agatha Fassett, the piano duo Ethel Bartlett and Rae Robertson had offered him a commission. Fassett, *The Naked Face of Genius*, 317.
49. Peter Bartók, *My Father*, 308.
50. Donald Maurice, *Bartók's Viola Concerto: The Remarkable Story of His Swansong* (Oxford: Oxford University Press, 2004), 11.
51. Peter Bartók, *My Father*, 312.
52. Peter Bartók, *My Father*, 315.
53. Peter Bartók, *My Father*, 314.
54. Peter Bartók, *My Father*, 316.
55. Peter Bartók, *My Father*, 319.
56. *BBL*, 348.
57. Peter Bartók, *My Father*, 320.
58. Ditta's birthday was on 31 October.
59. See Facsimile 8, Somfai, *Béla Bartók*, 55.
60. See Lenoir, *Folklore et transcendance*, 418.
61. Maurice, *Bartók's Viola Concerto*, 14.
62. Maurice, *Bartók's Viola Concerto*, 14.
63. Somfai, *Béla Bartók*, 112.
64. *BBL*, 349.
65. Vilmos Juhász, *Bartók's Years in America* (Washington, DC: Occidental Press, 2006), 18. The Kecskemétis are not explicitly identified in the text, though it is obvious that they are the interviewees.
66. *The New York Times*, 27 September 1945, 21.
67. Anon., 'Bela Bartok Dies in Hospital Here: Noted Hungarian Composer, Specialist in Music

Folklore, Played Own Works at 10', *The New York Times*, 27 September 1945, 21.

68. For a detailed discussion and reassessment of Bator's role in the Bartók estate, see Carl Leafstedt, 'Rediscovering Victor Bator, Founder of the New York Bartók Archives', *Studia Musicologica* 53, nos. 1–3 (2012), 349–72.

69. Robert T. Jones, 'From Bela to Ditta', *The New York Times*, 11 May 1969, D29.

## Postlude

1. Vilmos Juhász, *Bartók's Years in America* (Washington, DC: Occidental Press, 2006), 20.

2. Márton Gyöngyösi, Leader of Jobbik's foreign affairs committee, 'Azerbaijan: Hungary's Gate to the East – The Need for a Strategic Alliance' <http://www.jobbik.com/speech_m%C3%A1rton_gy%C3%B6ngy%C3%B6si_conference_embassy_azerbaijan> accessed 11 August 2014.

3. Alan P. Merriam, 'Definitions of "Comparative Musicology" and "Ethnomusicology": An Historical-Theoretical Perspective', *Ethnomusicology*, 21, no. 2 (1977), 189–204 (199).

4. <http://www.ethnomusicology.org/?page=WhatisEthnomusicol> accessed 26 August 2014.

5. Béla Bartók, *Slovenské L'Udové Piesne*, vol. 3, ed. Alica Elscheková and Oskár Elschek (Bratislava: ASCO art and science, 2007), 19.

6. László Dobszay, 'Folksong Classification in Hungary: Some Methodological Conclusions', *Studia Musicologica*, 30, no. 1 (1988), 235–80 (239).

7. Marilyn M. Garst, 'How Bartók Performed His Own Compositions', *Tempo* 155 (1985), 15–21.

8. Jonathan W. Bernard, 'Bartok and Traditional Form Description: Some Issues Arising from the Middle and Late String Quartets', in Dániel Péter Biró and Harald Krebs, eds., *The String Quartets of Béla Bartók: Tradition and Legacy in Analytical Perspective* (New York: Oxford University Press, 2014), 22–4.

9. <http://www.nytimes.com/2011/01/23/arts/music/23composers.html?pagewanted=all&_r=0> accessed 8 August 2014.

10. For an earlier consideration of this issue see Vera Lampert, 'Bartók's Music on Record: An Index of Popularity', *Studia Musicologica* 36, nos. 3–4 (1995), 393–412.

# Bibliography

Anon. 'Alice M. Ditson Fund, Research Award', *Columbia University Libraries/Information Services* <https://exhibitions.cul.columbia.edu/exhibits/show/music-centennial/ditson-fund/bela-bartok> accessed 30 December 2013.

Anon. 'Bartok Admits Jazz Influence in Compositions', *The Pittsburgh Press*, 23 January 1941, 15.

Anon. 'Bartok Talk Postponed', *The Harvard Crimson* (1943) <http://www.thecrimson.com/article/1943/3/8/bartok-talk-postponed-pthe-first-lecture/> accessed 10 January 2014.

Anon. 'B.B.C. Concert', *The Times* (London), 26 May 1934, 10. *The Times Digital Archive*, accessed 26 July 2013.

Anon. 'Bela Bartok at Queen's Hall', *The Times* (London), 9 November 1933, 10. *The Times Digital Archive*, accessed 26 July 2013.

Anon. 'Bela Bartok Dies in Hospital Here: Noted Hungarian Composer, Specialist in Music Folklore, Played Own Works at 10', *The New York Times*, 27 September 1945, 21.

Anon. 'Erdély etnikai és felekezeti statisztikája (1850–1992)' ('Transylvania's Ethnic and Denominational Statistics [1850–1992]'), *Varga E. Árpád* <http://varga.adatbank.transindex.ro/?pg=3&action=etnik&id=3625> accessed 18 November 2008.

Anon. 'Folk Music of Rumania from the Collection of Bela Bartok', Folkways Records album FE4419, 1950. Liner Notes <http://media.smithsonianfolkways.org/liner_notes/folkways/FW04419.pdf> accessed 19 January 2014.

Anon. 'HGC to Offer Modern Work: Compositions by Williams, Bartok in Sanders Concert', *The Harvard Crimson* (1943) <http://www.thecrimson.com/article/1943/2/18/hgc-to-offer-modern-work-pbesides/> accessed 10 January 2014.

Anon. 'Holló Gyula', *BANATerra* <http://www.banaterra.eu/magyar/H/hollo_gy.htm> accessed 31 December 2013.

Anon. 'International Festival', *The Times* (London), 21 June 1938, 14. *The Times Digital Archive*, accessed 17 September 2013.

Anon. 'Notes of Musicians Here and Afield: Bela Bartok to Return to the United States', *The New York Times*, 11 August 1940, 106.

Anon. 'Our Correspondent', 'Anti-Jewish Exhibition in Germany', *The Times* (London), 26 May 1938, 18. *The Times Digital Archive*, accessed 6 December 2013.

Anon. 'Purchasing Power of Money in the United States from 1774 to Present', *Measuring Worth* <http://www.measuringworth.com/ppowerus/> accessed 6 December 2013.

Anon. 'The Annual RPI and Average Earnings for Britain, 1209 to Present (New Series)', *Measuring Worth* <http://www.measuringworth.com/datasets/ukearncpi/result2.php> accessed 7 December 2012.

Anon. 'The Immigration Act of 1924' <http://www.upa.pdx.edu/IMS/currentprojects/TAHv3/Content/PDFs/Immigration_Act_1924.pdf> accessed 31 December 2013.

Anon. 'The Music Box', *The Harvard Crimson* (1943) <http://www.thecrimson.com/article/1943/2/12/the-music-box-pbela-bartok-noted/#> accessed 10 January 2014.

Anon. 'Value of the Gilder/Euro'. *International Institute of Social History* <http://www.iisg.nl/hpw/calculate.php> accessed 17 September 2013.

Antcliffe, Herbert. 'Musical Notes from Abroad: Holland'. *The Musical Times* 69, no. 1030 (December 1928), 1134.

Antokoletz, Elliott. *The Music of Béla Bartók: A Study of Tonality and Progression in Twentieth-Century Music*. Berkeley and Los Angeles: University of California Press, 1984.

Ashcroft, Bill, Gareth Griffiths and Helen Tiffin. *The Empire Writes Back: Theory and Practice in Post-Colonial Literatures*. London and New York: Routledge, 1989.

Baedeker, Karl. *Austria-Hungary, Including Dalmatia and Bosnia: Handbook for Travellers*. Leipzig: Karl Baedeker, 1905.

Balázs, Béla. *A vándor énekel – Versek és novellák*, ed. Sándor Radnóti. Budapest: Magyar Helikon, 1975.

Bán, András D. *Hungarian-British Diplomacy, 1938–1941: The Attempt to Maintain Relations*. London: P. Frank Cass Publishers, 2005.

Barati, George. *George Barati: A Life in Music*, interviewed and edited by Randall Jarrell <http://library.ucsc.edu/sites/default/files/userfiles/barati.pdf>, 18–19, accessed 26 October 2013.

Bárdos, Lajos. 'Heptatonia secunda – Egy sájastágos hangredszer Kodály műveiben'. *Magyar Zene* 3–4 (1962–3).

Barenscott, Dorothy. 'Articulating Identity through the Technological Rearticulation of Space: The Hungarian Millennial Exhibition as World's Fair and the Disordering of Fin-de-Siècle Budapest', *Slavic Review* 69, no. 3 (Autumn 2010), 571–90.

*Bartók Béla családi levelei* (*BBcl*). Budapest: Zeneműkiadó, 1981.

*Bartók Béla levelei* (*BBlev*). Budapest: Zeneműkiadó, 1976.

Bartók, Béla. *Bluebeard's Castle*. Full score. English trans. Christopher Hassall. Vienna, London and New York: Universal Edition, nd.

Bartók, Béla. 'Die Volksmusik der Araber von Biskra und Umgebung', *Zeitschrift für Musikwissenschaft* 9 (November 1920), 489–522.

Bartók, Béla. *First Suite*, pocket score. Budapest: Editio Musica Budapest, 1956.

Bartók, Béla. 'Hungarian Folk Songs (Complete Collection)'. Online publication by the Hungarian Academy of Sciences Institute for Musicology <http://db.zti.hu/nza/br_en.asp> accessed 13 September 2012.

Bartók, Béla. 'Parry Collection of Yugoslav Folk Music: Eminent Composer Who Is Working on It, Discusses Its Significance', *The New York Times*, 28 June 1942, x6.

Bartók, Béla. *Rumanian Folk Music, Volume One, Instrumental Melodies*, ed. Benjamin Suchoff. The Hague: Martinus Nijhoff, 1967.

Bartók, Béla. *Rumanian Folk Music, Volume Four, Carols and Christmas Songs (Colinde)*, ed. Benjamin , trans. E. C. Teodorescu. The Hague: Martinus Nijhoff, 1975.

Bartók, Béla. *Rumanian Folk Music, Volume Five, Maramureş County*, ed. Benjamin, trans. E. C. Teodorescu, preface trans. Alan Kriegsman. The Hague: Martinus Nijhoff, 1975.

Bartók, Béla. *Slovenské L'Udové Piesne,* vol. 3, ed. Alica Elscheková and Oskár Elschek. Bratislava: ASCO art and science, 2007.

Bartók, Béla. *The Hungarian Folk Song*. London: Oxford University Press, 1931.

Bartók, Béla. 'The National Temperament in Music', *The Musical Times* 69, no. 1030 (December 1928), 1079.

Bartók, Béla. *Turkish Folk Music from Asia Minor*. Princeton and London: Princeton University Press, 1976.

Bartók, Béla. *Village Scenes*. English trans. Martin Lindsay, new edn., Universal Edition, 1994, rev. Péter Bartók, UE8712.

Bartók, Béla, and Albert B. Lord, *Serbo-Croatian Folk Songs: Texts and Transcriptions of Seventy-Five Folk Songs from the Milman Parry Collection and a Morphology of Serbo-Croatian Folk Melodies*. New York: Columbia University Press; Oxford: Oxford University Press, 1951.

Bartók Jr., Béla. *Apám életének krónikája*. Szombathely: Helikon Kiadó, 2006.

Bartók Jr., Béla. 'Béla Bartók's Diseases', *Studia Musicologica Academiae Scientiarum Hungaricae* 23 (1981), 427–41.

Bartók Jr., Béla. 'The Private Man', in *The Bartók Companion*, ed. Malcolm Gillies. London: Faber and Faber, 1993.

Bartók Jr., Béla, ed. *Bartók Béla családi levelei*. Budapest: Zeneműkiadó, 1981.

Bartók, Peter. *My Father*. Homosassa, FL: Bartók Records, 2002.

Bechert, Paul. 'Musical Notes from Abroad: Vienna'. *The Musical Times* 63, no. 953 (July 1922): 515.

Bellman, Jonathan. *The 'Style hongrois' in the Music of Western Europe*. Boston: Northeastern University Press, 1993.

Berend, Iván Tibor, and György Ránki. *East Central Europe in the Nineteenth and Twentieth Centuries*. Budapest: Akademiai Kiado, 1977.

Bernard, Jonathan W. 'Bartok and Traditional Form Description: Some Issues Arising from the Middle and Late String Quartets', in Dániel Péter Biró and Harald Krebs, eds., *The String Quartets of Béla Bartók: Tradition and Legacy in Analytical Perspective*. New York: Oxford University Press, 2014.

Bettelheim, Bruno. *Uses of Enchantment: The Meaning and Importance of Fairy Tales*. London: Penguin Books, 1978.

Biró, Dániel Péter, and Harald Krebs, eds. *The String Quartets of Béla Bartók: Tradition and Legacy in Analytical Perspective*. New York: Oxford University Press, 2014.

Bődy, Pál. 'The Rumanian-Hungarian Confrontation, 1840–70', in *Transylvania: The Roots of Ethnic Conflict*, eds. John F. Cadzow, Andrew Ludanyi and Louis J. Elteto. Kent, Ohio: The Kent State University Press, 1983. At <http://www.hungarian-history.hu/lib/transy/transy10.htm> accessed 1 February 2009.

Bónis, Ferenc. *Béla Bartók: His Life in Pictures and Documents*, trans. Lili Halápy, rev. Kenneth McRobbie. Budapest: Corvina, 1972; New York: Belwin Mills Publishing Corporation, 1972.

Bónis, Ferenc. '*The Miraculous Mandarin*: The Birth and Vicissitudes of a Masterpiece', in *The Stage Works of Béla Bartók*. Opera Guide 44. Series editor Nicholas John. London: John Calder, 1991.

Bonavia (?), Ferruccio. 'London Concerts: Béla Bartók', *The Musical Times* 70, no. 1034 (April 1929), 51–2.

Bratuž, Damjana. 'On the Shaman's Trail: Béla Bartók's Szabadban (OUTDOORS)', *Ninth International Congress on Musical Signification 'Music, Senses, Body' 'La Musica, i Sensi, il Corpo'*, 19–23 September 2006, Università di Roma Tor Vergata, <http://www.damjanabratuz.ca/bartokiana/abstracts/on_the_ shamans_trail.htm> accessed 8 January 2013.

Brown, Julie. *Bartók and the Grotesque: Studies in Modernity, the Body and Contradiction in Music*. Aldershot: Ashgate, 2007.

Chisholm, Erik. *Béla Bartók* <http://www.erikchisholm.com/writings3.php> accessed 26 October 2013.

Citron, Pierre. *Bartok*. Paris: Éditions du Seuil, 1963.

Clegg, David. 'Das Englische Programm der *Kossuth-Symphonie*', in , vol. 1, ed. Denijs Dille. Budapest: Bartók Archiv, 1964.

Colles, H. C. 'Béla Bartók', *The Times* (London), 18 March 1922, 8. *The Times Digital Archive*, accessed 29 November 2012.

Congdon, Lee. 'The Making of a Hungarian Revolutionary: The Unpublished Diary of Bela Balazs' (sic). *Journal of Contemporary History* 8, no. 3 (1972), 55–74.

Cooper, David. *Béla Bartók: Concerto for Orchestra*. Cambridge Music Handbook. Cambridge: Cambridge University Press, 1996.

Cooper, David. 'Béla Bartók and the Question of Race Purity', in *Musical Constructions of Nationalism: Essays on the History and Ideology of European Musical Culture, 1800–1945*, eds. Harry White and Michael Murphy. Cork: Cork University Press, 2001.

Cooper, David. 'Béla Bartók's *Bluebeard's Castle*: A Musicological Perspective', in *Bluebeard's Legacy: Death and Secrets from Bartók to Hitchcock: New Encounters: Arts, Cultures, Concepts*, ed. V. Anderson and G. Pollock. London: I. B. Tauris, 2009.

Csáth, Géza. 'Bartók Béla és Kodály Zoltán'. *Nyugat* 3, no. 7 (1910) <http://epa.oszk. hu/00000/00022/00053/01450.htm> accessed 9 October 2012.

C.W.D. 'Benny Goodman and Clarinet Go Classical Here', *Daily Boston Globe*, 5 February 1941, 19.

Demény, János, ed. *Béla Bartók Letters (BBL)*. Budapest: Corvina Press, 1971.

Devitte, H. 'The Simple Life at Waidberg: An Extraordinary Colony', *The Advertiser* (Adelaide), Saturday 17 September 1910, 16–24.

D.H. 'London Concerts: Hungarian String Quartet', *The Musical Times* 70, no. 1034 (April 1929), 352.

*Diagnostic and Statistical Manual of Mental Disorders*, Fourth Edition (DSM-IV). Washington, DC: American Psychiatric Association, c. 1994.

Dille, Denijs. 'Bartók, lecteur de Nietzsche et de la Rochefoucauld'. *Studia Musicologica Academiae Scientiarum Hungaricae* 10, no. 3/4 (1968), 209–28.

Dille, Denijs. *Béla Bartók: Regard sur le passé*. Louvain-la-Neuve: Institut Supérieur d'Archéologie et d'Histoire de l'Art, Collège Érasme, 1990.

Dille, Denijs. *Genealogie Sommaire de la Famille Bartok*. Antwerp: Metropolis, 1977.

Dille, Denijs, ed. *Documenta Bartókiana*, 6 vols. Budapest: Akadémiai Kiadó, 1964–81.

Dobszay, László. 'Folksong Classification in Hungary: Some Methodological Conclusions', *Studia Musicologica*, 30, no. 1 (1988), 235–80 (239).

Downes, Olin. 'Dissension Marks Music Festival', *The New York Times*, 2 July 1927, 20.

Downes, Olin. 'New Quartet Gives Novelties', *The New York Times*, 18 March 1931, 33.

Downes, Olin. 'The Kolisch Quartet: Debut in Washington is Outstanding Event of Coolidge Festival', *The New York Times*, 14 April 1935, x5.

Downes, Olin. *The New York Times*. 29 October 1937, 18.

Downes, Olin. 'Bartok is Honored Here', *The New York Times*, 25 April 1940, 27.

Downes, Olin. 'Reiner Conducts Haydn Symphony; Performance of B-Flat Work is Feature of Concert by the Philharmonic; The Bartoks on Programme; Concerto for Two Pianos They Composed Presented in New Form', *The New York Times*, 22 January 1943, 24.

Downes, Olin. 'Rodzinski Directs Berlioz Symphony; Bartok Violin Concerto also Heard – Spivakovsky Soloist with The Philharmonic', *The New York Times*, 15 October 1943, 22.

Downes, Olin. 'Menuhin Thrills Capacity Crowd: Violinist Features New Bela Bartok Sonata in Recital at Carnegie Hall', *The New York Times*, 27 November 1944, 16.

Downes, Olin. 'Bartok Concerto Introduced Here: Boston Symphony, Directed by Koussevitzky, Plays New Work at Carnegie Hall', *The New York Times*, 11 January 1945, 18.

Durgin, Cyrus. 'Music, Symphony Hall, Boston Symphony Orchestra', *Daily Boston Globe*, 2 December 1944, 6.

Durgin, Cyrus. 'Music, Symphony Hall, Boston Symphony Orchestra'. *Daily Boston Globe*, 30 December 1944, 4

Eckhardt, Tibor. 'Proclamation', *The American Hungarian Federation* <http://www.americanhungarian-federation.org/images/AHFHistory/IndependentHungaryProclamation_Eckardt.gif> accessed 9 January 2014.

Elie Jr., Rudolph. 'Symphony Concert', *Boston Herald*, 30 December 1944, np.

Eötvös de Vásárosnamény, József. *The Village Notary: A Romance of Hungarian Life*, trans. Otto Wenckstern. London: Longman, Brown, Green, and Longmans, 1850.

Evans, Edwin. 'London Concerts: Contemporary Music Centre', *The Musical Times* 64, no. 964 (June 1923), 424.

Evans, Edwin. 'London Concerts: Jelly D'Aranyi and Bartók', *The Musical Times* 65, no. 971 (January 1924), 71.

Evans, Edwin. 'London Concerts: Contemporary Music', *The Musical Times* 73, no. 1070 (April 1932), 359.

Fassett, Agatha. *The Naked Face of Genius: Béla Bartók's Last Years*. London: Victor Gollancz Ltd, 1970.

Fitzgerald, Michael. *Autism and Creativity: Is There a Link between Autism in Men and Exceptional Ability?* East Sussex: Brunner-Routledge, 2004.

Fitzgerald, Michael. 'Did Bartok have High Functioning Autism or Asperger's Syndrome?', *Autism – Europe Link* 29 (2000), 21.

Frank, Julia. 'Great Composer Lived Here: Mrs Sageman Remembers the Bartoks', *Adirondack Daily Enterprise*. 18 August 1970 <http://localwiki.net/hsl/Bartok_Cabin> accessed 2 February 2014.

Freud, Sigmund. *On Sexuality: Three Essays on the Theory of Sexuality and Other Works*. The Pelican Freud Library, vol. 7. Harmondsworth: Penguin Books Ltd, 1997.

Fricsay, Ferenc. *Über Mozart und Bartók*. Copenhagen and Frankfurt am Main: Wilhelm Hansen, 1962.

Frigyesi, Judit. 'Béla Bartók and the Concept of Nation and Volk in Modern Hungary', *The Musical Quarterly* 78, no. 2 (Summer 1994), 255–87.

Frigyesi, Judit. *Béla Bartók and Turn-of-the Century Budapest*. Berkeley: University of California Press, 1998.

Garst, Marilyn M. 'How Bartók Performed His Own Compositions', *Tempo* 155 (1985), 15–21.

G.G. 'Goodman Assists in Szigeti Recital: Band Leader Carries Clarinet Part with the Violinist in Bartok Rhapsody', *The New York Times*, 10 January 1939, 23.

Gillies, Malcolm. *Bartók Remembered*. London: Faber and Faber, 1990.

Gillies, Malcolm. *Bartók in Britain: A Guided Tour*. Oxford: Clarendon Press, 1989.

Gillies, Malcolm. 'Stylistic Integrity and Influence in Bartók's Works: The Case of Szymanowski', *International Journal of Musicology* 1 (1992), 139–60.

Gillies, Malcolm, ed. *The Bartók Companion*. London: Faber and Faber, 1993.

Goddard, Scott. 'Review of *Hungarian Folk Music* by Bela Bartók, trans. M. D. Calvocoressi', *Music and Letters* 12, no. 4 (1931), 419

Gombocz, Adrienne, and László Somfai. 'Bartóks Briefe an Calvocoressi (1914–1930)', *Studia Musicologica Academiae Scientiarum Hungaricae* 24, nos. 1–2 (1982), 199–231.

Gombocz, Adrienne, and László Vikárius. 'Twenty-Five Bartók Letters to the Arányi Sisters, Wilhelmine Creel and Other Correspondents. Recently Acquired Autograph Letters in the Bartók Archives', *Studia Musicologica Academiae Scientiarum Hungaricae* 43, nos. 1–2 (2002), 151–204.

Gombosi, Otto. 'The Art of the Hungarian Composer Bartok: An Estimate of the Music of a Contemporary who is on a Visit Here', *The New York Times*, 5 May 1940, 160.

Harmans, W. 'Musical Notes from Abroad: Amsterdam', *The Musical Times* 64, no. 964 (June 1923), 433.

Hoensch, Jürg. *A History of Modern Hungary, 1867–1986*. London and New York: Longman, 1988.

Hooker, Lynn. 'Modernism on the Periphery: Béla Bartók and the New Hungarian Music Society of 1911–1912', *Musical Quarterly* 88, no. 2 (Summer 2005), 274–319.

Hopkins, Charles. 'Thomán, István'. *Grove Music Online, Oxford Music Online* <http://0-www.oxford-musiconline.com.wam.leeds.ac.uk/subscriber/article/grove/music/27855> accessed 9 July 2010.

Howes, Frank. 'Editorial Notes', *Journal of the Folk-Song Society* 8, no. 35 (1931), 304.

Jacobs, Melville. 'Survey of Pacific Northwest Anthropological Research, 1930–1940'. *Pacific Northwest Quarterly* 32, no. 1 (1941): 79–106.

James, Ioan. *Asperger's Syndrome and High Achievement: Some Very Remarkable People*. London and Philadelphia: Jessica Kingsley Publishers, 2006.

Jeszenszky, Géza. 'Hungary Through World War I and the End of the Dual Monarchy', in *A History of Hungary*, eds. Peter F. Sugar, Petér Hanák and Tibor Frank. New York: John Wiley & Sons, 1994.

John, Nicholas, series editor. *The Stage Works of Béla Bartók*, Opera Guide 44. London: John Calder, 1991.

Jones, Robert T. 'From Bela to Ditta'. *The New York Times*. 11 May 1969, D29.

Juhász, Vilmos. *Bartók's Years in America*. Washington, DC: Occidental Press, 2006.

Kárpáti, János. *Bartók's Chamber Music*. New York: Pendragon Press, 1994.

Kárpati, János. 'Early String Quartets', in *The Bartók Companion*, ed. Malcolm Gillies. London: Faber and Faber, 1993.

Kecskeméti, Paul. *Meaning, Communication and Value*. Chicago: The University of Chicago Press, 1952.

Kenneson, Claude. *Székely and Bartók: The Story of a Friendship*. New York: Amadeus Press, 1994.

Kiddle, Henry, and Alexander J. Schem, eds., *The Year-Book of Education for 1878*. New York: E. Steiger; London: Sampson Low & Company, 1878.

Konrád, Miklós. 'Jews and Politics in Hungary in the Dualist Era, 1867–1914', *East European Jewish Affairs* 39, no. 2 (2009), 167–86.

Koussevitzky, Serge. 'Justice to Composers: Koussevitzky Speaks for Need of Support for Those Who Create', *The New York Times*, 16 May 1943, x5.

Kroó, György. *A Guide to Bartók*. Budapest: Corvina Press, 1974.

Kroó, György. 'Duke Bluebeard's Castle'. *Studia Musicologica Academiae Scientarum Hungaricae* 1, parts 3/4 (1961), 251–340.

Kun, Béla. *Revolutionary Essays*. London: BSP, nd [1919?].

Laki, Peter. 'The Gallows and the Altar: Poetic Criticism and Critical Poetry about Bartók in Hungary', in *Bartók and His World*, ed. Peter Laki. Princeton: Princeton University Press, 1995.

Laki, Peter. 'Violin works and the Viola Concerto', in *The Cambridge Companion to Bartók*, ed. Amanda Bayley. Cambridge: Cambridge University Press, 2001.

Laki, Peter, ed. *Bartók and His World*. Princeton: Princeton University Press, 1995.

Lampert, Vera. 'Bartók at Harvard University as Witnessed in Unpublished Archival Documents', *Studia Musicologica Academiae Scientarum Hungaricae* 35, 1/3 (1993–4), 113–54.

Lampert, Vera. 'Bartók's Music on Record: An Index of Popularity', *Studia Musicologica* 36, nos. 3–4 (1995), 393–412.

Lampert, Vera. *Népzene Bartók műveiben – A feldolgozott dallamok forrásjegyzéke*. Budapest: Helikon Kiadó, 2005.

Leafstedt, Carl. 'Asheville, Winter of 1943–44: Béla Bartók and North Carolina', *The Musical Quarterly* 87, no. 2 (summer 2004), 219–58.

Leafstedt, Carl. *Inside Bluebeard's Castle: Music and Drama in Béla Bartók's Opera*. New York and Oxford: Oxford University Press, 1999.

Leafstedt, Carl. 'Rediscovering Victor Bator, Founder of the New York Bartók Archives', *Studia Musicologica* 53, nos. 1–3 (2012), 349–72.

Leibowitz, René. 'Bela Bartok: Or the Possibility of Compromise in Contemporary Music', *Transition Forty-Eight* 3 (1948), 92–122.

Leibowitz, René. 'Béla Bartók, ou la possibilité du compromis dans la musique contemporaine', *Les Temps modernes* 3, no. 25 (October 1947), 705–34.

Lenoir, Yves. *Folklore et transcendance dans l'oeuvre américaine de Béla Bartók (1940–1945)*. Louvain-la-Neuve: Institut Supérieur d'Archéologie et d'Histoire de l'Art Collège Érasme, 1986.

Lesznai, Lajos. *Bartók*, trans. Percy M. Young. London: J. M. Dent and Sons, Ltd, 1973.

Lewando, Ralph. 'City Symphony, Composer Give Brilliant Performance: Bela Bartok, Noted Hungarian, is Soloist for His Own Ultra-Modern Music', *The Pittsburgh Press*, 25 January 1941, 7.

Lukacs, John. *Budapest 1900: A Historical Picture of a City and its Culture*. New York: Grove Press, 1988.

'M'. 'London Concerts: BBC Symphony Concerts', *The Musical Times* 71, no. 1045 (March 1930), 259.

Maurice, Donald. *Bartók's Viola Concerto: The Remarkable Story of His Swansong*. Oxford: Oxford University Press, 2004.

McCartney, Carlile Aylmer. *Hungary: A Short History*. Edinburgh: Edinburgh University Press, 1962.

Menuhin, Yehudi. *Unfinished Journey*. London: Macdonald and Jane's, 1976.

M.M.S. 'London Concerts: Béla Bartók', *The Musical Times* 78, no. 1129 (March 1937), 267.

Moreux, Serge. *Béla Bartók*, trans. G. S. Fraser and Erik de Mauny. London: The Harvill Press, 1953.

Móricz, Klára. 'New Aspects of the Genesis of Béla Bartók's "Concerto for Orchestra": Concepts of "Finality" and "Intention"', *Studia Musicologica Academiae Scientarum Hungaricae* 35, no. 1/3 (1993–4), 181–219.

Móricz, Klára. 'Operating on a Fetus: Sketch Studies and their Relevance to the Interpretation of the Finale of Bartók's *Concerto for Orchestra*', *Studia Musicologica* 35, nos. 3–4 (1995), 461–76.

Nietzsche, Friedrich. *Human, All Too Human: A Book For Free Spirits*, trans. Alexander Harvey. Chicago: Charles H. Kerr & Company, 1908.

Nyerges, Anton N. (trans. and introduction). *Poems of Endre Ady*. Buffalo, NY: Hungarian Cultural Foundation, 1969.

Paddison, Max. *Adorno's Aesthetics of Music*. Cambridge: Cambridge University Press, 1993.

Parker, Sylvia. 'A Riverton Retreat: Royal Charter to State Forest', *Vermont Historical Society* (2010) <http://vermonthistory.org/journal/78/VHS780105_95-111.pdf> accessed 27 December, 2013.

Pearson, Raymond. *The Longman Companion to European Nationalism: 1789–1920*. Harlow: Longman, 1994.

Pegolotti, James A. *Deems Taylor: A Biography*. Boston: Northeastern University Press, 2003.

Phillips, Charles D. F. *Materia Medica and Therapeutics: Inorganic Substances*. New York: William Wood & Company, 1882.

Pollatsek, László. 'Béla Bartók and His Work: On the Occasion of His Fiftieth Birthday (Concluded)', *The Musical Times* 72, no. 1062 (1931), 699.

Pound, Ezra. 'Ligurian View of a Venetian Festival', *Music and Letters* 18, no. 1 (1937), 36–41.

Pound, Ezra. *Guide to Kulchur*. London: Faber & Faber, 1938.

Racy, Ali Jihad. 'Historical Worldviews of Early Ethnomusicologists: An East-West Encounter in Cairo, 1932', in *Ethnomusicology and Modern Music History*, ed. Stephen Blum, Philip Bohlman and Daniel Neuman. Chicago: University of Illinois Press, 1993.

R H. 'Florence Music Convention', *The New York Times*, 11 June 1933, x4.

Richards, Julie A. 'The Piano Quintet of Béla Bartók: Context, Analysis and Revisions'. DMA Dissertation. University of Houston, 2009.

Rosenberg, Donald. *The Cleveland Orchestra Story*. Cleveland: Gray & Company, 2000.

Rosenfeld, Paul. 'Bartok Soloist at Symphony Concert', *Daily Boston Globe*, 18 February 1928, 5.

Sármány-Parsons, Ilona. 'Hungarian Art and Architecture, 1896–1914', in *A Golden Age: Art and Society in Hungary, 1896–1914*, ed. G. Éry and Z. Jobbágyi. Budapest, London and Miami: Corvina, Barbican Art Gallery, Center for the Fine Arts, 1990.

Schmidt, Carl B. *Entrancing Muse: A Documented Biography of Francis Poulenc*. Hillsdale, NY: Pendragon Press 2001.

Schneider, David E. *Bartók, Hungary and the Renewal of Tradition: Case Studies in the Intersection of Modernity and Nationality*. Berkeley and Los Angeles: University of California Press, 2006.

Scholes, Percy, ed. *The Mirror of Music, 1844–1944: A Century of Musical Life in Britain as Reflected in the Pages of the Musical Times*. London: Novello & Co. Ltd and Oxford University Press, 1947.

Slonimsky, Nicolas. *Lexicon of Musical Invective: Critical Assaults on Composers Since Beethoven's Time*, 2nd edn. Seattle and London: University of Washington Press, 1969.

Smith, Barry, ed. *The Complete Letters of Peter Warlock*. Woodbridge: The Boydell Press, 2005.

Smith, Warren Story. 'Symphony Concert', *Boston Post*, 2 December 1944, np.

Somfai, László. 'Bartók Béla: 2. Hegedű-zongora szonáta'. *A hét zeneműve* (1977) <http://www.mr3-bartok.hu/component/option,com_alphacontent/section,5/cat,18/task,view/id,206/Itemid,52/> accessed 5 December 2012.

Somfai, László. *Béla Bartók: Composition, Concepts, and Autograph Sources*. Berkeley and Los Angeles: University of California Press, 1996.

Somfai, László. 'The "Piano Year" of 1926', in *The Bartók Companion*, ed. Malcolm Gillies. London: Faber and Faber, 1993.

Somfai, László, ed. *Documenta Bartókiana*, vol. 5. Budapest: Akadémiai Kiadó, 1977.

Stafford, William C. *A History of Music*. Edinburgh: Constable and Company, 1830; reprinted by the Boethius Press (New York), 1986.

Steed, H. Wickham, Walter Alison Phillips, and David Hannay. 'A Short History of Austria-Hungary and Poland', in *Encyclopaedia Britannica*, 11th Edition. London: The Encyclopaedia Britannica Company, Ltd, 1914.

Steinfirst, Donald. 'Bartok Work is Presented by Symphony', *Pittsburgh Post-Gazette*, 25 January 1941, 5.

Straus, Noel. 'Ovation to Bartok at Szigeti Recital', *The New York Times*, 22 April 1940, 18.

Straus, Noel. 'Bela Bartok Work Introduced Here', *The New York Times*, 29 January 1941, 21.

Suchoff, Benjamin. 'Bartók's Folk Music Publication', *Ethnomusicology* 16, no. 2 (1971), 220–30.

Suchoff, Benjamin. 'Bartók's Odyssey in Slovak Folk Music', in *Bartók Perspectives: Man, Composer and Ethnomusicologist*, ed. Elliott Antokoletz, Victoria Fischer and Benjamin Suchoff. Oxford: Oxford University Press, 2000.

Suchoff, Benjamin. *Béla Bartók: Life and Work*. Lanham, MD: Scarecrow Press, 2001.

Suchoff, Benjamin. 'Fusion of National Styles', in *The Bartók Companion*, ed. Malcolm Gillies. London: Faber and Faber, 1993.

Suchoff, Benjamin. 'Structure and Concept in Bartók's Sixth Quartet', *Tempo* 83 (Winter 1967-8), 2–11.

Suchoff, Benjamin, ed. *Béla Bartók Essays* (*BBE*). Lincoln, NE: University of Nebraska Press, 1992.

Suchoff, Benjamin, ed. *Béla Bartók Studies in Ethnomusicology*. Lincoln, NE, and London: University of Nebraska Press, 1997.

Szabolcsi, Bence. *A Concise History of Hungarian Music*. Budapest: Corvina, 1964.

Szász, Zoltán. 'Political Life and the Nationality Question in the Era of Dualism (1867–1918)', in *History of Transylvania*, vol. 3, ed. Zoltán Szász. New York: Columbia University Press, 2002 <http://mek. oszk.hu/03400/03407/html/431.html> accessed 9 October 2012.

'Szőllős'. *Kislexikon* <http://www.kislexikon.hu/szollos.html> accessed 26 February 2010.

Tallián, Tibor. *Béla Bartók: The Man and His Work*, trans. Gyula Gulyás, rev. Paul Merrick. Budapest: Corvina, 1981.

Taubman, Howard. 'Bela Bartok Plays Own Compositions', *The New York Times*, 14 April 1940, 44.

Taubman, Howard. 'Bartok Quartet Heard in Premiere', *The New York Times*, 21 January 1941, 18.

Taylor, Deems. *The New York Times*, 27 September 1945, 21.

Thomán, István. *The Technique of Piano Playing: Fundamental Exercises for the Mastery of Even and Virtuosic Playing* (*A zongorázás technikája*). Budapest: Editio Musica, 1982.

Thomson, David. *Europe Since Napoleon*. Harmondsworth: Penguin Books Ltd, 1970.

Tryon, Winthrop P. 'Dr Koussevitzky to Present Work at Symphony Concerts', *The Christian Science Monitor*, 30 December 1944.

Twain, Mark. 'Second Preface, in Three Parts: Paragraph 6', in *Autobiography of Mark Twain*, vol. 1 (2010,2008)<http://www.marktwainproject.org/xtf/view?docId=works/MTDP10362.xml;style=work;brand—tp;chunk.id=d1e9128#d1e9149> accessed 4 January 2014.

*Ugocsa*, 8 May 1892.

Ujfalussy, Jozsef. *Béla Bartók*. Budapest: Corvina, 1971.

Vambéry, Arminius. *Hungary in Ancient, Mediaeval, and Modern Times*. London: T. Fisher Unwin, 1886.

Várdy, Steven Béla. 'Hungarian Americans during World War II: Their Role in Defending Hungary's Interests', in *Ideology, Politics and Diplomacy in East Central Europe*, ed. M. B. B. Biskupski. Rochester, NY: University of Rochester Press, 2003.

Vasvári, Louise O. 'A Comparative Approach to European Folk Poetry and the Erotic Wedding Motif'. *CLCWeb: Comparative Literature and Culture* 1, no. 4 (1999) <http://docs.lib.purdue.edu/clcweb/vol1/iss4/1>, accessed 4 March 2012.

Vikárius, László. 'Béla Bartók's "Cantata Profana" (1930): A Reading of the Sources', *Studia Musicologica Academiae Scientarum Hungaricae* 35, no. 1 (1993–4), 249–301.

Vörös, Alexander. 'Agricultural Education in Hungary from Times Past Down to the Present', in *Agricultural Industry and Education in Hungary: Being an Account of the Visit of the Essex Farmers' Party to Hungary in May and June, 1902*, compiled by T. S. Dymond. Chelmsford: County Technical Laboratories, 1902.

Walker, Alan. 'Ernst von Dohnányi (1877–1960): A Tribute', in *Perspectives on Ernst von Dohnányi*, ed. James A. Grymes. Lanham, MD: Scarecrow Press, 2005.

Weiss, Emila, and Orsolya Szeibert. 'Grounds for Divorce and Maintenance Between Former Spouses: Hungary' <http://ceflonline.net/wp-content/uploads/Hungary-Divorce.pdf> accessed 12 December 2012.

Weiss-Aigner, Günter. 'The "Lost" Violin Concerto', in *The Bartók Companion*, ed. Malcolm Gillies. London: Faber and Faber, 1993.

Weiss-Aigner, Günter. 'Youthful Orchestral Works', in *The Bartók Companion*, ed. Malcolm Gillies. London: Faber and Faber, 1993.

Weiss-Aigner, Günter. 'Youthful Piano Works', in *The Bartók Companion*, ed. Malcolm Gillies. London: Faber and Faber, 1993.

Weissmann, Adolf. 'Musical Notes from Abroad: Germany', *The Musical Times* 64, no. 961 (March 1923), 211.

Wilson, Paul. 'Violin Sonatas', in *The Bartók Companion*, ed. Malcolm Gillies. London: Faber and Faber, 1993.

Ziegler, Márta. 'Bartók's Reise nach Biskra', *Documenta Bartókiana*, vol. 2, ed. Denijs Dille. Budapest: Akadémiai Kiadó, 1965.

Zsuffa, Joseph. *Béla Balázs, the Man and the Artist*. Berkeley, Los Angeles and London: University of California Press, 1987.

Zweig, Stefan. *The World of Yesterday*. London, Toronto, Melbourne and Sydney: Cassell and Company Ltd, 1943.

# Index

Page numbers in *italics* refer to figures and tables. Musical works are listed under composers; other works are listed by title.

Aachen 239
Abendroth, Hermann 227
Aberystwyth University 179, 182
Ábrányi, Emil 173
Abrudbánya (Abrud) 106, 107
Academia Română, Bucharest 107, 127
Accademia Nazionale di Santa Cecilia, Rome 239
acoustic scale 119, 133, 138, 142, 147, 148–9, 218, 223, *248*, 250, 294, 306, 312, 354, 363, 366
The Active Society for the Propagation of Contemporary Music 260, 264
Adana 283
Adenauer, Konrad 219
Adler, Guido 378
Adorno, Theodor 44
Ady, Endre 143–8, 167, 342
　Blood and Gold (*Vér és arany*) (1907) 99, 144, 147
　On Elijah's Chariot (*Az Illés szekerén*) (1908) 99, 122
　Longing for Love (1909) 144
　New Poems (*Új versek*) (1906) 99, 111
　'Régi énekek ekhója' ('Echo of Old Songs') 118
　see also Bartók, Béla: works: Five Songs
Aeolian/Dorian mode 205
Aeolian Hall, London 182, 187, 201
Aeolian mode 40, 72, 85, 106, 134, 138, 145, *164*, 177, 219, 247, 284, 312, 346
aesthetics xiii–xiv, 27, 99, 254, 296
AKM (performing rights society) 299
Albanian folk music 282
Albrecht, Sándor 12, 15, 246, 261, 262, 322
*Algemeen Handelsblad* (newspaper) 272
Algeria 122, 128–30, 196, 350
Algerian folk music xiv, 128–30, 288
Alice M. Ditson Foundation 329

Alkan, Charles-Valentin 118–19
　*Twelve Etudes in Major Keys* op. 35 118
all interval tetrachords 228, 229
alpine horns 107, 253, 353, *354–5*
Altdörfer, Keresztély 9
American Ballet Theatre 357
American Society of Composers, Authors and Publishers *see* ASCAP
Amherst College, Massachusetts 333
Amsterdam 194, 207, 234–5, 272, 285
anapaest-dactyl rhythm 251
anapaest rhythm 32, 47, 101, 228, 302, 305, 306, 312, 350
*Anbruch* (journal) 180
Andreae, Volkmar 103–4
Anger, near Graz 180
Ankara 283
Anklam 63
'Anna Molnár' (ballad) 110
Anschluss 298, 299, 309
Antcliffe, Herbert 235
anti-Semitism 2, 172, 173, 299, 310, 336
Antokoletz, Elliott 175
Appalachians, USA 76, 96
'Arab Folk Music from the Biskra District' (Bartók) 150, 157, 193
Arabic music 25, 28, 150, *165*, 193, 196, 197, 208, 213, 215, 232, 253, 254, 261, 279, 288, 293, 347, 358
Arad 23, 122, 154, 220, 395n. 8
Arad, Atar 372
Arányi, Adila d' 21, 178, 179–80, 189, 260
Arányi, Hortense Emilia d' (Titi) 180, 181, 188
Arányi, Jelly d' 179, 180, 181, 182, 187, 188, 189, 190, 194–5, 201, 225, 250
Ardeleana (Romanian tune) 138, 212, 371, 372
Argentière 88
Aristophanes, *Lysistrata* 172

ArkivMusic 380–1
Arnhem 207
Arolla 245, 246
Arts Theatre Club, London 238, 243
ASCAP (American Society of Composers,
    Authors and Publishers) 342, 344,
    355, 356, 364, 373
Ashcroft, Bill 27, 43
Asheville, North Carolina 356–7, 360, 367
Asperger syndrome 12–13, 188
atonality 148, 170–1, 203, 221, 227–8, 272,
    380
Auden, W. H. 334
Aug, Wilma 219
Auric, Georges 188
Auróra (journal) 108
Ausgleich ('compromise') (1867) 1–2, 22
Austria 3, 7, 257, 287
Austria-Hungary
    fall of 166, 167
    in the First World War 136, 151–2
Austrian national anthem ('Gott erhalte') 31,
    33, 34, 45, 53, 54
Austro-American Conservatory of Music 258
Autism Spectrum Disorders 12–13, 188, 376
axis theory 29, 55–6, 86, 280, 293, 346, 366
Az Est (newspaper) 298

Babits, Mihály 99
Bacău 136
Bach, Johann Sebastian
    influence on Bartók 20, 214, 218, 247
    works 207, 218, 326, 335, 358
        Chromatic Fantasy and Fugue 61, 69, 71
        St Matthew Passion 114, 247, 247
        The Well-Tempered Clavier 11, 218
Backhaus, Wilhelm 57
Baden Baden 221
Baedeker guides 75, 128
bagpipes 66, 117, 127, 138, 162, 212, 214, 260,
    368, 372
Balázs, Béla 67, 98, 99
    on Bartók 67, 121
    A fából faragott királyfi (The Wooden Prince)
        131–2, 153, 154
    A kékszakállú herceg vára (Duke Bluebeard's
        Castle) 109–12, 115, 162
    'Nocturne' 67
    political activity 167, 169, 172
    A vándor énekel (The Wanderer Sings) 82
Baldwin Piano Company 220, 334
Balinese Ceremonial Music (McPhee) 333
Balinese Tembung mode 334
Balkan folk music 268, 282
Ballard, Arthur C. 331
Baller, Adolph 356
Ballets Russes 133
Ballo, Ivan 262
Balog, János 232
Balogh, Ernő 220, 221, 260, 324, 327, 336, 342
Bánát region 1, 107, 122, 127, 136, 138, 139
Bánffy, Count 153

Bánffy-Hunyad (Huedin) 75
Baník, Anton 261
Baranyai, Gyula 67
Barati, George (György Braunstein) 263
Barbirolli, John 285
Barcelona 65, 220, 255, 315
Bárd Ferenc és Fia (publisher) 27
Bárdos, Lajos 148, 368
Baré, Emil 132
Barenscott, Dorothy 15
Barkaszó (Barkaszova, Ukraine) 122
Baroque music 214, 215, 218, 220, 242–3, 247,
    248, 251, 260, 312, 346, 350, 358, 368
Bartók, origins of name 3
Bartók, Béla
    collections
        'Arab Folk Music from the Biskra District'
            150, 157, 193
        Cântece poporale române şti din comitatul
            Bihor (Ungaria) (Romanian Folksongs
            from the Bihor District) (1913) 107,
            127–8, 130, 135–6
        The Hungarian Folk Song (A magyar népdal)
            39, 57, 88, 202, 205, 208, 239–43, 244,
            245, 255–6, 281, 320, 368
        Melodien der Rumänischen Colinde
            (Weihnachtslieder) 245–6, 273–4, 282
        Rumanian Folk Music 127, 138–9, 185, 212,
            217, 251, 254, 274, 338, 351, 357, 360,
            372, 373
        Serbo-Croatian Folk Songs (with Lord) 347,
            348, 349, 350, 360
        Slovenské Ľudové Piesne 262, 369
        Turkish Folk Music from Asia Minor 284,
            342, 373
    correspondence
        with Annie Müller-Widmann 285, 287, 298,
            299, 300, 308, 323, 326, 335
        with Ditta (second wife) 207, 237, 238, 239
        with Etelka Freund 76, 88, 89, 94, 95, 96,
            106, 115
        with Frederick Delius 69, 104, 106, 109, 126
        with Ion (János) Buşiţia 136, 144, 160–1,
            163, 168, 180, 205, 258, 259, 283
        with Irmy Jurkovics 58–60
        with István Thomán 36, 45, 61–2, 65, 89, 95
        with Márta (first wife) 93–4, 97, 107, 120,
            122, 153, 163, 180
        with mother 10, 20, 27, 29, 29–30, 33–4, 36,
            56, 58, 60–1, 64, 65, 66, 74, 75, 81–2,
            95, 102, 127, 168, 179, 180, 187, 194,
            200, 219, 225, 237–8, 257, 258, 276, 285
        with sister 42, 49–50, 52, 65, 102, 169, 258
        with son Béla 276, 296, 311, 328, 330, 331,
            332
        with son Péter 328, 353, 357, 360–1, 361,
            362, 363, 364
        with Stefi Geyer 76, 77–9, 95
    education 9–11, 12, 14–21, 27, 29, 152
    employment 271–2
        at Columbia University 329, 330, 331, 334,
            338

at Harvard University 338, 340–1, 342, 365
at the Hungarian Academy of Sciences 266,
    276–7, 297
at the Liszt Academy 74, 96, 104, 172, 201,
    221, 258, 266
at the University of Washington (proposed)
    330–1
folk music
    arrangements *see* works
    change in approach 43–4
    collecting of 57, 65–6, 74–5, 75–7, 88–9,
        94–6, 100, 102, 106–7, 110, 117, 122,
        127–30, 135–6, 137, 139–40, 152, 154,
        160, 161, 163, 175, 203, 232, 240, 244,
        245, 261–2, 266, 283, 320, 346, 368,
        378–9
    Székely ballads in *Ethnographia* 82–3
    views on 8, 42, 44, 59, 69, 76–7, 82, 95, 104,
        123, 161, 174–5, 179, 180, 185, 203–4,
        261, 264, 272, 277, 284, 337–8, 348
    *see also* Bartók, Bela: collections; folk music:
        methodology for collecting
honours 65, 205, 233, 250, 259, 262,
    275, 327
interview, 'The National Temperament in
    Music', *The Musical Times* 235–6
lectures 326, 331, 340–1
    Columbia University (1941 or 1942) 150
    Harvard (1943) 26
    'Liszt Ferenc/Liszt Problems', Hungarian
        Academy of Sciences (1936) 276–7
    'Népzenénk és a szomszéd népek népzenéje'
        ('Hungarian Folk Music and the Folk
        Music of Neighbouring Peoples')
        (1934) 265
    'The Relation between Contemporary
        Hungarian Art Music and Folk Music',
        Columbia University 258
    'Some problems of folk music research in
        East Europe', Harvard (1940) 324
    Stanford University (1941) 333
    in Turkey 283
life
    appearance 5, 121, 226, 323
    attachments: Adila Arányi 21, 180; Ditta
        Pásztory 199; Felicitás Fábián 18, 20,
        38, 62; Jelly d'Arányi 188; Jurkovics
        sisters 38–9; Klára Gombossy 139–41,
        203; Márta Ziegler 93; Stefi Geyer 74,
        77–9, 81, 82, 83, 87, 92
    attitude towards alcohol 118
    background 376
    birth 7
    childhood development 8
    clothing 33, 66
    death 372–3
    dieting 129, 163
    emigration to America 299–300, 309,
        310–11, 326, 326–7, 328, 332, 365
    at fifty 256
    final days 372–3
    financial situation 180, 195, 201, 220–1,

309, 329, 330, 331, 334, 340, 341–2,
    343, 355, 361, 363, 364
first flight 276
during the First World War 136–7
illnesses 8, 10, 15, 17–18, 19, 42, 95, 109,
    129, 166, 255, 261, 283, 322, 326, 331,
    333, 335, 338, 341–4, 353, 355, 356–7,
    360, 363–4, 372–3
love of collecting 12, 121, 128
love of walking and climbing 106, 120, 239,
    258, 265–6
marriage to Márta Ziegler
    courtship and wedding 93, 94, 96
    birth of Béla 94
    breakdown and divorce 140, 188,
        199–200
memorial plaque 255
not in 'Degenerate Music' exhibition 310
nudism 120–1
personality 8, 12–13, 42, 44, 58, 67, 121,
    226, 246, 263, 264, 272, 273, 334–5,
    340, 344, 361, 364, 373, 375–6
political activity 167, 169, 172, 173, 174–5,
    257, 336–7
political views 287, 297–8, 299, 303, 308,
    310
refusal to perform in Germany 262
relationship with Kodály 56–7, 62
relationship with mother 9, 78, 322–3
religion 12, 42, 60, 77–8, 114, 151, 367
as a smoker 364
at thirty 96–7
title 6
wedding with Ditta Pásztory 200
withdrawal from public life 122–3, 128, 143,
    152
as musician
    as accompanist xiv–xv, 58, 64, 116, 161, 194,
        244, 251, 259, 272, 273, 277, 286, 322,
        324–5, 330
    artistic block 207
    on board of UMZE 115
    cancellation of concerts 357
    commission fees 296–7, 300, 363, 365
    competitions 57, 121–2
    composition studies 14, 16–17, 29
    as conductor 89
    early abilities 9
    first public appearance 10
    harmony studies 12
    as own agent 63
    interest in jazz 258, 288
    orchestration studies 11
    as solo pianist xiv–xv, 10, 11, 16, 19–20,
        34, 36, 38–9, 41, 50–1, 56, 58, 61, 63,
        68, 69, 74, 109, 116, 168, 170, 182, 194,
        201, 220, 224–5, 225, 226, 227, 237–8,
        254–5, 258, 259–60, 262, 263, 265, 272,
        275, 276, 283, 285–6, 286, 299, 308,
        311, 322, 324–5, 326, 328, 333, 336
    piano duo recitals with Ditta 288, 298, 311,
        322, 326, 330, 331, 333, 334, 339

Bartók, Béla: as musician (*cont.*)
    piano studies 9, 10, 11, 12, 14, 15–16, 20, 29
    piano teaching 74, 93, 152–3, 180, 199, 220,
        328
    status as composer 380–1
    status as performer 379
    theoretical contribution xiv, 25
    radio broadcasts 220, 227, 238, 259, 265, 272,
        284, 285, 286, 299, 309, 324
    sketchbooks 345, 357, 358, 359
        Black Pocket-Book 76, 79, 80, 89–90, 104,
            154, 163
    style
        key points 28, 36, 41, 47–8, 87, 106, 112,
            150, 190, 259, 379–80
        orchestration 29, 32
        use of string techniques 123, 135, 184, 197,
            222, 224, 231, 267, 268–9, 301, 306
    views on
        abroad 34, 58, 64, 65, 88, 95, 181–2, 237,
            260, 276, 328, 360–1, 365
        art 58
        atonality 170, 272
        Claude Debussy 105, 179
        conducting himself 89
        Delius 108–9
        Erik Satie 188
        folk music *see* Bartók, Béla: folk music
        Franz Liszt 41
        Gypsy music 108
        his compositional style 72, 84, 137, 150
        father 7
        own works 52, 56, 69, 72, 90, 162, 196, 200,
            251, 252, 262, 286, 287, 345, 361
        own piano playing 16, 68
        own piano teaching 104
        Hungarians/Hungarian music 59, 77, 82, 106
        Kodály 57, 103
        lack of performances 339
        having a life partner 61
        Menuhin 356
        music 78, 93–4
        the Nazis 287
        opinion formers in Hungary 122–3
        philosophy 58, 59–60, 61, 255
        popular music 351–2
        religion 60, 77–8
        Richard Strauss 20–1, 39, 51
        Schoenberg 179
        Shostakovich 352
        society 161, 163, 187
        Stravinsky 179
        suicide 78
        Székely 190
        Thomán 15, 16
        tonality 304
        Wagner 39
        war 308, 312, 364, 365
        women's rights 50, 61
    works 38, 57, 298
        *Allegro barbaro* (1911) 118–20, 128, 149,
            168, 207, 208, 238, 260

Andante con Variazioni (1894) 11
Budapest gymnastics competition (*A
    budapesti tornaverseny*) (1890) 9
*Cantata profana. A kilenc csodaszarvas*
    (*Cantata Profana. The Nine Enchanted
    Stags*) (1930) 138, 245–50, 247, 249,
    265, 266, 320, 343
Changing piece (*Változó darab*) (1890) 9
childhood 9, 11
Concerto for Orchestra (1943) 18, 26, 44,
    47, 52, 53, 70, 71, 73, 248–9, 271, 305,
    307, 343, 345–55, 347, 349, 351, 354–5,
    361–3, 371, 380, 381
Concerto for Two Pianos and Orchestra
    (1940) 339
*Contrasts* (*Kontrasztok*) (1938) 288, 300–3,
    302, 318, 330, 336, 366
The Course of the Danube (*A Duna folyása*)
    (1891) 10, 11
Dance Suite (*Táncszvit*) (1923, 1925) 195–9,
    197, 200–1, 207, 225
Divertimento (1939) 312–15, 313, 326,
    329–30
Drei Klavierstücke (1898) 13–14, 17
*Duke Bluebeard's Castle* (*A kékszakállú
    herceg vára*) (1911 rev. 1912 & 1917)
    20, 105, 109, 112–15, 112, 114, 121–2,
    131, 133, 141, 142, 162, 188, 240, 346
Eight Hungarian Folk Songs (*Nyolc magyar
    népdal*) (1907, 1917) 160
Eight Improvisations on Hungarian Peasant
    Songs (*Improvizációk magyar
    parasztdalokra*) (1920) 175–8, 176, 182
'Est' ('Evening') (1903) 23, 24, 25–6, 27, 62
Fifteen Hungarian Peasant Songs (*Tizenöt
    magyar parasztdal*) (1914–18) 161–2
First Sonatina (1890) 9
*The First Term at the Piano* (*Kezdők
    zongoramuzsikája*) (with Reschofsky)
    (1913) 137
Five Hungarian Folk Songs
    (*Magyar népdalok*) (1933) 244, 263–4,
    299
Five Songs (*Öt dal*), E. Ady op. 16 (1916)
    143–8, 155, 159, 169–70, 182, 183–4,
    195, 238
Five Songs (*Öt dal*) op. 15 (1916) 135,
    140–3, 141, 143, 155, 182
'For Children' (*Gyermekeknek*) (1908–9) 89,
    137, 178
Forty-Four Duos (*Negyvennégy duó*), for
    two violins (1931–2) 254, 259, 299
Four Dirges (*Négy siratóének*) op. 9a
    (c.1909–10) 104–5
Four Hungarian Folk Songs (*Magyar
    népdalok*) (1930) 244–5, 247
Four Old Hungarian Folk Songs (*Négy régi
    Magyar népdal* (1910–12, rev. 1926)
    120
Four Orchestral Pieces (*Négy zenekari
    darab*) (1912, orch. 1921) 123–5,
    135, 180

Four Piano Pieces (*Négy zongora darab*)
DD71 (1903) 23, 27–9, *28*, 34, 35, 36,
39, 51, 102
Four Slovak Folk Songs (*Négy tót népdal*)
(1916 or 1917) 244
Four Songs to texts by Lajos Pósa (1902) 25
Fourteen Bagatelles (*Tizennégy zongora-
darab*) (1908) 79, 84–7, 89–90, 92, 96,
102, 103, 173
From Gyergyó. Three Folk songs from the
Csík District (*Gyergyóból. Három
csíkmegyei népdal*) (1907) 85
*From Olden Times (Elmúlt időkből)* (1935)
274, 275, 287
*Genesis Suite* movement (unrealised) 365
Hungarian Peasant Songs (*Magyar
parasztdalok*) (1933) 254
Hungarian Sketches (*Magyar képek*) (1931)
254
*Kossuth* (1903) 19, 23, 24–5, 27, 29,
30–4, *32*
Liebeslieder (1900) 17
*Mazurka* (1890) 9
*Mikrokosmos* (1926, 1932–9) 38, 218, 286–7,
324, 334, 351
*The Miraculous Mandarin (A csodálatos
mandarin)* (1918–19, orch. 1924)
124, 162–3, *163*, *164–5*, 168, 172, 182,
197, 198, 202–3, 205, 213, 216, 219,
256–7
*The Miraculous Mandarin* Suite (1818,
completed 1927) 260, 286
*Music for Strings, Percussion and Celesta
(Zene húros hangszerekre, ütőkre és
celestara)* (1936) 277–83, *278*, 285, 288,
309, 312
Nine Little Piano Pieces (*Kilenc kis
zongoradarab*) (1926) 207, 218, 19
Out of Doors (*Szabadban*), five piano pieces
(1926) 207, 210–13, 215
Piano Concerto No. 1 (*I Zongoraverseny*)
(1926) 207, 213–18, *215*, *216*, *217*, 219,
220, 242, 243, 250, 252, 255, 259, 287,
309
Piano Concerto No. 2 (*II Zongoraverseny*)
(1930–1) *252*, 250–4, 262, 263, 264,
265, 266, 272, 276, 285–6, 305, 307,
311, 328, 329, 333, 367
Piano Concerto No. 3 (1945) 363, 365–9,
*367*, *368*, 371, 372, 374
Piano Quintet (1903–4) 37–8, *38*, 39, 55,
57–8, 103
Rhapsody for Violin and Orchestra No. 1
(1929) 243
Rhapsody for Violin and Orchestra No. 2
(1928 rev. 1935 or 1944) 238, 243, 286
Rhapsody for Violin and Piano No. 1 (1928)
232–3, 323, 324
Rhapsody for Violin and Piano No. 2 (1828
rev. 1935 or 1944) 233–4, 286, 311,
335–6, 356
Rhapsody (*Rapszódia*) op. 1 (1904, orch.

1905) 40–2, *40*, 57–8, 69, 94, 103–4,
168, 207, 220, 225, 238, 239, 243, 244,
250, 260, 322
Romanian Christmas Carols (*Román
kolinda-dallamok*) (1915) 137, 138, 161
Romanian Folk Dances (*Román népi
táncok*) (1915) 137, 138, 207
Scherzo (Burlesque) op. 2 (1904)
(suppressed) 44–8, *46*
*Scherzo oder Fantasie* in B major (1897) 14,
55, 359
*Seherezáde (Scheherazade)* (unrealised) 172
Seven Sketches (*Vázlatok*) (1908–10) 93,
116–17
Slovak Folk Songs (*Tót népdalok*) (1917)
244
Sonata for Piano (*Szonáta*) (1926) 207,
208–10, *208*, *209*, *211*, 214, 221
Sonata for Solo Violin (1944) 356, 357–60,
361
Sonata for Two Pianos and Percussion
(1937) 215, 252, 287–96, *289*, *291*, *295*,
298–9, 310–11, 326, 327, 349
Sonata for Violin and Piano no. 1 (1921)
179–80, *181*–7, *183*, 189, 190, 192,
194–5, 201, 272, 286, 338, 356
Sonata for Violin and Piano no. 2 (1922)
189, 190–4, *191*, *192*, *193*, 197, 201,
221, 238, 239, 243, 255, 259, 272,
277, 323
Sonata in E minor for Violin and Piano
(1903) 23, 34–6, *35*, 58
Sonata No. 1 in G minor for Piano (1894) 11
Sonatina (*Szonatina*) (1915) 137, 138–9,
161, 254, 360
String Quartet No. 1 op. 7 (1908–9) 79,
89–92, *91*, 93, 94, *96*, 103, 188–9,
239, 324
String Quartet No. 2 (1915–17) 154–60,
*156*, *158*, *160*, 162, 170, 182, 185, 198,
321, 324
String Quartet No. 3 (1927) 221–4, *222*, *223*,
233, 238–9
String Quartet No. 4 (1928) 88, 227–32,
*228*, 239, 251, 256, 266, 346
String Quartet No. 5 (1934) 251, 265,
266–71, *271*, 273, 284–5, 315, 346
String Quartet No. 6 (1939) 303, 312,
315–22, *317*, *321–2*, 328, 335, 366
String Quartet No. 7 (unrealised) 373
Suite No. 1 (*I Svit*) (1905 rev. c.1920)
51–6, 69, 70, 71, 74, 143, 258, 260,
273, 275
Suite No. 2 (*II Svit*) (1905, 1907 rev. 1943)
62, 69–73, *70*, 71, 89
Suite (*Svit*) op. 14 (1916) 148–51, *149*, 155,
170, 182, 197, 208, 238, 360
Symphony in E♭ major (1902) (unfinished)
21, 45, 56
Székely Folk Song, *Piros alma (Székely
népdal)* (1904) 39
Székely Songs (*Székely dalok*) (1932) 254

Bartók, Béla: works (*cont.*)
  Ten Easy Piano Pieces (*Tíz könnyú
    zongoradarab*) (1908) 79, 87–8, 102,
    137, 178, 258
  Three Burlesques (*Három burleszk*)
    (1908–11) 93, 117–18, 173
  Three Hungarian Folk Tunes (*Három
    magyar népdal*) (1914–18 rev. 1941)
    161
  Three Studies (*Etüdök*) (1918) 170
  Transylvanian Dances (*Erdélyi táncok*)
    (1931) 254
  Twenty Hungarian Folk Songs (*Húsz
    magyar népdal*) (1929) 239–43, 244
  Twenty-Seven Two- and Three-Part
    Choruses (*27 két- és háromszólamú
    korus*) (1935–6,1937–41) 274–5,
    287
  *Two Elegies* (*Két elégia*) (1908–9) 79, 83–4,
    96, 170, 173
  Two Pictures (*Két kép/Deux Images*) (1910)
    105–6, 128, 161, 323
  Two Portraits (*Két portré*) op. 5 (1908–9)
    79, 82, 87, 132, 224, 356
  Two Romanian Dances (*Két román tánc*)
    op. 8a (1910) 100–2, *101*, 102
  Variations on a Theme by F. F. (*Változatok*)
    (1901) 18, 71
  Village Scenes (*Falun: Dedinské scény*)
    (1924) 203–5, 209, 286
  Viola Concerto (sketches; completed by
    Serly) (1945) 363, 369–72
  Violin Concerto No. 1 op. posth. (1907–8,
    pub. 1956) 79–82, *80*, *81*, 84, 87, 90, 91,
    306
  Violin Concerto No. 2 (1937–8) 296–7, 300,
    301, 302, 303–7, *304*, *305*, 308, 338,
    355, 356
  Wallachian piece (*Oláh darab*) (1890) 9
  Waltz (*Walczer*) (1890) 9
  *The Wooden Prince* (A fából faragott
    Királyfi) (1914–17) 105, 123, 131–5,
    *134*, 152, 153–4, 162, 188, 273
  *The Wooden Prince* (A fából faragott
    Királyfi) Suite (1921, 1924?) 258
  writings 257
    analyses of Seiber's quartets 90
    'Antwort auf einem rumänischen Angriff'
      ('Response to a Romanian Attack') 277
    'Comparative Music Folklore', *Népművelés*
      (1912) 125
    'Draft of the New Universal Collection of
      Folk Songs' (with Kódaly) (1913) 125
    'The Folk Songs of Hungary' (1928) 72
    'The Folklore of Instruments and their Music
      in Eastern Europe' (1911–41) 162
    'Gipsy Music or Hungarian Music?' (1930)
      352
    on Gypsy music, *Auróra* (1911) 108
    'Hungary in the Throes of Reaction',
      contribution, *Musical Courier* (1920)
      173

    'Der Musikdialekt der Rumänen von
      Hunyad', *Zeitscrift für
      Musikwissenschaft* 174
    'La Musique populaire Hongroise' 187
    'The Problem of the New Music', *Melos*
      (1920) 170–1
    'Race Purity in Music' 336–7
    'The Relation of Folk Song to the
      Development of the Art Music of Our
      Time' (1921) 179
    report on the International Congress of
      Arab Music, Cairo (1932) 261
    review in *Il Pianoforte* 189–90
    on Turkish folk singing, *Nyugat* 283
    'Die Volksmusik der Araber von Biskra und
      Umgebung' ('The Folk Music of the
      Arabs of Biskra and Surroundings')
      (1920) 129–30
    'What is Folk Music?' *Uj Idők* (1931) 257
Bartók, Béla (father) 4–5, 5–6, 7, 8
*Bartók, Béla hangszeres magyar népzenegyűjtése
  (Béla Bartók Hungarian Instrumental
  Folk Music Collection*) (Tari) 378
Bartók, Béla (son) 6, 8, 57, 94, 106, 122, 139, 151,
  152, 174, 200, 206, 258, 275, 334, 342,
  373, 376
Bartók, Ditta (née Pásztory; second wife) xiii,
  203, 265–6, 272, 274, 275, 334, 341,
  360, 365, 373, 374
  after Bartók's death 374
  background 199
  friendships 327, 333
  illnesses 221, 364, 372, 374
  as a pianist 326, 363, 365, 366, 374
    duo recitals with Bartók 288, 298, 311,
      322, 326, 330, 331, 333, 334,
      336, 339
  pregnancy 202
  wedding 6, 200
Bartók, Erzsébet Clementina Paula (later Tóth;
  'Elza' or 'Böske'; sister) 7, 23–4, 29, 30,
  42, 57, 61, 77, 95, 163, 200, 205, 239,
  334, 373
Bartók, Gergely (Gregorius; great-great-
  grandfather) 3
*Bartók in Britain* (Gillies) 187, 243
Bartók, János (grandfather) 4–5, 7
Bartók, János (great-grandfather) 3–4
Bartók, Mária (née Gondos; great-great
  grandmother) 3
Bartók, Márta (née Ziegler; first wife) 122,
  128–9, 139, 152, 153, 154, 180, 205
  courtship and marriage 93, 94, 96
  birth of Béla 94, 106
  as Bartók's copyist 120, 200
  breakdown of marriage and divorce 188,
    199–200
  marriage to Károly Ziegler 206
Bartók, Matild (née Ronkovics; grandmother) 5
Bartók, Paula (née Voit; mother) 6–7, 8–9, 10,
  15, 18, 19, 20, 29, 30, 67, 75, 168, 172,
  200, 239, 322, 373

Bartók, Péter (son) 7, 202, 205, 265–6, 274, 286, 309, 327, 332, 334, 335, 352, 360, 372, 374, 376
 on Bartók 298, 327, 342
Basilides, Mária 243, 244, 264, 273
Basle 255, 277, 298, 326
Basle Chamber Orchestra (Basler Kammerorchester) 277–8, 285, 312
Basle Conservatory of Music 277
Batka, János 34
Bator, Victor 372, 374
Bătută din pălmi (hand clapping) 185, 192
Baudelaire, Charles 24
Baugham, E. A. 187
Bayreuth 19, 33, 39, 45
BBC (British Broadcasting Corporation) 202, 224–5, 251, 286
 BBC Midland Orchestra 276
 BBC Symphony Orchestra 243, 251, 260, 265
 Concerts of Contemporary Music 238
Bechert, Paul 181
Bechstein Hall, Berlin 36
Beer, August 33
Beethoven, Ludwig van
 influence on Bartók 11, 20, 90, 125, 143, 269, 270, 290, 294
 influence on Dohnányi 33
 Pound on 285
 works 116, 182
  Kreutzer Sonata 189
  *Leonore No. 3* overture op. 72b 11
  piano concertos 16, 272, 322
  piano sonatas 10, 269, 290
  string quartets 90, 273, 367
  symphonies 15–16, 55, 125, 143, 270
  *Zwölf Contretänze* 294, *295*
Beethovensaal, Berlin 89
Beiuş *see* Belényes
Békés County 57, 66, 67–8, 95, 102, 194, 320
 *see also* Vésztő
Békéscsaba 194
*Béla Bartók Masterpieces for the Piano* (Bartók) (1945) 84, 85
Béla Bartók Memorial House, Budapest 75
Béldi, Izor 103
Belényes (Beiuş) 94–5, 107, 122, 154, 163
Belgium 308
Bellman, Jonathan 23, 25–6
Benedek 66
Berbers 128, 350
Bereg County 122
Berend, Iván 2
Berg, Alban 262, 310, 329, 381
 Violin Concerto 340
Berlin 35, 36, 102, 172–3, 227, 243
Berlin Philharmonic Orchestra 89
Berlioz, Hector
 *Fantastic Symphony* 93
 *Harold in Italy* 363
Bernard, Jonathan 380
Beszterce (Bistriţa, Romania) 8, 11, 95, 175

Besztercebánya 137, 139, 152
Bettelheim, Bruno 110–11
Beu, Octavian 196, 255
*Beyond Good and Evil* (Nietzsche) 78
Bible, St Matthew's Gospel 250
Bihar County 14, 94–5, 102, 107, 117, 122, 138, 149, 154, 163, 247, 284
 *see also Cântece poporale româneşti din comitatul Bihor*
Bihor County *see* Bihar County
birdsong 105, 114, 117, 212, 351, 353, 359, 367
Birlea, Ion 128
Birmingham 276
Biskra 128, 129–30, 179, 197, 213, 254
Bluebeard legend 110–11
Blüthner-Saal, Berlin 172–3
Bobál, Sámuel 127, 137
Bodenstedt, Friedrich 17
Bődy, Pál 5
Bologna 257
Bolshevism 173, 310
Bonavia, Ferruccio 238
Boosey & Hawkes (publishers) 69, 90, 144, 300, 303, 330, 335, 345, 363, 370
'Borbála Angoli' (ballad) 161
Borsodszirák 3
Bösendorfer Konzertsaal, Vienna 50
Boston, Massachusetts 226, 330, 361–2
*Boston Herald* (newspaper) 362
*Boston Post* (newspaper) 362
Boston Symphony Orchestra 343, 361–2
Boult, Sir Adrian 265
Bournemouth 201
Bowden 34
Brada, Ede 154
Brahms, Johannes 17, 33, 69, 218
 influence on Bartók xiv, 14, 17, 18, 20, 25, 34, 35, 37, 70
 Hungarian Dances 25
 Second Piano Concerto 20
 Third Symphony 311
 violin sonatas 207, 311, 359
 waltzes 138
Brăiloiu, Constantin 245, 246, 255, 354
Brand, Max 310
Brassó (Braşov) 75, 76, 151, 220
Bratislava *see* Pozsony
Bratuž, Damjana 211
Braunstein, György (George Barati) 263
Braunwald 300
Breitkopf & Härtel (publishers) 87
Bremen 243
Brenner, József (Géza Csáth) 103
Breuer, János 312
BBC 250
 Symphony Orchestra 250
Britten, Benjamin 306, 334, 381
Brodie, Diana (wife of Erik Chisholm) 264
Brown, Julie 45, 246
Brugnoli, Attilio 58
Brüll, Adél 147

Brussels 285–6
Bucharest 127
Budapest
  Bartók in 15, 16, 65, 74, 75, 107, 115, 120, 174,
    227, 258, 259, 261, 311, 322
  millennial celebrations (1896) 15
  political situation 152, 166, 167–9, 171–2
  society in 2, 15, 59, 143
Budapest City Council 195, 196
Budapest Concert Orchestra 258, 263, 322
Budapest Ethnographic Museum 107, 168
Budapest Municipal Council 65
Budapest Opera 21, 134, 153, 162, 168, 173, 202,
    219, 256–7, 258, 273
Budapest Philharmonic Orchestra 16, 32, 33, 44,
    51, 52, 56, 128, 143, 168, 174, 208, 227,
    264
*Budapesti Hírlap* (*Budapest News*) (newspaper)
    30, 33, 161
*Budapesti Napló* (newspaper) 19
Buesst, Aylmer 265
'Bulgarian' rhythm 38, 282, 300, 302, 347
Bull, Storm 333
burlesque 45, 46, 55, 71, 86, 92, 318, 320, 352
  *see also* Bartók, Béla: works: Scherzo
    (Burlesque); Three Burlesques
Bush, Nancy 144, 147, 245
Buşiţia, Ion (János) 94–5, 122, 126–7, 153, 154,
    163
Busoni, Ferruccio 34, 36, 69, 89, 96,
    116, 119, 171
  on Bartók 87
  influence on Bartók xiv
Buttykay, Ákos 115

Cacula, Ila 233
Cairo 260–1
Calvinists 75
Calvocoressi, Michel-Dimitri 180–1, 189, 202,
    205, 239, 245, 250, 255–6
cameras, Bartók's use of 139
Canada 332, 365
*Cântece poporale româneşti din comitatul Bihor
    (Ungaria)* (*Romanian Folksongs from
    the Bihor District*) (Bartók) (1913) 107,
    127–8, 130, 135–6
Carnegie Hall, New York 226, 285, 300, 323, 326,
    338, 339–40, 355, 356, 361, 362
Carroll, Grace 356
Carter, Elliott 228
Casella, Alfredo 233
Castelnuovo-Tedesco, Mario 365
Catholic church *see* Roman Catholic church
C. D. W. (critic) 330
Ceauşescu, Nicolae 255
celesta *165*, 277–83, *278*, 285, 288, 306, 309, 312
Cemal, Ulvi 283
Chamberlain, Neville 308
Chevillard, Camille 58
Chicago 323, 333
Chicago Philharmonic Society 345
Chicago Symphony Orchestra 333

Chiesa 205
children's songs
  'Der Esel ist ein dummes Tier' ('The Donkey
    is a Stupid Animal') 81
  'Gólya, gólya, gilice' 211
  taunting songs 282
Chisholm Erik 260, 264
Chisholm, Morag 264
Chopin, Frédéric
  influence on Bartók 11, 14, 20
  works 36, 51, 69
choriambus rhythm 23, 32, 37, 247
Chován, Kálmán 16
Christian Nationalists 173, 174, 179
*The Christian Science Monitor* (newspaper) 361
Christmas carols *see colinde*
Cieplinski, Jan 273
cimbalom 35, 37, 40, 183, 301
Cincinnati Symphony Orchestra 226
Citron, Pierre 10
Clark, Edward 225
Clementi, Muzio, *Gradus ad Parnassum* 11
Clerment-Tonnerre, Elisabeth, Duchesse de 187
*Cleveland News* (newspaper) 328
Cleveland Orchestra 328
*Cleveland Press* (newspaper) 328
Cluj *see* Kolozsvár
Coates, Albert 187
Cocke, Dr C. Hartwell 356
*col legno* technique 135, 197, 224
*colinde* (Romanian Christmas carols) 137, 138,
    192, 198, 210, 245, 245–6, 259, 268,
    273–4, 282, 312, 351
Colles, H. C. 182
Cologne 219, 227
Columbia University, New York 258, 325, 327,
    329, 330, 338
Columbia University Press 360
*Columbus*, SS 225
'Commission of the Arts and Sciences' of
    Independent Hungary 336
Concertgebouw Orchestra, Amsterdam 207,
    234–5
Congresso Internazionale di Musica, Rome
    (1911) 115
*Convorbiri* (journal) 135–6
Coolidge Foundation 265
Cooper, Gerald M. 179, 201
Copenhagen 238
Corvin Wreath 250
Couperin, François 116
Cowdray Hall, London 286
Cowell, Henry 264–5
Creel, Wilhelmine 297, 333, 334, 338, 361
Croats 1, 22
*csárdás* (dance) 10, 36, 39, 51, 55, 64
Csáth, Géza (József Brenner) 103
Cserny, József 169
Csík County 75, 76–7, 85, 175, 240, 244
Csík-Karczfalva 76
Csíkrákos (Racu) 75
Csíkszereda 151

Csongrád County 68
Csorba (Štrba, Slovakia) 274
Csorvás 7
Curtis Institute of Music, Philadelphia 324
Czech Philharmonic Orchestra 272
Czechoslovakia 3, 175, 298, 308
  see also Slovakia
Czechs 308
Czerny, Carl 10

D. H. (critic) 238–9
Daily Boston Globe (newspaper) 226, 330, 362
The Daily Dispatch (newspaper) 34
Dalmatian folk music 26, 348, 350
Dann, Dr Arnold 356–7
Danube River 10, 15, 136, 172, 177
Danzig 243
Darányi, Kálmán 298
Darázs (Dražovce, Slovakia) 93, 107–8
darbuka (drum) 193, 215, 216
davul (drum) 349
'De băut' (drinking tunes) 185, 192
De Telegraaf (newspaper) 272
Déak, Imre 274
Debussy, Claude 177, 179, 381
  Bartók on 179
  influence on Bartók xiv, 45, 72, 87, 90, 105,
    117, 118, 123, 141, 145, 293, 301, 325,
    348
  works 90, 108, 115, 117, 118, 189
'Degenerate Music' ('Entartete Musik')
    exhibition, Düsseldorf (1938) 310
Delani 117
Delius, Frederick 120, 178
  on Bartók 72
  Bartók's correspondence with 69, 104, 106,109,
    126
  influence on Bartók 105, 123, 125
  meeting with Bartók 104
  works 104, 108–9, 125, 187
Della Ciaja, Azzolino Bernardino 220
Demény, Dezső 115
Demény, János 23
Denver, Colorado 225, 330
Dessau 225
Detroit, Michigan 331
Deutsches Kammermusikfest, Baden
    Baden 221
Devitte, H. 120–1
Diabelli, Anton 10
Diaghilev, Sergei 133, 234
Dickenson-Auner, Mary 181
Dieren, Bernard van 178
Dietl, Lajos 39, 49, 68
Dille, Denijs 3, 5, 6, 13, 21, 56, 59, 62, 74, 119,
    139, 140
Diósy, Ödön 147
Ditson, Charles 329
dobă (drum) 349
Doboz 66, 68
Dobszay, László 378
Dohnányi, Ernő 14, 74, 82, 139, 168

awards 250
as a conductor 227, 243, 256, 258, 264
as director of the Liszt Academy 168, 172,
    266
political activity 167, 169, 173
post-war difficulties 174, 195
Sonata for cello and piano in B♭ minor (1899)
    20
students of 19, 300
style 33
works 102, 195
  Passacaglia 36
  Variations and Fugue on a Theme by G. E. 18
Dohnányi family 29
Doráti, Antal 338, 352
Dorian mode 40, 68, 118, 134, 139, 176, 205, 223,
    241, 247, 268, 282, 284, 346
Dósa, Lidi 39, 68
Downes, Olin 220, 225, 226, 256, 273, 324,
    339–40, 355, 361, 362
Drei Masken Verlag (publisher) 190
drinking tunes ('De băut') 185, 192, 242
drums / drumming 9, 158, 193, 211, 215, 252,
    278, 278, 287, 288, 349, 350
Dual Monarchy 22, 48, 49
Dubost, Madame 187
Dukas, Paul 177
Dumbrăviţa de Codru 284
Durgin, Cyrus 362
Durigo, Ilona 170, 238
Düsseldorf 310
Dvořák, Antonín, Suite for Orchestra
    op. 39 34

E. E. (Edwin Evans, critic) 194–5, 201, 260
Eastern Orthodox church 1
Eastman School of Music, New Yok 324
Eckhardt, Tibor 336
Edison Bell 26
education policies, Hungarian 2, 4–5
'Ég a kunyhó, ropog a nád' ('The Hut is Blazing,
    the Reed Crackles') (Hungarian song)
    38
Egressy, Béni 174
Egyetértés (Accord) (newspaper) 32–3
Egyházmarót (Kostolné Moravce, Slovakia)
    127, 137
Egypt 260–1
1848 revolution 22, 24, 25, 31
Einstein, Albert 344
Einstein, Alfred 262
El-Kantara 129
Elie, Rudolph, Jr. 362
Elschek, Oskár 378
Elscheková, Alica 378
'Entartete Musik' ('Degenerate Music')
    exhibition, Düsseldorf (1938) 310
Enyed 152
Eötvös College, Budapest 56, 67
Eötvös de Vásárosnamény, Baron József 4, 5
Erdélyi, Csaba 372
Erdélyi, József 246

'Erdők, völgyek, szűk ligetek' (Transyvanian folk
      song) 110
Erkel, Ferenc 10, 15, 51, 66, 121
Erkel, László 10, 11
Erkel, Sándor 32
'Der Esel ist ein dummes Tier' ('The Donkey is a
      Stupid Animal', German children's
      song) 81
Esti Újság (Evening News) (newspaper) 33
ethnic issues 1–3, 5, 8, 9, 15, 22, 59, 75–6, 98,
      100, 175, 255
Ethnographia (journal) 82–3, 125
Ethnographic Map of Hungary (Teleki) 98
Evans, Edwin 194–5, 201, 260
Evanston 333, 334

F. B. (Ferruccio Bonavia, critic) 238
Fábián, Felicitás (Felicie) 18, 20, 38, 62
Fachiri, Alexander 180, 260
Failoni, Sergio 272
Falk, Miksa 19
Farkasréti Cemetery, Budapest 373
Farmer, George 260
Farnaby, Giles, 'Quodlings Delight' (sic) 220
Fascism 257, 287, 297–8
Fassett, Ágota (Agatha) (née Illés) 246, 327, 332,
      339, 340, 341, 360
Fassett, Stephen 327
'Fehér László' (Hungarian song) 67, 68, 350
Fehérvölgy (Albac) 107
Fekete-ér puszta 66
Feketebalog (Čierny Balog) 140, 203
Felsőireg 85, 110, 346
Felsőrépa (Râpa-de-Sus) 139, 232
Felsőszászberek 163
Ferencsik, János 273, 326
Feresd (Feregi) 138
Festival Hongrois, Paris (1910) 102
Feuermann, Emanuel 273
Finno-Ugric tribes 196
First World War (1914–18) 136, 163/166
Fischer, Hedviga and Karl 39
Fitzgerald, Michael 13
Fitzwilliam Virginal Book 220
Fiume 65
Fleischer, Antal 243
Flemish Radio Orchestra 285–6
Flipse, Eduard 272, 273
Florence 262–3, 311, 322
flutes (folk) 129, 212
Földvár (Feldioara) 151
folk music
   methodology for collecting 65, 66, 107, 125–6,
         128, 130, 136, 235–6, 260–1, 274, 277,
         283–4, 377, 378–9
   see also under individual countries
'The Folk Songs of Hungary' (Bartók) 72
Foss, Hubert 274
France 65, 88, 136, 187, 361
Franck (farm manager) 66
Frankfurt-am-Main 250, 255, 262
   Opera House 189, 220

Frankfurt Radio Symphony Orchestra 251, 262
Frankl, Steve 385n10
Franz Ferdinand, Archduke 136
Franz Joseph, Emperor 22, 49, 65, 136, 320
Free Trade Hall, Manchester 61
Frescobaldi, Girolamo, Toccata in G for organ,
      F 3.05 368
Freud, Sigmund 110
Freund, Etelka 69, 76, 87, 88
Freund, Robert 69
Fricsay, Ferenc 352
Friedrich, István 171
friss (fast or fresh) tempo 23, 35, 36, 37,
      41, 185, 221, 232, 233, 234,
      240, 278
Fu'äd I, King 260
Függetlenség (Independence) (newspaper) 33
funeral laments 352
Furtwängler, Wilhelm 220

Galánta 57, 264
Gând Românesc (Romanian Thought) (maga-
      zine) 277
Ganz, Rudolph 94, 102
Garamvidék (journal) 139
Garay, Ákos 57, 175
Garfield, Viola E. 331
Garst, Marilyn 379
Gauk, Aleksandr 237
Gemer County 378
Genesis Suite (collective work) 365
Geneva 257, 311, 326
Genoa 220
gentry 2, 6, 22, 43, 59, 76, 95, 108
George Washington, SS 227
Gerlicepuszta 23, 37, 39, 67, 68, 71, 85
German language 8, 30, 48, 161
German music 17
Germans 1, 3, 9, 22, 59, 98, 167
Germany 251, 262
   Bartók's attitude towards 297, 303, 310
Geyer, Stefi 74, 76, 77–8, 81, 82, 83, 87, 90, 92,
         238, 255, 277, 299, 326, 356
   Stefi's motif 78, 79, 80–1, 83, 86, 88, 90, 96,
         113, 142, 184, 249, 301, 350
Gianicelli, Károly 19, 21, 33
Gillies, Malcolm 71, 183, 187, 243
'Giovinezza' (Fascist anthem) 257
'Gipsy Music or Hungarian Music?' (Bartók) 351
Giraud, Albert 24
Glasgow 259–60, 264
Gleiman, Ani 140
Gleiman, Wanda 140, 163, 199
Gluck, Christoph Willibald, Le Cadi dupe 154
Gmunden 29
Goddard, Scott 256
Godowsky, Leopold 36
golden section theory 296
Golgotha (site of Jesus's crucifixion) 114
Golschmann, Vladimir 326
'Gólya, gólya, gilice' (Hungarian children's song)
      211

Gömbös, Gyula 257
Gombosi, Otto 12, 325
Gombossy, József 139
Gombossy, Klára 139–41, 189, 203
    poems 139, 140–1
'Good wine, youth and good health' (Hungarian
    folk song) 52, 55
Goodman, Benny 288, 300, 330, 336
'Gott erhalte' (Austrian national anthem) 31, 33,
    34, 45, 53, 54
Grainger, Percy 104
Gray, Cecil 178, 179, 180
Graz 63, 106
Griffiths, Gareth 43
grotesquery 45, 48, 87, 124, 131, 132, 135, 162,
    301, 319
Gruber, Emma (née Sándor, later Kodály) 18, 19,
    20, 27, 28, 40, 56, 62
Gruber, Henrik 18
Guide to Kulchur (Pound) 285
Gürzenich Orchestra 227
Gyergyó 76, 95
Gyergyószentmiklós 76
Gyergyótekerőpatak 85
Gyöngyösi, Márton 377
Gypsies 1, 22, 75
Gypsy music/musicians 7, 9, 22, 26, 40, 41, 43,
    44, 53, 139, 232, 233, 234, 269, 273,
    276, 301, 307, 318
    Bartók on 108
    influence on Bartók 10, 25, 35, 41, 51
Gypsy scale 23, 25, 29, 32, 37, 40, 45, 62, 229,
    279, 295, 314, 315
Gyula 66, 67–8

Hába, Alois 260
Hajdu, István (Pista) 66
Hajós, Edit 121
Halkevi institution 283
Hallé Orchestra 31, 33, 61
hallgató ornamentation 23, 32
Hamerik, Ebbe 238
hand clapping (bătută din pălmi) 185, 192
Hannay, David 48, 49
Harangozó, Gyula 257
Haraszti, Emil 161
Harmans, W. (critic) 194
Harmat, Boriska 154
'Harmonie du soir' (Baudelaire) 24
Harsányi, Kálmán 23, 24, 25, 39, 45
The Harvard Crimson (newspaper) 340–1
Harvard University, Cambridge, Massachusetts
    26, 324, 337, 338, 340–1, 347, 365
Haselbeck, Olga 162
Hassall, Christopher 109
Hauer, Josef Matthias 310
Haupt-Stummer family 152–3
Haupt-Stummer, Baron Lipót 152
Hawkes, Ralph 335, 345, 373
Hawtrey, Sir Ralph 180
Haydn, Joseph
    influence on Bartók 10

Symphony no. 102 in B♭ 339
Haynau, General Julius Jacob von 25
Hebbel, Frigyes 99, 110
Hédel, Zólyom County 139
'Heiliger Dankgesang eines Genesenen an die
    Gottheit in der lydischen Tonart' (from
    Beethoven's String Quartet in A minor
    op. 132) 367
Heinsheimer, Hans 330, 363, 364
hemiola rhythms 14, 38, 54–5, 70, 359, 368
heptatonia secunda mode 148, 177, 186, 190, 192,
    198, 210, 212, 218, 247, 270
Herald Tribune (newspaper) 362
Herder, Johann Gottfried von 257
'Hërvadj, rózsám, hërvadj' ('Fade away, rose,
    fade away') (Hungarian folk song)
    368
Herzfeld, Viktor 14
Herzog, George 324, 329
Heseltine, Philip (Peter Warlock) 178–9,
    187, 201
    on Bartók 178, 179
Hevesi, Sándor 122
Heward, Leslie 276
Hindemith, Paul 260, 310
    Concerto for Orchestra 345
    Ludus Tonalis 218
History of Music (Stafford) 23
Hitler, Adolf 251, 257, 262, 298, 308, 334,
    336
HMV (record company) 261
Hoensch, Jürg 1–2
Hoffman-Stehlin, Maja (wife of Paul Sacher)
    277–8
Hoffmann, Emanuel 277–8
Hofmann, Hermann 265
Holland 272, 276, 308, 311
Holló, Dr Gyula 335, 341–2
    on Bartók 375–6
Holofernes (Assyrian general) 110
Honegger, Arthur 187
Hont County 127, 378
Hooker, Lynn 115, 116
Hopkins, Charles 15
hora (dance) 95, 354, 371
hora lungă melodies 190, 191, 192, 193, 196, 230,
    318
Hornbostel, Erich von 260, 324
Horthy, Admiral Miklós 171, 250, 336
Hotel Woodrow, New York 355, 360
Howes, Frank 256
Hubai, Gergely 145
Hubay, Jenő 16, 74, 123, 172, 174, 189, 250,
    266, 311
Huddersfield 195
Human, All Too Human (Nietzsche) 49–50
Hungarian Academy of Sciences (Magyar
    Tudományos Académia) 266, 272, 273,
    276, 297
Hungarian Democratic Republic 166, 167,
    168
Hungarian Ethnographic Society 82–3

Hungarian folk music 23–4, 25, 38, 52, 54, 55, 62, 85, 89, 95, 110, 119, 350
current situation 377
in Turkey 283
see also under Bartók, Béla: works
The Hungarian Folk Song (A magyar népdal) (Bartók) 39, 57, 68, 88, 112, 113, 202, 205, 208, 239–43, 244, 245, 255–6, 281, 320, 368
Hungarian Folk Songs (Magyar népdalok) (Bartók and Kodály) (1906) 62–3, 67, 67–9, 68
Hungarian language 2, 8, 22, 26, 30, 48, 75, 255
Hungarian national costume 23, 33, 48
Hungarian National Symphony Orchestra 115
Hungarian nationalism 21, 22, 29–30, 43–4, 59
Hungarian Quartet 238–9
Hungarian Red Army 171
Hungarian Royal Drawing School, Budapest 27
Hungarian Soviet Republic 168, 171, 173
Hungarian State Opera 272
Hungarian uprising (Aster Revolution) (1918) 166, 167
Hungarians 1, 9, 43, 67, 89, 98, 100, 167
Hungary
economic problems 261
effect of the Treaty of Trianon (1920) 175
map 3
national identity 377
plight of musicians in 173–4
political situation 48, 166, 167–9, 171–2, 364
Huntingdon, Pennsylvania 323
Hunyad County 75, 138, 174
Huszár, Károly 171
Hylton, Jack 258
Hyrtl, Anton 12

iambic rhythms 37, 229, 242, 269, 281, 307, 314, 318, 350, 358, 359, 371
Il Pianoforte (magazine) 174, 189–90
Illés, Ágota see Fassett, Ágota
Imperial Army Bill (1903) 27, 48–9
improvisation 37, 190, 196, 212
see also Bartók, Béla: works: Eight Improvisations
Independence Party (Hungary) 48, 49
Indonesian music 333–4
Indy, Vincent d' 96
influenza pandemic (Spanish flu) (1918–20) 163/166
Institute of Arabic Music, Cairo 261
International Congress of Arab Music, Cairo (1932) 260–1
International Music Convention, Florence (1933) 262–3
International Society for Contemporary Music see ISCM
Iraqi folk music 196
ISCM (International Society for Contemporary Music) 190, 194–5, 220, 257, 286, 298–9, 315, 335

Italy, Bartók's veto on broadcast of his music to 297

Jacobs, Melville 331
Jacques-Dalcroze, Emile, First Violin Concerto 32
Jászberény 74–5
jazz 258, 288, 310
Jeszensky, Géza 2
Jews 1, 2, 18–19, 19–20, 22, 59, 172, 173, 299, 310
Joachim, Joseph 180, 218
Jobbik Party, Hungary 377
Johnstone, Arthur 34
Jones, Robert T. 374
Jones, Trefor 265
Journal of the Folk-Song Society 256
Judith (Biblical figure) 110
Juhász, Gyula 99
Jung, Erwin (first husband of Stefi Geyer) 238
Juniata College, Huntingdon, Pennsylvania 323
Jurkovics, Emsy 29, 38–9
Jurkovics, Irmy 29, 38–9, 57, 58–60
'Justice to Composers' (Koussevitzky) 343

Kacsóh, Pongrác 115
Kálmán, Oszkár 162
Kansas City 225, 330
Kapp, Wofgang 173
Karlsruhe 239
Károlyi, Count Mihály 166, 168, 364
Kárpáti, János 92, 149, 183
Kassa (Košice, Slovakia) 194
Kazim, Necil 283
Kecskemét 220, 287
Kecskemét Choral Society 128
Kecskeméti, Erzsébet xiii, 360, 365, 373
Kecskeméti, Pál xiii–xiv, 260, 365, 373
'Kék nefelejcs' ('Blue Forget-Me-Not') (Hungarian folk song) 52, 54
Kenneson, Claude 296–7
Kentner, Louis (Lajos) 263
Kern, Aurél 33
Kerner, István 19, 21, 32, 33, 44, 51, 56, 69, 104
Kerpely, Jenő 103
Kerpenyes 106
Kersch, Ferenc 10
Keviszőllős (Seleuş) 139
Kezdők zongoramuzsikája (The First Term at the Piano) (Reschofsky) 137
Kharkov 237
Kibéd 68
Kilyénfalva 76, 95
Kingdom of Hungary, declaration of 171
Kiriac-Georgescu, Dumitru 107, 127
Kisfaludy Society of Budapest 275
Kisgaram (Hronec) 139
Kleiber, Erich 227
Klemperer, Otto 263
Klimt, Gustav, Judith and the Head of Holofernes 110

Kodály, Emma 116, 121, 169
  see also Gruber, Emma
Kodály, Zoltán 98, 109, 115, 262–3, 274
  advice to Bartók 46, 72, 107
  article on Bartók in *La Revue musicale* 187
  awards 250
  on Bartók's First String Quartet 92
  Bartók's introduction to 56
  birthplace (Kecskemét) 287
  concerts of his music 102, 103, 116
  correspondence with Bartók 329
  'Draft of the New Universal Collection of Folk
      Songs' (with Bartók) (1913) 125
  folk music collecting 56, 57, 160, 214, 235,
      266, 378
  folk-song arrangements 62–3
  marriage 116
  political activity 167, 169, 172, 173, 174
  post-war difficulties 179, 195
  relationship with Bartók 56–7, 121
  as a student 56, 67
  works played by Bartók 225, 227
  Cello Sonata 102, 172–3
  Concerto for Orchestra 345
  *Dances of Galánta* (*Galántai táncok*) 57, 264
  'Gólya-nóta' ('Stork Song') 211
  *Psalmus hungaricus* 200
  Sonata op. 8 for unaccompanied
      cello 358
Koessler, Hans (János) 14, 16–17, 19, 27, 29, 34
Kohner, Baron Adolf 163
Kolisch Quartet 273, 315, 328
Kolisch, Rudolf 336, 340
*kolo* (dances) 349
Kolozsvár (Cluj-Napoca) 76, 89, 152, 194, 220
Komárno, Slovakia 202
König, Peter 63, 120
Königsberg 243
Konrád, Miklós 19
Konzerthaus, Vienna 160–1
Korbay, Francis (Ferenc), arrangement of 'Good
      wine' 52, 55
Korda, Alexander 169
Körösfő (Izvoru Crişului) 75, 88
Kósa, György 163
Kossar, Antonia 286, 311
Kossuth, Ferenc 48
Kossuth, Lajos 24, 25, 31, 48
Kosztolányi, Dezső 99
Köteles, Zsuzsi 68
Koussevitzky Music Foundation 343, 345
Koussevitzky, Serge 226, 343, 361, 363
Kovács, Sándor 102, 103, 115
Krasner, Louis 340
Krenek, Ernst 262
Kristóf, Károly 9
Krohn, Ilmari 107, 115, 125, 130
Kroll Opera House, Berlin 227
Kroó, György 52
Kubrick, Stanley, *The Shining* 280
Kun, Béla 168–9, 171, 172
kuruc fourths 23, 32, 37, 40, 54

Lachmann, Robert 260
'Lady Isabel and the Elf Knight' (ballad) 110
Lajtha, László 57, 175
Lake Balaton 244
Laki, Peter 37
Lamoureux Orchestra 58
Láng, Pál Henry 336
*lassú* (slow) tempo 23, 25, 29, 36, 37, 40, 41,
      53, 184, 221, 232, 233, 240, 241,
      278, 307
Laurance Turner Quartet 335
Lausanne 311
Lax, Dr Henry 373
Leafstedt, Carl 82, 109, 114
League of Composers 324, 336
League of Nations International Committee on
      Intellectual Cooperation 257–8
Leetch, Dr Henry 344
Lehár, Franz 353
  *Die lustige Witwe* (The Merry Widow) 352
Leibowitz, René 254
Lenau, Nikolaus 17
Lendvai, Ernö 26, 29, 55–6, 119, 280, 296,
      346
Lengyel, Menyhért 167, 172
  *A csodálatos mandarin* (*The Miraculous
      Mandarin*) libretto 162–3
'Lenin Boys' 169
Leningrad 237
Leningrad Philharmonic Orchestra 237
Lenoir, Yves 347, 349, 371
Lesznai, Lajos 5
Lewando, Ralph 329
*Lexicon of Musical Invective* (Slonimsky) 226
Library of Congress, Washington, DC 265,
      273, 323
Lichtluftheim nudist colony, Waidberg 120–1,
      126
Ligeti, György 230, 253
'Ligurian View of a Venetian Festival' (Pound)
      284–5
Lipótváros Casino, Budapest 19–20, 121
Lisbon 255
Liszt Academy, Budapest 12, 14–21, 27, 34–5,
      56, 57, 60–1, 74, 93, 94, 96, 109,
      122–3, 152, 168, 169–70, 173, 180,
      194, 199, 201, 221, 239, 244, 258,
      263, 315
Liszt, Ferenc (Franz)
  Bartók on 276–7
  influence on Bartók xiv, 18, 28, 30, 35, 37, 40,
      41, 45, 51, 56
  Légion d'Honneur awards 259
  students of 10, 15, 16, 69
  studied by Bartók 11, 19, 20, 41
  works 51, 71, 83, 93, 109
      Hungarian Rhapsodies 32, 40
      Piano Sonata in B minor 19, 35, 71
      *Spanish Rhapsody* 34, 36, 51
      *Totentanz* 56, 61
Liverpool 182, 276

Locrian mode 102, 117, 125, 132, 133, 144–5, 247, 254
London 179, 250, 260, 265, 276, 299, 335
London Symphony Orchestra 187
l'Orchestre Symphonique de Paris 259
Lord, Albert B. 324
Los Angeles, California 225
Löwe, Ferdinand 56
Lugosi, Béla 169
Lukács, György 169, 172
Lukács, József 174
Lup, Iuon 233
Lupu, Radu 379
Lutosławski, Witold 253
Lydian/Mixolydian polymode 138, 301, 305, 312, 354, 371
Lydian mode 92, 101, 102, 106, 114, 116, 177, 205, 208, 234, 282, 306, 315, 317
Lydian/Phrygian polymode 223

macaronic verse 9
MacDowell Club, New York 335
Macleod, Joseph 188
McPhee, Colin 333–4
Madrid 255
madrigal tradition 245
Maeterlinck, Maurice 115
Magyar Hírlap (Hungarian News) (newspaper) 33
Magyar Lant (Hungarian Lyra) (journal) 39
Magyar Nemzet (newspaper) 9
A magyar népdal see The Hungarian Folk Song
Magyar Színpad (newspaper) 162
Magyarcsernye (Nova Crnja, Serbia) 4
Magyarisation 1–2, 15, 22, 98
Magyarism 29, 40, 99
Magyars 1–2, 2, 22, 30, 43, 48–9, 75–6, 95, 100
Mahler, Gustav 135, 381
  influence on Bartók 32
Malvern Wells 195
Manchester 31, 33, 34, 61
The Manchester Guardian (newspaper) 34
Manhattan, SS 325
Mann, Thomas 258
Máramaros County (Maramureş) 127, 130, 138, 139, 185, 190, 194, 232, 234
Máramarossziget (Satu Mare) 194
Maramureş see Máramaros
Marcello, Benedetto 220
Maria Christina, Queen of Spain 64
Maros River 151
Maros-Torda County 68, 152, 160, 163, 245
Marosvásárhely (Târgu Mureş) 152, 160, 163
Marteau, Henri 32
Mărunţel (Romanian tune) 371, 372
Marxism 168–9
Matica Slovenská 108, 189, 261–2, 310
Maupassant, Guy de 237
Maurice, Donald 370, 372
Meaning, Communication and Value (Kecskeméti) xiii–xiv

mechanical music 270–1
Melodien der Rumänischen Colinde (Weihnachtslieder) (Bartók) 245–6, 273–4, 282
Melos (journal) 170–1, 194, 203
Mendelssohn, Felix
  influence on Bartók 13
  works 13, 17
Mengelberg, Willem 225, 234
Menuhin, Yehudi 304, 338, 356, 361, 364
  on Bartók 338, 356, 359
Merritt, Arthur Tillman 340, 341–2, 365
Mersin 283
Messiaen, Olivier 170
microtones 359
Mihalovich, Ödön 14, 19, 102, 123, 152
Miklós, Jutka 139
Milan 205
Milhaud, Darius 187, 262, 365
Ministry of Culture, Hungary 115
Minneapolis Symphony 338, 356
Miquelle, Georges 331
The Mirror of Music, 1844–1944 (Scholes) 202
Mitropoulos, Dimitri 338, 356
Mixolydian mode 68, 85, 132, 133, 139, 161, 177, 198, 204, 209, 212, 275, 367, 371
Mixolydian/Phrygian mode 145
M. M. S. (Marion Margaret Scott) (critic) 286–7
Modern Music (journal) 336
modernist style 27, 34, 54, 116, 203, 224, 362, 380, 381
Moldavia 94, 136
Molnár, Antal 51, 52, 53, 57, 103, 167
MoMA (Museum of Modern Art), New York 324
Mondsee 258
Montana, Switzerland 239
Monteux, Pierre 207, 234–5
Moore, Douglas 329, 330
Moreux, Serge 9, 254
Móricz, Klára 345, 353
Móricz, Zsigmond 99
Morocco 65
Morris, William 27
Moş, Pătru 232
Moscow 237
Mosonmagyaróvár 5, 7
Mosonyi, Mihály 51
Mount Sinai Hospital, New York 341–3
Movement for Independent Hungary 336
Mozart, Wolfgang Amadeus
  influence on Bartók 10
  works 10, 25, 154, 207, 250, 311, 326, 328
Müller, Jørgen Peter 120, 121
Müller-Widmann, Annie 285, 287, 298, 299–300, 300, 308, 323, 326, 335
Müller-Widmann, Oskar 285, 299–300
Munich 225
Munich Agreement (1938) 308
Municipal Theatre, Budapest 272
Mureş-Turda see Maros-Torda

Murillo, Bartolomé 58
Murray, William 220–1
Museum of Modern Art (MoMA), New York 324
*Music and Letters* (journal) 256, 284–5
*Musical Courier* (journal) 173–4
*The Musical Times* (journal) 181, 194, 201, 202, 235, 238–9, 243–4, 256, 286–7
Musik Akademie, Basel 238
*Musikblätter des Anbruch* (journal) 219
Musikforeningen Orchestra, Copenhagen 238
Musikhistorisch Zentrale, Vienna 160–1
Musikverein, Vienna 263
Mussolini, Benito 30, 257, 284–5
Mussorgsky, Modest, *Pictures at an Exhibition* 53
*My Father* (Péter Bartók) 266, 298, 335
*My System* (*Mit System*) (Müller) 121

Nagy, Endre 9
Nagybecskerek 4
Nagymegyer 368
Nagyszeben 151
Nagyszentmiklós (Sânnicolau Mare) 1, 2–3, 4–5, 7, 8, 29, 38–9, 67, 100, 175, 255
Nagyszőllős (Vynohradiv, Ukraine) 8, 8–9, 10, 67, 122
Nagyvárad (Oradea) 9–10, 75, 95, 122, 144, 175, 194, 202, 220
*The Naked Face of Genius: Béla Bartók's Last Years* (Fassett) 327, 332
Nákó (Nacu), Kristóf 4
Naples 205, 323
National Museum, Budapest 66
*National-Zeitung* (newspaper) 288
nationalisation 169
nationalism 2, 22, 23–5, 26–7, 29–30, 59
  musical 21, 22–3, 25, 30–4, 43–4, 235–6
Native Indian ('Indian') music 331
Nazism 287, 297–8, 299, 310, 312, 336, 365
NBC Symphony Orchestra 363
Németh-Šamorínsky, Štefan 261
*Nemzeti Újság* (*National News*) (newspaper) 174
*Népmûvelés* (*Education of People*) (journal) 125
*Népszava* (newspaper) 195
The Netherlands 272, 276, 308, 311
Neue Sachlichkeit (New Objectivity) 218
New England Conservatory, Boston 330
New Hungarian Music Society (UMZE) 115–16, 257, 259
New Hungarian Quartet 315
New Jersey College for Women, Hackettstown 327
New World String Quartet 256
New York xiii, 221, 225, 226, 256, 258, 285, 300, 315, 323, 324, 325, 326, 327–8, 329, 330, 335, 338, 339–40, 341–3, 355, 356, 360, 361, 362, 365
New York Philharmonic Orchestra 225, 285, 338, 339, 355
*The New York Times* 220, 225, 226, 256, 262, 273, 300, 323, 324, 325, 326, 328, 329–30, 335, 337–8, 339–40, 343, 361, 364, 373, 374, 380

Nietzsche, Friedrich 49–50, 59–60, 61, 78
'night music' 53, 72, 123, *165*, 191, 212, 215, 222, 230, 231, 253, 280–1, 293–4, 301, 313–14, 350, 351, 359, 371
Nirschy, Emilia 154
Nitra County *see* Nyitra
nomads 261, 284
Normanhurst Court, Battle 195
North African music 130, 193, 196, 197, 198–9, 214, 215, 347
  *see also* Algerian folk music
Northwestern University, Evanston, Illinois 333
Norway 126
nudism 120–1
'Nun komm der Heiden Heiland' (chorale) 349–50
Nuremburg 262
Nyerges, Anton 111, 118, 147
Nyitra (Nitra) County 93, 107–8, 378
*Nyugat* (*West*) (journal) 67, 99, 103, 118, 131, 167, 169, 246, 276–7, 283

*Observer* (newspaper) 202
octatonic scale 87, 104, 150, 175, 190, 212, 213, 214, 224, 230, 232, 234, 240, 274, 293, 346, 347, 371, 372
Odd Fellow Palæet, Copenhagen 238
Odessa 237
Ojetti, Ugo 262
Oppenheimer, Dr Bernard S. 341–2
Oradea *see* Nagyvárad
Ormandy, Eugene 323, 326, 329–30, 336
Osmaniye 283
Ótátrafüred (Starý Smokovec, Slovakia) 283
Otterloo, Willem van 276
Ovieda 255
Oxford 259
Oxford University Press 202, 255, 274

P. R. (Paul Rosenfeld, critic) 226
*Pacific Northwest Quarterly* (journal) 331
Paddison, Max 44
Paganini, Niccolò, Ninth Caprice, 'La Chasse' 359
Palermo 205
Palestrina, Goivanni Pierluigi, Bartók's interest in 274
Pallay, Anna 154
Paris 96, 239, 259, 285, 311
Parker, Sylvia 327
Parma 311
parody 48, 271, 352
Parrish, Dorothy 310–11, 323, 325, 328, 334, 372
Parry Collection, Harvard University 324, 337, 347
Parry, Milman 324
Party of Hungarian Life 257
Passail 29
Passy-Cornet, Adél 16
Pásztory, Edith (Ditta) *see* Bartók, Ditta
Pásztory, Gyula (father-in-law) 199

Pásztory, Kornélia (née Petrovics, mother-in-law) 199, 202
Pegolotti, James 342
Penderecki, Krzsysztof 230, 253
Péntek, György Gyugyi 75
Perahia, Murray 379
percussion 215, 263, 278, 287–96, 349
Perera, Mrs Lionello 356
performing rights societies 299, 342
Perrault, Charles, *La Barbe bleue* 110
Persian folk music 196
Pest County 66, 68
*Pester Lloyd* (newspaper) 33
*Pesti Hírlap* (newspaper) 103
*Pesti Napló* (newspaper) 33, 297
Pethő, Bertalan 12
Petranu, Professor Coriolan 277
Petri, Endre 300
Petrie, George 337
Petrovoselo (Vladimirovac, Serbia) 127
Pfitzner, Hans, *Palestrina* 311
Philadelphia 324
Philadelphia Orchestra 225, 323, 326, 329–30
Philharmonic Quartet 324, 325
Phillips, Frank 265
Phillips, Walter 48, 49
phonographs 65, 66, 69, 107, 127, 136, 139, 172, 283–4, 377, 379
Phrygian mode 37, 84, 101, 106, 116, 118, 119, 123, 148, 185, 215, 216, 229, 230, 240, 241, 243, 244, 284, 317
*Pierrot Lunaire* (Giraud) 24
'Piros alma' ('The Red Apple') (Transylvanian folk song) 39–40, 68
Pittsburgh 323, 328–9
*Pittsburgh Post-Gazette* 328–9
*The Pittsburgh Press* (newspaper) 288, 329
Pittsburgh Symphony Orchestra 328
*The Plain Dealer* (newspaper) 328
Pollatsek, László 256
polymodality 84, 101, 116, 117, 142, 155, 223, 266, 279, 295, 301, 306, 312, 317, 371
Popovici, Ion 232, 233
Popper, Dávid 16
popular music 10, 22, 32, 37, 42, 51, 54, 55, 62, 196, 232, 234, 243, 252, 351, 377
    Bartók on 235, 351–2
Portland, Oregon 225
Portugal 63, 255
Posvék, Lajos 63
Poulenc, Francis 187, 188
    on Bartók 188
Pound, Ezra 284–5
Pozsony (Bratislava) 6, 10, 11, 34, 41, 63, 68, 153, 167–8, 175, 239, 261
Prague 225, 272
*Pravda* (newspaper) 168–9
Previtali, Fernando 285
Priegnitz, Hans 309–10
Primrose, William 363, 369, 370, 371
Princip, Gavrilo 136

Pro Arte Quartet 227
'Proclamation of the Hungarian Intelligentsia' (1918) 167
Prokofiev, Sergei 381
proto-Fascism 172
Provisional National Assembly, Hungary 364
Provo, Utah 330
Prunières, Henry 187

Queen's Hall, London 250, 265, 276

'Race Purity in Music' (Bartók) 336–7
Rachmaninov, Sergei 381
    Second Symphony 79
*Racial Problems in Hungary* (Seton–Watson) 161
Racy, Ali Jihad 261
Radio Budapest 265
Radvánszky, Baron Antal 199
Radvány (Radvaň, Slovakia) 199–200
Rafajna-Ujfalu 122
Rákóczi March 55
Rákoshegy 120, 122
Rákosi, Jenő 30, 33
Rákosi, Zoltán 139
Rákoskeresztúr, Pest 65–6, 67, 120, 137, 148, 152, 154, 172, 174, 176
Rameau, Jean-Philippe 116
Ránki, György 2
Râpa-de-Sus (Felsőrépa) 139, 232
Rappaport, Dr Israel 342, 355, 361, 364, 372
Rásonyi, László 275
Rathaus, Karol 310
Ravel, Maurice 94, 173, 177, 187, 381
Rebner, Adolf 189
Reed College, Portland, Oregon 333
Reger, Max 17
    influence on Bartók xiv, 80, 90
Reiner, Fritz 225, 226, 324, 325, 328, 339, 340
Reinhardt, Max 172
Reinitz, Béla 195
Reményi, Joseph 336
Renaissance music 274, 275
Reschofsky, Sándor 137
Respighi, Ottorino 262
Révész, Géza 195
*La Revue musicale* (journal) 177, 180, 187
Richards, Julie 37
Richter, Hans (János) 16, 33–4, 45, 61
Rimaszombat (Rimavská Sobata, Slovakia) 199
Riverton, Vermont 327, 332–3
Rodziński, Artur 328, 355
Roman Catholic church 1, 10, 12, 43, 151
Romania 2–3, *3*, 262
    effect of the Treaty of Trianon (1920) 175
    invasion of Transylvania 151–2
    *see also* Transylvania
Romanian Army, occupation of Budapest (1919) 171
Romanian folk music xiv, 94–6, *95*, 100, 106–7, 117, 119, 127, 185, 192, 196, 216, 232–3, 233–4

*see also* Bartók, Béla: works; *colinde*;
    *Rumanian Folk Music*
Romanian Government 205
Romanian language 8, 255
Romanians 1, 2, 22, 75–6, 100
Romanticism 21, 26, 218, 220, 379
Rome 205, 239, 311, 322
Rosbaud, Hans 251, 262
Rosenauer, Michi 140
Rosenfeld, Paul 226
Rossini, Gioachino, *The Barber of Seville*
    237
Roth Quartet 239
Rotterdam 272, 273
Rotterdam Philharmonic Orchestra 272, 273
Roussel, Albert 187, 262
    Concerto for Small Orchestra 345
Royal National Hungarian Academy of Music *see*
    Liszt Academy
Royal Philharmonic Society 187
Rózsavölgyi (publisher) 93, 94, 100, 105, 116,
    117, 121, 202
Rozsnyai Károly (publisher) 87, 89, 93, 96
Rubinstein Competition, Paris (1905) 57–8
Rühlig, Philip 298
*Rumanian Folk Music* (Bartók) 127, 138–9, 185,
    212, 217, 252, 254, 274, 338, 351, 357,
    360, 372, 373
Rushworth Hall, Liverpool 182, 276
Ruskin, John 27
Russia 237
Ruthenian folk music 234
Ruthenians 1, 9, 22

Saalbau, Frankfurt 188–9
Saanen 311
Sacher, Paul 277–8, 285, 287, 299, 311, 326
Sachs, Curt 260
*The Sackbut* (journal) 178, 179
Saerchinger, César 173
Sageman, Margaret 344
St Louis, Missouri 326, 330
St Louis Symphony Orchestra 326
St Paul, Minnesota 225
Saint-Saëns, Camille 64, 135
    *Danse macabre* 301
    Second Piano Concerto in G minor 69
Salakusz (Salakuzy, Slovakia) 214
Salle Pleyel, Paris 259
salons 19, 56, 62, 187
San Francisco, California 225, 330
San Sebastián 255
Sándor, György 352, 357
Sándor, Pál 18–19
Sankt Radegund bei Graz 8
Santpoort 276
Sanzogno, Nino 311
Saranac Lake, New York 343–4, 355, 360, 364,
    365, 372–3
Sargent, Malcolm 363
Sarkad 66
Satie, Erik 104, 177, 188

*Saturday Review* (periodical) 187
Sauer, Emil von 62
Saxons 75, 151, 152
saxophones 133–4
Saygun, Ahmed Adman 283, 284
S. B. (critic) 34
Scarlatti, Domenico 116, 220
Schaffhausen 275
Scherchen, Hermann 265, 275, 311
Scheveningen 311
Schiesser, Fritz 298
Schiff, András 379
Schneider, David 41, 208, 213
Schoenberg, Arnold xiv, 124, 254, 310, 329, 365,
    380, 381
    Bartók and 86, 145
    Bartók on 179, 304
    works 86, 116, 145
Scholes, Percy 201–2
Schott (publisher) 52
Schrecker, Franz 310
Schubert, Franz 34, 138, 328
Schulthess, Walter (second husband of Stefi
    Geyer) 238
Schuman, William 343
Schumann, Robert
    influence on Bartók 10, 14, 17, 35
    works 17, 35, 36, 51
Schuricht, Carl 311
scordatura tuning 301
'Scotch snaps' 26, 32, 54, 72, 371
Scott, Marion Margaret 286–7
Scottish music 372
Seattle, Washington 225, 330, 333
Sebestyén, Gyula 83
Seeger, Charles 379
Seemayer, Willibald 66
Seiber, Mátyás 90
Serb-Croat-Slovene State (Yugoslavia) 175
Serbia 127, 136
Serbian language 8
Serbo-Croatian folk music xiv, 324, 330,
    337–8
*Serbo-Croatian Folk Songs* (Bartók and Lord)
    347, 348, 349, 350, 360
Serbs 1, 2–3, 22, 29
Serly, Tibor 121, 365, 370–2
Seton-Watson, Robert William 161
Severance Hall, Cleveland, Ohio 328
*Sezătoarea (Gathering)* (journal) 135
Sharp, Cecil 76, 96
Shilkret, Nathaniel 365
*The Shining* (Kubrick) 280
Shostakovich, Dmitri 381
    Seventh Symphony parodied 271, 352
Sibelius, Jean 381
Sidi-Okba, Algeria 129
Sieg, L. P. 331
Simon, Eric 336
'The Singing Great Plain' festival, Kecskemét
    (1937) 287
Slonimsky, Nicolas 226, 259

Slovak folk music xiv, 89, 95, 100, 107–8, 119,
127, 137, 189, 203, 214, 261–2, 262,
310, 369, 378
*see also under* Bartók, Béla: works
Slovakia 93, 107–8, 127, 137, 139–40, 152, 167–8,
194, 199–200, 202, 203, 214, 274, 283,
378
*see also* Czechoslovakia
Slovaks 1, 22, 57, 67, 69, 93, 100, 137, 152
*Slovenské L'udové Piesne* (Bartók) 262, 369
Smetana Hall, Prague 272
Smith, Warren Story 362
Socialist Party of Hungary 168–9
soldiers' songs 160, 161, 244
Solomon, Larry 28
Somfai, László 41, 137, 170, 190, 210, 211, 218,
227, 316, 370
Sopron 63, 202
Sorabji, Kaikhosru 178
Sorbonne, Paris 187
Spain 63, 255
Spanish music 219
Spivakovsky, Tossy 355–6
Sprague-Coolidge, Elizabeth 265
Sprague-Coolidge Foundation 323
Stadthaus, Winterthur 238
Stafford, William 23
STAGMA (Staatlich genehmigte Gesellschaft
zur Verwertung musikalischer
Aufführungsrechte) 299
Stanford University, Palo Alto, California 333
Steed, Henry Wickham 48, 49
Steinfirst, Donald 328–9
Steuermann, Edward 181
Stevens, Halsey 183
Stock, Frederick 333
Strasser, István 132
Straus, Noel 324, 329–30
Strauss, Richard 135, 262, 263
influence on Bartók xiv, 17, 20–1, 26, 27–8, 30,
32, 34, 39, 45, 47, 56, 70, 73, 81, 90,
133, 135, 242, 352
*Alpine Symphony* 133
*Also sprach Zarathustra* 20, 47
*Death and Transfiguration* 21
*Don Quixote* 81
*Ein Heldenleben* 27–8, 34, 93
*Salome* 135
*Sinfonia Domestica* 51, 134
Stravinsky, Igor 174, 177, 187, 343, 365, 381
affinity with Bartók 102, 120, 158, 176, 197,
203, 207–8, 213, 213–14, 217, 218, 234,
251, 303, 320
Bartók on 179
campaign against 179
in 'Degenerate Music' exhibition 310
influence on Bartók xiv, 87, 124, 133, 229, 301
works 179, 203, 208, 218, 311, 345
Concerto for Piano and Wind Instruments
208, 213–14, 251
*The Firebird* 187, 251
*L'Histoire du soldat* 218, 320

*Petrushka* 120, 133, 134, 208
*Le Sacre du printemps* 124, 158, 179, 234
Strohbach, Hans 219
Stuttgart 225
*style hongrois* 25, 26, 27, 34–5, 39, 40, 44, 54, 81,
90, 113
Suchoff, Benjamin 53, 54, 83, 119, 316
suicide, Bartók on 78
*sul ponticello* technique 123, 184, 222, 224, 306
'Survey of Pacific Northwest Anthropological
Research, 1930–1940' (Jacobs) 331
Swarthmore College, Pennsylvania 327
Switzerland 88, 239, 300, 311, 326
symbolism, of red apples 39–40
symbolist drama 109–12, 114, 115
'Syria Mosque', Pittsburgh 328
Szabolcsi, Bence 22–3
Szamosújvár (Gherla) 107
Szantho, Enid 324, 325
Szász, Zoltán 151–2
Szecseleváros (Săcele, 'seven villages') 75
Szeged 67, 152
Szeged Music Conservatory 63, 120
Szeges 68
Szeibert, Orsolya 200
Székely, Arnold 199, 263
Székely family 259, 272, 285
Székely folk music 76–7, 82–3, 109–10, 240–1
Székely, Mientje 273, 309
Székely National Museum 220
Székely people 100
Székely, Zoltán 189, 194, 207, 233, 238, 243, 272,
276, 286, 296–7, 303, 307, 308, 311, 315
Székelyhidy, Ferenc 161
Székelylengyelfalva 177
Szeklence 234
Szeklers 75, 151
Szekszárd 206
Szendy, Árpád 102
Szenkár, Jenő 189, 219
Szentes 68
Szentirmai, Elemér, 'Just a Fair Girl' 92
'Szép a leány ideig' ('A girl is handsome awhile')
(Hungarian folk song) 112, *113*
'Szép vagy, gyönyörű vagy Magyarország' '(You
are beautiful, you are lovely Hungary')
(aria) 351
Szerém County 175
Szigeti, József 64, 221, 225, 232, 233, 239, 243, 259,
300, 323, 324, 325, 330, 343, 356, 357
Szigeti, Wanda 300
Sziladpuszta 66
*Színházi Élet* (*Theatre Life*) (weekly) 152
*Színják* (*Stageplay*) (journal) 109
Szőllőpuszta 205
*Szózat* (*The Voice*) (newspaper) 174
Szymanowski, Karol 187
*Notturno e tarantella* 183
*Trois mythes* 183

'The Taboo of Virginity' (Freud) (1917) 110
Talich, Václav 272

Tallián, Tibor 3, 5
Tango, Egisto 153, 154, 162, 173
Tansman, Alexandre 221, 365
Tápiószele 67
tar (drum) 215
Tari, Lujza 378
Tatabánya 152
Taubman, Howard 323, 328
Tausig, Carl 69
Taylor, Colin 178
Taylor, Deems 342, 373
Tchaikovsky, Pytor Ilyich, Swan Lake 279–80
Teatro La Fenice, Venice 311
The Technique of Piano Playing (Thomán) 16
Tecirli, Tüysüz 284
Teleki, Count Pál 98
Temes County 122, 127, 136
Temesvár (Timişoara) 63, 122, 152, 202
Temesváry, János 103
Tempo (periodical) 309
Teutsch, Bishop 152
The Hague 235
The Hague Philharmonic Orchestra 311
The Times (newspaper) 182, 250, 260, 265, 298–9, 310
Théâtre du Vieux-Colombier, Paris 187
Thomán, István 14, 15–16, 19, 20, 21, 36, 45, 61–2, 74
Thomson, David 22
Tiffin, Helen 43
Timisoara see Temesvár
timpani, pedal 263
Tisza, István 49
Toch, Ernst 310, 365
Tőkésújfalu (Klátova Nová Ves, Slovakia) 152
Toldy, László 65
Tolga, Algeria 129, 350
Tolna County 85, 110, 175, 244
Tolofean, Toma 233
Tommasini, Anthony 380, 381
tone clusters 264, 281, 302
Tonhalle Orchester, Zürich 103–4
Tonhalle, Zürich 238
Tonkúnstlerfest des Allgemeinen Deutschen Musikvereins, Zurich (1910) 103–4
Topánfalva 107
Toprakkale 284
Torda 152
Torda-Aranyos County 138
Torockó (Rimetea) 88–9
Torontál County 107, 127, 136, 138, 139
Toscanini, Arturo 257
Tóth, Árpád 99
Tóth, Emil Oláh (brother-in-law) 66, 169
Town Hall, New York 324, 327–8, 328
Transylvania 75–6, 100, 245
    demands for autonomy 2
    invasion by Romania 151–2
    see also under individual locations
Transylvanian folk music 39–40, 57, 68, 75–7, 100, 106–7, 108, 109–10, 122, 254, 352
Treaty of Trianon (1920) 2–3, 3, 27, 94, 100, 174,

175
Treitler, Leo 88
'Tristan chord' 36, 37, 45, 70, 80–1, 87, 105, 165
Tryon, Winthrop P. 361–2
Tudor, Antony 357
Tura 66, 68
Turin 322
Turkey 275, 283–4
Turkish folk music xiv, 25, 283
Turkish Folk Music from Asia Minor (Bartók) 284, 342, 373
Turócszentmárton (Martin) 6, 107
Twain, Mark (Samuel Langhorne Clemens) xii

Udvarhely County 175
Új Élet (journal) 125
Új Idők (New Times) (journal) 144, 257
Ujfalussy, József 26
Újtátrafüred 153
Ukraine 237
Ukrainian folk music 196
UMZE (Új Magyar Zene-Egyesület, New Hungarian Music Society) 115–16, 257, 259
Unfinished Journey (Menuhin) 338
Ungarische Jahrbücher (journal) 277
Unger, Hermann 219
Universal Edition (publisher) 140, 143, 162, 195, 201, 234, 239, 247, 250, 273–4, 299, 303
University of Oregon, Eugene 333
University of Washington (Seattle) 330, 331, 333
Utrecht 207, 276

Vágássy (bagpiper) 66
Vajna, Gábor Pávai 17–18
Valencia de Alcántara 255
Vámbéry, Ármin 25
Váncsfalva (Onceşti), Máramaros County 139
Várdy, Steven Béla 336
Városmajor Szanatórium, Budapest 144
Vaskoh (Vascău) 102
Vaskohmező (Câmp), Bihar County 138
Vaughan Williams, Ralph, The Lark Ascending 159
Vecsey family 65–6, 67
Vecsey, Ferenc 64, 74
Vecsey, Lajos 64
Venice 202, 220, 311
    Biennale 266, 285
verbunkos (recruiting dance) 26, 29, 35, 37, 44, 45, 51, 53, 55, 81, 184, 185, 190, 221, 232, 245, 278, 282, 300–1, 304, 314, 318, 346, 350–1, 366
    history and characteristics 22–3
Veszelka, Mihályné 68
Vésztő 57, 77, 95, 102, 163, 194
Vienna 49, 263
Vienna Conservatoire 14, 39, 49, 87
Vienna Philharmonic Orchestra 56, 69
Vigadó Concert Hall, Budapest 56, 263
Vikár, Béla 57, 65, 67, 68, 161, 175, 177, 232

Vikárius, László 246
Világ (The World) (newspaper) 167, 195
The Village Notary (Eötvös de Vásárosnamény) 4
Vincze, Zsigmond, A hamburgi menyasszony
  352, 353
Virgil, The Georgics 246
Voinovich, Géza 297
Voit, Emma (aunt) 9, 95, 102
Voit, Irma (aunt) 8–9, 30, 168, 239, 257, 258, 285,
  332
Voit, Lajos (uncle) 7
Voit, Moritz (grandfather) 6
Voit, Terézia (née Polereczky; grandmother) 6
Volkmann, Robert 15
  Piano Concerto in C 74
  Variations on a Theme by Handel 34
Volksmusik der Rumänen von Maramureş
  (Bartók) 190
Vörös, Alexander 5
Vörösmarty, Mihály 174
vörösterror (red terror) 169

Wagner family 33
Wagner, Richard 19, 21, 26, 33
  influence on Bartók 36, 39, 70, 72, 125, 133,
    164
  Götterdämmerung 125
  Die Meistersinger 93
  Parsifal 39, 164
  Das Rheingold 133
  Tristan und Isolde 39, 72, 81
  see also 'Tristan chord'
Waidberg 120–1, 126
Waldbauer, Imre 103, 189, 190, 194
Waldbauer-Kerpely Quartet 103, 155, 162, 170,
  194, 239
Walker, Alan 19
Wallachs 94–6, 357
Walton, William, Viola Concerto 363
Warlock, Peter see Heseltine, Philip
Warsaw 225
Washington, DC 265, 273, 323
Weber, Carl Maria von, Rondo Brillante in E♭
  major 10
Webern, Anton 381
Weill, Kurt 310
Weiner, Leó 102, 115, 263
Weiss-Aigner, Günter 11, 21
Weiss, Emila 200
Weissman, Adolf 194
Wellesz, Egon 187, 260
Wells College, Aurora, New York 333
Wenckheim family 66
Wenckheim, Count Géza 7

West Side Hospital, New York 372–3
West, the 99
White Terror 171–2
Wigmore Hall, London 238–9, 335
Wilson, Duncan 264
Wilson, Freda 264
Wilson, Paul 183, 184
Wilson, President Woodrow 167
Wilson, Sir Duncan and Lady 182
Winterthur 238, 265, 275
Wireless Chorus 265
Wireless Symphony Orchestra 225
With Strings Attached (Szigeti) 233
Wlassics, Baron Gyula 202
Wolf, Hugo 26
  influence on Bartók 17, 40, 242
Wood, Carl Paige 330, 331, 333
Wood, Sir Henry 243, 250, 260, 276
WQXR radio station 324

xylophones 135, 367

Yugoslav folk music 330
Yugoslavia 2–3, 3, 324, 337–8, 348, 350
  see also under individual regions

Z cells 88, 124, 135, 142, 145, 146, 148, 151, 155,
  156–7, 159, 175, 178, 190, 334
Zádor, Eugene (Jenő) 365
Zágon, Géza Vilmos 122–3, 128, 131
Zala County 175
Zalatna 107
Zathureczky, Ede 273, 311, 322
Zeiller, Gustav 219
Zeitlin, Lev 58
Zeitschrift für Musikwissenschaft (journal) 174,
  261
Zeneközlöny (Music Gazette) (journal) 51, 115,
  121–2
Ziegler, Dr Hans Severus 310
Ziegler, Herma (sister-in-law) 93
Ziegler, Dr Károly (cousin-in-law) 152
Ziegler, Károly (father-in-law) 93, 122
Ziegler, Károly (second husband of Márta)
  206
Zöbisch, Ottó 154
Zólyom County (Zvolenská, Slovakia) 137,
  139–40, 203, 378
Zsolt, Nándor 258
Zsuffa, Joseph 112
Zurich 265, 311
Zurich School of Music 69
Zvolen County see Zólyom County
Zweig, Stefan 7